The Selected Papers of
Elizabeth Cady Stanton and Susan B. Anthony

The Selected Papers of Elizabeth Cady Stanton and Susan B. Anthony

VOLUME I

IN THE SCHOOL OF ANTI-SLAVERY
1840 TO 1866

Ann D. Gordon, EDITOR

Tamara Gaskell Miller, ASSISTANT EDITOR

Stacy Kinlock Sewell, EDITORIAL ASSISTANT

Ann Pfau, EDITORIAL ASSISTANT

Arlene Kriv, EDITORIAL ASSISTANT

RUTGERS UNIVERSITY PRESS

NEW BRUNSWICK, NEW JERSEY, AND LONDON

THIRD PRINTING, 2001

LIBRARY OF CONGRESS CATALOGING-IN-PUBLICATION DATA

Stanton, Elizabeth Cady, 1815–1902.
    [Selections. 1997]
    The selected papers of Elizabeth Cady Stanton and Susan B. Anthony /
Ann D. Gordon, editor ; Tamara Gaskell Miller, assistant editor.
    p.   cm.
    Includes bibliographical references and index.
    Contents: v. 1. In the school of anti-slavery, 1840 to 1866
    ISBN 0-8135-2317-6 (alk. paper)
    1. Feminists—United States—Archives.   2. Suffragists—United States—
Archives.   3. Stanton, Elizabeth Cady, 1815–1902—
Archives.   4. Anthony, Susan B. (Susan Brownell),
1820–1906—Archives.   5. Feminism—United States—History—19th
century—Sources.   6. Women—Suffrage—United States—History—19th
century—Sources.   I. Anthony, Susan B. (Susan Brownell), 1820–
1906.   II. Gordon, Ann D. (Ann Dexter)   III. Miller, Tamara
Gaskell.   IV. Title.
HQ1410.A25   1997
016.30542—dc21   97-5666
                                                                CIP

BRITISH CATALOGING-IN-PUBLICATION information available

TEXT DESIGN: Judith Martin Waterman of Martin-Waterman Associates, Ltd.
Manufactured in the United States of America

⇗

Publication of this volume was assisted by a grant from the National Historical
Publications and Records Commission.

⇗

Frontispiece photographs are of Elizabeth Cady Stanton, *circa* 1848 (courtesy
of Rhoda Barney Jenkins) and Susan B. Anthony, *circa* 1850 (courtesy of the
Department of Rare Books and Special Collections, University of Rochester).

To the Memory of Corinne Ann Guntzel
Citizen of Seneca Falls, New York

❧ Contents

✎ ILLUSTRATIONS

Petition for Universal Suffrage

Letter by Elizabeth Cady Stanton

Susan B. Anthony

Membership certificate of the Women's New York State
Temperance Society

Cartoon by Elizabeth W. McClintock

Elizabeth Cady Stanton and child

Lucy Stone

Bloomer costume

Martha Coffin Wright

Lucretia Coffin Mott

Aaron Macy Powell

Sarah Parker Remond

Charles Lenox Remond

Antoinette Brown Blackwell and daughter Florence

Cartoon of Ninth National Woman's Rights Convention

Letter by Susan B. Anthony

Women's Loyal National League badge

White male abolitionists

❧ PREFACE

THIS IS THE FIRST IN A SERIES of volumes presenting selected papers of Elizabeth Cady Stanton (1815–1902) and Susan B. Anthony (1820–1906). The volumes will complete a three-stage project to collect and publish the papers of the preeminent advocates of women's legal and political rights in nineteenth-century America. Active reformers for fifty-five years each, Stanton and Anthony worked as lecturers, journalists, writers, organizers, petitioners, and lobbyists. Despite efforts by friends and family early in this century to assemble the documents they created, only a small proportion were discovered and available for research. Their personal and political correspondence remained dispersed. Their appeals to the American public lay hidden in ephemeral publications.

When this project began in 1982, the editors conducted an international search of archives, private collections, newspapers, and other printed sources to locate letters, diaries, and manuscripts as well as articles and reports of meetings and speeches. Their search, described in detail in *The Papers of Elizabeth Cady Stanton and Susan B. Anthony: Guide and Index to the Microfilm Edition* (1992), more than doubled the previously known sources. Documents were located and copied in two hundred libraries and archives in the United States, Canada, New Zealand, England, the Netherlands, France, and Germany and in nearly seven hundred different newspapers and periodicals.

The project next made this new, comprehensive collection available. Fourteen thousand documents were published in a microfilm edition of forty-five reels in 1991. The *Papers of Elizabeth Cady Stanton and Susan B. Anthony*, edited by Patricia G. Holland and Ann D. Gordon, integrates the records of both women from all sources into a single chronology, and it includes all issues of the *Revolution*, the weekly newspaper published by Anthony and Stanton during Reconstruction.

Now the project is bringing the most important documents to print.

Only a small percentage of the entire collection can be transcribed and annotated for publication, but these volumes will represent the collection in a form accessible to more readers. Of more than biographical interest, the papers are a valuable source for many kinds of research in American and women's history. Elizabeth Cady Stanton and Susan B. Anthony still amuse and invigorate us with their convictions and wit about women's rights, and their papers allow us to discover the rich political tradition left by woman suffragists. Their *Selected Papers* focuses on the public careers of two co-workers in the cause of woman suffrage, beginning with the start of their activism in the 1840s and pursuing the story of their ideas, tactics, reputations, and impact until the end of their lives, in the twentieth century. Volume one draws on the papers dating from 1840 to 1866; it documents the start of Stanton's and Anthony's careers as reformers, the early years of the movement to secure the rights of women, and the movement's transformation during the Civil War.

❦ Acknowledgments

IT IS A PLEASURE TO THANK our benefactors, whose intellectual, social, and financial contributions made this volume possible and pleasurable to complete. Most of all I want to acknowledge the staff of the *Papers of Elizabeth Cady Stanton and Susan B. Anthony*, microfilm edition, from which this edition derives. My coeditor on that project, Patricia G. Holland, and associate editors, Gail Malmgreen and Kathleen McDonough, not only completed the comprehensive collection of Stanton's and Anthony's papers and published it, but also kept meticulous research files that still inform our work on this further, selected edition.

The title page credits the people whose work is most evident in the pages of this volume. A special word of thanks is owed to the graduate assistants who worked to the highest professional standards for less than professional pay. Other students at Rutgers joined us for short stints. Elizabeth Smith, attorney at law and graduate student in American history, brought her legal skills to the project. Graduate students Mary Poole and Ann Marie Nicolosi contributed fine detective work and a serious commitment to order. Four undergraduate history majors joined the staff as interns and hourly assistants. We thank Jennifer Boutell, Terri Wells, Ilanit Sluzak, and Lynn D. Ritter for their help. A fellowship from the National Historical Publications and Records Commission allowed us to bring Mary K. Trigg onto the staff as a fellow scholar and student of historical editing. Her work contributed to this and subsequent volumes.

Beyond our offices, we received invaluable assistance in research from many generous people. Julie Pope, an independent researcher in Topeka, Kansas, tracked down information about people and places in Leavenworth. Judith Wellman, the leading authority on woman's rights activism at its birthplace in Seneca Falls, shared her research with us. Christopher Densmore demonstrated similar generosity with his knowledge about the Society of Friends in New York State. Dozens of archivists, librarians, and local historians answered our queries, but we asked the most of the staffs at Union College, Syracuse University, the Sophia Smith Collection, and the Schlesinger Library.

We also acknowledge the owners of manuscripts who allowed us to publish documents from their collections: the Arthur and Elizabeth Schlesinger Library on the History of Women in America, Radcliffe College; Sophia Smith Collection, Smith College; George Arents Research Library, Syracuse University; Vassar College Library; University of Rochester Library; Mabel Smith Douglass Library, Rutgers University; Houghton Library, Harvard University; Rare Books and Manuscript Library, Columbia University; Trustees of the Boston Public Library; William L. Clements Library, University of Michigan; Henry E. Huntington Library; Massachusetts Historical Society; American Antiquarian Society; Kansas State Historical Society; New Jersey Historical Society; Rare Book and Manuscript Division, Astor, Lenox and Tilden Foundations, New York Public Library; Buffalo and Erie County Public Library; Carl Albert Center Archives, University of Oklahoma; and the Robert A. Baum Trust.

Like students of Elizabeth Cady Stanton before us, we are especially indebted to Rhoda Barney Jenkins, a great-granddaughter of ECS, whose encouragement of historians and loyal support of this project are a joy.

This volume was produced with major financial support from the Research Division of the National Endowment for the Humanities, an independent federal agency; the National Historical Publications and Records Commission; the Barbara Lubin Goldsmith Foundation; the Gladys Krieble Delmas Foundation; and Rutgers, the State University of New Jersey. Within those institutions are countless individuals whose confidence in the edition earned our gratitude. We have also received generous gifts from the following individuals: Rhoda Barney Jenkins, Herbert C. Pollock, Kathleen Alaimo, Arlene Alda, Lois Banner, Lorie Barnum, Lisa Baskin, Elizabeth Bodine, Ann Braude, Carolyn De Swarte Gifford, Nancy Green, Susan Grigg, Patricia Holland, Honora Horan, Mary Huth, Lee and Susan Lane, Carol DeBoer Langworthy, Margaret Lyons, Barbara McMartin, Thomas C. Mendenhall, Carol Nadell, Mary Beth Norton, Rosemary Fry Plakas, Sherrill Redmon, Carol Roper, Priscilla Schuhmann, Shelah Scott, Lynn Sherr, Alice De Swarte Smith, and Dorothy Sterling.

Colleagues at Rutgers have provided the necessary material aid, appropriate intellectual stimulus, and welcome interest. Special thanks are due the staff of the circulation and interlibrary loan departments at the Alexander Library and to Alice Kessler-Harris, Mary DeMeo, John Salapatas, Harvey Waterman, Richard Foley, and David Rumbo. We also acknowledge the assistance of all the staff at the Rutgers University Press.

I also salute the staff children who share their mothers with Elizabeth Cady Stanton and Susan B. Anthony: Dan Marketti and Emily and Patrick Miller. Last but not least, I thank Rudy Bell and Jim Marketti, who each gambled in his own way that this project could float and made it possible.

ᷞ A. D. G.

INTRODUCTION

THIS VOLUME DOCUMENTS the lives of Elizabeth Cady Stanton (ECS) and Susan B. Anthony (SBA) from the start of 1840 through November of 1866. Young adults at the start of the story, they are leaders at its conclusion. In this period, they discovered their interest in reform, built a new woman's rights movement on the ideas, skills, and personnel of the older antislavery movement, and established themselves as valuable contributors to their own cause and to the crusade against slavery. Reformers welcomed ECS's strong, argumentative writing and speaking and SBA's skills as an organizer and lobbyist. By the end of the Civil War, their reputations rested chiefly on their mobilization of women in New York State, to win significant legislative victories for woman's rights, and in the nation, to petition Congress for the Thirteenth Amendment. Summing up the years from 1840 to 1866, ECS described herself and SBA as students "in the school of anti-slavery," who learned there the lessons of human rights.[1]

This volume closes with two reports of a November 1866 meeting called by the new American Equal Rights Association. The Civil War had transformed the woman's rights movement. Its leaders were no longer content to build a separate political force that asked solely for woman's rights. By taking up as their own the issues raised by the war—emancipation, presidential leadership, and reconstruction—their movement became as well a vehicle for women's political involvement. The turning point came in 1866, when ECS and SBA launched what Frederick Douglass called "the good ship *'Equal Rights Association.'*"[2] At the Eleventh National Woman's Rights Convention, in New York City in May, activists agreed to "bury the woman in the citizen, and our

[1] See document number 217 within.
[2] F. Douglass to ECS, 16 February 1866, in Patricia G. Holland and Ann D. Gordon, eds., *Papers of Elizabeth Cady Stanton and Susan B. Anthony* (Wilmington, Del., 1991, microfilm), 11:367. (Cited hereafter as *Film*.)

organization in that of the American Equal Rights Association."[3] In a bold attempt to redirect the course of Reconstruction, they resolved to "secure Equal Rights to all American citizens, especially the right of suffrage, irrespective of race, color or sex."[4] The equal rights association asserted, in effect, that women not only shared with white and black men the right to vote but also shared a right to set the radical political agenda. By the fall of the year, it was evident that this goal pitted them against their friends in both the American Anti-Slavery Society and the Republican party, who believed that manhood suffrage was the next objective of Reconstruction.[5]

Elizabeth Cady

Elizabeth Cady was the eighth child born to Daniel and Margaret Livingston Cady, the most prominent citizens of Johnstown, New York. At the time of her birth on 12 November 1815, only three of the older children still lived—Tryphena, age eleven, Eleazer, age nine, and Harriet, age five. Margaret and Catharine were added to their number in 1817 and 1820, before Eleazer died in 1826.[6]

Elizabeth attended the dame school of Maria Yost and the Johnstown Academy, and she studied Greek with a local minister. In 1830 her father sent her to Emma Willard's Troy Female Seminary, and three years there completed her formal training. Her education was a good one. Johnstown's academy had more than a local reputation as a place

[3] See document number 217.

[4] See document number 217.

[5] A word about terminology. This volume adheres to the nineteenth-century practice of referring to "woman's rights" and a "woman's rights movement." The singular form recalled the language of natural rights and placed the rights of woman alongside the rights of man. The reformers, granddaughters of soldiers in the American Revolution, argued that women too possessed inalienable rights that no social categories like slave or free, married or single, could remove. Some modern students of the era regard the singular form as symptomatic of the movement's inattention and insensitivity to social differences. The recent trend to rename this antebellum movement a struggle for *women*'s rights employs modern usage and, in some cases, protests the premise of natural rights.

[6] Elizabeth Cady Stanton, *Eighty Years and More: Reminiscences, 1815–1897* (1898; reprint, Boston, 1993), 20–24; Orrin Peer Allen, *Descendants of Nicholas Cady of Watertown, Mass., 1645–1910* (Palmer, Mass., 1910).

to prepare for college or complete a secondary education, and Emma Willard aspired to make her seminary the equal of New England's colleges.[7] At a ceremony in 1892 to dedicate a new building at the seminary, ECS recalled "good teachers, who took us through the pitfalls of logic, rhetoric, philosophy, and the sciences."[8]

Daniel Cady (1773–1859) was a lawyer with an interest in politics, a respected teacher of law, and the owner of extensive property. He served in the state assembly from 1808 to 1813, and in the year of Elizabeth's birth, he sat in Congress. After his daughters left home he won election to the bench of the state supreme court where he served from 1847 to 1855. His reputation for legal training drew young men to Johnstown, and they, in turn, spread his influence across the state. It also distinguished his household as a place for male companionship and an incidental legal education; law was part of one's upbringing and social life in this family. As ECS told it years later, her first lessons in the laws regarding women came from the students teasing her. Three of her sisters married Daniel Cady's students, and Henry Stanton studied with Cady after he and ECS were married.[9]

In her autobiography ECS crafted the character of her father to stand in for a patriarchal and orthodox society against which she and the woman's rights movement rebelled, and the caricature overwhelms the scant record of his personality. Did Daniel Cady restrain his daughter's political ambitions in the 1850s? The evidence from his daughter is suspect. Each time she recounted their conflict, she changed the story, and several versions are demonstrably erroneous. Her worst charges were that he threatened to leave her family homeless if she spoke in person to the legislature, but, even in that version, she softened the image by recounting how her father helped to select the best legal examples for the address he deplored. The indirect evidence is stronger. After Cady's death in 1859, ECS bolted into new political activities and public appearances.[10]

7 *History of Montgomery and Fulton Counties, N.Y.* . . . (1878; reprint, Interlaken, N.Y.,1981),197; Anne Firor Scott, "What, Then, is the American: This New Woman?" *Journal of American History* 65 (December 1978): 691.

8 E. C. Stanton, *Eighty Years*, 443–44.

9 *Biographical Dictionary of the American Congress, 1774–1971* (Washington, D.C., 1971); *History of Montgomery and Fulton Counties, N.Y.*, 200.

10 Ann D. Gordon, "Afterword," in E. C. Stanton, *Eighty Years*, 469–83;

Margaret Livingston (1785–1871), daughter of a hero of the American Revolution, married Daniel Cady in 1801. "My mother had the military idea of government," ECS wrote long after her mother's death, but strictness must have been balanced with warmth. Margaret Cady's daughters routinely came home to give birth to their babies, and her house was often full of very young grandchildren. A friend wrote of her old age, that she had "one of the liveliest of minds, and was the match of any of her children in wit and repartee."[11] As a widow in 1867 she placed her well-known name at the head of a petition for woman suffrage addressed to the state constitutional convention.

None of the Cady girls pursued a career, ECS's younger sister once explained, because "our father supported his five daughters."[12] What little is known of Elizabeth's years after she left school suggests a round of family duties and visits. She looked after the children of her sister Harriet and pursued her interest in music. No doubt she spent time in the state capital, as Daniel Cady moved his family between Johnstown and Albany. She also became friends with her cousin Gerrit Smith, who lived in Peterboro, New York.[13] On an extended visit to his house in the fall of 1839 she fell in love with another guest, Henry Stanton. At the start of 1840, she was twenty-four years old and in love with a man her father deemed an inappropriate match. Daniel Cady expected his sons-in-law to demonstrate the capacity at least to provide for his daughters, and Henry B. Stanton, at the height of his powers as an abolitionist orator, had neither profession nor capital. Elizabeth faced her predicament at home in Johnstown, while Henry Stanton resumed his work for the American Anti-Slavery Society.

SUSAN B. ANTHONY

At the opening of 1840, eighty miles to the southeast of Johnstown, in Greenwich Township, Susan B. Anthony faced an altogether different familial predicament as she approached her twentieth birthday. Since

---

"Reminiscences of Elizabeth Cady Stanton," undated typescript, and New York *Mail and Express*, 15 December 1894, both in *Film*, 33:39–43; E. C. Stanton, *Eighty Years*, 187–89.

[11] E. C. Stanton, *Eighty Years*, 4; *Golden Age*, 23 September 1871, in *Film*, 15:747.

[12] C. H. Cady file, Emma Willard School Archives, Troy, N.Y.

[13] *Film*, 6:85–88, 244–49, 305–8, 366–67.

the start of the nation's 1837 financial collapse, her father's fortunes had sunk inexorably. He lost business, home, household belongings, and still slid deeper into debt. Pulled out of boarding school in 1838, Susan returned home to help her family move and then set off to support herself as a teacher. The new year 1840 found her living at home again and working in local schools.[14]

Susan was born on 15 February 1820 to Daniel and Lucy Read Anthony in Adams, a town in the Berkshire hills of Massachusetts. Raised in a large Quaker family, Daniel Anthony (1794–1862) had attended the well-known Nine Partners Boarding School in Dutchess County, New York, and returned home to Adams to marry Lucy Read (1793–1880), a Baptist from neighboring Cheshire, in 1817. Their daughter Guelma was born one year later. After Susan's birth, Lucy Anthony bore five more children: Hannah in 1821, Daniel Read in 1824, Mary in 1827, Eliza (who died at age two) in 1832, and Jacob Merritt in 1834.[15] Despite their mother's religion, all the children were raised in the Society of Friends, but because of it, they learned music and spent time with relatives who grew up outside the society's discipline.

Soon after Susan's birth, Daniel Anthony built a small textile mill, said to be the first in Adams. The mill was successful, and, in about 1826, he was invited to move his family into Washington County, New York, where John McLean, a local politician and promoter, needed a manager for a larger mill he had built at Battenville. For the next decade Anthony did very well. He put up a large brick house, hired teachers for his children, and sent his two oldest daughters to Philadelphia to Deborah Moulson's Quaker boarding school for girls. The financial crisis of 1837 closed the mill and brought bankruptcy. The family moved into a neighborhood known as Hardscrabble, and for eight more years hung on in eastern New York, supported in part by their daughters. In 1845 further economic troubles led Daniel Anthony to plan a fresh start, and he settled on a farm, owned by his brother-in-law Joshua Read, near Rochester, New York. Although the family continued to farm, in the late 1840s Daniel Anthony opened an insurance

[14] Ida Husted Harper, *Life and Work of Susan B. Anthony*, (1898–1908; reprint, New York, 1969), 1:33–43.

[15] Charles L. Anthony, comp., *Genealogy of the Anthony Family from 1495–1904* (Sterling, Ill., 1904.)

agency in Rochester and eventually brought his sons-in-law into the business.

Daniel Anthony combined entrepreneurial zeal with a reformer's passion. Describing an argument of his, soon after his conversion to immediate emancipation, SBA wrote: "Father kept very cool, never talked once on his accustomed key."[16] As soon as the family moved to Rochester in the 1840s, it was Daniel who plunged into the radical community of abolitionists and dissident Quakers, and his children followed. Not only Susan, but also her brother Daniel Read learned, in this family, to make reform central to their lives.

Lucy Read Anthony is nearly invisible in the historical record, and an inordinate amount of the family's correspondence is preoccupied with raising her spirits, as if they all knew she was subject to anxiety and depression. Nonetheless, the Anthony household was a sociable place, where prominent reformers found rest and conversation, and three generations often lived together.

Susan B. Anthony's was the generation of girls who entered the textile mills in Lowell, Massachusetts, and made up a majority of the teachers of young children in New England and New York.[17] She might well have worked even without her family's financial problems. After boarding school, she moved to New Rochelle to teach at a Friends school run by Eunice Kenyon. Back with her family in 1839,[18] she taught for two years closer to home, where Washington County licensed her to work in its common schools. Although SBA retired from teaching at age twenty-nine, she never quite abandoned her identity as a teacher. For a decade she pressed the New York State Teachers' Association to accept women as equals in its own activities and demand equal pay for them in their jobs. Whenever she got the chance, she spoke about education and woman's rights at county teachers' institutes, the state-funded workshops where teachers continued their education. Teaching was the experience she brought to debates over women's work and wages throughout her life, and her attention to wage-earning women was more consistent than Elizabeth Cady Stanton's.

[16] See notes to document 28.

[17] See Thomas Dublin, *Transforming Women's Work: New England Lives in the Industrial Revolution* (Ithaca, N.Y., 1994.)

[18] *Film*, 6:198–243, 250–304, 309–65.

HENRY B. STANTON

Elizabeth Cady married Henry Brewster Stanton (1805–1887) in May 1840, and on their honeymoon to the World's Anti-Slavery Convention in London, the new bride found herself introduced immediately into the contentious leadership of the transatlantic antislavery movement. Born in Connecticut to Joseph and Susan Brewster Stanton, Henry Stanton moved to Rochester, New York, in 1826 and learned both journalism and law in the service of politics.[19] But his secular ambitions were interrupted by a religious revival in 1830, and he determined to enter the Lane Seminary in Cincinnati to study for the ministry. Under the influence of Theodore Dwight Weld, he also resolved to devote his life to opposing slavery. Within a few years, the abolitionist activities of students at Lane met opposition from the school's leaders, and in 1834 Stanton was one of the many students who left Lane in protest. The Lane Seminary rebels, as they were known, became some of the best workers against slavery, and Henry Stanton found work as an agent of the American Anti-Slavery Society in 1835. By the time he met Elizabeth Cady, Stanton had broken with the movement's most prominent figure, William Lloyd Garrison. Garrison thought that abolitionists should refuse to participate in a political system corrupted by slavery, while Stanton believed that slavery could be ended by forcing political parties to make it an issue. At the start of 1840, Stanton was in the thick of preparations for founding the Liberty party. Garrison not only disagreed with him, he also denounced him.[20]

Henry Stanton and Elizabeth Cady made an odd couple. One who met them in Dublin late in 1840 said Henry Stanton "does not appear to me to be easy of access," but ECS "is one in ten thousand"; "such eloquence, such simplicity of manner—such naïveté, a clearsightedness,

[19] The most complete biography of Stanton is Arthur Harry Rice, "Henry B. Stanton as a Political Abolitionist" (Ed.D. diss., Columbia University, 1968).

[20] Garrison's position is set forth in Aileen S. Kraditor, *Means and Ends in American Abolitionism: Garrison and His Critics on Strategy and Tactics, 1834–1850* (New York, 1969). More sympathetic to Henry Stanton is the account in Betty Fladeland, *James Gillespie Birney: Slaveholder to Abolitionist* (Ithaca, N.Y., 1955).

candor, openness, such love for all that is great and good," he raved.[21] Other abolitionists noted that ECS lacked Henry's religious intensity. Moreover, she was drawn to the accomplished women sent to London by their antislavery societies, most of whom sided with Garrison, not her new husband.

In this volume, after opening the story and introducing his wife into a new circle of friends, Henry Stanton recedes from view. His absence reflects, in part, the disappearance of his correspondence with his wife, but it is also a measure of how often he was away from home. When the Stantons returned from England, he agreed to study law with Daniel Cady, in order to have a profession. He would not, however, give up his convictions about slavery and politics.[22] While in Johnstown and then in Boston, where he practiced law, he worked tirelessly to build the Liberty party. Back in New York by 1847, he was involved in each turn of the state's antislavery political configuration. The Liberty party was followed by the Barnburner revolt in the Democratic party, which was followed, in time, by the Free Soil and Republican parties, and Henry Stanton stumped the state for them all. Three times he ran for office, twice winning a seat in the state senate and once conducting a largely symbolic campaign for lieutenant governor.

REFORM

Not until 1851 were ECS and SBA brought together by the interconnections of western New York reform. Thus, at the start of this volume, the documents tell separate stories about young women independently drawn to activism, while pursuing quintessentially female occupations, as wife and mother and as teacher. By 1848 ECS and SBA had friends in common; four years later they were political allies; by 1854 they had perfected a collaboration that made the New York State movement the most sophisticated in the country.

The influences on ECS in the 1840s are imperfectly documented. Questions about woman's rights had already arisen among abolition-

[21] Richard D. Webb to Elizabeth Pease, 4 November 1840, in Clare Taylor, *British and American Abolitionists: An Episode in Transatlantic Understanding* (Edinburgh, 1974), 119–20.

[22] See Reinhard O. Johnson, "The Liberty Party in Massachusetts, 1840–1848: Antislavery Third Party Politics in the Bay State," *Civil War History* 28 (September 1982): 237–65.

ists, when women insisted on an equal right to speak out against the evils of slavery, even though enjoined by the Bible to be silent and by society to leave public matters in the hands of men.[23] Her new social circle placed ECS among the women who led that struggle to establish an equal place for women in the movement. A regular reader of at least two antislavery papers, ECS also kept herself informed about the movement's beliefs and methods. Less evident in the documents is the impact of her acquaintance with lawyers and the law at a time when New Yorkers debated legal reform and the rights of individuals.[24] By 1848 she had transformed the antislavery conflict about individual responsibility and moral equality into a legal claim that women were endowed with the same natural rights as men, deserved equal protection of their individual liberty, and should organize themselves to secure their rights in the laws and institutions of the land. For that purpose she called a convention at Seneca Falls.

Not much is known about the jobs SBA held in the early 1840s. For two years she taught in the family of Lansing G. Taylor, a well-to-do farmer and entrepreneur at Fort Edward, and prepared his children for the male and female academies in Albany.[25] When her family moved to Rochester in 1845, Susan joined them, but she left again five months later to head the female department at the Canajoharie Academy. Susan stayed in that job until the summer of 1849. At Canajoharie, temperance brought her into reform. Had she stayed with her family in Rochester, her work might well have been different. The rest of the Anthonys were befriended by local radicals in the Western New York

[23] Gerda Lerner, *The Grimké Sisters from South Carolina: Pioneers for Woman's Rights and Abolition* (New York, 1971), and Jean Fagan Yellin, *Women and Sisters: The Antislavery Feminists in American Culture* (New Haven, 1989), provide good accounts of this early history. See also the essays in Jean Fagan Yellin and John C. Van Horne, eds., *The Abolitionist Sisterhood: Women's Political Culture in Antebellum America* (Ithaca, N.Y., 1994).

[24] Useful discussions of this influence on ECS are found in Judith Wellman, "Women's Rights, Republicanism, and Revolutionary Rhetoric in Antebellum New York State," *New York History* 69 (July 1988): 353–84; Peggy A. Rabkin, *Fathers to Daughters: The Legal Foundations of Female Emancipation* (Westport, Conn., 1980); and Norma Basch, *In the Eyes of the Law: Women, Marriage, and Property in Nineteenth-Century New York* (Ithaca, N.Y., 1982).

[25] *Film*, 6:515–18, 545–49, 553–57.

Anti-Slavery Society, Quakers who were leaving the Genesee Yearly Meeting to found the Congregational Friends, and advocates of equality between the sexes in all secular and religious activity. Those neighbors of the Anthonys were the people who responded to ECS's call for discussion of woman's rights.[26] Living with her non-Quaker relatives, in a town dominated by Democrats, SBA was isolated from these new influences for several years. She joined the Daughters of Temperance in Canajoharie. At the time, the temperance movement was managed by ministers, who delineated the role of women as auxiliary to the work of men. When she returned to Rochester in 1849, the city's Daughters of Temperance made her their presiding sister, but slowly, it seems, she moved into the more radical group, especially to work with the abolitionists. She had clearly absorbed messages about women's role in reform and found herself in a conflict within the temperance movement that paralleled the earlier antislavery struggle over the role of women in reform. By then she was working closely with ECS, and the two friends moved together against the problem.

[26] This community is carefully reconstructed in Nancy A. Hewitt, *Women's Activism and Social Change: Rochester, New York, 1822–1872* (Ithaca, N.Y., 1984).

✥ EDITORIAL PRACTICE

PRINCIPLES OF SELECTION

Though this first volume covers a longer period of time than the others in the series, the ratio of documents published to documents available is typical of the edition as a whole. Here the editors have selected 224 documents from 1,735 available, or roughly 8 percent. Documents are printed in their entirety with two exceptions: entries from diaries, journals, and account books are selected from the larger document; ECS's and SBA's contributions to meetings and pertinent discussion by other participants are excerpted from the fullest coverage available.

The high cost of producing and publishing historical editions creates an editorial imperative to bulldoze most of the trees while leaving an attractive and useful forest in place. The selection of which documents to include in each volume often boils down to arbitrary choices between equally valuable items. There are, however, guidelines. Selection is governed first by the mission to document the careers of the two co-workers. Drawn from the papers of two people, the selections must next represent differences in the documentation of each one. The dominant stories evident in the documents of any year or era are retained as well. For this volume additional decisions were made. First, although letters by ECS and SBA had priority, incoming mail was included if it supplied the only evidence about particular moments in the story or documented the other voice in longstanding friendships with ECS or SBA. Second, entries from SBA's diaries were included when they provided the only or best record of her experience. Third, speeches of this period were only sampled. The selections make available authoritative texts of important speeches and document significant contributions by ECS and SBA to the public debate over the rights of women. Fourth, the inclusion of discussions in which many people other than ECS and SBA participate reflects the editors' conviction that in the battle of ideas waged by these women, exchanges with opponents and allies give critical evidence about political style, intellectual influences, and differences of opinion that the principals might otherwise have failed to mention.

ARRANGEMENT

Documents are presented in chronological order according to the date of authorship, oral delivery, or publication of the original text. Documents dated only by month appear at the start of the month unless the context in surrounding documents dictates later placement. Documents dated only by year appear at year's end. Documents that cover a span of time, such as diaries and account books, are placed at the date of the earliest entry, and the longer text is interrupted for the placement of other documents that fall within the same period of time.

If a diary entry was written on the same date as another document, it is assumed that the entry was written at day's end. When two or more documents possess the same date, ECS and SBA authorship takes precedence over incoming mail, and SBA's papers appear before those of ECS unless the context dictates otherwise.

SELECTION OF TEXT

Most documents in this edition survive in a single version. When choices were required, original manuscripts took precedence over later copies, and the recipient's copy of correspondence was used. A speech reported by a stenographer took precedence over the manuscript. The newspaper to which SBA or ECS submitted a text took precedence over newspapers that reprinted it.

When letters survive only in transcripts made by editors and biographers, the earliest transcript was used as the source text. This rule gives precedence to Ida H. Harper's "Early Letters of Elizabeth Cady Stanton," published in 1903, over all transcripts by Harriot Stanton Blatch and Theodore Stanton; Harper was the more reliable editor, and it is safer to assume she worked from an original because she worked first. It also gives precedence to the Stanton children's typescripts over their published texts; considerable rewriting occurred between the two. Occasionally the editors created a composite text from two imperfect transcripts of the same missing original. The two sources of such a text are both indicated in the endnote, separated by a semi-colon, and textual additions from the second source are set off by angle brackets.

For the text of meetings and other oral events, the official report, or in its absence, the most comprehensive coverage, is the primary source text. If reports differ widely, composite reports were created. Additions to or substitutions from a second source are set off by angle brackets. The sources are separated by a semi-colon in the endnote.

FORMAT

Some features of the documents have been standardized when set into print. The indentation of existing paragraphs was consistently set. The dateline of each letter appears as the first line of text, flush to the right margin, regardless of its placement in the original. The salutation of letters was printed on one line, flush left. Extra space in the dateline or salutation indicates the author's line break. The complimentary close of letters was run into the text itself, regardless of how the author laid it out, and signatures were placed at the right margin beneath the text. The dash is uniformly rendered even though the lengths vary in the originals.

Each document is introduced by an editorial heading or title that connects the document to ECS or SBA, except in the case of meetings at which both women participated. Then, the heading identifies the occasion.

Following the text, an unnumbered endnote describes the physical character of the document and the source or owner of the original. The endnote also identifies variants of the text, explicates unusual physical properties of the document, and explains the uses made of square brackets in the transcription. In the case of diary entries, this note appears at the end of the series. Numbered notes follow the endnote, except that numbered notes for diary entries follow each entry.

TRANSCRIPTION

The editors strove to prepare for print the most accurate transcription that reproduces the format of the original as nearly as possible. However, the greater the remove from the author, the less literal is the representation.

LETTERS AND DIARIES. The editors retained the author's punctuation, which includes: the absence of customary symbols; emphasis by underlining, although not the occasional use of double or triple underlines; spelling and capitalization; abbreviations; superscripts; and paragraphing, or its absence. The author's form of dating was retained, including the Quaker practice to number the months. Closing quotation marks have been supplied in square brackets when the author neglected to enter them.

Emendations in the original text are marked by symbols to show cancelled text, interlineations, and other corrections and additions. A minimum number of exceptions were allowed when the interlineation obviously resulted from a slip of the pen or thought, as when an infinitive was clearly intended but the "to" was added above the line. Strike outs and other erasures are indicated with a line through the text. Interlineations, above or below the line, are framed in up and down arrows. Text from the margin has been moved into place with an editorial notation about the original location.

SBA's dashes can usually be distinguished as either pauses or full stops, and the distinction is represented by spacing. The em-dash is flush to the words on either side in a pause; extra space has been added after the dash at a full stop. SBA made no visible distinction when capitalizing letters "a," "m," and "w," and in haste, often lost the distinction for other letters. When her customary practice could not be found, the editors resorted to standard usage. Haste also affected SBA's ending syllables. Her rendition of "evening" became "evenng" and then something resembling "eveng." A similar evolution occurred with the "ly" ending. These compressions and contractions were ignored and the invisible letters supplied.

ECS's letters contain a form of implied punctuation; if a comma or period were required and she had reached the right margin of her paper, she omitted the punctuation. Rather than supplying what she left out, extra space was introduced into the text, larger for a full stop.

SPEECHES. Manuscripts of the earliest speeches given by ECS and SBA survive, and because these speeches were not reported in the press, there is but one possible source text. In order to preserve two very different kinds of evidence in these documents, indications of revisions, underlinings, and symbols were moved out of the text into textual notes. This practice allows experts concerned with composition and inscription to recover the writing process, while permitting the general reader to "hear" the speech. Despite the condition of their manuscripts, speakers introduce the necessary punctuation, pronounce the misspelled word, sound emphasis, place interlineations, omit strike outs, and expand abbreviations. In the textual notes, the alterations are listed by paragraph and line numbers, referenced to paragraph numbers printed beside the text. The textual notes employ the same editorial symbols in use elsewhere.

ECS's speech on the history of woman's rights, delivered by SBA in 1858, has not been treated in this fashion because her own manuscript cannot be found. The transcription of SBA's reading copy is clear, but details of *her* inscription are not recorded as textual notes. Substantial changes she made to her own copy are recorded in the numbered notes.

PRINTED TEXTS. In printed texts, obvious typographical errors have been silently corrected. When new words were substituted, the original wording was recorded in a numbered note. The original titles of articles and appeals were retained as part of the text. The practice of antebellum typesetters to use small capitals for emphasis and for highlighting the names of speakers has been ignored. To preserve the emphasis, italics have been substituted.

ANNOTATION

In numbered notes, the editors have provided the information they think necessary for readers to understand the documents. In occasional editorial notes placed between documents, the editors have explained events absent from the extant papers. Editorial notes placed either beneath a document's heading or interjected in the transcription, provide context for texts excerpted from reports of a meeting.

To incomplete place and datelines the editors have added, in italic type within square brackets, the best information available to complete the line. The basis for supplying dates is explained in a numbered note. New York State is assumed to follow the names of towns and counties in this volume.

The numbered notes principally identify references in the text, explain textual complexities, and summarize documents omitted from the edition. People are identified at the first occurrence of their names in the documents. The editors have tried to identify every person and reference, but they have not added notes simply to say "unidentified" or "not located."

Documents published in this volume may be found at their date in the microfilm edition of the *Papers of Stanton and Anthony*. A citation to the film (as *Film*, reel number:frame numbers) appears in the endnote only if the document is missing or filmed at a different date. *Film* citations are included for documents mentioned within the numbered notes.

TEXTUAL DEVICES

[roman text]	Text within square brackets in roman type is identified in the unnumbered endnote.
[roman text?]	The question mark indicates that the editors are uncertain about the text within the square brackets.
[roman date]	Date when a speech was delivered or an article published.
[*italic text*]	Editorial insertion or addition.
[*italic date*]	Date supplied by editors. In most cases, the basis is explained in a numbered note.
↑text↓	Authorial interlineation or substitution.
~~text~~	Text cancelled by the author.
~~illegible~~	Text cancelled by author that cannot be recovered.
<roman>	Addition to the source text from a second source.

✌ Abbreviations

Throughout the volume Elizabeth Cady Stanton is referred to as ECS and Susan B. Anthony as SBA.

Abbreviations Used to Describe Documents

AL ⌇ Autograph Letter
ALS ⌇ Autograph Letter Signed
AMs ⌇ Autograph Manuscript
Ms ⌇ Manuscript

Standard References, Newspapers, and Journals

ACAB ⌇   James Grant Wilson and John Fiske, eds., *Appletons' Cyclopaedia of American Biography*, 6 vols. (New York, 1886–1889)

Allibone ⌇   Samuel Austin Allibone, *A Critical Dictionary of English Literature and British and American Authors*, 3 vols. (Philadelphia, 1854–1871)

Allibone Supplement ⌇   John Foster Kirk, *A Supplement to Allibone's Critical Dictionary of English Literature and British and American Authors*, 2 vols. (Philadelphia, 1891)

American Women ⌇   Frances E. Willard, *American Women: Fifteen Hundred Biographies with over 1,400 Portraits*, 2 vols. (New York, 1897)

Anthony ⌇   Ida Husted Harper, *Life and Work of Susan B. Anthony*, 3 vols. (1898–1908; reprint, New York, 1969)

BDAC ⌇   *Biographical Dictionary of the American Congress, 1774–1971* (Washington, D.C., 1971)

BDAmerEd ⌇   John F. Ohles, ed., *Biographical Dictionary of American Educators*, 3 vols. (Westport, Conn., 1978)

BDTerrGov ❦ Thomas A. McMullin and David Walker, *Biographical Directory of American Territorial Governors* (Westport, Conn., 1984)

BDGov ❦ Robert Sobel and John Raimo, eds., *Biographical Dictionary of the Governors of the United States, 1789–1978*, 4 vols. (Westport, Conn., 1978)

Birney, *Letters* ❦ James Gillespie Birney, *Letters of James Gillespie Birney, 1831–1857*, ed. Dwight L. Dumond, 2 vols. (New York, 1938)

Black Abolitionist Papers ❦ C. Peter Ripley et al., eds., *The Black Abolitionist Papers*, 5 vols. (Chapel Hill, N.C., 1985–1992)

DAB ❦ Allen Johnson and Dumas Malone, eds., *Dictionary of American Biography*, 20 vols. (New York, 1928–1936)

DANB ❦ Rayford W. Logan and Michael R. Winston, eds., *Dictionary of American Negro Biography* (New York, 1982)

DBF ❦ J. Balteau et al., eds., *Dictionnaire de biographie française* (Paris, 1939–)

DNB ❦ Leslie Stephen and Sidney Lee, eds., *The Dictionary of National Biography*, 22 vols. (1885–1901; reprint, London, 1973)

Douglass, *Papers* ❦ Frederick Douglass, *The Frederick Douglass Papers. Series One: Speeches, Debates, and Interviews*, ed. John W. Blassingame et al., 5 vols. (New Haven, 1979–1992)

"D. R. Anthony," *KHQ* ❦ Edgar Langsdorf and R. W. Richmond, eds., "Letters of Daniel R. Anthony, 1857–1862," *Kansas Historical Quarterly* 24 (1958): 6–30, 198–226, 351–70, 458–75

"Early Letters" ❦ Ida Husted Harper, "Early Letters of Elizabeth Cady Stanton," *Independent* 55 (21 May 1903): 1188–94

Eighty Years ❧ Elizabeth Cady Stanton, *Eighty Years and More: Reminiscences, 1815–1897* (1898; reprint, Boston, 1993)

Film ❧ Patricia G. Holland and Ann D. Gordon, eds., *Papers of Elizabeth Cady Stanton and Susan B. Anthony* (Wilmington, Del., 1991, microfilm)

Garrison and Garrison, *Life* ❧ Wendell Phillips Garrison and Francis Jackson Garrison, *William Lloyd Garrison: The Story of His Life Told By His Children*, 4 vols. (New York, 1885–1889)

Garrison, *Letters* ❧ William Lloyd Garrison, *The Letters of William Lloyd Garrison*, ed. Walter M. Merrill and Louis Ruchames, 6 vols. (Cambridge, Mass., 1971–1981)

History ❧ Elizabeth Cady Stanton, Susan B. Anthony, Matilda Joslyn Gage et al., *History of Woman Suffrage*, 6 vols. (vols. 1–3, New York, 1881–1885; vol. 4, Rochester, 1902; vols. 5–6, New York, 1922)

Hoffman's Chancery Reports ❧ Murray Hoffman, *Reports of Cases Argued and Determined in the Court of Chancery of the State of New York* (New York, 1841)

Howard's Practice Reports ❧ Nathan Howard, *Practice Reports in the Supreme Court and Court of Appeals of the State New York*, 67 vols. (Albany, 1845–1884)

JAH ❧ *Journal of American History*

JNYA ❧ *Journal of the New York Assembly*

JNYS ❧ *Journal of the New York Senate*

KHQ ❧ *Kansas Historical Quarterly*

Lib. ❧ *Liberator* (Boston)

MVHR ❧ Mississippi Valley Historical Review

NASS ❧ *National Anti-Slavery Standard* (New York)

NAW ❧ Edward T. James, Janet Wilson James, and Paul S. Boyer, eds., *Notable American Women, 1607–1950: A Biographical Dictionary*, 3 vols. (Cambridge, Mass., 1971)

NCAB ❧ *National Cyclopaedia of American Biography*, 63 vols. (New York, 1891–1984)

Quaker Genealogy ❧ William Wade Hinshaw, *Encyclopedia of American Quaker Genealogy*, 3 vols. (Ann Arbor, Mich., 1936–40)

RSSNY, 1829 ❧ *The Revised Statutes of the State of New-York, Passed during the Years One Thousand Eight Hundred and Twenty-seven, and One Thousand Eight Hundred and Twenty-eight . . . Printed and Published under the Direction of the Revisers, Appointed for that Purpose*, 3 vols. (Albany, 1829)

RSSNY, 1836 ❧ *The Revised Statutes of the State of New-York; as Altered by the Legislature; . . . Prepared by and Published under the Superintendence of the Late Revisers*, 3 vols. (Albany, 1836)

RSSNY, 1852 ❧ *The Revised Statutes of the State of New-York, as Altered by Subsequent Legislation; . . . Prepared by Hiram Denio and William Tracy*, 2 vols. (Albany, 1852)

Sandford's Chancery Reports ❧ Lewis Halsey Sandford, *Reports of Cases Argued and Determined in the Court of Chancery of the State of New York*, 4 vols. (New York, 1846–1850)

SEAP ❧ Ernest H. Cherrington, ed., *Standard Encyclopedia of the Alcohol Problem*, 6 vols. (Westerville, Ohio, 1925–1930)

Stanton ❧ Theodore Stanton and Harriot Stanton Blatch, eds., *Elizabeth Cady Stanton, as Revealed in Her Letters, Diary and Reminiscences*, 2 vols. (1922; reprint, New York, 1969)

TroyFS ❧ Mrs. A. W. Fairbanks, ed., *Emma Willard and Her Pupils, or Fifty Years of Troy Female Seminary, 1822–1872* (New York, 1898)

Weld-Grimké, *Letters* ~ Gilbert H. Barnes and Dwight L. Dumond, eds., *Letters of Theodore Dwight Weld, Angelina Grimké Weld, and Sarah Grimké, 1822–1844*, 2 vols. (1934; reprint, Gloucester, Mass., 1965)

Wendell's Reports ~ John L. Wendell, *Reports of Cases Argued and Determined in the Supreme Court of Judicature: and the Court for the Trial of Impeachments and the Correction of Errors of the State of New York*, 26 vols. (Albany, 1829–1842)

Whittier, *Letters* ~ John Greenleaf Whittier, *The Letters of John Greenleaf Whittier*, ed. John B. Pickard, 3 vols. (Cambridge, Mass., 1975)

WWW1 ~ *Who Was Who in America*, vol. 1, *1897–1942* (Chicago, 1942)

WWW4 ~ *Who Was Who in America*, vol. 4, *1961–1968* (Chicago, 1968)

WWWCW ~ Stewart Sifakis, *Who Was Who in the Civil War* (New York, 1988)

WWWH ~ *Who Was Who in America, Historical Volume, 1607–1896*, rev. ed. (Chicago, 1967)

ARCHIVES AND REPOSITORIES

CSmH ~ Henry E. Huntington Library, San Marino, Calif.

CtY ~ Yale University Libraries, New Haven, Conn.

DLC ~ Library of Congress, Manuscript Division (unless otherwise noted), Washington, D.C.

DNA ~ National Archives and Records Service, Washington, D.C.

KHi ~ Kansas State Historical Society, Topeka, Kan.

MB ~ Boston Public Library, Boston, Mass.

MCR-S ~ Radcliffe College, Arthur and Elizabeth Schlesinger Library on the History of Women in America, Cambridge, Mass.

MH-Ar ❧   Harvard University Archives, Cambridge, Mass.

MH-H ❧   Harvard University, Houghton Library, Cambridge, Mass.

MHi ❧ Massachusetts Historical Society, Boston, Mass.

MNS-S ❧   Smith College, Sophia Smith Collection, Northampton, Mass.

MWA ❧   American Antiquarian Society, Worcester, Mass.

MiU-C ❧   University of Michigan, William L. Clements Library, Ann Arbor, Mich.

N ❧ New York State Library, Albany, N.Y.

NBu ❧   Buffalo and Erie County Public Library, Buffalo, N.Y.

NJost ❧   Johnstown Public Library, Johnstown, N.Y.

NN ❧   New York Public Library, Astor, Lenox and Tilden Foundations, New York, N.Y.

NNC ❧   Columbia University, New York, N.Y.

NNFL ❧   Religious Society of Friends (Quakers), New York Yearly Meeting, Haviland Records Room, New York, N.Y.

NPV ❧   Vassar College Library, Poughkeepsie, N.Y.

NRU ❧   University of Rochester Library, Rochester, N.Y.

NSchU ❧   Union College Library, Schenectady, N.Y.

NSyU ❧   Syracuse University Libraries, Syracuse, N.Y.

NjHi ❧   New Jersey Historical Society, Newark, N.J.

NjR ❧   Rutgers University Libraries, New Brunswick, N.J.

NjVHi ❧   Vineland Historical and Antiquarian Society, Vineland, N.J.

OHi ❧   Ohio Historical Society, Columbus, Ohio.

OO-Ar ❧   Oberlin College Archives, Oberlin, Ohio.

OkU ❧   University of Oklahoma at Norman, Okla.

PHi ⇜ Historical Society of Pennsylvania, Philadelphia, Pa.

PSC-Hi ⇜ Friends Historical Library of Swarthmore College, Swarthmore, Pa.

UkLQ ⇜ Friends House Library, London, U.K.

UkOxU-Rh ⇜ Oxford University, Rhodes House Library, Oxford, U.K.

MANUSCRIPT COLLECTIONS

Blackwell Papers, DLC ⇜ Blackwell Family Papers

Blackwell Papers, MCR-S ⇜ Blackwell Family Papers

ECS Papers, NjR ⇜ E. C. Stanton Papers, T. Stanton Collection, Mabel Smith Douglass Library

Garrison Papers, MB ⇜ William Lloyd Garrison Papers, Department of Rare Books and Manuscripts

Garrison Papers, MNS-S ⇜ Garrison Family Papers

Letters of Daniel R. Anthony, KHi ⇜ Letters of Daniel Read Anthony, Manuscript Department

Post Papers, NRU ⇜ Post Family Papers

Smith Papers, NSyU ⇜ Gerrit Smith Papers, George Arents Research Library

The Selected Papers of
Elizabeth Cady Stanton and Susan B. Anthony

·⟨⸺⟩·

1 ❧ HENRY B. STANTON TO ELIZABETH CADY

Philadelphia Jany. 1, 1840.

"A happy new Year" to thee, my own beloved Elizabeth! I hope this bright but cold morning finds thee cheerful & brilliant as usual, and encircled with the affectionate admiration of many warm friends. But, among them all thou shalt not find one who loves thee more devotedly, or would do more to render this & all thy future years "happy," than him whose hand traces these lines. Their prayer is, that the same kind Being who has caused thy path thus far in life to bloom with such sweet flowers, & has crowned thy years with His loving kindness, may continue to spread the banner of His guardian care over thee and lead thee into pleasant bowers and by the side of still waters, till, at a period far remote, He shall gently call thee to a brighter world & more enduring joys. And <u>where</u> & <u>how</u> shall <u>we</u> be at the beginning of the next new Year? Will these hearts be still united, and, like kindred drops, mingled into one? Of myself, I can say in the words of Moore:—[1]

> "<u>This</u> heart, like a tendril accustomed to cling,
>   Let it ~~glow~~ ↑grow↓ where it will cannot flourish alone;
> But will lean to the nearest and loveliest thing,
>   It can twine with itself, and make closely its own."

I need not tell ~~you~~ ↑<u>thee</u>↓ who that "nearest and loveliest thing" is. And will <u>it</u> ever falter in its affection? Let the same sweet poet answer.

> "The heart that loves truly, love, never forgets,
>   But as truly loves on to the close,
> As the sun-flower turns to her god as he sets,
>   The same look that she turned when he rose."

With what deep pathos does my heart respond Amen! to these lines.

If I seem to be uncommonly <u>poetical</u> & <u>pointed</u> in my address to <u>thee</u> this morning, dear E, attribute it to the fact, that I am writing in the room of John G. Whittier, "<u>the Quaker poet</u>."[2]

I have just parted with Mr. & Mrs. & Miss Smith & Miss Cochran,[3] who have gone out of the city to Germantown to dine. Elizabeth & I have sung Cork Leg, the Gypsey ballad,[4] & a dozen others, besides having a chat about you. Let me tell you a little incident, to show that I am "still harping on my" Lizzy. On our way to the depot of the Germantown Rail-road this morning, we stopped a few moments [this is a wretched pen] at Mr. Webb's, of whom you have heard Miss Stewart speak. Miss Webb inquired after Mr. Stewart's family.[5] I told her I had seen them recently, and that Miss <u>Elizabeth</u> told me if I saw Miss Webb, to give her love to her. Miss Webb stared interrogatively. I repeated, "Miss Elizabeth sent her love to you." Miss Webb seemed not to understand me, and "cousin Nancy" and "Lib Smith" laughed. I asked for an explanation. Says Lib Smith, "Was it <u>Elizabeth</u> who sent her love to Miss Webb?" I saw I was caught; & turning to Lib, said, "I hope you will excuse me for thinking so constantly of you, as to use your name thus involuntarily? You must not lay it to heart." "Certainly not," said she, laughing. The affair afforded those of the party who are in the secret, no little amusement. If your father had been present, I think he would have said with the venerable Polonius in Hamlet, "<u>Still harping on my daughter</u>!" But, I am quite sure, since this receipt of your father's letter (of which, more by & by)[6] I shall not mistake him for a <u>rat</u>, & therefore shall not kill him, Hamlet-like. Nor do I believe you will drown yourself, like Ophelia; but live to bless me. And, as to myself, I can not only say with Hamlet, "I <u>did</u> love you, fair Ophelia," but can add, with all my soul, "I <u>do</u> love you"; and if I be abolition-mad, all parties shall yet know that "there's method in my madness."[7] So much for Hamlet & Miss Webb! [I am interrupted, and shall not be able to conclude this, till I reach New York; whence I go this P.M.]

<u>New York, Thursday</u>. [*2 January*]

I arrived in this city about 1 o'clock last night, half frozen to death. But, I was warmed with the expectation of meeting a letter ("sleepy of course") from you, & slept soundly till 9 this morning. On going to the office[8] I inquired, and found ———! The loveliest correspondant I ever had, once commenced a letter to me thus:—"How cruel! Dear Henry, not to write to me in so long a time; nearly two weeks (all but four days) passed, & not one line from you!" But, I did not <u>positively</u> expect a letter from you, dearest E, & therefore I am not much disappointed. But, it does afford me so much pleasure to get a few lines dictated by your great heart & penned by your little hand, that the hours pass slowly till they come. I know there is a letter for me somewhere in the snow drifts between this & Johnstown.[9]

❧ AL, ECS Papers, DLC. Square brackets in original.

1. Thomas Moore (1779–1852), Irish poet and lawyer. Stanton modifies stanzas from "'Tis Sweet to Think" and "Believe Me, If All Those Endearing Young Charms."

2. John Greenleaf Whittier (1807–1892), abolitionist and poet from Massachusetts, boarded in Philadelphia while he edited the *Pennsylvania Freeman* for the Anti-Slavery Society of Eastern Pennsylvania. Local antislavery meetings had taken Stanton from New York to Philadelphia on 26 December. (Whittier, *Letters*, passim; H. B. Stanton to Gerrit Smith, 25 December 1839, Smith Papers, NSyU.)

3. Gerrit Smith (1797–1874) was Elizabeth Cady's first cousin and the person who introduced her to Henry Stanton. He and his wife Ann Carroll Fitzhugh Smith (1805–1875), known as Nancy, were in Philadelphia to visit their daughter Elizabeth (1822–1911) at school and were joined by a daughter of Cornelia Wynchie Smith Cochran, Gerrit's sister. Philanthropists and activists, Gerrit and Ann Smith committed themselves to the immediate abolition of slavery in 1835, at an antislavery meeting in Utica, New York. Gerrit Smith presided over the New York State Anti-Slavery Society from 1836 to 1839, and Ann Smith served as a vice president of the Anti-Slavery Convention of American Women at New York City in 1837. The Smiths lived at Peterboro, New York, where they entertained most of the reformers of the day. (*DAB*, s.v. "Smith, Gerrit"; *NAW*, s.v. "Miller, Elizabeth Smith"; Ralph Volney Harlow, *Gerrit Smith: Philanthropist and Reformer* [New York, 1939]; Smith Papers, NSyU.)

4. "The Cork Leg" was a popular comic song by British songster Jonathan Blewitt; the "Gypsey Ballad" is unidentified.

5. Samuel Webb (1794–1869) was a Philadelphia Quaker and early abolitionist. The daughter may have been his oldest, Rebecca Webb (1824–1899), a poet who published under her married name of Artois. (Mary Webb Artois, *Poems of Rebecca Couch . . . Poems of Samuel Webb* [n.p., 1921].) Jane E. Stewart was a friend of both Elizabeth Smith and Elizabeth Cady who lived in Utica. Rumor said she might have become Mrs. Stanton. She married Luther Rawson Marsh in 1845. Her father Alvan Stewart (1790–1849) was an antislavery leader and lawyer in New York. One of the first to argue that the Constitution allowed the federal government to destroy slavery, he believed in independent political action by abolitionists. (David McAdam et al., eds.,

History of the Bench and Bar of New York [New York, 1897], 1:486, 2:266–69; Gerald Sorin, *The New York Abolitionists: A Case Study of Political Radicalism* [Westport, Conn., 1971], 47–52; *Eighty Years*, 58.)

6. The words from "since this" to the closing parenthesis were struck out with hatch marks at a later date. It is not known if Daniel Cady wrote directly to Stanton or if Stanton refers to Cady's letter of 14 December to Gerrit Smith, which said in part: "I understand he has no trade or profession that he is not now and never has been in any regular business and if so—and he willing to marry—he cannot in my judgment be overstocked with prudence—or feel much solicitude for her whom he seeks to marry— . . . I understand Mr Stanton now has some employment in an Abolition society which yields him a living— . . . Mr Stantons present business cannot be regarded as a business for life— If the object of the Abolitionists be soon accomplished he must be thrown out of business—and if success does not soon crown their efforts—the rank and file will not much longer consent to pay salaries—" (Smith Papers, NSyU.)

7. Stanton draws from several parts of *Hamlet*: "harping on my daughter" in act 2, sc. 2, line 188; "rat" in act 4, sc. 1, lines 10–11; "love" in act 5, sc. 1, lines 236, 263; and "madness" in act 2, sc. 2, lines 206–7.

8. The office of the American Anti-Slavery Society at 143 Nassau Street.

9. The manuscript ends here without signature. Stanton may have continued his letter on 4 January, again from New York. In a typed transcript, prepared by the Stanton children from an unknown source, Henry reviews his financial history since he was "thrown entirely upon [his] own resources" at age thirteen. Despite refusing "a dollar's gratuitous aid from anyone," he had met the costs of his own schooling, the "liberal education" of two brothers, a modest library, "generous contributions" to reform causes, and he still managed to save $3,000. Aid from others, he wrote, "would relax my perseverance and detract from my self-reliance"; "if I would be a man, I must build on my own foundation with my own hands." (*Film*, 6:372–73. Revised in *Stanton*, 2:4–5.)

·⊂═════⟩⟩·

2 ⇝ ELIZABETH CADY TO ANN FITZHUGH SMITH

Seneca Falls March 4th [*1840*]

My very dear Cousin,

Papa, Tryphena & I passed Wempsville on Friday evening & we all regreted that we had not determined at Utica to stop & make you a visit, but as Papa had paid his fare to Auburn, he would not listen to our earnest entreaties to go to Peterboro.[1] Did George Birney deliver our messages?[2] I feared he might not remember my name. I saw Jane

Stewart at Utica She told me that cousin Garrit had been very ill. I am very sorry. I do believe the Homeopathists could ease him[3] Mr Bayard says his physicians do not understand his constitution nor disease Dear cousin Nancy do induce him to go to New York this spring & consult Dr. Vandenburgh.[4] he is quite celebrated. Cousin G. ought to take better care of himself. We cannot afford to lose such a champion for negroes & womans rights, particularly at this crisis—when, (as <u>they</u> say) the antislavery cause is on the wane its friends having proved its enemies by their "political action."[5] I cannot tell you dear cousin with how much pleasure, & how often, in memory I go back & enjoy again the many weeks I spent with you—[6] And if I have thought of you—& with much affection, why (say you) have I never written before? Because I have not known where to direct. I shall never forget those happy days,—the rides—the walks—the races, the games, the head scratching & ear picking—the warm baths & cold showers—the music & mail days, the arrivals & departures—"the kisses & cream" & those happy mornings & evenings when we all met round the family altar & sang together those sweet hymns of praise—memories like these bind me to the dear ones who shared those joys with me, with a spell that cannot soon be broken. You have heard dear Cousin I suppose that my engagement with S. is dissolved, & I know you wonder, & so do I. Had anyone told me at Peterboro that what has occurred would occur I would not have believed it but much since then has convinced me that I was too hasty. We are still friends & correspond as before & perhaps when the storm blows over we may be dearer friends than now.[7] The oak stands straight ~~amidst~~ though the winds rage fierce, & the rains beat heavy upon it—for it has the strength to oppose them all—not so the gentle flowers they droop their heads, & when the storm is passed they rise again. Do write me a few lines dear cousin and tell me where Lib is & I will write to her. Stanton gave me her direction once but I have forgotten it.— tell us too how cousin Garrit is—give my love to him. All join with me in love. Tell Laura I have after many experiments succeeded in making or preparing rather potatoes in her peculiar style.—[8] adieu from your affectionate cousin

⇜ *Elizabeth*

When you write to Lib, please remind her that she promised to write to me as soon as she arrived in Philadelphia   did she do so? I will take it for granted she did, blame the Loco foco post-masters that I have never received it[9]   ⟍

P.S. What was the result of Mrs Weld's accouchment I am really desirous to know, whether the prodigy (for such I think it must be if mental qualities are hereditary & I believe they are) came in the form of man or woman[10]

⤙ ALS, ECS Papers, DLC.

1. She accompanied Daniel Cady and her sister Tryphena Cady Bayard (1804–1891) from Johnstown to the Bayards' home in Seneca Falls, where, according to Henry Stanton, she expected to visit for a couple of months. The oldest Cady daughter, Tryphena married Edward Bayard (1806–1889) in 1827. From a distinguished Delaware family, Bayard graduated from Union College in 1825 before studying law with Daniel Cady. He and Tryphena lived in Johnstown until 1834. While they lived in Seneca Falls, Bayard developed an interest in the medical practice of homeopathy, leading to a change in professions. He was qualified as a physician in 1845 and enjoyed a distinguished career in New York City. Tryphena Bayard shared his interest, and she was, along with ECS, a trustee of the homeopathic New York Medical College and Hospital for Women and Children in 1864. The Bayards had no children. Wempsville (now Wampsville) was the station nearest the Smiths' house at Peterboro on the Syracuse and Utica Railroad. (*Cleave's Biographical Cyclopaedia of Homeopathic Physicians and Surgeons* [Philadelphia, 1873], 51; Orrin Peer Allen, *Descendants of Nicholas Cady of Watertown, Mass., 1645–1910* [Palmer, Mass., 1910], 173; *Historical and Biographical Encyclopaedia of Delaware* [Wilmington, Del., 1882], 226–27; Gravestones, Johnstown, N.Y.; William Harvey King, ed., *History of Homeopathy and Its Institutions in America* [New York, 1905], 3:128, 143–44; *Eighty Years*, 26–32; *New York Times*, 1 October 1889; *Woman's Tribune*, 10 May 1891.)

2. Only eight years old at the time, George (1832–185?) was the fifth son of the abolitionist James G. Birney. After his mother's death in 1838, he and the other Birney children lived with the Smiths at Peterboro. (Betty Fladeland, *James Gillepsie Birney: Slaveholder to Abolitionist* [Ithaca, N.Y., 1955], 165.)

3. An alternative to the era's "heroic" medical treatments, introduced to America in 1825, homeopathy encouraged healthy living and prescribed minute doses of remedies that would produce symptoms of the disease in a healthy person.

4. Federal Vanderbergh (1788–1868), a longtime resident of Geneva, New York, practiced homeopathic medicine at New York City. (*Cleave's Biographical Cyclopaedia*, 414.)

5. A reference to the critique by William Lloyd Garrison and his followers of the decision by Stanton, Smith, and other American Anti-Slavery Society members to establish a third, antislavery party and run candidates for office. A

meeting of the Liberty party to nominate candidates was scheduled for 1 April 1840.

6. This was EC's visit to Peterboro in October 1839, when she met Stanton.

7. On 27 February 1840 Henry Stanton described their relationship in similar terms to Gerrit Smith: "We continue to correspond, & our relations are of the most friendly character." However, he went on, "I dread the influence of Mr. Bayard upon her. She has been too much under the influence of such people." She risked wasting her fine powers "in the giddy whirl of fashionable follies." (Smith Papers, NSyU).

8. Laura Bosworth (1796–1883) came to live with the Smiths in 1809 and stayed, occupying her own house after 1833. She seems to have been part domestic help, part family member, and part ally in reform. In 1867 her name headed a petition for woman suffrage submitted to the New York constitutional convention. (Octavius Brooks Frothingham, *Gerrit Smith: A Biography*, 2d ed. [New York, 1879], 27–28; "Verses of G. Smith," p. 160, G. Smith to Laura Bosworth, September 1849, will of Laura Bosworth, proved 8 October 1883, all in Smith Papers, NSyU; *History*, 2:286.)

9. A reference to postmaster general Amos Kendall who restricted abolitionists' use of the mail. Loco-Foco Democrats, like Kendall, supported President Martin Van Buren's subtreasury bill.

10. Angelina Emily Grimké Weld (1805–1879) gave birth to her first child, Charles Stuart Weld, on 13 December 1839. Angelina and her older sister Sarah Moore Grimké (1792–1873) left their slaveowning family in South Carolina in the 1820s to live in Philadelphia and, by 1835, began to work for the abolition of slavery. Eloquent speakers with first-hand knowledge of their subject, they found audiences in female antislavery societies but soon attracted large, mixed audiences. Their unseemly behavior of preaching to men elicited sharp attacks from the New England clergy and precipitated the crisis over women's role in antislavery work. Undaunted by opposition, the sisters continued to lecture and advocated woman's liberation while presenting the case for liberating the slave. Since Angelina's marriage in 1838 to Henry Stanton's teacher and close friend Theodore Dwight Weld (1803–1895), she and Sarah had retired from the platform. Living legends by 1840, the sisters had written important statements about women's duties and capacities that continued to influence abolitionists. For the Anti-Slavery Convention of American Women in 1837, Angelina Grimké wrote *An Appeal to the Women of the Nominally Free States* (1837), about woman's responsibility to help end slavery and her duty to participate in this public and political cause. In 1838 Sarah Grimké published *Letters on the Equality of the Sexes and the Condition of Woman* (1838), in which she denied any biblical justification for women to occupy an inferior position and called for woman's rights. (*NAW*; Gerda Lerner, *The Grimké Sisters from South Carolina: Pioneers for Woman's Rights and Abolition* [New York, 1971]; Benjamin P. Thomas, *Theodore Weld: Crusader for Freedom* [New Brunswick, N.J., 1950].)

·✠————✠————✠·

EDITORIAL NOTE: A significant turn of events occurred which no contemporary documents explain. Elizabeth Cady married Henry B. Stanton at Johnstown, New York, on 1 May 1840. According to her autobiography, published in 1898, she had broken her engagement to end "months of anxiety and bewilderment"; then, "suddenly I decided to renew it, as Mr. Stanton was going to Europe as a delegate to the World's Anti-Slavery Convention, and we did not wish the ocean to roll between us." Neither her letters after March 4 and before June 25 nor information about Daniel Cady's appeasement have been found. Theodore Weld knew their plans by April 10. Henry Stanton, who had not collected his salary from the antislavery society for two years, was "now in circumstances which imperatively demand the whole of it or nearly all by the first of May. I am not at liberty to explain," Weld wrote to Lewis Tappan. On April 17 Stanton swore Gerrit Smith to secrecy about his hopes to visit Peterboro on May 2 with Elizabeth. "We may come in chains," he wrote, "& much as you abhor thralldom, we shall totally dissent from any proposition of emancipation, immediate or gradual, present or prospective!" "A few friends," ECS recalled, witnessed the ceremony performed by Johnstown's Presbyterian minister. The newlyweds traveled to New York City and prepared to leave for England, making a last-minute change to sail on May 11 with Henry's good friend and Liberty party presidential candidate James G. Birney. (Genealogical files, notes from Presbyterian Church records, NJost; *Eighty Years*, 71–72; T. D. Weld to L. Tappan, 10 April 1840, Weld-Grimké, *Letters*, 2:828; H. B. Stanton to G. Smith, 17 April, 10 May 1840, Smith Papers, NSyU.)

·✠————✠————✠·

3   ∽   ECS TO SARAH M. GRIMKÉ AND ANGELINA GRIMKÉ WELD

London June 25th 1840

Dear sisters, Sarah & Angelina

    Yesterday the convention closed, & I hasten to redeem my promise, to tell you something about it.[1] We send you papers containing a minute account of all the proceedings, therefore I shall be very general in what I write. All things considered the convention has passed off more smoothly than any of us anticipated. The woman's rights question besides monopolizing one whole day has by being often referred to, created some little discord, for on this point we find a difference of opinion among the men & women here as well as with us in America. Garrison arrived on the fourth day of the meeting, but as the female delegates were not received and were not permitted to take their seats as delegates, he refused to take his, consequently his voice was not heard throughout the meeting.[2] However last evening he opened his mouth, & forth came, in my opinion, much folly,—a party was given to foreign delegates at the Crown & anchor Hotel (a famous place for whig celebrations to which we all adjourned from Exeter Hall—there in a spacious room, where Fox[3] used to give great dinners to his whig friends, a feast was spread for us after which instead of toasts & jokes we had antislavery speeches. Garrison took this opportunity to relieve his full heart. This being a social occasion, & in no way connected with the convention he thought he might do so without sacrificing principle. This was his first appearance & he was received with many cheers, but oh! how soon by his want of judgement did he change the current of feeling in his audience,—a general look of disappointment was visible among the English ere he had spoken long. The chairman (for these social meetings which are frequent here are conducted with great order) was obliged to call him to order for wandering from the subject of conversation, which by general consent was to be slavery. Garrison touched dwelt I might rather say, on woman's rights, poor laws, temperance, &c &c and last of all stirred up the ire of Dr Hoby, he accused him of having proved recreant to the cause of abolition when in America—up jumped Dr Hoby red in the face, & declared that he had always acted right (would that all men could say that)—then came a scene which ended by the two gentlemen complimenting e[ach] other, shaking hands & then at the request of the chairman sitting down. George Bradburn attacked Dr Cox one day in the convention, he unlike Dr Hoby acknowledged that his course in America had not been magnanimous.[4] Mr Birney thinks his confession does him great honour.[5] Thomas Clarkson has been our chairman occassionally for a short time. He took the chair at the opening of the meeting & said a few words. Sunday evening he called on the American ladies[6] (we are all staying at the same house) each one of us had the pleasure of taking the hand of that venerable man, & conversing with him a few minnits. His daughter gave us each a lock of his hair. Thomas Clarkson Jun. is a fine lad of nine years of age, the only remaining representative of his worthy grandfather. We have been very kindly received here, & treated with great attention. I have seen your dear friend Elizabeth Peas, she complains very much that you do not write to her.[7] I made your apologies but I do not think that they satisfied her. Anna Braithwaite an old friend of your family, has made many kind inquiries after you.[8] Lucretia Mott[9] has just giving me a long message for you, which condensed is that she thinks you have both been in a state of retiracy long enough, & that it is not right for you to be still, longer, that you should either write for the public or speak out for oppressed woman. Sarah in particular she thinks should appear in public again as she has no duties to prevent her. She says a great struggle is at hand & that all the friends of freedom for woman must rally round the Garrison standard. I have had much conversation with Lucretia Mott & I think her a peerless woman. She has a clear head & a warm heart—her views are many of them so new & strange that my causality[10] finds great delight in her society. The quakers here have not all received her cordially, they fear her heretical notions. I am often asked if you have not changed your opinions on woman's rights & I have invariably taken the liberty to say no, though John Scoble[11] has always contradicted me. who is right? I heard a very interesting discussion between him & Elizabeth Peas last evening on woman's rights.— She fairly vanquished him I thought for he took refuge under man's strongest weapon in contest with woman—flattery. I have seen Amelia Opie & Elizabeth Fry[12] & had the pleasure of a long talk in a corner with each of them. They are both interesting to me. They converse in a plain way, not fluently & their language not elegant, but they talk as those who have been accustomed to think. These women all know Angelina W[eld] & I am often called upon to describe the dear lady. Your names are always mentioned with great enthusiasm. You would laugh I am sure to see the look of surprize when to the list of virtues I add your great skill in discharging all your domestic avocations. Dear friends how much I love you!! What a trio! for me to love. You have no idea what a hold you have on my heart. The two green spots to me in America are the peaceful abodes of cousin Garrit & Theodore Weld. oh! I cannot tell you with what delight I look forward to the many hours I hope to spend in those places of pleasant memories. Do dear friends write a few lines to me & ask dear Theodore to lay down his hoe & add one line. My heart was very sad in parting with him. He reminded me so much of my dear Brother Bayard, the same originality & freedom of thought characterizes both, though I think Theodore the greater of the two, for he is morally as well as intellectually great. But I must tell you about our voyage. We had a pleasant passage of twenty one days, no storms, nor gales, nor anything to frighten us   Mr Birney was sick all the time, Henry & I not at all. I grew very weary after a week passed away, for we had no pleasant companions on board & Mr Birney kept to himself like a clam in his shell all the time. We saw no wonders except the nautilus & mother Carey's chickens.[13] Henry wishes me to say that he attributes his freedom from sea-sickness <u>to his strict observance of the Graham system</u>.[14] Your dear friends Charles Stewart & George Thompson[15] are well I see them often. O'Connell has spoken several times in the convention. I like him very much   He intends to address a letter to his country-men in America on slavery. I hope it may have a good effect. He wrote a long letter to Mrs Mott, showing, by many good reasons that the convention had no right to refuse any delegates that were sent to the <u>world's convention</u>.[16] Guizot the French minister made a short speech in Exeter Hall. Have you read his work on civilization?[17] my brother used to get his strongest arguments against immediate abolition from that work. I wish dear Theodore would pick him to pieces. Amelia Opie told me that he was a gradualist. It was said you know that the French had acknowledged the independance of Texas, their delegates deny it[18] [*concluded sideways in margin of first page*] I fear dear friends this will not be a satisfactory letter to you, my excuse is that there is so many things to tell that I do not what to tell first. I leave the external world for Henry to describe. I feel more interest in Amelia Opie than in Westminster Abbey. I feel that I should tell you much more about the convention but I have so many letters to write that I must refer you to the papers for information   Henry sends love to all adieu dear friends.— Pray for us—kiss Charly for me   Yours in love

✒ *Elizabeth C. Stanton*

✒ ALS, Weld-Grimké Papers, MiU-C. Words obscured by damage are supplied in square brackets.

1. The Stantons arrived in London on 3 June 1840 to prepare for Henry's participation in the General (or World's) Anti-Slavery Convention that opened

on 12 June in Freemason's Hall. Called together by the British and Foreign Anti-Slavery Society, four hundred delegates considered a full agenda on slavery and the slave trade before adjourning on 23 June. On the first day, the delegates voted to reject the credentials of women from American antislavery societies and provided them with tickets to the visitors' gallery. (General Anti-Slavery Convention, *Proceedings of the General Anti-Slavery Convention Called by the Committee of the British and Foreign Anti-Slavery Society and Held in London from Friday, June 12th, to Tuesday, June 23rd, 1840* [London, 1841]; Lucretia Mott, *Slavery and "The Woman Question": Lucretia Mott's Diary of Her Visit to Great Britain to Attend the World's Anti-Slavery Convention of 1840*, ed. Frederick B. Tolles [Haverford, Pa., 1952].)

2. William Lloyd Garrison (1805–1879), the most influential American abolitionist, arrived triumphant from the annual meeting of the American Anti-Slavery Society in New York, where his followers routed the opposition to their radical platform. Beginning in 1831, he had defined the standard for opponents of slavery as immediate emancipation of slaves and recognition that the sin of slavery was its violation of the human rights of its victims. Antislavery societies coalesced around that standard. By 1840 a belief in immediate emancipation was not in itself enough to hold together the complex movement that grew rapidly in its first decade. Garrison's commitment to women's right to be antislavery activists precipitated a series of divisions over the movement's relationship to churches, the Constitution, and political action, and over the authority of Garrison himself. (*DAB*; Garrison, *Letters*, passim; Aileen Kraditor, *Means and Ends in American Abolitionism: Garrison and His Critics on Strategy and Tactics, 1834–1850* [New York, 1969].)

3. The meeting at Exeter Hall and the reception at the Crown and Anchor occurred after the convention's adjournment. Charles James Fox (1749–1806), member of Parliament and foreign secretary, opposed regulatory measures to improve the British slave trade, insisting that it be abolished instead.

4. Garrison and George Bradburn recalled the behavior of two Baptist ministers, James Hoby (1788–1871) and Francis Augustus Cox (1783–1853), on an American tour in 1835. Though they were instructed by the Board of Baptist Ministers in London to urge American Baptists to support emancipation, they refused to convey that message. Bradburn (1806–1880), an American delegate and a Unitarian minister, was elected to the Massachusetts legislature in 1839. Despite his close association with Garrison, in 1844 he joined the Liberty party to work alongside Henry Stanton. (Garrison, *Letters*, 2:113n, 588, 3:19n, 653.)

5. Well known in England for his dramatic decision to free his family's slaves in 1834 and become an outspoken advocate of abolition, James Gillespie Birney (1792–1857) was a southern lawyer and an accomplished writer and speaker. He worked as agent and executive secretary of the American Anti-Slavery Society in the late 1830s, but, like Henry Stanton, he believed in political action and the need for a third, antislavery party. On the eve of his

departure from New York for the London convention, he accepted the presidential nomination of the new Liberty party. (Fladeland, *James Gillespie Birney*.)

6. Thomas Clarkson (1760–1846) campaigned relentlessly to abolish the British slave trade. His only son, Thomas, died in an accident in 1837, leaving a widow, Mary Clarkson, and their five-year-old son Thomas. Clarkson brought his daughter-in-law and grandson to visit the American women. (Ellen Gibson Wilson, *Thomas Clarkson, A Biography* [New York, 1990]; Mott, *Slavery and "The Woman Question,"* 32–33.)

7. Elizabeth Pease (1807–1897), later Nichol, was an important link in the chain that joined British and American abolitionists, and she had corresponded with the Grimkés for several years. Living with her father, a Quaker manufacturer and reformer at Darlington, she became a leader of women in the antislavery cause. In 1840 she still resisted American advocacy of woman's rights, though in other respects she was an ardent partisan of William Lloyd Garrison. Pease married John Pringle Nichol, a professor at the University of Glasgow, in 1853, and lived the rest of her life in Scotland. She was later active in the Edinburgh woman suffrage movement. (Anna M. Stoddart, *Elizabeth Pease Nichol* [London, 1899]; Clare Midgley, *Women Against Slavery: The British Campaigns, 1780–1870* [London, 1992]; Clare Taylor, ed., *British and American Abolitionists: An Episode in Transatlantic Understanding* [Edinburgh, 1974].)

8. Anna Lloyd Braithwaite (1788–1859), a minister of the Society of Friends, toured the United States three times in the 1820s and knew Sarah Grimké from her stays in Philadelphia. (J. Bevan Braithwaite, *Memoirs of Anna Braithwaite* [London, 1905].)

9. Lucretia Coffin Mott (1793–1880) sailed to London with credentials from the Pennsylvania Anti-Slavery Society and the Philadelphia Female Anti-Slavery Society. She was one of the country's most respected abolitionists and a leader and minister among Hicksite Quakers. There were strong suspicions that she was the prime target of the movement to reject women, that orthodox Friends in England insisted she be barred from the convention for her heretical views. "It is a pity," a liberal Friend in London wrote her on 27 June, "that you were excluded on the plea of being women; but it is disgusting that under that plea you were actually excluded as heretics. That is the real ground, and it ought to have been at once proclaimed and exposed by the liberal members of the Convention." (William Howitt to L. C. Mott, *History*, 1:434.) Born on Nantucket and educated at the Nine Partners School of the Society of Friends, she was married in 1811 to her fellow student James Mott (1788–1868), who became a merchant in Philadelphia. There she raised six children. Intensely religious but an independent thinker, she left the orthodox Friends because she believed that responsibility for a righteous life rested on the individual, guided by an unmediated understanding of the word of God. That commitment to individualism carried her into the antislavery movement where she

was noted for her work for racial justice in the North as well as abolition in the South. Just as she would purge religion of its customs and hierarchies, she would purge the world of superstition and intolerance. She was, ECS wrote, "emancipated from all faith in man-made creeds, from all fear of his denunciations. Nothing was too sacred for her to question, as to its rightfulness in principle and practice." (*History*, 1:422.) Mott provided the bridge between the abolitionist and woman's rights movements, both by the example of her own intellect and by her network of friends. (*NAW*; Anna Davis Hallowell, ed., *James and Lucretia Mott. Life and Letters* [Boston, 1884]; Otelia Cromwell, *Lucretia Mott* [Cambridge, Mass., 1958]; Margaret Hope Bacon, *Valiant Friend: The Life of Lucretia Mott* [New York, 1980]; Lucretia Mott, *Lucretia Mott: Her Complete Speeches and Sermons*, ed. Dana Greene [New York, 1980]; *History*, 1:407–40; Whittier, *Letters*, 1:439–49, 458–59, 466–68.)

10. One of the mental faculties identified by phrenologists, "causality" was defined as the "ability to reason and comprehend first principles; the why and wherefore faculty." According to the science of phrenology, each mental faculty conformed to a part of the skull and could be identified and measured in a person's character by the shape and bumps of the skull. (*American Phrenological Journal* 15 [January 1852]: 23.)

11. John Scoble (c. 1810–c. 1868), British clergyman and an early worker in the transatlantic antislavery movement, visited the Weld and Grimké household in 1839, after completing an enquiry into the apprenticeship system in the West Indies. He opposed giving women a greater role in agitation. Scoble, James Birney, and Henry Stanton toured the British Isles after the convention. (Douglass, *Papers*, 2:338n; Weld-Grimké, *Letters*, 2:791–92; Annie Heloise Abel and Frank J. Klingberg, eds., *A Side-Light on Anglo-American Relations, 1839–1858* [Lancaster, Pa., 1927].)

12. Amelia Alderson Opie (1769–1853) was a poet and, before becoming a Quaker in 1825, a novelist, who had known Mary Wollstonecraft in London. She entertained the Stantons at Norwich in November 1840 and corresponded with ECS. Her friend Elizabeth Gurney Fry (1780–1845), an English Quaker, was well known as a prison reformer, especially for her efforts to help female prisoners at Newgate. (*DNB*.)

13. Since ancient times, sailors described one of the maritime mollusks as a nautilus sailing on the ocean's surface. Alexander Pope listed it among nature's models for human behavior: "Learn of the little Nautilus to sail,/Spread the thin oar, and catch the driving gale." ("Essay on Man," epistle 3, lines 177–78.) Mother Carey's Chickens was a popular name for the birds seen skimming the water in a ship's wake, often specifically the Wilson's Petrel.

14. Sylvester Graham (1794–1851), health reformer, advocated a diet of whole wheat flour and no stimulants. The Welds followed his regimen, as ECS discovered on a visit just before she sailed for London. The "peculiar table arrangements," she recalled, consisted of "cold dishes without a whiff of heat,

or steam" and no tea or coffee. "There was no catering in this household to the weaknesses of those who were not weaned from the flesh-pots of Egypt." (*History*, 1:392.)

15. Charles Stuart (not Stewart) and George Thompson were both well known in England and America for their passionate opposition to slavery. Stuart (1781–1865) retired from military service in India to teach in Utica, New York, where his students included Theodore Weld. Despite his conservatism about women's role in the movement, he remained a close friend of Weld. (Anthony J. Barker, *Captain Charles Stuart, Anglo-American Abolitionist* [Baton Rouge, 1986].) Thompson (1804–1878) was Garrison's chief ally in Great Britain and a fiery, fearless orator, whose American tour against slavery in 1834 and 1835 touched off riots in northern cities. His reformism extended to the British anti-corn law movement and British rule in India. He returned to the United States to lecture in 1850. (*DNB*.)

16. Daniel O'Connell (1775–1847) was the first Irish Catholic to take his seat in Parliament, a brilliant spokesman for Irish rights, and an opponent of slavery. He made several visits to the women delegates at their gallery seats during the convention and responded to Lucretia Mott's request for a letter protesting their exclusion. (*DNB*; Mott, *Slavery and "The Woman Question,"* 34; *Lib.*, 4 September 1841.)

17. François Pierre Guillaume Guizot (1787–1874) first published his *Histoire de la civilization en Europe depuis la chute de l'Empire romain jusqu'à la révolution française* in 1828. He had just become France's ambassador in London. ECS probably refers to her brother-*in-law* Edward Bayard. Eleazer Cady, her only brother to live past childhood, died in 1826 at age twenty.

18. ECS misunderstood the discussion; France had already recognized the independent republic of Texas. After a debate led by James G. Birney, the convention resolved that Texas "ought not to be received into the family of nations" while its constitution upheld slavery. (*Proceedings of the General Anti-Slavery Convention, 1840*, 454–59.)

4　⇒　ECS TO GERRIT SMITH

York August 3rd [*1840*]

Dear Cousin,

We hear that in America you abolitionists are sad & depressed, there are so many clouds darkening your horizon & I wonder not. The thought that three millions of our fellow beings and country men groan in bondage & the day of their freedom yet uncertain (though it will surely come) is enough to sadden any heart. Would that you were here you would find much to cheer you. Mr Birney   Mr Scoble, Henry & myself are going through all the principle towns in the Kingdom.[1] These three gentlemen lecture almost every evening—horrifying the British public with the enormities of our slavery system. Loud cries of shame! shame! fill the House whenever the negro pew[2] is mentioned, & the bursts of indignation that follow some of Henry's graphic descriptions are music to an antislavery ear. We are kindly & warmly received everywhere,—we find it is no disgrace to be an abolitionist in England, but requires some moral courage not to be one, as many of our eloquent clergy have proved. What does cousin Margaret say of Mr Kirks course.[3] Night after night we hear many of the British clergy of all sects, declare most solemnly that no American clergyman who is not an abolitionist in <u>America</u> both in theory & practise, shall ever[4] enter their pulpits again. At all these meetings we have some great personage in the chair, some member of the royal family, or a sir or the mayor of the town, in which we may be. Tell Libby Mr Birney is much admired by all the ladies young & old, & indeed he is a noble man & I like him very much, though he lectures me occasionally through Henry for my want of discretion. He is almost too discreet I think, too fearful of what "the people" may say. When we were at sea the Captain dared me to be hoisted to the top of the mast in a chair, so for a piece of ↑fun↓ one day when all the passengers were at dinner I went up, & would you believe it—it quite distressed Mr Birney, he thought it very undignified on my part. However it will do me no harm to be checked occasionally, & as we are among strangers & on such a mission we cannot be too serious. I feel that I am a little too gay, & much too ignorant on the subject of slavery for the circumstances in which I am placed. I hope cousin Nancy will write me one of her long serious letters often. Henry often wishes that I was more like her. I console him by telling him that cousin Nancy was quite gay & frolicksome once. We are going to Scotland & Ireland. I received a letter from home a few days since, saying that Cousin Garrit had pub[lish]ed an letter saying that nothing more could be done in America by the abolitionists. I am sure it must be a mistake.[5] You will have seen James C. Fuller before you receive this,— & he will no doubt give you much pleasing information about the state of public feeling here, & his success in raising funds, for the free slaves who have escaped to Canada.[6] As Henry wishes to add a few lines I must bid you adieu. Much love to cousin Nancy & Libby. I am glad to hear that your health is improving—your cousin

↣ *Elizabeth C Stanton*

↣ ALS, Smith Papers, NSyU. Words obscured by a tear are supplied in square brackets. In a short note following this letter, Henry Stanton described the same aspects of his tour and spoke enthusiastically about returning to work in America.

1. Under the auspices of the British and Foreign Anti-Slavery Society, Henry Stanton lectured for several months after the convention's close, holding four or five meetings a week in most of the principal cities. He described American slavery, emphasized the complicity of the churches in its survival, and pointed out how Britain could help to overthrow it. ECS traveled with him part of the time. (Abel and Klingberg, *Side-Light on Anglo-American Relations*, 71–77; Fladeland, *James Gillespie Birney*, chap. 10; H. B. Stanton to G. Smith, 22 September 1840, Smith Papers, NSyU.)

2. The emblem of racial segregation in American churches.

3. Margaret Smith of Albany, who addressed Gerrit Smith as "cousin." The revivalist pastor of Albany's Fourth Presbyterian Church from 1829 to 1837, Edward Norris Kirk (1802–1874) was one American preacher who declared his opposition to slavery, and he had welcomed Gerrit Smith, Alvan Stewart, and George Thompson to deliver their abolitionist views at his church. After an extended European tour, Kirk returned in 1839 to begin a series of revivals in the major cities along the East Coast. By summer he had reached Boston, where he later settled to lead the Mount Vernon Church. (David O. Mears, *Life of Edward Norris Kirk, D.D.* [Boston, 1877].)

4. Another hand added an "n" to this word: "shall never enter."

5. In private Smith wrote that he was sick of the quarrels among abolitionists and unwilling to line up with either the American Anti-Slavery Society or its new rival the American and Foreign Anti-Slavery Society; "*for the present* at least, these organizations will be the occasion of keeping up and aggravating these quarrels." (G. Smith to Theodore Weld, 11 July 1840, Weld-Grimké, *Letters*, 2:849–50.)

6. James Cannings Fuller (1793–1847), of New York, attended the convention in London while in England raising money for a manual training school, intended to benefit blacks living in Canada West. Opened in 1842, the British-American Institute became the center of a community called Dawn, near Dresden. Fuller moved his family from England in 1834 and settled at Skaneateles where various radicals tried to establish a communal farm. (William H. Pease and Jane Pease, *Black Utopia: Negro Communal Experiments in America* [Madison, Wis., 1963], 63–83; *Lib.*, 10 December 1847; Garrison, *Letters*, 4:378n; Lester Grosvenor Wells, *The Skaneateles Communal Experiment, 1843–1846* [Syracuse, N.Y., 1953].)

5   ECS TO ELIZABETH J. NEALL[1]

Johnstown Jan 25th [*1841*][2]

Dear Lizzy

The "<u>invitation</u> <u>extraordinary</u>" came to me & I gave it a warm welcome as a token of remembrance from a dear friend, & most gladly will I obey its call & fulfill my promises at some future time, not far distant. Perhaps I will return home with thee after the meeting in May at New York,[3] when I sincerely hope to meet you all. Henry & I are quite undecided as to our future occupation & place of residence. We shall pass the winter in visiting our friends, beyond that we have no plans. To morrow morning we are going to Peterboro, where we shall probably meet Mr Birney. Cousin Gerrit is blowing a little flame between Mr Birney & cousin Nancy's sister, Elizabeth Fitzhue. She is a woman of years & fortune. I think it would be a very suitable match, & I do hope his honour the "Judge" may succeed.[4] I did not see the Weld's tho' I spent a fortnight in New York. I regretted very much not seeing them, but we had a letter from Theodore saying that Angelina was on the eve of her confinement, (her son Charles Stuart is not much over a year old) that of course prevented us from visiting them[5] I had a letter from Angelina at New York among other things she says their views on the woman question are <u>un</u>changed & <u>un</u>changeable. I used to tell John Scoble so, but he invariably contradicted me. Our visit to England has been of much use to the women there.— They are now forming large societies in many towns, not for <u>sewing</u> but for raising funds in various ways to aid us in our struggle. They assemble once a week to get & impart what information †they can↓ on the subject of slavery as it exists the world over. Charles Stuart is the active agent in forming these societies.[6] I found many many women fully & painfully convinced of our present degradation as women. Oh! Lizzy what a voyage we had from Liverpool to Boston, head winds & storms all the time. I suffered dreadfully ~~all the time~~, for seventeen days & nights, except the few hours I spent in Halifax I have resolved "to tempt the seas no more" But oh! what bliss did I know when we entered the beautiful harbour at Boston one bright & sunny afternoon, it more than repaid me for all my ocean woes, & oh! what a supper I did eat that night & how I did caper on terra firma. Depend it upon the ocean was never made for man nor woman. I have been very happy & very busy ever since my return & have not felt any of that loneliness of which you complain. So you are studying German & French, well I am not behind you in the way of new occupations. I am mending shirts &c, & knitting grey socks. I trust we shall both be much improved ere we meet again. The subduing influence of German upon your tongue will not surpass the effect of "lessons in economy" upon my extravagant nature   I met a Mr Collins in London from Boston & enjoyed many long conversations with him   I thought him a "clever" man, but I heard sad tales of him in New York. do you know him?[7] I read an article of John G's in the "friend of man" about the convention. I am sorry he is not right on the woman question.[8] You must never say yea Lizzy until he renounces all divine right to govern you or decide in all cases where you differ. dear me! what a mighty shadow some of Paul's private opinions have afforded, under which all the "Lords of Creation" may shelter their cruelties & wrongs towards woman & make injustice a divine command[9] [*sideways on first page*] I have written to Sarah Pugh.[10] Henry joins me in much love to you. I shall be happy to hear from you often Direct to Johnstown, Fulton Co. N.Y. I shall be here again in a few weeks. —adieu your friend

⟡ *Elizabeth Cady Stanton*

[*at top of first page*] Much love to my dear friends Mr & Mrs Mott

⟡ ALS, Sydney Howard Gay Papers, Rare Book and Manuscript Library, NNC.

1. Elizabeth Johns Neall (1819–1907), later Gay, attended the London convention as a delegate of Philadelphia's Female Anti-Slavery Society. Her Quaker family was distinguished for its abolitionism; her grandfather Warner Mifflin freed his slaves in the eighteenth century; Daniel Neall, Sr., her father, was an effective speaker and local leader; at age seventeen, in 1837, she attended the Anti-Slavery Convention of American Women in New York. An invaluable member of her antislavery society, she resisted efforts to make her a lecturing agent. Despite rumors she would marry John G. Whittier, she married Sydney Howard Gay in 1845. (Whittier, *Letters*, vol. 1, passim; *Quaker Genealogy*, 2:757, 811, 902; *Friends' Intelligencer* 64 [1907]: 816; Dorothy Sterling, *Ahead of Her Time: Abby Kelley and the Politics of Antislavery* [New York, 1991], 166–67.)

2. The Stantons landed on 21 December 1840 on board the *Acadia*. They reached Johnstown on 7 January 1841, after visiting New York City. (H. B. Stanton to Gerrit Smith, 8 January 1841, Smith Papers, NSyU.)

3. ECS anticipates anniversary week in New York City, when antislavery societies held their annual meetings.

4. James Birney married Elizabeth P. Fitzhugh on 25 March 1841. He attended Princeton with her brother Daniel and knew her sister Ann Smith through his friendship with Gerrit Smith. In calling Birney "the Judge," ECS may refer to an incident in Dublin, when Daniel O'Connell introduced "Judge Birney" to a meeting. To Birney's protest that he had no claim to the title, O'Connell replied, "If you are not one, you well deserve to be one." (Fladeland, *James Gillespie Birney*, 204, 207; [Elbridge J. Cutler], *Fitzhugh Birney. A Memoir* [Cambridge, Mass., 1866].)

5. The Welds' second child Theodore Grimké Weld was born 3 January 1841.

6. Rival antislavery organizations targeted British women after the London convention, and Stuart organized societies into alliance with the British and Foreign Anti-Slavery Society, while attacking the "woman intrusion" that spoiled Garrisonian societies. (Midgley, *Women Against Slavery*, 124, 162; John A. Collins to Maria Weston Chapman, 3 December 1840, and Sarah M. Grimké to Elizabeth Pease, 11 February 1842, in Taylor, *British and American Abolitionists*, 128, 163.)

7. John Anderson Collins (1810–1879) neglected to tell ECS that his mission to England entailed promoting the Garrisonian wing of American abolitionism at the expense of Henry Stanton's reputation. In England to raise money for the American Anti-Slavery Society, he dogged Stanton, Birney, and Scoble on their tour and accused them, in a letter to Garrison, of "sow[ing] discord & retail[ing] falsehood & calumny." (*DAB*; J. A. Collins to W. L. Garrison, 27 December 1840, in Taylor, *British and American Abolitionists*, 134.)

8. ECS probably mistook one antislavery paper for another. Whittier's letter appeared in the *Pennsylvania Freeman*, 19 November 1840. "The rejection of the women delegates," he wrote, "seems to me to afford no just grounds or even excuse for a general and sweeping condemnation of that great and important meeting. . . . Whatever may be our opinions of the disposal of the question of 'women's rights' or of any other distinct and extraneous matter,— let us see to it that we do not gladden the heart of the slave-holder, by depreciating and undervaluing its really glorious anti-slavery character." (Whittier, *Letters*, 1:439–49.)

9. As Sarah Grimké phrased it, the "principle support of the dogma of woman's inferiority, and consequent submission to her husband is found in some passages of Paul's epistles." Much of the New Testament is about or by the apostle Paul, who converted to Christianity after Jesus' death and dedicated his life to preaching the faith. Paul directed wives to "submit yourselves

unto your own husbands, as it is fit in the Lord." (Col. 3:18.) As man had been made in the image of God, so woman was "the glory of man," and "neither was the man created for the woman; but the woman for the man." (1 Cor. 11:7–9.) In addition, Paul commanded women to "keep silence in the churches"; "if they will learn anything, let them ask their husbands at home: for it is a shame for women to speak in church." (1 Cor. 14:34–35.) Paul's teachings on women influenced both canon and civil law and were used in arguments against granting women an equal voice in church and state. (Sarah M. Grimké, *Letters on the Equality of the Sexes and the Condition of Woman* [1838; reprint, New York, 1970], 91; *History*, 1:81–82.)

10. Sarah Pugh (1800–1884) was another delegate to the London meeting from Philadelphia who toured France with the Stantons in July. A former Quaker and a teacher, Pugh was the mainstay of the Philadelphia Female Anti-Slavery Society. In cooperation with Lucretia Mott, she joined the local agitation for woman's rights and helped to organize the national convention at Philadelphia in 1854. After the war she continued to be active in the woman suffrage movement. (*NAW; Eighty Years*, 93; *Memorial of Sarah Pugh. A Tribute of Respect From Her Cousins* [Philadelphia, 1888]; *History*, 1:327, 337, 376, 814.)

·⊂══════⊃·

6 ⤳ LUCRETIA COFFIN MOTT TO ECS

Philada. 3 mo. 23rd. 1841

My dear Eliz^h

With Sarah Pugh and Lizzy Neall for thy correspondents, I cannot hope to convey much that will be new or interesting; but for the love I bear thee, my dear girl, thy cousins must not go without a line, expressive of my interest in you both;[1] for let me assure Henry, that from the hour he came here—an unsophisticated "Lane Seminary boy," he has had our best wishes; as well as ⌜of late⌟ our fears, lest he would give too much aid to new-organization. But we'll let that pass— He and J. G. W.[2] too must not forget their first love. If such a thing is possible as an honest & <u>Christian</u> lawyer, in this day of over-reaching, I hope he may be successful in his new pursuit.[3]

And my dear, what is the result of all the enquiries of thy open, generous confiding spirit? Art thou settled on the sure foundation, of the revealed will of God to the inner sense? Or is thy mind still perplexed with the schemes of salvation, and plans of redemption which are taught in the schools of Theology? It is lamentable, that the simple & benign religion of Jesus should be so encumbered with the creeds & dogmas of sects— Its primitive beauty obscured by these gloomy appendages of man— The investigations of the honest inquirer checked by the cry of heresy—infidelity! Thou knows how it was in London—thou knows too, that I have no wish to proselyte to any speculative opinions I may hold; but all may know, for I proclaim it abroad, that I long to see obedience to manifested duty—leading to practical righteousness, as the christian's standard—the test of discipleship—the fruit of faith. Then large liberty—unbounded toleration—yes "Religious right," as to forms of worship and abstract theories.[4]

This most excellent Charity will not forbid our calling the attention of those, who are superstitiously dwelling in the shadows & figures of the true, to what we may deem a more enlightened and better understanding of the law of Christ.— But this is not what I took the pen for. It was to tell thee how well I love you both, and how much we want to see you. When are we to have this said visit? It must be soon or we fear not at all, this year. Dont let peculiar circumstances discourage.[5] We are all "own folks" here, at least we feel so, & it will give us the most sincere pleasure to welcome you at 136 North 9th st. Thou must not feel as thou did in England when travelling with Henry & stopping at fr^{ds} houses. But was'nt that, take it altogether a pleasant visit & tour?

I ever dwell on it with delight. George Combe, in a letter to us, speaks of Henry's call as giving him pleasure. He has presented me a copy of his "Notes" on this country.[6] The work will be out in a week or two. I have a nice letter from Dr Channing acknowl^g Lady Byron's present—[7] Come and see it. We have also a lot of beautiful gifts from our anti-S. fr^{ds} in England—the Ashurst's—Wade's &c[8]

We regret much that we have had so little of the company of thy cousins. We have been waiting for the returning health of Gerritt Smith, so as to enjoy their society—and here now they are going away to leave us.

Eliz^h kindly called with thy letter this morn^g. And thou art a Homeopathist—a believer in Animal magnetism too!—[9] Well there is no harm in investigation—and surely the 'Faculty' have need to be distrustful of their conflicting theories. Tell Henry to remember the anniversary of our state society is approaching.[10] He must not let the study of Law be all-absorbing—forget not that he early dedicated himself to the slave's cause. How glad we were that you went to Dublin & saw our dear friends there;[11] come & talk about them. My Husband dont know that I am writing, but he loves thee dearly & often talks about thee. Most fondly thine

⤜ *L. Mott*

⤜ ALS, ECS Papers, DLC. Transcript in ECS Papers, NjR.

1. Gerrit, Nancy, and Elizabeth Smith were again in Philadelphia and carried this and a letter from Sarah Pugh to ECS at Johnstown. (S. Pugh to ECS, 24 March 1841, *Film*, 6:423.)

2. That is, John Greenleaf Whittier.

3. Henry Stanton began to study law with Daniel Cady on 23 February 1841.

4. These phrases appear in one of Mott's sermons, reported at Marlboro Chapel, Boston, in September 1841. (Mott, *Complete Speeches*, 25–34.)

5. Mott alludes to the division in antislavery ranks that put Henry Stanton at odds with Garrisonians like herself.

6. George Combe (1788–1858), a Scottish phrenologist, published *Notes on the United States of North America During a Phrenological Visit* in 1841. He described a visit with the Motts in Philadelphia and their visit to his home in Scotland. Stanton called on Combe sometime after he and ECS arrived in Edinburgh on 13 October 1840. (*DNB*.)

7. Anna Isabella Milbanke, Lady Byron (1792–1860), also known as Lady Noel Byron, married the poet Lord Byron in 1815 and separated from him a year later. She befriended Mott in London and asked her to carry an engraving to William Ellery Channing (1780–1842), a leading Unitarian preacher in Boston and author of the influential *Essay on Slavery* (1835). (Joyce Bellamy and John Saville, eds., *Dictionary of Labour Biography* [London, 1972–1979]; Mott, *Slavery and "The Woman Question,"* 54; *DAB*.)

8. William Henry Ashurst (1792–1855), a London lawyer and reformer of many interests, supported the right of American women to be seated at the convention in 1840 and urged that their exclusion be protested. One daughter, Elizabeth A. Ashurst (c. 1820–1850), accompanied him to the antislavery meetings. Mott may also refer to John Wade, a delegate to the convention from the Midland Association of Baptist Churches. (*DNB*; Mott, *Slavery and "The Woman Question,"* 34; Joseph O. Baylen and Norbert J. Gossman, eds., *Biographical Dictionary of Modern British Radicals*, vol. 2, *1830–1870* [Brighton, U.K., 1984].)

9. ECS wrote to her cousin that she intended "to commence life on Homeopathic principles" after witnessing "wonders in Homeopathy & Animal magnetism" at Seneca Falls. Essentially hypnotism, animal magnetism was a rage in medical experiments and in entertainment. (ECS to Elizabeth Smith, 17 March 1841, *Film*, 6:415.)

10. The Anti-Slavery Society of Eastern Pennsylvania convened on 6 May 1841 without Henry Stanton.

11. The Stantons stayed with the president of the Hibernian Anti-Slavery Society James Haughton (1795–1873) and visited Mott's good friends Richard Davis Webb (1805–1872) and his wife Hannah Waring Webb (1809–1862). They were co-workers and leaders among Irish reformers. (Abel and Klingberg, *Side-light on Anglo-American Relations*, 75n; Samuel Haughton, *Memoir of James Haughton. With Extracts From His Private and Published Letters* [Dublin, 1877]; Douglas C. Stange, *British Unitarians Against American Slavery, 1833–65* [Rutherford, N.J., 1984]; Garrison, *Letters*, 4:56n.)

·❮———— ❯❮ ————❯·

7 ➳ ECS to Elizabeth J. Neall

Johnstown Nov. 26th [*1841*]

Dear Lizzy,

Your letter dated Phil. July 18th was mailed at St Johnsville August 30th for Johnstown & about the last of September I received it at Seneca Falls, where I was until last week when I returned home,[1] & found a long interesting letter from dear Sarah Pugh. "Well" Lizzy the bright summer & autumn have passed & none of you have visited me, & now many months must necessarily pass ere we can meet, to talk over the wonderful things that have transpired during the last year or two, of our eventful lives. Oh! how much I have to tell you all of what happened to me after parting with you all in the old world, of facts, & of feelings since my return to my native land. It has been a sore trial to me not to have had for so long a time any opportunity of seeing or talking to my dear Philadelphia friends.— Your letter is before me, & as I read along, one sentence causes me to pause. You say, "How much I have regretted your absence from our business meetings during your stay in New York. We wished to ask you to go with us, but feared that you might be disinclined to do so & that you certainly would attend them had you cared for or been interested in them" Let me assure you that nothing would have pleased me more than to have been present at a womans business meeting, where I might have seen the faces & heard the voices of Abbey Kelly & Lydia M Child.[2] How could I know of the existence of such meetings no one told me. Had I known of them why should I have been disinclined to go? because Henry might not have wished me to go?— You do not know the extent to which I carry my rights. I do in truth think & act for myself deeming that I alone am responsible for the sayings & doings of E. C. S. I did not go to any business meetings with Henry because I knew I would have no voice in those meetings, & had I known of A.S. business meetings in which I should have been considered as an independant morally responsible being I should have been there if possible. Since I met you in New York be it known unto you that I have made my debut in public. I made a Temperance speech at Seneca Falls, & was so eloquent in my appeals as to affect not only my audience but myself to tears. The room in which I spoke was large & about an hundred women were present. I infused into my speech an Homeopathic dose of woman's rights, as I take good care to do in many private conversations. I intend to "keep it before the people"[3]   I have succeeded in getting two copies of Sarah Grimkè's letter, one is circulating in Seneca Falls & on in our village.[4] Do go round to the friends houses & collect all the copies of that work that you can find & send them forth to do good, if you will send me one I should be glad. I find that little book does "execution" what a pity that it is out of print. If you find any good articles in papers on the subject I wish you would send them to me. I do not take the A.S. Standard but a frien[d] of mine here takes it & I have the reading of it, & Sarah Pugh you know sends me the Liberator regularly, & that is the only woman's rights food I have for myself & disciples.[5] Charles Burleigh I see by the papers is in Ohio. I hope if he passes home this way he will stop & see us. His reception at Cincinnatti was rather troubled. I thought the age for abolition mobs had passed.[6] Are you among those who rejoice at the success of the "liberty party" I do very much.[7] The question of no ↑civil↓ government is so grea[t] a one that I cannot decide upon it just now. [*word torn away*] taking it then for granted that civil government [is?] right—it is important that our good men shoul[d] regulate this government, now our abolitionists are the best men in our country, & I should be unwilling that as a body they should exert no political influence. Slavery is a political question created & sustained by law, & must be put down by law. One great advantage of forming a party over that of scatteration is that in voting the abolitionists show their numbers, & make our corrupt politicians fear & tremble. There is great danger on the other hand of abolitionists themselves being corrupted, but it would take many years methinks to make them as a party so corrupt as either of our great national parties now are. I had a letter from Sarah Grimkè a short time since, they were all well when she wrote. I heard that Angelina & Sarah had made some public addresses this fall—Sarah did not mention it in her letter. I hope it is so— I spent a week at Peterboro on my way down. Mrs Smith expects to welcome a little stranger there in April—it is twelve years since a similar event occured under that roof.[8] Mrs Birney has been more expeditious, she will produce a new work in January, to her admiring husband & the public. I am looking learned too these days, as if I had conceived some great idea   <u>if my domestic cares are not too great</u> I shall come out with my first production in March. If the true sentiments of an author appear in his works [*sideways on first page*] then will my work ever breath love & justice equality for woman   I will write to Sarah Pugh soon. Mary Grew wrote me a long interesting & kind letter last winter which I am ashamed to say I have not yet answered. Give my love to her & tell her I have not forgotten her.[9] Remember me warmly to James & Lucretia Mott. I had the pleasure of meeting several agreeable friends at Waterloo & among the rest Lydia Mott, she is a charming woman.[10] She was [*sideways on second page*] under the care of my brother in law some time. He has abandoned the law & commenced the practice of Homeopathy.[11] [*sideways on third page*] Write to me often. Henry joins with me in much love to you & all your friend

   Elizabeth Cady Stanton.

[*sideways on fourth page*] You need not direct my letters to Henry unless you intend them for both of us   I am as well known here as he is

   ALS, Sydney Howard Gay Papers, Rare Book and Manuscript Library, NNC. Brackets surround words torn at margin.

     1. ECS spent the fall with her sister Tryphena Bayard. (H. B. Stanton to Gerrit Smith, 9 September 1841, Smith Papers, NSyU.)

     2. Neall referred to the American Anti-Slavery Society anniversary that opened on 11 May 1841. Now entirely Garrisonian, the society placed women on its business and executive committees. ECS accompanied Henry Stanton to New York for the rival American and Foreign Anti-Slavery Society meeting, also on 11 May, where opponents of women's collaboration prevailed. Abigail Kelley and Lydia Maria Child were prominent abolitionists. Kelley (1810–1887), later Foster, was a Quaker school teacher in Lynn, Massachusetts, when William Lloyd Garrison convinced her of the need for immediate eman-

cipation. After several years in the leadership of female antislavery societies, she began in 1839 to lecture to mixed audiences and became one of the movement's foremost speakers. Her encouragement of other, younger women to become antislavery agents brought both Lucy Stone and SBA to the platform. She was also respected for her strategic sense about where to concentrate resources and expand the movement. The decision to appoint her to the business committee of the American Anti-Slavery Society in 1840 precipitated the walkout by clerical and conservative abolitionists. In 1845 she married Stephen S. Foster, with whom she lived on a farm near Worcester, Massachusetts. Lydia Maria Francis Child (1802–1880), a professional writer, was also won over to abolitionism by Garrison and thereafter put her literary reputation and talent into service to the cause. *An Appeal in Favor of That Class of Americans Called Africans* (1833) influenced many people to oppose slavery and drew attention to the laws and customs by which the North practiced racial discrimination. Two years later she published *The History of the Condition of Women, in Various Ages and Nations*, in two volumes, a work that supplied Sarah Grimké, ECS, and a generation of activists with illustrations of women's oppression and achievement. She was named to the executive committee of the American Anti-Slavery Society in 1840, and in 1841 she became editor of the *National Anti-Slavery Standard*. (*Lib.*, 28 May 1841; *New York Herald*, 12 May 1841; *NAW*; Sterling, *Ahead of Her Time*; Carolyn L. Karcher, *The First Woman in the Republic: A Cultural Biography of Lydia Maria Child* [Durham, N.C., 1994].)

3. No record of this speech survives. Lucretia Mott copied this passage, beginning at "made a temperance speech," into a letter to Richard and Hannah Webb, 25 February 1842, Anti-Slavery Collection, MB.

4. *Letters on the Equality of the Sexes, and the Condition of Woman.*

5. The *National Anti-Slavery Standard*, organ of the American Anti-Slavery Society, began weekly publication on 11 June 1840. From 20 May 1841 to 4 May 1843, Lydia Maria Child was its editor. William Lloyd Garrison edited the *Liberator* weekly in Boston from 1 January 1831 to 29 December 1865.

6. Charles Calistus Burleigh (1810–1878) was mobbed at Cincinnati on 12 and 13 October. At the end of 1841 he returned east from a two-month tour in Ohio and Indiana through New York and apparently did meet up with the Stantons. (*DAB*; *NASS*, 4 November 1841, 13 January 1842; *Lib.*, 22 October, 12 November 1841; H. B. Stanton to Gerrit Smith, 4 December 1841, Smith Papers, NSyU; Lucretia Mott to Richard and Hannah Webb, 25 February 1842.)

7. Organized early in 1840, the Liberty party ran antislavery candidates for national and state offices until most of its supporters moved into the Free Soil party in 1848. Its first slate was headed by James G. Birney for president and Thomas Earle, a lawyer from Philadelphia, for vice president. At this date, Henry Stanton was active in the New York Liberty party, which ran state and local candidates in 1841, but he made his biggest contribution in Massachusetts

from 1842 to 1847. ECS defends the party against Garrisonian criticism. The "no-human-government" abolitionists argued that a moral stand against slavery necessitated withdrawing from politics and politicians under the proslavery Constitution of the United States. Their differences on the role of political action in overthrowing slavery caused Henry Stanton and William Lloyd Garrison to part company in the late 1830s, and many of the men who withdrew from the American Anti-Slavery Society in 1840 endorsed and worked for the Liberty party. (Arthur Harry Rice, "Henry B. Stanton as a Political Abolitionist" [Ed.D. diss., Columbia University, 1968], 229–66; Fladeland, *James Gillespie Birney*, 175–89; Harlow, *Gerrit Smith*, 136–92; Reinhard O. Johnson, "The Liberty Party in Massachusetts, 1840–1848: Antislavery Third Party Politics in the Bay State," *Civil War History* 28 [September 1982]: 237–65.)

8. Gerrit and Nancy Smith lost two young children, born after their daughter Elizabeth: Fitzhugh Smith (1824–1836) and Ann Smith (1830–1835).

9. Mary Grew (1813–1896), a pillar of Philadelphia's Female Anti-Slavery Society, attended the London antislavery convention, where her father, the Reverend Henry Grew, a delegate, spoke against accepting the credentials of women, including his daughter. From 1845 to 1850, she served on the editorial board of the *Pennsylvania Freeman*, and for six months in 1849 and 1850 she edited the paper. Grew campaigned for woman's rights with her friends Lucretia Mott and Sarah Pugh and helped to organize meetings in Pennsylvania. She served as president of the state's woman suffrage association from 1869 until 1892. (*NAW*; Ira V. Brown, *Mary Grew: Abolitionist and Feminist, 1813–1896* [Selinsgrove, Pa., 1991].)

10. A few miles west of Seneca Falls, Waterloo was home to several prominent Quaker families, including cousins of Elizabeth Neall. Lydia Mott (1807–1875) lived on Maiden Lane in Albany. At this address, famous among reformers and politicians, she provided a home for her sisters, fugitive slaves, and traveling abolitionists. A capable organizer, she had charge of conventions and legislative hearings for the antislavery movement; she was also, ECS wrote, "one of the quiet workers who kept all things pertaining to the woman's rights reform in motion at the capital." A distant relative of James Mott and the daughter of Long Island Quakers, she moved to Albany in 1824 to teach school. She also taught briefly in Philadelphia where SBA was her pupil. (SBA diary, 19 February, 8 March 1838, *Film*, 6:133ff; Thomas Clapp Cornell, *Adam and Anne Mott: Their Ancestors and Descendants* [Poughkeepsie, N.Y., 1890], 134, 219; *History*, 1:744–45n; *Woman's Journal*, 28 August 1875; obituaries in SBA scrapbook 8, Rare Books, DLC.)

11. That is, Edward Bayard.

·❮━━━━❧❮━━━━❯·

8 ❧ ECS TO ELIZABETH PEASE

Johnstown Feb 12th [*1842*]

Dear friend Elizabeth

As I set me down to write Henry says, "now Lizzy tell Miss Pease <u>all</u> the antislavery news," but as I glance at this small sheet, & remember what an amount of news there is to tell, & moreover that you take several American papers, I shall ↑not↓ enter into particulars, but merely say that our cause in this country is onward. I think the division so far from injuring the cause has been a decided benefit, if we except the bitter personal feeling which in some few cases has arisen between those of opposite opinions. There is in fact a third party, which is a sort of connecting link between the two grand divisions composed of those who have strong sympathies with both in many particulars. I am one of this party. I am an admirer of Garrison. He is a great reformer an honest, upright man, ever ready to sacrifice present interest to stern principle, & having no fear of man. I have full confidence in him, he would be Garrison & no one else the world over. Most men will compromise a little sometimes, for policy, as they miscall dishonesty, but Garrison not a hairs breadth where principle is involved. What a noble exhibition of his character, we had at the London Convention. At the time I did not fully appreciate the sacrifice he made, but the more I think of it the more I admire that one act. Being <u>the</u> champion of antislavery in this country he would have undoubtedly received more attention & had more influence in the Convention than any other delegate.— he knew that, & yet single & alone he dared (by refusing to take his seat) to say to that august assembly, you have made a false decision, & I shall take no lot nor part with you so long as you withhold justice from my friends. He is an advocate of "Human Rights" not black man's merely. His religious opinions are summed up in Christs sermon on the mount & I believe he tries to obey those plain commands in all his dealings with the world, hence his seeming folly, "the children of this world are wiser than the children of light"[1] & how supremely ridiculous to them would be one who imitated the example of Christ. How think you would one of your Lords interpret the command "do justice, love mercy" or one of our worldly minded Divines, the command "Be ye perfect"?—[2] Would that people were as willing to take Christs commands literally, as they are the figurative language of Paul. By telling you what I love in Garrison you may see wherein I sympathize with his party. It may be that my great love for Henry may warp my judgement in favour of some of his opinions, but I claim the right to look at his actions & opinions with the same freedom & impartiality that I do at those of any other men. Well, then as I am not ↑yet↓ fully converted to the doctrine of no human government I am in favour of political action, & the organization of a third party as the most efficient way of calling forth & directing action. So long as we are to be governed by human laws, I should be unwilling to have the making & administering of those laws left entirely to the selfish & unprincipled part of the community, which would be the case should all our honest men, refuse to mingle in political affairs. Many of the Garrison party are in favour of political action, but not of the third party. A party formed & candidates nominated afford a rallying point, a neucleus round which the mass may gather, ↑which↓ gives a reality to antislavery principles which "no voting" & scatteration cannot boast. O'Con[nell] has written a letter to the Irish in this country[,] now when one of our exciting elections come round which think you would be the most easily done—to keep these Irishmen from the polls altogether, or to induce them to vote aright?[3] We all love action & when all around us are busy we like to do something too. Then too, by organization we show our force The leading parties already begin to regard with anxious looks the rapidly increasing antislavery party. In the county in which I live, but 25 antislavery votes were given last year, this year 125 were given Our whole country has increased in proportion, cities excepted.— But I did not intend to dwell so long on my sympathies. It was a great disappointment to me not seeing you before I left England. Your kind note I received from Mr More on board the steamer as we were leaving Liverpool, & often did I read it over on our dreary passage.[4] I have written to Mrs Sarah Wigham[5] of all my <u>domestic afflictions</u>, since I left England, if you feel any curiosity to know them as you often visit Edinburgh, she will show you my letter, which contains too my apologies for so long neglecting to write to my English, Scotch & Irish friends. Henry joins with me in kind regards to our Darlington friends. The Bachus's, & your brother & sister with whom we stayed. Our regards also to your Mother & Father & much love for yourself.[6] May we not hope to hear from you soon? it would give us great pleasure   We see by the papers that your good people are making great efforts to repeal the corn laws. I was much pleased with George Thompson's eloquent speech at the great Manchester meeting of the 700 clergy[7] [*sideways on first page*] what blindness to the best interests of your country your rulers exhibit can it be they are in truth so blinded, or are they not governed by some selfish motive.— You will see by our papers that we too, are having exciting times—caused tho' by the prominent place the slavery question is taking in our public debates. [*sideways on second page*] Theodore Weld & Joshua Leavitt are spending the winter at Washington, observing & reporting all important movements.[8] Sarah, Angelina & her two little boys are well I hear from them occasionally. I have spent several days with them at [*sideways on third page*] different times since my return. I told them what John Scoble said that night at Mr Ball's in London, about their changing their opinions on woman's rights.[9] You remember he contradicted me flatly, as he did on many other occasions. They have not changed— I wish [*page torn*] send you some of their letters to me. Let me [*sideways on fourth page*] assure you that they are woman's rights to the core. As Angelina said to me in one of her letters, "How could any one visit in our family & not learn our opinions on that subject—do we not live out principles"   It is even so. At family worship Sarah & Angelina as often lead as Theo. & so in every-thing. John Scoble visited them. They think of him very much as we do. It was a sore trial to me to be so much with him when in your country. [*added at top of first page*] Our Philadelphia friends were all well when I last heard from them. Dear Lucretia Mott is as active as ever. To morrow Henry is going to Boston to attend a Convention I hope he will see Charles Remond & many other of our good Boston friends.[10] But I must say Farewell   Yours in love

⇘ *Elizabeth Cady Stanton*

Direct my letters Elizabeth Cady Stanton   Johnstown, Fulton. Co. State of New York

⇝ ALS, Garrison Papers, MB.

1. Luke 16:18.

2. Micah 6:8, ". . . what doth the Lord require of thee, but to do justly, and to love mercy, and to walk humbly with thy God?"; and Matt. 5:48, "Be ye therefore perfect, even as your Father which is in heaven is perfect."

3. Brought over from Ireland by Charles Remond in December 1841, the "Address From the People of Ireland, To Their Countrymen and Countrywomen in America," called upon Irish-Americans "to unite with the abolitionists" and exercise their moral and political power "for the sake of humanity." The names of sixty thousand inhabitants of Ireland followed Daniel O'Connell's. The letter was read to a Boston audience at an antislavery meeting on 28 January and reported in the press. The text was published in March. (*Lib.*, 4 February, 25 March 1842.)

4. Probably Mark Moore at whose lodgings, No. 6 Queen Street Place, the Stantons stayed in London.

5. Sarah Nicolson Wigham and her husband John Wigham, Jr., hosted the Stantons at Edinburgh in October 1840. Part of a large Quaker family, they were active in the Edinburgh Anti-Slavery Society. (Garrison, *Letters*, 4:36n; John Wigham, Jr., to J. H. Tredgold, 6, 14 October 1840, Anti-Slavery Papers, UkOxU-Rh; John Scoble to J. H. Tredgold, 14 October 1840, Abel and Klingberg, *Side-Light on Anglo-American Relations*, 73.)

6. The Stantons visited Darlington before sailing from England. Many members of the Backhouse (not Bachus) family of Quaker philanthropists lived there; the Stantons met Jonathan Backhouse (1779–1842), a delegate to the convention, in London. Of the Pease family, ECS mentions Elizabeth's father Joseph Pease (1772–1846), stepmother Anna Bradshaw Pease (1782–1856), brother John Beaumont Pease (1803–1873), and sister-in-law Sarah Fossick Pease (1801–1877). (Stoddart, *Elizabeth Pease Nichol*, 33, 38, 104; Mott, *Slavery and "The Woman Question,"* 25, 32; "Dictionary of Quaker Biography," typescript, UkLQ.)

7. Loaned to the Anti-Corn Law League by the British India Society, George Thompson assembled the clergy on 17 August 1841 for a training session to make of each minister a local agitator for free trade. (Norman Longmate, *The Breadstealers: The Fight Against the Corn Laws, 1838–1846* [New York, 1984], 122–26; Archibald Prentice, *History of the Anti-Corn Law League* [London, 1853], 1:247.)

8. Weld joined Joshua Leavitt at Washington in December 1841 to conduct research for John Quincy Adams and other abolitionists in Congress, who stepped up their attacks on slavery during the second session of the Twenty-seventh Congress. Weld stayed in the capital until spring. Leavitt (1794–1873), editor of the Liberty party organ, the *Emancipator*, was in Washington to cover the session. (Thomas, *Theodore Weld*, 192–96; Weld-Grimké, *Letters*, 2:879–938, 947–75.)

9. William Ball (1801–1878), an English Quaker, entertained delegates to the World's Anti-Slavery Convention at his house in Tottenham on 25 June 1840.

10. Henry Stanton attended the Massachusetts Liberty party convention on

16 February 1842. (*Emancipator*, 24 February, 4 March 1842.) Charles Lenox Remond (1810–1873), a delegate to the London convention, protested the exclusion of women by refusing to take his seat. After the meeting, he stayed abroad for a year and a half as a lecturer on slavery and racial prejudice. Born in Salem, Massachusetts, Remond was the first African-American lecturing agent hired by the American Anti-Slavery Society and was active from 1838 until the Civil War. In the 1850s he traveled in New York and Ohio with SBA. He was also a consistent advocate of women's equal rights. (*DANB*; *Black Abolitionist Papers*, 3:318–19n.)

---

9 ⤳ ECS TO ELIZABETH SMITH

Johnstown May 28th [*1842*]

Dear Lib,

We are all very desirous to hear particularly about your Mother & brother Jonah[1]   Write us everything, for instance a description of Jonah's appearance, <u>diet</u> & all his physical habits. Is he treated according to Combe?[2] Has Cousin Nancy plenty of nourishment for Jonah? Is Jonah good? Does he ever have the <u>belly ache</u> & do you then administer the quack remedies, such as cat-mint. Does he like his bath. Did you find his antislavery wardrobe abundantly supplied?[3] Cate[4] wishes to know what ~~his~~ colour his eyes are & how his moral sentiments are developed. Mama wishes to know why you have retired from the city of Peterboro?—[5] but to continue with Jonah & his mother. How many times does Jonah nurse during the night? Is cousin Nancy thin? Are you not coming down this summer? Cate wishes you to send by Papa her Homeopathic Journal. We have weighed Daniel this morning & he weighs 17 pounds.[6] How much does Green weigh? Tell us about the Birney's when you write.[7] Cate is here   she & Jonah are well & expect to remain so until the 1st of July. good morning your Cousin

⤳ *E. C. Stanton*

⤳ ALS, Papers of ECS, NPV. Transcribed in part in ECS Papers, Douglass Library, NjR.

1. Green Smith was born to Ann Smith on 14 April 1842. "Jonah," doubtless from the biblical story of a man swallowed by a whale, refers herein to various unborn babies.

2. Andrew Combe (1797–1847), brother of George Combe, wrote medical

books for the lay reader, and his *Treatise on the Physiological and Moral Management of Infancy* (1840) was very popular among American reformers. (*DNB.*)

3. A reference to the search for cotton produced by free labor. Gerrit Smith presided over the American Free Produce Association in 1838 and boycotted goods like cotton and sugar produced by slave labor. (Ruth Ketring Nuermberger, *The Free Produce Movement: A Quaker Protest Against Slavery* [Durham, N.C., 1942], 24–25, 114.)

4. Catharine Henry Cady (1820–?), the youngest of ECS's sisters, married Samuel Wilkeson on 14 June 1841, and their daughter Margaret Livingston Wilkeson, the first of five children, was born in 1842. Catharine entered the Troy Female Seminary in 1835 and graduated in 1837. In her words, she "Had not any professional life, or work. My father supported his five daughters." Wilkeson (1817–1889) was her father's student after his graduation from Union College in 1837, and he married Cate the year after he qualified for the bar. He practiced law in Albany until about 1848. From a prominent Buffalo family, Wilkeson took over the family's iron mills after his father's death in 1848 and founded a daily newspaper, the Buffalo *Democracy*, published in 1854 and 1855. He then bought the *Albany Evening Journal* from its legendary editor Thurlow Weed to become a powerful voice in building New York's Republican party. In 1859 he left Albany for New York City where he worked primarily for the *New York Tribune* and was an acclaimed war correspondent. After the war, Wilkeson worked for Jay Cooke and became secretary of the Northern Pacific Railroad until his death. (*TroyFS*; C. H. Cady file, Emma Willard School Archives; Genealogical files, notes from Presbyterian Church Records, NJost; *ACAB*; Hendrik Booraem, *The Formation of the Republican Party in New York: Politics and Conscience in the Antebellum North* [New York, 1983], 75–76, 170–71; Louis M. Starr, *Bohemian Brigade: Civil War Newsmen in Action* [New York, 1957], 66–73, 212–14, 359; Eugene V. Smalley, *History of the Northern Pacific Railroad* [New York, 1883], 282–86.)

5. To cut his expenses and reduce his debts, Gerrit Smith put his house in Peterboro up for sale and moved to a cottage in the summer of 1842. The house did not sell, and the Smiths returned home in 1845.

6. Daniel Cady Stanton, called "Neil" by family members, was born 2 March 1842 at Johnstown.

7. The Birneys had moved to Saginaw, Michigan, where Elizabeth Birney gave birth to Fitzhugh Birney on 9 January 1842.

·⟨══════⟩·

10 ❧ HENRY B. STANTON TO ECS

Boston, Thursday Afternoon. [*23 June 1842*]

My dearest daughter,

If you knew how happy it makes me feel to get a letter from you, you would not let a fortnight pass away without writing to me. Two weeks to day since I heard from you![1] I have been fearful that you or the Kiddy are ill; & you do not like to let me know it. Now, dearest, if you or the dear boy are sick, you must not fail to send me information forthwith. For, if either of you should be very ill & I not be informed of it, I should feel much worse than to know the worst. Do promise me, then, that you will not fail to let me know immediately if either of you are unwell. Pledge me this, & then I shall not feel so anxious when these long intervals pass away. Will you dearest?

Last night I dreamed of being with you. Oh how sorry was I when I awoke & found it was but a dream! I do think of you very, very often; & I long to be with you again, to enjoy your smiles & kisses. I suppose you hardly think of me for a week together. You have the sweet little Kiddy to play with & embrace, & so you forget all about "the peppy." But, reflect: where would the Kiddy have been but for me?! I am anxiously waiting to hear from dear Cate. I hope she will get thro her trials safely, & be blessed with a stout, healthy <u>daughter</u>! You must not frighten her half to death, by telling her constantly what "a horrid affair" it is. You must remind her of the royal courage of Victoria.[2]

Speaking of trials & deliverences reminds me of what I am to pass through next month. I shall probably be ready for my examination before the "grave and reverend seignors" of the law, by the middle or last of July—I hope by the middle. I think I shall go through the ordeal without getting scathed—tho they are pretty rigid in their tests. They examine their candidates quite thoroughly in all the ancient & modern law of real property, & go pretty considerably into personal property, mercantile law, the various sorts of actions & remedies, &c. &c. I shall prepare myself pretty faithfully in Blackstone & Kent, ↑& one two other authors↓ & run the risk. I study very closely—much more so than usual.[3]

If brother Wilkeson is at Johnstown, give my love to him, & tell him I wish, on his return to Buffalo, he would ~~petition~~ circulate a petition among the members of the Buffalo bar, praying the legislature at its August session, to pass a law extending to lawyers who have been admitted to the highest courts of our sister states, the same rights & privileges ↑on coming into New York↓ which a New York lawyer would be entitled to on removing into almost every State of the Union— viz, <u>an admission to the same rank & standing in the Courts of those states which he had in his own</u>. Tell him New York is in bad repute in other states because of her want of comity in this respect. Read this paragraph to S. W. & he will understand what I am at.[4]

Will you ask your father to send me a certificate of the time I studied law with him—also, stating that four years were allowed for classical studies? Say to him that his certificate of my commencement to study with him, bears date on the 23. February, 1841, & was filed in the Supreme Court Clerk's office the same day. I left his office May 23. 1842. So that I studied with him precisely 15 months.— When he makes out the certificate, let him do it on a sheet of paper, & then,[5] unless he wishes to fill it up with good advice, will you?

For the last two weeks, it has rained nearly every day. We are now <u>enjoying</u> a northeast storm. The country around the city looks green & beautiful, & things grow finely. I hope Mr., Mrs., & Miss Cady[6] will make a visit here the last of July. They would be delighted with a look at the capital of New England & its environs. What say <u>you</u> to settling down here?— Kiss the dear Kiddy, & tell his mother that I long to kiss him & her (especially the latter) for myself & not by proxy. Tell [Mom?] to beware of the youth!— Write me, dear love, every week. For I delight to hear from you. Ah, verily,

                                    ❧ *Henry.*

When you write, tell me something of the news. How the License excitement is—whether growing or abating.[7] I shall send the family a newspaper now & then, to let them know that the end of the world is not yet; at least in Boston; altho the Millerites & Mormons are increasing. The Mormons & Millerites hold meetings in the city every week.—[8] Ask Mr. Leaton[9] if a Mr. Hawley is lecturing in Fulton Co., & let me know what Mr. L. says.— I occasionally see some of the Southwicks. Saw Isaac Winslow recently. He has just returned from France. Emily has been in Havre since we left her there.[10] Mr. W. inquired particularly after you.

[*in margin of first page*] ☞ Do not let the Kiddy catch cold. See that he is not held by the window in the evening. He must get older before we toughen him. We must take great care of our precious treasure.— I find many in this region are adopting Homeopathy.— The Boston Whigs think Webster will adhere to Capt. Tyler, even tho the captain goes over to the Locos. Webster is in bad repute here.[11]

⤙ ALS, ECS Papers, DLC. Postmarked 23 June.

1. None of the letters that ECS wrote to Henry Stanton in Boston has been found. Stanton left Johnstown on 23 May, "to read law and preach immediate emancipation," in the words of his father-in-law. The *Emancipator* announced that he was available for lectures near Boston on weekends. By 2 August, out of money, he returned to Johnstown and completed his reading there. Back at Boston in the fall he passed the bar examination on 4 October. (D. Cady to Gerrit Smith, 23 May 1842, Smith Papers, NSyU; H. B. Stanton to James G. Birney, 2 August 1842, Birney, *Letters*, 2:707–9; H. B. Stanton to ECS, 4 October 1842, *Film*, 6:465–69; *Emancipator*, 30 June 1842.)

2. He proposes Queen Victoria as a model of courage for Catharine Wilkeson's impending childbirth. The Queen had a profound dread of childbirth, but her courage in the face of two attempts on her life—while the Stantons were in London in June 1840 and again on 30 May 1842—won her great respect. (Elizabeth Longford, *Victoria R.I.* [London, 1964], 144–70.)

3. Stanton took advantage of new, simplified rules for admission to the Massachusetts bar by passing an examination. He names staples of the lawyer's education: James Kent (1763–1847), *Commentaries on American Law*, 4 vols. (1826–1830), and William Blackstone (1723–1780), *Commentaries on the Laws of England*, available in numerous American editions. (Anton-Hermann Chroust, *The Rise of the Legal Profession in America* [Norman, Okla., 1965], 2:231–32.)

4. In Massachusetts an attorney qualified in another state needed only to establish residency before being admitted to practice.

5. At the margin, Stanton drew a seal to indicate his meaning and then added to his sentence.

6. The last of ECS's sisters to marry, Margaret Chinn Cady (1817–1902) graduated from Troy Female Seminary in 1836 and lived with her parents. On 5 September 1842 she married Duncan McMartin (1817–1894), a student of Daniel Cady's from Johnstown. The McMartins lived alternately in Johnstown and Albany before the war and settled in Grundy County, Iowa, in the late 1860s. (Allen, *Descendants of Nicholas Cady*, 174; *TroyFS*; *Portrait and Biographical Record of Jasper, Marshall and Grundy Counties, Iowa* [Chicago, 1894], 371–72; genealogical notes courtesy of Barbara McMartin, Canada Lake, N.Y., and Barbara Wood McMartin, Beaman, Ia.)

7. New York's temperance movement intensified in 1841 and 1842 with a new focus on political and legal ways to stop the liquor trade. Reasoning that government protected the industry by granting licenses for the manufacture and sale of liquor, temperance advocates sought the repeal of licensing laws at the state level and the denial of licenses at the local level. (Harlow, *Gerrit Smith*, 80–83.)

8. Millenarianism, a part of Mormon teaching, inspired followers of William Miller as well. Millerites, who anticipated Christ's second coming in 1843, published a newspaper in Boston.

9. Abel L. Leaton, a resident of Johnstown, was organizing a Baptist church there and superintending the Baptist Sunday School in nearby Gloversville. (*History of Montgomery and Fulton Counties, N.Y.* [1878; reprint, Interlaken, N.Y., 1981], 196, 202.)

10. The Southwicks and the Winslows, Quaker families prominent in New England's abolitionist circles, were related through the marriages of sisters from Portland, Maine. Sarah Hussey married Isaac Winslow; her younger sister Comfort Hussey married Isaac's brother Nathan; and Thankful Hussey married Joseph Southwick. The Southwicks lived in Boston, where Thankful (1792–1867) and her daughters were active in the Female Anti-Slavery Society. Emily Annette Winslow (1822–1904) was named a delegate to the London convention in 1840. Her father Isaac Winslow, also a delegate to London, was a sea captain and whaler who lived for a time in France. Emily married Franklin Taylor in 1851 and moved to Germantown, Pennsylvania. (David Parsons Holton and Frances K. Holton, *Winslow Memorial. Family Records of Winslows and Their Descendants in America* [New York, 1888], 2:885–87; Garrison, *Letters*, 2:209n, 393n; *History*, 1:341n; Debra Gold Hansen, *Strained Sisterhood: Gender and Class in the Boston Female Anti-Slavery Society* [Amherst, Mass., 1993]; Frank Barkley Copley, *Frederick W. Taylor: Father of Scientific Management* [New York, 1923], 1:44–50.)

11. Secretary of State Daniel Webster (1782–1852) and President John Tyler (1790–1862). Webster was the only cabinet member who did not resign in 1841 to protest Tyler's veto of banking bills, and Whigs in Massachusetts were divided about the wisdom of his decision. Though he faced new pressure to resign in the summer of 1842, in anticipation of the Massachusetts Whig party convention, Webster stayed in the cabinet until May 1843. To Stanton such divisions among the state's Whigs created opportunities for the Massachusetts Liberty party. (Maurice G. Baxter, *One and Inseparable: Daniel Webster and the Union* [Cambridge, Mass., 1984], 310–17, 360–61.)

11 ∝ SARAH M. GRIMKÉ TO ECS

Belleville, [*N.J.*] December 31, 1842.

Dear Elizabeth:

I have thought much of thee since thou left us, of thy situation [an]d thy conduct in Boston.[1] There is much, very much there, to gratify the [t]aste and the intellect, and thou wilt greatly enjoy the high mental im[p]rovement which exists there, I presume in a greater degree than in any [o]ther of our cities. This is delightful. It is right to value these attain[m]ents and to derive all the blessings from them which they are calculated [t]o confer. But too often they take the place of better things and leave [t]he heart unpenetrated by the love of God, uninfluenced by the love of our [f]ellow creatures. What we do in the cause of humanity is not done because [w]e love holiness and are aiming at its attain- ments, but because it gratifies [o]urselves to exercise the feelings of benevolence. We are not governed by [p]rinciple, but by impulse. Now, my sister, I greatly fear this contact for [th]ee, because thou has not given thy heart to God, and therefore this [p]reserving power cannot uphold thee. He has blessed thee with talents [w]hich if de- voted to his service will be a blessing to thy self, to thy [h]usband and family and to the world. Henry greatly needs a humble, holy [c]ompanion, and thou needst the same. In Boston, there will be little to [m]ake you so, much to draw your hearts away from God. I long to see you [s]itting at the feet of Jesus, hearing his words and doing his will. This [i]s all you need to place you among the choicest instruments for doing good.

I hope the sad divisions in the anti-slavery cause in Boston will [n]ot deprive you of the pleasure of being acquainted with the noble women [w]ho are on the other side. Let me know how this is and tell me all about [y]ourself. Affectionately thine,

∝ *S. M. Grimké.*

∝ Typed transcript, ECS Papers, Douglass Library, NjR. Square brackets surround letters obscured by the binding of a notebook.

1. Presumably ECS saw Sarah Grimké when she passed through New York City en route to Boston in November 1842. To say she moved to Boston at this

date would be misleading; ECS spent nearly equal amounts of time with her sisters and parents in New York and with her husband in Boston between the end of 1842 and 1846. (Ellen Cochran Walter to Gerrit Smith, November 1842, Smith Papers, NSyU.)

·◦=========∞=========◦·

12 ❧ ECS to Elizabeth J. Neall

[*Boston*] Friday Feb 3rd [*1843*]

Dear Lizzy

Anna Southwick read your letter to me this afternoon,[1] it called up a desire to write you. I obey the impulse. I have spent two winters in the region where you now are, why were we not there at the same time? However I am glad that we have been in the same place & known so many of the same scenes & people.[2] I know you must be happy   children of nature such as you & I find ↑in↓ the purity & freedom of the country life an atmosphere more congenial to us than that of the city, with all its moral & physical impurity, its constant excitement about trifles. This smoke & noise seems a kind of barrier, keeping ones spirit down, we must go out into the open fields or forests to have a full communion with divinity. How beautifully Emerson in his "Nature"[3] extols the country. And you have been sitting at the feet of Parker[4] & drinking in wisdom. I too have taken deep draughts from the same source & feel refreshed. I have heard a course of lectures from him & am now reading his discourses of last winter. He feasts my soul—he speaks to me or rather God (through him) to me. Harriet Minot[5] called to see me a few days since. I read her from Parker "How to move the world"[6] she was much pleased with the idea, tho' she laughed somewhat at first. "Move myself why here I am   now what can I do["] said she to Hatty Winslow,[7] why you must make your thoughts pure, your motives   your actions, all noble & lofty. Well said she   that is a most difficult matter,—if you should tell me to get up & turn a great black dog out of this room why I should know how to set about the work, but as to driving the devils out of my heart when I can see neither heart nor devils is a process I know not how to commence, & so she went on materializing our spiritualities for a time, & then chimed in with Hatty & myself & we talked like three young philosophers on the science of spiritual existences, for you know these Boston Transcendentalists have reduced the phenomenon of spirit to a fixed science & its wanderings can now be calculated upon with as much certainty as the appearance of comets by astronomers. The two Hattys are sweet girls. They go next week to their respective homes & I ↑shall↓ see no more of them for a time. I spent this morning in the House of Representatives hearing the intermarriage law discussed[8] it passed to the third reading this morning. Yeas 187. nays 116. that infamous law will no doubt be repealed ↑now.↓ we looked for a larger majority in its favour of repeal however we must be satisfied to get what we want by small majorities. "The old Bay State" is doing nobly. O! Lizzy we had a grand meeting at Faneuil Hall, such freedom & such sweet music from the Hutchinson family. Garrison as you will see by the papers spoke several times.[9] I am so glad to see him well again. He is the freeest man I know. I see he often surprises his own clique, this shows that he does not take counsel on every thought he gives to the world. We get his clear simple views of right in his impolitic speeches & resolutions, tho' to me he gives the strongest evidences of wisdom & sound policy by discarding altogether what the world calls policy. I am enjoying myself more than I ever did in any city. I attend all sorts & sizes of meetings & lectures. I consider myself in a kind of moral museum & I find that this Boston affords as many curiosities in her way as does the British museum in its. I have seen & heard Foster, Beech, Abigal Fulsom &c. &c.[10] I do wish we could have met here, but we did not & now the question is where can we meet. I will tell you, at Johnstown. I shall be there when come east in the spring & then I shall claim a visit from you & whoever is with you at that time. I should be very very happy to see you there & you can have no excuse for not making your arrangements with reference to me next spring. I wish to see & know more of you dear Lizzy, that when hereafter I am seated som winters evening in my family with children & grandchildren all about me, I may have some anecdotes to tell of "Lizzy Neal," a name destined to excite a deep interest in the hearts of the coming generation. You have visited Scotland & the birth place of the sweet poet Robert Burns, & who that goes there does not think & speak of Highland Mary. The love of a poet always makes its object immortal, who would not be willing to be the "femme covert" of a poet, to be immortalized among all future generations.[11] Latimers wife has a baby six weeks old, the baby & mother are visiting the

Southwicks much to Anna's annoyance,[12] as she hates all babies speaking of a baby reminds me that I wrote this to free my little innocent from all reproach. You say in your letter to Anna that I have never written to you since the birth of my baby. All I have to say is that neither baby nor mother are to blame but on the Devil's head fall the blame, for he it is who has tempted me to a long course of neglect of those I love through sheer laziness, as the poet truthfully remarks in his own sweet & forcible words,

> Idle boys & girls are found
> Standing on the devils ground.

Do remember me kindly to your uncles family[13] & Mrs Prior,[14] & to the Philadelphia friends when you write to them & tell me something about them when you answer this which I expect will be very soon Farewell dear Lizzy yours in love,

❧ Elizabeth C. S.

❧ ALS, Sydney Howard Gay Papers, Rare Book and Manuscript Library, NNC. Addressed c/o Thomas McClintock, Waterloo, New York.

1. Anna R. Southwick (1823–1911) was the youngest daughter of Joseph and Thankful Southwick. (Garrison, *Letters*, 6:271n; Hansen, *Strained Sisterhood*, 21, 66.)

2. Neall spent the winter with her cousins at Waterloo. (Sterling, *Ahead of her Time*, 166–67.)

3. *Nature* (1836) was the first book published by Ralph Waldo Emerson (1803–1882), the philosopher of transcendentalism. It celebrated the lover of nature as one who retained youthfulness and overcame egotism.

4. Theodore Parker (1810–1860) was a Unitarian clergyman, author, and lecturer in Boston, whose work helped to define transcendentalism. He published *A Discourse of Matters Pertaining to Religion* in 1842.

5. Harriet Minot (1815–1888), later Pitman, was a childhood friend of John G. Whittier and his sister Elizabeth, from Haverhill, Massachusetts, and an abolitionist. In 1844 she married Boston businessman Isaac Pitman and lived in Cambridge. She was a founder of the New England Woman's Club in 1868. (Whittier, *Letters*, 1:85n, 528-30; Garrison, *Letters*, 1:210, 215–16; *History*, 3:304n; *Woman's Journal*, 10 November 1888.)

6. "How to Move the World," published in *The Critical and Miscellaneous Writings of Theodore Parker* (Boston, 1843), counsels that the humblest person can "work a Revolution in the affairs of men, . . . This Gospel of God is writ for all. *Let him that would move the world move first himself.*" (220–21.)

7. Harriet Winslow (1819–1889), the daughter of Nathan and Comfort Hussey Winslow, was a cousin of both Emily Winslow and Anna Southwick and, like

them, a member of the Boston Female Anti-Slavery Society, though she lived with her father in Portland, Maine. Her poems appeared in the antislavery press, and she was another good friend of the Whittiers. In 1848 she married Charles List and moved to Boston. After List's death in 1856, she married Samuel E. Sewall, the widower of her older sister and a prominent abolitionist lawyer. Harriet Sewall was active in the suffrage movement in Massachusetts. (*NCAB*, 10:347; Whittier, *Letters*, 1:512.)

8. Abolitionists had campaigned in Massachusetts since 1831 to repeal a law of 1786 that barred interracial marriages. On 25 February 1843, the governor signed the bill of repeal. (David H. Fowler, *Northern Attitudes Towards Interracial Marriage: Legislation and Public Opinion in the Middle Atlantic and the States of the Old Northwest, 1780–1930* [New York, 1987], 149–53, 387–89.)

9. The annual meeting of the Massachusetts Anti-Slavery Society, 25–27 January 1843, was held at Faneuil Hall, the public meeting place and market in Boston known as the "Cradle of Liberty" for its association with protests leading up to the American Revolution. The Hutchinson Family Singers here made their first appearance at an antislavery meeting. The four brothers from New Hampshire—Jesse (1813–1853), Judson J. (1817–1859), John Wallace (1821–1908), and Asa Burnham (1823–1884)—were established entertainers whose repertoire included temperance and antislavery songs. Their success at this meeting created a demand for their music at other gatherings of reformers. Abigail Hutchinson apparently did not join her brothers on this occasion. (*Lib.*, 3 February 1843; Dale Cockrell, ed., *Excelsior: Journals of the Hutchinson Family Singers, 1842–1846* [Stuyvesant, N.Y., 1989], x–xi, 95–97.)

10. Thomas Parnell Beach, Stephen Symonds Foster, and Abigail H. Folsom were well known for their rowdiness in the cause of abolition and free speech. Beach (1808–1846), a minister and antislavery agent, joined Foster in disrupting religious meetings and services to talk about slavery, and authorities jailed him several times in 1841 and 1842. (Parker Pillsbury, *Acts of the Anti-Slavery Apostles* [Concord, N.H., 1883], 92–95, 302–3; Garrison, *Letters*, 3:101n; Garrison and Garrison, *Life*, 3:22, 4:250.) Foster (1809–1881) prepared for the ministry at Dartmouth College but broke with organized religion while a student at Union Theological Seminary and campaigned against slavery. He made it his special mission to confront churches with their failure to condemn slavery. In *The Brotherhood of Thieves; or a True Picture of the American Church and Clergy*, published in 1843, he attacked the churches and justified the abolitionists' call for leaving, or coming out from, churches to protest slavery. To hold fellowship with slaveholding churches was, he argued, to uphold slavery. Foster married Abby Kelley in 1845. (*DAB*; Jane H. Pease and William H. Pease, *Bound with Them in Chains: A Biographical History of the Antislavery Movement* [Westport, Conn., 1972], 191–217; Sterling, *Ahead of Her Time*.) Abby H. Folsom (c. 1792–1867), dubbed "that flea of conventions" by Emerson, was an extreme advocate of free speech at antislavery

meetings who resisted the authority of presiding officers to silence her. (Garrison, *Letters*, 2:727n; *NCAB*, 2:394)

11. An allusion to the love between Whittier and Neall, celebrated in his poem, "To a Friend, On Her Return From Europe," published in the *Pennsylvania Freeman*, 10 March 1841. ECS equates it with the poems to Mary Campbell, or "Highland Mary," by the popular Scottish poet Robert Burns (1759-1796), born at Alloway in Ayrshire. Though Neall and Whittier remained friends, he had, by this date, transferred his affections to another young Philadelphia abolitionist, Elizabeth Lloyd. By "femme covert" ECS means marriage. The term in common law indicated a woman whose identity was subsumed in that of her husband, who lost her individual standing in law. (Alan Norman Bold, *A Burns Companion* [New York, 1991], 29-30; Whittier, *Letters*, 1:324-25n; Sarah Pugh to ECS, 24 March 1841, *Film*, 6:423.)

12. At the center of a highly publicized fugitive slave case, Rebecca Latimer escaped from slavery with her husband George in October 1842. They were followed to Boston by George's owner who had him arrested. A Latimer committee mounted a legal defense, and the case roused the public to win passage of a law that barred state officials from aiding a slaveholder who seized a fugitive. Latimer's freedom was purchased, and the family settled in the Boston area. (Thomas D. Morris, *Free Men All: The Personal Liberty Laws of the North, 1780-1861* [Baltimore, 1974], 109-11; correspondence with Bayla Singer, Palm Beach Gardens, Fla.)

13. No doubt a reference to Thomas McClintock, although the connection between Elizabeth Neall's family and his is unclear. Neall's grandmother was related to his wife. McClintock (c. 1792-1876), from Philadelphia, was an abolitionist, a minister among Hicksite Quakers, and a leader in the free produce movement before he moved to Waterloo in 1836. There he ran a drug and book store on free produce principles and became influential in the Junius Monthly Meeting and the Genesee Yearly Meeting, where opinions about antislavery activism were dividing the society. In 1848, working closely with Lucretia Mott, McClintock led a separation from the yearly meeting and wrote the *Basis of Religious Association*, the rationale for establishing the Congregational Friends. He married Mary Ann Wilson, of Burlington, New Jersey, in 1820, and together they attended the woman's rights convention at Seneca Falls. He left Waterloo for Easton, Pennsylvania, early in the 1850s and returned to Philadelphia by 1859. (*Quaker Genealogy*, 2:240, 274, 941; *Friends' Intelligencer* 33 [1877]: 89; John E. Becker, *A History of the Village of Waterloo, New York, and Thesaurus of Related Facts* [Waterloo, N.Y., 1949], 135-36; Nuermberger, *Free Produce Movement*, 14-15.)

14. Margaret Wilson Pryor (c. 1785-?) was a Quaker abolitionist in Waterloo, originally from Burlington, New Jersey, and related to both the Neall and McClintock families. After marrying George W. Pryor (1779-?) in 1816, she moved to Philadelphia and into New York State. In Skaneateles in the 1830s, George Pryor led a Quaker seminary for girls, and in 1843, the Pryors were

associated with the experimental community in that town. Margaret Pryor attended the women's antislavery convention in 1837, and the Pryors were moving spirits in establishing the Garrisonian Western New York Anti-Slavery Society. Like other members of the Congregational Friends in Junius, the Pryors attended the woman's rights convention at Seneca Falls and signed its declaration. It was also Margaret Pryor who helped ECS organize her domestic life in Seneca Falls by introducing her to Amelia Willard, the housekeeper who stayed with the Stantons for thirty years. Willard was, ECS wrote, "trained by [Pryor] in all domestic accomplishments." By 1868, Margaret Pryor had retired to Vineland, New Jersey, where she took part in annual protest votes on election day. (*Quaker Genealogy*, 2:181, 251, 274; Garrison, *Letters*, 3:115n; Wells, *Skaneateles Communal Experiment*, 3; Sterling, *Ahead of Her Time*, 164–66; *History*, 3:476–78.)

---

13 ᵻ SBA TO AARON R. VAIL[1]

Centre Falls Oct 22, 1843.

Dear Cousin

Having come to the conclusion that our Danby friends had entirely forgotten us I could not forbear troubling you with a few lines, for the purpose of showing Semantha, that I can, (with great effort) refrain from penning a half a dozen letters to her, while she thus continues this long and I fear lasting silence.— Father was at New-York about a week since, and heard from Cousin Anson L. of the death of Uncle Nathan Lapham. I had hoped that Father & Mother would have visited Danby, while the only Brother of our dear Grand-Mother Anthony was living, but they have procrastinated until it is too late.[2] They are now thinking of making a short visit at Adams, but doubt their getting started some, as the Mill business is very confining at this season.[3]

I accompanied Father as far as Troy. Semantha must know I called at Mrs Willards, but did not succeed in becoming an inmate of the Seminary on credit,[4] which I did not so much lament after spending one half-day in different classes at the school. Think I should prefer getting the substantial part of an education at a less popular institution.— Sister M.[5] is still at Adams, received a letter from her yesterday. ~~The people~~ Our friends there are well. E. Hoxie was married very soon after Mary arrived there & they had an abundance of wedding cake at

Edwards Fathers of course.[6] Semantha do you not wish we could have had a good chunk.

Sister Hannah's[7] school continues two or three weeks. She has taught about eight months. She is going to have a short vacation and then commence teaching a family school in Easton, consisting of 6 scholars, at $1.75 per. week. I should think from appearances she had about concluded to make Easton her permanent residence. They wish her to teach the District school again next summer, which she probably will unless she prefers to take the charge of a <u>Widower</u> and <u>three children</u> which there is danger of as the Widower has been highly recomended and would have been <u>exhibited</u> to the household to day like any other <u>great</u> <u>curiosity</u>, had not providence interfered by causing the rain to fall so incessantly through the day. Thus you will perceive she is in great demand out round while I stand back amazed. Tell Semantha to have her Sunday go to meeting gound[8] all <u>starched</u> up nice, for she shall have a bid and we ~~will~~ single, happy ones will have nice times. Well said, cant I tell quite a long yarn when I set myself about it. You'll take it all for truth of course.

Reuben Bakers little girl has been very sick for some time & is no better.[9] If Semantha only knew it, I have a great deal of knews (as usual) to tell her, but shall not, until she can ~~devote~~ ↑spend↓ time to write to me. I shall probably be at home this winter as our folks think they cannot spare both of us & I hope to receive a visit from you and Saphrona without fail. Saphrona I wish you would ~~even~~ write a few words ~~if~~ & tell me what S. V. is up to. do come down and bring the children too. I have not forgotten the pleasant little visits I enjoyed with you last winter. Give my love to your Mother and all the rest of our friends, C. White in particular. I often think of her in her lonely situation,[10] & finally take a large share for yourselves and excuse these lines   From your affectionate Cousin

~ Susan B Anthony

~ ALS, SBA Papers, MCR-S.

1. Aaron Rogers Vail (1810–1888) lived at Danby, Vermont, with his wife Sophronia Lapham Vail (1814–1858) and their children; his sister Semantha (1826–1905) kept house nearby for their father John. Aaron, a businessman and Danby's postmaster, and Semantha were SBA's second cousins and good friends with all the Anthonys. In 1853 Aaron moved his family to Buffalo to go into business with his brother. Semantha Vail boarded with the Anthonys in

1839, and SBA studied algebra at Danby in the winter of 1843. Semantha married her cousin Henry Griffith Lapham (1822–?) in 1846 and moved to Brooklyn, New York, where SBA continued to visit her. Years later she helped to finance distribution of the *History of Woman Suffrage* to libraries. (Moses Vail to SBA and Hannah Anthony, 13 February 1843, and Semantha Vail to SBA, 3 September 1843, *Film*, 6:475–76, 487–90; William Penn Vail, *Moses Vail of Huntington, L.I.* [n.p., 1974], 221–25; Bertha Bortle Beal Aldridge, *Laphams in America* [Victor, N.Y., 1952], 49–50, 53, 94–95, 182–83; *Quaker Genealogy*, 3:198, 332; J. C. Williams, *History and Map of Danby, Vermont* [Rutland, Vt., 1869].)

2. Nathan Lapham, the brother of Hannah Lapham Anthony (1773–1841), died 25 September 1843, at age eighty-two. He was grandfather to Sophronia Lapham Vail, and his sisters were the grandmothers of the Vails and the Anthonys. With other family members he had moved from Adams, Massachusetts, to Danby about 1809. His son Anson Lapham (1804–1876) moved to New York City about 1833 and became a successful businessman and philanthropist. He retired to Skaneateles in 1861. (Aldridge, *Laphams in America*, 53; *Quaker Genealogy*, 3:198; *Friends' Intelligencer* 33 [1877]: 682.)

3. At this date Daniel Anthony ground plaster and feed at his grist mill near Centre Falls in Greenwich Township. (D. Anthony to John Anthony, 29 July 1841, SBA Papers, MCR-S.)

4. The Troy Female Seminary was the premier school for girls, especially those training to be teachers. Founded in 1822 by Emma Hart Willard (1787–1870), the school educated the daughters of well-to-do and powerful families like ECS and her sisters, alongside young women from poorer families. To attend the seminary "on credit" would enable SBA to repay her tuition out of her future wages as a teacher and assure her of the seminary's help in finding a job. (Anne Firor Scott, "What, Then, is the American: This New Woman?" *JAH* 65 [December 1978]: 679–703.)

5. Mary Stafford Anthony (1827–1907) made the round of relatives at Curtisville and Adams, Massachusetts. Mary Anthony moved to Rochester with her parents in 1845 and stayed there the rest of her life, working as a teacher and principal in the city's schools; keeping house for her mother, sister, and various nieces and nephews; and taking what part she could beside SBA as a reformer. She joined her sister as an agitator at New York teachers' meetings and accompanied her to woman's rights conventions. In her retirement Mary was an officer of the New York State Woman Suffrage Association, and she managed the state headquarters for the suffrage amendment campaign of 1894. According to her obituary, "If the elder [sister] had more oratorical ability, the younger certainly had more executive ability; but there the marked differences ended." (M. S. Anthony to SBA, 1 October 1843, *Film*, 6:491–94; Charles L. Anthony, comp., *Genealogy of the Anthony Family From 1495–1904* [Sterling, Ill., 1904], 173; Rochester *Post Express*, 6 February 1907.)

6. A first cousin of SBA's, Eliza H. Hoxie (1823–1898) grew up in Adams in

the large family of Hannah Anthony Hoxie, Daniel Anthony's sister and a Quaker minister. Eliza married Edward B. Shove (1821–1854), son of Joseph Shove, in 1843, and they farmed at Easton, New York. Active locally in reforms, she joined SBA in Albany for the first woman's temperance meeting in 1852. After Edward Shove's death, Eliza married Merritt Cook and moved to his farm in Middle Granville, New York, where she lived for the rest of her life. She earned a medical degree from the Woman's Homeopathic Medical College of New York in 1880. (Anthony, *Anthony Genealogy*, 195; Federal Census, New York, 1850; Leslie R. Hoxie, *The Hoxie Family: Three Centuries in America* [Ukiah, Ore., 1950], 80; Aldridge, *Laphams in America*, 157.)

7. Hannah Lapham Anthony (1821–1877) taught school for several years before she married Eugene Mosher on 4 September 1845. She stayed in Washington County when her family moved west, and she and Eugene had five children. In the 1860s the Moshers settled in Rochester. Hannah's one public act was to register and vote with SBA in 1872. (Mildred Mosher Chamberlain and Laura McGaffey Clarenbach, comps., *Descendants of Hugh Mosher and Rebecca Maxson Through Seven Generations* [n.p., 1980], 311–12; *Ballot Box*, June 1877.)

8. SBA's spelling of "gown."

9. Reuben Baker (1795–1866) was a prominent member of Easton Monthly Meeting. (*Friends' Intelligencer* 23 [1867]: 729.)

10. By "mother" SBA means Elizabeth Griffith Lapham, mother of Sophronia Vail. C. White is probably Cynthia Lapham White, a daughter of Nathan Lapham. (Aldridge, *Laphams in America*, 53.)

·◁══════❦══════▷·

14 ❧ HENRY B. STANTON TO ECS

Boston June 11.—Tuesday. [*1844*]

Dear Elizabeth:—

I recieved your letter of Sunday morning, last evening. You say you have recieved no letter from me since you have been at Canaan.[1] I wrote you last Thursday (I think) in reply to your letter of the previous Monday morning, & which you ought to have recieved by Saturday morning. I directed it to you at Canaan, Columbia County, New York,— not to the care of any one—for, you did not direct me to do so. I intended to have sent you money in this letter, but, you not having recieved the other letter in due time, induces me to not send money till I hear that you get my letters regularly—for, it may be lost. When you get this, let me know immediately, & I will send the necessary funds—

or, if I get a letter, in the mean time, announcing that you have recd my first letter to Canaan, I will immediately send money. I do not know how much to send, tho. I suppose $20 will be hardly enough—for, the fare on the rail road will be $11, I suppose, besides way expenses, & provided you dont stop over.[2] Then $8 or $9 will not be enough perhaps to pay your Canaan bills. And yet, a twenty dollar bill is the most convenient to send. However, I will decide when I get your letter. You may state in your next, how much you will need & I will forward it, whether it require one or two bank bills.

Mrs. O. read me your letter to her, last night.[3] She will (so she said) write you in the same mail which carries this, & tell you all about how things are at Chelsea. In my letter which I sent to Canaan, I told you how my office was arranged. I have got a neat one, & by adding 4 yards to the old carpet we had in the upper room, it fitted the front room of my office. Mr. Bishop has carpeted the back-room.[4] I am getting some handsome new furniture, & when completed, shall have the finest office at No. 10 Court St.— You see I am sending out some circulars to the temperance & antislavery men in the city, to let them know that I am in the way of business, & can be found if they wish. I am glad to hear that dear little Henry the second, is well & as good & black as ever. Why did you not let Neil the precious, write a line in my last letter? You would, if you had known how much pleasure it gives to read his scribblings—especially, when his hand is guided by his darling mother! I had a letter from Wilkeson yesterday. He says Cates leg is no better. You speak of staying at Canaan till the last of this month. I hope you will do no such thing. You can be just as well off for air & roaming-grounds both for yourself & the boys, at Chelsea as at Canaan. We can interchange letters, so that you can get here early next week, or certainly during the week; & you must not delay beyond that. Indeed, the last of next week will carry us to the 22d, & you must come & see by that time. In truth, I am almost resolved to send money in this letter & insist that you come this very week. I will see the Southwicks, & look out for a girl. As to your mother, I will write to her to-morrow, at the latest & urge her to come. Kiss the precious chubs for me, & in your next, I charge you to let Neil write. Give my best love to Uncle, Aunt & all the family at Canaan. <u>Write</u>   Your own

❧ *Henry.*

[*on address leaf*] Since I wrote the within, I have written a long letter to

Mrs. Cady, urging her to come with you & spend some weeks at Chelsea

❧ ALS, on printed circular, ECS Papers, DLC.

1. ECS gave birth to Henry Brewster Stanton, Jr., known as "Kit," on 15 March 1844. She and her children were visiting her uncle Eleazer Cady (1775–1856) and aunt Lucy Backus Cady (?–1846) on their farm at Canaan, in Columbia County, New York. Stanton's previous letter is not located. (Allen, *Descendants of Nicholas Cady*, 92, 174.)

2. Canaan was served by the Hudson and Berkshire Railroad, terminating at West Stockbridge, Massachusetts, and there intersecting with a rail line to Boston.

3. Mary Livingston Olmstead (1812–1885) was a first cousin of ECS who married John Wesley Olmstead (1816–1891) in 1837 and had three children by 1844. John Olmstead was a Baptist clergyman in Chelsea, Massachusetts, and Henry Stanton boarded with his family. In 1846 Olmstead became editor of the *Christian Reflector* and began a long career in religious publishing. (Henry King Olmsted, comp., *Genealogy of the Olmsted Family in America* [New York, 1912], 282; *ACAB*.)

4. Stanton's first law partnership broke up in a dispute over representing liquor dealers. He wrote this letter on a circular announcing his solo practice as attorney and counsellor at No. 10 Court Street, Boston. After working as a student in Stanton's office, Joel Prentiss Bishop (1814–1901) was admitted to the Massachusetts bar 9 April 1844. He became a noted legal author, beginning with his *Commentaries on the Law of Marriage and Divorce, and Evidence in Matrimonial Suits* (1852). (*DAB*; Henry B. Stanton, *Random Recollections*, 2d ed. [New York, 1886], 65; H. B. Stanton to Gerrit Smith, 20 May 1844, Smith Papers, NSyU.)

15 ❧ ECS TO ELIZABETH SMITH MILLER AND CHARLES D. MILLER[1]

Albany Feb 3rd [*1845*]

Dear Cousins,

We were all pleased to hear of your happiness—a fine large boy & all fears & suffering past! dear Lib you must be filled with joy.—& then too "he introduced himself with ease" & to a circle of strangers!! he must indeed be "well bred"   How much I should like to see the little gentleman—no doubt he will in time manifest all the suaviter in modo

& fortiter in re² that so distinguishes his illustrious Grand-father from the rest of <u>his sex</u>.

Gerrit Smith Miller welcome to this land of ours!—that you may be just such another fanatic as he is whose name you bear, is my best wish for you. Cousin Charly I hope you will exercise your authority in keeping Lizzie in her room for one month at least   Do write us again & describe the boy more particularly. All join with me in hearty congratulations to the parents, grand-parents & youthful uncle of little Gerrit.³ We have had sad times here for some weeks—as all the children have been sick   Maggie & Neil are better but we fear the babies have the whooping cough.⁴ Cousin Nancy must write us a letter of particulars— We shall wish to hear from Lib often until she is well & then <u>she</u> must write us her opinion on the subject of introducing well bred young gentlemen into good society⁵   All join in love. I just received a letter from Henry describing the Texas annexation in Boston.⁶ He says the Wigs did all the managing, wrote the address &c & the abolitionists did all the talking—he says the Whigs were horribly scared—none of the Honourables took a long breath until the convention adjourned. Abigail Fulsome was the first speaker!⁷ good night

ॐ   *Cousin Lee*⁸

ॐ AL, Papers of ECS, NPV, and facsimile fragment in *Stanton*, 2:12.

1. Elizabeth Smith married Charles Dudley Miller (1818–1896) on 18 October 1843. Their son Gerrit Smith Miller was born at Peterboro on 30 January 1845. From a prominent Utica family, Charles Miller attended Hamilton and Harvard colleges, studied law in Rome, New York, and worked at a bank in Cazenovia at the time of his marriage. In 1845 Gerrit Smith asked him to work in the business office at Peterboro, and the Millers settled into their own house near the Smiths. In 1868 they moved into a large, lakeside house in Geneva, New York, where Charley Miller kept a stable of race horses. (Genealogical scrapbook, Smith Papers, NSyU.)

2. "Gentle in manner, resolute in deed."

3. That is, Green Smith, son of Gerrit and Ann Smith.

4. Margaret Wilkeson and Daniel Stanton. Candidates for "the babies" include Bayard Wilkeson, born in Albany on 17 May 1844; Flora McMartin, born on 17 June 1843; and Henry B. Stanton, Jr.

5. The manuscript ends at this point. The letter's conclusion is reproduced as a facsimile in *Stanton*.

6. H. B. Stanton to ECS, 31 January 1845, *Film*, 6:519–20. Stanton described the Convention of the People of Massachusetts, held at Faneuil Hall, Boston, on 29–30 January 1845, to protest the annexation of Texas. Though

Whigs called the meeting, prominent abolitionists were elected delegates from their wards and did, as ECS retells it, do much of the speaking. (*Lib.*, 31 January, 7 February 1845; Baxter, *One and Inseparable*, 375-76.)

7. That is, Abby Folsom.

8. "Lee" may have been her name inside her family; Henry Stanton also used it occasionally.

---

16 ❧ SBA TO THE ANTHONY FAMILY

Canajoharie Aug. 12, 1846[1]

Dear Friends at the Cottage

It is now noon of that awful day, that day of days. Do I not carry a pretty steady hand considering. Well I have examined 4 classes before Mr. Hagar,[2] & Trustees Sholl, McFarlane, Vanalstine, Wilcox[3] etc. succeeded far better than I had even hoped. Mr. C[aldwell] says this noon, "Well School marm you have got on a little too much paint this time." My face looks as if the blood might easily ooze through. I do not feel more than one half as much frightened no I mean excited as I had anticipated. I feel that my credit as a Teacher is at stake & I must not stop to be alarmed. Well last eve I came home from school exhausted, my nerves all on fire &c. thought to try on my new dress, had got it fairly hooked, when ding went the bell, well Mr. Hagar it was. I had my dress to Change   E[leanor] went in & entertained him, while Kate[4] tried to hook me   "God["] said she & went on & swore & worked away & after a long time travelled the whole length & I presented myself before the gent, he staid & made arrangments. Mr. C. came up & we had a very sociable time & my mind would get a little off the subject now & then. half past 9. I went to bed no sleep for me though, I got up walked the room, sat on the floor & went to bed again until between 12 [*and*] 1 I lost [*illegible*], & slept until the Roosters crowed then opened my eyes & could not close them again, got up as soon as it was light, washed as Lewis says all over, Put on some new shoes Mr. C. got me in Albany Patent Leather heels & toes & blue prunella, half gaters, set like ribbon   after breakfast combed my hair down in the oldfashioned way not over my ears, braided it in 4 braids, then went down & E. sowed them together put in he[r] shell comb, then I put on my new gound which is plaid, white, blue, purple & brown, has two puffs around the skirt, cups to the sleeves, with puffs & buttons where they end & puff at the rist   sleves cup up like M[ary]s[5] Cashimere, & ~~wristlets~~ ↑undersleeves↓ I have made out of my linen wristlets & some linen off Mr. C's ruffled shirts & a new colaret about my neck, Mags[6] Gold pencil with a pen it, & Susan watch & black chain   That makes up the costume & in fine all say the School marm looks beutiful & I heard some of the Scholars expressing fears lest some one might be smitten & they thus be deprived of their teacher   Well there goes the first bell & I must to my business again

[*Easton*] Aug 16. Well mother I have survived the examination & am now Sunday afternoon seated at Hannah's kitchen table.[7] Eleanor, Hannah & Charlotte[8] are chatting away but after all I cannot but regret that I am where I cannot see ~~me~~ my dear Parents. We left Canajoharie Friday P.M. staid all night at Albany. Came to Troy Saturday morn & found a boy there, with Eugenes horse & waggon, we piled in the boy sat on the trunk & I drove   we had a pretty good, the day being some cloudy & some windy

I find H. very happily situated, says she should be perfectly happy, if she could only know that mother enjoyed herself. I cannot say quite as much, but I do feel that I could enjoy life far better than now, did my mother write me a cheerful letter now & then. Could I know that my Parents were happy I would be glad. We have had quite a good time, last eve after E. got to bed it was necessary for us to take a walk & we had a good old fashioned chat & cried because we could not all be together. oh we are such foolish silly creatures, we used to have far greater troubles & still when all as far as location is concerned is pleasant, we are yet sighing for something more. why can we not be happy with what we have

Monday [*17 August*] 11 oclock   I have been washing dishes, rubbing a little &c. Tomorrow we are going to the Ville,[9] I would like to be there this moment. This is pleasant here, but Rochester holds the preference with me, that beautiful yard that snug, new little house all seem more like home than does Easton. I intended to have sent this this morning but the mail does not go until tomorrow. H. will write this eve. E[leanor] will go home Friday. H. is talking & thinking about visiting you, thinks she will go, when I return to Canajoharie. do you write & Mary too all, how does Father is he better. H. & I have shed a few briny tears, that we could not all be under the roof of our loved Parents. I should have come to Rochester alone, had it not been for the expense. I rather deny myself & save the money to pay your & M[ary]s expenses down, feeling, that for you to visit old washington would afford you so much pleasure, but you will go back satisfied if you are like me.

Tuesday morn [*19 August*]. We are all in trim for Battenville, waiting for Eugene. Eleanor seems to enjoy herself. I cannot say much this morn, but will give you a long yarn after I have seen the Scrabblers[10] & Ville folks. There is nothing here that seems any more pleasant than Rochester. I think of you often & all the time & wish you were with us to talk & chat. I am in the store writing. Eugene wants Han to waite until January then says he will go west with her. I tell her not to do it, unless Mother will come down here.

Eleanor thinks Eugene a clever fellow, says he is good looking &c. I cant write now wait until I have seen the old homestead & then the ides will flow & the pen fly. I have made up my mind that we take just about so much comfort let us be where we will, it is the disposition not the presence or absence of this or that supposed happiness. I have every reason to be encouraged in my school business. The prospect is thought very flattering, they say Miss Anthony's classes acquitted themselves nobly, that ought to make you & Father feel happy & it makes me happy that I am able to do my parents thus much honor. ‡ My love to all Father Mother Mary Daniel Merritt & Lorinda,[11] & Rhoda & Elias.[12] I had hoped to see you all this vacation but not so & I must be content & I hope we may all strive to enjoy the present blessings & not sigh for impossibilities   Write immediately every thing how you feel & what you think about H going west or your coming down. Uncle & Aunt Howe are going west very soon.[13] Well good bye. You shall soon hear again from your affectionate Daughter.

~ *Susan B. Anthony*

H. could not get time to write. You not worry about my things. There will be chances by & by.

~ ALS, SBA Papers, MCR-S. Printed in part in *Anthony*, 1:50–51. Addressed to Lucy Anthony.

1. On 11 May 1846 SBA took up the duties of head teacher in the female department of the Canajoharie Academy, for which work she would earn the

tuition money paid by her students less 12.5 percent. Her parents and the youngest children—Daniel R., Mary, and Merritt—were living on a farm west of Rochester in the town of Gates. SBA boarded with George Caldwell (c. 1808-?), a merchant, academy trustee, and husband of her first cousin Eleanor J. Read Caldwell (c. 1812-?). Canajoharie and Palatine Bridge, on opposite shores of the Mohawk River, were inhabited by numerous members of the Read and related families, including Joshua Read, Eleanor's father and SBA's uncle. (Joshua Read et al. to SBA, 25 April 1846, *Film*, 6:568-70; Daniel Anthony to John Anthony, 12 May 1846, SBA Papers, MCR-S; Palatine Bridge and Canajoharie Methodist Church, Subscribers to the First Centenary of Methodism and List of Families, compiled in 1960, Montgomery County Department of History and Archives, NN; Federal Census, 1850.)

2. Daniel Barnard Hagar (1820-1896) was the academy's principal and his wife Mary Bradford McKim Hagar one of its teachers until the end of 1848. After graduating from Union College in 1843, Hagar pursued a distinguished career in education and became principal of the Salem State Normal School in Massachusetts in 1865. (*BDAmEd.*)

3. A partial list of the trustees. The Reverend William Nace Scholl (1805-1889), widowed since 1845 and father of several children, courted SBA when she arrived in Canajoharie, to her considerable amusement and confusion. Minister to the English Evangelical Lutheran congregation of St. Mark's, Scholl remarried in 1850. (SBA to M. S. Anthony, 19 July 1846, *Film*, 6:594-601; Harry V. Bush, *The Story of St. Mark's Evangelical Lutheran Church and Congregation* [Canajoharie, N.Y., 1935]; Records of the English Evangelical Lutheran Church of Canajoharie, N.Y., 1840-1882, copied by Gertrude A. Barber, typescript, 1941, NN.) The Reverend James McFarlane preached to the town's Reformed Church from 1845 to 1848. (*History of Montgomery and Fulton Counties, N.Y.*, 99.) It is not evident which Mr. Van Alstine served as a trustee. The last named was probably Lester Wilcox, an attorney, born in Massachusetts about 1810. (Federal Census, 1850.)

4. A servant in the Caldwell household. SBA mentioned Kate in a letter to her sister Mary, writing "Dutch Kate short & dirty is here," and later lumped Kate with the "Cattle they call girls here." In 1850 the Caldwell household included Catharine Donnelly, age thirty-eight, born in Poland. (Federal Census, 1850; SBA to M. S. Anthony, 19 July 1846, and SBA to L. R. Anthony, 9 August 1846, *Film*, 6:594-611.)

5. Her sister Mary.

6. Probably Margaret Read Caldwell, Eleanor's sister.

7. Eleanor Caldwell and SBA visited Hannah Anthony Mosher in Easton, where Hannah moved after her marriage to Eugene Mosher. Mosher (1819-1894) was the youngest child of a Quaker doctor who moved into Washington County about 1786. He ran a store in Easton. (Chamberlain and Clarenbach, *Descendants of Hugh Mosher*, 128-29, 311-12; Federal Census, 1850.)

8. Probably Eugene Mosher's sister, born in 1814.

9. Battenville, Greenwich Township. The Anthony family lived there when they first settled in Washington County, and it was home to SBA's sister Guelma Anthony McLean.

10. Residents of Hardscrabble, a section of Greenwich Township to which the Anthony family moved in 1839. It was renamed Centre Falls.

11. Daniel Read Anthony (1824–1904) was educated at the academies in Union Village and Canajoharie, served as a clerk to an uncle, and spent several years teaching and working in Washington County and western Massachusetts before joining his father in business in Rochester. In 1854 he boarded the train of young abolitionists sent by the New England Emigrant Aid Society to Kansas and lived briefly at Lawrence. Three years later he left Rochester for Kansas again. Settling at Leavenworth, he dove into the territory's impassioned politics and frontier economy to become a successful newspaper publisher. (Anthony, *Anthony Genealogy*, 185–91; Eli Thayer, *A History of the Kansas Crusade, Its Friends and Foes* [New York, 1889], 69–71; "D. R. Anthony," *KHQ*; *United States Biographical Dictionary: Kansas Volume* [Chicago, 1879], 56–63; Daniel Anthony to Guelma Anthony, 2 October 1837, SBA Papers, MCR-S.) Jacob Merritt Anthony (1834–1900), the youngest of SBA's siblings, was known always as Merritt. He spent one term in the preparatory department of Oberlin College before moving to Kansas. He farmed at Osawatomie until 1860, and after a short-lived attempt to farm at Pike's Peak, Colorado, he returned to enlist in the Seventh Kansas Cavalry, Company A, in 1862. At the end of the war he stayed in Leavenworth until 1869, when he moved to Fort Scott, Kansas. (Alfred Theodore Andreas, *History of the State of Kansas, Containing a Full Account of Its Growth*, [Chicago, 1883], 2:1076; *Woman's Journal*, 23 June 1900; alumni files, OO-Ar.) Lorinda, a young girl, whose mother SBA saw several times in Canajoharie, lived with the Anthonys. Possibly she was a daughter of Carlos Read, another of SBA's cousins, who died in disgrace in 1837, leaving two children. (Joshua Read to Daniel Anthony, 16 July 1837, SBA Papers, MCR-S; Ruth Story Devereux Eddy, *The Eddy Family in America* [Boston, 1930], 198.)

12. Elias DeGarmo and Rhoda DeGarmo (?–1873) farmed next door to the Anthonys and provided introductions to Rochester's radical community. Hicksite Quakers, the DeGarmos were founding members of the Western New York Anti-Slavery Society, and Rhoda was among the women who emerged as its leaders. Joining the McClintocks and other disaffected Friends from Waterloo, the DeGarmos helped to found the Yearly Meeting of Congregational Friends in 1848 and were active members through the 1850s. Rhoda DeGarmo also served on the committee to arrange a woman's rights convention at Rochester in August 1848. Still a friend of woman's rights in the year before her death, she joined SBA in the attempt by women to vote in 1872. (Nancy A. Hewitt, *Women's Activism and Social Change: Rochester, New York, 1822–1872* [Ithaca, N.Y., 1984], 61, 120, 143, 211, 230; Hewitt, "Feminist Friends: Agrarian Quakers and the Emergence of Woman's Rights in America," *Feminist Studies* 12 [Spring 1986]: 26–49.)

13. Lucy Anthony's older and only sister, Amy Read Howe (1777–1865) and her husband Joseph Howe (1777–1862) moved to New York from Massachusetts about 1806, settling first at Deerfield, in Oneida County near Utica, and then, late in life, at Phelps, in Ontario County, near several of their children. (Read Genealogy Ms., SBA Papers, MCR-S; Daniel Wait Howe, *Howe Genealogies* [Boston, 1929], 200.)

·⟨⟩·

17 ⇝ SBA TO THE ANTHONY FAMILY

Canajoharie Nov. 6, 1846

Dear Mother & Sister,

What recollections rush over me. Nov. 6th was the day I bid adieu to Battenville friends & the 7th that awful day of days, on which we left our home, to seek a better in the beautiful plains of the west. How differently do we now feel, at least I do. Would circumstances permit me to remain under the same roof with my Parents, in our new home, I would now, methinks, be content but I do not know though, these minds of ours, would be, but are not content. I do not look with regret upon that day, I can but rejoice our Father almost tore us away from those familiar scenes. I would not that we had been inactive & suffered that burden to have rested upon our minds until the present, when had the same casuality befallen that gristmill, we must have been left without a ray of hope, oh happy am I that such a misfortune has not awaited us.[1]

Sunday P.M. [*8 November*] A pleasant Sunday for a rarity this is. Margaret little Mary[2] & myself went to Lutheran Church this morning, heard Mr. Sholl preach, did very well. The boys returned from Washington Co. last Monday.[3] they spent a week with H[annah] did not go up to the Ville, had joyous times they say. H. killed chickens & cooked them for breakfast, very often & I guess fixed up the good things most of the time. They had new light mixed pants & blue roundabouts,[4] & Joshua a new circular cloak & felt O.K. I can assure you, new cloth caps too. They saw Aaron who was passing on his way from Troy,[5] they, like the old Coks,[6] think Eugene the best fellow

Eight weeks of this Term are now gone. 4 Pupils entered the school ↑during↓ the last week, which makes the number 25. 11 of the $5 & 14 of the $3. My Tuition money will be nearly the same as last Term. That Salary business runs in my head I can tell you, & I am striving diligenty, hoping my pupils may make such advancment as to induce others to come in. I have never heard of the least fault-finding either with scholar or Parent, but not a few remarks of commendation. Helen Berbeck entered the school last week. She is said to be unmanagable, but I hope to find her otherwise. I have already been obliged to show some motions & performances that cannot be in my school & she sorta stared at me, as much as to say thats queer, but I think, seeing she hopes to be a sort of a cousin she will carry herself rather strait.[7] I have to day been writing to Mrs. T. Mr. Caldwell hast just returned from Albany, says there is great rejoicing about the Whig Victory. he is an Old Hunker & rejoices with the whigs in the defeat of Silas.[8] I have heard Father talk politicks, but never seen folks <u>electionier</u> before now. Mr. C. to night tells me to give Justice,[9] one of the Clerks, the uncollected ↑Tuition↓ bills & he shall collect them for me. I can hardly feel sufficiently thankful for the many kindnesses I receive.

Saturday P.M. the 14th. A year ago how we piled into that waggon & old grey dragged us to the Carrot bed etc & then Catharines Supper, Mary & my visit to Lewis etc, etc, all passed though.[10] I am now moved & in the kitchen chamber, where it is nice & warm   I do not have to travel over the Carpets, nor feel that I am out of the world. I have nothing from Washington since the boys returned, now two weeks. Shall try & write ↑to A.↓ tomorrow, but 5 weeks more & I expect to be with sister Gula. Shall give H[annah] timely notice, that if she visits much with me during that week, it must be at Aarons. I called up to Jo's just dusk, they had been putting up stoves, in the Parlor they have a self regulator & says he <u>hoss</u> I have fixed stove for you, shall I have the pleasure of showing you the room? I declined. he has told M[argaret] I <u>must</u> come there this winter any way, but I guess the <u>women</u> think I had better not.[11] to <u>day</u> it seems as though E[leanor] had rather have me than not. She is alone & Mr C[aldwell] gone very often, but she is so much the creature of circumstance, you can not but feel constantly how fleeting are calm & happy moments. I every day say to myself distrust none so much as thy owwn selfish heart, for that [*written sideways in centerfold*] most assuredly is the prompter to so much ill speaking of others   Dont mention the lots of love I enclose to you all. I would give a cookee to see you all & hear Merritt laugh etc etc—dont he never think of Susan & Mother are you never going to write again—

Sunday eve. 15th I attended Church this A.M. then went over the River & staid until 4 P.M.[12] Uncle had been ↑very much↓ perplexed and to finish off with, when he got home from Church & went into the barn he found his corn crib burst & some of his corn in the barn yard & some on the barn floor with hens & geese hard at work. The pigs also <u>neighbors pigs</u> had rooted up a large bed of parsnips. Well his feelings were very much tried; he seemed striving very hard to hush his passions, finally said he, It seems as though the Devil was trying to see if he could not tempt me to day. he walked to the barn & back again then took his concordance & from that, turned to some passage in luke where read for a long time. What a change there must be in that man, in olden times, he, insted of thus struggling with & quelling the storm of passion, would have burst forth in uncontrollable wrath and the most bitter oaths. O that we all might thus wrestle & conquer every unruly passion of the heart.

Mary will you copy the Indian Students lament & send me   Kate Wetmore[13] plays it but does not know the words & promises to sing it for me if furnish the words. She sang a few lines of the tune the other night I felt as though I were home. O how I wish I could fly there & be at no expense & then you might expect me a Friday eve. Jacob Anthony[14] has failed, Mabe Tymeson was his Clerk. Daniel why dont write & tell a body what you are about, & Father whether he has sold the wheat, & what the prospect is about coming out even the first year, you know we thought we would be contented to be able to say even   I had rather hear about living matters, than any thing else. Mr. C. & Uncle spend this week at Johnstown, Uncle has lawsuit. O how comes on that Johnson affair.[15] Well you have got all if you can only unriddle it.

~ *S B. A.*

~ ALS, SBA Papers, MCR-S. Though written on a single sheet and filed separately, the fragment dated "Sunday the 15th" appears to conclude this otherwise incomplete letter. Addressed to Daniel Anthony. Letters in square brackets expand initials.

1. The anniversary of her family's move from Washington County to the farm, where they arrived on 14 November 1845. SBA alludes to the burden of

her father's bankruptcy and the news that his gristmill in Washington County had recently burned down.

2. Margaret A. Read Caldwell (c. 1820–1849) and her daughter Mary Eleanor, age six. (Palatine Bridge and Canajoharie Methodist Church subscribers; Federal Census, 1850.)

3. The boys of George and Eleanor Caldwell: Joshua Read Caldwell (1834–1865) and Elisha S. Caldwell (c. 1837–?). They visited Hannah and Eugene Mosher at Easton but did not proceed to Battenville to visit the McLeans. (Federal Census, 1850; *Canajoharie Radii and Tax-Payers' Journal*, 14 September 1865.)

4. A short, close-fitting jacket.

5. Aaron M. McLean (1812–1896) married SBA's older sister Guelma in 1839. His grandfather John McLean moved into Washington County before 1800 and built the mill that Daniel Anthony managed in Battenville. Aaron's father Thomas King McLean was born in 1784 and married Mary Perine in 1812. Aaron grew up with SBA and her sisters and stayed in Battenville as a merchant, until moving to Rochester in the late 1850s or early 1860s. Guelma Penn Anthony McLean (1818–1873), known to her family as Gula, attended Deborah Moulson's school in Philadelphia with SBA. When she married the Presbyterian McLean, she was disowned from the Society of Friends. Though not evidently active in the woman's rights movement, Guelma McLean attempted to vote with SBA in the election of 1872. (Baker Genealogical Ms., SBA Papers, MCR-S; Anthony, *Anthony Genealogy*, 173, 182; Crisfield Johnson, *History of Washington County, New York* [Philadelphia, 1878], 352; Federal Census, 1850.)

6. This nearly illegible word is unexplained.

7. Helen Jane Burbeck (1831–1849), the daughter of Joseph Burbeck, a physician, and his wife J. Adaline Burbeck, expected to become a cousin when her sister Sarah married Daniel Stafford Read, SBA's cousin. (Bush, *Story of St. Mark's*.)

8. John Young, a Whig, defeated the incumbent Silas Wright in the race for governor of New York. The "Hunkers" of the Democratic party opposed Wright, a Democrat, chiefly because he vetoed an appropriation for improvements to the Erie Canal. The Democratic *Albany Argus*, 26 April 1847, referred to George Caldwell as "an efficient democrat, and capable officer." (DeAlva Stanwood Alexander, *A Political History of the State of New York* [1909; reprint, Port Washington, N.Y., 1969], 2:114–25.)

9. A clerk for George Caldwell.

10. "Carrot bed" refers to stories about a carrot crop of mythical proportions grown on the Anthonys' farm by its previous occupants. Friends in Washington County heard that the family felt "less disposed to doubt the reports of the famous 'carrot crop' since you find so rich and beautifull a land." (P. H. C. Remington to SBA, 8 March 1846, *Film*, 6:562–66.) Lewis B. Burtis (c. 1793–1868) married Sarah Anthony, a distant cousin of SBA's, for

his second wife. They removed from the Saratoga Monthly Meeting in eastern New York in 1839 to settle near Rochester, and at some point farmed the land later occupied by Daniel Anthony. With the DeGarmos and Sarah's brother Asa Anthony and his wife, Lewis and Sarah Burtis were part of the rural, radical Quaker community that welcomed Daniel Anthony's family. Released from the Genesee Yearly Meeting for their abolitionism, Lewis and Sarah A. Burtis (1810–1900) became active in the Congregational Friends, the woman's rights movement, and spiritualism. (Anthony, *Anthony Genealogy*, 123; Records of Saratoga Monthly Meeting, NNFL; Garrison, *Letters*, 4:259n; Hewitt, *Women's Activism and Social Change*, 61, 170; H. D. Barrett and A. W. McCoy, eds., *Cassadaga: Its History and Teachings* [Meadville, Pa., 1891], 232.)

11. Joseph W. Caldwell (c. 1814–?), younger brother of George, married the younger Read daughter. He and Margaret Read Caldwell moved into their own house on the Palatine Bridge side of the river in June 1846. In October SBA wrote home that she needed to be on the Canajoharie side because crossing the river in bad weather was too difficult. Her letters indicate that deciding where to board raised many questions: of personality, marital stability, household size, domestic help, traffic patterns within the house, distance to work, and even heat. Each move received full discussion with her female relatives in town *and* with her family in Rochester. She moved to Joseph Caldwell's in January 1847 to make way at George Caldwell's for his sisters. (Federal Census, 1850; SBA to Lucy Anthony, 18 June, 22 October 1846, *Film*, 6:627–30.)

12. Joshua Read (1783–1865) lived in Palatine Bridge. An older brother of Lucy Read Anthony, he was a well-to-do farmer and sometime businessman, an academy trustee, and the person who rescued the Anthonys from the effects of bankruptcy. He purchased and returned to them their household and personal goods and then leased them the farm near Rochester. He and his wife Mary Stafford Read (1787–1866) had three children: Eleanor Read Caldwell, Margaret Read Caldwell, and Daniel Stafford Read. (Read Genealogical Ms., SBA Papers, MCR-S; Ernest Nean Stafford, *Laban Stafford, His Ancestors and Descendants; A Genealogy* [n.p., 1962], 220; *Anthony*, 1:35; Federal Census, 1850; *Canajoharie Radii and Tax-Payers' Journal*, 29 November 1865.)

13. Though often mentioned in SBA's letters, this member of the large Wetmore family is unidentified.

14. Jacob C. Anthony was among the trustees of the English Lutheran Church when it organized in Canajoharie in 1839 and he had left town by 1850. His connection, if any, to SBA's family is not evident. (*History of Montgomery and Fulton Counties, N.Y.*, 99; Federal Census, 1850.)

15. One of many references to a protracted lawsuit between Daniel Anthony and Chester or Chet Johnson, a farmer and businessman of Washington County. Stemming from Anthony's bankruptcy, the case was in the courts by 1843 and still on appeal in 1850. (SBA to family, 15 April 1847, SBA to Lucy R.

Anthony, 31 October, 19 November 1848, all in *Film*, 6:654–57, 841–43, 845–48; Joshua Read to D. Anthony, 11 June 1843, D. Anthony to Lucy R. Anthony, 28 January 1850, in SBA Papers, MCR-S; Federal Census, 1840; Johnson, *History of Washington County, N.Y.*, 353.)

·⟨⸺⸻⸺⟩·

18 ❧ ECS TO ELIZABETH SMITH MILLER

[*Albany*] Thursday afternoon [*15? April 1847*][1]

Dear Lizzie,

We were very glad to see his honour Mr Caukins[2] last evening   We asked him a great many questions about all of you & had he been a woman we should have asked him a great many more. Papa left a bundle for you at Wempsville last week. Have you received it yet?— We are glad that Cousin Gerrit is trying the efficacy of Homeopathy and thinks of trying Hydropathy also   I fear for him however, the drunkard will return to his cups, & he perchance to his Iodine & oitments & to the strong excitment of some painful operation, tho' I will hope for the best. We are all well here   The moving is to commence next week.[3] Mrs Bayard will be here in a few days. On Monday I take up the line of march for Boston where I hope to meet the Eaton tribe[4] about the third week in April as their last letters said they should sail from Liverpool the 4th of April. I suppose you have heard of Mary Delavan's engagement to Clarkson Potter.[5] Dr Sprague's church is to be opened on Sunday—it has been closed during the winter for repairs.[6] Mrs Morris' son Owen has an appointment in the army,[7] Lieut. of the artillary, I see some of your relations occasionally   I believe they are all flourishing. We spent a very pleasant evening with Sarah[8] on her return from Peterboro. She speaks very highly of your domestic accomplishments & of your discipline both of yourself & boy. I have—the greatest desire to see you in your own house & I certainly shall before the 1st of June. Tell Charlie that I shall parley & reason no more with him but we shall meet in fair fight in the groves of Peterboro before long. The direction of his last letter to me caused such violent & continued outbreaks of laughter among the post office boys that they all lost their situations, only think of their sorrowing parents, & their own young hopes so suddenly & strangely blasted. In Henry's last letter to me he says he is much better than he has been during the winter—he dreads the change from Boston to Seneca, & I fear he will long for the strong excitement of a city life, tho' I hope after a time he will be happy & contented there I am sure I shall, for I the country & that climate is very delightful   at all events Henry will have rest there & health too I hope when we get beyond the reach of those east winds. Mama sends much love to you, Charley Cousins Nancy & Gerrit & I join with her. Do write & tell us how you are, & what you are doing reading &c, your Cousin

🙠 Lib.

P.S. Tell cousin Gerrit that he will no doubt be toasted by the Paddies at all their public dinners for years to come.[9] What indescribeable suffering the poor Irish must be now undergoing. It seems to me the best way to relieve them is to bring them here to our land of plenty. I think instead of mourning over the increase of emigration, we should rejoice for surely their condition is improved   The tigers send love to Green tell him they have not yet turned into lambs.

[*on address leaf*] Cousin Charley observe the direction E. C. Stanton— Albany—

🙠 ALS, Papers of ECS, NPV. Variant transcript in ECS Papers, NjR.

1. Dated with reference to the reopening of the Second Presbyterian Church on Sunday, 18 April 1847. (*Daily Albany Argus*, 15 April 1847.)

2. Caleb Calkins (not Caukins) worked for Gerrit Smith in the land office at Peterboro from 1840 until Smith's death. (Harlow, *Gerrit Smith*, 40.)

3. Though this sentence has been read as a reference to the Stantons' move from Boston to Seneca Falls, moves of the Cady clan are more probable. The arrival of "Mrs. Bayard," presumably Edward's mother, Ann Bassett Bayard, suggests the move might involve the relocation of Edward and Tryphena Bayard from Seneca Falls to New York City, though Edward had studied homeopathy in the city earlier than this date. Another possibility is a move of Daniel Cady's household back to Johnstown; the family moved routinely in and out of Albany. ECS describes below that she will head east to Boston, not west to Seneca Falls, and meet her sister. She later recalled that from Boston she and her sister moved with their children to Johnstown. ECS took title to the house in Seneca Falls from her father on 22 June 1847 and then oversaw an extensive remodeling before she or the children moved in. Henry Stanton stayed in Boston until December 1847, but he returned to New York for a

month in mid-October—a time when the move probably occurred. (Deed, *Film*, 6:665–67; *Eighty Years*, 143–44; H. B. Stanton to Joshua Reed Giddings, 15 November, 11 December 1847, Giddings Papers, OHi.)

4. Her sister Harriet Eliza Cady Eaton (1810–1894), brother-in-law and cousin Daniel Cady Eaton (1804–1855), and their children Harriet Cady Eaton (1835–?) and Daniel Cady Eaton (1837–1912). The son of Daniel Cady's sister Sally and her husband Amos Eaton, the naturalist and founder of Rensselaer Institute, Daniel Cady Eaton grew up in the Cady household and clerked for a local merchant in Johnstown. Under his uncle's patronage, he went to New York City in 1825 for additional experience in trade and, in time, had his own firm in the city, importing dry goods. Business took him abroad often, and he died in Paris. Eaton married his cousin Harriet in 1831. Their daughter Harriet married George Stewart Brown in 1857. Their son Cady graduated from Yale College and, after a brief stint as a lawyer, returned to Yale as a professor of art history. (Allen, *Descendants of Nicholas Cady*, 174–75; Ethel M. McAllister, *Amos Eaton: Scientist and Educator* [Philadelphia, 1941], 39, 472–73; Gravestones, Johnstown, N.Y.; Genealogical files, notes from Presbyterian Church Records, NJost; *ACAB*; D. Cady Eaton Papers, CtY.)

5. Clarkson Nott Potter (1825–1882) in fact married Virginia Mitchell in 1851. After studying law in Milwaukee, he returned to Albany in 1847. Mary Delavan was probably a daughter of Edward Cornelius Delavan, a wealthy wine merchant of Albany who repented and poured his fortune into the temperance movement. (*New York Times*, 22 January 1882; *SEAP*.)

6. William Buel Sprague (1795–1876) served as pastor of Albany's Second Presbyterian Church from 1829 to 1869. (*ACAB*.)

7. Lewis Owen Morris (1824–1864) received a commission in the United States Army on 8 March 1847, after the death of his father, Lewis Nelson Morris, in the Mexican War. Young Morris continued his military career and was killed at Cold Harbor in 1864. (*ACAB*; *New York Times*, 9 June 1864.)

8. Probably Sarah Miller (1815–1853), older sister of Charles D. Miller.

9. In the wake of the Great Famine of 1846, Albany's leading citizens, including the governor and Daniel Cady, sponsored a drive to raise money and commodities for shipment to Ireland. Gerrit Smith's gift of $2,000 was the largest individual donation. (*Daily Albany Argus*, 11–15 February, 25 March 1847.)

·(⊂━━━━━◓◓◓◓━━━━⊃)·

19   ⇝   SBA TO THE ANTHONY FAMILY

Canajoharie May 28/48.

Dear Parents

I have not written you but once since the commencement of this Term.[1] And a long time it seems too. I had intended to have spent a part of last Sunday in talking to you with my pen, but could not steal time. Joseph and Margaret left for New-York on Saturday the 20th inst. The office of care taker was assigned to me. M. has the same girl that she did when you were here. She presided in the kitchen. Theodore went with them to New-York. Mary E. & Albert remained with me.[2] It was the first time M. has slept away from her own home since she went to house keeping   We were very lonely Albert in particular. They were gone six days, had a very pleasant time. I got along with my family cares as well as I had anticipated, knowing my want of practice. Albert is an uncommon boy for smartness & sweetness. I do not know any difference in my love for him & my Sisters' children. In fact I feel an interest in the prosperity & success of the whole family not much if any inferior to that for our own. Has it not been Uncles fortune to act the part of real friend to those around him. His heart & hand are ever ready to assist the unfortunate. Would that it were in our power to return some small pre= cious token of the deep gratitude we feel for the sympathy and benefits confered when we were in the deep waters of affliction. He is still feeble, yet has he been enabled to go through with all the excitement & fatigues of these trying times, much to the astonishment of all the family. How sadly different the feelings now from those indulged a year ago. Then all hearts were elate with hope, now are all those bright dreams blighted.[3] Ah fickle fortune how dost thou play thy pranks e'en when reason sits enthroned and wields her mighty sceptre.

I had the pleasure of reading a short letter from Aaron last week also one from H[annah]   Nothing new from either. It is but ten weeks to Summer vacation. I told M. yesterday that I thought of nothing but getting fixed & ready to go to Rochester in August. Sometimes I can hardly wait for the time to come. If I could only spend the Sundays under the roof of my Parents home, I now think I would be content. They have talked of building a new Academy this Summer but I do not believe they will. My room is not fit to stay in & I have promised myself that I would not pass another winter in it. If I must forever teach, I will seek at least a comfortable house to do pennance in. A weariness has come over me that the short spring vacation did not in the least dispel. I have a pleasant school of 20 scholars, but I have to manufacture the interest duty compels me to ~~feel~~ exhibit ~~for the advancement of my pupils~~. I am anxious they should learn, but feel almost to shrink from the task, energy & something to stimulate is wanting; but I expect the long summer vacation spent with my dearest & truest friends will give me new life & fresh courage to persevere in the arduous path of duty.

Do not think me unhappy with my fate, no not so, I am only a little tired & a good deal lazy, that is all. Margaret now thinks of going west with me and I guess she will not give it up again.

Writing letters does not afford any satisfaction, I want something more real to feast upon. I am out of sorts with the whole world, I want a new ↑$5.00↓ fancy hat, $15.00 pin, $20.00 mantilla, dresses, shoes, gloves, pocket hankerchiefs &c &c. oh yes ↑& a↓ nice fan. Every one of which I am resolved to deny myself. I am going to have my straw bleached & trimmed with my old ribbon, my blue lawn dress I have had made over, which is as handsome as when new, the black braise[4] is being made, which will be as nice as new & is very much worn, & for the rest I am determined to banish even the desire.

H[annah] had just had a letter from D. R. he continues pleased with his situation & I hope they are suited with him.[5]

All my happifying thoughts are of the anticipated joys of next vacation. Willet the Clerk was down to the Canal a week ago to day,[6] a line boat was there he heard a man & woman talking about a stor[e &] house with green blinds & the Academy on the hill, he stepped up & asked them about whom they were talking, they told him, said you were well but gave him no card or name. I know from description that it must be none other than Lewis Burtis.

Do write very soon, tell about the strawberries & peaches, cherries & plums. Joseph talks some of going with us & going to his fathers with M[argaret]   Joshua & Elisha want to come too. I guess I will come home & live this winter & let Mary & Merritt go to Washington Co. H[annah] wants J. M[erritt] to come there & stay & go to school &

Aaron & Gula do not feel at all satisfied with Marys visit G. said Aaron could not be reconciled to M's going home last winter. How I wish J. M. would send me or us some Strawberries by Express, or some merchant or body coming down on the Cars, guess I can stand it though till I come out   Now be all ready to visit. O can it be I shall be with you in ten weeks. Now Merritt write tell me how the yard looks, what flowers are in blossom & all about the farming business. Love to all

⇌ *S B A.*

⇌ ALS, SBA Papers, MCR-S. Letters in square brackets expand initials and complete a word obscured by an inkblot.

1. A gap in the letters stretches from 23 September 1847 to this date. A letter dated 6 January 1848 should be 1849. (*Film*, 6:674-76.)
2. The children of Joseph and Margaret Caldwell. Theodore was about six years old, Mary Eleanor about eight, and Albert Story about three. (Federal Census, 1850.)
3. The misfortunes remain unexplained.
4. Ida Harper understood this word to be "barége," a light, silky dress fabric, resembling gauze. Alternatively, it might be "baize," a coarse, woolen or cotton fabric napped to imitate felt. (*Anthony*, 1:52.)
5. Daniel R. Anthony had gone east to Lenox and Adams, Massachusetts, to learn business.
6. Willet was one of three clerks working for George Caldwell. The Erie Canal passed through the town of Canajoharie.

·⟨⟩⟨⟩·

Editorial note: On 11 July 1848, the *Seneca County Courier* published an unsigned call to a "Convention to discuss the social, civil, and religious condition and rights of woman," to open at Seneca Falls on 19 July. The first day's sessions were, it read, "exclusively for women," but the public was urged to attend on the second day, "when Lucretia Mott, of Philadelphia, and other ladies and gentlemen, will address the convention." Nothing written at the time documents the planning or authorship of this announcement, but ECS recalled three decades later that Lucretia Mott, Martha C. Wright, and Mary Ann McClintock, sitting with her "around the tea-table of Richard Hunt, a prominent Friend near Waterloo, decided to put their long-talked-of resolution into action, and before twilight deepened into night, the call was written." Later she added Jane Hunt's name to the list. As an historian, ECS set this event in the context of New York's debate over the property rights of married women. Since Thomas Herttell first proposed in 1836 that state law allow married women to hold title to property as if they were single, the subject of women's rights had received considerable attention from lawyers, legislators, and reformers. Laws that gave husbands control of their wives' property, it was argued, violated women's natural rights, and, some reformers continued, the disfranchisement of women allowed men to perpetuate the injustice. By 1846 some women petitioned the state's constitutional convention for property law reform and suffrage; their disfranchisement, they said, violated principles of the Declaration of Independence. But delegates defeated a constitutional clause recognizing married women's property rights, and the discussion moved back to the legislature. ECS had many personal links to this debate. Though her extant papers of the period are silent on the subject, she recalled discussions in Albany with the governor and Judge Hurlbut; she argued with Ansel Bascom, Seneca County's delegate to the constitutional convention; and by one account she also petitioned the legislature. Bills to reform the law came before the legislature in 1847 and 1848, and on 7 April 1848, the governor signed the Married Women's Property Act. A modest measure that fell short of Herttell's goals, that left unchanged the husband's control of joint earnings and women's wages, the act gave women separate control of the real and personal property they brought into marriage or acquired by gift while married. "Thus," ECS wrote in the *History of Woman Suffrage*, "the discussions in the constitutional convention and the Legislature, heralded by the press to every school district, culminated at last in a woman's rights convention." (*History*, 1:63-68, 98-100; *Eighty Years*, 144-45, 148-51; Judith Wellman, "The Seneca Falls Women's Rights Convention: A Study of Social Networks," *Journal of Women's History* 3 [Spring 1991]: 9-37; Norma Basch, *In the Eyes of the Law: Women, Marriage, and Property in Nineteenth-Century New York* [Ithaca, N.Y., 1982], 113-61; Elizabeth Bowles Warbasse, *The Changing Legal Rights of Married Women, 1800-1861* [New York, 1987], 100-108, 205-14; Peggy A. Rabkin, *Fathers to Daughters: The Legal Foundations of Female Emancipation* [Westport, Conn., 1980], 85-99.)

•⊂======✖✕======⊃•

20 ✒ ECS TO ELIZABETH W. McCLINTOCK[1]

Grassmere [*Seneca Falls*] Friday morning [*14? July 1848*][2]

Dear Lizzie,

Rain or shine I intend to spend Sunday with you that we may all together concoct a declaration   I have drawn up one but you may suggest any alterations & improvements for I know it is not as perfect a declaration as should go forth from the first woman's rights convention that has ever assembled. I shall take the ten o'clock train in the morning & return at five in the evening, provided we can accomplish all our business in that time. I have written to Lydia Maria Child Maria Chapman[3] & Sarah Grimkè, as we hope for some good letters to read in the convention. Your friend

✒ *Elizabeth C. Stanton*

✒ ALS facsimile, in *Heirlooms of History* 7 (November 1992): 38; location not known; not in *Film*.

1. Elizabeth Wilson McClintock (1821–1896), later Phillips, was a daughter of Thomas and Mary Ann McClintock and a friend as well as relative of Elizabeth Neall. Living with her parents in Waterloo and working in the family's store, she was part of the circle of abolitionists and radical Quakers linked through the Western New York Anti-Slavery Society and the Genesee Yearly Meeting. She spoke at both the Seneca Falls and later Rochester meetings. In 1852 she married Burroughs Phillips of Syracuse but was widowed shortly thereafter. She settled at Vineland, New Jersey, where both ECS and SBA kept in touch with her. (*Quaker Genealogy*, 2:815; ECS, "In Memoriam," *Woman's Journal*, 21 November 1896, *Film*, 36:85; research by Judith Wellman.)

2. Dated by the statement in the *History of Woman Suffrage* that the meeting to draw up the Declaration of Sentiments occurred later than the meeting to write the call, on a Sunday morning. "Grassmere" was ECS's name for her house on Washington Street, a tribute to the poet William Wordsworth who named his home "Grasmere." (*History*, 1:67–68; *Eighty Years*, 90.)

3. Maria Weston Chapman (1806–1885) was an early member of the Boston Female Anti-Slavery Society, a member of the business and executive committees of the Massachusetts and the American societies, and an extraordinary fund-raiser. At her command, antislavery women from Scotland to Ohio

supplied the goods to be sold at the annual fairs that raised several thousand dollars each year. A supporter of the Grimkés' right to speak and a believer in women's equality as abolitionists, Chapman steered clear of woman's rights when separately considered. In July 1848 she left Boston for Europe in order to educate her children. (*NAW*; Pease and Pease, *Bound With Them in Chains*, 28-59.)

·⊂══════⋙⋘══════⊃·

21 ⋙ DANIEL ANTHONY TO SBA

Rochester July 16, 1848

Dear Daughter

Yours of the 12 Inst by Wm Davis was handed us the next Day after he left Canajoharie—[1] He came up and brot it himself— We regret to learn that sickness & death are giving our Friends in that vicinity such an amount of trouble & sorrow— Death being one of natures grand operators to carry on the depopulation of the Earth will forever be casting his darts in a way to bring Grief to our hearts untill we are educated to view all things relating to death & even that itself in a very diferent light from what we now do— I see no good reason why we should be so deeply afflicted about that which we can not help— Were we to be so trained as to consider nothing a source of trouble to the mind but the neglect of doing all in our power to relieve the miseries of the afflicted and improve in every way posible the condition of man— Then were we called to mourn the <u>cause</u> of such call would be at our controll—and the removeall of which would not only dry up our tears but send joy & hapiness to the destitute millions who are now suffering under tortures of every description heaped upon them by what is termed the more Christian & enlightened part of community— Farmington Yearly Meeting at thier last getting together divided—[2] That portion of its members who take the liberty of holding up to view the wickedness of War—Slavery Intemperance—Hanging &^c & who take the liberty of steping just over the line drawn two hundred years since—up to which all the members may walk—but no further—That portion of the society who are not exactly satisfied to confine thier opperations for ameliorating the condition of man within the compass of an old shriveled up nutshell *illegible* [a]nd who are of opinion that each individual should have a right to even think as well as act for himself & in his own way to assist in rooling on the wheel of reform has left the more orthodox—wise and self righteous part of the society to attend to nothing but matters of pure & undefiled religion—this latter portion of Friends not wishing to have thier holy & most devout meditations any longer disturbed by the intercessions of the friend of the bondman for aid to restore to himself the three millions of human beings which the inactivity & silence of that society as well as all others ~~has~~ continues to be the cause of thier remaining thus chattelized— I do not learn ~~what~~ how large a part of the members have in this way withdrawn—I suppose something towards half— In Rochester they have commenced a new meeting under the dictation of niether Priest deacon nor Elder—[3] As respects your continuing in Can[ie] longer than the present term we think we must leave mostly to yourself— We are to some extent aware of the labour & fatigue of mind you have to undergo in order to do justice to your patrons—pupils & yourself— You are or must be also aware that we are abundantly able as well as willing to bear the tremendious "Burden" that all our old maids & young maids will be able to throw upon us— Your Mother thinks & says while I am writing this that you will probably enjoy yourself in school through the winter better after making a visit to Rochester—and thinks you had better come at the close of this term on a visit even should you conclude to finish the present year in teaching— Mary also leaves the whole matter of your teaching through the winter or not wholly to you—says she is not determined whether she would go East to spend the winter in case you should come home to remain   I have only to say that when you get tired of teaching try something else—or if you get tired of teaching there & wish a rest & then to try it again elswhere—come home whenever you think best & look out for another chance whenever you think best if ever— Should you however determine—<u>with consent of the Trustees</u> to teach there no longer than this term—I should think much of your making the Eastern visit you name—but if you conclude to continue your school & come home now on a visit only—you will write us about a week before you leave—naming the time of day you leave or rather at what time you will arrive here—as you may have some calls to make on the way— We are all in first rate plight for company & hope you will take with you as many of our relatives from C & Palatine as you can enlist to undertake such a campaign

We have understood that some one suggested to your Uncle Joshua that it would be a satisfaction to your Mother to have a letter from him— Now this ↑is↓ most accurately correct   She thinks as well as myself that such a production from her only Brother would be a most soothing & spirit reviveing matter as well as a very great rarity.

Your Mother thinks you would like to hear about or Money Making Matters

Firstly—I have farmed here three years each & every year has been very dry in this place & vicinity— No further off than the City—there has been five times the rain this summer that there has here & so all arround us— Some crops have suffered much— Wheat we are now cutting is midling—corn good potatoes want rain very much—carrots fair—Onions & other garden stuff D°—Oats pretty good—have sold some vegetables—some eggs—some Butter & <u>some Butter Milk</u>—$20 worth of scullions not worth diging last fall were left in ground till they grew this spring—then took them to market to the above amount— Peach ↑trees↓ well loaded— Have just recd letter from Danl R— He gives a full description of a pleasent visit to Adams—is well suited with his location—thinks he could not have done better— Guelma tells us all about Batten^le— Aunt Amy Wier died lately after a three hours illness   My Chet Johnson is in Salem jail for stealing $85— Aaron thinks he will have a chance to do a job for the State unless he can <u>squirm out</u>   Have bot a three years old colt $55 33/100—works well—is heavier than old Gray—have three cows—4 hogs & no cat— Love to all

& D. A.

[*across top of second and third pages*] Your mother & self & Merritt returned last tuesday from Vienna[4]—went to visit your Uncle & Aunt Howe your Aunt Howe thought she could not come any further   L Clark & Nancy & thier two children were there just before us—staid with us going & coming—the old folks are quite smart—tell your Uncle Read— Eastern friends all well—

[*upside down at top of fourth page*] If you conclude to come direct from C to Rochester without stoping—you can name the time so that I can meet you at the depot

& ALS, SBA Papers, MCR-S. Letters in square brackets obscured by ink smudge.

1. The most recent of SBA's letters home is dated 11 June 1848, *Film*,

6:684–87. William H. Davis (1825–?), a nephew of Mary Stafford Read, traveled regularly between his parents' home in Canajoharie and his apprenticeship to a grocery and wine merchant in Rochester, and the Anthonys relied on him to carry letters and packages. (*History of Montgomery and Fulton Counties, N.Y.*, 158; Washington Frothingham, ed., *History of Montgomery County* [Syracuse, N.Y., 1892], 41–42.)

2. Daniel Anthony recounts the first step in the organization of the Yearly Meeting of Congregational Friends at Waterloo. At Farmington in the week of 11 June, the Genesee Yearly Meeting of the Society of Friends divided, the Hicksites retaining the structure and discipline of the Friends, the liberals and abolitionists endorsing the autonomy of each congregation. As Anthony explains, abolitionism precipitated the crisis, when Friends who worked in secular antislavery societies were disciplined. That power to discipline was at the heart of the dispute. The dissidents agreed that no true church could restrict a Christian's liberty of conscience. According to the principles drafted in June and signed in October, "the recognition of the right of every member to act in obedience to the evidence of Divine Light, in its present and progressive unfolding of truth and duty to the mind, must be a fundamental principle in every right organization." A congregation of equals would also recognize the perfect equality of men and women, manifested in the decision to "meet together and transact business jointly." The June meeting called Friends to convene again in October 1848, when Thomas McClintock's Basis of Religious Association was adopted. (Hallowell, *James and Lucretia Mott*, 298–325; Benjamin F. Gue, *Diary of Benjamin F. Gue in Rural New York and Pioneer Iowa, 1847–1856*, ed. Earle D. Ross [Ames, Ia., 1962], 33–34; *Basis of Religious Association, Adopted by the Conference Held at Farmington, in the State of New York, on the Sixth and Seventh of Tenth Month, 1848* [Waterloo, N.Y., 1848]; Wellman, "Seneca Falls Women's Rights Convention," 24–27; A. Day Bradley, "Progressive Friends in Michigan and New York," *Quaker History* 52 [1963]: 95–103; Hugh Barbour et al., eds., *Quaker Crosscurrents: Three Hundred Years of Friends in the New York Yearly Meetings* [Syracuse, N.Y., 1995], 134–35, 174–75.)

3. The Basis of Religious Association proposed to discontinue meetings of ministers and elders in order to prevent "the abuses and evils of ecclesiastical organizations"; "a true church organization does not admit of placing one or more persons over a congregation as the stated spiritual teacher, or teachers." Congregational Friends would "meet together as brethren."

4. The Rochester and Auburn rail line passed through Vienna, within the village of Phelps, where the Anthonys visited Joseph and Amy Read Howe, who were, in turn, visiting their children. Daniel Anthony also mentions one of the Howe daughters, Nancy Howe Clark (1811–1897); her husband Lemuel Clark, a Presbyterian minister; and their young daughters, Emily and Susan. The Clarks probably lived in Brockport at this time. (Howe, *Howe Genealogies*, 200; *ACAB*, s.v. "Griggs, Emily Clark"; and obituary tipped into SBA diary, 1897, *Film*, 36:247ff.)

22 ✎ LUCRETIA COFFIN MOTT TO ECS

Auburn[1] 7 mo. 16th 48—

Dear Elizabeth

I ought to have answered thy first kind letter of information &
invitation, other than by verbal message sent by our mutual friend
Mary Ann M'Clintock, who hoped to see thee a few minutes, on her
return from Deruyter—[2] I requested her to tell thee how poorly my
husband was, and that it was not likely I should be able to go to Seneca
Falls, before the morning of the Convention. James continues quite
unwell—I hope however that he will be able to be present the 2nd day.

My sister Martha[3] will accompany me on 4th day morn^g—& we will
with pleasure accept thy kind invite to your house that night if you
should not be too much crowded with company. My daughter Martha[4]
thinks she is not quite enough of a reformer, to attend such a Convention. The true reason however, I presume is, that she is more interested
just now, with her cousins here, & her time being short she dont
incline to leave them.

James says thy great speech thou must reserve for the second day, so
that he & others may be able to hear it. I was right glad to hear of thy
resolve, & hope thou wilt not give out—

The convention will not be so large as it otherwise might be, owing
to the busy time with the farmers, harvest &c— But it will be a
beginning & we may hope it will be followed ↑in due time↓ by one of a
more general character.

I have just returned from a meeting with the prisoners & many
others—have another appointment this evening @ 6 o['clock] at the
Universalist Church—[5]

Are you going to have any reform or other meeting during the
sittings of the Convention?

We shall go from the Cars directly to the meeting on 4th day

Give thyself no trouble about meeting us. There will be enough to
conduct us thither. Lovingly thine

✎ *Lucretia Mott*

❦ ALS, ECS Papers, DLC. Transcript in ECS Papers, NjR, and in *Stanton*, 2:17–18. Letters in square brackets were torn from a corner.

1. Home of her sister Martha Coffin Wright. Lucretia and James Mott spent much of the summer of 1848 in New York and Canada, with visits to the Seneca tribe at the Cattaraugus Reservation and African-American refugees in Canada West, attendance at Genesee Yearly Meeting, and participation in two woman's rights conventions. (L. C. Mott to Edmund Quincy, *Lib.*, 6 October 1848.)

2. Mary Ann Wilson McClintock (1800–1884) moved to Waterloo with her husband Thomas in 1836, and like him was a leader among Quakers and an abolitionist. She and Lucretia Mott were visiting Quaker communities, like the one at De Ruyter, in Madison County east of Auburn, about the Congregational Friends. (*Quaker Genealogy*, 2:240, 274, 807; *History*, 3:454; *Friends' Intelligencer* 41 [1885]: 250.)

3. Martha Coffin Pelham Wright (1806–1875) had married, at age eighteen, an army captain from Kentucky named Peter Pelham and moved with him to Florida. Two years later she was back in Philadelphia, a widow and a mother. After a stint teaching, she married David Wright (1805–1897), a lawyer, in 1829, moved to New York, and had six children in addition to the daughter from her first marriage. Though she did not share her sister's religious faith, Martha Wright was a stalwart of the state antislavery society and, after attending the meeting at Seneca Falls, one of the inner circle of woman's rights leaders until the end of her life. An avid letter writer and a wit, she left a valuable archives of correspondence on woman's rights and woman suffrage. (*NAW*; Hallowell, *James and Lucretia Mott*.)

4. Martha Mott (1828–1880) was the youngest of Lucretia Mott's children. In 1853 she married George W. Lord. (Hallowell, *James and Lucretia Mott*, 337, 376, 404, 421.)

5. The New York State prison at Auburn, completed in 1820.

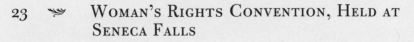

23 ❧ WOMAN'S RIGHTS CONVENTION, HELD AT SENECA FALLS

[19–20 July 1848]

A Convention to discuss the Social, Civil, and Religious Condition of Woman, was called by the Women of Seneca County, N.Y., and held at the village of Seneca Falls, in the Wesleyan Chapel,[1] on the 19th and 20th of July, 1848.

The question was discussed throughout two entire days: the first day by women exclusively, the second day men participated in the deliberations. Lucretia Mott, of Philadelphia, was the moving spirit of the occasion.

On the morning of the 19th, the Convention assembled at 11 o'clock. The meeting was organized by appointing Mary M'Clintock[2] Secretary. The object of the meeting was then stated by Elizabeth C. Stanton; after which, remarks were made by Lucretia Mott, urging the women present to throw aside the trammels of education, and not allow their new position to prevent them from joining in the debates of the meeting. The Declaration of Sentiments, offered for the acceptance of the Convention, was then read by E. C. Stanton. A proposition was made to have it re-read by paragraph, and after much consideration, some changes were suggested and adopted. The propriety of obtaining the signatures of men to the Declaration was discussed in an animated manner: a vote in favor was given; but concluding that the final decision would be the legitimate business of the next day, it was referred.

Adjourned to half-past two.

In the afternoon, the meeting assembled according to adjournment, and was opened by reading the minutes of the morning session. E. C. Stanton then addressed the meeting,[3] and was followed by Lucretia Mott. The reading of the Declaration was called for, an addition having been inserted since the morning session. A vote taken upon the amendment was carried, and papers circulated to obtain signatures. The following resolutions were then read:

Whereas, the great precept of nature is conceded to be, "that man shall pursue his own true and substantial happiness," Blackstone, in his Commentaries, remarks, that this law of Nature being coeval with mankind, and dictated by God himself, is of course superior in obligation to any other.[4] It is binding over all the globe, in all countries, and at all times; no human laws are of any validity if contrary to this, and such of them as are valid, derive all their force, and all their validity, and all their authority, mediately and immediately, from this original; Therefore,

Resolved, That such laws as conflict, in any way, with the true and substantial happiness of woman, are contrary to the great precept of nature, and of no validity; for this is "superior in obligation to any other."

Resolved, That all laws which prevent woman from occupying such a station in society as her conscience shall dictate, or which place her in a position inferior to that of man, are contrary to the great precept of nature, and therefore of no force or authority.

Resolved, That woman is man's equal—was intended to be so by the Creator, and the highest good of the race demands that she should be recognized as such.

Resolved, That the women of this country ought to be enlightened in regard to the laws under which they live, that they may no longer publish their degradation, by declaring themselves satisfied with their present position, nor their ignorance, by asserting that they have all the rights they want.

Resolved, That inasmuch as man, while claiming for himself intellectual superiority, does accord to woman moral superiority, it is preeminently his duty to encourage her to speak, and teach, as she has an opportunity, in all religious assemblies.

Resolved, That the same amount of virtue, delicacy, and refinement of behavior, that is required of woman in the social state, should also be required of man, and the same transgressions should be visited with equal severity on both man and woman.

Resolved, That the objection of indelicacy and impropriety, which is so often brought against woman when she addresses a public audience, comes with a very ill grace from those who encourage, by their attendance, her appearance on the stage, in the concert, or in the feats of the circus.

Resolved, That woman has too long rested satisfied in the circumscribed limits which corrupt customs and a perverted application of the Scriptures have marked out for her, and that it is time she should move in the enlarged sphere which her great Creator has assigned her.[5]

Resolved, That it is the duty of the women of this country to secure to themselves their sacred right to the elective franchise.[6]

Resolved, That the equality of human rights results necessarily from the fact of the identity of the race in capabilities and responsibilities.

Resolved, therefore, That, being invested by the Creator with the same capabilities, and the same consciousness of responsibility for their exercise, it is demonstrably the right and duty of woman, equally with man, to promote every righteous cause, by every righteous means; and especially in regard to the great subjects of morals and religion, it is self-evidently her right to participate with her brother in teaching them, both in private and in public, by writing and by speaking, by any instrumentalities proper to be used, and in any assemblies proper to be held; and this being a self-evident truth, growing out of the divinely implanted principles of human nature, any custom or authority adverse to it, whether modern or wearing the hoary sanction of antiquity, is to be regarded as self-evident falsehood, and at war with the interests of mankind.

Lucretia Mott read a humorous article from a newspaper, written by Martha C. Wright. After an address by E. W. M'Clintock, the meeting adjourned to 10 o'clock the next morning.

In the evening, Lucretia Mott spoke with her usual eloquence and power to a large and intelligent audience on the subject of Reforms in general.[7]

THURSDAY MORNING.

The Convention assembled at the hour appointed, James Mott, of Philadelphia, in the Chair. The minutes of the previous day having been read, E. C. Stanton again read the Declaration of Sentiments, which was freely discussed by Lucretia Mott, Ansel Bascom,[8] S. E. Woodworth,[9] Thomas and Mary Ann M'Clintock, Frederick Douglass,[10] Amy Post,[11] Catharine Stebbins,[12] and Elizabeth C. Stanton, and was unanimously adopted, as follows:

DECLARATION OF SENTIMENTS.

When, in the course of human events, it becomes necessary for one portion of the family of man to assume among the people of the earth a position different from that which they have hitherto occupied, but one to which the laws of nature and of nature's God entitle them, a decent respect to the opinions of mankind requires that they should declare the causes that impel them to such a course.

We hold these truths to be self-evident: that all men and women are created equal; that they are endowed by their Creator with certain inalienable rights; that among these are life, liberty, and the pursuit of happiness; that to secure these rights governments are instituted, deriving their just powers from the consent of the governed. Whenever any form of Government becomes destructive of these ends, it is the right of those who suffer from it to refuse allegiance to it, and to insist upon the institution of a new government, laying its foundation on such principles, and organizing its powers in such form as to them shall seem most likely to effect their safety and happiness. Prudence, indeed, will dictate that governments long established should not be changed for light and transient causes; and accordingly, all experience hath shown that mankind are more disposed to suffer, while evils are sufferable, than to right themselves by abolishing the forms to which they are accustomed. But when a long train of abuses and usurpations, pursuing invariably the same object, evinces a design to reduce them under absolute despotism, it is their duty to throw off such government, and to provide new guards for their future security. Such has been the patient sufferance of the women under this government, and such is now the necessity which constrains them to demand the equal station to which they are entitled.

The history of mankind is a history of repeated injuries and usurpations on the part of man toward woman, having in direct object the establishment of an absolute tyranny over her. To prove this, let facts be submitted to a candid world.

He has never permitted her to exercise her inalienable right to the elective franchise.

He has compelled her to submit to laws, in the formation of which she had no voice.

He has withheld from her rights which are given to the most ignorant and degraded men—both natives and foreigners.

Having deprived her of this first right of a citizen, the elective franchise, thereby leaving her without representation in the halls of legislation, he has oppressed her on all sides.

He has made her, if married, in the eye of the law, civilly dead.[13]

He has taken from her all right in property, even to the wages she earns.[14]

He has made her, morally, an irresponsible being, as she can commit many crimes with impunity, provided they be done in the presence of her husband. In the covenant of marriage, she is compelled to promise obedience to her husband, he becoming, to all intents and purposes, her master—the law giving him power to deprive her of her liberty, and to administer chastisement.

He has so framed the laws of divorce, as to what shall be the proper causes of divorce; in case of separation, to whom the guardianship of the children shall be given; as to be wholly regardless of the happiness of women—the law, in all cases, going upon the false supposition of the supremacy of man, and giving all power into his hands.

After depriving her of all rights as a married woman, if single and the owner of property, he has taxed her to support a government which recognizes her only when her property can be made profitable to it.

He has monopolized nearly all the profitable employments, and from those she is permitted to follow, she receives but a scanty remuneration.

He closes against her all the avenues to wealth and distinction, which he considers most honorable to himself. As a teacher of theology, medicine, or law, she is not known.

He has denied her the facilities for obtaining a thorough education—all colleges being closed against her.[15]

He allows her in Church as well as State, but a subordinate position, claiming Apostolic authority for her exclusion from the ministry, and, with some exceptions, from any public participation in the affairs of the Church.

He has created a false public sentiment, by giving to the world a different code of morals for men and women, by which moral delinquencies which exclude women from society, are not only tolerated but deemed of little account in man.

He has usurped the prerogative of Jehovah himself, claiming it as his right to assign for her a sphere of action, when that belongs to her conscience and her God.

He has endeavored, in every way that he could to destroy her confidence in her own powers, to lessen her self-respect, and to make her willing to lead a dependant and abject life.

Now, in view of this entire disfranchisement of one-half the people of this country, their social and religious degradation,—in view of the unjust laws above mentioned, and because women do feel themselves aggrieved, oppressed, and fraudulently deprived of their most sacred rights, we insist that they have immediate admission to all the rights and privileges which belong to them as citizens of these United States.

In entering upon the great work before us, we anticipate no small amount of misconception, misrepresentation, and ridicule; but we shall use every instrumentality within our power to effect our object. We shall employ agents, circulate tracts, petition the State and national Legislatures, and endeavor to enlist the pulpit and the press in our behalf. We hope this Convention will be followed by a series of Conventions, embracing every part of the country.

Firmly relying upon the final triumph of the Right and the True, we do this day affix our signatures to this declaration.[16]

Lucretia Mott,	Hannah Plant,
Harriet Cady Eaton,	Lucy Jones,
Margaret Pryor,	Sarah Whitney,
Elizabeth Cady Stanton,	Mary H. Hallowell,
Eunice Newton Foote,	Elizabeth Conklin,
Mary Ann M'Clintock,	Sally Pitcher,
Margaret Schooley,	Mary Conklin,
Martha C. Wright,	Susan Quinn,
Jane C. Hunt,	Mary S. Mirror,
Amy Post,	Phebe King,
Catharine F. Stebbins,	Julia Ann Drake,
Mary Ann Frink,	Charlotte Woodard,
Lydia Mount,	Martha Underhill,
Delia Mathews,	Dorothy Mathews,
Catharine C. Paine,	Eunice Barker,
Elizabeth W. M'Clintock,	Sarah R. Woods,
Malvina Seymour,	Lydia Gild,
Phebe Mosher,	Sarah Hoffman,
Catharine Shaw,	Elizabeth Leslie,
Deborah Scott,	Martha Ridley,
Sarah Hallowell,	Rachel D. Bonnel,
Mary M'Clintock,	Betsey Tewksbury,
Mary Gilbert,	Rhoda Palmer,
Sophrone Taylor,	Margaret Jenkins,
Cynthia Davis,	Cynthia Fuller,
Mary Martin,	Eliza Martin,
P. A. Culvert,	Maria E. Wilbur,
Susan R. Doty,	Elizabeth D. Smith,
Rebecca Race,	Caroline Barker,
Sarah A. Mosher,	Ann Porter,
Mary E. Vail,	Experience Gibbs,
Lucy Spalding,	Antoinette E. Segur,
Lavinia Latham,	Hannah J. Latham,
Sarah Smith,	Sarah Sisson.

The following are the names of the gentlemen present in favor of the movement:

Richard P. Hunt,
Samuel D. Tillman,
Justin Williams,
Elisha Foote,
Frederick Douglass,
Henry W. Seymour,
Henry Seymour,
David Salding,
William G. Barker,
Elias J. Doty,
John Jones,
William S. Dell,
James Mott,
William Burroughs,
Robert Smalldridge,
Jacob Matthews,

Charles L. Hoskins,
Thomas M'Clintock,
Saron Phillips,
Jacob Chamberlain,
Jonathan Metcalf,
Nathan J. Milliken,
S. E. Woodworth,
Edward F. Underhill,
George W. Pryor,
Joel Bunker,
Isaac Van Tassel,
Thomas Dell,
E. W. Capron,
Stephen Shear,
Henry Hatley,
Azaliah Schooley.

The meeting adjourned until two o'clock.

AFTERNOON SESSION.

At the appointed hour the meeting convened. The minutes having been read, the resolutions of the day before were read and taken up separately. Some, from their self-evident truth, elicited but little remark; others, after some criticism, much debate, and some slight alterations, were finally passed by a large majority.[17] The meeting closed with a forcible speech from Lucretia Mott.

Adjourned to half-past seven o'clock.

EVENING SESSION.

The meeting opened by reading the minutes, Thomas M'Clintock in the Chair. As there had been no opposition expressed during the Convention to this movement, and although, after repeated invitations, no objections had presented themselves, E. C. Stanton volunteered an address in defence of the many severe accusations brought against the much-abused "Lords of Creation."

Thomas M'Clintock then read several extracts from Blackstone, in proof of woman's servitude to man; after which Lucretia Mott offered and spoke to the following resolution:

Resolved, That the speedy success of our cause depends upon the zealous and untiring efforts of both men and women, for the overthrow of the monopoly of the pulpit, and for the securing to woman an equal participation with men in the various trades, professions and commerce.

The Resolution was adopted.

M. A. M'Clintock, Jr. delivered a short, but impressive address, calling upon woman to arouse from her lethargy and be true to herself and her God. When she had concluded, Frederick Douglass arose, and in an excellent and appropriate speech, ably supported the cause of woman.[18]

The meeting was closed by one of Lucretia Mott's most beautiful and spiritual appeals. She commanded the earnest attention of that large audience for nearly an hour.

M. A. M'Clintock, E. N. Foote,[19] Amy Post, E. W. M'Clintock, and E. C. Stanton, were appointed a Committee to prepare the proceedings of the Convention for publication.

❧ *Report of the Woman's Rights Convention, Held at Seneca Falls, N.Y., July 19th and 20th, 1848* (Rochester, 1848). The resolutions were also published in *Seneca County Courier*, 4 August 1848. The report was reprinted in 1870 by Robert J. Johnston of New York within *Proceedings of the Woman's Rights Conventions at Seneca Falls and Rochester, N.Y., July and August, 1848*. Though he reset the type, Johnston reproduced the original title page that named John Dick, at the North Star Office, as printer. Also in *History*, 1:70–73.

1. The First Wesleyan Society of Seneca Falls broke away from the Methodist Episcopal Church in 1843 and built its chapel at the corner of Mynderse and Falls streets.

2. Mary Ann McClintock (c. 1823–1880), sometimes designated "Jr.," was a daughter of Thomas and Mary Ann McClintock. She married James Truman of Philadelphia in 1852, and after he completed his medical training, they lived in Waterloo, Philadelphia, and for a time in Germany. (*Quaker Genealogy*, 2:824; *NCAB*, 24:299–300; research by Judith Wellman.)

3. None of the speeches made at the convention was reported, despite the presence of at least three newspapermen: Nathan J. Milliken of the *Seneca County Courier*, Frederick Douglass of the *North Star*, and E. W. Capron of the *National Reformer*. On the problem of recovering what ECS said, see editorial note below at September 1848.

4. This entire paragraph and the sense of the one following are taken from the section, "Of the Nature of Laws in General," in the introductory book of William Blackstone, *Commentaries on the Laws of England in Four Books* (New York, 1841), 1:27-28. The quotation marks are in Blackstone.

5. From a resolution by Angelina Grimké adopted at the female antislavery convention of 1837. (*Turning the World Upside Down: The Anti-Slavery Convention of American Women, Held in New York City, May 9-12, 1837*, ed. Dorothy Sterling [New York, 1987], 13.)

6. New York's constitution of 1846, like that of many states, defined eligible voters as "males." For white men it guaranteed universal suffrage. Black men could vote only if they owned sufficient property. Prior to 1848, claims that women shared an equal right to the franchise arose not only in debates about their property rights but also in connection with efforts to amend the constitution and grant equal political rights to African-American men. The restriction on black voting remained in place until after the Civil War. (N.Y. Const. of 1846, art. II, sec. 1; Judith Wellman, "Women's Rights, Republicanism, and Revolutionary Rhetoric in Antebellum New York State," *New York History* 69 [July 1988]: 353-84.)

7. E. W. Capron described Lucretia Mott's address as "one of the most eloquent, logical and philosophical discourses we ever listened to." Speaking on a similar topic to the American Anti-Slavery Society in 1848, she urged each reformer to "be as the Jesus of the present age"; "Let us no longer be blinded by the dim theology that only in the far seeing vision discovers a millennium, when violence shall no more be heard in the land—wasting nor destruction in her borders; but let us behold it now, nigh at the door—lending faith and confidence to our hopes." (Auburn *National Reformer*, 3 August 1848, in ECS Papers, DLC; Mott, *Complete Speeches*, 71-79.)

8. Ansel Bascom (1802-1862), a lawyer, reformer, and local political leader, was the Free Soil party's candidate for Congress. He represented Seneca County in the constitutional convention of 1846, where he urged equal suffrage for blacks, and propounded a radical view of the laws of marriage and property. Marriage, he argued, should not vest in either party the property of the other, nor should it impose liabilities for debts acquired before marriage. Bascom was also a member of the legislature that passed the Married Women's Property Act of 1848. (Edward Doubleday Harris, *A Genealogical Record of Thomas Bascom and His Descendants* [Boston, 1870], 61-62; Glenn C. Altschuler and Jan M. Saltzgaber, *Revivalism, Social Conscience, and Community in the Burned-Over District: The Trial of Rhoda Bement* [Ithaca, N.Y., 1983], 22-27, 81; Wellman, "Seneca Falls Women's Rights Convention," 18; Basch, *In the Eyes of the Law*, 151, 168; *Eighty Years*, 144-45, 153.)

9. Stephen E. Woodworth (1816-?), a member of the Baptist Church, owned a general store in Seneca Falls. A bachelor in the summer of 1848, he was married soon after the convention either to signer Mary Gilbert or to a sister of hers. (Research by Judith Wellman.)

10. Frederick Douglass (1818–1895), the only African American at the meeting, escaped from slavery in Maryland in the fall of 1838 and settled in Massachusetts. Early in the 1840s he began to lecture and swiftly became one of the most persuasive and appealing witnesses against slavery. William Lloyd Garrison encouraged him, and Douglass toured with agents of the American Anti-Slavery Society. After two years in England, he returned in 1847 with the idea of publishing his own paper, an act of independence opposed by Garrison and his friends in Boston. Douglass moved to Rochester and issued the first number of the *North Star* on 3 December 1847. He tried to straddle the division between local Garrisonians, among whom he found close friends like Amy Post and Daniel Anthony, and the region's political abolitionists, like Gerrit Smith, whose ideas he shared and whose support made his newspaper possible. Though Douglass disagreed with elements of the antebellum woman's rights platform, particularly with the demand for equal property rights within marriage, he was a consistent supporter of woman's right to vote, and he maintained a friendship with ECS and SBA until his death. (William S. McFeely, *Frederick Douglass* [New York, 1991]; Benjamin Quarles, *Frederick Douglass* [1948; reprint, New York, 1968]; Douglass, *Papers*, 2:451.)

11. Amy Kirby Post (1802–1889), well known as an abolitionist in Rochester, was joined at the convention by her sister Sarah Kirby Hallowell and her stepdaughter Mary Post Hallowell. She and her husband Isaac Post (1798–1872) were founding members of the Western New York Anti-Slavery Society. Like other antislavery Friends in the region, the Posts parted company with the Genesee Yearly Meeting to join the dissidents who organized the Congregational Friends in 1848. There was little of radical reform in Rochester that did not pass through their house; spirit communication was studied and authenticated there; radical lecturers and fugitive slaves stayed there; campaigns against capital punishment met there; and Amy Post helped to arrange Rochester's woman's rights convention on 2 August 1848. (*NAW*; *ACAB*; Nancy A. Hewitt, "Amy Kirby Post," *University of Rochester Library Bulletin* 37 [1984]: 4–21.)

12. Catharine Ann Fish Stebbins was the daughter of Rochester abolitionists and radicals and wife of the antislavery lecturer Giles Badger Stebbins. Her marriage took place while her family lived in a utopian community at Sodus Bay on Lake Ontario, but the couple settled in Rochester for many years. Active in the Congregational Friends, they were also early believers in spiritualism. Catharine Stebbins was identified with woman's rights and woman suffrage the rest of her life. In 1871, when women in many parts of the country tried to vote, she made a well-publicized attempt to register in Detroit. She held numerous offices in the National Woman Suffrage Association, and she contributed to the *History of Woman Suffrage*, writing a reminiscence of Josephine Griffing and a chapter on Michigan. (Hewitt, *Women's Activism and Social Change*, 130, 192–93, 214; *History*, 2:26–39, 3:47–48, 523–25; Giles Badger Stebbins, *Upward Steps of Seventy Years. Autobiographic, Biographic, Historic* [New York, 1890].)

13. With this passage and the list of legal wrongs that follows, the authors join a debate about reforming American law to remove remnants of English common law. They point to the infamous passage in Blackstone's *Commentaries* about the effect of marriage on the woman: "By marriage, the husband and wife are one person in law: that is, the very being or legal existence of the woman is suspended during the marriage, or at least is incorporated and consolidated into that of the husband; under whose wing, protection, and *cover*, she performs every thing." From a considerable literature about married women's rights, legal reform, and the common law, the authors appear to have known the work of Elisha Powell Hurlbut especially well. Hurlbut (1807–?) was born and practiced law in Herkimer County, until he moved to New York City in 1835. His *Essays on Human Rights, and Their Political Guaranties*, published in 1845, is an extreme statement of inalienable individual rights, informed by phrenology and legal history and laced with sarcasm. Reformers kept the book in print. The Scottish phrenologist George Combe added preface and notes for an edition published in Edinburgh in 1847, and the American firm of Fowlers and Wells reprinted Combe's edition between 1848 and 1853. Hurlbut was elected a judge of New York's Supreme Court at the same time as Daniel Cady in 1847, and ECS met him in Albany in the 1840s. Like other legal reformers, Hurlbut rejected the English common law as a feudal artifact unsuited to modern America, but his criticism included a scathing portrait of male domination that is echoed in the Declaration of Sentiments. The common law, he wrote, was "the law of the male sex gathering unto themselves dominion and power at the sacrifice of the female." Its influence rendered the laws "touching the Rights of Woman, . . . at variance with the laws of the Creator; and the question is, Which shall stand?" In his chapter on "The Rights of Woman," he described woman's civil death; "in the eye of the law" the woman who marries "exists not at all," she is placed in a "legal tomb." Her property is conferred upon her husband because "every body knows that the dead cannot keep their property—and the wife is legally dead." The authors of the Declaration followed Hurlbut in all their examples. Of woman's criminal impunity, he asked, "Hath not woman a *right* to be ever regarded as a free moral agent?" He condemned any coercion of a wife "as an inferior and dependent," no matter how mild, and he singled out the male-defined laws of divorce and custody as proof that women needed a voice in legislation. (Blackstone, *Commentaries on the Laws of England*, 1:355; Elisha P. Hurlbut, *Essays on Human Rights, and Their Political Guaranties* [New York, 1848], 120–21, 148, 161, 163, 167; Henry H. Hurlbut, *The Hurlbut Genealogy, or Record of the Descendants of Thomas Hurlbut, of Saybrook and Wethersfield, Conn.* [Albany, 1888], 232, 350–51; ECS to Editor, Boston *Index*, 16 October 1876, *Film*, 18:1055–56.)

14. This statement omits the new Married Women's Property Act of 1848.

15. Oberlin College was the exception; it admitted women at its founding and granted them bachelor degrees in 1841.

16. One hundred names appear in this list. ECS recalled that some people later removed their names. Signers who appear elsewhere in this volume are identified at the dates listed below. E. W. Capron, 14 April 1854; Jacob P. Chamberlain, 27 September 1860; Harriet Cady Eaton, 15 April 1847; Mary H. Post Hallowell, 25 May 1852; Jane C. and Richard P. Hunt, 3 October 1848; Elizabeth W. McClintock, 14 July 1848; Mary Ann Wilson McClintock, 16 July 1848; Thomas McClintock, 3 February 1843; Nathan J. Milliken, 23 July 1848; James and Lucretia Mott, 25 June 1840; George W. and Margaret Wilson Pryor, 3 February 1843; Martha Wright, 16 July 1848.

Most of the signers took no further public part in the movement for woman's rights. Historian Judith Wellman has identified eighty-three of the sixty-eight women and thirty-two men. By and large, she writes, they were drawn to the convention by local ties. The majority lived in Seneca Falls and nearby Waterloo; others traveled from Rochester, Auburn, and surrounding counties. Not only did ECS bring her sister Harriet Eaton, and Lucretia Mott accompany her sister Martha Wright, but more than half of the signers attended the convention in the company of a sister, parent, child, cousin, or spouse. Wellman describes public networks that drew people to the Wesleyan Chapel as well. Every church in Seneca Falls was represented by someone, but dissident Quakers made up the largest group. The Junius Monthly Meeting in Waterloo, a center of the Congregational Friends, was well represented, and Quakers traveled the longest distances to attend. Another network consisted of local Free Soilers, proponents of a new political party to unite antislavery Democrats and Whigs, who held a series of meetings in Seneca Falls in the summer of 1848. Eighteen of the twenty-six people from the village had family members who supported the Free Soil movement, including ECS, whose husband was out of town lecturing for the new party. The third network was made up of legal reformers, whose ideas shaped discussion, but Ansel Bascom, the most conspicuous among them, did not sign the Declaration. (Wellman, "Seneca Falls Women's Rights Convention.")

17. Of this discussion and its outcome, E. W. Capron reported, the resolutions "were finally adopted, nearly as they were originally drawn up" by the women meeting alone on Wednesday morning; not even the lawyers who opposed "the equal rights of women, and who were present," dissented. In the *History of Woman Suffrage*, ECS wrote that only the resolution about the elective franchise "was not unanimously adopted." "Those who took part in the debate," she recalled, "feared a demand for the right to vote would defeat others they deemed more rational, and make the whole movement ridiculous." She and Frederick Douglass, who saw that suffrage "was the right by which all others could be secured," carried the resolution "by a small majority." (Auburn *National Reformer*, 3 August 1848; *History*, 1:73.)

18. Though no record of his speech survives, Douglass wrote in the July 28 issue of the *North Star*, that from atop "the watch-tower of human freedom," he applauded all movements "to improve and elevate the character and condition

of any members of the human family." "In respect to political rights, we hold woman to be justly entitled to all we claim for man. We go farther, and express our conviction that all political rights which it is expedient for man to exercise, it is equally so for woman. All that distinguishes man as an intelligent and accountable being, is equally true of woman; and if that government is only just which governs by the free consent of the governed, there can be no reason in the world for denying to woman the exercise of the elective franchise, or a hand in making and administering the laws of the land. Our doctrine is, that 'Right is of no sex.'" (Clipping in SBA scrapbooks, Rare Books, DLC; also in ECS Papers, DLC; reprinted in *History*, 1:74–75.)

19. Eunice Newton Foote (1819–?) came to the convention and signed the Declaration with her husband Elisha Foote (1809–1883). She married Foote in 1841 after he completed his legal studies with Daniel Cady, and they settled in Seneca Falls. There he served as district attorney, judge of the county's court of common pleas, and village president in the 1840s. The Footes shared an interest in science and technology and took part in meetings of the American Association for the Advancement of Science in the 1850s. One of their daughters, Mary Newton Foote Henderson of Missouri was a prominent suffragist after the Civil War. (*NCAB*, 21:339–40; *New York Times*, 27 October 1883; research by Judith Wellman.)

·◖▬▬▬▭▬▬▬◗·

24 ⪼ ECS AND ELIZABETH W. McCLINTOCK TO
THE EDITORS, *SENECA COUNTY COURIER*

[*after 23 July 1848*][1]

Messrs. Editors: If your columns are open to the women of Seneca county, we throw down the glove to any one who will meet us, in fair argument, on the great question of Woman's Rights. Depend upon it, this soon will be *the* question of the day. All other reforms, however important they may be, cannot so deeply affect the interests of humanity, as this one. Let it therefore be fairly and candidly met. Ridicule will not have any effect on those who seriously feel themselves aggrieved; argument is far better.

We have recently had the pleasure of listening to a sermon on this subject, and we feel truly grateful that the pulpit is, at length, calling public attention to this important question.[2] In the course of this sermon the Bible argument was *touched upon*. We hope it may yet be gone into more fully; for the Bible is the great Charter of human rights, when it is taken in its true spiritual meaning; though its great, immortal, life-giving truths can be perverted by narrow, bigoted, sectarian teachers so as to favor all kinds of oppression, and to degrade and crush humanity itself. No reform has ever been started but the Bible, falsely interpreted, has opposed it. Wine-drinking was proved to be right by the Bible. Slavery was proved to be an institution of the Bible. War, with its long train of calamities and abominations is proved to be right by the Bible. Capital punishment is taught in the Bible. Now, it seems to us, the time has fully come for this much abused book to change hands. Let the people no longer trust to their blind guides, but read and reason for themselves—even though they thus call down on themselves the opprobrious epithet of "infidel," than which no word in our language is more misunderstood and misapplied. We throw back the charge of infidelity on the religionists of the present day, for though they assert their belief in the Divinity of Christ, they deny, in theory and practice, his Divine commands. Do they not rally around and support all the great sins of this guilty nation? What say they to the golden rule, and the injunction, "Resist not evil"?[3] Why, the self-styled christians of our day have fought in and supported the unjust and cruel Mexican war,[4] and have long held men, women, and children in bondage. Oft-times, when no conclusive arguments can be brought to bear upon a subject, a cry of "infidelity" is raised, that the mind of the public may be prejudiced against it. In the sermon referred to, the speaker endeavored to make still stronger the fetters that bind the spirit of woman, and one of his most effective instrumentalities, or one that he seemed to consider the most effective, from its many repetitions, was this charge of infidelity; as if a regard for the rights of any portion of God's children can merit such an epithet; as if a belief in and a desire to act in accordance with the truth, that, there is "neither Jew nor Greek, male nor female, bond nor free, but all are one in Christ Jesus"[5] can be so termed; as if a conviction that woman possesses a conscience, active and clear, which proves for her as able a guide as that of man, can be called infidelity. Rather let the term apply to him who, in direct opposition to the spirit of Christianity, endeavors, by isolated passages of Scripture, to destroy the conscience and the sense of moral accountability in one half the people of the earth; to make it their duty to look up to and obey man instead of that Divine Being who claims the reverence and obedience of all his sons and daughters. It is time this charge should rest where it rightfully belongs—upon those who are infidel to truth; upon those who,

> Torture the pages of the hallowed Bible
> To sanction crime, and robbery, and blood;
> And in oppression's hateful service, libel
> Both man and God.[6]

The great truth uttered by our Revolutionary fathers, that "no government can be formed without the consent of the governed," refers of course to human government. We can in no wise control God's government, and we would not if we could, for as far as we understand His laws, they are in perfect harmony with the nature of him whom they are to control. His laws, engraven on the heart of man, made manifest in all nature, and written in his revealed word, do but re-echo the same great truths.

The speaker broadly asserted that the customs and government of our day were established by God. Every nation has claimed the same, in all past times. When have any people been willing to believe themselves unfavored and unapproved by God? The wicked Jews made God the author of all their wars and calamities. They claimed for themselves His peculiar guidance. "Thus saith the Lord" was not more falsely used then than now, to bind heavy burthens and lay grievous commands in His name, on the innocent and confiding. No doubt the spiritual Fathers stand up in old England this day and declare that "the powers that be are ordained of God."[7] Honor the King (or Queen)[8] say they, but we, having "gone in advance of the Bible," have rebelled against the King; cast his crown under foot, set aside his laws, and declared all men free and equal. Was this treason against God and man? Was this "blotting out the Bible and trampling it under foot"? Was this "rank infidelity"? Certainly, if these passages of Holy Writ, "The powers that be are ordained of God," and "Honor the king," are to be taken literally. But all see the absurdity of this position. Let go the letter of the Bible and seize hold of the true, spiritual meaning that runs through every page. It is very clear, to every thinking mind, that there is no government on the face of the earth, established by God. Ours is certainly better than any other, yet, think you, that, with our slavery and war; our political rioting; the lamentable condition of our church, whose priests tithe mint, annise, and cummin, and neglect the weightier matters of the law, justice, mercy, and truth;[9] think you, I say, that the God of love smiles complacently or approvingly on our republican experiment? Verily! no!

Before we can reverently bow down, either to man or his government, you must first prove both to be divine. "Wives obey your husbands."[10] We place this injunction in the same category with, "Honor the King." Let those who consider these commands binding, marry *wise* men, and get them to Belgium with all possible expedition, as that is one of the few, little corners of God's green earth where the species of gentleman called King is allowed to breathe.[11] The greatest nation in the world is at this moment under the government of a woman, and we may travel through the length and breadth of her dominions and no priest will tell you that it is a sin for a woman to reign and rule over a mighty people, prorogue parliament, review her armies in person, and *hold her own husband as a subject*. For ourselves, we believe no one worthy of being called master, but God himself, and to Him alone will we stand or fall. Christ, the greatest of Teachers, from whom the Divinity shone forth most clearly when on earth, says nothing degrading or derogatory to woman. His commands are alike to man and woman. He laid aside the miserable formalisms, traditions, and customs of the Jews; but not so with all the writers of the Epistles. We must not make God responsible for all they have said. Paul, himself, admitted that he spoke sometimes by permission and sometimes by commission.[12]

One thought seemed to sit heavy on the soul of the speaker. He feared that if woman should be admitted to all the rights and privileges of citizens, she might be drafted and enrolled as a common soldier. Vain fear! What woman! the follower of the meek and lowly Jesus, who commands his disciples to "Resist not evil," shedding her brother's blood, plunging the deadly weapon into the heart of the Seminole chief,[13] or the poor, jaded, harassed Mexican. Oh no, she has not so learned Christ. *Her* conscience man has not yet wholly perverted. She *knows* that war is a sin. And why cannot the law exempt her from this bloody crime as well as the whole sect of Quakers, and the Priesthood, too, for she, as well as they, is "subject to many weaknesses and infirmities." The law does not compel any one to fight who considers it a sin, and who that believes in the Divinity of Christ's commands can advocate war?

It was remarked, during the sermon, that the Bible is filled with the doctrine of woman's subjection; and Sarah's obedience to Abraham, was brought forward as an example for us. Through her obedience to him she was made to utter a falsehood.[14] Such a consequence would prevent a conscientious woman from yielding herself to the guidance of another, even if it were one of the *stronger* sex. The Bible is full of instances where the women obeyed not the injunction, "Let your women keep silence."[15] Miriam and Judith, Deborah[16] and Anna the Prophetess, the four daughters of Philip, and Priscilla, Tryphena and Tryphosa,[17] many of whom Paul (who did well for one of the single brotherhood) greeted as fellow-laborers; and there were many "devout and honorable women,"[18] whose names are not given, who were recognized as co-workers by the Apostles. Can this, sanctioned as it is by God himself, be called "beastly heathenism."

One consolation was given us, one ray of light allowed to pierce the gloom, one golden edge to the dark cloud. We were told that it may be, the order will be reversed in Heaven; that the precedence will there be accorded to woman as here it has been to man. If this be the Heavenly order is it not the duty of every Christian to endeavor to render Earth as near like Heaven as possible?

But there were two most potent reasons why woman should be in subjection:

1st. Adam was made before Eve.

2nd. Eve sinned before Adam. Now, there is no escape for woman here, for if she be older than her husband, then of course she must be subject to him, because she must have sinned first. If on the contrary she be younger, she must be subject to him because he was made first. From this part of the discourse there is no appeal. It is unanswerable; and unless by a profound attention to and diligent study of the garden scene we discover some opening for woman, we shall have to say, in the truly eloquent words of the speaker, "It is the centre and the circumference, the Alpha and Omega of Woman's Rights, to remain in that sphere which Providence has assigned her, and under the control of those guardians whom God, in his wisdom, may see fit to appoint."

∽ *Elizabeth Cady Stanton,*
∽ *Elizabeth W. M'Clintock.*

∽ *Seneca County Courier*, n.d.; from ECS Papers, DLC; on *Film* at September 1848.

1. Written in response to a sermon delivered on Sunday, 23 July 1848, the letter, the editors noted, "has been in our possession for some time"; we "hope that the ladies will pardon our delay in printing it." It appeared before the woman's rights convention in Rochester on Wednesday, 2 August. The *Courier*'s publishers in July were Nathan J. Milliken and T. J. Mumford, but its editors changed over the summer with the start of a paper for the Free Soil party. Milliken (1822–?), a supporter of the Free Soil movement, signed the Declaration of Sentiments. He left Seneca Falls for Canandaigua in 1849. (*History of Seneca Co., New York. With Illustrations Descriptive of Its Scenery, . . .* [Philadelphia, 1876], 54–55; Harrison Chamberlain, "The Seneca Falls Press," *Occasional Papers of the Seneca Falls Historical Society* [1905], 2–3; Dexter C. Bloomer, *Life and Writings of Amelia Bloomer* [1895; reprint, New York, 1975], 13–15.)

2. At the Rochester convention, while urging the audience to debate woman's rights, ECS asked anyone who disagreed with the "notions of the Rights of Woman," to object now, "and not, as at Seneca Falls, keep silent through all our deliberations, and afterwards, on the Sabbath day, use the pulpit throughout the town to denounce them, when they could not, of course, be allowed to reply." Elizabeth McClintock read from notes of the sermon. (*Proceedings of the Woman's Rights Convention, Held at the Unitarian Church, Rochester, N.Y., August 2, 1848, To Consider the Rights of Woman, Politically, Religiously and Industrially* [New York, 1870], 4–5, 12, *Film*, 6:723ff.)

3. Matt. 7:12, the "Golden Rule" reads: "Therefore all things whatsoever ye would that men should do to you, do ye even so to them: for this is the law and the prophets." ECS also cites Matt. 5:39: "But I say unto you, That ye resist not evil: but whosoever shall smite thee on thy right cheek, turn to him the other also."

4. The Mexican War ended in February 1848 and brought California and the New Mexico territory under the control of the United States. Support for the war came largely from the South, and its conduct and outcome were understood to demonstrate southern control of national politics.

5. ECS adapts Gal. 3:28.

6. John G. Whittier, "A Summons," stanza 6.

7. Rom. 13:1.

8. 1 Pet. 2:17.

9. Matt. 23:23 reads: "Woe unto you, scribes and Pharisees, hypocrites! for ye pay tithe of mint and anise and cummin, and have omitted the weightier matters of the law, judgment, mercy, and faith."

10. 1 Pet. 3:1.

11. Leopold I (1790–1865), the first King of the Belgians, came to the throne in 1831.

12. An allusion to 1 Cor. 7:6: "But I speak this by permission, and not of commandment."

13. Osceola, leader of the Seminole at the start of the tribe's wars with the United States died in army custody in 1839, after he was promised safe conduct to a peace conference.

14. Allusions to Abraham's orders that Sarah identify herself as his sister and thus trick Abimelech into taking her for his wife. Gen. 20:2, 13.

15. 1 Cor. 14:34.

16. Miriam and Deborah are Old Testament prophets. (Exo. 15:20; Judg. 4.) In the Apocrypha, Judith too is a prophet and a military hero. (Jth.)

17. In the New Testament, these women are identified as prophets and preachers. (Luke 2:36; Acts 21:9, 18:26; Rom. 16:12.)

18. Acts 13:50.

·⊂══════⋙⋘══════⊃·

25 ❧ ADDRESS BY ECS ON WOMAN'S RIGHTS

Editorial note: The manuscript of an address ECS delivered after the conventions of 1848 was handed down to her daughters, who gave it to SBA, who in turn deposited it in the Library of Congress. Writing to her daughters, ECS called it her "first speech," one "delivered several times immediately after the first Woman's Rights Convention." She spoke on two occasions, at least: in September at Waterloo and on 6 October to the Congregational Friends at Farmington.

Between 1848 and 1850, ECS turned to this address as a source for short articles, and then she lost track of the manuscript. Emma Robinson Coe borrowed it, according to SBA's notations on a cover sheet, probably when she visited ECS in the fall of 1851. It was back in ECS's possession by 1866, when Theodore Tilton saw the "old and tattered" manuscript while he interviewed ECS for a biography. He understood this to be "the first 'set speech' which Mrs. Stanton ever delivered," one that she "repeated at several places in the interior of the State of New York, during the first months that followed the first convention."

However, since 1870, on the basis of a title page printed by Robert J. Johnston, the same speech with modifications has been identified as the address ECS delivered *to* the conventions in Seneca Falls and Rochester. There are obstacles to accepting that identification. First, there is no evidence that ECS made any speech at the Rochester convention, let alone one of this length. Second, no contemporary report of Seneca Falls noted a major speech by ECS, though small parts of the address might match her several contributions to the meeting. Finally, Lucretia Mott, present at both conventions, referred to ECS's speech in September at Waterloo as "thy maiden speech." Johnston's publication is more likely an artifact of 1870 than a document of 1848.

ECS is no doubt implicated in the publication of the *Address of Mrs. Elizabeth Cady Stanton, Delivered at Seneca Falls & Rochester, N.Y., July 19th & Aug. 2d, 1848* in 1870. Though the title page might reflect a printer's misunderstanding about events, someone carefully adjusted the text to eliminate the scene set in the opening paragraphs and convert to present tense all references to the conventions and their demands. It is unlikely that Robert Johnston issued an unauthorized text; he knew ECS well, as an officer of the American Equal Rights Association and printer of the *Revolution*. ECS, SBA, and Amy Post collaborated on other pamphlets he issued in 1870 to celebrate two decades of woman's rights agitation. But if ECS created the *Address*, she neither quoted from nor referred readers to it in histories of the conventions that she wrote after 1870.

The text published here is based upon the manuscript. In the numbered endnotes, major differences in the later, published text of 1870 are noted. (Lucretia Mott to ECS, 3 October 1848, see below; Gue, *Diary of Benjamin F. Gue*, 40; Theodore Tilton, "Mrs. Elizabeth Cady Stanton," in James Parton, et al., *Eminent Women of the Age* [Hartford, Conn., 1868], 332–61; SBA to Mary P. Hallowell, 11 April 1867, *Film*, 12:118–21; *History*, 1:69.)

[September 1848]

¶1   Ladies and gentlemen, when invited some weeks ago to address you I proposed to a gentleman of this village to review our report of the Seneca Falls convention and give his objections to our Declaration, resolutions and proceedings to serve me as a text on which to found an address for this evening—the gentleman did so, but his review was so laconic that there was the same difficulty in replying to it as we found in replying to a recent sermon preached at Seneca Falls—there was nothing of it.

¶2   Should that gentleman be present this evening and feel disposed to give any of his objections to our movement, we will be most happy to answer him.[1]

¶3   I should feel exceedingly diffident to appear before you wholly unused as I am to public speaking, were I not nerved by a sense of right and duty—did I not feel that the time had fully come for the question of woman's wrongs to be laid before the public—did I not believe that woman herself must do this work—for woman alone can understand the height and the depth, the length and the breadth of her own degradation and woe. Man cannot speak for us—because he has been educated to believe that we differ from him so materially, that he cannot judge of our thoughts, feelings and opinions by his own. Moral beings can only judge of others by themselves—the moment they give a different nature to any of their own kind they utterly fail. The drunkard was hopelessly lost until it was discovered that he was governed by the same laws of mind as the sober man. Then with what magic power, by kindness and love, was he raised from the slough of despond and placed rejoicing on high land. Let a man once settle the question that woman does not think and feel like himself and he may as well undertake to judge of the amount of intellect and sensation of any of the animal creation as of woman's nature. He can know but little with certainty, and that but by observation.

¶4   Among the many important questions which have been brought before the public, there is none that more vitally affects the whole human family than that which is technically termed Woman's rights.[2] Every allusion to the degraded and inferior position occupied by woman all over the world, has ever been met by scorn and abuse. From the man of highest mental cultivation, to the most degraded wretch who staggers in the streets do we hear ridicule and coarse jests, freely bestowed upon those who dare assert that woman stands by the side of man—his equal, placed here by her God to enjoy with him the beautiful earth, which is her home as it is his—having the same sense of right and wrong and looking to the same Being for guidance and support. So long has man exercised a tyranny over her injurious to himself and benumbing to *her* faculties, that but few can nerve themselves against the storm, and so long has the chain been about her that however galling it may be she knows not there is a remedy.

¶5   The present social, civil and religious condition of women is a subject too vast to be brought within the limits of one short lecture. Suffice it to say for the present, that wherever we turn the history of woman is sad and drear and dark, without any alleviating circumstances, nothing from which we can draw consolation. As the nations of the earth emerge from a state of barbarism, the sphere of woman gradually becomes wider but not even under what is thought to be the full blaze of the sun of civilization is it what God designed

it to be. In every country and clime does man assume the responsibility of marking out the path for her to tread,—in every country
does he regard her as a being inferior to himself and one whom he is
to guide and controul. From the Arabian Kerek whose wife is obliged
to steal from her Husband to supply the necessities of life,—from the
Mahometan who forbids pigs dogs women and other impure animals to enter a mosque, and does not allow a fool, madman or
women to proclaim the hour of prayer,—from the German who
complacently smokes his meerschaum while his wife, yoked with
the ox draws the plough through its furrow,—from the delectable
gentleman who thinks an inferior style of conversation adapted to
women—to the legislator who considers her incapable of saying
what laws shall govern her, is this same feeling manifested.[3] In all
eastern countries she is a mere slave bought and sold at pleasure.
There are many differences in habits, manners, and customs, among
the heathen nations of the old world, but there is little change for the
better in woman's lot—she is either the drudge of man to perform all
the hard labour of the field and the menial duties of the hut, tent, or
house, or she is the idol of his lust the mere creature of his ever
varying whims and will. Truly has she herself said in her best estate,

> I am a slave, a favoured slave
> At best to share his pleasure and seem very blest,
> When weary of these fleeting charms and me,
> There yawns the sack and yonder rolls the sea,
> What! am I then a toy for dotards play
> To wear but till the gilding frets away?[4]

In christian countries, boasting a more advanced state of civilization
and refinement, woman still holds a position infinitely inferior to
man. In France the Salic law[5] tells much although it is said that
woman there has ever had great influence in all political revolutions.
In England she seems to have advanced a little— There she has a
right to the throne, and is allowed to hold some other offices and
some women have a right to vote too— But in the United States of
America[6] woman has no right either to hold office, nor to the elective franchise, we stand at this moment, unrepresented in this government—our rights and interests wholly overlooked.

¶6   Let us now glance at some of the popular objections to this whole question. There is a class of men who believe in the natural inborn, inbred superiority both in body and mind and their full complete Heaven descended right to lord it over the fish of the sea, the fowl of the air, the beast of the field[7] and last tho' not least the immortal being called woman. I would recommend this class to the attentive perusal of their Bibles—to historical research, to foreign travel—to a closer observation of the manifestations of mind about them and to an humble comparison of themselves with such women as Catharine of Russia, Elizabeth of England distinguished for their statesman-like qualities, Harriet Martineau and Madame de Stael for their literary attainments, or Caroline Herschel and Mary Summerville for their scientific researches, or for physical equality to that whole nation of famous women the Amazones.[8] We seldom find this class of objectors among liberally educated persons, who have had the advantage of observing their race in different countries, climes, and under different phases, but barbarians tho' they be in entertaining such an opinion—they must be met and fairly vanquished.

MAN SUPERIOR, INTELLECTUALLY, MORALLY AND PHYSICALLY.

¶7   1st Let us consider his intellectual superiority.[9] Man's superiority cannot be a question until we have had a fair trial. When we shall have had[10] our colleges, our professions, our trades, for a century a comparison may then be justly instituted. When woman instead of being taxed to endow colleges where she is forbidden to enter, instead of forming societies to educate young men shall first educate herself, when she shall be just to herself before she is generous to others—improving the talents God has given her and leaving her neighbour to do the same for himself we shall not then hear so much of this boasted greatness. How often now we see young men carelessly throwing away the intellectual food their sisters crave. A little music that she may while an hour away pleasantly, a little French, a smattering of the sciences and in rare instances some slight classical knowledge and a woman is considered highly educated. She leaves her books and studies just at the time a young man is entering thoroughly into his—then comes the cares and perplexities of married life.[11] Her sphere being confined to her house and children, the burden generally being very unequally divided, she knows nothing beside and whatever yearning her spirit may have felt for a higher existence, whatever may have been the capacity she well knew she possessed for more elevated enjoyments—enjoyments which would not conflict with these but add new lustre to them—it is all buried beneath the weight that presses upon her. Men bless their innocence are fond of representing themselves as beings of reason—of intellect—while women are mere creatures of the affections— There is a self conceit that makes the possesser infinitely happy and one would dislike to dispel the illusion, if it were possible to endure it. But so far as we can observe it is pretty much now-a-days as it was with Adam of old. No doubt you all recollect the account we have given us. A man and a woman were placed in a beautiful garden. Every thing was about them that could contribute to their enjoyment. Trees and shrubs, fruits and flowers, and gently murmuring streams made glad their hearts. Zephyrs freighted with delicious odours fanned their brows and the serene stars looked down upon them with eyes of love.

¶8   The Evil One saw their happiness and it troubled him. He set his wits to work to know how he should destroy it. He thought that man could be easily conquered through *his affection for the woman*. But the woman would require more management. She could be reached only through her intellectual nature. So he promised her the knowledge of good and evil. He told her the sphere of her reason should be enlarged, he promised to gratify the desire she felt for intellectual improvement, so he prevailed and she did eat. Did the Evil One judge rightly in regard to man? Eve took an apple went to Adam and said "Dear Adam taste this apple"—"if you love me eat." Adam stopped not so much as to ask if the apple was sweet or sour. He knew he was doing wrong, but his love for Eve prevailed and he did eat. Which I ask you was the "creature of the affections"?[12]

¶9   2nd Let us consider man's claims to superiority as a moral being.[13] Look now at our theological seminaries, our divinity students—the long line of descendents from our apostolic Fathers and what do we find here? Perfect moral rectitude in every relation of life, a devoted spirit of self sacrifice, a perfect union in thought opinion and feeling among those who profess to worship the one God and whose laws they feel themselves called upon to declare to a fallen race? Far from it. These persons all so thoroughly acquainted with the character of God and of his designs made manifest by his words and works are greatly divided among themselves—every sect has its God, every sect has its own Bible, and there is as much bitterness, envy, hatred and malice between these contending sects yea even more than in our political parties during periods of the greatest excitement. Now the leaders of these sects are the *priesthood* who are supposed to have passed their lives almost in the study of the Bible, in various languages and with various commentaries, in the contemplation of the infinite, the eternal and the glorious future open to the redeemed of earth. Are they distinguished among men for their holy aspirations—their virtue, purity, and chastity? Do they keep themselves unspotted from the world? Is the moral and religious life of this class what we might expect from minds (said to be) continually fixed on such mighty themes? By no means, not a year passes but we hear of some sad soul sickening deed perpetrated by some of this class. If such be the state of the most holy we need not pause now to consider those classes who claim of us less reverence and respect. The lamentable want of principle among our lawyers generally is too well known to need comment—the everlasting bickering and backbiting of our physicians is proverbial— The disgraceful riots at our polls where man in performing so important a duty of a citizen ought surely to be sober minded. The perfect rowdyism that now characterizes the debates in our national congress—all these are great facts which rise up against man's claim to moral superiority.

¶10   In my opinion he is infinitely woman's inferior in every moral virtue, not by nature, but made so by a false education. In carrying out his own selfishness, man has greatly improved woman's moral nature, but by an almost total shipwreck of his own. Woman has now the noble virtues of the martyr, she is early schooled to self denial and suffering. But man is not so wholly buried in selfishness that he does not sometimes get a glimpse of the narrowness of his soul, as compared with women. Then he says by way of an excuse for his degradation, God made woman more self denying than us, it is her nature, it does not cost her as much to give up her wishes, her will, her life even as it does us. We are naturally selfish, God made us so. No! think not that he who made the heavens and the earth, the whole planetary world ever moving on in such harmony and order, that he who has so bountifully scattered, through all nature so many objects that delight, enchant and fill us with admiration and wonder, that he who has made the mighty ocean mountain and cataract, the bright and joyous birds, the tender lovely flowers, that he who made man in his own image, perfect, noble and pure, loving justice, mercy, and truth, think not that He has had any part in the production of that creeping, cringing, crawling, debased selfish monster now extant, claiming for himself the name of man. No God's commands rest upon man as well as woman, and it is as much his duty to be kind, gentle, self denying and full of good works as it is hers, as much his duty to absent himself from scenes of violence as it is hers. A place or a position that would require the sacrifice of delicacy and refinement of woman's nature is unfit for man, for these virtues should be as carefully guarded in him as in her.

¶11   The false ideas that prevail with regard to the purity necessary to constitute the perfect character in woman and that requisite for man have done an infinite deal of mischief in the world. We would not have woman less pure, but we would have man more so. We would have the same code of morals for both. Moral delinquencies which exclude women from the society of the true and the good should assign to man the same place. Our partiality towards man has been the fruitful source of dissipation and riot, drunkenness and debauchery and immorality of all kinds. It has not only affected woman injuriously by narrowing her sphere of action, but man himself has suffered from it. It has destroyed the nobleness, the gentleness that should belong to his character, the beauty and transparency of soul—the dislike of every thing bordering on coarseness and vulgarity, all those finer qualities of our nature which raise us above the earth and give us a foretaste of the beauty and bliss, the refined enjoyments of the world to come.

¶12   3rd Let us now consider man's claims to physical superiority.[14] Methinks I hear some say, surely you will not contend for equality here. Yes, we must not give an inch lest you claim an ell, we cannot accord to man even this much and he has no right to claim it until the fact be fully demonstrated, until the physical education of the boy and the girl shall have been the same for many years. If you claim the advantage of size merely, why it may be that under any course of training in ever so perfect a developement of the physique in woman, man might still be the larger of the two, tho' we do not grant even this. But the perfection of the physique is great power combined with endurance. Now your strongest men are not always the tallest men, nor the broadest, nor the most corpulent, but very often the small man who is well built, tightly put together and possessed of an indomitable will. Bodily strength depends something on the power of will. The sight of a small boy thoroughly thrashing a big one is not rare. Now would you say the big fat boy whipped was superior to the small active boy who conquered him? You do not say the horse is physically superior to the man—for although he has more muscular power, yet the power of mind in man renders him his superior and he guides him wherever he will.

¶13   The power of mind seems to be in no way connected with the size and strength of body. Many men of Herculean powers of mind have been small and weak in body. The late distinguished Dr Channing of Boston was very small and feeble in appearance and voice, yet he has moved the world by the eloquence of his pen. John Quincy Adams was a small man of but little muscular power, yet we know he had more courage than all the northern dough faces[15] of six feet high and well proportioned that ever represented us at our Capitol. We know that mental power depends much more on the temperament than the size of the head or the size of the body. I have never heard that Daniel Lambert was distinguished for any great mental endowments.[16] We cannot say what the woman might be physically, if the girl were allowed all the freedom of the boy in romping, climbing, swimming, playing hoop and ball. Among some of the Tarter tribes of the present day the women manage a horse, hurl a javelin, hunt wild animals, and fight an enemy as well as the men.[17] The Indian women endure fatigue and carry burthens that some of our fair faced, soft handed, mustachoed, young gentlemen would consider it quite impossible for them to sustain. The Croatian, and Wallachian women perform all the agricultural operations, (and we know what physical strength such labours require) in addition to their own domestic concerns;[18] and it is no uncommon sight in our cities to see the German immigrant *with his hands in his pockets*, walking complacently by the side of his wife, whilst she is bending beneath the weight of some huge package or piece of furniture,—physically as well as intellectually it is use that produces growth and developement. But there is a class of objectors who say they do not claim superiority, they merely assert a difference, but you will find by following them up closely that they make this difference to be vastly in favour of man. The Phrenologist says that woman's head has just as many organs as man's and that they are similarly situated. He says too that the organs that are the most exercised are the most prominent. They do not divide heads according to sex but they call all the fine heads masculine and all the ill shaped feminine, for when a woman presents a remarkably large well developed intellectual region, they say she has a masculine head, as if there could be nothing remarkable of the feminine gender and when a man has a small head very little reasoning power and the affections inordinately developed they say he has a woman's head thus giving all glory to masculinity.

> Some say our heads are less.
> Some men's are small, not they the least of men;
> For often fineness compensates for size;
> Beside the brain is like the hand and grows,
> With using—[19]

¶14 We, the women of this state have met in convention within the last few months both in Rochester and Seneca Falls to discuss our rights and wrongs.[20] We did not as some have supposed assemble to go into the detail of social life alone, we did not propose to petition the legislature to make our Husbands just, generous and courteous, to seat every man at the head of a cradle and to clothe every woman in male attire, no none of these points however important they may be considered by humble minds, were touched upon in the convention. As to their costume the gentlemen need feel no fear of our imitating that for we think it in violation of every principle of beauty taste and dignity and notwithstanding all the contempt and abuse cast upon our loose flowing garments we still admire their easy graceful folds, and consider our costume as an object of taste much more beautiful than theirs. Many of the nobler sex seem to agree with us in this opinion for all the Bishops, Priests, Judges, Barristers, and Lord Mayors of the first nation on the globe and the Pope of Rome too, when officiating in their highest offices, they all wear the loose flowing robes, thus tacitly acknowledging that the ordinary male attire is neither dignified nor imposing. No! we shall not molest you in your philosophical experiments with stocks, pants,[21] high heeled boots and Russian belt. Yours be the glory to discover by personal experience how long the knee pan can resist the terrible strapping down which you impose—in how short time the well developed muscles of the throat can be reduced to mere threads by the constant pressure of the stock, how high the heel of the boot must be to make a short man tall and how tight the Russian belt may be drawn and yet have wind enough to sustain life. Our ambition leads us neither to discovery or martyrdom of this sort.

¶15 But we did assemble to protest against a form of government existing without the consent of the governed, to declare our right to be free as man is free—to be represented in the government which we are taxed to support—to have such disgraceful laws as give to man the right to chastise and imprison his wife—to take the wages which she earns,—the property which she inherits and in case of separation the children of her love—laws which make her the mere dependent on his bounty—it was to protest against such unjust laws as these and to have them if possible forever erased from our statute books, deeming them a standing shame and disgrace to a professedly republican, christian people in the nineteenth century. We met

> To uplift woman's fallen divinity
> Upon an even pedestal with man[22]

¶16 And strange as it may seem to many we then and there declared our right to vote according to the Declaration of the government under which we live. This right no one pretends to deny. We need not prove ourselves equal to Daniel Webster to enjoy this privilege for the most ignorant Irishman in the ditch has all the civil rights he has, we need not prove our muscular power equal to this same Irishman to enjoy this privilege for the most tiny, weak, ill shaped, imbecile stripling of 21 has all the civil rights of the Irishman. We have no objection to discuss the question of equality, for we feel that the weight of argument lies wholly with us, but we wish the question of equality kept distinct from the question of rights, for the proof of the one does not determine the truth of the other. All men[23] in this country have the same rights however they may differ in mind, body, or estate. The right is ours. The question now is, how shall we get possession of what rightfully belongs to us. We should not feel so sorely grieved if no man who had not attained the full stature of a Webster, Van Buren, Clay[24] or Gerrit Smith could claim the right of the elective franchise, but to have the rights of drunkards, idiots, horse-racing, rum selling rowdies, ignorant foreigners, and silly boys fully recognised, whilst we ourselves are thrust out from all the rights that belong to citizens—it is too grossly insulting to the dignity of woman to be longer quietly submitted to. The right is ours, have it we must—use it we will. The pens, the tongues, the fortunes, the indomitable wills of many women are already pledged to secure this right. The great truth that no just government can be formed without the consent of the governed, we shall echo and re-echo in the ears of the unjust judge until by continual coming we shall weary him.

¶17   But say some would you have woman vote? What refined delicate woman at the polls, mingling in such scenes of violence and vulgarity—most certainly—where there is so much to be feared for the pure, the innocent, the noble, the mother surely should be there to watch and guard her sons, who must encounter such stormy dangerous scenes at the tender age of 21. Much is said of woman's influence, might not her presence do much towards softening down this violence—refining this vulgarity? Depend upon it that places that by their impure atmosphere are rendered unfit for woman cannot but be dangerous to her sires and sons. But if woman claims all the rights of a citizen will she buckle on her armour and fight in defence of her country? Has not woman already often shown herself as courageous in the field as wise and patriotic in counsel as man? But for myself—I think all war sinful. I believe in Christ—I believe that command Resist not evil to be divine. Vengeance is mine and I will repay saith the Lord—[25]   Let frail man, who cannot foresee the consequences of an action walk humbly with his God—loving his enemies, blessing those who curse him and always returning good for evil. This is the highest kind of courage that mortal man can attain to and this moral warfare with ones own bad passions requires no physical power to achieve. I would not have man go to war. I can see no glory in fighting with such weapons as guns and swords whilst man has in his possession the infinitely superior and more effective ones of righteousness and truth.

¶18   But what would you gain by voting. Man must know the advantages of voting for they all seem very tenacious about the right. Think you if woman had a voice in this government, that all those laws affecting her interests would so entirely violate every principle of right and justice?[26] Had we a vote to give might not the office holders and seekers propose some change in woman's condition? Might not "woman's rights" come to be as great a question as "free soil"? But are you not already sufficiently represented by your Fathers, Husbands, Brothers and Sons. Let your statute books answer the question. We have had enough of such representation. In nothing is woman's true happiness consulted, men like to call her an angel—to feed her with what they think sweet food nourishing her vanity, to induce her to believe her organization is so much finer more delicate than theirs, that she is not fitted to struggle with the tempests of public life but needs their care and protection.[27] Care and protection? such as the wolf gives the lamb—such as the eagle the hare he carries to his eyrie. Most cunningly he entraps her and then takes from her all those rights which are dearer to him than life itself, rights which have been baptized in blood and the maintenance of which is even now rocking to their foundations the kingdoms of the old world. The most discouraging, the most lamentable aspect our cause wears is the indifference indeed the contempt with which women themselves regard our movement. When the subject is introduced among our young ladies among those even who claim to be intelligent and educated it is met by the scornful curl of the lip and by expressions of disgust and ridicule. But we shall hope better things of them when they are enlighted in regard to their present position, to the laws under which they live—they will not then publish their degradation by declaring themselves satisfied nor their ignorance by declaring they have all the rights they want.

¶19　They are not the only class of beings who glory in their bondage. In the Turkish Harem where woman is little above the brute of the field, where immortal mind is crushed and the soul itself is as it were blotted out, where beings God has endowed with a spirit capable of enjoying the beauties which he has scattered over the broad earth—a spirit whose cultivation would fit them for a never ending existence, in those Seraglios where intellect and soul are buried beneath the sensualism and brutality which are the inevitable result of the belief in woman's inferiority, even here she is not only satisfied with her position but glories in it.[28] Miss Martineau in her travels in the East recently published says referring to the inmates of the Harems:

Every where they pitied us European women heartily, that we had to go about travelling and appearing in the streets without being properly taken care of, that is watched. They think us strangely neglected in being left so free and boast of their spy system and imprisonment as tokens of the value in which they are held.[29] Can women here, although her spiritual and intellectual nature is recognized to a somewhat greater degree than among the Turks, and she is allowed the privilege of being in her nursery and kitchen, and although the Christian promises her the ascendancy in Heaven as man has it here, while the Mahomedan closes the golden gates of the Celestial city tight against her—can she be content notwithstanding these good things to remain debarred from an equal share with man in the pure enjoyments arising from the full cultivation of her mind and her admission into the rights and privileges which are hers. She must and will ere long, when her spirit awakens and she learns to care less for the

> Barren verbiage current among men
> Light coin the tinsel clink of compliment[30]

She must and will demand

> Every where
> Two heads in counsel, two beside the hearth
> Two in the tangled business of the world
> Two in the liberal offices of life
> Two plummets dropped to sound the abyss
> Of science and the secrets of the mind.[31]

¶20 Let woman live as she should, let her feel her accountability to her Maker— Let her know that her spirit is fitted for as high a sphere as man's and that her soul requires food as pure as refreshing as his—let her live *first* for God and she will not make imperfect man an object of reverence and idolatry— Teach her her responsibility as a being of conscience and of reason—that she will find any earthly support unstable and weak, that her only safe dependence is on the arm of omnipotence.[32] Teach her there is no sex in mind, that true happiness springs from duty accomplished and she will feel the desire to bathe her brow heated from the struggles of an earthly existence in the cool stream that flows fresh and sparkling from the

Divine fountain. She will become conscious that each human being is morally accountable for himself that no one can throw upon another his burden of responsibility, that neither Father, Husband, Brother nor son, however willing they may be, can relieve woman from this weight, can stand in her stead when called into the presence of the searcher of spirits.

¶21   Methinks I hear some woman say, We must obey our Husbands!![33] Who says so. Why the Bible. No you have not rightly read your Bible. In the opening of the Bible at the creation of our first parents, God called their name Adam and gave them dominion over the fish of the sea, the fowl of the air and the beast of the field, but he says nothing to them about obedience to each other. After the fall after Noah came out of the ark he addresses them in like manner.[34] The chief support that man finds in the Bible for this authority over woman he gets from the injunctions of Paul. It needs but little attention to see how exceedingly limited that command of St Paul must be even if you give it all the weight which is usually claimed for it. Wives obey your Husbands in the Lord.[35] Now as the command is given to *me*, I am of course to be the judge of what is in the Lord and this opens a wide field of escape from any troublesome commands. There can be no subordination where the one to whom the command is given is allowed to sit in judgement on the character of the command. The Bible argument on this subject would afford of itself sufficient material for an entire lecture. I shall not therefore attempt to go into it at this time, enough now to say that that best of Books is ever on the side of freedom and we shrink not from pleading our cause on its principles of universal justice and love.

¶22   Let me here notice one of the greatest humbugs of the day, which has long found for itself a most valuable tool in woman. The education society.[36] The idea to me is monstrous and absurd of woman in her present condition of degradation and ignorance, forming a society for the education of young men—an order of beings above themselves—claiming to be gifted with superior powers of mind and body—having all the avenues to learning, wealth, and distinction thrown freely open to them and if they have but the energy to avail themselves of all these advantages—they can easily secure an education. Whilst woman poor and friendless robbed of all her rights, oppressed on all sides, civilly, religiously, and socially, must needs go ignorant herself—the idea of such a being working day and night with her needle stitch, stitch, stitch, (for the poor widow always throws in her mite for she is taught to believe that all she gives for the decoration of churches and their black coated gentry is unto the Lord) to educate a great strong lug of man.

¶23 I think a man who under the present state of things has the moral hardihood to take an education at the hands of woman and at such an expense to her, ought as soon as he graduates with all his honours thick upon him take the first ship for Turkey and there pass his days in earnest efforts to rouse the inmates of the Harems to a true sense of their present debasement and not as is his custom immediately enter our pulpits to tell us of his superiority to us "weaker vessels"[37] his prerogative to command, ours to obey—his duty to preach, ours to keep silence. Oh! for the generous promptings of the days of chivalry—oh! for the poetry of romantic gallantry,—may they shine on us once more—then may we hope that these pious young men who profess to believe in the golden rule, will clothe and educate themselves and encourage poor weak woman to do the same for herself—or perchance they might conceive the happy thought of reciprocating the benefits so long enjoyed by them and form societies for the education of young women of genius whose talents ought to be rescued from the oblivion of ignorance. There is something painfully affecting in the self sacrifice and generosity of women who can neither read or write their own language with correctness going about begging money for the education of men. The last time an appeal of this kind was made to me I told the young lady I would send her to school a year if she would go, but I would never again give one red cent to the education society, and I do hope every christian woman who has the least regard for her sex will make the same resolve. We have worked long enough for man and at a most unjust, unwarrantable sacrifice of self, yet he gives no evidence of gratitude but has thus far treated his benefactors with settled scorn ridicule and contempt. But say they you do not need an education as we do. We expect to shine in the great world, our education is our living. What let me ask is the real object of all education? Just in proportion as the faculties which God has given us are harmoniously developed, do we attain our highest happiness and has not woman an equal right with man to happiness here as well as hereafter and ought she not to have equal facilities with him for making an honest living whilst on this footstool?

¶24 One common objection to this movement is that if the principles of freedom and equality which we advocate were put to practise, it would destroy all harmony in the domestic circle. Here let me ask how many truly harmonious households have we now? Take any village circle you know of and on the one hand you will find the meek, sad looking, thoroughly subdued wife who knows no freedom of thought or action—who passes her days in the dull routine of household cares and her nights half perchance in making the tattered garments whole and the other half in slumbers oft disturbed by sick and restless children— She knows nothing of the great world without—she has no time for reading and her Husband finds more pleasure in discussing politics with men in groceries, taverns or Depots than he could in reading or telling his wife the news whilst she sits mending his stockings and shirts through many a lonely evening, nor thinks he selfish being that he owes any duty to that perishing soul, beyond providing a house to cover her head, food to sustain life and raiment to put on and plenty of wood to [burn?].

¶25 As to her little world within she finds not much comfort there. Her wishes should she have any must be in subjection to those of her tyrant—her will must be in perfect subordination, the comfort of the wife, children, servants one and all must be given up wholly disregarded until the great head of the house be first attended to. No matter what the case may be he must have his hot dinner. If wife or children are sick—they must look elsewhere for care, he cannot be disturbed at night, it does not agree with him to have his slumbers broken it gives him the headache—renders him unfit for business and worse than all her very soul is tortured every day and hour by his harsh and cruel treatment of her children. What mother cannot bear me witness to anguish of this sort? Oh! women how sadly you have learned your duty to your children, to your own heart, to the God that gave you that holy love for them when you stand silent witnesses to the cruel infliction of blows and strips from angry Fathers on the trembling forms of helpless infancy— It is a mothers sacred duty to shield her children from violence from whatever source it may come, it is her duty to resist oppression wherever she may find it at home or abroad,[38] by every moral power within her reach. Many men who are well known for their philanthropy, who hate oppression on a southern plantation, can play the tyrant right well at home. It is a much easier matter to denounce all the crying sins of the day most eloquently too, than to endure for one hour the peevish moanings of a sick child. To know whether a man is truly great and good, you must not judge by his appearance in the great world, but follow him to his home—where all restraints are laid aside—there we see the true man his virtues and his vices too.

¶26 On the other hand we find the so called Hen-pecked Husband, oftimes a kind generous noble minded man who hates contention and is willing to do anything for peace. He having unwarily caught a Tarter tries to make the best of her. He can think his own thoughts and tell them too when he feels quite sure that she is not at hand,— he can absent himself from home as much as possible, but he does not feel like a free man. The detail of his sufferings I can neither describe nor imagine never having been the confident of one of these unfortunate beings.[39] Now in such households as these there may be no open ruptures—they may seemingly glide on without a ripple upon the surface—the aggrieved may have patiently resigned themselves to suffer all things with christian fortitude—with stern philosophy—but can there be harmony or happiness there? oh! no far from it. The only happy households we now see are those in which Husband and wife share equally in counsel and government. There can be no true dignity or independence where there is subordination, no happiness without freedom.[40]

¶27 Is it not strange that man is so slow to admit the intellectual power the moral heroism of woman. How can he with the page of history spread out before him doubt her identity with himself. That there have been comparatively a greater proportion of good queens than of good kings is a fact stated by several historians.[41] "Zenobia the celebrated queen of the East, is not exceeded by any king on record, for talent, courage, and daring ambition. The Emperor Aurelian while besieging her beautiful city of Palms, writes thus: The Roman people speak with contempt of the war I am waging with a woman. They are ignorant both of the character and the power of Zenobia." She was possessed of intellectual attainments very unusual in that age and was a liberal patron of literature and science. No contemporary sovereign is represented as capable of such high pursuits.[42]

¶28 Margaret Queen of Denmark, Norway and Sweden, justly called the Semiramis of the north, by her talent energy, firmness and foresight raised herself to a degree of power and grandeur then unequalled in Europe.[43] No monarch has ever rivalled Isabella of Spain in bravery sagacity political wisdom and a proud sense of honour. Yet these characteristics were united with the purest modesty and the warmest feminine affections. Ferdinand, her husband, was her inferior in mind, heart and nobility of character; but as a wife and a mother she seems to have been a more perfect model than of a queen.[44] Her treaty with the queen of Portugal when they met on the frontiers of the two kingdoms is probably the only one of which it could be truly said: "The fair negotiators experienced none of the embarrassments usually incident to such deliberations, growing out of jealousy, distrust and a mutual desire to over reach. They were conducted in perfect good faith and a sincere desire on both sides to establish a cordial reconciliation."[45] Austria has produced no wiser or better sovereign than Maria Theresa to whose strength of character her nobles paid involuntary homage when they unanimously exclaimed "We will die for our King Maria Theresa." She too was the most affectionate of wives and most devoted of mothers.[46] "In England it was common to hear the people talk of King Elizabeth and Queen James. Catharine of Russia bears honourable comparison with Peter the Great. The annals of Africa furnish no example of a monarch equal to the brave intelligent and proud hearted Zinga, the negro Queen of Angola. Blanche of Castile evinced great ability in administering the government of France, during the minority of her son, and similar praise is due to Caroline of England, during the absence of her Husband."[47] What did woman not do what did she not suffer in our revolutionary struggle. In all great national difficulties her heart has always been found to beat in the right place. She has ever been loyal to her country and her tyrants. He has said it and it must be right was the remark of Josephine in her happy days, when her own judgement suggested a change of course from the one marked out to her by Napoleon, but she lived long enough to learn that her tyrant might both do and say much that was not right.[48]

¶29 It has happened more than once that in a great crisis of national affairs, woman has been appealed to for her aid. Hannah More one of the great minds of her day, at a time when French revolutionary and atheistical opinions were spreading—was earnestly besought by many eminent men to write something to counteract these destructive influences—[49] Her style was so popular and she had shown so intimate a knowledge of human nature that they hoped much from her influence. Her village politics by Will Chip, written in a few hours showed that she merited the opinion entertained of her power upon all classes of mind. It had as was expected great effect. The tact and intelligence of this woman completely turned the tide of opinion and many say prevented a revolution, whether she did old Englands poor any essential service by thus warding off what must surely come is a question—however she did it and the wise ones of her day gloried in her success. Strange that surrounded by such a galaxy of great minds, that so great a work should have been given with one accord to a woman to do.

¶30 Where was the spirit found to sustain that mighty discoverer Christopher Columbus in his dark hours of despair? Isabella of Arragon may be truly said to be the mother of this western world. It was she who continued the constant friend and protector of Columbus during her life, although assailed on all sides yet she steadily and firmly rejected the advice of narrow-minded, timid counsellors and generously bestowed her patronage upon that heroic adventurer. In all those things in which the priests had no interest and consequently did not influence her mind, she was ever the noble woman loving justice—the christian loving mercy. The persecution of the Jews and the establishment of the Inquisition cannot be said to have been countenanced by her, they were the result of priestly impudence. Torquemada the confessor of the Queen did not more fatally mislead her than do the priests of our day mislead us, the cry of heretic was not more potent in her day than that of Infidel in ours.[50] They burned the bodies of all those who differed from them we consign their souls to Hell fire.[51]

¶31 The feeling we so often hear expressed of dislike to seeing woman in places of publicity and trust is merely the effect of custom—very like that prejudice against colour that has been proved to be so truly American.[52] What man or woman of you has a feeling of disapproval or disgust in reading the history of Joan of Arc. The sympathies of every heart are at once enlisted in the success of that extraordinary girl.[53] Her historian tells us that when all human power seemed unavailing, the French no longer despised the supernatural aid of the damsel of Dom Remy. The last stronghold of the Dauphin Charles was besieged, the discouraged French were about to abandon it when the coming of this simple girl paralyzed the English and inspired the followers of Charles with the utmost courage. Her success was philosophical in accordance with the laws of mind. She had full faith in herself and inspired all those who saw her with the same. Let us cultivate like faith, like enthusiasm and we too shall impress all who see and hear us with the same confidence which we ourselves feel in our final success.

¶32 There seems now to be a kind of moral stagnation in our midst. (Philanthropists have pulled every string. War, slavery, drunkeness, licentiousness and gluttony have been dragged naked before the people and all their abominations fully brought to light. Yet with idiotic laugh we hug these monsters to our arms and rush on. Our churches are multiplying on all sides, our Sunday schools and prayer meetings are still kept up, our missionary and tract societies have long laboured and now the labourers begin to faint—they feel they cannot resist this rushing tide of vice, they feel that the battlements of righteousness are weak against the mighty wicked, most are ready to raise the siege.[54] And how shall we account for this state of things? Depend upon it the degradation of woman is the secret of all this woe,—the inactivity of her head and heart. The voice of woman has been silenced, but man cannot fulfill his destiny alone—he cannot redeem his race unaided, there are deep and tender chords of sympathy and love in the breasts of the down fallen the crushed that woman can touch more skillfully than man. The earth has never yet seen a truly great and virtuous nation, for woman has never yet stood the equal with man.[55] (As with nations so with families. It is the wise mother who has the wise son, and it requires but little thought to decide that as long as the women of this nation remain but half developed in mind and body, so long shall we have a succession of men decrepit in body and soul, so long as your women are mere slaves, you may throw your colleges to the wind, there is no material to work upon, it is in vain to look for silver and gold from mines of copper and brass. How seldom now is the Fathers pride gratified, his fond hopes realized in the budding genius of the son—the wife is degraded—made the mere creature of his caprice and now the foolish son is heaviness to his heart. Truly are the sins of the Fathers visited upon the children. God in his wisdom has so linked together the whole human family that any violence done at one end of the chain is felt throughout its length.)

¶33　Now is the time, now emphatically, for the women of this country to buckle on the armour that can best resist the weapons of the enemy, ridicule and holy horror. "Voices" were the visitors and advisers of Joan of Arc, "voices" have come to us, oftimes from the depths of sorrow degradation and despair,—they have been too long unheeded. The same religious enthusiasm that nerved her to what she deemed her work now nerves us to ours, her work was prophesied of, ours too is the fulfilling of what has long since been foretold. In the better days your sons and your daughters shall prophesy.[56] Her struggle and triumph were alike short, our struggle shall be hard and long but our triumph shall be complete and forever. We do not expect that our path will be strewn with the flowers of popular favour—that our banner which we have flung to the wind will be fanned by the breath of popular applause, no we know that over the nettles of prejudice and bigotry will be our way, that upon our banner will beat the dark stormcloud of opposition from those who have entrenched themselves behind the strong bulwark of might, of force and who have fortified their position by every means holy and unholy, but we steadfastly abide the result. Unmoved we will bear it aloft—undaunted we will unfurl it to the gale,—we know the storm cannot rend from it a shred, that the electric flash will but more clearly show to us the glorious words inscribed upon it, "Equality of rights" and the rolling thunder will be sweet music in our ears, telling us of the light [rest of line torn away] of the purer clearer atmosphere [rest of line torn away]

¶34　A new era is dawn<ing upon the world,> when old might to right <must yield—the battle blade> to clerkly pen, when the m<illions> now under the iron heel of <the tyrant will assert> their manhood, when woman <yielding to the> voice of the spirit within her will <demand the> recognition of her humanity, when <her soul, grown> too large for her chains, will burst th<e bands> around her set and stand redeemed regenerated and disenthralled.[57]

> The slumber is broken and the sleeper has risen
> The day of the Goth and the Vandal is o'er
> And old earth feels the tread of freedom once more

While the globe resounds with the tramping of legions who roused from their lethargy are resolved to be free or perish—while old earth reels under the crashing <of> thrones and the destruction of despotisms, hoary with age, while the flashing sunlight that breaks over us <makes> dark so much that men have before revered <and> shows that to be good that had scarcely been dreamed of—while mind is investigating anxiously so much in politics, in science, in morals, while even the Indian rejoices in the bright light and throws from him his chieftainship shall we the women of this age be content to remain inactive and to move in but a narrow and circumscribed sphere, <a> sphere which man shall assign us?[58] Shall we forget that God has given <us the same powers and faculties> that he has conferred <on him—the same desires,> the same hopes—the same trust in immortality—that the same voice called us into being, that the same spark which kindled us into life is from the Divine and ever burning Fire—that we are responsible to Him alone for the right cultivation and employment of our minds and hearts and that it is not for man to say "Thus far shalt thou go and no far<ther>." Poor fallible man [*rest of line torn away*] up to him a [*rest of line torn away*] before him—as [*word torn away*] juror? while the spirit within constantly whispers, Fools! will ye look to that that cannot satisfy you. Will you waste your time and strength on lowering buckets into empty wells. Will you reverence that, that is of like nature with yourselves?

> Then fear not thou to wind thy horn,
> Though elf and gnome thy courage scorn.
> Ask for the castles King and Queen,
> Though rabble rout may rush between,
> Beat thee senseless to the ground,
> In the dark beset thee round,
> Persist to ask and it will come,
> Seek not for rest in humbler home
> So shalt thou see what few have seen
> The palace home of King and Queen.

✒ AMs, ECS Papers, DLC.

1. The revised text published in 1870 (referred to hereafter as 1870) omits the first two paragraphs of the manuscript text.

2. ECS published paragraphs 4–6 as "Woman," *Lily*, January 1850, and the Address to the Women of the State of New York, from the Yearly Meeting of Congregational Friends at Waterloo, in June 1850, opened with variants of this and the next paragraph. ECS served on the committee to draft the address, along with Charles Lenox Remond, Eliab W. Capron, and Lydia Ann Jenkins. (*Film*, 6:1032, 1056–65.)

3. ECS's chief source for historical and cross-cultural information about women in this sentence and throughout the speech was the two volume *History of the Condition of Women, in Various Ages and Nations*, published in 1835 by Lydia Maria Child. Child's work supplied examples as well for Sarah Grimké, *Letters on the Equality of the Sexes*. Both the Kerek and Mohammedan examples are in Child's volume about women of Asia and Africa (1:41, 68). ECS may have coined the image of a German couple, though Grimké attributes similar behavior to a number of nationalities (42–43). Child viewed European society more positively: it "differs from that of Asiatic nations or savage tribes in the comparative equality of labor between the sexes; if poor women are obliged to work hard, poor men are so likewise; they do not, like Orientals, sit in idleness, while women perform nearly all the drudgery" (2:181).

4. On the title page of Child's *History of the Condition of Women*, from Lord Byron, "The Corsair," the first two lines are found in canto 2, pt. 14, and the last four in canto 3, pt. 8. Neither author copied Byron's lines precisely. The "sack" alludes to purging the harem by tossing an unwanted woman into the Bosphorus in a sack.

5. By the Salic law, females were excluded from the line of succession to the throne of France.

6. Inserted here in 1870: "in a republic based on the theory that no just government can be formed without the consent of the governed . . . ."

7. Gen. 1:28.

8. This standard list of capable women can be found in both Child and Grimké. Monarchs in Russia and England, Catherine II or Catherine the Great (1729–1796) ruled from 1762 to her death, and Elizabeth I (1533–1603) ruled from 1558 to 1603. In the field of letters, Harriet Martineau (1802–1876), a British writer and ardent abolitionist, visited the United States from 1834 to 1836 and, under the influence of the Grimké sisters, became an advocate of woman's rights. Germaine de Stael (1766–1817), a French writer and leader of an intellectual and political salon, went into exile during Napoleon's reign. British astronomers, Caroline Lucretia Herschel (1750–1848) and Mary Fairfax Somerville (1780–1872) were honored for their discoveries by the Royal Astronomical Society. For evidence of women's physical potential, the most

popular example was the Amazons, a tribe of warrior women in antiquity who fought the Greeks.

9. This paragraph was included in "Man Superior—Intellectually—Morally—Physically," pt. 1, *Lily*, February 1850, *Film*, 6:1037.

10. Inserted here in 1870: "our freedom to find out our own sphere, when we shall have had . . . ."

11. Revised in 1870 to read: "Then comes the gay routine of fashionable life, courtship and marriage, the perplexities of house and children, and she knows nothing beside."

12. Sarah Grimké observed that Eve's temptation came from "a being with whom she was unacquainted." Adam fell "not through the instrumentality of a supernatural agent, but through that of his equal"; "it appears to me," she wrote, "that to say the least, there was as much weakness exhibited by Adam as by Eve." (Grimké, *Letters on the Equality of the Sexes*, 6)

13. "Man Superior—Intellectually—Morally—Physically," pt. 2, *Lily*, March 1850, *Film*, 6:1039, contains paragraphs 9–11.

14. "Man Superior—Intellectually—Morally—Physically," pt. 3, *Lily*, April 1850, *Film*, 6:1044, contains paragraphs 12–13.

15. That is, William Ellery Channing. John Quincy Adams (1767-1848), sixth president of the United States and congressman, opposed the extension of slavery and the gag rule that stopped expressions of antislavery views. Northerners who voted with the South to protect slavery were dubbed "doughfaces."

16. Daniel Lambert, a Londoner of immense weight who exhibited himself as a curiosity, also appeared as a character in Charles Dickens, *Nicholas Nickleby* (1839).

17. This sentence from Child, *History of the Condition of Women*, 1:176.

18. To this point the sentence from Child, *History of the Condition of Women*, 2:167.

19. Alfred Lord Tennyson, "The Princess," pt. 2, lines 131-35.

20. In 1870, the sentence reads: "We have met here to-day to discuss our rights and wrongs, civil and political, and not, as some have supposed, to go into the detail of social life alone." "Woman's Rights," *National Reformer*, 14 September 1848, contains paragraph 14, and "The Convention," *Lily*, June 1850, consists of paragraphs 14, 15, and most of 16, *Film*, 6:764-65, 1066.

21. Elements of men's fashionable attire, the stock was a close-fitting cloth wrapped about the neck, and pants were strapped down beneath the instep to retain a snug fit.

22. Tennyson, "The Princess," pt. 2, lines 207-8.

23. Both "The Convention" and 1870 read "All white men."

24. Martin Van Buren (1782-1862), a New Yorker, was eighth president of the United States and the Free Soil party candidate for president in 1848. Henry Clay (1777-1852), senator, Speaker of the House of Representatives,

secretary of state, and Whig candidate for president in 1848, was regarded as one of the great politicians of the age.

25. Matt. 5:39 and Rom. 12:19.

26. "Should Women Vote," *Lily*, July 1850, *Film*, 6:1077–78, begins here and continues through most of paragraph 19.

27. This and the two sentences following were used in the address of the Congregational Friends.

28. Shortened in 1870 to read: "In the Turkish harem, in those Seraglios, where intellect and soul are buried beneath the sensualism and brutality which are the inevitable results of woman's degradation, even there, she declares herself not only satisfied with her position, but glories in it."

29. A paraphrase of Harriet Martineau, *Eastern Life, Past and Present* (London, 1848), 2:164.

30. Tennyson, "The Princess," pt. 2, lines 40–41.

31. Tennyson, "The Princess," pt. 2, lines 155–60.

32. From this point, 1870 reads: "omnipotence, and that true happiness springs from duty accomplished. Thus will she learn the lesson of individual responsibility for time and eternity. That neither father, husband, brother or son, however willing they may be, can discharge her high duties of life, or stand in her stead when called into the presence of the great Searcher of Hearts at the last day."

33. An "X" is lightly drawn across paragraph 21, though the text is retained in 1870.

34. Gen. 9:2. This paragraph leans on Grimké, *Letters on the Equality of the Sexes*, especially pages 10–11, 94–95.

35. Eph. 5:22.

36. ECS closely follows the discussion in Grimké, *Letters on the Equality of the Sexes*, 120–21 in this and the next paragraph.

37. 1 Pet. 3:7.

38. In 1870 sentence reads: "It is woman's mission to resist oppression wherever she may find it, whether at her own fireside, or on a Southern plantation, by every moral power within her reach." The plantation is removed from the next sentence about men.

39. Here in 1870 is added: "but are not his sorrows all written in the book of the immortal Caudle, written by his own hand, that all may read and pity the poor man, though feeling all through that the hapless Mrs. Caudle had, after all, many reasons for her continual wail for substantial grief." She refers to *Mrs. Caudle's Curtain Lectures*, written by Douglas Jerrold for the British magazine *Punch* and published in book form in 1845.

40. Sentence added at end of paragraph in 1870: "Let us then have no fears that this movement will disturb what is seldom found a truly united and happy family."

41. Sentence from Child, *History of the Condition of Women*, 2:206.

42. Zenobia, queen of Palmyra, came to the throne after the death of her husband and conquered Egypt, but the Roman Emperor Aurelian defeated and captured her in 272. Child praised her as "the most remarkable among Asiatic women," but omitted Aurelian's well-known tribute (1:30–31). ECS could find it in the classic textbook, Emma Willard, *Universal History in Perspective*, 12th ed. (New York, 1854), 158. She also consulted Samuel L. Knapp, *Female Biography; Containing Notices of Distinguished Women, in Different Nations and Ages* (New York, 1834).

43. Both Child, *History of the Condition of Women*, 2:206, and Willard, *Universal History*, 348, link the names of these two queens. Margaret I (1353–1412) consolidated the crowns of Denmark, Norway, and Sweden by 1398 and ruled a short-lived empire until her death. Semiramis was a mythical Assyrian queen credited with founding the city of Babylon and conquering many lands.

44. Isabella (1451–1504), Spanish queen of Castile and Léon from 1474, married Ferdinand V of Castile, also known as Ferdinand II of Aragon, (1442–1516), in 1469 and reigned with him as sovereign of Castile. The glorification of Isabella as grand but feminine, brave but modest, and superior to her husband is consistent with Willard's interpretation in *Universal History*, 276. ECS also read William H. Prescott, *History of the Reign of Ferdinand and Isabella, the Catholic*, first published in 1837.

45. Quotation from Prescott, *History of Ferdinand and Isabella*, in 1872 edition at 1:268. Isabella negotiated with Dona Beatriz of Portugal, her aunt, a mediator for the queen of Portugal.

46. ECS follows Samuel Knapp, *Female Biography*, 406, in translating the Latin as "king." Maria Theresa (1717–1780) came to the Hapsburg throne in 1740. The pledge of the Hungarian nobles enabled her to fight the war of Austrian succession against the monarchs of Europe who disputed her claim to the throne.

47. Quotation from Child, *History of the Condition of Women*, 2:206–7. Several queens are named. While Elizabeth I ruled England, James VI ruled Scotland. He later became James I of England. Catherine the Great is measured against Peter the Great (1672–1725.) Queen Zhinga (1582–1663) of Ndongo in western Angola led her people in resistance to Portuguese domination. In France Blanche of Castile (1185?–1252), wife of Louis VIII, was regent during the minority of their son Louis IX and again when her son departed on a crusade. Caroline of Ansbach (1683–1737), wife of England's George II, served as her husband's regent repeatedly between 1729 and 1737.

48. Josephine (1763–1814) was empress of France until Napoleon Bonaparte arranged with the Pope for their marriage to be annulled in 1809. Victim of selfish manhood, she became something of a sentimental heroine in the 1830s and 1840s. Napoleon broke "the heart of the best of his friends," Willard's *Universal History* (456) explained.

49. Hannah More (1745–1833), English author and reformer, wrote *Village Politics, Addressed to All the Mechanics, Journeymen, and Day Labourers in*

Great Britain (1792) under the name of "Will Chip, a country carpenter." In a dialogue two laborers dismiss the revolutionary ideas reaching England from France and celebrate monarchy, deference, the gentry, and religious faith as the strengths of the English system. (Mary Alden Hopkins, *Hannah More and Her Circle* [New York, 1947], 205-9.)

50. Again, Isabella of Castile, who supported the explorations of Christopher Columbus (1451-1506). This willingness to regard Isabella as more victim than sovereign when considering the Inquisition prevailed in Prescott's biography and was echoed in Willard, *Universal History*. Tomas de Torquemada (1420?-1498), a Dominican monk, was made inquisitor general.

51. Added at close of this sentence in 1870: "we consign their souls to hell-fire and their lives to misrepresentation and persecution."

52. Inserted here in 1870: "Where men make no objections to women or negroes to serve or amuse them in public, but the claim of equality is what chagrins the tyrant. Man never rejects the aid of either, when they serve him in the accomplishment of his work."

53. Joan of Arc (1412?-1431), national heroine of France, claimed divine inspiration for her decision to rally the people to the aid of the dauphin, the future Charles VII (1403-1461) of France, who was kept from the throne by English armies. There were scores of books available about Joan, most of them interpreting her story as a test of faith. A few shared ECS's humanistic interpretation of her charisma as self-confidence. Willard wrote: "Her own solemn persuasion of the reality of her mission,—which was, she said, communicated in visions,—together with the intrepidity of her manner, made an impression of awe,—even on the minds of the gay courtiers." (*Universal History*, 254.)

54. Added in 1870: "Verily, the world waits the coming of some new element, some purifying power, some spirit of mercy and love."

55. This paragraph underwent considerable revision in 1870 and became the final paragraph of the speech, followed by the closing verse.

56. Joel 2:28.

57. The address of the Congregational Friends used paragraph 34, without the verse, as its penultimate paragraph, and the text marked by angle brackets is restored to the torn manuscript from that source.

58. The Friends omitted this reference to the work of Hicksite Friends with the Seneca Nation in western New York. In a constitution adopted in 1845 on the recommendation of the Friends, the Seneca replaced government by chiefs with representative government. (Barbour, *Quaker Crosscurrents*, 96-99.)

TEXTUAL NOTES

¶1	*l.*7	replying to recent sermon
¶3	*l.*1	appear ~~thus~~ before you
¶3	*ll.*13-14	the sober man then with what magic
¶3	*ll.*15-16	rejoicing on high land let a man once

¶4   *l*.10   as it is—having
¶5   *l*.10   marking ↑out↓ the path
¶5   *ll*.18–19   delectable gentlemen who thinks
¶5   *l*.20   the ~~legislature~~ ↑legislator↓ who considers
¶5   *l*.28   whims & will truly has she herself
¶7   *l*.1   his intellectual~~ly~~ superiority
¶7   *ll*.5–6   enter, ~~shall first educate herself~~ instead of
¶7   *l*.11   throwing ↑away↓ the intellectual
¶7   *ll*.11–12   sisters crave, a little music
¶7   *l*.22   lustre to them it is all burried
¶9   *l*.7   to a fallen race?—far from it
¶10 *l*.8   compared with women   then he says
¶10 *l*.12   he who ↑made↓ the heavens
¶10 *l*.16   the mighty ↑ocean↓ mountain &
¶10 *l*.22   as much ~~your~~ ↑his↓ duty
¶10 *l*.25   would ↑require↓ the sacrifice
¶11 *l*.3   man has done an infinite
¶12 *l*.4   no right to claim ↑it↓ until
¶12 *ll*.9–10   tho' we grant even this
¶12 *l*.17   You do no say the horse
¶13 *ll*.27–28   they do ↑not↓ claim superiority
¶13 *l*.31   & they all lie ~~in the same place~~ ↑and that they are similarly situated↓
¶14 *l*.15   opinion for all ↑the↓ Bishops
¶17 *l*.12   woman ↑already↓ often shown
¶17 *ll*.21–22   go to war I can see no
¶17 *ll*.23–24   superior ↑& more effective↓ ones
¶18 *l*.19   baptized blood
¶18 *l*.26   disgust ridicule
¶18 *l*.29   satisfied ~~with the laws under~~ nor their
¶19 *l*.3   soul ↑itself↓ is as it were
¶19 *l*.4   where ~~one half the human beings God has made &~~ ↑those beings God has↓ endowed with
¶20 *ll*.9–10   she will ↑feel↓ the desire
¶21 *ll*.17–18   afford ↑of itself sufficient↓ material ~~enough~~ for
¶22 *l*.1   me hear notice
¶22 *l*.2   has long ~~made~~ ↑found↓ for itself
¶22 *l*.13   with her needle stitch, stich, stich,
¶23 *l*.4   thick upon take the
¶24 *ll*.1–2   principles ↑of freedom & equality↓ which
¶24 *l*.17   put on ↑and plenty of wood to [burn?]↓
¶25 *l*.19   may find ~~it~~ ↑at↓ home
¶25 *ll*.19–20   moral ↑power↓ within her reach
¶26 *l*.13   harmony or happiness there oh! no

¶28   *l*.9   to have ↑been↓ a more perfect

¶29   *ll*.4–5   spreading—↑was earnestly besought by↓ many eminent ↑men↓ ~~men earnestly besought her~~ to write

¶29   *l*.15   in her success, strange

¶30   *l*.12   to have ↑been↓ countenanced

¶32   *l*.15   race unaided there are deep

¶33   *ll*.7–8   was prophesied ↑of↓, ours

¶33   *ll*.10–11   short, ↑our struggle shall be hard & long↓ but

¶33   *l*.20   undaunted~~ly~~ we will

¶33   *ll*.21–22   will ~~not~~ ↑but↓ more clearly

¶34   *l*.6   large for ~~the~~ ↑her↓ chains,

¶34   *l*.15   before ~~deemed light~~ ↑revered↓

¶34   *ll*.16–17   while ↑mind↓ is investigating

¶34   *l*.25   into ~~being is~~ life is from the

·◁────━☓━────▷·

26 ✑ ECS TO AMY KIRBY POST

Grassmere [*Seneca Falls*] Sept 24th [*1848*]

Amy Post Dear friend,

I have often thought of you all since our Rochester convention[1] & desired to hear from you, as to what you were thinking, doing, & your plans for the future. Our conventions both went off so well that we have great encouragement to go on. What are we next to do?— We have declared our right to vote— The question now is how shall we get possession of what rightfully belongs to us?— Ought there not to be a simultaneous petitioning for this right among the women of the several states? We wish this movement to be as general as possible— Do you not think we ought to have an agent to travel all over the country & lecture on this subject. Lucy Stone[2] I think might be engaged for that purpose She has an engagement now with the antislavery society in Massachusetts, but that will soon end I have understood she said she wished to devote herself to the cause of woman. Do any of the Rochester friends know her personally? if so, it would be well to ascertain how she feels on this subject. I received a letter of <u>congratulation</u> from Paulina Wright yesterday[3] She is much pleased with the action of the women of western New York— She says they intend to hold a convention in Philadelphia shortly— I hear you have communication with the spiritual world in Rochester.[4] Do ask the spirits if we shall accomplish anything by our recent movement. Remember me kindly to all the friends. I have so often regretted my foolish conduct in regard to the President of the convention at R.[5] The result proved that your judgement was good, & Mrs Bush discharged her duties so well that I was really quite delighted that we were able through her to do up our business so well without depending on any man. My only excuse is that woman has been so little accustomed to act in a public capacity that she does not always know what is due to those around her. Let me hear from you soon   your friend & co-worker

⬥ *Elizabeth Cady Stanton*

⬥ ALS, HM 10499, Ida Harper Collection, CSmH.

1. Amy Post was in charge of arrangements for the convention on 2 August 1848. The large crowd included James and Lucretia Mott, ECS, Mary Hallowell, Frederick Douglass, and the McClintocks, as well as local activists, Sarah Anthony Burtis, Rhoda DeGarmo, and, it was later said, Daniel, Lucy, and Mary Anthony. New resolutions pledged to "petition our State Legislature for our right to the elective franchise, every year, until our prayer be granted," and urged "That those who believe the laboring classes of women are oppressed ought to do all in their power to raise their wages, beginning with their own household servants." ECS read the Declaration of Sentiments, which this convention adopted, and joined several discussions. (*Film*, 6:723–40, 742–57; *History*, 1:75–87, 456; *Anthony*, 1:59; Hewitt, *Women's Activism and Social Change*, 131–35.)

2. Lucy Stone (1818–1893) grew up on a farm in West Brookfield, Massachusetts, taught school, and supported herself through Oberlin College, graduating in 1847. Determined to become a public speaker and aided by Abby Kelley Foster, she was made a lecturer for the Massachusetts Anti-Slavery Society. Lecturing became her career. Typical of reports on her style were the words of the *National Era*, after a speech in Washington in 1854. "Every heart was taken captive by the grace, modesty and propriety of her manner, and the melody and richness of her voice. . . . Miss Lucy is an admirable speaker, fluent, yet forcible; her mind teems with apposite facts and illustrations of her thought, which pour forth in an uninterrupted stream of beautiful elocution." (*Lib.*, 24 February 1854.) She delivered speeches on women and abolitionism in the Northeast and Midwest, earning a very good income from the work. In Ohio, Massachusetts, and Wisconsin, she launched state campaigns for legal reform, and she assumed responsibility for organizing several of the national conventions. After her marriage to Henry Browne Blackwell in 1855, her career slowed down, but she was still sought after as a speaker, and the public recognized her as a symbol of woman's rights agitation, for keeping her own

name and protesting taxes on her property. She worked closely with ECS and SBA until 1867. Thereafter she became their chief critic and rival. (*NAW*; Andrea Moore Kerr, *Lucy Stone: Speaking Out For Equality* [New Brunswick, N.J., 1992]; Carol Lasser and Marlene Deahl Merrill, eds., *Friends and Sisters: Letters Between Lucy Stone and Antoinette Brown Blackwell, 1846–93* [Urbana, Ill., 1987].)

3. Presumably she refers to Paulina Wright's letter of 19 September 1848, extant only as a transcript, but the available text omits mention of a meeting in Philadelphia. (*Film*, 6:772.) Paulina Kellogg Wright (1813–1876), later Davis, lived in Utica until 1844 and became a reformer through antislavery activity. The Wrights' house was a target of mobs against abolitionists in 1835 and provided a home for Abby Kelley during her tours of New York in 1842. In Philadelphia because she had taken her ailing husband there and stayed after his death in 1845, Wright educated herself to lecture on physiology. She acted as midwife for Abby Kelley Foster at the birth of a daughter named Paulina Wright Foster in 1847. Remarried in 1849 to Thomas Davis of Providence, Rhode Island, Paulina Davis was a member of the committee that called the First National Woman's Rights Convention in 1850, and she presided for several years over the central committee, charged with organizing subsequent conventions. From 1853 to 1855, she published the *Una*, the first newspaper established to promote woman's rights. A fashionable life at Providence, Newport, and Washington, eroded her zeal for reform; she shunned dress reform because it alienated fashionable people and promoted literary women over reformers in the movement. She maintained a commitment to individual rights, free from the restraints of church and state, and for a time after the Civil War, she was a leader in the National Woman Suffrage Association. (ECS, "Reminiscences of Paulina Wright Davis," *History*, 1:283–289; *NAW*; Sterling, *Ahead of Her Time*; *Eighty Years*, 150; Yuri Suhl, *Ernestine L. Rose and the Battle for Human Rights* [New York, 1959], 59.)

4. The interest shown by Amy and Isaac Post in the rappings communicated by the dead through the mediumship of the Fox sisters, Kate and Margaret, of Hydesville, New York, created a core of believers in Rochester, who sponsored the young girls in public demonstrations and popularized a belief in spiritualism. At this date, the demonstrations were confined to the Posts' house, where reformers came to communicate with the dead. (Ann Braude, *Radical Spirits: Spiritualism and Women's Rights in Nineteenth-Century America* [Boston, 1989], 10–13.)

5. When officers of the convention were selected at a preliminary meeting on 1 August, disagreement surfaced about the propriety and ability of women to serve. According to the revised report of the convention, when it was decided to make Abigail Bush president, Elizabeth McClintock declined to be secretary, "on the ground of being unprepared to have a woman the presiding officer." "To our great surprise," the account continues, "two or three other women—glorious reformers, well deserving the name—coming from a distance

to attend the meeting, at first refused to take their seats upon the platform, or otherwise co-operate with the Convention, for the same cause." In the *History of Woman Suffrage*, ECS added: "Mrs. Mott, Mrs. Stanton, and Mrs. McClintock, thought it a most hazardous experiment to have a woman President, and stoutly opposed it." Abigail Norton Bush (c. 1810–c. 1898) was active in the Western New York Anti-Slavery Society in the forties. A close friend of the Posts, she witnessed the earliest demonstrations of the spirit rappings and became a believer. She moved to California after 1850, and at age 86 became involved in that state's suffrage referendum campaign. For her pioneering role at the Rochester meeting she was honored at anniversaries held in 1878 and 1898. Suffragists noted her death at the annual meeting in April 1899. (*Proceedings of the Woman's Rights Conventions, Held at Seneca Falls & Rochester, N.Y., July & August, 1848* [New York, 1870], 3; unidentified clipping, 19 July 1896, SBA scrapbook 1876–1903, DLC; *History*, 1:75, 3:120; 4:298, 345; *Film*, 6:723–40, 20:319, 38:148, 458–61, 542; Hewitt, *Women's Activism and Social Change*, 106–7, 121–22, 131, 144; Braude, *Radical Spirits*, 11, 195.)

---

27 ☙ Lucretia Coffin Mott to ECS

Philada. 10 mo. 3rd. 1848

My dear Eliz^h

The letter or parcel sent to the M'Clintocks, by my daughter 3 weeks ago—I find was kept at Auburn, until last week. You must have thought me very remiss in acknowledging yours, so acceptable—and so I have been, thy last, which I have read again & again to my own & others' entertainment.[1] <u>I am now trying to awaken sufficient interest to hold a Woman's Rights' Meeting in this City</u>— It is far more difficult than we found it out West— Still there are numbers here, who feel a deep interest in the cause. Few however are accustomed to public speaking. Thou asks if Sarah Pugh & Mary Grew will not take hold & work— Mary has been very feeble all summer—and continues so much so, as to be obliged to withhold her active aid in the publication of the Freeman, and rarely meets with our Ex. Com.[2] We could not therefore depend upon her for anything more than perhaps a short production of her pen. Abby Kimber[3] is much at home with her aged & feeble Mother, and Sarah with hers. But they would both give all the aid in their power. We have been looking around for a suitable place to hold a

Meeting or Convention in— There will be difficulty in obtaining one for that object—or such an one as we should like— <u>Why cant thou & the M'Clintocks come on here to attend such a meeting? You are so wedded to this cause, that you must expect to act as pioneers in the work</u>— The writer of that letter from ↑near↓ Boston, which I sent for your perusal, & which I should be glad to have again, when you have done with it, would probably come & aid in a meeting— Paulina Wright expects to leave here soon for Boston, so that we may not depend upon her— There may however be some unknown "Mrs Sandfords"[4] to come upon our platform, so we will be of good courage— <u>If there is any probability of having your company on such an occasion, we could make the time suit your convenience</u>. Please consult Mary Ann & daughters & let me know. <u>I had thought of the last week in this month, but some time in next would do as well, if you could better come then</u>.

The Book that thou & Eliz^h M'Clintock are "concocting" I hope will be forth-coming. It is just what is needed— <u>But you must not depend upon me for a single chapter</u>. It is not in my line. You can <u>borrow</u> from S. M. Grimke's all the historical part of hers—Bible & all—and from Mary Woolstonecraft[5] much that is excellent—

As to the generality of the works extant on that subject, it is ~~only~~ ↑more↓ surprising that they saw & wrote as far as they did, than that they did not embrace the whole—

The progress that we see in every work of truth & reform ought to lead us to hail each step in the advance-field of Woman's duties & rights. Look back to the days of our Grandmothers & be cheered—

Oliver Johnson is here.[6] He tells me that an orthodox minister in the town in Mass. where he has lived the last year, a stranger to me, took occasion lately, to hold me up to his congregation, as the worst of women— I send a low, vulgar scrap, from a Paper, published here, which I never see;[7] this & that article from the Boston Paper sent in the other parcel, give evidence of some of the misrepresentation & ridicule we anticipated.

Richard Hunt speaks very favorably of thy maiden speech at Waterloo.[8] He says some of their respectable inhabitants were well pleased— He would have preferred the head-dress a little different— It looked rather Theatrical he thought—"a kind of turban & bows"— When thou comes here we can give thee an example of Quaker simplicity. I

rejoiced however, that thou wast willing to ~~deliver~~ write that lecture—
& hope thy talents in that way will be well "exercised by reason of
use"—and that Eliz^h and Mary M'Clintock will not let their's rust, but
will follow thy example & "speak to my people that they go forward."[9]
<u>Do you write to Rochester & stir up those women to their duties</u>?

As to the Grimkes, I have little hope of them, after such a flash &
such an effecetual extinguishment—we must not depend upon them.
Nor upon any who have been apostles before us—but be ready for
"those things which shall hereafter appear unto" us—[10]

We are now in the midst of a Convention of the colored people of
this City—Douglass & Delany, Remond & Garnet[11] are here—all taking an active part—and as they include women—& <u>white</u> women too, I
can do no less, with the interest I feel in the cause of the slave, as well
as of woman, than be present & take a little part— So yesterday, in a
pouring rain, Sarah Pugh & self, walked down there, & expect to do
the same today—still raining— So ever in a hurry I conclude, with the
dearest love to you all—

❧ *Lucretia Mott*

The letter sent with this,[12] I found on our arrival home from the west—
Thou wilt see by the date, that the writer had no knowledge of our
doings— I presume she has not a thorough acquaintance with our
language, by wh I account for a blindness of style— I was interested in
it—please return it—

We have been begging "a lot" of second hand winter clothing, with
some pieces new goods to send to the Refugees in Canada— My
husband had two large boxes packed & forwarded last week— We
learn by letter from Hiram Wilson & the Female Teacher, that the
steam saw mill is in operation & doing well—they appear encouraged—[13]

❧ ALS, ECS Papers, DLC. Variants in ECS Papers, NjR, and *Stanton*, 2:22.
The underlinings may be marks by ECS to draw Elizabeth McClintock's
attention to portions of the letter.

1. ECS's letter may be the source for the transcript and printed text dated
30 September 1848 in *Film*, 6:772.
2. Mary Grew joined the editorial board of the *Pennsylvania Freeman* in
1845. She and Mott served together on the executive committees of the Female
Anti-Slavery and Pennsylvania Anti-Slavery societies.
3. Abby Kimber (1804–1871), active in the Philadelphia Female Anti-Slavery
Society, attended the London convention in 1840. She and her sister taught in

a Quaker school founded by their father. As friend and co-worker of Lucretia Mott and Mary Grew, she was active in the city's early woman's rights meetings. (Garrison, *Letters*, 4:443n, 5:44n; *History*, 1:376.)

4. Rebecca M. M. Sanford, a young bride, arrived at the convention in Rochester a stranger and made a speech uniformly described as eloquent. She spoke for twenty minutes "in a voice whose pathos thrilled every heart." Her husband stood nearby, "a most delighted, nay, reverential listener. It was a scene never to be forgotten." Itinerant publishers, the Sanfords issued a weekly *Gem of Science* at Ann Arbor, Michigan, and moved next to Chagrin Falls, Ohio, where they published the *True Kindred*, a paper for women. By 1853 they had moved to New London, Ohio. The editors of the *History of Woman Suffrage* identified her as then (about 1880) the postmaster of Mount Morris, New York. (*History*, 1:77-78, 819; *National Reformer*, 17 August 1848; *Lib.*, 15 September 1848; Crisfield Johnson, comp., *History of Cuyohoga County, Ohio* [Cleveland, 1879], 190; *History of Washtenaw County, Michigan* [1881; reprint, Ann Arbor, 1990], 1:441.)

5. There is no further talk of a book by ECS until 1855. Mott refers her to Sarah Grimké, *Letters on the Equality of the Sexes*, and to Mary Wollstonecraft (1759-1797), author of *A Vindication of the Rights of Women*, published in London in 1792 and issued in numerous American editions thereafter.

6. Oliver Johnson (1809-1889), one of Garrison's earliest collaborators, served the antislavery movement principally as an editor. In addition to assisting at the *Liberator*, he edited the *Anti-Slavery Bugle* (Salem, Ohio), the *Pennsylvania Freeman*, and the *National Anti-Slavery Standard*. Horace Greeley also employed him at the *New York Tribune*. While living in Ohio from 1849 to 1851, Johnson and his wife Mary Ann White contributed to the campaign for woman's rights in the state's new constitution. (*DAB*.)

7. Enclosure missing. Clippings of reactions to the woman's rights conventions of 1848 are compiled in ECS Papers, DLC. Selections appear in *History*, 1:802-5.

8. Richard Pell Hunt (1797-1856) was a wealthy Quaker living at Waterloo, where he constructed commercial buildings and invested in the town's woolen factory. He was also an abolitionist, a Congregational Friend, and a supporter of woman's rights. At his house, the call to the convention of Seneca Falls was written, and the Hunts both attended the meeting and signed the Declaration of Sentiments. Jane C. Master Hunt (1812-1889), a native of Philadelphia and Richard's fourth wife, stayed in Waterloo after her husband's death. (*Friends' Intelligencer* 13 [1857]: 569, 46 [1889]: 777; Becker, *History of the Village of Waterloo, New York*, 136, 151-52; research by Judith Wellman.)

9. Mott adapts Exo. 14:15.

10. Rev. 1:19.

11. Frederick Douglass spent two weeks in Philadelphia meeting with African-American congregations about "the subject of our duties to the slave and ourselves." In addition to Douglass and Charles Lenox Remond, Mott heard

Martin Robison Delany (1812–1885) and Henry Highland Garnet (1815–1882). Delany coedited the *North Star* and traveled widely to lecture and sell subscriptions. Garnet was pastor of the Liberty Street Presbyterian Church in Troy, New York, and prominent in the conventions of black citizens. (*NASS*, 19 October 1848; *DANB*; *Black Abolitionist Papers*, 2:397–98n, 440–41n.)

12. Enclosure missing.

13. Mott refers to the community of Dawn, near Dresden in Canada West, where Hiram Wilson (1803–1864), an Oberlin graduate, established the British-American Institute to provide manual training for African Americans who fled from slavery. In addition to classes for adults and children, the institute offered jobs, and its sawmill was its most successful enterprise. Though he was no longer in charge, Wilson and his wife taught school at Dawn until 1850. By female teacher, Mott may refer to Mrs. Lorena Parker of Oneida County, New York, who taught alongside the Wilsons in 1848. (*Lib.*, 27 October 1848; *National Era*, 18 November 1847; Pease and Pease, *Bound With Them in Chains*, 115–39; Pease and Pease, *Black Utopia*, 63–83.)

·◁=====※=====▷·

28 ❧ SBA TO LUCY READ ANTHONY

Canajoharie Oct. [29], 1848.

Dear Mother

Your letter of the 24th & 25th inst. was received, read & has been forwarded to Eugene. Father arrived here yesterday A.M. before breakfast.[1] After breakfast he went over the river & I followed as soon as I could put my room in order & wash & dress. We took dinner at Uncles, then Uncle came to Josephs & took tea. Father at first intended to take the evening Packet, but after much persuasion consented to wait until this A.M. Packet, he left before breakfast this A.M., I heard the horse & opened the north blind, waved my handkerchief & he shook his umbrella in return. The briny waters would come in spite of me. I can endure to part with friends, going in any direction, save towards my home. I have felt rather long faced to day. Did not go to Church. I have been really glad to have Father express his sentiments with regard to reform.[2] Though the good folks call us crazy fanatics now, the day will come when they must acknowledge their stupidity. The way in which the Law-suit has been decided is too much to put up with, but Father has done all that could be done & feels but too keenly, this ill fated decision. I would that, that disagreeable, purse draining peace destroying affair might be brought to a final resting place. It now is the only barrier, to our family enjoyments   Perhaps though we would become proud & forget to be charitable, were we gratified in all wordly wishes. Let us do the best we can & remember not to blame others for our own discontent & disquietude. I see no Fathers or Mothers that I would exchange my own for, & I hope my Father & Mother feel the same way with regard to their children. I did not tell Father to write, but be sure & do so very soon after his return, he is going to Uncle John's tomorrow.[3]

That sample of calico you sent is beautiful, I wish I had the dress have not yet purchased even a calico since my return. Margaret sent a little red dress for Lorinda, & I sent my old rubbers for Merritt to make balls of. M[ary]'s are out of the same pack, therefore she be careful about leaving them near the stove. Write often. Aaron says I must surely go down there, but I will see about it. There is nothing new here with much love I subscribe myself your daughter

➣ *Susan*

Monday A.M. [*30 October*] There is nothing new! only I took supper at Georges, he thinks Cass is O.K.[4] I asked him if there was no other smart man in the country, Oh yes Fred Douglas. Said I you do think my Father a little crazy on the subject of slavery, no said he not a little, but a good deal, he never saw a man so wrapped up in a nigger as Father is in Douglas. Dont mind if you dont get a chance to send that dress. It is not likely you will unless you should leave it with Mr Davis & that would hardly be best I guess

Father will tell you about my Financial matters, for two years board up to end of this Term have stipulated to pay $96.00 & have paid $45.00 leaving $51. yet due & I have between $80. & $90 to collect but is almost 9 oclock & I am not dressed for the worse than pig pen, so good bye, write soon to   S. B. A.

➣ ALS, SBA Papers, MCR-S. SBA erroneously dated it "Oct. 31."

1. En route to Rochester. Daniel Anthony visited SBA on his eastbound journey earlier in October.

2. SBA described her father's conversations with relatives during his earlier visit: "Uncle is Old Hunker to the back bone, and would not allow that the

North had any more right to interfere with Southern Slavery, than the South had with the Northern system of manufacturing. Father kept very cool, never talked once on his accustomed key. I was glad to have Father express his mind. Many people are so afraid of disturbing the repose of those engaged in inhuman traffick." (SBA to L. R. Anthony, 10 October 1848, *Film*, 6:830–33.)

3. John Anthony (1800–1882), one of Daniel's brothers, lived at Auburn, about halfway between Canajoharie and Rochester. (Anthony, *Anthony Genealogy*, 198–99.)

4. Lewis Cass (1782–1866), the Democratic nominee for president in 1848 and a former senator from Michigan, thought that decisions about the extension of slavery into new territories should be local and left to the settlers.

·(⊏━━━━━⊐)·

29 ～ PHOEBE HATHAWAY[1] TO ECS

Farmington 11. mo. 11. '48

Dear friend

I send thee another letter which I received from Lucy Stone by last mail. Thou wilt be glad to hear she can come to this state so much sooner than she expected.[2]

Perhaps thou hast written her before this, and told her something definite relative to the plans of the society. I have written her but once, and then little more than to ask her if she would be willing to enter this field, and if so, upon what terms. I suppose she wishes to know definitely what her work is to be, and as nearly as possible <u>where</u>.

My love to Lizzie McClintock, please, when thou sees her, and say to her Ann Adams is with me, and also sends much love. In haste— Thine truly

～ *Phoebe Hathaway*

～ ALS, Scrapbook 1, Papers of ECS, NPV.

1. Phoebe Hathaway (1819–1902) lived all her life in Farmington, New York, where her Quaker parents settled and her older brother Joseph Comstock Hathaway raised his family. Both brother and sister were active in the Western New York Anti-Slavery Society and thus linked to the Garrisonians in Massachusetts and in Rochester. (Elizabeth Starr Versailles, *Hathaways of America* [Northampton, Mass.,1965],162; Hewitt, *Women's Activism and Social Change*, 117; Gue, *Diary of Benjamin F. Gue*, 40; Garrison, *Letters*, 3:111n.)

2. Enclosure missing. At Oberlin, Antoinette Brown heard about this plan and wrote Lucy Stone, "How glad I am that you are going to lecture for the Womans Rights Convention or Soc. rather." (Lasser and Merrill, *Friends and Sisters*, 46.)

<hr/>

30 ❧ SBA TO LUCY READ ANTHONY

Canajoharie Feb 7, 1849

Dear Mother

I intended to have written you on Sunday but wished to wait a little to hear from Easton & to day the news has arrived. Charlotte is marrie, well I rejoice with her, and hope she may see no cause for regret.[1] H[annah] seems to feel quite cheerily & I feel that I shall now feel more at home when visiting her. how I would like to spend one night with her as in olden times, and talk over matters & things in general. Must not Edward looked pretty, oh dear, dear I laughed until the tears ran down my cheeks, but after all there may be real worth beneath an awkward exterior. H. is looking forward to spring as well as myself. This Term will close nine weeks from to day. Mother (& Merritt if he can leave his business) must be ready & come down, to make an Eastern tour with me. Margaret will not hear a word of my leaving Canajoharie for good, as the saying is, but I dont know. I am tired, would like a rest & am inclined to think I shall take one.

The new Principal is an Alabama gent of the age of 19, is in the Senior Class of Union College.[2] his Father is a slave holder. he sways his school as a master would govern, implicit obedience, not one whisper or the rod is administered. Mr. Hagar drew on his Students by the gentle cords of love, & government of that sort is mild & pursuasive. Mr Bradly makes no conversation about matters just says, this is right, do it & it must be done, there is no other way. he has the most perfect order.— A colored man by the name of Bibb, ~~has~~ delivered two letures in the Methodist Church last week.[3] I could not attend   Every one says, Miss Anthony did you hear that colored gentleman lecture, (yes in Canajoharie they begin to speak somewhat respectfully of the being blessed with a darker hue). I heard that Bradly said that Bibb for the space of 40 minutes poured forth a stream of the most stirring Eloquence, that America could not produce his superior. Bibb, the last evening, gave his narative. I heard one lady remark, she never thought the slaves ought to bee freed until she heard Bibb. I very much regret I did not hear him as I understand he spoke of Douglas. We have Public Temperance Lectures Semi monthly. Two weeks from last eve Gauph[4] is expected here. The retrograde march of the Temperance cause is truly alarming—

Uncle is better, but has a bad cough, very short breath & is so lame as to be hardly able to walk from one room to another. Aunt M[ary] about the same. I went over Sunday A.M. after Church & staid 2 or 3 hours. She talked about your coming   said she was happy that felt willing to have me here, that they or M[argaret] could not get along without me.— Joseph is now in Albany on Official business he says no more about California, but I have many doubts about his having given up the expedition.[5] George went to N.Y. last week to see about purchasing shares in a California enterprise, do not know what he did. Dr Dewitt Rile leaves for the Gold mines in about two weeks. I wish I had about $100,000 of the precious dust. I would no longer be School marm. I was a man would'nt I be off. I was ten oclock when I commenced writing & I rather guess it must be bed time   So Good night, with much love to all.

⮜ AL, SBA Papers, MCR-S. SBA overwrote the opening of a letter to Mary Hagar. Letters in square brackets expand initials.

1. Probably Charlotte Mosher, who married Archie Rogers.

2. Daniel Hagar was replaced in December 1848 by Thomas Bibb Bradley (1826–1857), class of 1849 at Union College. After graduation, Bradley returned to Alabama to teach school for one year and practice law. By 1855 he edited a literary magazine in Mississippi. (Alumni files, NSchU.)

3. Henry Walton Bibb (1815–1854) ranked with Frederick Douglass as an effective antislavery speaker in the late 1840s. After escaping from slavery in 1842, he lectured widely in the Northeast and published his *Narrative of the Life and Adventures of Henry Bibb, An American Slave* in October 1849. Passage of the Fugitive Slave Act in 1850 caused him to move to Canada, where he became a leader among African-American refugees. (*DANB.*)

4. John Bartholomew Gough (1817–1886) was a reformed drunkard and accomplished orator whose lectures against drink moved countless people to sign a pledge of abstinence.

5. Gold fever began in December 1848, when President James K. Polk brought to public attention the discovery of gold in California, made earlier in the year.

·(⟐━━━━━⟐━━━━━)·

31 ⇒ SPEECH BY SBA TO THE DAUGHTERS OF TEMPERANCE

Editorial note: On 2 March 1849 SBA delivered her first public address to an audience of women assembled by the Montgomery Union, No. 29, of the Daughters of Temperance at Canajoharie. She notes below that women formed the local union in 1848, and in a letter that follows, she identifies herself as its Presiding Sister, or "P.S." In letters home she never foreshadowed her prominence in this movement. Founded in 1843, the Daughters of Temperance comprised local unions of women fifteen years of age or older who pledged total abstinence and mutual benefit. Guided by the motto "Virtue, Love and Temperance," Daughters directed their attention to improving "the female character" and discountenancing the use of liquor in their communities to influence male behavior. SBA's allusions to opposition are vague. That temperance advocates met resistance is the most obvious explanation of her meaning. Her audience knew, too, that like the Sons of Temperance, the Daughters met criticism for their secret rituals. But the more telling tensions by 1849 arose over definitions of woman's place. Though separated from the Sons, the Daughters sanctioned a female role in maintaining public morality that stopped short of public action. As the male temperance movement relied less on moral and more on legal reform at the end of the decade, however, female activists were preparing to join the Sons of Temperance in politics. (George F. Clark, *History of the Temperance Reform in Massachusetts, 1813–1883* [Boston, 1888], 67–71; John A. Krout, *The Origins of Prohibition* [1925; reprint, New York, 1967], 213–15.)

[2 March 1849]

¶1   Welcome Ladies, to this, our Hall of Temperance. You have been invited to meet with us this afternoon and for what purpose have you come hither? Are you here to listen to the advancement of new truths, or to hear old ones eloquently portrayed? Permit me *timely* to advise you, that you are destined to disappointment and tell you as nearly as I can, what were our motives in soliciting our friends to mingle with us this afternoon.

¶2 We feel that the cause we have espoused, is a common cause, a cause in which you, with us are deeply interested, and we would that some means were devised, by which our brothers and sons shall no longer be allured from the *right*, by the corrupting influence of the fashionable sippings of wine and brandy, those sure destroyers of mental and moral worth, and by which our Sisters and daughters may no longer be exposed to the vile arts of the gentlemanly appearing gallant but really half inebriated seducer. Our motive is to ask of you, council in the formation, and cooperation in the carrying out, of *plans*, which may produce a radical change in our moral Atmosphere.

¶3 We, who call ourselves Daughters of Temperance, and who are united into one Sisterhood, for the promotion of our great cause, the cause of Virtue, Love and Temperance, do from week to week meet here, to encourage each other in the way of well doing.

¶4 While we have thus met together, one year has sped its course, one sun has rolled its circuit round, and the question is asked us, What good have you done, what better is society, that you have thus sacrificed your time. What do you propose doing? You can find no intemperate females in Canajoharie, whom you may reform and surely there can be no possible necessity of your Order being longer sustained, nor need we be asked to join with you and like you sacrifice our time for naught.

¶5 I would that I were capable of answering such questions in a manner that would carry conviction to the minds of all present, and cause them to feel that wherever a great and public evil exists, there individual effort can avail but little in its removal.

¶6 But to the question, What good our Union has done? I will say, that the circumstances under which we organized were indeed unpropitious, and that the influence of those circumstances are still felt. Our numbers have increased but slowly. Those only have joined us, who have been so fortunate as to have the first and false impression of the object of our association, supplanted by a knowledge of our real purpose. Though we may not be able to tell you, or ourselves to discover, where we, in any signal manner, have advanced our noble cause, though we at times have been almost disheartened in our hope of benefitting our fallen fellow beings, though we both as a society and individually, have been scandalized as being deficient in mental and moral capacity to farther the great cause we profess to love. Though our Order has been strongly opposed, by ladies professing a desire to see the moral condition of our race elevated. And though we still see some of our thoughtless female friends whirling on in the giddy dance, with an intoxicated partner at her sides, and we more than this, see her accompany her reeling companion to some secluded nook and there quaff with him from that virtue destroying cup. Still may we not hope that an influence, though now unseen and unfelt, has gone forth, which shall tell upon the future, which shall convince us that our weekly resort to these meetings has not been in vain, and which shall cause the friends of humanity to admire and respect, nay venerate this now despised little band of Daughters of Temperance. It is the assurance that "God will speed the Right" that inspires us with courage to go onward. "Truth will prevail." Is not the Cause of Virtue, love and Temperance, on the side of Truth? It is and must be. Then why doubt its ultimate triumph, or why hesitate to do all in your power to hasten the day when Intemperance, with its slow and noiseless step, shall no more be permitted to enter our family circles, to bind its first cords with a touch too gentle to be felt. If such an influence has gone forth, then have we not sacrificed our time in vain, No! Happy are we to be thus privileged to spend a swiftly passing hour of each week in the society of those who profess a fellow feeling of sympathy for suffering humanity.

¶7   We count it no waste of time, to go forth through our streets, thus proclaiming our desire for the advancement of our great cause. You, with us no doubt feel that Intemperance is the blighting mildew of all our social connexions. You would be most happy to speed on the time, when no wife shall watch with trembling heart and tearful eye the slow, but sure descent of her idolized companion, down to the loathsome haunts of drunkenness. You would hasten the day when no mother shall have to mourn over a darling son, as she sees him launch his bark on the circling wave of this mighty whirlpool.

¶8   How is this great change to be wrought, who are to urge on this vast work of reform, shall it not be we who are most aggrieved by the foul destroyers inroads. Most certainly. Then arises the question how are we to accomplish the end desired. I answer, not by confining our influence to our own home circle, not by centering all our benevolent feelings upon our own kindred, not by caring naught for the culture of no minds, save those of our own darlings. No, No, the gratification of the selfish impulses *alone*, can never produce a desirable change in the moral aspect of society.

¶9   Would we cause a social change, we must nourish and invigorate the social affections. We must learn to estimate the worth of a human soul. We must feel, that wherever we behold a being wearing the impress of his Maker, there is one brother and there is one who claims from us, kindness and protection. How can we feel an interest about those of whom we know nothing, and how are we to know unless we associate together and inform ourselves of their wants and dangers. Could we truly estimate the extent of combined influence, then could we calculate, how much the state of society may be advanced by even the most inferior organization.

¶10   It is generally acceded that it is our sex that fashions the social and moral state of society, and when we look around us do we not see much that we are unwilling to believe *is so* through our influence? We do not presume that females possess unbounded power, in abolishing the evil customs of the day, but we do believe that were they en masse to discountenance the use of wine and brandy as a beverage at both their public and private parties, not one of the opposite sex, who has any claim to the title of Gentleman, would so insult them as to come into their presence after having quaffed of that foul destroyer of all true delicacy and refinement.

¶11   I am not aware that we have any inebriate females among us, but have we not those, who are fallen from *Virtue*, and who claim our efforts for their reform, equally with the inebriate, and while we feel it our duty to extend the hand of sympathy and love to those who are wanderers from the path of Temperance, should we not be also zealous in reclaiming those poor deluded ones, who have been robbed of their most precious gem, virtue, and whom we blush to think belong to our sex.

¶12   Now ladies, all we would do, is to do all in our power, both individually and collectively to harmonize and happify our social system. And we are fully persuaded, after having been organized one year, that for females to unite, and carry out the principles of our Order, is the most effectual method of establishing those customs in our social intercourse, which shall better conduce to the greatest good of the whole. We must remember that we live not for self alone, and that we are accountable to the great Author of all, not only for our own *actions*, but for the influence which they may have upon those with whom we associate.

¶13 We now ask of you candidly and seriously to investigate the matter, and decide for yourselves, whether the object of our Union be not on the side of right, and if it be, then one and all, for the sake of erring humanity, come forward and *speed* on the right. If you come to the conclusion that the end we wish to attain is right, but are not satisfied with the plan adopted, then I ask of you to devise means by which this great good may be more speedily accomplished, and you shall find us ready with both heart and hand to cooperate with you. In my humble opinion, all that is needed to produce a complete Temperance and Social reform in this age of moral suasion, is for our sex to cast their united influence into the balance.

¶14 Ladies! there is no neutral position for us to assume. If we avow not our desire to promote this noble enterprise, both by precept and example then is our influence on the side of Intemperance. If we say we love the cause and then sit down at our ease, surely do our actions speak the lie.

¶15 And now permit me once more to beg of you to lend your aid to this great Cause, the Cause of God and all mankind. If we who are now organized, few in number and possessed of comparatively little individual influence, may dare to hope that by our united efforts, some *small* good has been done, what vast results might we not anticipate, could we secure the active cooperation of all our more influential Ladies. For most assuredly, when all our mothers become zealous and active in our noble cause, then will they no longer have to mourn over their children's departure from the path of Temperance and Virtue, and when all our young ladies come forth and boldly declare themselves on the side of reform, then will they no longer experience the mortification of seeing their dear brothers, lost to all true refinement of soul. And when this anxiously looked for time shall have arrived, and not till then, will the great object be accomplished for which our Union has been instituted.

❧ AMs, SBA Papers, DLC. Endorsed at a later date by SBA, "Susan B. Anthonys First Public Address delivered before the Canajoharie Union of the Daughters of Temperance," and, later still, "in 1848—I think—" Ida Harper marked the manuscript for the revised text she published in *Anthony*, 1:53–55.

TEXTUAL NOTES

¶2	*l*.2	interested↑, and↓ We
	l.4	be ~~exposed~~ allured
	l.5	sippings, of ↑wine brandy↓ those sure
	ll.7–8	appearing ↑gallant↓ but ↑really↓ half inebriated
¶3	*ll*.3–4	Temperance, ~~have~~ ↑do↓ from week to week ~~met~~ ↑meet↓ here
¶4	*l*.2	~~query~~ ↑question↓ ~~arises~~
	ll.3–4	have ↑thus↓ sacrificed
	ll.4–5	find ↑no↓ intemperate
¶5	*l*.3	exists, ~~no~~ ↑there↓
	l.4	avail ~~aught~~ ↑but little↓ in
¶6	*l*.2	under ↑which↓ we organized
	ll.5–6	first ↑and false↓ impression of the object
	ll.7–8	or ~~to discover~~ ourselves to discover
	ll.9–10	in ↑our↓ hope
	l.10	though ↑we↓ both
	l.13	our ~~way~~ ↑Order↓ has
	l.15	see ↑some of↓ our
	ll.16–17	at ~~their~~ ↑her↓ sides, ~~though~~ ↑and↓ we
	l.17	her accompany~~ing~~ her
	l.27	side of Truth, it ~~is~~ must be, then
	l.28	or ↑why↓ hesitate
	l.28	your ↑power↓ to
	l.29	Intemperance with ~~a~~ ↑its↓
	l.30	circles, ~~and~~ ↑to↓ bind
	ll.31–32	~~What better is Society that you have thus from week to week,~~ ↑If such an influence has gone forth, then have we not↓ sacrificed ~~your~~ ↑our↓ time ↑in vain,↓ ~~Ladies we call it not a sacrifice of time.~~ ↑No!↓
	l.33	hour of each weak
¶7	*ll*.1–2	streets, ↑thus↓ proclaiming
	l.3	with us ↑no doubt↓ feel
	l.4	connexions, ~~and~~ ↑You↓ would

	ll.6–7	down ↑to↓ the loathsom
¶8	*l*.1 beg.	~~You would that~~ How is
	ll.1–2	~~the great~~ ↑this vast↓ work
	l.8	selfish ~~passions~~ ↑impulses↓ <u>alone</u>,
¶9	*ll*.2–3	worth of ~~the~~ ↑a↓ human soul,
	l.8	of ~~individual~~ ↑combined↓ influence,
¶10	*l*.1	that ↑it is↓ our sex ~~possesses~~ that ~~power of~~ fashioning↑'s↓ the
	l.2	we ~~view~~ look around us ↑do↓ we ↑not↓
	l.5	in ~~breaking~~ abolishing
	l.7	at ↑both↓ their ~~private~~ ↑public↓
	l.8	the ↑title of↓ Gentleman,
¶11	*l*.1	am ↑not↓ aware
	l.2	fallen ~~to~~ ↑from↓ <u>Virtue</u>, and
	ll.2–3	claim ↑our↓ efforts
	l.6	in ~~the~~ reclaiming ~~of~~ those
	l.6	ones, ↑~~of our own sex~~↓ who
¶12	*l*.2	to ~~render~~ harmonize
	l.3	↑And↓ We are ↑fully↓ pursuaded,
	l.5	of ~~brining about~~ establishing
	l.6	social intercouse,
	l.6	better ~~conform~~ ↑conduce↓ to
¶13	*l*.1	you ↑candidly &↓ seriously
	ll.4–5	If ↑you↓ come
	ll.7–9	accomplished, ↑and you shall find us ready with both heart and hand to cooperate with you↓. In
¶14	*l*.4	ease, ~~then~~ ↑surely do↓ our

[*cancelled paragraph from verso*] If you can devise means by which, our wish may be better and ↑more↓ speedily accomplished then surely you↑r↓ ~~will have the~~ generosity ↑will prompt you↓ to enlighten us, ~~and~~ ↑but↓ and if no better method presents itself to your mind, ~~then~~ will you not with us unite and give your influence to aid on this great work ~~of Temperance reform~~. In my opinion, all that is needed to ~~produce make~~ ↑produce↓ a complete temperance reform, is for ~~the our sex~~ ↑woman in a united body↓ ~~to show to the world~~ us to cast our united influence into the balance.

¶15	*l*.1 beg.	~~Ladies ↑will↓ you not Ladies~~ ↑And no↓w permit
	ll.1–2	you ↑to↓ lend ↑your aid to↓ this great
	ll.3–4	little ↑individual↓ influence,
	l.5	done, [*cancelled passage*] what ↑great↓ results might not be expected, were you, with many of our influential ladies, who ~~have not honoured~~ ↑are not present this afternoon were to give by your active Cooperation hearts↓ the

Cause of Virtue Love Temperance with their presence
this afternoon, to give it ↑to the↓ a hearty God Speed us,
by your active cooperation, a hearty God Speed. [*end of
cancelled passage*] What

*l.*13   soul. ~~And Until this~~ And

*l.*14   shall ↑have↓ arrive

*ll.*14–15   object ↑be accomplished↓ for

·⊂━━━━━━⊃·

32 ❧ SBA TO LUCY READ ANTHONY

Canajoharie March 7ᵗʰ 1849

Dear Mother,

I now take my pen in hand to inform you that <u>we</u> have a sweet little
girl[1] & that I have assisted in the performance of the various duties.
M[argaret] has been anxiously waiting, since one week yesterday. The
babe was born Tuesday (yesterday) A.M. at 2½ oclock. M. had a pretty
hard ~~part~~ time. I was with her through the whole, had Dr. White,[2]
Eleanor & a Mrs. Snyder. It is rather tough business is it not Mother.
Oh I am so glad she is through with it. I never slept a wink, went to
school next A.M. every time one of the girls would speak, I imagined it
was M's groan. it was a nervous forenoon, in the P.M. I staid home &
went to bed, have a Miss Snyder to assist me, who can take charge of
school matters.

I wanted to write you last night but could not   M. has suffered a
good deal with after pains, is a little easier now, Aunt M[ary Read] was
not invited to the Party, she does not like it much, but all ↑thought↓
that ~~she~~ her presence would only make her self sick & M. worse. she
came up early yesterday A.M. & staid until to night about 9 oclock, then
went down to Eleanors   they have been ↑there↓ two weeks to day.
Sarah & Dan keep the Castle.[3] Uncle is gradually improving, says
when it gets pleasant weather, he shall write to Uncle Howe to meet
him & Aunt at Utica and go on to Rochester that he had business with
Father & rather be there to transact it—

Friday Evening 5 oclock [*9 March*]. Now Mother this is too bad. I
intended to have sent what I had written on ~~Wednesday~~ ↑Thursday↓,
but in the morning I had so many ways to go that I forgot it until it was
too late

This afternoon I went down to Georges, ~~where~~ for Albert Story, he had been there since Tuesday A.M. Uncle said he must witness the meeting, so he went out harnessed old Tin to the wagon & I mounted, with my old shawl & hood & rode through the square. Albert said a great deal, his Ma asked him what we should call the baby, he says Aunt Eleanor. Well said M. that is Mary's name, well then he would call it Margaret no Susan. Mary says its name must be Susan Gertrude. I asked J[oseph] if he would not name it after me, he said no, he would have no Suse about his house. Stopped to tend baby fix M. &c.

It is now ten oclock, but I must scribble a little more. M. is pretty smart. I should think her about like Gula, but O dear if you could, there I've been & cleaned M's teeth & fixed her for sleep. She has a nurse but Susan must do the little extras when at home, but as I was saying you would laugh & then get out of patience to see Aunt Mary. You dont feel so well Margaret do you, you look bad, I am afraid you ant agoing to have a good getting, you seem just as you did when Theodore was a baby, &c &c. This noon she says ↑to me↓ I dont know but you will have to give up school & stay here, Margaret is so much more cheerful, the minute you come in   Mrs. Snyder told her that it was my cheerfulness that made M. feel so much better. Aunt Mary seems determined to have it all her own way & that is on the gloomy side. she however seems better at present, than she has for a long time. She comes up early mornings & goes home nights. This Term closes 4 weeks from next Wednesday. I am decided that I shall not teach another Term. The new teachers are not very popular. M[argaret] I suppose will move in April or May into one of the new houses she says I must certainly stay with her until she gets moved & settled, which I suppose I had better do. Joseph brought me Fathers letter to night when he came to tea, I had begun to feel that I ought to hear from you, but still judging you from myself I concluded you could find no time to write   I guess it is two months since I wrote Aron & Gula & H[annah] & E[ugene] & Dan. Our Jane went off about 7 weeks ago, then M with my help got along about a week before the Irish Wine came,[4] she was here 6 weeks, could not cook at all, nor could M. go into the kitchen very often. I would get up dress part of the children & sometimes the whole & then go down & superintend the breakfast, then & noon run home & broil the Steak or fix the dinner, at night work &c. this week we have made another exchange, got a colored woman named Dina that has always lived at Blind Mr Van Alstines   She can get up the dinners now I tell you, but I am too sleepy to write.

The celebrated Mr. Gough lectured here last evening, I did steal away & go. O what a lecture, what arguments, how can a man or woman remain neutral or be a <u>moderate</u> drinker. One week ago this P.M. the Daughters of T. invited the ladies of the Village to meet with them at their room & listen an address from their P.S. S. B. Anthony the story was written on about 8 sheets, the import was the necessity for all to help, & do something more than merely say your cause is good we wish you well—

Dan S. [Read] came here the next day said that he had that day heard it remarked that Miss Anthony was the Smartest woman that ~~was~~ ↑is↓ now or ever was in Canajoharie. Oh there is lots of little thoughts & things I would like to tell you, but oh my eyes refuse to stay open. I have not had any good sleep since ~~Monday~~ ↑Sunday↓ night. M. said oh Susan this is too bad that you should go through with all this, how can I ever pay you for all yo do for me. When she got in bed she put her arms around my neck & kissed me, sh felt so thankful. She had the greatest imaginable trouble about a Doctor. Dr. Stafford[5] she would like to patronize but he was so young & inexperienced, she hated to offend him, but when the time came she sent for White & when he first came she could not bear him she sported about his long hair & slouchy looks but when she got through she loved him the best of any Doctor she ever had. to bed I will go, all are asleep save me, to night I stewed some of Aunt Lucy's peaches for M. they tasted so good to her & I sorta reckon I took a dive into them, every time I tasted them I could see just how mother looked when she was cutting them   good night says

⮜ *S B A*

Saturday A.M. I went to bed at 12 & slept till after sunrise this A.M. Margaret slept first & is real smart now. Aunt M. is frightened to death if any of <u>her</u> folks have slight turn of the bellyache   Mother dont ↑let us not↓ allow ourselves to be unmindful <u>of the</u> blessings we receive, when we think of our troubles   Write soon to your Susan B.

[*at top of first page*] I would like to write lots more but must wait a few days. I want to hear how Mary is

⮜ ALS, SBA Papers, MCR-S. Letters in square brackets expand initials.

1. Margaret Caldwell gave birth to Margaret Read Caldwell on 6 March 1849.

2. Joseph White, born in Connecticut in 1800, moved to Canajoharie in 1838 and opened a drugstore. He was a physician and the treasurer of Canajoharie Academy. (Frothingham, *History of Montgomery County*, 160–61.)

3. Daniel Stafford Read (c. 1824–?) and Sarah Adeline Burbeck Read (1829–1904) married in 1847 and lived next door to Joshua Read in Palatine Bridge. Daniel farmed his father's land. SBA stayed in touch with Daniel and Sarah and stopped to see them in her later travels. (Federal Census, 1850; Bush, *Story of St. Mark's*.)

4. These servants have not been identified.

5. John H. Stafford (1823–?), a nephew of Mary Stafford Read, practiced medicine and established the pharmacy of Hodge and Stafford at Canajoharie. (Stafford, *Laban Stafford*, 226; *History of Montgomery and Fulton Counties, N.Y.*, 101.)

---

33 ⮝ SBA TO DANIEL R. ANTHONY

Palatine Bridge May 11,/49

Dear Brother

At the time your last letter was received, my every moment was occupied in the performance of painful yet pleasurable duties

Our Cousin Margaret was then very low & I acted the part of nurse & house-wife. She died on the 26th of April, leaving a babe seven weeks old[1]

Oh dear brother it is a glorious death, to die a Christian. May we all follow the departed as she followed Jesus, so that our last end may be like hers, so that when our mortal frames shall have been lain in the cold Earth, naught but good may be repeated of us.

Daniel I would say much to you, but I have neither time nor energy to write   All around me bears so sad an aspect.

I am at Uncles in No. 1. Aunt Mary, Theodore & the baby (Margaret R.) are here, Mary E. & Albert Story & Joseph are at George's   I had intended to have been with you ere this, but Aunt will not give me up yet. Theodore has had the Ague & is sick yet, also the whooping cough, the baby has the whooping cough too, very hard, & Aunts health is very poor[2]   Sarah has not been here since I came, they say she is coming soon. I dont know how Aunt could do without me, I ought to be at home but I know our Mother will readily yield any enjoyment, if

by so doing she can contribute to the happiness of her only brother &
his family.

I had anticipated going to New-York but must forego that pleasure.
Daniel S. is in the store, they have one clerk, John Jenkins[3]   is it not
better to be a clerk & be sure of a good salary, than run any risk.

Sunday P.M. [*May 13*] This was a rainy morning, so I could not go
↑over↓ to Church. It is nearly three months since I have attended
Church. Theodore has a fit of the Ague to day. Joseph has been over &
made a call   It no doubt seems sad to him to see his two motherless
children sick. Mary & Albert are very well.

How I wish I could be seated with you and have a good long chat,
but I at present must be content to forego the pleasures of the presence
of those nearest and dearest to me, that I may if possible in some slight
degree cheer by my presence the family of our much loved & venerated
Uncle. I would ↑not↓ wish to be selfish, but it is human nature to love
to gratify self. I now think I shall be with you before many weeks roll
around. I have thought I would come to Stockbridge, then go to Uncle
Alberts & so around, will that be the best way think you.[4] Mother has
about given up coming down at present   Their new arrangement for
living seems to make it impossible for her to leave home, which I very
much regret—[5]

I must now write to Hannah. I ↑guess↓ she has concluded to keep
silence, Aaron & Gula also   I have ↑not↓ had a line from any of them in
a long time, should think they might write me—

It seems to me that no ↑one↓ feels that it is any thing out of the
common course of things, for me to sacrifice my every feeling, almost
principle, to gratify those with whom I chance to mingle.

I would like the good will of all, but I wish to have right on my side,
in the endeavor to obtain it. Write soon & tell me if you are going to
Yearly meeting & if there is any strong inducement for me to go.[6]

Daniel let us strive to have right on our side come what will, & then
we shall have one comfort which the guilty know not, & that is a
conscience void of offence, an inward joy which none but the doers of
good can know. That I may not be permitted to deviate from the path
of duty is my daily & hourly prayer to God— With much love I am
Your Sister

✉ *S. B. Anthony*

write soon.

❧ ALS, SBA Papers, MCR-S. Addressed to West Stockbridge, Massachusetts.

1. SBA wrote her mother about Margaret Caldwell's death and funeral on 25 April 1849, *Film*, 6:904–5.

2. The census taker in 1850 found the children still divided, with Theodore at his grandparents' house in Palatine Bridge. Across the river Joseph Caldwell lived with his brother George, his sister-in-law, their children, and his own Mary E. and Albert S. The baby presumably died.

3. Born in New Jersey and about twenty-six years old. (Federal Census, 1850).

4. SBA describes a circuit among relatives in western Massachusetts: her brother at Stockbridge; Albert Dickinson, married to SBA's aunt Ann Eliza Anthony, at Curtisville; and, no doubt, her grandfather and numerous other relatives at Adams.

5. Daniel Anthony spent most of his time in Rochester, establishing himself as an insurance agent, while Lucy Anthony oversaw the farm.

6. No doubt the Hicksite branch of New York Yearly Meeting at New York City.

·❨══════❩·

34 ❧ ECS to Lucretia Coffin Mott

Grassmere [*Seneca Falls*] Sept 26th [*1849*]

Dear Lucretia,

As I am deeply interested in having all womankind who are dependent on themselves for their support strike out some new path to wealth & distinction, beside the needle, & marriage as a necessity, & as I have hung out my sign as the she pilot to guide & direct all young maidens who wish to launch their bark on an untried sea, I have had several applications for advice & assistance. Emily Winslow & Abby Southwick[1] at my suggestion have just established a school for young girls in Buffalo. The spirit of enterprize has seized Elizabeth McClintock & Anna Southwick, & they have decided to be famous silk merchants, in Philadelphia making their annual visits to Paris & other great cities of the old world. Preparitory to the realization of these bright hopes they would fain get a clerkship in the establishment of thy noble son Edward Davis.[2] I believe he made Elizabeth an offer of a situation in his House some years ago—she had not the courage to accept it at that time but now she has the hardihood to sue for it— ah! me those woman's rights conventions, have spoiled our lovely maidens now instead of remaining satisfied with the needle & the school room they would substitute the compass & the exchange. If Edward Davis cannot give them a situation in his House, perhaps he might get them into some other silk establishment. Will you inquire & let me know as soon as possible. The climate of Boston is too severe for Anna or she might get into some establishment there, tho it would be pleasanter for her to commence her new life in a strange city & with so agreeable a companion as Elizabeth McClintock. How often I have thought of you dear Lucretia since our pleasant visit at Peterboro, & how sad I felt in hearing of your deep affliction in the loss of an only brother.[3] you must feel the void—but he has no doubt passed to a higher & more congenial sphere than the one in which he moved on earth. Cousin Gerrit has taken another new step since you saw him. He now keeps the Jewish Sabbath. His servants say they have two sabbaths—they do no work on their own sabbath & he will not allow it on his. I think under this new arrangement the servants are much more pleased & benefited than either Gerrit or his God. Gerrit enjoyed your visit very much & regretted that it could not have been longer. Is he not very liberal for one so bound by forms?— Now Lucretia do not take the trouble to answer this letter yourself make one of the youngsters do it for you, reserve your strength for something of more importance. Remember me kindly to you Husband & children. Henry is now in N.Y. getting out his book. The little boys are all well[4] good night yours in love

⤙ *E. C. Stanton*

⤙ ALS, Garrison Papers, MNS-S.

1. Abigail Southwick (1819–1904), later Stephenson, was the sister of Anna and the oldest daughter of Joseph and Thankful Southwick of Boston. She attended the convention of antislavery women in 1838 and was a delegate to the London convention in 1840. Married to John Hubbard Stephenson in 1859, she moved to New York City and stayed in touch with ECS. (Garrison, *Letters*, 4:687n, 5:134n, 6:271; Hansen, *Strained Sisterhood*.)

2. Edward Morris Davis (1811–1887) married Maria Mott (1818–1897) in 1836. E.M. Davis & Company, with offices in Philadelphia and New York, imported silk. A Quaker and an abolitionist, Davis worked closely with his mother-in-law, especially in Pennsylvania's antislavery society. After serving in the Civil War, he was active in both the Radical Club and the Citizens' Suffrage Association, where woman suffragists found strong allies. (Hallowell, *James and Lucretia Mott*; Taylor, *British and American Abolitionists*; *History*,

3:461–64; *Philadelphia Inquirer*, 28 November 1887; *Friends' Intelligencer* 54 [1897]: 582.)

3. Thomas Mayhew Coffin, the only brother of Lucretia Mott and Martha Wright, died of cholera on 12 July 1849 at age fifty-one. (E. M. Davis to David Wright, 12 July 1849, Wright genealogical files, Garrison Papers, MNS-S.)

4. Henry B. Stanton, *Sketches of Reforms and Reformers, of Great Britain and Ireland*, was published by John Wiley in 1849. The boys numbered three: Daniel, or Neil, now seven; Henry, or Kit, now five; and Gerrit Smith Stanton, or Gat, born at Chelsea, Massachusetts, on 18 September 1845.

---

35 ❧ ECS TO LUCRETIA COFFIN MOTT

Grassmere [*Seneca Falls*] Nov 12th [*1849*]

Dear Lucretia

I need not tell you that the Philadelphia documents surprised me not a little— Not so much, that the application was unsuccessful, as the manner in which it was refused. I hesitated in sending the drama & caricatures to the Girls,[1] so fearful am I of doing anything to discourage the first dawnings of independence in the heart of woman— Woman is already so degraded—so afraid of what man may think and say of her,— She has so long been the butt of every jest, for parlour, Bar-room & newspaper, that her love of approbation is sufficiently developed without any further application of ridicule or caricature— However having great confidence in your judgement, as you sent them to me—I sent them on, & the result has proved you as I always knew you to be—the wiser of the two.— The effect produced was the opposite of what I had looked for. Combativeness[2] seemed to receive the blow & forthwith came a Drama of some intellectual vigour, which I backed up with a little of my irony, just enough to show our incapacity, to use that <u>manly</u> weapon <u>ridicule</u>. Excuse us for making our first attack on those of thine own household. But we did it from personal regard to you— We thought to give thy son the opportunity of immortalizing himself, by laying the first stone in this country, for woman to stand upon, on her way to wealth & fame—but it seems he declines the honour—however this does not end the scheme with us— The letter of the New-York house seemed favourable, tho' in the teeth of the caricature— How shall we take it? Is it ironical do you think? What are Hallowell's conditions?[3] They might not seem so atrocious to us, as to you metropolitans— You must write us what you think of the drama, & caricatures & if they equal those sent by the "Lords of creation" & if the individuals served up preserve their good nature & equanimity under this western flagellation—

The devotion of Edward's clerks to the interest of the house is quite refreshing it speaks well for Edward—, however I think they have mistaken the effect that would be produced by the proposed innovation— In my opinion it would increase rather than diminish the trade of any house— Depend upon it, all kinds of business will move on more successfully when we have

> Every where
> Two heads in counsel, two beside the hearth
> Two in the tangled business of the world
> Two in the liberal offices of life
> Two plummets dropt for one to sound the abyss
> Of Science and the secrets of the mind.[4]

Fear not that we shall be discouraged, no, we have full faith in "the good time coming." Truth is mighty & I know woman will yet stand on an even pedestal with man.

We are glad to hear that there is some probability of your coming west soon—do let us see the light of your countenance this side of Cayuga bridge, when you come to Auburn again—[5] We think quite seriously of sending all this concern, dramas, caricatures &c, (names changed) to Jane Swisshelm—[6] What do you think of it? As we are in a hurry to do up the package for Saml Wells,[7] I cannot say all I wish to in this epistle— Do let us hear from you as soon as you get all the old carpets mended & your house cleaned. Kind regards to your dignified husband & those mischievous children   your friend

⇜ *E C Stanton*

Friend Mary Ann[8] wishes to see that letter I wrote to you, which created such a sensation among the silk merchants. She considers it a spoke in the wheel. If it is in existence, please give it to Sarah.[9] E. C. S.

⇜ Copy in unknown hand, Garrison Papers, MNS-S.

1. Addressing "The Two Elizabeths," Mott replied to the previous letter on 25 October and sent a package of documents generated by discussions in

Edward Davis's firm. Davis, she explained, "laid the subject before his partner and the house here" and "consulted the New-York house." In a letter to
Mott, sent on to Seneca Falls, Davis explained that he could not take the
women on because they did not qualify. Staff in his New York office reported
their discussions to Philadelphia; they would affirm women's right to the work
but referred the decision to Davis, concluding, "Nothing is impossible." They
also enclosed cartoons of women at work in a warehouse while men idly
watched them. More cartoons were drawn by the Philadelphia staff, and Maria
Mott Davis recorded their discussion somewhat humorously. "You will not be
at all discouraged, I hope, by the result," Mott wrote. "There must be a
beginning to every thing." ECS sent this "bundle of nonsense" to Elizabeth
McClintock with an indignant cover letter. "Good Heavens!! what fools these
Quakers are!" she began. All of the material provided ECS and McClintock
with words and attitudes to write the drama that follows. (*Film*, 6:936-53.)

2. A faculty of the mind identified by phrenologists as self-defense, resistance, and "the energetic go-a-head disposition." Elizabeth McClintock described herself as "very much pained" by the evidence that she and Anna
became "subjects for caricature and ridicule." (E. McClintock to L. C. Mott,
13 November 1849, Garrison Papers, MNS-S.)

3. Morris L. Hallowell (1809–1881) was a member of Philadelphia Monthly
Meeting and a partner in Morris L. Hallowell & Co., merchants of silk and fancy
goods. He indicated a willingness to receive the women but with (unspecified)
conditions. (City directory, 1849; *Friends' Intelligencer* 37 [1881]: 298.)

4. Alfred Lord Tennyson, "The Princess," pt. 2, lines 155-60.

5. Mott had written that in November she would go to Dutchess, Ulster,
and Westchester counties to help "congregationalize" the Society of Friends
and join Abby Kelley Foster at antislavery meetings. Crossing the northern
end of Cayuga Lake and facilitating travel west of Auburn, the Cayuga bridge
was regarded in New York as a dividing line between east and west. (*History
of Seneca Co., N.Y.*, 12.)

6. Jane Grey Cannon Swisshelm (1815–1884) published and edited the
weekly *Saturday Visiter*, at Pittsburgh, Pennsylvania, to promote abolition
and women's legal rights. The paper began in 1848, and though Swisshelm
recalled publishing it until 1857, when she moved to St. Cloud, Minnesota, no
issues later than January 1854 have been located. Swisshelm turned against the
suffrage movement and, in her autobiography, mocked the woman's rights
movement she had joined. (*NAW*; Jane Grey Swisshelm, *Half a Century*, 2d
ed. [1880; reprint, New York, 1970]; *History*, 1:387-88.)

7. Possibly the Samuel Wells among the Lane Seminary rebels, an antislavery agent in the 1830s, and a friend of the Welds. (Weld-Grimké, *Letters*,
1:84, 178-80, 2:674.)

8. That is, Mary Ann McClintock.

9. Sarah McClintock was a daughter of Mary Ann and Thomas McClintock,
living in Philadelphia.

·⫘————※※————⫸·

36 ❧ DRAMA BY ECS AND ELIZABETH W. McCLINTOCK

[*c. 12 November 1849*]

DRAMATIS PERSONAE[1]

E^d M. Davis	A Merchant Prince
C^h W. Wharton	Junior Partner
Rush Plumley	First Salesman
E^d Walton	Clerk
H. Earle	Book keeper
J. Janney	Salesman
Remmington ⎱ Tal^n Wright ⎰	Boys
Lucretia Mott	Mother-in-law to Edward
Spirit	

SCENE 1ST.

Philadelphia

A handsomely furnished apartment. E^d M. Davis *seated in a luxurious arm-chair. He looks around the room & soliloquizes.*

	Here have I, by long years of patient toil,
The	Gathered around me much to make life pleasant.
soliloquizer	By constant traffic in the crowded mart
feeleth	Of trade, I have won all that ministers
very	To sense & spirit. Not for me the slow,
comfortable	The tedious road to wealth—the handing out
	The skein of silk, the yard of tape. Not mine
	The penny & the fip. My ambition
	Grasped a wider realm, and box and bale,
	Gold-filled coffers & clerks obsequious,

Attest my rich success. My name stands high
On Change—and for fair deeds of charity
Men give me praise.

(*Enter* B. Rush Plumley.)

How does thee do, Rush?

RUSH: Oh, Edward, my heart
Is stirred within me. Most indignantly
The strong pulse bounds. Inspired by mighty words
From lips glowing with new fire from Heaven,
Stronger & deeper has grown my hatred
Of oppression. That Being, great and good,
Whose watchful care the meanest insect feels,
Looks not with kindly smile on deeds that throw
O'er our fair earth, a shadow deep and drear.
The dark-browed slave, who toils on Southern
     plains;
The pale-faced, sickly boy, from whose wan cheek
Our Northern factories' poisoned air
Its early bloom has stolen; the dwellers
On green Ireland's shores; and England's crushed
And sorely-suffering sons; the shrieks, the groans,
What from broad Europe's fierce, unsanguined
     fields
Fill the earth with anguish—all these demand,
The sympathetic tear—the helping hand.

EDWARD: And woman, too,
Rush, thou must not forget <u>her</u> degradation.
Fast-closed to her are all those pleasant paths
Which most do lead to profit and renown.
Toiling from early morn to latest eve,
She scarce can win her daily food. Grieve want
Attends her—tired and worn her strong spirit
Sinks—vice and ruin claim her for their prey.

(Lucretia Mott *enters with an open letter in her hand.*)

*Rush
hath received
new life
at
Norristown
&
groweth
philanthropical*

*Edward
joggeth
Rush's
memory*

LUCRETIA: This letter by a swift messenger
Has just been brought to me. Read it, Edward,
And tell me—canst thou gratify a wish
So new?

(Edward *takes the letter and reads.*)

"Moved by the spirit of enterprize, Anna Southwick & E. W. M'Clintock desire to open for themselves a new & broader road to fortune. A wholesale business will be much to their taste, and one in which silks and ribbons are the articles of merchandise being peculiarly fitted for woman, they desire thee to ask Edward M. Davis, who once offered Elizabeth a situation in his store, if it can be obtained now."

(*He starts up & exclaims,*)

*Edward
is so
taken by
surprise
that he
forgetteth
himself
& his
blank verse.*

It is very true, some four or five years ago, I did offer E. W. M'Clintock a situation in my store, as saleswoman, with a salary of $500. but, Lord bless me! did she think I was in earnest? I never dreamed she would accept it. I did it for effect. For a while I trembled at what I had done—but so long a time has passed I thought all danger over. I cannot grant it. It would not do. What can have induced these girls to step so far beyond their accustomed limits.

*Lucretia
remembereth
old
times.*

LUCRETIA: Not twice our earth
Her annual course has made, since among
The white villages that make bright the shores
Of New York's fair lakes—with the magic might
Of eloquence, I labored to awaken
In the heart of woman, the strong desire,
The earnest wish for freedom. I told her,
Too long had she remained the slave or toy
Of man—her faculties of mind and soul
Allowed to rust unused. With unwonted fire
My own heart burned and with the pleading tones
Of entreaty, I conjured her to demand

A wide field of action—that places
Of emolument & trust shall not be
Filled by man alone. And in that cold clime
Good seed scattered comes to quick blossoming.

She
changeth
to plain
prose

To think that our Edward M. Davis should be
the first one tried! But, look round, my son, and
find "reasons of some weight" to satisfy these
Western girls.

RUSH: In the olden time
When high among priests and elders, my name
Was placed, to my sisters in the gospel,

He
telleth
what he
hath
been.

I gave the glad hand of equality.
Moved by the same Divine spirit, we took
Sweet counsel together. The memory
Of those days is precious to me. But this
Cannot be. "Our House" has not foundation
Firm enough to bear these rude shocks; her fall
Would surely come, and we be left to weep
Over the shapeless ruins. We cannot
Afford this deed of mercy & of truth.[2]

EDWARD: My soul is sick. Would that
Right & policy did not so conflict.
But I will go & with my clerks consult.

(*Exeunt severally.*)

SCENE 2ND.

Counting House—27 Church Alley, at dusk— Store closed.

EDWARD DAVIS: Honored partner, young men & boys— I have lately received a letter of great importance from the Empire State which I wish to lay before you—and as it is the custom of merchants to take no step without the counsel of their clerks from the first salesman even to the errand boy, I would fain learn the opinion of each before I venture to decide on this novel proposition.

(Plumley *reads an extract from the letter.*)

"Now the spirit of enterprise has seized
Two maidens fair who fain would famous be
In trade. In your great city they would lay
The foundations of an extensive House,
Whose heads might bravely make their frequent trips,
To crowded cities far beyond the sea.
But for the realization of these hopes
They humbly sue for them a fitting place
In the House of the noble-hearted man,
Who, with flattering promise, bade them leave
Their wanted walks—to wealth, to follow him."

E. DAVIS: Thy place in our House, friend Wharton, gives thee the first right to speak. What sayest thou to this strange request?

WHARTON: I object to the whole proposition.[3] In the first place our House might suffer. We might as well have a row of tall Othellos[4] behind our counter as so many women—either would draw down upon us scorn, ridicule & perchance a mob. It is better far to spout our humanity in the forum than to live it out in our trade. In the second place, it would be subversive of the delicacy & refinement of woman to bring her into daily contact with thee & these coarse men. Ah, no, let her remain in the lofty position assigned her in our statute books—on a full equality with Afric's noble sons.

RUSH PLUMLY: I bid the applicants God speed— Would they already had a House whose tall shadow might darken ours. But we cannot afford to be generous. Principle is one thing, policy quite another.

E. DAVIS: Well, Walton what is thy opinion?

WALTON: As regards the "interests of the House" or the applicants?[5]

E. DAVIS: Both.

WALTON: I consider such a step to be against the "interests of our House" (& that thee will allow should always be our first, our highest consideration) & of doubtful propriety for the applicants. Society is not prepared for such an innovation. She is too sacred to be thus rashly violated—and far be it from <u>thee</u> to do aught to prepare her for a change. Leave her alone—& no doubt, in due time, she will, in some miraculous way, change herself.

E. DAVIS: What has thee to say, friend Earle?

HENRY: My mother thinks women are inferior.[6]

SPIRIT: Henry: does thy mother know thee's out?

E. DAVIS: Well, Janney, what does thee think?

JANNEY: To me there is sex in mind.[7] I cannot think of woman as a moral & intellectual being—hold converse with her as I would with you. Be she ever so gifted, refined & spiritual, in the presence of that lovely being I cannot, for my life, forget she is a woman. I say, let the fair ones come. How my eyes would feast themselves on those graceful beings, lightly gliding round midst piles of goods & boxes & these stalwart men—but ask me not to turn aside from this bright vision, to seduce any of Adam's sons into the purchase of a roll of silk or ball of ribbon—

SPIRIT: When the daughters of earth come to buy of thee, Oh! most voluptuous Janney, dost thou forget the "interests of the House"—turn from the cerulean blue of thy costly silk & in lieu of praises of its lustrous beauty, fine fiber & French dye dost thou stand dumb in admiration of thy lovely purchaser?

E. DAVIS: Thy turn has come, brave Tallman, say thy say outright.

WRIGHT: I, too, have a mother, but naught have I heard from her lips, naught have I witnessed in her daily life to impress on me the belief of woman's inferiority.[8] I am interested in her elevation, but it is not for me to say which thine honor shall hold most dear, "the interests of the House" or those of woman. But I think in our debates thus far we have dwelt too much on expediency rather than right. It is not well to sacrifice principle to a perverted public sentiment.

SPIRIT: Far off in our realms of bliss there comes up to us from this nether sphere much boasting of progress—but lo! in coming down I find it not. You chide the sons of Israel because forsooth they made a golden calf & then did worship it.[9] Even so do you who claim the higher, inner light to know by instinct what is right & wrong. Ye, too, have made an idol which you call sometimes society, sometimes public sentiment—but in this case the "interests of the House."

E. M. DAVIS: Well, Remmington, what says thee? Why droops thy head & wherefore look so sad?

REM: This day am I made old indeed. The bright dreams of my youth are passed my budding hopes are blighted. My heart is still, no longer shall it bound with joy in view of the opening future. The dark cloud of restraint, like an incubus sits heavy on my soul & shadows all my coming days. How patiently have I through weary childhood endured the tyranny of nursery & schoolroom sustained by the belief that in manhood I should be free. Then thought I, I can stand upright—then shall my heart flow out to all humanity—then shall this strong arm put down all oppression— But, lo! to-day I learn that man, too has his tyrants—monsters who stalk about in the noon-day and make earth hideous with their war.

SPIRIT: Young man, thou mayest still be free & live out the dream of thy childhood. To do this thou must take no counsel of thy kind, or of thy lower nature, but early learn to heed not the applause of man—

"To scorn delights & live laborious days."[10]

WALTON: Come, Edward what has thee to say?

E. DAVIS: "Man, that is born of woman, is of a few days & full of trouble"[11]

SPIRIT: Would that this group could, Minerva-like have sprung from the brains of their fathers[12]—then might they prate of woman's weakness & not abuse themselves.

OMNES [All]: As it is—oh cruel fate the mother stamps her sons.

SPIRIT: Even so— The All wise hath so linked together the human race that any violence done at one end of the chain is felt throughout its length. Enslave your women then look not for brave sons.

E. DAVIS: I rejoice at the noble stand taken by my coadjutors in New

York and if you with whom I here associate could but respond how promptly would I stretch forth the helping hand to those brave girls.

OMNES: Let us not bound the overflowings of thy generous heart— Let them come. We shall not forget that we are gentlemen & can in our intercourse with them bemean ourselves as such.

> (*With the chivalry of the 14th century they all give 3 cheers for woman—& retire.*)

SCENE 3RD.

*A luxurious chamber—lights dimly burning—*Edward M. Davis*stretched on a couch, just recovering from a severe attack of palpitation of the heart. Conscience keen.*

SPIRIT: Now, Edward, rouse thy spirit's strength. Much depends on this decision.

EDWARD: I should like to know more particularly the views of the applicants.[13] If they come as women, with what we are accustomed to regard the privileges of the sex, I should decide against the request. If as human beings, they would be obliged to open store, sweep out run to bank, collect notes & go to the Union line to receive goods, open cases, hoist boxes &c &c. they would decide against it.

SPIRIT: Wisdom teaches us division of labor. You do not require a single clerk now in your employ to perform this long line of duties. If your book-keeper or salesman is perfect in his department, you do not require of him the performance of the menial offices of the house. Do you not as a man, owe something to woman for the years of oppression she has quietly endured at your hands. Can you not grant her a few privileges whilst you deny her all her rights. Come to you as human beings! In what other guise, pray could they come. That you fully recognize their humanity is all that is desired.

E. DAVIS: But is society prepared for this innovation?

SPIRIT: Hast thou labored so many years to reform the evils of thy day, slavery, war, Capital Punishment &c. & now, in thy manhood, when the noble qualities of head & heart which Heaven has bestowed upon thee, should be in their full vigor & activity, dost thou pause & hesitate to offend or outrage a wicked and oppressive public sentiment? What higher object can there be in life than to set a false world right? You admit woman to be equal to man in all respects. Facts have proved her so. None but the ignorant & unthinking deny it. We have seen her at different times occupying every variety of station in life with dignity & ability. She has shown her equality & identity with man.

E. DAVIS: Yes—the question now is shall we recognize her as such? Shall we remove all restraint and run with her a fair and manly race.

(*Spirit vanishes.*)[14]

⪻ Ms in hand of E. W. McClintock, Garrison Papers, MNS-S. While layout follows the original, inconsistencies in the form have been eliminated, and the conventions of typesetting plays have been introduced.

1. The cast list identifies staff at E.M. Davis & Co., located at 27 Church Alley, Philadelphia, nearly all of them Quaker abolitionists and reformers. Charles W. Wharton (c. 1823–1902), who married in 1849, was a partner in the firm and a member of the Hicksite Philadelphia Monthly Meeting. (City directory, 1849; *Quaker Genealogy*, 2:938; *Friends' Intelligencer* 59 [1902]: 535.) Benjamin Rush Plumley (1816–1887), also spelled Plumly, married into the extended Wilson family that included the McClintocks. An executive committee member of the Pennsylvania Anti-Slavery Society, Plumley, like Edward Davis, broke with his religious training to serve in the military during the Civil War. (*Quaker Genealogy*, 2:815, 911; *ACAB*.) There were several Edward Hicks Waltons among the city's Quakers, and this one remains unidentified. Henry Earle (1829–?) was son of Thomas Earle, a Quaker lawyer in Philadelphia and the Liberty party's vice-presidential candidate in 1840. He became a banker and broker. (*Quaker Genealogy*, 2:792, 858; Edwin B. Bronner, *Thomas Earle As a Reformer* [Philadelphia, 1948], 19.) Jacob Janney is unidentified. Matthew Tallman Wright (1832–1854), known as Tallman, was the son of David and Martha Coffin Wright. A troubled boy, he left home to live with the Motts in the summer of 1849, but ran away to California in 1851 and died in San Francisco. (Wright genealogy, Garrison Papers, MNS-S; Bacon, *Valiant Friend*, 131–32, 139, 147, 155.) No mention is made of a Remington in the letters sent from Philadelphia to Seneca Falls.

2. Maria Mott Davis's summary of Rush Plumley's comments concludes: "If any injury or loss should arise from such experiment, the 'House' should be above that contingency, and strong enough to make the effort successfull. Therefore if we had ½ a million capital & the applicants were qualified they should come—" (At 25 October 1849 in *Film*, 6:941–42.)

3. Maria Davis reported Wharton's objections "to the whole proposition, as unwise for our House or any other and injurious to the applicants, because without the sphere of woman, and subversive of her delicacy and refinement."

4. That is, an African man, from Shakespeare's play of that name.

5. According to Maria Davis, Walton acknowledged "that as a matter of principle women had an undoubted right" to work in the importing business, but with him it was "only a question of policy, and he should regard such an arrangement as hostile to the interests of the 'House.'" Disapproval "would be felt in diminished trade."

6. Henry Earle ventured "that he did not think them naturally strong enough in mind, to conduct such a concern" and that women's duties were domestic and social. His remarks, according to Maria Davis, met with emphatic dissent from "all the House, who were 'born of woman.'"

7. Jacob Janney feared that "the social influence of the applicants might be too strong upon the young of the store, and lessen their attention to business."

8. Tallman Wright dissented from Wharton's belief that trade would diminish if the firm hired women but he "thought women not adapted to the duties of our business."

9. Exod. 32; Acts 7:41.

10. John Milton, "Lycidas," line 73.

11. Job 14:1.

12. The goddess of wisdom, she was born from her father's brow.

13. In the discussion, Davis opined that "he would shut his eyes to sex," but the applicants would need to surrender "any privileges of sex." To succeed they needed an apprenticeship, performing the "menial offices of the House" for several years, and, starting at their age, the applicants would always lag behind the men who began in the business as boys. "[W]ould they be satisfied to spend valuable years of womanhood in acquiring what their girlhood might have learned?" "Therefore—while he recognized the principle & policy of employing human beings—as such—irrespective of sex, in every department of business for which they were qualified, the circumstances of this case would oblige him to refuse the application, for the benefit of all concerned—"

14. Lucretia Mott replied on 27 November. "I need not say, how much amusement the returns you made afforded. . . . I took them to our A.S. Ex. Com. mg. Edwd & Rush were present at the readg. there, & at first, with rather an ill grace, bore the 'flagellation' regarding it undeserved, if you 'could only have known how very respectfully your proposal was received—no ridicule—nothg. to wound unless indeed, their view of the impossibility of carrying out the intent by beginning so high.'. . . I was delighted at the evidence of a determination to act, as well as to call conventions to talk." (*Film*, 6:979-89.)

37 ⮜ ARTICLE BY ECS[1]

[April 1850]

DIVORCE.

I see there is a bill before the Legislature providing some new doors, through which unhappy prisoners may escape from the bonds of an ill assorted marriage. Among other things, drunkenness is made a ground of divorce. I hope that bill may pass.[2] Were public sentiment right on this question of divorce, I think too much of woman's instinctive love of what is true, good, and beautiful to believe, that she would willingly come in daily contact, with a coarse, beastly, disgusting Drunkard, and consent to be the partner of his misery and rags through a long weary life. The Legislature, so far from placing any barrier in the way of a woman wishing to leave a drunken husband, ought to pass laws, compelling her to do so. As the state has to provide homes for idiots, it certainly has a right to say how many there shall be.[3] The Spartans had some good laws, in relation to marriage and children.[4] Would that we of the nineteenth century had the humility to believe that lessons of wisdom might be drawn from the past. If Legislators think they have the right to regulate marriage in any particulars, would it not be better to exercise their legislative talent, on those without the "charmed circle?" Let them say who shall and who shall not be legally married. Instead of compelling a woman by law, to live with a Drunkard, they ought to pass laws forbidding Drunkards to marry. If, as at present, all can freely and *thoughtlessly* enter into the married state, they should be allowed to come as freely and *thoughtfully* out again.

⮜ S. F.[5]

⮜ *Lily*, April 1850.

1. ECS's contributions to the *Lily* began in November 1849. Published monthly at Seneca Falls in the interest of temperance, the *Lily* was edited by Amelia Jenks Bloomer (1818–1894), a governess and tutor in Waterloo in 1840 when she married Dexter Bloomer, a lawyer and newspaperman of Seneca Falls. In 1848, her Ladies' Temperance Society decided to publish a paper. Though left to do the job on her own, she produced the first issue of the *Lily*

in January 1849. She relocated the paper to Mount Vernon, Ohio, in 1853, but sold it to Mary Birdsall in 1855, when she moved to Council Bluffs, Iowa. As the popularizer of the reform costume, consisting of shortened skirt worn over trousers, Bloomer's name became synonymous with dress reform. (*NAW*; Bloomer, *Amelia Bloomer*; E. Douglas Branch, "The Lily & the Bloomer," *Colophon*, pt. 12 [December 1932].)

2. On 21 January 1850 the state assembly received a petition "of sundry inhabitants of the city of New-York, praying for an amendment of the law respecting divorces" and referred it to a select committee. Since 1787, when the first statute was passed granting jurisdiction over divorce to the courts, adultery had been the only grounds for complete divorce in New York. Later legislation allowed for divorce from bed and board, or legal separation, for cruel treatment or abandonment. Parties seeking divorce in unusual cases could petition the legislature, but the constitution of 1846 prohibited legislative divorces. By the mid-nineteenth century only South Carolina had more restrictive divorce laws. On 13 February 1850 Silas M. Burroughs, assemblyman for Orleans County and later a Republican member of Congress, reporting for the committee, proposed amendments to the statute: that the causes of divorce include "wilful desertion and abandonment for five years—sentence and confinement in a state prison or penitentiary for three years—habitual drunkenness for 5 years—and insanity leading to partial idiocy." On 1 April Burroughs twice tried to schedule a vote on the amendment and was twice voted down. He reintroduced the proposal in 1851. (*JNYA*, 21 January, 13 February, 1 April 1850, pp. 160, 355, 1065, 1067; 8 January 1851, p. 40; *Daily Albany Argus*, 14 February 1850; *BDAC*; Hendrik Hartog, "Marital Exits and Marital Expectations in Nineteenth Century America," *Georgetown Law Review* 80 [1991]: 115–17.)

3. In the same issue of the *Lily*, in "A Startling Fact," ECS reported figures about idiocy supplied by Governor George N. Briggs of Massachusetts at a recent temperance meeting: that of 1,200–1,300 idiots in the Commonwealth, 1,100–1,200 were children of drunken parents. (*Film*, 6:1045.)

4. Governed by laws from the legendary Lycurgus, ancient Sparta provided models of relative equality in marriage and of state responsibility for children.

5. "Sun Flower" was one of several noms de plume employed by ECS in the *Lily*.

·❮━━━━❯❮━━━━❯·

38 ❧ ECS TO MARY ANN WHITE JOHNSON AND
THE OHIO WOMEN'S CONVENTION[1]

Seneca Falls, N.Y., April 7th [1850].

Dear Mary Anne: How rejoiced I am to hear that the women of Ohio
have called a Convention preparatory to the remodeling of their State
Constitution. The remodeling of a Constitution, in the nineteenth
century, speaks of progress, of greater freedom, and of more enlarged
views of human rights and duties. It is fitting that, at such a time,
woman, who has so long been the victim of ignorance and injustice,
should at length throw off the trammels of a false education, stand
upright, and with dignity and earnestness manifest a deep and serious
interest in the laws which are to govern her and her country. It needs
no argument to teach woman that she is interested in the laws which
govern her. Suffering has taught her this already. It is important, now
that a change is proposed, that she speak, and loudly too. Having
decided to petition for a redress of grievances, the question is *for what
shall you first petition?* For the exercise of your right to the elective
franchise—nothing short of this. The grant to you of this right will
secure all others, and the granting of every other right, whilst this is
denied, is a mockery. For instance: What is the right to property,
without the right to protect it? The enjoyment of that right to-day is no
security that it will be continued to-morrow, so long as it is granted to
us as a favor, and not claimed by us as a right. Woman must exercise
her right to the elective franchise, and have her own representatives in
our national councils, for two good reasons:

1st. Men cannot represent us. They are so thoroughly educated into
the belief that woman's nature is altogether different from their own,
that they have no idea that she can be governed by the same laws of
mind as themselves. So far from viewing us like themselves, they seem,
from their legislation, to consider us their moral and intellectual an-
tipodes; for whatever law they find good for themselves, they forthwith
pass its opposite for us, and express the most profound astonishment if
we manifest the least dissatisfaction. For example: our forefathers, *full*

of righteous indignation, pitched King George, his authority and his tea chests, all into the sea, and because forsooth, they were forced to pay taxes without being represented in the British government. "Taxation without representation" was the text for many a hot debate in the forests of the new world, and for many an eloquent oration in the parliament of the old. Yet, in forming our new government, they have taken from us the very rights which they fought, and bled, and died, to secure to themselves. They have not only taxed us, but in many cases they strip us of all we inherit, the wages we earn, the children of our love; and for such grievances we have no redress in any court of justice this side of Heaven. They tax our property to build Colleges, then pass a special law prohibiting any woman to enter there. A married woman has no legal existence; she has no more absolute rights than a slave on a Southern plantation. She takes the name of her master, holds nothing, owns nothing, can bring no action in her own name; and the principle on which she and the slave is educated is the same. The slave is taught what is considered best for him to know—which is nothing; the woman is taught what is best for her to know—which is little more than nothing; man being the umpire in both cases. A woman cannot follow out the impulses of her own immortal mind in her sphere, any further than the slave can in his sphere. Civilly, socially, and religiously, she is what man chooses her to be—nothing more or less—and such is the slave. It is impossible for us to convince man that we think and feel exactly as he does, that we have the same sense of right and justice, the same love of freedom and independence. Some men regard us as devils, and some as angels; hence one class would shut us up in a certain sphere for fear of the evil *we* might do, and the other for fear of the evil that *might be done to us*; thus, except for the sentiment of the thing, for all the good it does us, we might as well be thought the one as the other. But we ourselves have to do with what *we are* and what *we shall be*.

2d. Man cannot legislate for us. Our statute books and all past experience teach us this fact. His laws, where we are concerned, have been, without one exception, unjust, cruel, and aggressive. Having denied our identity with himself, he has no data to go upon in judging of our wants and interests. If we are alike in our mental structure, then there is no reason why we should not have a voice in making the laws which govern us; but if we are not alike, most certainly we must make laws for ourselves; for who else can understand what we need and desire? If it be admitted in this government that all men and women are free and equal, then must we claim a place in our Senate Chambers and Houses of Representatives. But if, after all, it be found that even here we have classes and caste—not "Lords and Commons," but Lords and Women—then must we claim a lower House, where our Representatives can watch the passage of all bills affecting our own welfare or the good of our country. Had the women of this country had a voice in the government, think you our national escutcheon would have been stained with the guilt of aggressive warfare upon such weak defenceless nations as the Seminoles and Mexicans? Think you we should cherish and defend, in the heart of our nation, such a wholesale system of piracy, cruelty, licentiousness and ignorance, as is our slavery? Think you that relic of barbarism, the gallows, by which the wretched murderer is sent with blood upon his soul, uncalled for, into the presence of his God, would be sustained by law? Verily no, or I mistake woman's heart, her instinctive love of justice and mercy, and truth.

Who questions woman's right to vote? We can show our credentials to the right of self-government; we get ours just where man got his; they are all Heaven-descended, God-given. It is our duty to assert and re-assert this right, to agitate, discuss and petition, until our political equality be fully recognized. Depend upon it, this is the point to attack, the stronghold of the fortress—*the one* woman will find most difficult to take—*the one* man will most reluctantly give up; therefore let us encamp right under its shadow—there spend all our time, strength and *moral* ammunition, year after year, with perseverance, courage and decision. Let no sallies of wit or ridicule at our expense, no soft nonsense of woman's beauty, delicacy and refinement, no promise of gold and silver, bank stock, road stock, or landed estate, seduce us from our position, until that one stronghold totters to the ground. This done, the rest will they surrender *at discretion*. Then comes equality in Church and State, in the family circle, and in all our social relations.

The cause of woman is onward. For our encouragement, let us take a review of what has occurred during the last few years. Not two years since, the women of New York held several Conventions. Their meetings were well attended by both men and women, and the question of woman's true position was fully and freely discussed. The proceedings of those meetings and their Declaration of Sentiments were all published and scattered far and near. Before that time, the newspapers said but little on that subject. Immediately after, there was scarcely a newspaper in the Union that did not notice these Conventions, and generally in a tone of ridicule. Now, you seldom take up a paper that has not something about woman; but the tone is changing—ridicule is giving way to reason. Our papers begin to see that this is no subject for mirth, but one for serious consideration. Our literature also is assuming a different tone. The heroine of our fashionable novel is now a being of spirit, of energy, of will, with a conscience, with high moral principle, great decision and self-reliance.

Contrast Jane Eyre with any of Bulwer's, Scott's or Shakespeare's heroines, and how they all sink into the shade compared with that noble creation of a woman's genius![2] The January No. of the Westminster Review contains an article on Woman, so liberal and radical, that I sometimes think it must have crept in there by some mistake.[3] Our fashionable lecturers, too, are now, instead of the time-worn subjects of "Catholicism," "The Crusades," "St. Bernard," and "Thomas a Becket," choosing Woman for their theme. True, they do not treat this new subject with much skill or philosophy; but enough for us that the great minds of our day are taking this direction. Mr. Dana, of Boston, lectured on this subject in Philadelphia. Lucretia Mott followed him, and ably pointed out his sophistry and errors.[4] She spoke to a large and fashionable audience, and gave general satisfaction. Dana was too sickly and sentimental for that meridian. The women of Massachusetts, ever the first in all moral movements, have sent, but a few weeks since, to their Legislature, a petition demanding their right to vote and hold office in that State.[5] Woman seems to be preparing herself for a higher and holier destiny. That same love of liberty which burned in the hearts of our sires, is now being kindled anew in the daughters of this proud Republic. From the present state of public sentiment, we have every reason to look hopefully into the future. I see a brighter, happier day yet to come; but Woman must say how soon the dawn shall be, and whether the light shall first shine in the East or the West. By her own efforts the change must come. She must carve out her future destiny with her own right hand. If she have not the energy to secure for herself her true position, neither would she have the force or stability to maintain it, if placed there by another. Farewell! yours, sincerely,

ᗒ *E. C. Stanton.*

∽ *Proceedings of the Ohio Women's Convention, Held at Salem, April 19th and 20th, 1850; with an Address by J. Elizabeth Jones* (Cleveland, 1850), 15-19, in *Film* at 19 April. Also in *Anti-Slavery Bugle*, 27 April 1850; *NASS*, 9 May 1850; *Lib.*, 17 May 1850; and *History*, 1:810-12. ECS published a large portion of this as "Why Must Women Vote," *Lily*, May 1850 (*Film*, 6:1055).

1. Called to "secure to all persons the recognition of Equal Rights, and the extension of the privileges of Government without distinction of sex or color," the convention met at Salem on April 19 and 20. Five hundred women answered the call and agreed that no men would speak during the sessions. ECS's letter was read on the first day, as were letters from Lucretia Mott, Lucy Stone, Sarah Pugh, and a number of women in Ohio. The upcoming state constitutional convention presented "a most favorable opportunity for the agitation of this subject," and texts of an appeal to the women of Ohio and a memorial to the constitutional convention were adopted. Despite a flood of petitions for the enfranchisement of women and black men, Ohio's new constitution retained the state's provision for white male suffrage. (*Anti-Slavery Bugle*, 30 March, 6, 27 April 1850; Isaac F. Patterson, *The Constitutions of Ohio* [Cleveland, 1912]; Ohio, Constitutional Convention, 1850-51, *Report of the Debates and Proceedings*, 2 vols. [Columbus, 1851].)

Mary Ann White Johnson (1808-1872) lived in Salem for three years while her husband Oliver edited the *Anti-Slavery Bugle*, and she was an organizer and officer of the convention. In the 1840s she worked as assistant matron in the women's prison at Sing Sing, New York, under the direction of Eliza W. Farnham. Mary Ann Johnson (whose name also appears as Mary Anne or Marianne) remained active in the cause of woman's rights; she attended the first national convention at Worcester, Massachusetts, in October 1850, and presided over the first convention in Pennsylvania, held at West Chester in 1852. (*DAB*, s.v. "Johnson, Oliver"; *Woman's Journal*, 22 June 1872; Georgiana Bruce Kirby, *Years of Experience* [New York, 1886], 190-209; *History*, 1:350-52.)

2. By Charlotte Brontë (1816-1855), published at London in 1847. ECS contrasts Brontë's writing to the romantic, historical novels of Edward George Earle Bulwer-Lytton (1803-1873) and Walter Scott (1771-1832).

3. "Woman's Mission," *Westminster Review* 52 (January 1850): 181-96. Though the author regarded demands for woman's rights to be "as unwomanlike as they are useless," (190) he or she believed that "all women will eventually be taught from their childhood that the world asks work from all," and "that women should be brought up independent of man for subsistence, brought up to constant daily labour of some kind for her bread, or to promote the general well-being" (192).

4. On 17 December 1849 Lucretia Mott delivered a public lecture on woman to answer one by Richard Henry Dana (1815-1882), a lawyer, literary man, and adventurer. Dana delivered a distinguished series of lectures about Shakespeare's plays in the winter of 1849 and 1850, and to a lecture on Desdemona, he added

an address that ridiculed women whose names appeared in print for their achievements and celebrated women who adhered to the precepts of the Bible. After he spoke in Philadelphia, friends of Mott arranged for her to speak, and her *Discourse on Women* was immediately published. ECS heard Dana's "nauseous sentiments" in New York and observed that his "poetical" views overlooked "the stern realities" of how men treated women. (*DAB*; Hallowell, *James and Lucretia Mott*, 301-2, 487-506; Cromwell, *Lucretia Mott*, 148-49; Mott, *Complete Speeches*, 143-62; ECS to L. C. Mott, March? 1849?, *Film*, 6:894-97.)

5. The legislature took no action as a result of this campaign, led by Lucy Stone. (*History*, 1:208-15, and *Lib.*, 1, 8 February 1850.)

---

39 ❧ ARTICLE BY ECS

[May 1850]

LEGISLATIVE DOINGS.

Well, dear Lily, the Legislature of this state has at length adjourned.[1] The members have gone to their respective homes, with their money and two or three bushels of documents, each. The proceedings of the session are now to be published. This whole performance will cost the state about $200,000. Those women who hold property will be taxed in common with the men, to help raise this sum. But we will not grumble; for one bill alone, which they have passed, is of itself worth double this whole sum.[2] The substance of this bill is, that whatever money a married woman puts into a savings bank, she may draw it out again *herself*; no one else shall draw it, not even her liege lord, be he drunk or sober, wise or foolish, sane or insane. Heretofore, you know, no married woman could of herself invest money in any way. Under the new laws in relation to property, some rights were granted to women, but still no married woman could deposit money in a bank. So this winter it seems a bill sprung up in the lower House to this effect, that a married woman might work hard and put for instance $1000 in a bank, and then she should have a perfect right to draw out $250, the remainder should be at the disposal of her husband, whoever or whatever he might chance to be. This was *magnanimous!!* $250 is a great sum for a woman to have at her disposal, particularly if she have the skill to make more, and the providence to save what she earns. This bill passed the Assembly and went to the Senate; and what do you think that august body said to this outburst of chivalry from the lower House? In their amendment they surpassed their coadjutors, and themselves even, in generosity. They said a married woman might not only deposit money in a savings bank, but she might also draw it *all* out again *herself*. Thus amended, the bill passed the two Houses unanimously. One great principle is thus settled. Let the women of the Empire State return countless thanks to their sires and sons. Only think of it! *A woman!!* be she married or single, can now deposit her *own* money in a bank, and draw it *all* out again *herself*. The length, the breadth, the height and the depth of this act of mercy and justice is only equalled by the fact that our Legislatures have been but fifty short years in arriving at its truth.

☙ S. F.

☙ *Lily*, May 1850.

1. Henry Stanton won election to the New York senate at the November elections in 1849.

2. An act for the protection of savings banks and institutions receiving deposits from married women passed 25 March 1850. Section one of the statute stipulated that "it shall be lawful for the trustees or officers" of banks to pay to a married woman "such sum or sums as may be due such female, and the receipt or acquittance of such depositor shall be a sufficient legal discharge to the said corporation therefor." (*Laws of New York, 1850*, chap. 91, sec. 1.)

---

40 ☙ PAULINA WRIGHT DAVIS[1] TO ECS

Providence [*R.I.*] July 7th [*1850*]

Mrs Stanton   Dear Madam

You are already I presume fully aware of our movements in relation to a womans rights convention to be held in Worcester Oct 16th & 17th.[2] I find your name on my list and am most happy that it is so, for it is very pleasant to write to those who know their own positions and are willing others should also.

The convention is not designed to be a New England con—but a general one just so far as we can enlist attention to it, hence we ask your name and your husbands to ~~our~~ the call and any others in that part of

the state which you may think desirable to send me   We anticipate
your presance with us with confidence. I know of no one here who is as
earnestly interested in some points as your letters indicate that you are,
and each one must take the ground on which they feel most strongly
and press that point. I do not feel that in addressing you it is necessary
for me to go into a long explanation or argument to urge the claims of
the convention upon your attention   therefore I will only say that as to
progress so far as I have corresponded, it is of the most encourageing
nature. One gentleman said to me make any demands you please upon
my purse to further the object of the con— When I asked Mr Channing[3]
for his name, "Yes with all my heart" was the response, so also Mr
Alcott Dr Elder of Pda[4] and many others ~~illegible~~ ↑whose names↓ do
not now occur to me. I shall hope to hear soon that we are at liberty to
use your name and any others that you may send. I ask this as a favour
as we wish for more names from New York than we are able from
personale knowledge to obtain[5]   Yours very truly

❧ *Paulina W Davis*

❧ ALS, ECS Papers, DLC. Transcribed in part in ECS Papers, NjR. At the
bottom of this letter ECS wrote to persons unknown: "This is the distinguished Paulina Wright who married Thomas Davis a wealthy & influential
merchant in Providence, about a year ago. Send this back immediately."

1. Paulina Kellogg Wright remarried in April 1849 and moved with her new
husband, Thomas Davis, to Providence, Rhode Island.

2. Davis, Lucy Stone, and six others formed a committee, named at the May
antislavery meetings in Boston, to call the meeting known as the First National
Woman's Rights Convention. It met at Worcester on 23 and 24 October 1850.
(Paulina W. Davis, comp., *A History of the National Woman's Rights Movement, For Twenty Years* . . . [New York, 1871], 12–13.)

3. William Henry Channing (1810–1884), of Boston, was a reformer, author, Unitarian clergyman, and a nephew of William Ellery Channing. His
pursuit of a suitable and useful career had taken him to New York City,
Cincinnati, Brook Farm, and back to Boston. He was elected a vice president
of the woman's rights convention at Worcester in 1850, and at the meeting of
1851 he presented a report on woman's social relations. In 1852 Channing
accepted a call to preach to the Rochester Unitarian Society, where he stayed
until August 1854. He became, in that time, a staunch ally of the region's
radical women, assisting in their woman's rights, temperance, and antislavery
activities. Channing and his family settled in England from 1854 to 1861 and
again after the Civil War. (*DAB*; Octavius Brooks Frothingham, *Memoir of
William Henry Channing* [Boston, 1886], 254–76; *History*, 1:221–46, 509–10.)

4. Amos Bronson Alcott (1799–1888), best known today as the father of Louisa May, was a somewhat dreamy reformer with innovative ideas about education and recurrent interest in utopian communities. William Elder (1806–1885), of Philadelphia, was a physician and writer, known for his abolitionist views. He and his wife Sara Maclean Elder signed the call to the woman's rights convention. (*DAB*; *ACAB*.)

5. In an undated fragment, ECS replied, "Yes, with all my heart I give my name to your noble call." (*Film*, 6:1073.) The list of signers to the call also included her sister Catharine Wilkeson, Gerrit and Nancy Smith, and Charles D. and Elizabeth Smith Miller. ECS did not attend the convention but sent a letter. (*Lib.*, 7 September 1850, and *Proceedings of the Woman's Rights Convention, Held at Worcester, October 23d & 24th, 1850* [Boston, 1851], 51–54, *Film*, 6:1083, 7:1–13.)

---

41 ∽ ARTICLE BY ECS

[September 1850]

HOUSEKEEPING.

"A place for every thing, and every thing in its place."[1]

There is no point, on which men, simple souls, are more mistaken in regard to women, than in supposing, that the mass of us are perfect martyrs, to order and cleanliness, when the fact is, the general run of housekeepers offer themselves up, daily and hourly, living sacrifices, to the demons of dirt and disorder. Now there is my Cousin Barbary;[2] she has a kind husband, several fine children, a good house and furniture, servants and money, and yet poor Barbary is always in a ferment, and neither she, nor her house, ever have an air of ease and comfort. Barbary has the most complex way of housekeeping. She keeps it herself, and from the mysterious manner in which the whole domestic machinery moves on, one might think, that at some time, Barbary had been confidential adviser to the Autocrat of Russia. She lets no one into the secret of the hiding places of any of the domestic utensils; from the fine linen pillow cases, down to the knife cloth, no one but Barbary, can lay their hands upon anything; and she cannot go straight to what she wants. Oh! no, I have seen her many a time, chase round after the dish cloth, peering into every closet, pot, and pan, like some devoted wife in search of a drunken spouse, through all his accustomed haunts of idleness and ease and then, in despair, tear some old towel in two and take one half for her present necessity. Barbary has no one implement, or dish, for each particular purpose, but wood, iron and glass in her hands, are at once endowed with a kind of universal genius. Their individuality is wholly merged in the general good. A junk bottle may be called upon, in one revolution of the earth, to hold a quart of molasses, to roll out a piecrust, to perform various evolutions on the floor for the amusement of the baby, or its neck used to set out a muslin puff, or hold a tallow candle, through an entire evening. Poor Barbary knows no repose,—she is always on the go. If husband, children or servants wish anything, they must all go to Barbary. "Dear, where are my razors?" Down drops Barbary's work, and away she goes in search of the razors, and, after a thorough overhauling of the knife box, escritoire, and all the drawers in the side board, with a joyous bound, she brings them down from the top of the looking glass, all bound round with a strong hemp thread, to prevent, as she said, "little Jenny" from cutting herself, as she had had them to play with, contrary to paternal orders the night before; as neither her doll, rattle box, or big shell could be found. They had probably gone the day before under a great lounge, which served Barbary, in her fits of righting up the house, as a kind of Botany Bay,[3] where she banished every thing, that had the misfortune to fall in her way, at so important an epoch.

"Now," said Barbary, seating herself once more "I must mend Tommy's pantaloons." She had just got her thimble on, and her needle threaded, when the door opened and a broad face was presented by one of the daughters of Erin.[4] "Mrs. B., where is the bluing bag?"[5] "The bluing bag; Bridget? I'll see." Down go the pantaloons, and away goes Barbary, and after half an hour's search, she triumphantly brings forth the bluing bag from the box of starch. Poor Barbary! she accomplished so little and yet she was so tired when night came. I once ventured to say to her, that she might save a great deal of time and many steps if she would have a place for everything. She promptly replied, "I have no time to be orderly." I saw by her manner, that Barbary was not prepared to take any suggestions, so I pitied her in silence. But to you who read about Barbary, let me say: have one place for every thing, and train your household to put things in their proper places. Then husband, children and servants can all wait on themselves. In an orderly house a child five years old can tell where every thing is. If you would save time and labor cultivate order. Perhaps I will tell you more about Barbary another time; and I must tell you too, about my cousin Sobriny Jane, who is the pink of order and neatness.[6] She has nine pages of written directions for her servant to set the dinner table, and all her bundles are classified, hung up in linen bags, and duly labelled.

⇜ *E. C. S.*

⇜ *Lily*, September 1850.

1. An old English and American proverb.
2. If ECS had in mind a specific cousin, her identity is not known.
3. Where the British banished convicts, in New South Wales, Australia.
4. A servant. ECS employs a common stereotype that identified the Irish immigrant with domestic service. By the 1840s young Irish women constituted the majority of servants in eastern cities and found work in small towns as well. It is rare, in ECS's writings and elsewhere, that the employer represents disorder. More commonly the "daughter of Erin" betokens ignorance and clumsiness.
5. A bag of blue indigo in the rinse water, brightened the white laundry.
6. "My Cousin Sobriny Jane," *Lily*, November 1850, *Film*, 7:17–18.

·⊂══════⊃·

42 ⇝ ECS TO THEODORE D. WELD

Grassmere [*Seneca Falls*] Sept 22nd [*1850*]

Dear Theodore,

My heart leaps to embrace you in behalf of the eight or ten miserable little undeveloped vandals, that by your strong right arm are to be rescued from the "fumbling of the schools."[1] Most gladly would we consign all our boys to your care at once but Daniel is the only one who is old enough to leave home at present. And for him we desire a place when your spring term opens. He will be nine years old the second day of March. He is a large strong healthy boy, & I intend to teach him myself during the winter, to prepare him for the Weld institution. He needs a little urging along in spelling reading writing geography & arithmetic. He needs too some theological training. I wish to send him to you with a knowledge of the ten commandments,—of the locality of hell, & the personality of the devil, & a full belief in the great truths, that evil is not positive, that truth is absolute, & that there is a true standard of right wrong— With such an amount of mental & moral furnishment as a basis, I shall look to you for a glorious superstructure. Henry & I talked the matter all over on receiving your letter & at first thought to send the little fellow to you at once, but when I thought of the cold winter, the long nights, the cold feet & chapped hands & the four hundred unamiable miles stretching between me & my dear boy my maternal heart caved right in & I said we will not send him until the genial spring comes again when he will be nine years old.

But if his not being with you at the commencement of the year will forfeit his place for the spring I shall give up the mother, act the philosopher, & send him as soon as I can get him ready, for I fully appreciate the advantages a boy will have under your roof. What you say of schools generally is true, & I find most people say the same thing. Our schools are so many humbugs. You little know what a relief it is to me that you have decided to investigate this teaching business, & that there is now a strong probability that all our sons are to be in turn under your influence. But I hope dear Theodore, you will <u>allow</u> Angelina to attend to the childrens chirography, for I think I should be puzzled, at some future day, when sitting with spectacles on my nose, at a communication from one of my sons, penned in a style similar to one now before me, tho' for your encouragement let me say, your last letter to me is a great improvement on one of yours, that I keep as an autograph.[2] It was given me by Henry's mother, written to Dr. W. W. Bird in 34. & is a "wonderful & mysterious epistle," as wise ones say about things they cannot fathom. It is a sealed book to me tho' I take great comfort in two or three words which I have dug out, such glorious ones as "freedom," "philanthropy" & "unceasing exertions." Much love to each & all under your roof, as Henry wishes to write in this I must leave the remaining space for him   I wish Angelina & Sarah would write to us occasionally. I shall be quite anxious to hear how many boys you have & how you get on with the experiment. I shall go right to work polishing up my oldest born to fit him for the March winds of New Jersey. When does the second term commence?— good night   your friend

⚜ *E. C. Stanton*

≈ ALS, Weld-Grimké Papers, MiU-C. Henry B. Stanton added a note at the end of this letter.

1. Weld invited the Stantons to enroll their children in school on his farm at Belleville, New Jersey, where he and Angelina Weld and Sarah Grimké were the teachers. The school found a ready supply of pupils in the families of abolitionists; Martha Wright, Gerrit Smith, James Birney, Samuel Wilkeson, and the Stantons were among the parents who enrolled children. When the Welds joined the Raritan Bay Union at Perth Amboy, New Jersey, late in 1852, they moved the school to the new, experimental community. Their Eagleswood School continued until 1861. (Lerner, *Grimké Sisters*, 315-16; Thomas, *Theodore Weld*, 224-34; Account Book of Theodore Dwight Weld, 1850-1860, Manuscript Division, NN.)

2. Embarrassed by ECS's criticism of anyone's handwriting, Henry Stanton wrote in his addition to this letter: "As to chirography, if either of my sons ever reaches the perfection in the art to which you have attained, I think his mother will have as little trouble in deciphering his epistles as you will have in deciphering hers!—"

---

43 ≈ ABIGAIL KELLEY FOSTER TO ECS

Syracuse Jan. 11—1851

Mrs. Stanton

Esteemed friend— Allow me thus to address you, for altho' personally, almost a stranger to you I feel that I know you and I regard you with feelings of high esteem.

I am told by the anti slavery friends that you are the person in Seneca Falls whom I should address in reference to anti slavery business, and so I take the liberty to do so, as the friends whom I used to know in your place, may have removed from the place—as some of them certainly have—or possibly may have lost their interest in the cause;[1] I most earnestly hope, however, the latter evil may not have befallen them.

My husband and myself are on our way to attend the annual meeting of the Western N.Y.A.S. Society,[2] and propose stopping at your place to hold a meeting on Tuesday evening next, 14 inst. if there is nothing in the way to prevent it. If there is, we would like for you to ask our friends, McClintock at Waterloo, to appoint a meeting †for us↓ at their place for the same evening.

You will oblige us by ~~asking~~ leaving a note with the ticket master, at the Depot, informing us whether we are to go to Waterloo, as we shall have no time to wait, but shall want to go directly on in the same train. We shall be there in the cars which leave this place at 2 o'clock ↑P.M.↓ on Tuesday. On second thought, will you drop us a line at this place, Care of Stephen Smith,[3] ~~that~~ in case you get this in time to write so that we can get the letter on Monday. The cars stop so short a time I fear we should not be able to read a note at your depot before the cars would be off. Thine truly

❧ *Abby Kelley Foster*

❧ ALS, ECS Papers, DLC.

1. When Abby Kelley spoke at Seneca Falls in 1842 and 1843, she advocated that abolitionists come out of all proslavery churches or at least challenge their ministers to teach the sinfulness of slavery. One of her local supporters faced church discipline for taking Kelley's advice. (Sterling, *Ahead of Her Time*, 181–86; Altschuler and Saltzgaber, *Revivalism, Social Conscience, and Community*.)

2. The Fosters were en route to the Western New York Anti-Slavery Society meeting at Rochester on 16–17 January 1851, after which they lectured in New York through the winter and spring.

3. Stephen Smith (1776–1854) was a Quaker businessman and reformer at Syracuse who often hosted traveling abolitionists. (Garrison, *Letters*, 3:115n, 4:429n; Thomas E. Finegan, *Free Schools: A Documentary History of the Free School Movement in New York State* [1921; reprint, New York, 1971], 359.)

·❮━━━◆━━━❯·

44 ❧ ECS TO ABIGAIL KELLEY FOSTER

Grassmere [*Seneca Falls*] Sunday 12 ↑o'clock↓ [*12 January 1851*]

My dear Mrs Foster,

I have this moment received your letter. I shall send a messenger to the village immediately to proclaim the glad tidings that the dry bones of the Senecas are to be breathed upon by a mighty down easter, on the coming Tuesday night. You can no doubt have a meeting here as the Wesleyan chapel is always open & I will see that your approach is duly heralded. Now as a reward for the labour of sending this missive to you & of stirring up the faithful here, I claim the pleasure of making your acquaintance under my own roof. I can neither meet you at the depot nor attend your meeting in consequence of a kind of biennial clumsiness to which I have been subject many years.[1] Let the omnibus bring you directly to our house where I shall be most happy to welcome you & your Husband at any & all times. yours sincerely

≈ *Elizabeth Cady Stanton*

≈ ALS, Abigail Kelley Foster Papers, MWA.

1. ECS refers to pregnancy.

·⟨══════◦✶◦══════⟩·

45 ≈ ECS to Elizabeth Smith Miller

[*Seneca Falls*] Monday morning [*10 February 1851*]

Dear Liz,

Laugh in your turn I have actually got my fourth son. Yes, Theodore Weld Stanton[1] after two long mighty flourishes of his royal crown bounded upon the stage of life, with great ease <u>comparatively</u>!! I was sick but a few hours, did not lie down half an hour before he was born, but worked round as hard as I could all night to do up the last things I had to do at 7 o'clock Sunday morning he was born. I was bandaged up in cold water[2] & walked to my bed from the front parlour to the back. This morning I got up bathed myself in cold water & have sat by the table writing several letters. Has Mrs Burwell set sail yet. I wrote you Saturday night about her. adieu your cousin

≈ *Lib*

P.S. The baby weighs 10½ & looks like Gattie.

≈ ALS, ECS Papers, DLC.

1. Theodore Weld Stanton was born on 9 February 1851.
2. ECS refers to the methods recommended by practitioners of water-cure for reducing the pain and duration of labor and childbirth. Cold water acted like a tonic to the nervous system. According to Mary Gove Nichols, daily packing in wet sheets reduced the length of labor to anywhere "from 20 minutes to 4½ hours." Her patients also could walk the day after birth, be about the house during the first week, and ride out in a week or two. (Mary Gove Nichols, *Experience in Water-Cure: A Familiar Exposition of the Principles and Results of Water Treatment, In the Cure of Acute and Chronic Diseases* [New York, 1850], 74–75.)

·⟨══════✳══════⟩·

46 ☞ Lillian Muir Mynderse[1] to ECS

[*Seneca Falls, 10 February 1851*]

Miss Lillias Mynderse compliments & a hearty welcome to Theodore Weld Stanton, but she is quite surprised that he was allowed to live long enough to send greeting to his friends

Mrs Stanton will please accept a bottle of temperance wine, and drink to better luck next time.

❧ AL, ECS Papers, DLC; addressed to Theodore Weld Stanton.

1. Lillian Muir Mynderse writes in the name of her three-year old daughter Lillias. Edward Mynderse was a stove and pump manufacturer in Seneca Falls and a partner in a large distillery. He, Lillian, and their small children lived on Fall Street in 1851. (Research by the late Corinne Guntzel, Seneca Falls.)

·⟨══════✳══════⟩·

47 ☞ Article by ECS

[March 1851]

SOBRINY JANE.[1]

Some time ago, dear reader, I told you about my cousin Sobriny Jane, and from what I have already said I am sure that you must feel sufficient interest in this remarkable woman to listen with pleasure to some of her late sayings and doings. Well, she has just made an entire new manifestation of character; one that has filled *me*, even—and I have known her long and intimately—with wonder and surprise. I had always thought that Sobriny was sensitive to public sentiment; too much so, ever to strike out for herself a new path, unaided and alone. But of late the very spirit of her sire seems to have inspired her anew. During the short cold days of December, in the presence of her liege lord and all her sons, she assembled together her whole inheritance of petticoats, and, by a skillful surgical operation, separated those parts which were forever groveling in the dust, from those nearest the heart.

She then slipped her neatly turned foot and ankle into a masculine boot, leaped into a pair of Turkish trowsers,[2] and walked forth a mile and a half, through sleet and snow, to the home of her childhood. There having received the paternal nod of approval, she shrinks not, now, from encountering the vacant gaze, the vulgar laugh, and idle jeers, of ill-bred men, women and children.

Sobriny prophecies that henceforth the votaries of Fashion shall worship at a Turkish shrine; for the French having proved themselves incapable of forming a model Republic, are of necessity unfit to invent costumes worthy the imitation of daughters of the Pilgrim Fathers. Is it not better, voluntarily to imitate the Turkish nobility, than meekly bow to the dictation of a vulgar French milliner?

And to think, that Sobriny, with all her originality and daring, whilst learned editors were discussing the propriety of a change in our dress, should just do the deed, and in this costume appear here in our very midst! And what is still more worthy of our consideration, is, that a respectable dozen of the women of our village have decided to assume this costume at once. So prepare yourselves, ye Lords of Seneca, to see the idols of your affections soon flitting about your muddy streets, with as much ease and freedom as you do yourselves. And you, Mr. Courier,[3] please write another stirring article and talk up the fashion as fast as possible. If Mrs. Bloomer will persist in talking lightly of ten or twenty pounds of petticoats, console yourself with the reflection that she feels their weight as grievous as the least of us. *Entre nous*, I have every reason to think she is already perpetrating some mutilations on her own wardrobe. She had several interviews with Sobriny, and has an exact pattern of the costume.

≻ *E. C. S.*

≻ *Lily*, March 1851.

1. That is, Elizabeth Smith Miller.

2. So named for their similarity to the pants worn by Turkish women, the trousers were pleated or gathered in at the ankle.

3. Isaac Fuller, founder of the *Seneca County Courier* in 1837, was both owner and editor from 1851 to 1865. An editorial critical of female attire in his paper prompted Amelia Bloomer to write about dress reform in the *Lily*, and another article dared her to practice what she preached. (Chamberlain, "Seneca Falls Press," 2–3, 15; Bloomer, *Amelia Bloomer*, 13–15, 65–66, 144; *History of Seneca Co., N.Y.*, 54–55.)

48 ❧ ANGELINA GRIMKÉ WELD TO ECS

[Belleville, N.J., c. 1 April 1851][1]

[. . .] nursery with 3 other boys—it is a large room you may remember, but as soon as Green Smith came, I took the large boys out of the North Chamber & put them in the room immediately under & put up two single bedsteads in it for Neal[2] & Green, as they both wished to bathe, for I thot it was not best for boys to expose themselves daily before several others   And here you may see them ensconsed very comfortably & <u>peaceably</u> together for Green is too lovely to quarrel with any one— T[heodore] goes in every night & attends to Neal, but notwithstanding this he has once ——— It is well I had a gum elastic cloth to put under him or my new mattrass w^{ld} have been ruined— I had anticipated this difficulty with some of ~~my~~ ↑the↓ boys, for I have a neighbor who is greatly troubled in this way with all her children, one of them older than [Nea]l—

But here he comes & says I must send love to you & Kit & Gerrit & Theo—& two other persons, but I cant make out their names—he has just been cleaning his own & two or three other boys shoes & boots one cent for shoes & two for boots. He says I must tell you he wants to stay here, he likes this place

Theodore has formed a third, intermediate class for Green   Neal, Ch Chandler, Fitz Hugh[3] & 2 or 3 others— I am the writing & Sister the drawing teacher, and I hope between the three justice will be done— And now dear Lizzy, I hope you will forgive my apparent neglect & I will <u>try</u> to write once in two weeks & oftener, if sickness or any thing else in Neal should make it dutiful—so rest assured that no news will be good news. How are the babe & yourself— With our united love I am Yrs Truly

❧ *A G W*

❧ ALS, incomplete, scrapbook 1, Papers of ECS, NPV; addressed to Seneca Falls and forwarded to Peterboro. Letters torn by the seal are supplied in square brackets.

1. The opening of this letter was cut away, preserving primarily a note from Amelia Bloomer to ECS, written on the address leaf. The letter was postmarked at New York on 1 April, but ECS had taken her baby on a visit to Peterboro. Before forwarding the letter, Bloomer, the assistant postmistress, added a note: "shorten your visit as much as possible people have nothing to talk about while you are gone." She postmarked it again on 3 April.

2. Daniel, or "Neil," Stanton was enrolled in the Welds' school on 14 March 1851. (Account Book of Theodore Dwight Weld, 1850–1860, Manuscript Division, NN.)

3. Charles Chandler enrolled on 4 March 1851. Fitzhugh Birney, the son of James and Elizabeth Birney, was born in Michigan on 9 January 1842. He stayed at Belleville and moved with the school to Eagleswood at Perth Amboy. ([Cutler], *Fitzhugh Birney*.)

·❨════◆════❩·

Editorial note: ECS and SBA met in 1851, on or about May 13, when George Thompson, the fiery British orator, on a second American tour, lectured in and around Seneca Falls. The guest of Amelia Bloomer while in town to hear Thompson and William Lloyd Garrison, SBA was introduced to ECS by her hostess on a street corner after the lectures. The occasion was not documented at the time, and the story is pieced together from what Bloomer, ECS, and SBA recalled years later about an encounter that had become historic.

In her first telling of the history in 1868, ECS said only that temperance work brought SBA to her attention in 1851. Not until 1881 did she add the details about Thompson, Garrison, and Bloomer, and she retained those details in her autobiography, published in 1898. Simultaneously, she became hazy about the date. In 1868 she had told Theodore Tilton that her friendship with SBA dated from 1850, and as soon as he published that information, she began to quote his account in her own histories. It was after ECS constructed the narrative that Amelia Bloomer recorded her recollections. She repeated the 1850 date, described SBA as her houseguest, and set the scene on a street corner. When Ida Harper wrote SBA's biography, all the earlier versions were available to her. Because she emphasized the impact on SBA of the American Anti-Slavery Society's six-month campaign in 1851 to win new supporters in New York State, Harper observed the discrepancy in the year and returned the story to 1851.

With the exception of two newspaper accounts of temperance meetings that SBA led for the Daughters of Temperance in Rochester in February 1851,

Harper's biography is the sole source on SBA's activities between the time she left Canajoharie in 1849 and the fall of 1851. SBA's continued commitment to the temperance cause accounts for her acquaintance with Amelia Bloomer. But Harper explains a new interest in abolitionism, a direct outgrowth of Abby Kelley Foster's campaign. In Rochester several times between January and April and always on the look out for women who could become antislavery agents, Foster invited SBA to join her antislavery troupe for a week on the road, and SBA traveled to Syracuse for the American Anti-Slavery Society's annual meeting.

In this slippery story, Thompson's trip is a fixed point but it may not be the right point. When ECS added the detail that the encounter coincided with George Thompson's presence in Seneca Falls, she elaborated further to say that Thompson and Garrison stayed at her house. A contemporary account by a man traveling with Thompson indicates that the two men returned to Waterloo after their lectures, to spend a second night with the McClintock family. In an account so detailed as to indicate who met their trains, served them tea, and housed them, ECS is not named. Touring New York since February, Thompson had lectured a number of times in Rochester. After a short trip to Ontario, he attended the annual meeting on May 7 and left Syracuse three days later to speak in eight towns near the Finger Lakes, including Seneca Falls, before concluding his tour on May 18. SBA, it was said, wanted to hear him one more time. ECS, alone with her children in Seneca Falls, told Henry Stanton she would hear Thompson herself.

There is no documentary trace of how the acquaintance matured. (Harper's story that the two women met again in the summer of 1851 is in error.) Late in the year SBA worked in an unprecedented campaign of women for temperance legislation. Inspired by a law passed that year in the State of Maine making it illegal to manufacture or sell liquor, temperance men and women in New York mobilized for a similar law. The Daughters of Temperance amassed one hundred thousand signatures on their petitions for the "Maine law," and they called a meeting of women in Albany during the legislative session. On 28 January 1852 SBA stepped forward at that meeting to read aloud a letter from ECS. Clearly the two women had been in touch between May and January. But more than a month later, ECS still began a letter to SBA with the formal "Miss Susan B. Anthony." (ECS, "The Woman's Rights Movement and Its Champions in the United States," *Eminent Women of the Age*, ed. James Parton [Hartford, Conn., 1868], 397–98; Theodore Tilton, "Mrs. Elizabeth Cady Stanton," in ibid., 349; *History*, 1:456–57; *Eighty Years*, 162–63, 184;

Bloomer, *Amelia Bloomer*, 54–55; *Anthony*, 1:63–64; *Lib.*, 30 May 1851; ECS to H. B. Stanton, misdated 2 September 1851, *Film*, 7:105; *Lily*, November 1851, July 1852; Ian R. Tyrrell, *Sobering Up: From Temperance to Prohibition in Antebellum America, 1800–1860* [Westport, Conn., 1979], 252–89; and *Film*, 7:34–35, 48–52, 54, 58.)

·◁════━━════▷·

49 ❧ ARTICLE BY ECS

[July 1851]

MRS. SWISSHELM

Is a very queer woman, but all genuises are so. We like her, although she is forever saying something we wish unsaid. Women of intellect should do all in their power to raise woman to her true position, to make her feel the dignity of self-reliance and a noble independence, and not encourage her weaknesses, by talking to her about her "delicacy," "helplessness" and "physical disabilities."[1] It is very trying, every now and then to have Mrs. S. quoted against positions we think very important to be maintained. She is down on our holding conventions, passing resolutions, or taking care of ourselves. She seems to think the All-wise did not give us a complete outfit for the voyage of life,—that there are foes to be subdued and dangers to be encountered, which we have no will or muscle to meet, and no chart or compass to guide us. At our next convention we shall vote Mrs. Swisshelm a pair of horns, for self-defence, unless she recall the present claim she has set up against the *whole* male sex—and just say that in case of difficulty or danger to her precious person, she would call upon any one, stronger and more able bodied than herself. That in case she fell into a ditch she would not reject the stout arm of an Hibernian girl, because some effeminate little man was at hand, whose protection she had a right to claim. We wish, too, if Mrs. S. persists in making this claim on men only, she would limit it to the large and strong, and take the frail, little men in the same category with herself. I would ask Mrs. S. what "physical disability" has a strong, vigorous, well developed woman? If a woman has her ribs lapped from tight lacing, her spine crooked from stooping, her feet covered with corns, from tight shoes, why she is as much disabled as a *little man* with gout, inflammatory rheumatism, and a broken leg; and the little man is as much disabled as she; and if Mrs. Swisshelm, chased by a wild bull, claimed "protection" of either, it seems to me her safety would be more certainly ensured by the prosecution of her natural claim on her own feet.[2]

❧ E. C. S.

❧ *Lily*, July 1851. Swisshelm reprinted all but first sentence in *Pittsburgh Saturday Visiter*, 12 July 1851.

1. No doubt a response to reports of Jane Grey Swisshelm's actions in the Ohio women's convention at Akron on May 28 and 29. In the *Pittsburgh Saturday Visiter*, 7 June 1851, Swisshelm noted that she lacked space to discuss the meeting's resolutions and would do so in the next issue, but the *Visiter* of 14 June is missing. According to the *Anti-Slavery Bugle*, 7 June 1851, Swisshelm objected on the first day to a resolution that attributed inequalities between the sexes to "criminal injustice and cruel tyranny on the part of man, and reprehensible submissiveness . . . on the part of woman." On the second day she moved to amend the preamble to reflect her belief that women's "intellectual and moral endowments" were "as high as" but not "the same as" men's.

2. For more of this exchange see *Pittsburgh Saturday Visiter*, 12 July 1851, and *Film*, 7:101–2.

·◁══════◆══════▷·

50 ❧ Lucretia Coffin Mott to ECS

Philada. 9 mo. 11th. 1851—

My dear Eliz[h] C. Stanton

The seeming neglect of thy kind letter of invitation to visit you, and meet with our fr[d] Sarah Grimke, I would make the best apology for— It was handed me at Auburn, when on the eve of leaving there to return home, and when I had just written to Tho[s] & M. A. M'Clintock, answering a similar invitation to visit them, in which I had sent a special message to thee.

It would have given me unmingled pleasure to see & hold converse with you all; but public speaking seemed out of the question, from the state of my throat and general health. Indeed during the last week of my stay at Auburn, sickness, with a high fever confined me to bed several days, and I was really not well able to command nerve to write an answer to thy letter—especially as it must have been a negative one. I am now quite well, owing to such a fine rest from attending meetings— not going to one of any kind for 6 weeks. If I go to Auburn again next summer, I do promise myself the treat of seeing you all—either at Seneca Falls & Waterloo, or at b^r David Wright's at Auburn.

It seems the next Convention is advertised to be at Worcester—on the 15th Prox.[1] I have no expectation of being there. How I wish thou could go & take part in its proceedings! The M'Clintocks too ought to go, with one of their well written addresses. Thou wilt of course, send a letter, if thou cant be there in person.

We ought early to consider where will be the best place for the next National gathering, and when the best time. Amy Post wrote me that the Rochester friends of the cause had met & conferred together, & were united in desire to meet at that place. They were aware at the same time, that Syracuse would be the choice of some, as being more likely to secure the aid of Saml J. May—[2] It would also be more central for New-Eng. & Penn^a fr^ds— If held at either place, an earlier time in the season than October would be better—as many would like in taking a summer excursion to Niagara, &c to "kill 2 birds"— So confer with our Waterloo friends an with Rochester's too, and be prepared with a proposition to the Worcester Convention this year. There will be great advantages in fixing on the place thus early. Lucy Stone wrote me a few days ↑or weeks↓ ago, desiring that we might aid them in deciding on the next best place— As to Penna., with the exception of a few radical Quakers—Hicksits, whose names are cast out as evil, there is too much darkness on the subject, to bear such a glare as a National Convention would throw around. We must labor more in a smaller way. We want forerunners to come "crying in the wilderness."[3]

I have had great pleasure in reading the Westminster Review of our last year's Convention at Worcester, as reported in the Tribune—[4] It is from the pen of a woman too, in great part, which adds to the interest of the article—for no man can write on Woman's wrongs, as an intelligent sufferer of our own sex can— A Mr Taylor ↑of London↓ called on me a day or two ago,[5] a son of the author of the article—she was a widow, and lately married J. S. Mill, one of the conductors of that Review, as you know. He assisted her in writing it—altho' he says she wrote it. She sent me a copy, printed in pamphlet form. Her son gave me a few for distribution. I can only spare one for thee, which I herewith send. I have seen extracts from it in the Tribune, I think, but have not before read the whole article. It is beautifully written. I wish it could be reprinted & extensively circulated. I have sent one to Garrison, asking its publication entire, in the Liberator.[6]

I left one with the Truman girls last eve[g]—asking when they had done reading it, that their b[r] James send it to his Waterloo friends.[7] While there, they as well as we, were surprised agreeably by the arrival of Richard & Jane Hunt—by whom I send thee the pamphlet— With all manner of love, in which my James unites—thy fr[d]

⇝ *Lucretia Mott*

⇜ ALS, ECS Papers, DLC. Partial transcript in ECS Papers, NjR.

1. The call to the Second National Woman's Rights Convention at Worcester in October was published in the *National Anti-Slavery Standard*, 11 September 1851. ECS's letter to the convention is in *Film*, 7:123-24.
2. Samuel Joseph May (1797-1871) became pastor of the Unitarian church in Syracuse in 1845 and a year later published his sermon, *The Rights and Condition of Women*. He and Lucretia Mott held similar religious views; he would purify Christianity of a theology imposed upon it and return to the words of Jesus. From those words he learned a reformer's mission. Though a Garrisonian at the outset, May was able to work with the political abolitionists of New York State and be a moderating influence between the movement's contending factions. He was, as well, a valuable co-laborer of New York's woman's rights activists through the 1850s. A former principal of a normal school and a school committee member in Syracuse, he spoke with authority when, allied with SBA, he urged the New York State Teachers' Association to support racial equality in the schools and equal pay for teachers. (*DAB*; Pease and Pease, *Bound With Them in Chains*, 276-307; Samuel A. Eliot, ed., *Heralds of a Liberal Faith* [Boston, 1910], 3:239-49; Donald Yacovone, *Samuel Joseph May and the Dilemmas of the Liberal Persuasion, 1797-1871* [Philadelphia, 1991].)
3. Isa. 40:3.
4. "The Enfranchisement of Women," *Westminster Review* 55 (July 1851): 149-61. This anonymous article expanded the coverage given to the woman's rights convention of 1850 at Worcester by the *New York Tribune for Europe* into a stunning argument for the fundamental justice of allowing women their right to vote, not only in the United States, with its revolutionary tradition and Constitution, but also in Britain. The author was Harriet Hardy Taylor Mill (1807-1858), the wife of John Stuart Mill (1806-1873). (Olive Banks, *Biographical Dictionary of British Feminists*, vol. 1, *1800-1930* [Brighton, U.K., 1985]; F. A. Hayek, *John Stuart Mill and Harriet Taylor: Their Friendship and Subsequent Marriage* [London, 1951], 166-67.)

5. The first of Harriet Taylor's children by her first husband, born in 1827, Herbert Taylor conducted his father's wholesale drug business and made many trips to the United States.

6. The *New York Daily Tribune* published the article on 18 July 1851. Though Garrison omitted it from the *Liberator*, the article was the fourth of the Woman's Rights Tracts published at Syracuse in 1852, the third of the Woman's Rights Tracts published at Rochester in 1853, and a standard pamphlet for distribution by the woman's rights and suffrage movements for several decades.

7. James Truman (1826–1914), a medical student and Philadelphia Quaker, had four sisters living at home at this date: Mary Master, Anna, Sarah Pearson, and Catherine Hickman. Truman, who married Mary Ann McClintock in 1852, taught dentistry in and around Philadelphia and advocated women's entry into his profession. (*Quaker Genealogy*, 2:824; *NCAB*, 25:299–300; *History*, 3:452; *New York Times*, 27 November 1914.)

·❮━━━━━━❯·

51 ❧ ECS TO DANIEL C. STANTON

Johnstown Dec. 10th [*1851*]

Dear Neil

Your letter was sent to me from Seneca Falls.[1] I am at Johnstown & I shall stay here about one month so write to me here until I tell you I am going. We have had a very gay time here in the new house for a few days. Cousin Charley, Lizzy & Dudley & Aunty Cate & Bayard have all been here.[2] We danced one evening in the great hall & played all sorts of pranks. We have had several sleigh rides as there is plenty of snow here. Aunty Cates visit was cut short by a message from Buffalo that one of her little boys was very ill. Amelia has gone to visit her friends in the Black River country.[3] Gattie goes to Miss Yosts school.[4] You say that you & Henry wish to come home. Now Neally if you wish to stay at home when you do come, study hard, so that you & Henry can go to the Academy   Learn to be a good boy & learn all your lessons well & whenever Mr Weld is teaching you, give him all your thoughts. You know we have no good schools for boys that cannot read. You say if I will let you come home you will study all the time, well, just as soon as Mr Weld writes me that you study all the time & he thinks you would learn anywhere, that you behave like a gentlemen in every particular in habits, manners & language you shall come right home. Now set to work you & Henry & do your best. I should love to have you always with me, if I could manage you as well as Mr Weld does, but if you will learn to manage yourselves then we need never part again. It is very hard for me my dear boys to be separated from you & I feel worse since I visited you, but I feel that it is best you should be where you are. The days & months will soon glide away & we shall meet again in our own quiet home. Try to return to me better & wiser boys. I am glad that you are together & that you help each other   Keep yourselves clean mind & body. Do take care of your teeth. A word about your clothes   Mrs Weld thought your cloth jackets would not be sufficiently warm. Be sure & wear your collars all the time there is a good deal of warmth in them. The under part must not be starched. Lay those loose velvet jackets away for spring & wear your plaid jackets for great occasions & always put on an extra waist with them, as they are a little thinner than the cloth jackets. Did you get the stockings I sent you from New York? Have you got your sleds & skates? Neil have you ever recited on speaking night any of the peices I taught you? You know, "The slaves dream" "Excelsior," & "The blind Harper"[5]   If you should study either of those a little you could say them. One thing Neally I hope you will try to be more frank. What you do, do openly. Never again deceive, either by word, or act. When you have been a whole week without one sly or deceitful manifestation, do write & tell me? I hope you & Henry will be kind & loving to one another. Gattie says you may have his marbles divide them between you.

Ask Mrs Weld to put an under bed under your mattress, if she has one. These cold nights the caloric will pass off through a thin mattress very rapidly. Mrs Weld has covered you boys all most generously   My shoulders would ache under such an avalanche of bedding. I should prefer more under me & less over me. The weather here is intensely cold. I think of you every night when I tuck Gattie up & wish I could take you under my wing till morning. The boys here have gay times with their sleds. Have you any snow? You must tell me all about the sleds. Did Fitz keep the large sled?[6] Tell Fitz I hope he will study his lessons. The day I was in the school room I watched him & I noticed when the boys of his class were all studying their lessons, he held his book in his hand but let his eyes wander all over the room. I guess that the little organ on yours & Fitz heads called concentrativeness,[7] is too small. Now you ask Mr Weld to find that spot on your head & when you sit down to study give that spot a sound rubbing & keep scratching it, tell Fitz to do the same & I dare say you will improve in fixing your mind on your lessons. There Neil I have written four pages to you & Henry. What about the monkey talk?[8] Love to all. I hope little Joe has got well by this time. Have you & Kit been sick at all. Grandmama sends love to you. Do you need any more stockings. good night your

≈ *Mother*

≈ ALS, ECS Papers, DLC.

1. ECS closed up the house at Seneca Falls for much of the winter of 1851 and 1852, taking Gat and Theo with her on a series of visits, while Henry joined Neil at the Welds' school. In November she visited her sisters in New York City and her sons in New Jersey. Early in December she moved to her father's new house in Johnstown and stayed until late February. Henry Stanton was in Albany for most of this time. (ECS to D. C. Stanton, 14 October 1851, ECS to Editor, *Lily*, December 1851, and ECS to D. C. Stanton and H. B. Stanton, Jr., 20 December 1851, 1 January 1852, all in *Film*, 7:116, 128, 135–39, 144; Daniel Cady to Gerrit Smith, 15 September 1851, Smith Papers, NSyU; H. B. Stanton to D. C. Stanton and H. B. Stanton, Jr., 22 February 1852, ECS Papers, DLC.)

2. That is, Charles and Elizabeth Smith Miller, their son Charles Dudley, born in 1847, Catharine Cady Wilkeson, and her son Bayard. The younger Wilkeson boys were Samuel, Jr., born c. 1846, and Frank, born in 1848.

3. Amelia Willard (c. 1835–c. 1920) was, in the words of Gerrit Stanton, she "to whom the women of this country are in a measure indebted for the franchise." A young Quaker woman, she worked for Margaret and George Pryor before coming to the Stantons at age sixteen. Though the family regarded her as a part of their household from 1851 onward, Willard often went her own way. She was in Michigan at this time, but rejoined ECS at Johnstown in January. When in residence as the housekeeper, she supervised the servants inside and out. "She was," Gat Stanton wrote, "not only the overseer of the inside help, but the garden help had to suit her as well." There are suggestions that she shared the family's interest in reform. When Elizabeth Miller introduced the short dress to Seneca Falls, Willard copied her model and wore it for work at home and in town. Years later, according to Gerrit Stanton, she contributed a sizeable sum from her savings to underwrite publication of the *History of Woman Suffrage*. She died in Ypsilanti, Michigan, at age ninety-six. (*History*, 3:477n; *Eighty Years*, 203–5; G. Smith Stanton, "How Aged Housekeeper Gave Her All To Cause Of Woman Suffrage," unidentified and undated clipping, Seneca Falls Historical Society.)

4. ECS and her sisters had also studied with Miss Yost, "the good spinster,

Maria Yost, who patiently taught three generations of children the rudiments of the English language." She "was plump and rosy," ECS recalled, "with fair hair, and had a merry twinkle in her blue eyes, and she took us by very easy stages through the old-fashioned schoolbooks." (*Eighty Years*, 9.)

5. Henry Wadsworth Longfellow (1807–1882) wrote the poems "Excelsior" and "The Slave's Dream." "The Blind Harper" has not been identified.

6. That is, Fitzhugh Birney.

7. This "bump" on the head, identified by phrenologists, was not uniformly listed among the faculties of the brain, but its meaning and utility are clear. (Madeleine B. Stern, *Heads & Headlines: The Phrenological Fowlers* [Norman, Okla., 1971] 187.)

8. This unexplained activity was referred to again in a later letter to the boys. She asked, "How does the monkey talk come on? Did Henry ever get punished for talking like that long tailed animal?" (ECS to D. C. Stanton and H. B. Stanton, Jr., 20 December 1851, *Film*, 7:135–39.)

·⟨━━━━✕━━━━⟩·

52　⟫　ECS to Women's Temperance Meeting, Albany[1]

[*before 28 January 1852*]

Dear Friends

Though I cannot attend the coming convention   I take pleasure in sending a letter expressing the deep interest I feel in the question of temperance. I hail every movement on the part of woman that shows a determination to remedy the evils she has so long supinely endured There are two lines of action for the true reformer to pursue at the same time. One is to mitigate as far as possible existing evils; the other & far higher duty is to prevent their recurrence, by removing if possible their cause   The one is superficial & fragmentary   the other reaches down to the fundamental principles of society   For our present surface work I would suggest two points for your consideration

1st   That woman exercise her right to the elective franchise   Inasmuch as Intemperance is in part protected by law, we who are the innocent victims of the license system,[2] should [*have*] a voice in pulling it down

2nd   It is our duty to create a higher public sentiment in regard to the marriage obligations of drunkards wives. We must raise a new

standard of virtue heroism, & true womanhood   Hitherto it has been
declared the duty of woman, to love, honor, & obey her husband, no
matter what his transformation might be from the lover to the tyrant,
from the refined man, to the coarse licentious inebriate, or silly simper-
ing fool.

Loud & long have been the praises bestowed on those wives who
have faithfully loved & lived on in filth poverty & rags, the wretched
companions of a drunkard's sorrows; & the more wretched mother of
his ill starred children. It is pitiful to see how many excellent women
are dragging ⁺out↓ a weary existence in such relations; from mistaken
ideas of duty; from a false sense of religious obligation.

Think you God ever joined together, virtue & vice, beauty & deformity, a being with ⁺of↓ pure & heavenly aspirations, with one enslaved
by his animal appetites? It is love & sympathy that ⁺constitutes and↓
sanctifies true marriage; & she who consents to live in the relation of
wife with any man, whom she has ceased to love & respect, sacrifices
all claim to virtue & nobility   Such companionship call it what you
may is nothing more or less than legalized prostitution. Let us encourage   yea urge those stricken ones who are kept suffering in such
degrading bondage, held there by crude notions of Gods laws & the
tyranny of a false public sentiment, to sunder all such holy ties, to save
themselves from such demoralizing influences, & to escape the guilt of
stamping on the brow of innocence the low carnal nature of the confirmed
drunkard

What is the cause of drunkenness gullot intemperance, licentiousness & gluttony?—for all these are but different manifestations of the
same internal malady. Is it not the preponderance of the appetites over
the reason? And so long as by excessive self indulgence, we cultivate
the already overgrown animal nature, we may look for the continuance
of all these vices in our children. If we would begin a lasting work, if we
would take onward steps that need never be retraced we must give up
our idle luxurious habits & begin a life of self denial & activity. Let us
but cultivate the nobler elements of our being, our moral & intellectual
faculties with one half the assiduity that we have the mere animal
appetites, & we should soon see a change not only in our homes our
nurseries, but in the world at large. "An ounce of prevention is better
than a pound of cure"3

For all these drunkards gluttons & criminals, that meet the eye on all sides, mothers are responsible. Let woman live simply, occupy her mind & hands with worthy employments   subjects of practical utility & lofty speculation, with an ambition to develope all her own powers, & to make the race better & happier, nobly & independently living out her highest ideas of right regardless of the world's dread frown

Such a mother will of necessity stamp virtue & nobility on the brow of her child, inspire him with a love of the grand & the beautiful   the good & the true, ever present safeguards against the vices & temptations, that ~~surround~~ ↑beset↓ him in the outside world. With my best wishes for the success of the convention   Yours sincerely

              ❧ *Elizabeth Cady Stanton*

❧ ALS, ECS Papers, DLC; in *Film* at 28 January 1852. Headed by ECS "Mrs Stanton's letter to the Temperance Convention at Albany, Jan 28th," with year added in SBA's hand. SBA pasted the manuscript into a scrapbook and noted "Read by Susan B. Anthony—at the meeting held in the session room of the Hudson Street Presbyterian Church—where the dozzen women & Rev Samuel J. May & David Wright of Auburn & Lydia Mott of Albany [*illegible*] most valiantly—S. B. A." Revised text in *Lily*, March 1852, *Film*, 7:146-51.

1. At Albany's First Presbyterian Church on 28 January 1852, Mary C. Vaughan presided, and SBA shared secretarial duties with Lydia Folger Fowler. The *History of Woman Suffrage* describes this as a meeting called after women were denied a right to speak at the men's meeting, but contemporary evidence makes clear it was planned and announced in advance. Letters were received from Clarina Nichols of Vermont, Amelia Bloomer, and ECS. SBA read ECS's letter. At the end of the meeting, SBA, H. Attilia Albro, and Mary Vaughan were named to a central committee "to correspond with Temperance Women in different cities and villages of the State, to invite them to co-operate and combine their energies in this great Temperance Cause." (*Albany Evening Journal*, 30 January 1852, *Film*, 7:145; *Lily*, February 1852; Bloomer, *Amelia Bloomer*, 37; *History*, 1:476.)

2. That is, the licenses issued by state and local governments to control but also to legalize the liquor traffic.

3. An old adage traced to Benjamin Franklin's essay, "On Protection of Towns from Fire," published in 1735.

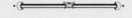

53   ECS TO SBA

Seneca Falls March 1st [1852][1]

Miss Susan B Anthony   Dear friend,

I do not know that the world is quite willing or ready to discuss the question of marriage. I feel in my innermost that the thoughts I sent your convention are true. It is in vain to look for the elevation of woman, so long as she is degraded in marriage. I say it is a sin, an outrage on our holiest feelings to pretend that anything but deep, fervent love & sympathy constitutes marriage. The right idea of marriage is at the foundation of all reforms. How strange it is, man will apply all the improvements in the arts & sciences to everything about him animate & inanimate, but himself. A child conceived in the midst of hate, sin, & discord, nurtured in abuse & injustice cannot do much to bless the world or himself. If we properly understand the science of life—it would be far easier to give to the world, harmonious beautiful, noble, virtuous children, than it is to bring grown up discord into harmony with the great divine soul of all. I ask for no laws on marriage I say with Father Chipman,[2] remove law & a false public sentiment & woman will no more live as wife with a cruel, beastly, drunkard, than a servant, in this free country will stay with a pettish, unjust mistress. If law makers insist upon exercising their perogative in <u>some</u> way on this question, let them forbid any woman to marry until she is twenty one. Let them fine a woman fifty dollars for every child she conceive by a Drunkard. Women have no right to saddle the state with idiots to ↑be↓ supported by the public. Only look at the statistics of the idiot asylums, nearly all the offspring of Drunkards.[3] Woman must be made to feel that the transmitting of immortal life is a most solemn responsible act & never should ↑be↓ allowed, except when the parents are in the highest condition of mind & body. Man in his lust has regulated this whole question of sexual intercourse long enough; let the mother of mankind whose perogative it is to set bounds to his indulgence, rouse up & give this whole question a thorough, fearless examination. I am glad Father Chipman said what he did of my letter,—it will call attention to that subject—& if by martyrdom I can advance my race one step I am ready for it. I feel this whole question of woman's rights turns on the pivot of the marriage relation, & sooner or later it will be the question for discussion. I would not hurry it on neither would I avoid it.—

I was much pleased with Mrs Fowler[4] but her framed-waist lined with whale-bones was a sad commentary on her lectures. The present artificial form of woman is an offense to my eyes— What a startling fact! the testimony of every surgeon I have ever asked—that no perfect woman can be found for anatomical purposes—the false ribs are always compressed in the female skeleton, some more, some less, & many actually lapped! As a consequence every vital organ displaced some-what Think of it,—talk of it,—& breath freely yourself,—good night yours truly

⤙ *E. C. Stanton*

I wish you would send my letter & Father Chipmans commentary to Mrs Swisshelm & ask to comment[5]

⤙ ALS, ECS Papers, DLC.

1. An archivist marked this manuscript "[1853]," and the date stuck; in *Film*, it appears at that date. But the events—"your convention," Samuel Chipman's response, and Lydia Fowler's visit to Seneca Falls—and the formal salutation place it in 1852. This is the earliest letter between ECS and SBA to be located.

2. Samuel Chipman (1786-?) was a professional "temperance" man, editor of the *Temperance Journal* published at Rochester, and author of an influential study about the "effects of intoxicating drinks in producing taxes, pauperism and crime," commissioned by the New York State Temperance Society. Later in 1852, he endorsed the call for women to organize a society, but he criticized the Albany meeting as a woman's rights gathering. (Krout, *Origins of Prohibition*, 234–35; Tyrrell, *Sobering Up*, 276.)

3. See note at April 1850, above.

4. Lydia Folger Fowler (1822-1879) delivered two lectures in Seneca Falls in February 1852. She was a physician and health reformer who, in 1844, married the leading phrenologist, Lorenzo Niles Fowler, and became a part of the family firm, Fowlers and Wells. After several years of lecturing and writing about physiology for women and children, she enrolled in Central Medical College at Syracuse in 1849 and earned her degree in 1850, the second woman in the country to do so, after Elizabeth Blackwell. She became active in the temperance and woman's rights movements, while she built a medical practice in New York City. In 1863 she and her husband moved to England. (*Lily*, March 1852; *NAW*.)

5. No extant issue of the *Saturday Visiter* mentions ECS's letter or Chipman's response. In fact, Jane Swisshelm criticized the Albany meeting and plans for a state society on grounds that women would divide the ranks of Maine law supporters by raising the extraneous matter of woman's rights. (*Pittsburgh Saturday Visiter*, 20 March 1852.)

·⸝⸝⸝⸝⸝·

54 ⮚ SBA TO THE EDITOR, *LILY*

Batavia,[1] May 25, 1852.

Dear Mrs. Bloomer: Your readers will doubtless expect to hear that the Women's New York State Temperance Society has adopted some efficient means for the revolutionizing of public sentiment on the great question of the Liquor traffic. Allow me to inform them that that Society proposes to accomplish its work through the "Foolishness of Preaching"[2] and has already *two* Lecturing agents in the field, and intends as soon as practicable to largely increase the number, so that previous to the time of the next election of Town and State officers, they may thoroughly canvass our state and rouse the women of every City, Village and School district to active efforts for the suppression of the Liquor traffic. It is said that woman's influence over man is all powerful; then let us exert it for the enactment of the "Maine Liquor Law."

Miss Clark addressed the people of Batavia last evening, in a most earnest and truthful manner; and was listened to with marked attention. After the address the Secretary of the Society stated its objects and the means by which it is proposed to effect them, and called upon the friends present to co-operate with the Women's New York State Temperance Society.[3] Several constituted themselves members, and large numbers will, without doubt, join and form an auxiliary society, which shall have for its object the purchase of Temperance newspapers, tracts, &c., for gratuitous distribution among those classes of persons who most need temperance light and truth, and are least likely to furnish themselves with it. I would like to give your readers the plan recommended for auxiliary societies, but it is now nearly mail time so I must bid them wait one month longer when we hope to be able to show them that we are at work in earnest, and in a manner that shall cause the downfall of the Liquor Traffic.

⤞　*S. B. Anthony.*

⤞ *Lily*, June 1852.

1. SBA was on the road as an agent of the Women's New York State Temperance Society. The committee named at the January meeting in Albany called a convention in Rochester for 20–21 April. Five hundred women attended the opening session, and the audience swelled to one thousand when men were admitted. After addresses by ECS, Amelia Bloomer, and Mary Vaughan and several hours of debate dominated by the men, the convention voted to form this new temperance society and elected ECS its president. An executive committee appointed SBA an agent on 23 May, and she joined agent Emily Clark at Batavia, west of Rochester. Emily Clark is identified only through her work for the society. She was single, and the press described her as of LeRoy, in Genesee County. She was elected an officer at the founding meeting in April 1852, and on 21 January 1853, when the year's petitions for the Maine law were presented, she addressed the New York State Assembly in the capitol. She won reelection to office at the society's annual meeting in 1853. (*Film*, 7:217.)

2. 1 Cor. 1:21.

3. SBA herself. See manuscript that fits this description, marked "Delivered for the First, at Batavia—N.Y. in company with Emily Clark," in *Film*, 7:221–33.

55　⤞　ECS TO SBA

[*Seneca Falls*] Sunday evening, [*after 25 May 1852*][1]

Dear Susan,

I will gladly do all in my power to aid you. Work down this way, then you come & stay with me, & Miss Clarke with Mrs Bloomer & I will assist you in getting up such a lecture as you desire. We will get up a meeting here & do what we can to advance the interests of the society. I think that you & Mrs Hallowell[2] & I have as good a right to infuse what we choose of the radical principle into the proceedings of the society, as the miserable time serving conservatives have to infuse their principles of policy & expediency. I think that address of Mrs V. is altogether too small,[3] too mamdy pamdy[4] to go forth from any society claiming the view we as a society do. Let the thing drop. I will address the women of the state as an individual, in due time, but this is between us. I am not astonished at what you write me of Mrs Gould.[5] The church is the great engine of oppression in our day, & you will always find church members truckling & politic. If my address would serve you as a kind of skeleton for a lecture I will send it to you & you can fill out the heads, more fully.[6] I am hoping to hear a good account of Miss Clarke, I have no doubt a little practice will make you an admirable lecturer. I will go to work at once & write you the best lecture I can. Dress loose, take a great deal of exercise & be particular about your diet, & sleep enough, the body has great effect upon the mind. In your meetings if attacked be good-natured & cool, for if you are simple & truth loving no sophistry can confound you.

Try & get subscribers for the Lily wherever you go, & make Mrs B. pay you something for your trouble. I will talk to her about you ⌐as⌐ an agent for the Lily, she needs an agent & you see you could easily attend to that in your meetings. I have a book just adapted to your wants a prize essay on Temperance going over the whole ground, which I will send you if you tell me where, or keep it until you come. I send you the report of the Temperance anniversary, read it closely & you will see that many are already prepared to carry this question into the churches. You will see in Clarke of Boston & Brainard of Philadelphia, the idea hinted at.[7] Shall our society lead or follow public sentiment,—I say lead. Have [*sideways in margin*] you read Emerson's speech to Kossuth?— read it & note what h[e] says of majorities.—[8] good night

❧   *E.*

❧ ALS, Papers of ECS, NPV. Letter in brackets torn from margin. Paragraphs rearranged and combined with others to create text dated 2 April 1852, *Film*, 7:189.

1. Written after SBA became an agent of the temperance society, this letter no doubt responds to a description of her tour and falls after May 25. In *Film*, it appears after May 23.

2. Mary H. Post Hallowell (1823–1913) served on the executive committee of the temperance society. The stepdaughter of Amy Post, Mary married William R. Hallowell (1816–1882), a Quaker businessman from Philadelphia, and they stayed in Rochester. In 1848 she accompanied Post to the Seneca Falls convention, signed the Declaration of Sentiments, and took part in the

Rochester convention as well. Like other members of her family, Mary Hallowell found her abolitionism and her commitment to woman's rights in conflict with the Genesee Yearly Meeting. She and William left the Society of Friends and joined Rochester's Unitarian church. For the rest of their lives, they remained local reformers. (*Quaker Genealogy*, 3:434; William F. Peck, *History of Rochester and Monroe County, New York, From the Earliest Times to the Beginning of 1907* [New York, 1908], 2:1243–44; Hewitt, *Women's Activism and Social Change*, 131, 162, 209, 214; research by Judith Wellman.)

3. ECS refers to the speech Mrs. Mary C. Vaughan of Oswego delivered at the Rochester temperance convention, urging women to use their "*moral power*." Vaughan presided at the meeting of temperance women in Albany in January 1852 and was the first agent appointed by the women's temperance society in May. Though illness forced her to resign in June, she returned to the field in December 1852 and won election as president of the society at its first annual meeting in June 1853. A firm believer in restricting the leadership to women, she defeated ECS for the post. This Mary Vaughan is probably the same woman who became known as a writer, working with Anne McDowell on the *Woman's Advocate*, published in Philadelphia, and coauthoring *Woman's Work in the Civil War* (1867) with Linus P. Brockett. (*Lily*, May 1852, 15 June 1853, *Film*, 7:195ff, 714ff; *NAW*, s.v. "McDowell, Anne.")

4. ECS misspeaks. "Namby pamby," a nickname given to poet Ambrose Phillips (1671–1749), came to mean insubstantial or insipid.

5. Sarah Thomas Seward Gould (?–1875), of Rochester, served on the executive committee of the temperance society. After studying at the Troy Female Seminary, she moved to Rochester in 1834 to open her own school for girls, Seward Seminary. When she married businessman and one-term mayor Jacob Gould in 1842, she left the seminary but retained her interest in education. With Gould's financial support she tried to open a women's college in 1852 and affiliate it with the University of Rochester. (*TroyFS*; Blake McKelvey, *Rochester: The Water-Power City, 1812–1854* [Cambridge, Mass., 1945], 269–71, 345; Blake McKelvey, "Rochester Mayors Before the Civil War," *Rochester History* 26 [January 1964], 4–5.)

6. Probably her opening remarks at Rochester, which included actions that "will tell directly on" the cause. These were: that women separate themselves from drunkards, petition the legislature to gain custody of children, eliminate liquor from their households, agitate and educate, promote temperance in all things, honor labor in order to counter idleness and vice, and divert their donations away from foreign missions to projects meeting the needs of poor neighbors. SBA's address on June 17 shows signs of ECS's outline and examples. (*Lily*, May 1852, also in *History*, 1:481–83; *Carson League*, 24 June 1852, *Film*, 7:269.)

7. At the anniversary of the American Temperance Union, in New York City on 13 May 1852, Rufus W. Clarke decried a clergy who preached against

sins of the past but not against sins of the present. They dared not tell their congregations, "Thou art the man." Thomas Brainerd defended the clergy's role in campaigns for the Maine law. It was their job to direct the people in their moral duties, even at the ballot box. (*Journal of the American Temperance Union*, 1 June 1852.)

8. Ralph Waldo Emerson welcomed the exiled Hungarian leader, Louis Kossuth (1802–1894) to Concord, Massachusetts, on 11 May 1852 and cautioned him about growing popular. Since his arrival in the United States in December 1851, Kossuth's appeal for American support of a Hungarian republic had sparked intense political debate. Advocates of American intervention in Europe took up his cause, but abolitionists, who had championed Kossuth and the Hungarian uprising of 1848 as emblems of universal liberty, turned against him when he vowed to remain neutral about American slavery. In New England Kossuth was concluding his tour to great acclaim on, what Emerson called, "the pilgrimage of American liberty." After acknowledging the controversy that Kossuth had generated, Emerson said: "We are afraid you are growing popular, sir; you may be called to the dangers of prosperity. But hitherto you have had, in all countries and in all parties, only the men of heart. I do not know but you will have the million yet. Then, may your strength be equal to your day! But remember, sir, that everything great and excellent in the world is in minorities." (*Kossuth in New England: A Full Account of the Hungarian Governor's Visit to Massachusetts; With His Speeches, and the Addresses That Were Made to Him, Carefully Revised and Corrected* [Boston, 1852], 222–24.)

·⟨⟞══⟜〓⟝══⟞⟩·

56 ⟳ ARTICLE BY ECS

[June 1852]

JAMES, THE BARBER,

Has just had a room neatly fitted up for ladies,—where he will cut off the hair, and shampoo the head for the small sum of one shilling. It would delight all physiologists and lovers of comfort, to see the heaps of beautiful curls and rich braids that have fallen beneath James' magic touch, from the over heated aching heads of about one dozen of our fair ones. If all the women could know the luxury of short hair, there would soon be a general leave taking of hair-pins, combs, braids and knots.[1]

⟳ E. C. S.

⟞ *Lily*, June 1852.

1. The *Rochester Daily Democrat* wrote of ECS: "Her hair, which is slightly silvered, was cut short, and 'shingled.'" (21 April 1852, *Film*, 7:207.)

---

57 ～ APPEAL BY ECS

[1 July 1852]

TEMPERANCE—WOMAN'S RIGHTS

An Appeal to the Women of the State of New York: By the President of the Women's New York State Temperance Society.

Some of the women of this State met in Convention at Rochester on the 20th of April, 1852, to consult each other as to what Woman might do in the present crisis of the Temperance movement. The subject was fully discussed throughout the greater part of two days, and we then decided to form ourselves into a State Temperance Society, admitting all as members on paying the sum of fifty cents. We thought it unwise to receive men as equals, eligible to any of the offices of our Society, inasmuch as we wished, in starting, to have the funds, lectures and doctrines to be preached under the control and at the suggestions of Woman, and to throw on her the whole responsibility of action.

Man has so much intrigue and worldly wisdom, and the best of them do so continually sacrifice principle to expediency, that we had great fears in taking him as a counsellor on any moral question. We are happy to say that many excellent men came forward on that occasion, gave us their names and fees, and seemed quite willing to be excused from all the labors and honors of our organization.

We already have three agents of our own sex[1] lecturing with great success, and we need more, that every part of this State—every county and town—may be thoroughly canvassed, and fully roused to do its duty at the coming Election.

The Gospel of Temperance with Woman, is not one of compromise. We say, let this question be carried wherever it legitimately belongs. We are tired of the tardy justice and false representation that we have thus far experienced at the hand of Government. Thousands of drunkards' wives, with no hope on earth, are raising their helpless hands to Heaven and pleading for mercy and for bread. Governments have no ears, corporations have no souls, and Man, claiming to be the natural protector of Woman, transformed into a demon by the vile drugs of the rum-seller, becomes her most cruel oppressor and tyrant. To these suffering ones, natural protectors, like estates in Chancery,[2] are unavailable, and the sooner they cease to look to them for comfort and support, and learn to stand alone, relying on their own God given powers for a noble independence and virtue, the better for themselves and the race. It has been left for Woman to preach the doctrine of Divorce—a doctrine which is to strike the most effective blow at the sin of drunkenness. Let man cease to persuade woman by his sophistry and logic, or compel her by his cruel and unnatural statutes, to act in violation of her will and conscience, and let him silently bow before the holy instincts of her nature, when she declared that God never joined together the pure and the vile, the virtuous and the vicious, the holy and the unholy. Such as these could never have been one in *spirit*, and they ought, therefore, never to be one in *flesh*.

We preach too, the doctrine that this question should be carried into the churches and into politics. We say to our Spiritual Fathers and bloated Legislators, sitting up in high places, "Hold! Enough! We want no more emanations from brains befogged with wine and brandy, we ask for no more drugged jurisprudence and theology, for we would now fain try the effect of cold water in ushering in a new dispensation of justice, mercy and peace."

For the promulgation of these doctrines we ask for the aid of true men and women. We ask support for the "Woman's State Temperance Society," in preference to all other organizations, for two reasons: First, because we take the highest moral ground on the Temperance question. Second, because on our platform, man and woman may alike be heard; whereas, in the old State Temperance Society, no woman is allowed to open her mouth—a fact fully demonstrated by the recent disgraceful occurrences in its Annual Meeting at Syracuse.[3]

What say you, after their repeated appeals to Woman, for aid and encouragement—after clearly announcing in their call, that they wished delegates from every Temperance Society in the State, did they refuse our delegates a seat on their platform? A voice in their counsels? Yes! verily. And in so doing, have fully explained to us the nature of their past appeals. They wished us to become members of their Society, by paying into its treasury the sum of One Dollar annually, to do all we could to clothe, feed and get up meetings for their fat agents, scattered through the State to distribute tracts, get up petitions, beg and work in any way and every way to fill their treasury, but always remembering, with due humility, that God never meant to place woman on an even pedestal with man!

I earnestly conjure the women of this State to withdraw from all societies and churches, under the exclusive jurisdiction of Man, where Woman is not allowed to speak or not recognized as an equal in counsel. Waste no more time in petitioning, until we have men with clear heads and sound hearts in our halls of legislation. Let woman never again be guilty of the folly of asking wine and beer-drinkers to put down the liquor traffic.

When we fill our Senate Chambers with men of our own choosing, it will be full time to petition. Nevertheless, let us carry our temperance principles into politics. But, say you, how can we, inasmuch as we have no voice in making the laws, no influence in the creation of a single law-giver, and our right to petition, even, sneered at,[4]—pray what can we do for Temperance in politics? Why, man has no more right to make a State Constitution, excluding us from all share in the government, than we have to get together and make one excluding *him*. Just so soon as all the women of this State say they will vote on the Temperance question, the work is done—for we shall not only be a majority in ourselves, but we shall be sustained by the greatest and best men of the State,—such as Judge Hurlbut,[5] of the Supreme Court, Gerrit Smith, Samuel J. May, &c., &c., and put our opposers into a most contemptible minority. Did Woman but know her power, we should soon see a change on the face of affairs. Our position is every year assuming greater importance. The new property law is going to make a mighty change. We do not see its effects yet, but time will make it manifest. Full half the property of this State, in less than ten years, will be in the hands of Woman. She, from her education, being more prudent, and less given to speculation than man, will be continually extending her possessions. Money is power, and Women will see the necessity then, if not before, of protecting their property by vote. Our colleges, rising up on all sides, thus securing to Woman a thorough education, will soon make intellectual equality a fact—not a point for speculation. Woman's eyes being now open to the necessity of physical development, she will soon add a more vigorous muscle and steady nerve to a more enlightened mind, and she will then have less fear of "mobs," "stygian" pools,[6] "ballot-boxes and caucuses." These will cease to be scarecrows to frighten her from rich harvests and substantial feasts, driving her to live on "airy nothings," 'mid earth and heaven. Let the Women of the Empire State talk no more of *Man's* indifference to the Temperance question, so long as they, having the power to settle it themselves, do from an ignoble indolence and servile reverence for custom, refuse to come forth now, and read the death doom of this monster evil.

⮜ *E. C. Stanton.*

⮜ *Carson League*, 1 July 1852. Also published in *Lily*, July 1852, and *Anti-Slavery Bugle*, 10 July 1852.

1. That is, SBA, H. Attilia Albro, and Emily Clark. Albro (whose name also appears as Atillia) lived in Rochester, where SBA worked with her first in the Genesee Union of the Daughters of Temperance. Apparently a widow, she lived in 1850 with two daughters in the household of S. Hutchinson, a physician in Rochester. In 1851 Albro could boast of four years of activism in the temperance cause. She was named to the central committee in January 1852, charged with calling the meeting at Rochester, and in April she was elected secretary of the Women's New York State Temperance Society. Hired as an agent in June, she worked through the year. At the annual meeting in 1853, Albro opposed changing the society's constitution to allow men to hold office, and she was reelected secretary. Many years later SBA located Albro in Austin, Minnesota, apparently remarried; in her diary SBA recorded her name in 1876 as Albro-Davidson and described her as the sister of Mr. O. S. Hutchinson of Bellefontaine, Ohio. (Federal Census, 1850; *Temperance Journal*, n.d., from SBA scrapbooks, *Lily*, 15 June 1853, and SBA diary, 22 March 1876, all in *Film*, 7:58, 714ff, 18:516ff.)

2. That is, money held in trust.

3. When the State Temperance Society convened in June, conservative clergymen disrupted the meeting to protest a sentence in the annual report that welcomed the Women's New York State Temperance Society. The Reverend Henry Mandeville of Albany explained that "when a woman goes out of her sphere, when she goes miles attended or unattended, to make speeches in Bloomer costume or not, I say she unsexes herself, she is hybrid, and I for one wish to do nothing in approbation of it." By a vote of 61 to 49, the delegates amended the report to remove any mention of women, and by a vote of 63 to 59 reversed the chair's ruling that the constitution allowed women to be delegates to the meeting. The "progressive party," in Amelia Bloomer's phrase, withdrew to a church. With Samuel J. May presiding, SBA and Bloomer spoke, and the large crowd adopted resolutions written by ECS. (*Carson League*, 24 June 1852, and *Lily*, July 1852, in *Film*, 7:263–72.)

4. A reference to the reception given women's petitions in the legislature,

especially by Assemblyman Moses D. Gale, during debates on the Maine law. Amelia Bloomer told the story in April. "After stating—whether truly or not, we have no means of knowing—that the remonstrants against the [Maine] law outnumbered the petitioners, if they excluded the females, he argued that they, our representatives, were not accustomed to listen to the voice of woman in legislating upon great public questions; and that the constitution of the female mind was such as to render woman incapable of correctly deciding upon those questions which he contended were involved in the passage of the proposed bill." (*Lily*, May 1852, *Film*, 7:195–205.)

5. That is, Elisha P. Hurlbut.

6. The hellish image of politics as a stygian pool, used sarcastically by many woman's rights activists in 1852, originated with Horace Mann, who described politics as a "black and sulphurous lake" of "tumultuous and howling waters," emitting both "roar and stench." In a popular lecture that favored better schools for women, Mann prayed: "May God save our wives, our mothers and our daughters, from the uncleanness and the rancorousness, from the savagery and the temptations, of politics; . . ." (Horace Mann, *A Few Thoughts on the Powers and Duties of Woman, Two Lectures* [Syracuse, N.Y., 1853], 97, 103.)

·❨═══❩·

58 ❧ SBA TO THE EDITOR, *CARSON LEAGUE*[1]

Manlius, Sept. 20th, 1852.

Mr. Thomas, During the past week, Mrs. Albro and myself have spoken in the villages of Jordan, Elbridge, Cardiff, Tully, Fabius, Lafayette, Fayetteville and Manlius.[2] The meetings were well attended. Men, women and children, all turn out, curious to see the women lecturers, and hear what they may have to say. In many places the people seem unwilling to commit themselves with regard to the propriety of woman's publicly advocating the Temperance Reform, and that unwillingness is greatly increased where the clergy refuse to give countenance to the movement. The power of the clergy over the minds of the people, particularly the women, is truly alarming. I am every day, more and more made to feel the importance of woman's being educated to "*lean not upon man but upon her own understanding.*"[3] The question now, with the masses of the women, is not whether they may be instrumental in doing good to society by engaging in the temperance work we propose to them, but, will the minister approve of the plan of action. It affords me much pleasure to state, that, in most of the villages we visited last week, the ministers of several of the churches, gave public testimony in favor of the Women's New York State Temperance Society, and heartily recommended to the women to form auxiliary Temperance Societies and set themselves earnestly and energetically about the work of enlightening the masses and causing them to feel that our only hope in the ultimate triumph of the temperance cause lies in the enactment of the Heaven born "Maine Law." This work, (as your readers doubtless are aware,) we propose to the women to accomplish, by means of banding themselves together, raising a fund and expending it in purchasing temperance tracts and news papers, and distributing them gratuitously, throughout their respective villages and towns, also by holding frequent public meetings. I do wish the women of every town and village of the state would form such societies. We want the right sort of a public sentiment: and the most efficient means of obtaining it, is to place the right sort of reading in every family, that the women and children may be informed, and keep up such an incessant talking about voting for temperance men, that their husbands and fathers will be compelled for *peace's sake*, if no other, to cast their votes for honest, humane, total abstinence men.

There seems to be a strong determination on the part of the Presbyterian Clergy, to crush this public movement of woman in the temperance cause. It is very seldom that a Presbyterian Church is opened for our meetings, and more seldom that a Presbyterian Priest attends them. All of which is perfectly consistent with the church dogma of theirs, which says woman must keep silence in the churches.

Our most enthusiastic meetings were those at Fabius. Indeed the woman element seemed to be just what was there needed to rouse the people to action. The Baptist, Methodist disciple[4] and clergymen all said they had preached plain temperance truths to the people, but all to no effect, except that the Baptist clergyman is thereby compelled to seek a new home, where the good cause is better loved. Most certain it is, that if the Minister proclaims other truths than those agreeable to his contributing members, his support will be withdrawn and he be left to go hungry until he may chance to find another situation. The Baptist Church retains among its members a rum-seller, who probably pays as much or more money toward sustaining it than any other member, and since the church does not possess the moral power to excommunicate this vile rum-seller, rum has shown itself quite capable of rendering the position of a temperance clergyman so uncomfortable as to compel him to leave it.

The connexion of the churches with the liquor traffic is truly fearful. We can hardly find one but is in some way connected with it. It is my solemn duty to speak against this monster vice of rum drinking wherever it may be found. The place that is not too holy to give shelter to this abomination, is not too exalted to be attacked by both man and woman. I hope the day not far distant when those professing to be the light of the world shall absolve all connexion with the liquor traffic and all who sanction or sustain it. Yours for Temperance,

✍ *S. B. Anthony.*

✍ *Carson League*, 30 September 1852.

1. John Thomas, of Syracuse, was an ally of Gerrit Smith and an editor. From 1849 to 1851 he edited the *Liberty Party Paper*, and when it merged with the *North Star* to form *Frederick Douglass' Paper*, Thomas was listed as contributing editor. The *Carson League* began weekly publication in June 1851, with Thomas as editor until at least 1854. It was the paper of the Carson League, an association of temperance reformers committed to using the law, the courts, and political action to defeat the liquor traffic. Under Thomas's editorship, the paper reported favorably on a wide range of reforms and encouraged women's activism in the temperance movement. (Douglass, *Papers*, 5:163n; *SEAP*, s.v. "Carson, Thomas L." and "Carson League.")

2. All towns and villages in Ononodaga County, circling Syracuse on the east, south, and west.

3. A revision of Prov. 3:5.

4. This should, no doubt, read "Methodist, Disciples," as the two denominations were unrelated. Known first as the "Campbellite" and later as the "Christian" church, the Disciples sought to restore Christianity to its primitive form.

59 ᭟ REMARKS BY SBA TO WOMEN'S NEW YORK
STATE TEMPERANCE SOCIETY

Editorial note: In the absence of ECS, who expected to deliver her fifth child any day, Attilia Albro presided over the meeting of the Women's New York State Temperance Society in the Wesleyan Chapel at Seneca Falls on 14 October, and Lucy Stone made the principal address. Delegates were present from eleven counties. The resolutions considered in the afternoon session offered neither controversy nor activity. They called upon men to vote their temperance principles, endorsed the Maine law, and approved, retroactively, the executive committee's decision to send delegates to the state temperance convention in June. After a recess, SBA and Lydia Ann Jenkins introduced additional resolutions.

[14 October 1852]

S. B. Anthony offered the following resolutions:

Resolved, That inasmuch as the Church in the present undeveloped state of the race, has the sole direction of the religious element in man, it is clearly its duty to take cognizance of the existing evils of the day, and among others that of intemperance, by banishing from its sacrament the poisonous cup, and denying fellowship to wine-bibbers, Rumsellers and Distillers.

Resolved, That if it be a violation of scripture for man to put asunder those whom God has joined together, it is equally a violation of holy writ for man, by his unjust laws, to hold together those whom God has never joined.

Mrs. Fish, of Victor,[1] read a short address which was well received; after which S. B. Anthony took the stand. She said it required no apology for a woman's appearing before a public audience. Jenny Lind,[2] and other great vocalists, actresses, &c., could appear with bare necks and arms before admiring audiences and be praised for their performances. It is only when woman appears as an advocate for the good of her race that she was pointed at as being out of her sphere, and ridiculed by the other sex, and many of her own. Shall women tamely submit to be the slaves of rum-drinking, rum-voting men? Men have no right to arrogate to themselves all the law-making, and make laws which so grievously curse woman. Woman has no longer a right to remain idly at home and allow her husband, brothers and sons to go down to drunkard's graves. She must refuse to be the bride of the moderate drinker, or to meet Tobacco-smoking, Rum-drinking young men with smiles in the social circle, or to go with them to places of amusement. She must no longer consent to entail upon her offspring the taste for alcoholic drinks. A large portion of the prevalent scrofulous diseases arise from intemperance. Many of the Idiots were the result of the same terrible and pernicious habit.

Many object to the ground that habitual drunkenness should be cause of divorce; that it is contrary to the Bible doctrine on this point. She referred to the present laws for divorce, the imprisoning a man for five years, wilful desertion, &c.,[3] and contended that these are, at least, equally opposed to the Bible. Should a woman be bound to live with a man that daily threatens to murder herself and children, until actual murder was committed? Does it ever occur to you that those who are the greatest sticklers for this Bible doctrine, and lift up their hands in holy horror at the mention of divorce, never mention the wholesale divorce going on south of Mason and Dixon's line?[4] If we are to be so strict on this point let us begin where the evil most exists.

Woman must withdraw from all churches which tolerate rum-drinkers and distillers. We can scarce find a community, where there is not a rum-making deacon or prominent member; and he remains quietly in the church because he has money and contributes to the pay of the minister. In a neighboring town a prominent member of the Methodist church was a distiller notwithstanding the Methodist discipline against it. The church that retains such men, is none of Christ's. The clergyman who does not speak out against it, and who administers the sacrament to such, is worse than the rum-seller himself. Think of a deacon watching the poison flowing from the "worm of the still," singing

> Come thou fount of every blessing,
> Streams of mercy never ceasing &c.

Better, far better take the pure waters of the earth for the communion than to feed a congregation the drugged whiskey that passes for wine.

Woman must carry these temperance principles into politics. If we cannot vote we can influence voters. If man assumes to vote for us, it is time we instruct him how we want voting done.

Mrs. L. A. Jenkins,[5] of Waterloo, offered the following resolution:

Inasmuch as the right to petition is the safeguard of the rights of the people, and as our petitions as women of the State of New York have been cast aside, and our right as memorialists been called in question, therefore

Resolved, That we will go by the hundreds, if not by the thousands, at the coming of our next legislature, and present a petition for the Maine Law, at our own hands.

Mrs. Jenkins ably sustained the resolution, and it was adopted.

The question on Miss Anthony's resolutions was then called for. The first was adopted without discussion. The second elicited a spirited discussion. Miss Anthony's well known position relative to the propriety of drunkenness being made a ground for legal divorce, was opposed by Mary C. Vaughan, who said that though agreeing with her friend that no woman should consent to remain in the relation of wife with the confirmed drunkard, nor to stamp upon the minds of her children the impress of the drunkard's beastly nature, or to rear them to an inheritance of his fatal appetite, yet the case called only for separation, not for divorce. The laws should be so modified that all property of the family, and her children, should belong to the wife, then she might if she chose, and could, care for the inebriate husband. Or if his example and conduct were too gross to be endured, she might have the power of ridding herself entirely of his presence. But there was always hope of his reform, and a home and a heart should be ready for him if he should ever regain the dignity of his manhood.

S. B. Anthony said that true marriage was a union of soul, of spirit, not a legalized form of words binding man and woman together. God never joined virtue and vice; the contract was no longer binding when one party became morally corrupt. The scripture said "Be ye not unequally yoked together." "Ye cannot serve both God and Mammon."[6] The drunkard's wife must serve him, she is his, the victim of his depraved passions and imbruted nature.

Mrs. Vaughan replied that we could not decide whom God had joined. There might have been at the period of marriage the true union of soul spoken of, which she agreed only sanctified the marriage relation. That true union though lost when the man became the victim of drunkenness, might be remembered if he reformed. The wife had no right to cast him off altogether for this vice alone. The scripture, the words of Christ admit of but one cause for divorce:[7] a separation from any other cause will admit of no second marriage.

<D. C. Bloomer, of Seneca Falls, sustained the arguments of Mrs. Vaughan. There was a wide difference between separation and divorce, the former only was admissible on account of drunkenness on scriptural grounds.>

Mrs. Gildersleeve, of Clyde, sustained the position of Miss Anthony, but was not heard with distinctness, and her argument could not be reported.

The vote on the resolution was called for, and it was adopted by a small majority.

A motion was made to appoint a committee to prepare a draft for a petition to the Legislature for the Maine Law, and to arrange a plan of action for the women of the State. Carried, and Amelia Bloomer, of Seneca Falls, Mary C. Vaughan, of Oswego, and Hannah S. Shute, of Fairport[8] appointed that Committee.

The Convention then adjourned *sine die*.

ᴈ *Lily*, November 1852; *Carson League*, 28 October 1852. Also reported in *Frederick Douglass' Paper*, 29 October 1852, *Film*, 7:442.

1. Angelina Fish (c. 1811–?) lived in Victor, Ontario County, with her husband Daniel Fish, a school teacher, and three children. She was named a vice president pro tem at this meeting, and she was placed on the executive committee of the society in 1853. (Federal Census, 1850.)

2. Jenny Lind (1822–1887), the Swedish nightingale, arrived in the United States in September 1850 for an extended singing tour. Five thousand people heard her premier concert in New York, and comparable crowds heard her in all the major cities.

3. SBA refers to conditions sufficient for limited divorce, or legal separation.

4. Known as the dividing line between slavery and free soil, the Mason and Dixon Line ran north of Delaware, Maryland, and Virginia.

5. Lydia Ann Moulton Jenkins (1824?–1874) was active in the Waterloo Congregational Friends with her husband Edmund S. Jenkins, and attended the woman's rights convention at Syracuse. She became a skillful lecturer on woman's rights. In 1853, wearing the "Bloomer costume," she addressed the national convention in Cleveland, and SBA counted her among the useful team of speakers in New York State. Jenkins was ordained by the Ontario Association of Universalists in Geneva, New York, and shared a ministry with her husband in Clinton. From 1866 until her death she and her husband conducted the Hygienic Institution, a water-cure, in Binghamton, New York. (David Robinson, *The Unitarians and the Universalists* [Westport, Conn., 1985], 282–83; Harry B. Weiss and Howard R. Kemble, *The Great American Water-Cure Craze: A History of Hydropathy in the United States* [Trenton, N.J., 1967], 168; *History*, 1:145.)

6. 2 Cor. 6:14 and Luke 16:13.

7. That is, adultery.

8. Hannah S. Shute, of Fairport, Monroe County, was named a vice president pro tem at this meeting, and she attended the Whole World's Temperance Convention in September 1853.

·(⟶※⟶)·

60   ❧   ECS TO LUCRETIA COFFIN MOTT

Seneca Falls Oct 22nd '52

Dear Lucretia

I am at length the happy mother of a daughter.[1] Rejoice with me all Womankind, for lo! a champion of thy cause is born. I have dedicated her to this work from the beginning. I never felt such sacredness in carrying a child as I have this one, feeling all the time strongly impressed with the belief that I was cherishing the embryo of a mighty female martyr— Glorious hope! may she wear the crown of martyrdom bravely & patiently, and leave her impress on the world for goodness & truth. She is the largest and most vigorous looking child I have ever had, weighing 12 lbs. with her clothes, and yet my labor was short & easy: I laid on a lounge about 15 minutes, and alone with my nurse & one female friend, brought forth this noble girl. I sat up immediately, changed my own clothes, put on a wet bandage, & after a few hours repose sat up again. When the child was 20 hours old I took a sponge bath, a sitz bath,[2] put on a wet bandage, and then walked out on the piazza, and the day being fine I took a drive on the plank road of three miles. Today, the third day, I am dressed and about the house as usual. All things are right with me & the baby thus far. Am I not a savage almost, for what refined, delicate, genteel, civilized woman wd. get well in so indecently short a time?[3] Dear me! How much cruel bondage of mind, and suffering of body, poor woman will escape when she takes the liberty of being her own physician of both soul & body.

I have been wishing to write to you ever since the Convention, to say how pleased I was with the whole proceedings, even to the death & resurrection of Brigham & the utter annihilation of the Rev. Hatch.[4] As to the Presidency it is a matter of rejoicing, & argues a great advance in our movement, that we now have competitors for that office, when, at our first convention no woman could be found with the moral hardihood to take that post of honor. The papers say, & I have no doubt they are right that you presided with great dignity—thank you in the name of woman.[5] My whole soul rejoices in every thing that is well done by Woman. I was greatly pleased that a Bloomer should have been the pet of the Convention.[6] Depend upon it Lucretia, that woman can never be developed in her present <u>drapery</u>, she is a slave to her <u>rags</u>—but I cannot prove that to you now. I must write about my daughter to a dozen other friends, so adieu for the present.

If Sallie Holly[7] is in Phil[a] give my love to her & tell her of my bliss— Adieu, Yr. frd. as ever

⇜   *E. C. Stanton*

I shall send this thro Martha Wright that she may read the news.[8]

⇜ Copy in hand of Martha C. Wright, in collection of Rhoda Barney Jenkins, Greenwich, Conn. On verso is ECS to Margaret Stanton Lawrence, 1882?, explaining that the Wright family had returned the copy and suggesting that Margaret paste it in her scrapbook. A variant is in *Stanton*, 2:44–45.

1. Margaret Livingston Stanton was born at Seneca Falls on 20 October 1852.

2. A further recommendation of water-cure practitioners, a sitz (or sitting) bath called for submerging the lower portion of the trunk into water.

3. In the literature of women's physiological reform, the comparison between "civilized" and "savage" women was common. Civilized women suffered more because their luxuries and fashions increased disease. "God has made of one blood all the people who dwell on the face of the earth," Mary Gove Nichols argued. But the slaves, Indians, and common Irish "have little suffering in child-bearing." "The Indian woman bears her babe, washes herself and her infant in the next running stream, and the travelling party to which she belongs seldom waits more than half a day for her." (Nichols, *Experience in Water-Cure*, 74.)

4. ECS refers to incidents at the woman's rights convention in Syracuse. J. R. Brigham, described as a school teacher, warned that women should keep to their domestic, superior sphere lest they become masculine. Lucretia Mott responded, and in the words of the *Standard*, "Mrs. M. settled the case for him most decidedly. The audience thought him used up, but he did not think so himself." He was back in the evening to argue his point again. The Reverend Junius Hatch caused considerably more disruption, when he asked if the convention recognized the authority of the Bible and ignored Lucretia Mott's answer, that the question was not before the meeting. Later, he returned to his theme when Lucy Stone showed insufficient respect for the Bible. Reports of the convention described him as "Mr. Hatch," "a vagrant priest, from Massachusetts," "Rev. Mr. Hatch, Congregational Minister," and "the Rev. Junius L. Hatch of Massachusetts." (*NASS*, 16 September 1852, *Film*, 7:424–25.)

5. ECS refers to the candidacy of Elizabeth Oakes Prince Smith for president of the convention. Promoted by Paulina Wright Davis, Smith was rebuffed

in favor of Lucretia Mott. This contest apparently occurred in a private meeting before the convention began; in public, Mott was the sole candidate. The incident was elaborated later, most notably in Ida Harper's unsubstantiated but detailed account of Smith's fashionable and revealing attire to which SBA objected, halting the nomination. Smith (1806–1893) was a popular writer who enjoyed success as well on the lyceum circuit. ECS and Elizabeth Miller were reading her novel *Shadow Land* (1852). After attending the national woman's rights convention in 1851, Smith adopted the cause as her own for a few years and presided over the central committee that conducted business between conventions. Of Mott's performance, one reporter wrote, "we have never known an assembly ruled with more good sense, grace and propriety. She anticipated the effect of every diverging motion and sentiment, and with admirable skill turned them in line of order." (*Anthony*, 1:72; Lucy Stone to Antoinette Brown, 24 November 1852, in Lasser and Merrill, *Friends and Sisters*, 124; *NAW*; ECS to E. S. Miller, 21 November 1852, E. O. Smith to ECS, 17 February, 2 March, 11 June 1852, in *Film*, 7:457–62, 157–60, 167–78, 253–61; *Frederick Douglass' Paper*, 17 September 1852.)

6. A reference to Lucy Stone, who wore the reform costume and, the press reported, "carried her audience above the earth, thrilled their hearts, and made herself their favorite." (*Frederick Douglass' Paper*, 17 September 1852.)

7. Sallie Holley (1818–1893), an abolitionist and woman's rights supporter, graduated from Oberlin in 1851 and lectured for the American Anti-Slavery Society. She visited ECS in the spring of 1852 and attended the women's temperance meeting at Rochester in April. (*NAW*; S. Holley to ECS, 26 May 1852, *Film*, 7:235–37.)

8. Mott sent her copy of this letter to the Weld-Grimké household. (A. G. Weld to ECS, 9 December 1852, *Film*, 7:467.)

·(⸻)·

61 ⪼ ECS TO PAULINA WRIGHT DAVIS

Seneca Falls Dec 6 [*1852*]

Dear Pauline

Many thanks for the beautiful presents which reached us in safety. I would have responded to your recent letters sooner but the truth is I am bound hand & foot with two undeveloped Hibernians in my kitchen a baby in my arms & four boys all revolving round me as a common centre. My eyes turn longingly to "the Association" as a truer mode of life. Woman must ever be sacrificed in the isolated household. It did rejoice me to see your names appended to the Prospectus of the Raritan

Bay Union, for I am resolved to go there.[1] But how I am to reach the goal is the question. I have nothing yet that I can call my own except the house I live in of which I have a deed. This is worth 2000$. Could I go there with my five children by taking so small a share? would my firm health, strength my capacity for & love of work be considered as capital? I should be a <u>jewel</u> in an Association for <u>they</u> <u>say</u> I am good natured, generous, & always well & happy. Oh what bliss is yet in store for us. All our talk about womans rights is mere moonshine, so long as we are bound by the present social system. Henry has a horror of all associations of the kind proposed—what shall I do with him?—as he seemed greatly pleased with you when you last met, as well as on the previous occasion when he kept you blushing in the stage coach, I think I shall hand him over to your eloquence. I had a letter a few days since from Mrs Spring which I will answer some time when the wigwam is quiet.[2] What of the paper? You ought to have some business to occupy you all of your time until we get to the Raritan Bay Union.— Mrs E. O. S.[3] has yet to learn the first great lesson of the true reform— to stand alone patiently & cheerfully & endure with an undisturbed spirit the jibs & jeers of the gaping crowd— "Let the weal & the woe of Humanity be everything to us, but their praise & their blame of no account."[4] The truly noble soul is not puffed up with praise or cast down by ridicule. But Dear E. O. S. will learn it all step by step—as prop after prop is swept away one learns self reliance.— My baby has no name yet, what does Pauline signify?— What do you think of Edith? Good night—Your friend

❧ E.

❧ Copy in unknown hand, Raritan Bay Union, Manuscript Group 285, NjHi; Rebecca Spring added, "This letter from Elizabeth Staunton I thought would interest you very much. She is a noble woman. Such a family would be worth a great deal. I hope to have a letter from her. I am glad I wrote."

1. ECS refers to the ideas popularized by Albert Brisbane and Horace Greeley for "associations" or utopian communities whose residents shared ownership and work. The Raritan Bay Union, at Eagleswood, near Perth Amboy, New Jersey, scheduled to take residents in 1853, was organized as a joint-stock company, with common facilities for eating and education, but private quarters for families. (Robert S. Fogarty, *Dictionary of American Communal and Utopian History* [Westport, Conn., 1980], 108-9, 158-59; Maud Honeyman Greene, "Raritan Bay Union, Eagleswood, New Jersey," *Proceedings of the New Jersey Historical Society* 68 [January 1950]: 1-20.)

2. Rebecca Buffum Spring (1811–1911) founded the Raritan Bay Union with her husband Marcus Spring (1810–1874), after many years of affiliation with other communal experiments. Quakers, philanthropists, and abolitionists, the Springs lived at Eagleswood until Marcus Spring's death. Rebecca Spring moved to California in 1874. (Women's Project of New Jersey, *Past and Promise: Lives of New Jersey Women* [Metuchen, N.J., 1990], 84–86.)

3. That is, Elizabeth Oakes Smith. Paulina Davis thought women needed their own, woman's rights newspaper, and she encouraged Smith to start one in Brooklyn, to be called *Egeria*. At the Syracuse convention in September 1852 Davis and Smith sought subscribers, saying they had raised half the funds needed to begin. Smith, it seems, lost interest, and it fell to Davis to begin the *Una*, published monthly at Providence from February 1853. Davis moved the paper to Boston at the end of 1854, and Caroline Dall shared editorial duties until the paper folded after the issue dated October 1855. (P. W. Davis to ECS, 9 February 1852, E. O. Smith to ECS, 17 February, 2 March 1852, and *Proceedings of the Woman's Rights Convention, Held at Syracuse, September 8th, 9th & 10th, 1852* [Syracuse, 1852], all in *Film*, 7:154–56, 157–60, 167–78, 322ff.)

4. A motto of Hugues Félicité Robert de Lamennais.

62 ❧ LUCY STONE TO SBA

West Brookfield [*Mass.*] Jan. [*1*] 1853[1]

Dear Susan

Since I wrote you at Seneca Falls, I have recieved your other letters— You say there is not a <u>woman</u> in all the state who can <u>speak</u>, at the meeting at Albany—[2]

You forget Antoinette Brown.[3] I think you would do well to have her, as she is a state's woman. She is now at Henrietta; It <u>is</u> important that some <u>speaking</u> woman, should be there, and if Antoinette <u>cant</u> go, I will try to do so, and make a speech either afternoon, or evening, of Friday the 21— But it will be vastly better for your <u>cause</u>, to have a woman from your own state—

I cant, in conscience speak in favor of the Maine Law— It does not seem to me, to be based on a sound philosophy. A law will not amount to much, so long as there is not a temperance public sentiment— Such a sentiment would be stronger than law, written on parchment—

My speech would have to go <u>behind</u> laws to the people's hearts

I hope you can get Antoinette, and then, I shall not be needed— But if not, and if you still think it best for me to go, I will. (Deo volente)[4]

Drop me a line at <u>West</u> Brookfield ↑Mass.↓— I think <u>you</u>, and not Mrs. Albro, should go before the Legislators— Yours Sincerely

⪼ *Lucy Stone*

⪼ ALS, Blackwell Papers, DLC.

1. Endorsed "Jan 3/53" by SBA, an indication that by "7" Stone meant "1." Stone's family lived in West Brookfield.

2. Called for 21 January 1853, this mass meeting would deliver temperance petitions to the legislature.

3. Antoinette Louisa Brown (1825–1921), later Blackwell, lived in Henrietta with her parents. A close friend of Lucy Stone, she graduated from Oberlin College in 1847 and stayed to complete its theological course in 1850. SBA met her in Rochester in 1852. Brown became the minister to South Butler's Congregational Church in the spring of 1853 and was ordained in August. Though recognized as the first woman to be ordained, Brown left her church after one year and became a freelance lecturer, writer, and preacher. She married Samuel Charles Blackwell in January 1856. (*NAW*; Elizabeth Cazden, *Antoinette Brown Blackwell: A Biography* [Old Westbury, N.Y., 1983]; Lasser and Merrill, *Friends and Sisters*.)

4. God willing.

·◖═══◗·

63 ⪼ SBA TO LUCY STONE

Albany Jan. 24, 1853

My Dear Lucy

I hope you are better, yes quite well. We were indeed very sorry that you could not be at our temperance Convention. The meetings passed off well considering the material we had, Samuel J. May, Lucy Stone & C. I. H. Nichols[1] <u>all</u> were <u>absent</u>, Antoinette L. Brown was our <u>stay</u>. Miss Clark, Bloomer Vaughan & Albro, were the speakers, no <u>man</u> of any celebrity indentified himself with us. I made no speech, was the Financier took by means of collections & memberships $90. Antoinettes address in the Capitol was a grand one, the friends felt that she <u>outdid</u> herself even. If we could only have had Lucy's speech in the Church Friday evening.[2] Your letters to L. Mott[3] & self did not come until the A.M. of the 22[d]   We <u>hoped</u> until the last moment. I enclose Mrs.

Stanton's Appeal, the paragraph on <u>Divorce</u>[4] is calling down the condemnation of our <u>pious presses</u>, Political papers, ↑who have↓ nothing to say against divorcing such as Cassey & Archy—Uncle Tom & Aunt Chloe,[5] but <u>horrified</u> at the idea of allowing the wife of a bloated drunkard, to be released.[6] Antoinette & I are going to New York & the intermediate cities next week— A. will tell you what a plan we now have on foot—[7] Yours Truly in haste

❧ *Susan B. Anthony*

❧ ALS, Blackwell Papers, DLC. Antoinette L. Brown to L. Stone on same sheet.

1. Clarina Irene Howard Nichols (1810–1885) was an early advocate of married women's legal rights and a pioneer in journalism. Raised in Vermont, she spent her early married life in Herkimer, New York, where she ran a seminary while raising three children. About 1839 she left her first husband, returned to Vermont, and began to write for the *Windham County Democrat* in Brattleboro. Divorced in 1843, she married George W. Nichols, publisher of the *Democrat*, and bore one more child. She spoke about the need for legal reform at the First National Woman's Rights Convention and became a temperance lecturer. In 1854 she settled in Kansas and was a leader of the territory's woman's rights movement. (*NAW*; "Reminiscences by Clarina I. Howard Nichols," in *History*, 1:171–200; Joseph G. Gambone, ed., "The Forgotten Feminist of Kansas: The Papers of Clarina I. H. Nichols, 1854–1885," *KHQ* 39 [1973]: 12–57, 220–61, 392–444, 515–63.)

2. The women convened at Albany's State Street Baptist Church on 21 January, at the end of a week of temperance meetings in the city. While a crowd at the church considered resolutions, Amelia Bloomer and Emily Clark delivered petitions with 28,000 names to the assembly and spoke briefly. In the evening, Attilia Albro and Bloomer conducted a meeting at the church, and SBA and Antoinette Brown went to the Assembly Chamber. There, "the cloak room, the lobbies and the galleries were at an early hour packed with a solid mass of human beings, and many were outside in the halls, unable to crowd inside the doors" to hear Brown's two-hour address. SBA read ECS's appeal, goading legislators who "hug the delusion" that they represent women, to "at least permit us, from time to time, to tell you of our wants and needs." (*Lily*, 1 February 1853, *Albany Evening Journal*, 21 January 1853, *Carson League*, 27 January 1853, and *New York Daily Tribune*, 24 January 1853, all in *Film*, 7:507–15.)

3. That is, Lydia Mott.

4. It read in part: "Suppose we have the Maine Law to-day—you have then disposed of all intoxicating drinks: but you have, still, the animal natures—the morbid appetites for stimulants and excitement entailed on generation after generation, which will work themselves out in some direction. But, back up

the Maine Law by the more important one on Divorce, and you make a permanent reform, in so regulating your laws on marriage, that the pure and noble of our sex may be sustained by the power of Government in dissolving all union with gross and vicious natures." (*New York Daily Tribune*, 24 January 1853, *Film*, 7:513–14.)

5. A reference to the forced separation of slaves in two novels. Cassy and Archy are the principal characters in *The Slave: or, Memoirs of Archy Moore*, by Richard Hildreth, published in 1838. Uncle Tom and Aunt Chloe appear in *Uncle Tom's Cabin*, by Harriet Beecher Stowe, published in March 1852.

6. In 1852, a select committee of the assembly advocated liberalizing New York's divorce laws but could not agree on a rule about divorce for drunkenness that would not be "liable to wanton abuse." Instead it proposed to increase the court's discretion in granting divorce in "cases of peculiar hardship and inconvenience wherein a divorce is manifestly proper"; its aim was to "embrace every proper case of gross and confirmed habitual drunkenness." This bill and a similar one introduced into the assembly on 26 January 1853 both died. ("Report of the Committee on the Judiciary, on the Subject of Divorce," *New York Assembly Documents*, 2 March 1852, No. 73; *JNYA*, 26 January, 2 March 1852, pp. 127, 390, and 26 January, 1 March 1853, pp. 157, 398.)

7. The plan was Lydia Mott's, to hold a woman's rights convention at Albany. In her addition to this letter, Antoinette Brown also explained her intention "to speak a few times with Miss Anthony on the Maine Law. She is a driving business woman." The time stretched into weeks. Joined on the first leg of their tour by Amelia Bloomer, they held meetings in New York City, worked their way northward through Poughkeepsie, Hudson, and Troy, and headed west to Utica and home. After a short break in mid-March, they lectured in Rochester, Lockport, and Buffalo at the end of the month. (*History*, 1:490–91; Bloomer, *Amelia Bloomer*, 98–113; and *Film*, 7:525–59, 565–67, 573–87.)

---

64 ⇝ SBA TO LUCY STONE

Rochester, May 1, 1853.

Dear Lucy:

I rejoice with you that the New York meetings are over, & I rejoice too that they were so good. If the reports are to be relied on, you made two most convincing speeches.[1]

When it rained so, last Monday night, I was at Syracuse, & had all sorts of sorry feelings lest your meeting would be so small as to disinspirit you; & when Sarah Pellet[2] brought me the Tribune on Tuesday P.M., I read the report most eagerly & joyously, I can assure you. Nettie & I had a meeting in Syracuse Tuesday night, the 26th, one in Utica Wednesday the 27th, both good—Mrs. Bloomer not in company.[3] Nettie & I both said over & over again that we felt as happy that Lucy had done s[uch] a glorious work in Metropolitan Hall, as though we ourselves had been the instruments. I am <u>very</u>, <u>very</u> <u>glad</u> you went to New York. Those speeches were not only spoken to the thousands in the Metropolis, but are carried to the remotest parts of this nation, & will in a few days be wafted across the Atlantic & be read by vast numbers of the inhabitants of the old world. Verily, those lectures have been given to the whole civilized world. I know something of the exhaustion you are now suffering, after such intense excitement, & really hope you may be able to take some quiet rest. Nature demands it at your hands. Lucy, <u>do</u> live a <u>long</u> life. There is a vast deal of work for you to do; therefore be prudent, that you may have strength to accomplish it.

I have a letter from Mrs. Fowler.[4] She says you express some doubts about being at our annual meeting. Mrs. Stanton desires me to say to you that she hopes you will not fail to be here. She wants to write you; but oh dear, Lucy, what can she do with <u>five</u> children & two raw Irish girls— Nettie & I staid all night with her last Thursday night. They got into a discussion on the divorce question. I think the right of divorce can be most clearly proved. Now, Lucy, do come, & if you can manage to stay <u>after</u> our meeting, I will get you up some meetings here that shall be profitable both spiritually & pecuniarily. One thing I want to say is, don't let <u>money</u> hinder you from coming. Trust me that you shall be compensated for your time.

Some of our "Little Fry," as Mrs. Stanton calls them, wish to stave off the divorce question, & we of course are the more anxious to have those present who can discuss it fully & ably. Mr. Channing is with us.[5] I am going to the city to hear him lecture on the Clergy & their influence, this eve.

Tuesday A.M. [*3 May*] I hope you will attend the Anniversary on the 11th inst., & also the meeting of Temperance Delegates on the 12th, & help us Tem. women claim our right to be represented in the World's Temperance Convention.[6] I expect the <u>brothers</u> will feel very much disturbed at <u>our</u> <u>presence</u>. Surely there is no peace for them until woman's equality is fully recognized.

I shall be at the annual meeting in N. York. If you are there, you can learn my whereabouts at the office of Fowler & Wells, 131 Nassau St.[7]

I do wish I could make you feel how important it is that you be at our Temperance Convention June 1.

I saw your friend Mr. Dewey a few days since. He wished me to say to you that they should be happy to have you come on in time to make them a visit before the meeting—but do come, Lucy. I hope to see you "face to face" in New York, then I can explain matters to you.

We intend to place our society on higher ground, admit all on terms of perfect equality.[8]

I leave home tomorrow or next day, & shall stop a few days in Washington Co. previous to going to N.Y. I look to the Antislavery friends to sustain us in a our claim that woman shall be represented at the World's Convention. Were it not for the hope of their presence, I should shrink from going into that meeting. Your Constitutional Convention comes off the 5th inst.[9] I hope your winter's labors may not have been in vain, but that Mass. will take the lead in granting to woman her equality. Yours truly,

⇝ *Susan B. Anthony.*

⇝ Transcript in hand of A. S. Blackwell, Blackwell Papers, DLC. Letters in square brackets were torn at margin.

1. Lucy Stone delivered her lectures, "Woman's Rights" and "The Legal Disabilities of Woman," at Metropolitan Hall on April 25 and 26. (*New York Daily Tribune*, 25, 26, 27 April 1853.)

2. Sarah Pellet (1824–1898) grew up as a neighbor of Lucy Stone and followed her to Oberlin, where she completed her studies in 1851 and earned her degree in 1858. For several years after college she lived in New York and studied theology. She attended the women's temperance meeting at Seneca Falls in 1852, and joined SBA in campaigns for woman's rights, before going to California in the fall of 1854 to lecture for two years. Later she taught school and worked for a time as a reporter. (*Woman's Journal*, 28 May 1898; Lasser and Merrill, *Friends and Sisters*, 26–29, 122, 125, 142.)

3. Brown and SBA held temperance meetings at Utica and Syracuse in late April. There are hints that after weeks of touring together SBA and Bloomer had a falling out. SBA's description of the disagreement is missing, but in response, Stone wrote: "I am sorry that Mrs. Bloomer has treated you so, but it takes everybody 40 years to get out of the wilderness, and we must be patient with those who have much of this pilgrimage yet to make." (L. Stone to SBA, 12 April 1853, and A. L. Brown to SBA, 14 April 1853, *Film*, 7:589, 591–94; Lasser and Merrill, *Friend and Sisters*, 130–31.)

4. Lydia F. Fowler. The Women's New York State Temperance Society's annual meeting was scheduled to begin in Rochester on 1 June.

5. That is, William Henry Channing.

6. The American Anti-Slavery Society met on 11 May during anniversary week, and on the next day delegates from temperance societies met to plan a World's Temperance Convention in September. This meeting, which came to be known as "the Brick Church meeting," broke into a shouting match over the right of women to help with the planning. Supporters of the women withdrew to a nearby water-cure to organize "a World's Convention, which shall be true to its name." (*Lib.*, 27 May 1853, *New York Daily Tribune*, 16 May 1853, and *Lily*, 15 June 1853, all in *Film*, 7:703–9, 714–19.)

7. The business offices of the publishing firm.

8. Advocates of woman's rights criticized the society's requirement that its officers be women. At the woman's rights convention in Syracuse, when SBA called the society "an offspring of this movement," Catharine Stebbins disagreed. A society that "excluded men from becoming officers, or controlling the funds" was "not in accordance with the principles of this Convention." At the society's annual meeting in 1853, ECS called the requirement a temporary expedient, designed to awaken women to their responsibility. It had worked, she told the members; women had "learned how to stand and walk alone." But the majority of members disagreed that it met only a temporary need, defeated an amendment to the society's constitution that would open the leadership to men, and replaced ECS as president. (*Proceedings of Woman's Rights Convention, 1852*, 77–78; Lasser and Merrill, *Friends and Sisters*, 113–19; *Lily*, June 1853.)

9. Stone lectured and circulated petitions for woman's rights in Massachusetts in advance of the constitutional convention that met from 4 May through 1 August 1853. (*History*, 1:247–54.)

·⊂══════⟩⊃·

65 ⤳ ANTOINETTE L. BROWN TO SBA

South Butler Aug 2nd, 53

Susan B. Anthony Very Respected Madam

There! isnt that a truly scientific and exemplary way of commencing a letter!

Mrs. H.[1] said you were in the city Friday expecting me there. I learned that the best way for me to go to Pultneyville was to take the cars to Palmyra, then the stage. In this way did not have to leave Rochester till after 10 Ock.[2] So I had plenty of time in the morning, to reach the city. If I had thought you would really have expected me would have written you about it.

Saw a number of your old friends from various parts of Wayne Co. All asked after you & your present doings; & the result was that I began to feel that you must speak at N.Y. both at the Temperance & Woman's Rights Conventions.[3] Do, for your own sake & your friends, as well as the causes, be as well prepared as you have the ability to be; then after those meetings are over go to lecturing at least for a few months in right good earnest　You ought to do it, & of course ↑its↓ what you are willing to do.

I talked on Temperance Sat. evening at Williamson & Sab. eve at Pultneyville. Thence red eyes & a heavy head to day.

Am just reading Fanny Fern.[4] Like her better & better! Good by. Very obligedly

≪ *Nette*

≪ ALS, Blackwell Papers, MCR-S.

1. Probably Mary Hallowell of Rochester.
2. Towns in Wayne County. Palmyra lies along the Erie Canal and a rail line, and Pultneyville and Williamson are north, near the shore of Lake Ontario.
3. The Whole World's Temperance Convention was scheduled for 1–2 September 1853, and what Lucy Stone called "an independent meeting" for woman's rights was to follow it on 6–7 September.
4. Sara Payson Willis Farrington (1811–1872), later Parton, wrote under the name Fanny Fern. *Fern Leaves from Fanny's Portfolio* (1853) was a best-selling collection of the popular articles she had written since 1851. Known for her unconventional wit and satiric style, Fern became a successful novelist and a well-paid newspaper columnist who sought economic independence and wider opportunities for women. (*NAW*; Joyce W. Warren, *Fanny Fern: An Independent Woman* [New Brunswick, N.J., 1992], 104–19.)

·⊂═════≍⊃·

66　≫　Lucy Stone to ECS

Aug. 14, 1853

Dear Mrs. Stanton

I do not think, let Truth come from what source it may, that any one, has a right to keep it. But I do think, that a premature announcement of it, is possible. As Jesus said, "I have many things to tell you, but hitherto, ye were not able to bear it."[1]

One who is in total darkness, finds his eyes pained by the sudden admission of bright light—and closes ↑them↓. So too with many, who are thinking on the Woman question;—broach in their hearing, these thoughts, that we must think, and feel, and their progress is yet so little, that they will be frightened from further investigation. Such at least, has been my fear. I do not care for any damnation, that may come from any quarter, when I am sure that the full time has come. I know that the abuse in question is perfectly appalling. I know that scripture, & customs and "husband's rights"[2] are all pleaded to cover the existing wrong— One noble woman told me how she fled from her husband, to the Shakers,[3] because he gave her no peace either during mensturation, pregnancy, or nursing, and on the application of such a brute to our legislature, the law of divorce was so modified, that that man, and others like him, might sooner be enabled, under cover of a legal marriage, to claim "a husbands rights."[4] I know many similar cases. Shall we keep silence when such curses are inflicted through woman upon the race? There is, I confess, much force in your reasoning upon the subject. I wish that dear Lucretia Mott, whose name & age, would add weight to her words, were ready to do justice to this department of our Cause. I believe that the Free Love theories grow out of this wrong. I mean that of Mary Gove Nichols & S. P. Andrews.[5]

If nothing happens, I will see you before the Cleveland Convention, and we will talk this whole subject over. I think that we agree, in all, except it be the time to strike. I shall be glad to get your thoughts for there is not another woman in our ranks, who thinks or who dares speak what she thinks on this topic, so far as I know—

I can see how difficult it will be for you leave home, or to prepare to leave, but, we shall sadly miss the brave, true words you have been wont to send us. When your children are a little more grown, you will surely be heard, for it can not be possible to repress what is in you. If I make any speech at the Temperance Convention in N.Y. it will be on the right of divorce for drunkenness.[6] That plea ought to be heard there, and I was feeling very safe, since that subject was in your hands. But if you do not go, your mantle must fall on me, or Susan Anthony.

Every thing is promising finely, for both conventions—

The Women, who asked our Constitutional Convention, for the

right to ~~withdraw~~ vote, were coolly "allowed to withdraw"7— We shall do it, and renew our forces, to such an extent that they will not again dare so insult us. Aff & truly yours

✑ *Lucy Stone*

[*sideways on first page*] I go to Vermont tomorrow, for a fortnights labor with the Freesoilers.[8]

✑ ALS, ECS Papers, DLC.

1. In missing letters, Stone and ECS discussed placing divorce on the agenda of the upcoming woman's rights convention. Though the words are spoken by Paul, not Jesus, Stone quotes 1 Cor. 3:2.

2. His rights to sexual intercourse.

3. The religious society of Shakers required celibacy, even of married couples.

4. Kentucky and New Hampshire granted divorce when one partner in a marriage joined a Shaker community and thus willfully stopped performing marital duties. ("Report of the Committee on the Judiciary, on the Subject of Divorce," *New York Assembly Document*, 2 March 1852, No. 73, p. 11.)

5. Mary Sargeant Neal Gove Nichols (1810–1884) was a health reformer and writer. Born Mary Neal in New Hampshire, she discovered a talent for teaching women about anatomy and physiology while she supported her husband Hiram Gove and their daughter. After she left Gove about 1842, she opened a medical practice and water-cure establishment in New York City, wrote articles about health, and published novels and short stories. In 1848 she married another medical reformer, Thomas Low Nichols (1815–1901), and the Nicholses wrote, taught, and edited together. Mary Nichols turned her attention to free love because she believed that many of women's health problems derived from bad marriages.

Stephen Pearl Andrews (1812–1886), among the most vocal proponents of "free love," laid out his views in articles for the *New York Tribune* late in 1852. A New Englander, he went south to practice law in New Orleans, moved into Texas during its years as an independent republic, and became an outspoken abolitionist. His passion became sociology, finding a science of life that would reveal the essential oneness of everything social and economic. He found the key in "individual sovereignty," and on that idea he based his definition of free love.

In 1853 Nichols and Andrews raised similar criticisms of marriage. They both believed that no amount of law could sanctify a loveless sexual union, and they put especial emphasis on the need for a woman to choose the father of her child. Nichols believed a woman's health often required ending her marriage, and Andrews observed that there were "*as many fugitives from matrimony as there are fugitives from slavery.*" (John B. Blake, "Mary Gove Nichols,

Prophetess of Health," in *Women and Health in America*, ed. Judith Walzer Leavitt [Madison, Wis., 1984], 359–75; Madeleine B. Stern, *The Pantarch: A Biography of Stephen Pearl Andrews* [Austin, Tx., 1968]; Stephen Pearl Andrews, *Love, Marriage, and Divorce. A Discussion Between Henry James, Horace Greeley, and Stephen Pearl Andrews* [Boston, 1889], 6, 13, 16–17, 69, 88–89.)

6. At the Whole World's Temperance Convention, Stone said: "Drink the intoxicating cup, and . . . you shall not be entitled to the marriage relation. And I would say to the man or woman who is a drunkard, and who has a husband or wife, you shall forfeit the marriage relation." (*New York Times*, 2 September 1853.)

7. Responding to petitions for woman suffrage, a committee of the Massachusetts constitutional convention reported, "That the petitioners have leave to withdraw." The committee reported that a majority of women consented to their political condition, and thus their disfranchisement met the test of the Declaration of Independence, that a government's just powers derive from the consent of the governed. (*Una*, 20 August 1853.)

8. For a report of Stone's tour in Vermont, see *Lib.*, 2 September 1853.

---

67   ❧   SPEECH BY SBA TO THE NEW YORK WOMAN'S RIGHTS CONVENTION

Editorial note: Known as the "Mob Convention," the woman's rights meeting on 6 and 7 September 1853 filled Broadway Tabernacle, one of New York City's largest churches, seating 2,500 people. Lucretia Mott presided. No stranger to disorderly crowds, Mott thought "that never, at any meeting, was public propriety more outraged, than at ours last evening." Despite a rumpus, hisses, boos, and shouts, Mott noted, "not a scream was heard from any woman." SBA spoke at the afternoon session of the second day. (*History*, 1:546–77.)

[7 September 1853]

During my attendance at the New York State Teachers' Convention, lately held in Rochester, my attention was attracted to the condition of that class of women who teach in our public schools.[1] Five hundred delegates were enrolled as members of that Convention, of whom three hundred were women; and yet men alone occupied all the offices of the Convention; they constituted the business committees, prepared the reports, and were entrusted exclusively with the management of the various subjects which came before the Convention; nor did any of the reports, until the close of the second day, allude to women as having any interest whatever in the profession of teaching. Nearly at the close of the first day's proceedings, an appeal was made to the teachers present to sustain the "New York Teacher," which is the organ of the New York State Teachers' Association. Ladies were not then forgotten; their existence was at once recognized when the pecuniary aid was to be solicited, and they were appealed to to be liberal in contributing to the support of that paper.

On the morning of the third day, which was the last, the president,[2] on taking the chair, remarked that it was frequently asked why women were not appointed on the Committees, to bring in reports, and take part generally in the business of the meeting. He said, "I will answer only for one." Then, standing in a very dignified position, meant to enforce every word he uttered, he said: "Look at this beautiful hall— behold each pilaster, each pedestal, each shaft, and each entablature, the crowning glory of the whole—all contributes, each in its proper place, to the strength, symmetry, and beauty of this magnificent structure. Could I aid in bringing this beautiful entablature from its proud elevation, and placing it in the dust and dirt which surrounds the pedestal? Never!" Now, what do you suppose was the effect of this oration on the women present? There was a general look from woman to woman; and, as they surveyed their ribbons, laces, brooches, and pins, the look said, as plainly as possible, "beautiful! really beautiful!!" They, no doubt, thought themselves sisters of the angels. Not a woman rose to speak till toward the close of the last session.

During the whole time, the great burden upon the souls of those men seemed to be their anxiety to take measures for elevating the profession of teaching to a level with the clerical, medical, and legal professions. The various details to this consummation were considered. The low compensation of teachers, which had the effect in many instances of making the profession a mere stepping-stone to the others, was reviewed. At last a member remarked, that it seemed to *her* that the great obstacle was entirely overlooked.[3] She said: "The public sentiment holds woman to be incapable of becoming acquainted with the mysteries of law, medicine, and theology; and yet, it is granted to her to fill the highest offices as a teacher. So long, then, as you, men teachers, consent to compete with women, you must be content to be considered as occupying no more than the level of her mental capacity." Next came

the election of new officers. A motion was made that a lady should fill
the office of Vice-President, but it was lost. There was an attempt made
to have a lady chosen as Secretary, but this also failed.[4] A few words
spoken by one woman seemed to give others courage; and one of the
teachers of our city rose and said that the Convention had been called
in order that the teachers of the State might take counsel together, to
aid the cause of education; but the result would seem to show that a few
men came for the purpose of elevating themselves, while the large
number of women present were entirely forgotten.[5] "I am," she said,
"teacher and principal of one of the free schools in this city, performing the same labor as gentlemen who fill a like office. I receive two
hundred and fifty dollars a year, while my brother receives six hundred
and fifty dollars a year, for the same services."

While she was making these remarks, the President called her to
order! I acknowledge she *was* out of order, there not being a motion
before the house; but, it seems, women are always out of order; therefore, she might as well be standing as sitting. She had given resolutions
to the Secretary: they were read, but not acted on; neither did there
seem to be any disposition to call them up; and she judged, from that
fact, that the Convention did not design paying attention to subjects
interesting women. However, they were subsequently brought forward.

In this State there are eleven thousand teachers, and of these, four-
fifths are women. By the reports it will be seen that, of the annual State
fund of $800,000, two-thirds are paid to men, and one-third to women;
that is to say, two-thirds are paid to one-fifth of the laborers in the
cause of education, while four-fifths of these laborers are paid with
one-third of the fund! And yet, they are satisfied. A gentleman said:
"The majority of the women here would nor prepare reports, nor act in
the Convention, even if voted for, just as it happened in the Massachusetts Convention." Thus, because *all* were not in favor of it, *none*
would be permitted to exercise the right.

❧ *Proceedings of the Woman's Rights Convention, Held at the Broadway
Tabernacle, in the City of New York, on Tuesday and Wednesday, Sept. 6th and
7th, 1853* (New York, 1853), 81–83.

1. The annual meeting of the New York State Teachers' Association convened on 2 August 1853. A year earlier SBA sat in on the meeting at Elmira and
noted "dissatisfaction and disgust" in the faces of female teachers who lis-

tened to the association's president address them as "brothers." Accompanied by Mary Anthony and dozens of local teachers, she returned to agitate in 1853. (SBA to Editor, *Carson League*, 9 August 1852 and [after 4 August 1853], *Film*, 7:314, 805; Hyland C. Kirk, *A History of the New York State Teachers' Association* [New York, 1883].)

2. Charles Davies (1798–1876) was educated at the United States Military Academy and spent most of his career teaching college mathematics. SBA's account of his comments on the meeting's third day is close to the official report. (*BDAmerEd*; *New York Teacher* 1 [September 1853]: 364, *Film*, 7:792–802.)

3. SBA paraphrases herself. (Unidentified clipping from SBA scrapbooks, *Film*, 7:803.)

4. SBA nominated Emma Willard for vice president, and D. H. Cruttenden nominated SBA for recording secretary. Willard declined, and Cruttenden's motion lost. (*New York Teacher* 1 [September 1853]: 367–68.)

5. A reference to Clarissa Northrop or Northrup of Rochester, whose resolutions were hurriedly adopted. One recognized "the right of female teachers to share all the privileges and deliberations of this body"; the second acknowledged the inadequacy of women's salaries and committed the association, "to remove the existing evil." (Unidentified clipping from SBA scrapbooks, *Film*, 7:803.)

·⟨==========⟩·

68 ⤳ FROM THE DIARY OF SBA

[early November 1853][1]

During the three weeks following the National Woman's Rights Convention held at Cleveland, Oct. 5, 6 & 7th 1853,[2] I travelled through the Southern tier of Counties in N.Y. State, & held meetings in some eight or ten different villages. I talked upon the subject of Temperance.

One year previous to this Miss Emily Clark of LeRoy N.Y. had passed over the same ground, Lecturing upon the same subject, & had aided the Ladies of several of the villages in forming Womens Temperance Societies. In every place, except Elmira, those societies had never existed after the evening of their beginning. The reason given, by very nearly all the ladies with whom I conversed, for the failure of their societies, was womans want of time & money to meet their demands. Their Temperance meetings could be made interesting & useful to their members, or others, ~~unless~~ only by securing the attendance of persons who could speak to the edification of the People. Those of their own number who possessed <u>ability</u> to prepare essays, found they had not the command of the <u>leisure hours</u> necessary for their preparation. And to secure the attendance of speakers & Lecturers from abroad, required money & money they possessed not— Thus as I passed from town to town was I made to feel the great evil of womans entire dependency upon man, for the necessary means to aid on any & every reform movement. Though I had long admitted the wrongs I never, until this time, so fully took in the grand idea of pecuniary & personal independence

It matters not how overflowing with benevolence toward suffering humanity [↑]may be the heart of woman,[↓] it avails nothing so long as she possesses not the power to <u>act</u> in accordance with those prompting. Woman must have a <u>purse</u> of her own, & how can this be, so long as the [↑]<u>wife</u>[↓] is denied the right to her <u>individual</u> & <u>joint</u> <u>earnings</u>. Reflections like these, caused me to see & really feel that there was no <u>true</u> <u>freedom</u> for woman without the possession of all her property rights, & that these rights could be obtained through <u>legislation</u> only, & if so, the sooner the demand was made of the Legislature, the sooner would [↑]we[↓] be likely to obtain them— This demand must be made by Petitions to the Legislature, & that too at its very next session— How could the work be started, why, by first holding a Convention & adopting some plan of united action.

On my return to Rochester on the A.M. of Nov. 8th I dined at W. R. Hallowell's & then went directly to Mr. Channing, told of the work I had planned, he answered <u>Capital</u>, <u>Capital</u>, & forth[3]

1. In the notebook that served as her diary in 1854 and her copybook thereafter, SBA wrote this incomplete statement about the end of her temperance work. Either she intended to explain the new work she launched with the state woman's rights convention in November and later detailed in the same book, or she drafted a speech. A summary of her remarks at the convention on 30 November 1853 covers the same ground. (*Frederick Douglass' Paper*, 16 December 1853, *Film*, 7:844ff.)

2. With Antoinette Brown, Sarah Anthony Burtis, and William Lloyd Garrison for companions, SBA left Rochester on 4 October 1853 to attend the national convention. (Garrison, *Letters*, 4:258–61)

3. The text ends here, at the bottom of a page.

∽ Bound volume, SBA Papers, MCR-S.

·⊂══════×══════⊃·

69 ~ SBA TO ECS

Rochester Nov. 11, 1853

My Dear Mrs. Stanton

Enclosed is a Call for a Woman's Rights Convention,—N.Y. State Con, to be held in Rochester the 1ˢᵗ or 2ᵈ week of S̶e̶p̶t̶ ↑Dec.↓ next—[1] Will you sign the Call—isn't it beautifully written, by Mr. Channing— I know you'll sign it, but then you must tell me by return mail—if I get no letter I ↑shall↓ take silence as consent— I have long letter commenced to you, but have not been able to finish it, for want of time— I will try & mail it ere long—it is relative to some new developements on Marriage & Divorce— I hope you will be able to attend this Convention, the question ↑upon↓ which you have commenced an address is emphatically a practical one, & you ought to present it, so it seems to me— I know of others who will talk upon that vital question—

We won't make President if you'll only come— What do you say to having a man for President— Would it be any more than equality to have a man President now & then—[2] We must make an appeal to employers in the various Trades to open their shops to women—also a statement of the Legal disabilities of Woman, with a petition to the Legislature praying for their removal—

The redress of our Legal wrongs can only come through Legislation, & our Legislators will not be likely to act upon them, before we are wide enough awake to ask them to do so—

Mrs. Nichols Lectures to night on the Maine Law— Don't you hope she will feel more sprightly than last Spring[3]—do write me by Mondays mail, & say that you will for the time ↑waive↓ household & baby cares & come to Rochester at the time of the Convention & open your mouth for the Good of the race   Yours full of Hope

~ *S. B. Anthony*

I haven't asked Dame Bloomer to sign her world wide name to the Call, if you think best you can ask her— S. B. A.

~ ALS, ECS Papers, DLC.

1. Enclosure missing. The call announced a convention to plan "prompt and efficient action" to correct abuses of woman's rights at the next legislative session. The text noted the need for equality in the areas of pay, access to occupations, widows' rights, rights to property, trial by jury, and suffrage. ECS signed the call but did not attend the convention on 30 November and 1 December. (*Film*, 7:840–41.)

2. Samuel J. May presided at the convention.

3. A reference to Clarina Nichols's speech at the Women's New York State Temperance Society meeting in June 1853.

---

70   ⮞   SBA TO LUCY STONE

Rochester, Dec. 13, 1853.

Dear Lucy

Your note from Indianapolis, dated Nov. 28, was duly received, & should have been answered long ere this.[1]

We are all greatly rejoiced at your success in Ky., & also that you are laboring in Indiana. Much as we wished your presence at our recent convention in this city, we could but feel that it was better for you to be in the South & West.[2] I send you by same mail with this our Democrat's report of the convention, & enclose a copy of the Call for the meeting, & the Appeal to the friends of Woman's Rights, relative to circulating the Petitions.[3] The Call, Resolutions, Petitions & Appeal are all of Channing's writing.

I think our convention passed off most gloriously for the cause. How could it be otherwise, with such spirits present as S. J. May, W. H. Channing, E. L. Rose,[4] & A. L. Brown? Mrs. Coe[5] & Mrs. Jenkins did not arrive until the P.M. of the last day.

Mrs. Stanton was just weaning her baby, & it was hardly recovered from fever & ague. She longs to be free from household cares, that she may go into the reform work.

Nettie has been in Mass. the last two weeks, was to speak in Worcester & Providence. She had a severe attack of rush of blood to the head after her return from Cleveland, & has not yet fully recovered from it.

Mrs. Jenkins & myself are going to do what we can to canvass the State & circulate petitions. I have written Mrs. Nichols to come into the eastern part of the State & help us on with our work. Mr. Channing has gone to Washington to preach the coming five Sundays in the Unitarian church of that city by invitation from its members. Is not that ominous of the times? His course here has been one of unexampled nobility. I think him the most Christ like man I ever knew. Mrs. Rose did herself & the cause great honor here. She was the favorite of the audiences. Several asked the privilege of entertaining Lucy Stone, & expressed great surprise that she was not to be here. I very much wish you could come into the State & hold meetings in the larger cities, & stir up the people to roll up a long list of signatures to Petitions.

We shall hold a convention in Albany in Feb., when the petitions will be presented. I wish we had 40 of the right sort of women, who would volunteer in the work before us. We sent our box of goods to the Boston Bazar last night. It inventoried $50., & then a beautiful herbarium of 710 varieties of flowers.[6]

Douglas is uncovering what has long been lurking beneath a smooth exterior. I hope you see the Liberator & the Douglas paper now & then.[7]

Can't you come into this State & lecture? It seems to me the object of our State convention is defeated unless we can carry up to Albany a host of petitions. We don't want our legislators to say only 2000 women desire their rights, & they shall be denied because the majority do not ask them.

The Cleveland Reports are tardy in their appearance, & Mrs. Severance says the reports are very imperfect.[8] I have paid Wells[9] for the N.Y. Reports, & have some $2 of that convention money yet in my possession. Mr. Higginson[10] ordered the whole W. Tem. Con. money to be sent to LeBaron[11] to be expended for reports to be sent, as I understood, to the <u>members</u> of the Con.—have heard nothing from LeBaron since. Do let me hear from you often, don't fail to stop in R.

⇒ S. B. A.

⇒ Transcript in hand of A. S. Blackwell, Blackwell Papers, DLC.

1. One paragraph of this letter is in *Film*, 7:842.

2. After the convention in Cleveland, Lucy Stone made a profitable lecture tour through Kentucky, Missouri, and Indiana. (Kerr, *Lucy Stone*, 73–74.)

3. The Rochester convention named committees to research and draft an address specifying "the remaining legal disabilities of women," and to report on women's industrial disabilities. Petitions to the legislature sought woman

suffrage and just and equal rights. William H. Channing's appeal was dated 8 December 1853. (*Film*, 7:844–54, 865.)

4. Ernestine Louise Siismondi Potowski Rose (1810–1892) left Poland in 1827, after renouncing her Jewish faith and rebelling against an arranged marriage. Adrift in Europe for several years, she settled in England in 1831 and found friends among the radicals gathered around Robert Owen. In 1836 she married British radical William Ella Rose and moved with him to New York. An exceptional education, her commitment to social reform, her advocacy of free thought, and her skill as a public speaker earned her rapid recognition among American reformers. In the 1840s, with Paulina Kellogg Wright, she petitioned the New York legislature for property law reform; she lectured against slavery; and she was an outspoken anticlerical. Rose attended the First National Woman's Rights Convention in 1850 and for the next decade was one of the movement's busiest lecturers and advocates. After the Civil War, she returned to England. (*NAW*; Suhl, *Ernestine Rose*.)

5. Emma Robinson Coe was a prominent lecturer in the woman's rights movement from 1850 to 1855, identified at different times as of Ohio, Michigan, and Buffalo. The *Anti-Slavery Bugle* tracked her lectures in Ohio and Michigan in 1851, and she spoke in Rochester and around Boston when she traveled east for the Second National Woman's Rights Convention. She also stopped to visit ECS at Seneca Falls on that trip. Late in 1854 she became a law student in the office of William T. Peirce of Philadelphia. By then Coe was a widow, with a small legacy from her husband and a young daughter named Alice. In 1858, Martha Wright, in an elaborate pun on the names of women who remarried, called her "Mrs. Emma R. Coe <u>Still</u>." Wright had also learned that she was ready to launch another lecture tour. (Garrison, *Letters*, 4:324n; Lasser and Merrill, *Friends and Sisters*, 109, 115, 121; *History*, 1:111, 123, 146–48, 232, 383, 824–25; *Anti-Slavery Bugle*, 1 February, 15 March, 5, 11, 26 April, 17 May 1851, 26 March 1853; Martha Wright to SBA, 9 July 1858, *Film*, 9:25–27.)

6. A reference to the contribution sent by the Western New York Anti-Slavery Society to the annual antislavery fair in Boston.

7. SBA refers to the open conflict between Frederick Douglass and William Lloyd Garrison that erupted late in 1853 in both the *Liberator* and the *North Star*. (William H. Pease and Jane H. Pease, "Boston Garrisonians and the Problem of Frederick Douglass," *Canadian Journal of History* 2 [September 1967]: 29–48.)

8. Caroline Maria Seymour Severance (1820–1914) grew up in northern New York and married Theodoric Cordenio Severance, a banker, in 1840. The couple moved to Cleveland, and there she entered antislavery circles and rose to leadership in the state woman's rights movement. In 1855 she moved to Boston and gained national attention, becoming a good lecturer and building such well-known institutions as the New England Hospital for Women and Children and the New England Woman's Club. In the fall of 1853 Severance

took charge of publishing the report of the national convention because she had complained loudly that the reports of previous conventions were of poor quality. (*NAW*.)

9. Samuel Robert Wells (1820–1875) joined the firm of Fowlers and Wells in 1844, when he married Charlotte Fowler, a phrenologist and sister of the firm's founders. At this time, he edited the *Water-Cure Journal*, in addition to running the publishing business. He published the report of the woman's rights convention held in New York in September. (*DAB*.)

10. Thomas Wentworth Higginson (1823–1911) was an abolitionist minister in Worcester, Massachusetts, and a conspicuous figure in the woman's rights movement. Prominent in the conflict over women's participation at the planning meeting for the World's Temperance Convention, he assumed leadership in the Whole World's Convention of September 1853. Higginson liked direct action. In 1856 he went twice to Kansas to help the antislavery settlers; he raised money in support of John Brown's raid on Harper's Ferry; and during the Civil War he commanded the first black regiment, the First South Carolina Volunteers. (Tilden G. Edelstein, *Strange Enthusiasm: A Life of Thomas Wentworth Higginson* [New Haven, 1968].)

11. C. B. LeBaron, a broker in New York and a temperance activist, seceded from the planning meeting for the World's Temperance Convention and helped to plan the Whole World's Convention. (City directory, 1858.)

71　❧　WILLIAM H. CHANNING TO ECS

Washington Dec 28th 1853

Dear Mrs Stanton

Let me add my word of earnest request to that of Judge Hay—given in the enclosed letter[1]—that you will draft the Address to the Legislature, on the Legal Disabilities of Women. On all accounts you are the person to do it, at once from your sex, talent, knowledge of the subject, and influence. There is not a man of us, who could tell the story of Woman's wrongs as strongly, clearly, tersely, eloquently, as yourself. Some woman, too ought to be the voice of her sisterhood,—at once to prove woman's sagacity and justice & power to right herself, and because men will listen to a woman's claim in her own behalf as they will not to any words of men. There is an air of earnest reality in such an address, from a representative of the aggrieved party,—which cannot be given by any friend outside the circle, however zealous. And then as to the time,—requisite for gaining & moulding materials aid can readily be commanded. Judge Hay will send a contribution; Mr Burroughs Phillips of Syracuse,[2] who at Mr May's request drew up a paper for the Convention will send one; Mr Wright of Auburn[3] will doubtless gladly give his help & advice; and other lawyers will do the like. I propose too if necessary, that you should employ the services of some one to study the details thoroughly out for your use,—at the expense of the Committee & Friends. Miss Anthony will be able to suggest, I doubt not yet other ways of shorting your labor. We want from you the Preface, the closing Appeal, and the general form and style; the materials will easily fall into place. Please then to enter into correspondence with Mr May; and I will on my return to Rochester give all assistance in my power.

I have been here for a week and a half, having preached two sundays, and am to leave Jan 9th for Rochester. I came on to see men, for myself, & form clearer impressions than I could gain through the press of the real state of feeling on the Slavery question. On the whole I am much encouraged. Trouble may grow out of this Nebraska question, to be sure;[4] & bargaining politicians are ready to throw millions of "niggers" in to the scale to add weight to their claims for party. Yet after all a good mutual understanding, a higher sense of justice and clearer view of the duties of the whole Nation are rapidly growing. We have entered on a better era. You of course have read of and rejoiced in the grand debut of Gerrit Smith.[5] It was a rare triumph. The scene was worth a journey from Rochester to look at; and I cannot but draw happy auguries from his reception. His health too constantly improves. Day before yesterday,—when I last saw them,—I was told that Mr & Mrs Preston[6] had just been there to call on Mrs Miller. But I am at the end of my paper. With cordial respect   Yrs,

❧ *W H Channing*

❦ ALS, ECS Papers, DLC.

1. Enclosure missing. William Hay, in a letter to SBA on 10 December 1853, offered to help identify unjust laws, but added that "the person who arranges and condenses our suggestions into an address should, from every consideration, be Mrs. Stanton, because her style is admirably suited to such a subject." Hay (1793–1870), who lived in Saratoga Springs after 1840, began the practice of law in 1812 and served in the state assembly in 1822. He was regarded as a scholar in the legal profession, and he published a book of

poetry in 1832. A champion of woman's rights, he joined in lobbying at Albany, and he helped to organize meetings held in Saratoga Springs. (*Film*, 7:855; Nathaniel Bartlett Sylvester, *History of Saratoga County, New York* [Philadelphia, 1878], 193.)

2. Burroughs Phillips married Elizabeth W. McClintock in 1852 and lived in Syracuse, where, judging by this and other brief references, he practiced law. He attended the national woman's rights convention at Syracuse in 1852 and the state convention at Rochester in 1853, and he had died by 1855. (*Quaker Genealogy*, 2:815; research by Judith Wellman.)

3. For David Wright's response, on 21 November 1853, to SBA's request for a list of unjust laws, see *Film*, 7:837-39.

4. A bill to organize the territory of Nebraska was introduced in the Senate on 14 December. By the terms of the Missouri Compromise of 1820, Nebraska would be free of slavery, but in the previous session southerners refused to support an identical bill unless it repealed that compromise. Channing's fears proved to be well grounded, when Senator Stephen A. Douglas of Illinois accepted southern terms and amended the bill to allow the territory's settlers to decide the future of slavery. Douglas (1813-1861) began his career in national politics in the House of Representatives in 1843, won election to the Senate in 1847, and ran unsuccessfully as the Democratic candidate for president in 1860. (James C. Malin, *The Nebraska Question, 1852-1854* [Lawrence, Kan., 1953]; David M. Potter, *The Impending Crisis, 1848-1861*, ed. Don E. Fehrenbacher [New York, 1976], 145-76; *BDAC*.)

5. Gerrit Smith won election to the Thirty-third Congress that convened in December 1853. Smith took his seat on or about 12 December, after an illness, and delivered his first speech on 20 December during discussions of the president's message to Congress. Ostensibly a criticism of the administration's Austrian policy, Smith made it an antislavery address. Both Ann Smith and Elizabeth Smith Miller joined him in the capital. (*Congressional Globe*, 33d Cong., 1st sess., Appendix, 50-52; Harlow, *Gerrit Smith*, 317-20.)

6. Possibly Congressman William Preston (1816-1887) and his wife Margaret Wickliffe Preston. On 20 December Preston defended slavery in reply to Smith's address. A Whig from Kentucky, he earned a law degree at Harvard in 1838. (*DAB*; *Congressional Globe*, 33d Cong., 1st sess., 72-73.)

72 ⇝ ECS TO SBA

<Seneca Falls, January 16, 1854>[1]

I find there is no use saying "no" to you. Women have grievances without number, but I want the exact wording of the most atrocious laws. I can generalize and philosophize by myself, but I have not time to look up statistics. While I am about the house, surrounded by my children, washing dishes, baking, sewing, I can think up many points, but I cannot search books, for my hands, as well as my brains, would be necessary for that work. <If I can, I shall go to Rochester as soon as I have finished my Address and submit it—and the Appeal too for that matter—to Channing's criticism. But prepare yourself to be disappointed in its merits, for> I seldom have one hour to sit down and write undisturbed. Men who can shut themselves up for days with their books and thoughts know little of what difficulties a woman must surmount.

⌫ "Early Letters," 1189; typed transcript, ECS Papers, NjR. Variant dated 1 December 1853, *Film*, 7:945.

1. Date is that assigned to the transcript. The letter falls between letters from Channing to ECS at 28 December above and an incomplete one dated 3 February 1854, *Film*, 7:956–59.

·(⊃━━━━◗◖◗━━━━⊂)·

73 ✽ WILLIAM H. CHANNING TO ECS

Feb 8th 1854, Rochester

Dear Mrs Stanton

I have made a few pencil marks in and about your pages, which may go for what they are worth. Some of the hints are probably good suggestions. But you will see.

Unless you wholly agree with the poet, who says

> "I walk through the azure,
> Unfond of erasure,"

I would commend Emerson's method of striking out now & then, a word or two. Some such seeming redundancies I have noted.

But now let me say that I like your address much more in reading it over, than when I heard it. It did not correspond quite to the form of address which had presented itself to my mind; but probably it will answer a better end. At any rate,—with the addition of a specification of Laws, either under each head or at the end, as shall finally appear best, this Address will be a good "Cathartic,"—I fancy to the body politic. It will surely cause a sensation, and stir up, if not carry off, the bile of our Legislators. Pardon my metaphors. But verily I cannot but think of that unfortunate Legislature, except as a Patient, about to swallow a very bitter pill,—can<u>died</u> on the outside maybe, but can<u>did</u> within

But I must close for the mail— So hoping to meet you on Monday—[1] faithfully yrs

~ *W H Channing*

~ ALS, ECS Papers, DLC.

1. The Albany convention was called for Tuesday, 14 February.

·⟨⟨══════⟩⟩·

74 ~ SBA TO LUCY STONE

Albany, Feb. 9, 1854.

Dearest Lucy:

Your note came to hand when I was at Seneca Falls.[1] Your name, with the others had been sent on to Albany and announced in the papers. I am so sorr[y] you are ill and cannot come. I will not urge you, for you must take care of your own health. I regret to have announced you in the Albany papers again, when you cannot be here. I am happy to say Mrs. Stanton is coming to Albany and will read her own address to the Legislature. Her petticoats have assumed their former length, and her wardrobe cleared of every short skirt. I am sorry, but still feel a great deal of sympathy for her. She stood all alone, without Father, Mother, Sister, Brother or Husband. She imagines now that she will be <u>less</u> <u>persecuted</u> by them all, but I tell her that the dress is not a matter of trouble to them, her ultraisms will become more obvious to them. Every one who <u>drops</u> the dress, makes the task a harder one for the few left.

Lucy there are a thousand things I want to say to you, indeed, I have been so pressed by those who are perhaps better and wiser than myself, to lay aside the short dress, so implored for the sake of the Cause, &c, &c, that for the last ten days my heart has almost failed me, and but for my reliance on my own convictions of right and duty, must have sat down disheartened and discouraged. It is hard to stand alone, but no doubt good discipline for us. Lucy if you are able to come here, do so. We will not ask you to make but just <u>one</u> speech, and that may be as short as you please, but we do all feel very anxious to have you with us. Lucy there are but few spirits that can stand the test. If you dont come, I will explain myself after the convention. May you soon be well again.

❦ *S. B. A*

❦ Transcript in hand of I. P. Boyer, Blackwell Papers, DLC.

1. From West Brookfield, Lucy Stone wrote on 2 February that headaches prevented her from attending the Albany convention. The call, dated 23 January, promised Stone, Wendell Phillips, and Clarina Nichols as speakers. (*Film*, 7:947, 954–55.)

· ⊂━━━━━━⟩·

75 ❧ ADDRESS BY ECS TO THE LEGISLATURE OF NEW YORK

Editorial note: On the evening of 14 February 1854, at the Young Men's Association Hall in Albany, ECS read her speech about New York's laws to the woman's rights convention. She did not, as is often stated, speak to the legislature. Rather, on the motion of William Channing, the convention adopted her speech as its address to the legislature and ordered the text printed. Senators and assemblymen received copies on 20 February, when the women's petitions were presented and referred to select committees in both houses. The first printings—in the *Albany Atlas*, 15 February 1854, that received by legislators, and the text used by the *Una* and the *Lily* to set their type in March and April—have not been found. In May 1854 SBA published the address as a tract, and that is the source text. It remained in print for many years, sometimes advertised as "The Position of Woman as Woman, Wife, Widow, Mother." Years later ECS created the confusion over audience; in recounting a dramatic scene with her father, to whom she read the address in advance of going to Albany, she called this "my first speech for the New York legislature." Not until 1860, however, did she speak *to* the legislature. (*Albany Evening Journal*, 15 February 1854, and SBA to L. Stone, 23 May 1854, in *Film*, 7:1040–46; *JNYA*, 20 February 1854, p. 320; *JNYS*, 20 February 1854, p. 228; *Eighty Years*, 187–89.)

[14 February 1854]

The thinking minds of all nations call for change. There
is a deep-lying struggle in the whole fabric of society; a
boundless, grinding collision of the New with the Old.

The tyrant, Custom, has been summoned before the bar of Common
Sense. His Majesty no longer awes the multitude—his sceptre is broken—his crown is trampled in the dust—the sentence of death is pronounced upon him. All nations, ranks and classes have, in turn,
questioned and repudiated his authority; and now, that the monster is
chained and caged, timid woman, on tiptoe, comes to look him in the
face, and to demand of her brave sires and sons, who have struck stout
blows for liberty, if, in this change of dynasty, she, too, shall find relief.

Yes, gentlemen, in republican America, in the 19th century, we, the
daughters of the revolutionary heroes of '76, demand at your hands
the redress of our grievances—a revision of your state constitution—a
new code of laws. Permit us then, as briefly as possible, to call your
attention to the legal disabilities under which we labor.

1st. Look at the position of woman as woman. It is not enough for us
that by your laws we are permitted to live and breathe, to claim the
necessaries of life from our legal protectors—to pay the penalty of our
crimes; we demand the full recognition of all our rights as citizens of
the Empire State. We are persons; native, free-born citizens; property-
holders, tax-payers; yet are we denied the exercise of our right to the
elective franchise. We support ourselves, and, in part, your schools,
colleges, churches, your poor-houses, jails, prisons, the army, the
navy, the whole machinery of government, and yet we have no voice in
your councils. We have every qualification required by the constitution, necessary to the legal voter, but the one of sex.[1] We are moral,
virtuous and intelligent, and in all respects quite equal to the proud
white man himself, and yet by your laws we are classed with idiots,
lunatics and negroes; and though we do not feel honored by the place
assigned us, yet, in fact, our legal position is lower than that of either;
for the negro can be raised to the dignity of a voter if he possess himself
of $250; the lunatic can vote in his moments of sanity, and the idiot,
too, if he be a male one, and not more than nine-tenths a fool; but we,
who have guided great movements of charity, established missions,

edited journals, published works on history, economy and statistics; who have governed nations, led armies, filled the professor's chair, taught philosophy and mathematics to the *savans* of our age, discovered planets, piloted ships across the sea, are denied the most sacred rights of citizens, because, forsooth, we came not into this republic crowned with the dignity of manhood! Woman is theoretically absolved from all allegiance to the laws of the state. Sec. 1, Bill of Rights, 2 R.S., 301, says that no authority can, on any pretence whatever, be exercised over the citizens of this state but such as is or shall be derived from, and *granted by, the people of this state.*[2]

Now, gentlemen, we would fain know by what authority you have disfranchised one-half the people of this state? You who have so boldly taken possession of the bulwarks of this republic, show us your credentials, and thus prove your exclusive right to govern, not only yourselves, but us. Judge Hurlbut, who has long occupied a high place at the bar in this state, and who recently retired with honor from the bench of the Supreme Court, in his profound work on human rights, has pronounced your present position rank usurpation.[3] Can it be that here, where are acknowledged no royal blood, no apostolic descent, that you, who have declared that all men were created equal—that governments derive their just powers from the consent of the governed, would willingly build up an aristocracy that places the ignorant and vulgar above the educated and refined—the alien and the ditch-digger above the authors and poets of the day—an aristocracy that would raise the sons above the mothers that bore them? Would that the men who can sanction a constitution so opposed to the genius of this government, who can enact and execute laws so degrading to woman-kind, had sprung, Minerva-like, from the brains of their fathers,[4] that the matrons of this republic need not blush to own their sons! Woman's position, under our free institutions, is much lower than under the monarchy of England. "In England the idea of woman holding official station is not so strange as in the United States. The Countess of Pembroke, Dorset and Montgomery held the office of hereditary sheriff of Westmoreland, and exercised it in person. At the assizes at Appleby, she sat with the judges on the bench. In a reported case, it is stated by counsel, and substantially assented to by the court, that a woman is capable of serving in almost all the offices of the kingdom, such as those of queen, marshal, great chamberlain and constable of England, the champion of England, commissioner of sewers, governor of work house, sexton, keeper of the prison, of the gate house of the dean and chapter of Westminister, returning officer for members of parliament, and constable, the latter of which is in some respects judicial. The office of jailor is frequently exercised by a woman. In the United States a woman may administer on the effects of her deceased husband, and she has occasionally held a subordinate place in the post office department. She has therefore a sort of post mortem, post mistress notoriety; but with the exception of handling letters of administration and letters mailed, she is the submissive creature of the old common law."[5] True, the unmarried woman has a right to the property she inherits and the money she earns, but she is taxed without representation. And here again you place the negro, so unjustly degraded by you, in a superior position to your own wives and mothers; for colored males, if possessed of a certain amount of property and certain other qualifications, can vote, but if they do not have these qualifications *they are not subject to direct taxation*; wherein they have the advantage of woman, she being subject to taxation for whatever amount she may possess. (Constitution of N.Y., article 2, sec. 2.)[6] But, say you, are not all women sufficiently represented by their fathers, husbands and brothers? Let your statute books answer the question.

Again we demand, in criminal cases, that most sacred of all rights, trial by jury of our own peers.[7] The establishment of trial by jury is of so early a date that its beginning is lost in antiquity; but the right of trial by a jury of one's own peers is a great progressive step of advanced civilization. No rank of men have ever been satisfied with being tried by jurors higher or lower in the civil or political scale than themselves; for jealousy on the one hand, and contempt on the other, has ever effectually blinded the eyes of justice. Hence, all along the pages of history, we find the king, the noble, the peasant, the cardinal, the priest, the layman, each in turn protesting against the authority of the tribunal before which they were summoned to appear. Charles the First refused to recognize the competency of the tribunal which condemned him: For how, said he, can subjects judge a king?[8] The stern descendants of our Pilgrim Fathers refused to answer for their crimes before an English Parliament: For how, said they, can a king judge rebels?[9] And shall woman here consent to be tried by her liege lord, who has dubbed himself law-maker, judge, juror, and sheriff, too?—whose power, though sanctioned by Church and State, has no foundation in justice and equity, and is a bold assumption of our inalienable rights. In England a parliament-lord could challenge a jury where a knight was not empanneled. An alien could demand a jury composed half of his own countrymen; or, in some special cases, juries were even constituted entirely of women. Having seen that man fails to do justice to woman in her best estate, to the virtuous, the noble, the true of our sex, should we trust to his tender mercies the weak, the ignorant, the morally insane? It is not to be denied that the interests of man and woman in the present undeveloped state of the race, and under the existing social arrangements, are and must be antagonistic. The nobleman cannot make just laws for the peasant; the slaveholder for the slave; neither can man make and execute just laws for woman, because in each case, the one in power fails to apply the immutable principles of right to any grade but his own. Shall an erring woman be dragged before a bar of grim-visaged judges, lawyers and jurors, there to be grossly questioned in public on subjects which women scarce breathe in secret to one another? Shall the most sacred relations of life be called up and rudely scanned by men who, by their own admission, are so coarse that women could not meet them even at the polls without contamination? and yet shall she find there no woman's face or voice to pity and defend? Shall the frenzied mother, who, to save herself and child from exposure and disgrace, ended the life that had but just begun, be dragged before such a tribunal to answer for her crime? How can man enter into the feelings of that mother? How can he judge of the mighty agonies of soul that impelled her to such an outrage of maternal instincts? How can he weigh the mountain of sorrow that crushed that mother's heart when she wildly tossed her helpless babe into the cold waters of the midnight sea? Where is he who by false vows thus blasted this trusting woman? Had that helpless child no claims on his protection? Ah, he is freely abroad in the dignity of manhood, in the pulpit, on the bench, in the professor's chair. The imprisonment of his victim and the death of his child, detract not a tithe from his standing and complacency. His peers made the law, and shall law-makers lay nets for those of their own rank? Shall laws which come from the logical brain of man take cognizance of violence done to the moral and affectional nature which predominates, as is said, in woman? Statesmen of New-York, whose daughters, guarded by your affection, and lapped amidst luxuries which your indulgence spreads, care more for their nodding plumes and velvet trains than for the statute laws by which their persons and properties are held—who, blinded by custom and prejudice to the degraded position which they and their sisters occupy in the civil scale, haughtily claim that they already have all rights they want, how, think ye, you would feel to see a daughter summoned for such a crime—and remember these daughters are but human—before such a tribunal? Would it not, in that hour, be some consolation to see that she was surrounded by the wise and virtuous of her own sex; by those who had known the depth of a mother's love and the misery of a lover's falsehood; to know that to these she could make her confession, and from them receive her sentence? If so, then listen to our just demands and make such a change in your laws as will secure to every woman tried in your courts, an impartial jury. At this moment among the hundreds of women who are shut up in prisons in this state, not one has enjoyed that most sacred of all rights—that right which you would die to defend for yourselves—trial by a jury of one's peers.

2d. Look at the position of woman as wife. Your laws relating to marriage—founded as they are on the old common law of England, a compound of barbarous usages, but partially modified by progressive civilization—are in open violation of our enlightened ideas of justice, and of the holiest feelings of our nature. If you take the highest view of marriage, as a Divine relation, which love alone can constitute and sanctify, then of course human legislation can only recognize it. Man can neither bind nor loose its ties, for that prerogative belongs to God alone, who makes man and woman, and the laws of attraction by which they are united. But if you regard marriage as a civil contract, then let it be subject to the same laws which control all other contracts. Do not make it a kind of half-human, half-divine institution, which you may build up but cannot regulate.[10] Do not, by your special legislation for this one kind of contract, involve yourselves in the grossest absurdities and contradictions.

So long as by your laws no man can make a contract for a horse or piece of land until he is twenty-one years of age, and by which contract he is not bound if any deception has been practiced, or if the party contracting has not fulfilled his part of the agreement—so long as the parties in all mere civil contracts retain their identity and all the power and independence they had before contracting, with the full right to dissolve all partnerships and contracts for any reason, at the will and option of the parties themselves, upon what principle of civil jurisprudence do you permit the boy of fourteen and the girl of twelve, in violation of every natural law, to make a contract more momentous in importance than any other, and then hold them to it, come what may, the whole of their natural lives, in spite of disappointment, deception and misery?[11] Then, too, the signing of this contract is instant civil death to one of the parties. The woman who but yesterday was sued on bended knee, who stood so high in the scale of being as to make an agreement on equal terms with a proud Saxon man, to-day has no civil existence, no social freedom. The wife who inherits no property holds about the same legal position that does the slave on the southern plantation. She can own nothing, sell nothing. She has no right even to the wages she earns; her person, her time, her services are the property of another.[12] She cannot testify, in many cases, against her husband. She can get no redress for wrongs in her own name in any court of justice. She can neither sue nor be sued. She is not held morally responsible for any crime committed in the presence of her husband, so completely is her very existence supposed by the law to be merged in that of another.[13] Think of it; your wives may be thieves, libellers, burglars, incendiaries, and for crimes like these they are not held amenable to the laws of the land, if they but commit them in your dread presence. For them, alas! there is no higher law than the will of man. Herein behold the bloated conceit of these Petruchios of the law, who seem to say:

> Nay, look not big, nor stamp, nor stare, nor fret,
> I will be master of what is mine own;
> She is my goods, my chattels; she is my house,
> My household stuff, my field, my barn,
> My horse, my ox, my ass, my anything;
> And here she stands, touch her whoever dare;
> I'll bring my action on the proudest he,
> That stops my way, in Padua.[14]

How could man ever look thus on woman?—She, at whose feet Socrates learned wisdom—she, who gave to the world a Saviour, and witnessed alike the adoration of the Magi and the agonies of the Cross.[15] How could such a being, so blessed and honored, ever become the ignoble, servile, cringing slave, with whom the fear of man could be paramount to the sacred dictates of conscience and the holy love of Heaven? By the common law of England, the spirit of which has been but too faithfully incorporated into our statute law, a husband has a right to whip his wife with a rod not larger than his thumb, to shut her up in a room, and administer whatever moderate chastisement he may deem necessary to insure obedience to his wishes, and for her healthful moral development![16] He can forbid all persons harboring or trusting her on his account. He can deprive her of all social intercourse with her nearest and dearest friends. If by great economy she accumulates a small sum, which for future need she deposit, little by little, in a savings bank, the husband has a right to draw it out, at his option, to use it as he may see fit.

"Husband is entitled to wife's credit or business talents (whenever their intermarriage may have occurred); and goods purchased by her on her own credit, with his consent, while cohabiting with him, can be seized and sold in execution against him for his own debts, and this, though she carry on business in her own name."—7 *Howard's Practice Reports*, 105, *Lovett agt. Robinson and Witbeck, sheriff, &c.*[17]

"No letters of administration shall be granted to a person convicted of infamous crime; nor to any one incapable by law of making a contract; nor to a person not a citizen of the United States, unless such person reside within this state; nor to any one who is under twenty-one years of age; nor to any person who shall be adjudged incompetent by the surrogate to execute duties of such trust, by reason of drunkenness, improvidence, or want of understanding, nor any married woman; but where a married woman is entitled to administration, the same may be granted to her husband in her right and behalf."[18]

There is nothing that an unruly wife might do against which the husband has not sufficient protection in the law. But not so with the wife. If she have a worthless husband, a confirmed drunkard, a villain or a vagrant, he has still all the rights of a man, a husband and a father. Though the whole support of the family be thrown upon the wife, if the wages she earns be paid to her by her employer, the husband can receive them again. If, by unwearied industry and perseverance, she can earn for herself and children a patch of ground and a shed to cover them, the husband can strip her of all her hard earnings, turn her and her little ones out in the cold northern blast, take the clothes from their backs, the bread from their mouths; all this by your laws may he do, and has he done, oft and again, to satisfy the rapacity of that monster in human form, the rumseller.

But the wife who is so fortunate as to have inherited property, has, by the new law in this state, been redeemed from her lost condition.[19] She is no longer a legal nonentity. This property law, if fairly construed, will overturn the whole code relating to woman and property. The right to property implies the right to buy and sell, to will and bequeath, and herein is the dawning of a civil existence for woman, for now the "femme covert" must have the right to make contracts. So, get ready, gentlemen; the "little justice" will be coming to you one day, deed in hand, for your acknowledgment. When he asks you "if you sign without fear or compulsion," say yes, boldly, as we do.[20] Then, too, the right to will is ours. Now what becomes of the "tenant for life?"[21] Shall he, the happy husband of a millionaire, who has lived in yonder princely mansion in the midst of plenty and elegance, be cut down in a day to the use of one-third of this estate and a few hundred a year, as long as he remains her widower? And should he, in spite of this bounty on celibacy, impelled by his affections, marry again, choosing for a wife a woman as poor as himself, shall he be thrown penniless on the cold world—this child of fortune, enervated by ease and luxury, henceforth to be dependent wholly on his own resources? Poor man! He would be rich, though, in the *sympathies* of many women who have passed through just such an ordeal. But what is property without the right to protect that property by law? It is mockery to say a certain estate is mine, if, without my consent, you have the right to tax me when and how you please, while I have no voice in making the tax-gatherer, the legislator or the law. The right to property will, of necessity, compel us in due time to the exercise of our right to the elective franchise, and then naturally follows the right to hold office.

3d. Look at the position of woman as widow. Whenever we attempt to point out the wrongs of the wife, those who would have us believe that the laws cannot be improved, point us to the privileges, powers and claims of the widow. Let us look into these a little. Behold in yonder humble house a married pair, who, for long years, have lived together, childless and alone. Those few acres of well-tilled land, with the small white house that looks so cheerful through its vines and flowers, attest the honest thrift and simple taste of its owners. This man and woman, by their hard days' labor, have made this home their own. Here they live in peace and plenty, happy in the hope that they may dwell together securely under their own vine and fig tree for the few years that remain to them, and that under the shadow of these trees, planted by their own hands, and in the midst of their household gods, so loved and familiar, here may take their last farewell of earth. But, alas for human hopes! the husband dies, and without will, and the stricken widow, at one fell blow, loses the companion of her youth, her house and home, and half the little sum she had in bank. For the law, which takes no cognizance of widows left with twelve children and not one cent, instantly spies out this widow, takes account of her effects, and announces to her the startling intelligence that but one-third of the house and lot, and one-half the personal property, are hers.[22] The law has other favorites with whom she must share the hard-earned savings of years. In this dark hour of grief, the coarse minions of the law gather round the widow's hearthstone, and, in the name of justice, outrage all natural sense of right; mock at the sacredness of human love, and with cold familiarity proceed to place a moneyed value on the old arm chair, in which, but a few brief hours since, she closed the eyes that had ever beamed on her with kindness and affection; on the solemn clock in the corner, that told the hour he passed away; on every garment with which his form and presence were associated, and on every article of comfort and convenience that the house contained, even down to the knives and forks and spoons—and the widow saw it all—and when the work was done, she gathered up what the law allowed her and went forth to seek her another home! This is the much talked of widow's dower. Behold the magnanimity of the law in allowing the widow to retain a life interest in one-third the landed estate, and one-half the personal property of her husband, and taking the lion's share to itself! Had she died first, the house and land would all have been the husband's still. No one would have dared to intrude upon the privacy of his home or to molest him in his sacred retreat of sorrow.[23]

How, I ask you, can that be called justice, which makes such a distinction as this between man and woman?

By management, economy and industry, our widow is able, in a few years, to redeem her house and home. But the law never loses sight of the purse, no matter how low in the scale of being its owner may be. It sends its officers round every year to gather in the harvest for the public crib, and no widow who owns a piece of land two feet square ever escapes this reckoning. Our widow, too, who has now twice earned her home, has her annual tax to pay also—a tribute of gratitude that she is permitted to breathe the free air of this republic, where "taxation without representation," by such worthies as John Hancock and Samuel Adams,[24] has been declared "intolerable tyranny." Having glanced at the magnanimity of the law in its dealings with the widow, let us see how the individual man, under the influence of such laws, doles out justice to his helpmate. The husband has the absolute right to will away his property as he may see fit. If he has children, he can divide his property among them, leaving his wife her third only of the landed estate, thus making her a dependent on the bounty of her own children. A man with thirty thousand dollars in personal property, may leave his wife but a few hundred a year, as long as she remains his widow.

The cases are without number where women, who have lived in ease and elegance, at the death of their husbands have, by will, been reduced to the bare necessaries of life. The man who leaves his wife the sole guardian of his property and children is an exception to the general rule. Man has ever manifested a wish that the world should indeed be a blank to the companion whom he leaves behind him. The Hindoo makes that wish a law, and burns the widow on the funeral pile of her husband;[25] but the civilized man, impressed with a different view of the sacredness of life, takes a less summary mode of drawing his beloved partner after him; he does it by the deprivation and starvation of the flesh, and the humiliation and mortification of the spirit. In bequeathing to the wife just enough to keep soul and body together, man seems to lose sight of the fact that woman, like himself, takes great pleasure in acts of benevolence and charity. It is but just, therefore, that she should have it in her power to give during her life, and to will away at her death, as her benevolence or obligations might prompt her to do.

4th. Look at the position of woman as *mother*. There is no human love so generous, strong and steadfast as that of the mother for her child; yet behold how cruel and ruthless are your laws touching this most sacred relation.

Nature has clearly made the mother the guardian of the child; but man, in his inordinate love of power, does continually set nature and nature's laws at open defiance. The father may apprentice his child, bind him out to a trade or labor, without the mother's consent—yea, in direct opposition to her most earnest entreaties, her prayers and tears.[26]

He may apprentice his son to a gamester or rumseller, and thus cancel his debts of *honor*. By the abuse of this absolute power, he may bind his daughter to the owner of a brothel, and, by the degradation of his child, supply his daily wants; and such things, gentlemen, have been done in our very midst. Moreover, the father, about to die, may bind out all his children wherever and to whomsoever he may see fit, and thus, in fact, will away the guardianship of all his children from the mother. The Revised Statutes of New-York provide that "every father, whether of full age or a minor, of a child to be born, or of any living child under the age of twenty-one years, and unmarried, may by his *deed or last will*, duly executed, dispose of the custody and tuition of such child during its minority, or for any less time, to any person or persons, in possession or remainder." 2 R.S., page 150, sec. 1.[27]

Thus, by your laws, the child is the absolute property of the father, wholly at his disposal in life or at death.

In case of separation, the law gives the children to the father; no matter what his character or condition.[28] At this very time we can point you to noble, virtuous, well educated mothers in this state, who have abandoned their husbands for their profligacy and confirmed drunkenness. All these have been robbed of their children, who are in the custody of the husband, under the care of his relatives, whilst the mothers are permitted to see them but at stated intervals. But, said one of these mothers, with a grandeur of attitude and manner worthy the noble Roman matron in the palmiest days of that republic, I would rather never see my child again, than be the medium to hand down the low animal nature of its father, to stamp degradation on the brow of another innocent being. It is enough that one child of his shall call me mother. If you are far sighted statesmen, and do wisely judge of the interests of this commonwealth, you will so shape your future laws as to encourage woman to take the high moral ground that the father of her children must be great and good.

Instead of your present laws, which make the mother and her children the victims of vice and license, you might rather pass laws prohibiting to all drunkards, libertines and fools, the rights of husbands and fathers. Do not the hundreds of laughing idiots that are crowding into our asylums, appeal to the wisdom of our statesmen for some new laws on marriage—to the mothers of this day for a higher, purer morality?

Again, as the condition of the child always follows that of the mother, and as by the abuse of your laws the father may beat the mother, so may he the child.[29] What mother cannot bear me witness to untold sufferings which cruel, vindictive fathers have visited upon their helpless children? Who ever saw a human being that would not abuse unlimited power? Base and ignoble must that man be, who, let the provocation be what it may, would strike a woman; but he who would lacerate a trembling child is unworthy the name of man. A mother's love can be no protection to a child; she cannot appeal to you to save it from a father's cruelty, for the laws take no cognizance of the mother's most grievous wrongs. Neither at home nor abroad can a mother protect her son. Look at the temptations that surround the paths of our youth at every step; look at the gambling and drinking saloons, the club rooms, the dens of infamy and abomination that infest all our villages and cities—slowly but surely sapping the very foundations of all virtue and strength.

By your laws, all these abominable resorts are permitted. It is folly to talk of a mother moulding the character of her son, when all mankind, backed up by law and public sentiment, conspire to destroy her influence. But when woman's moral power shall speak through the ballot-box, then shall her influence be seen and felt; then, in our legislative debates, such questions as the canal tolls on salt, the improvement of rivers and harbors, and the claims of Mr. Smith for damages against the state, would be secondary to the consideration of the legal existence of all these public resorts, which lure our youth on to excessive indulgence and destruction.

Many times and oft it has been asked us, with unaffected seriousness, "what do you women want? What are you aiming at?" Many have manifested a laudable curiosity to know what the wives and daughters could complain of in republican America, where their sires and sons have so bravely fought for freedom and gloriously secured their independence, trampling all tyranny, bigotry and caste in the dust, and declaring to a waiting world the divine truth that all men are created equal. What can *woman* want under such a government? Admit a radical difference in sex and you demand different spheres—water for fish, and air for birds.

It is impossible to make the southern planter believe that his slave feels and reasons just as he does—that injustice and subjection are as galling as to him—that the degradation of living by the will of another, the mere dependent on his caprice, at the mercy of his passions, is as keenly felt by him as his master. If you can force on his unwilling vision a vivid picture of the negro's wrongs, and for a moment touch his soul, his logic brings him instant consolation. He says, the slave does not feel this as I would. Here, gentlemen is our difficulty: When we plead our cause before the law makers and *savans* of the republic, they cannot take in the idea that men and women are alike; and so long as the mass rest in this delusion, the public mind will not be so much startled by the revelations made of the injustice and degradation of woman's position as by the fact that she should at length wake up to a sense of it.

If you, too, are thus deluded, what avails it that we show by your statute books that your laws are unjust—that woman is the victim of avarice and power? What avails it that we point out the wrongs of woman in social life; the victim of passion and lust? You scorn the thought that she has any natural love of freedom burning in her breast, any clear perception of justice urging her on to demand her rights.

Would to God you could know the burning indignation that fills woman's soul when she turns over the pages of your statute books, and sees there how like feudal barons you freemen hold your women. Would that you could know the humiliation she feels for her sex, when she thinks of all the beardless boys in your law offices, learning these ideas of one-sided justice—taking their first lessons in contempt for all womankind—being indoctrinated into the incapacities of their mothers, and the lordly, absolute rights of man over all women, children and property, and to know that these are to be our future Presidents, Judges, Husbands and Fathers; in sorrow we exclaim, alas! for that nation whose sons bow not in loyalty to woman. The mother is the first object of the child's veneration and love, and they who root out this holy sentiment, dream not of the blighting effect it has on the boy and the man. The impression left on law students, fresh from your statute books, is most unfavorable to woman's influence; hence you see but few lawyers chivalrous and high-toned in their sentiments towards woman. They cannot escape the legal view which, by constant reading, has become familiarized to their minds: *"Femme covert,"* "dower," "widow's claims," "protection," "incapacities," "incumbrance," is written on the brow of every woman they meet.

But if, gentlemen, you take the ground that the sexes are alike, and, therefore, you are our faithful representatives—then why all these special laws for woman? Would not one code answer for all of like needs and wants? Christ's golden rule is better than all the special legislation that the ingenuity of man can devise: "Do unto others as you would have others do unto you."[30] This, men and brethren, is all we ask at your hands. We *ask* no better laws than those you have made for yourselves. We need no other protection than that which your present laws secure to you.

In conclusion, then, let us say, in behalf of the women of this state, we ask for all that you have asked for yourselves in the progress of your development, since the *May Flower* cast anchor side Plymouth rock; and simply on the ground that the rights of every human being are the same and identical. You may say that the mass of the women of this state do not make the demand; it comes from a few sour, disappointed old maids and childless women.

You are mistaken; the mass speak through us. A very large majority of the women of this state support themselves and their children, and many their husbands too. Go into any village you please, of three or four thousand inhabitants, and you will find as many as fifty men or more, whose only business is to discuss religion and politics, as they watch the trains come and go at the depot, or the passage of a canal boat through a lock; to laugh at the vagaries of some drunken brother, or the capers of a monkey, dancing to the music of his master's organ. All these are supported by their mothers, wives or sisters.

Now, do you *candidly* think these wives do not wish to control the wages they earn—to own the land they buy—the houses they build? to have at their disposal their own children, without being subject to the constant interference and tyranny of an idle, worthless profligate? Do you suppose that any woman is such a pattern of devotion and submission that she willingly stitches all day for the small sum of fifty cents, that she may enjoy the unspeakable privilege, in obedience to your laws, of paying for her husband's tobacco and rum? Think you the wife of the confirmed, beastly drunkard would consent to share with him her home and bed, if law and public sentiment would release her from such gross companionship? Verily, no! Think you the wife, with whom endurance has ceased to be a virtue, who through much suffering has lost all faith in the justice of both Heaven and earth, takes the law in her own hand, severs the unholy bond and turns her back forever upon him whom she once called husband, consents to the law that in such an hour tears her child from her—all that she has left on earth to love and cherish? The drunkards' wives speak through us, and they number 50,000. Think you that the woman who has worked hard all her days, in helping her husband to accumulate a large property, consents to the law that places this wholly at his disposal? Would not the mother, whose only child is bound out for a term of years, against her expressed wishes, deprive the father of this absolute power if she could?

For all these, then, we speak. If to this long list you add all the laboring women, who are loudly demanding remuneration for their unending toil—those women who teach in our seminaries, academies and common schools for a miserable pittance; the widows, who are taxed without mercy; the unfortunate ones in our work houses, poor houses and prisons; who are they that we do not now represent? But a small class of fashionable butterflies, who, through the short summer days, seek the sunshine and the flowers; but the cool breezes of autumn and the hoary frosts of winter will soon chase all these away; then, they too will need and seek protection, and through other lips demand, in their turn, justice and equity at your hands.

≈ *Address to the Legislature of New-York, Adopted by the State Woman's Rights Convention, Held at Albany, Tuesday and Wednesday, February 14 and 15, 1854* (Albany, 1854). Also in *Lily*, 15 March 1854, and *Una*, April and May 1854. Published as well in *History*, 1:595–605.

1. The constitution specified that white male voters be twenty-one years of age, citizens for at least ten days, state residents for one year, and county residents for four months. Men "of color" could vote if they had resided in the state for three years and possessed two hundred and fifty dollars of property for at least one year. ECS also refers below to the provision that no man would lose his right of suffrage "while kept at any almshouse or other asylum, at public expense" or "while confined in any public prison." (N.Y. Const. of 1846, art. II, secs. 1, 3.)

2. The quotation from the 1852 edition of the *Revised Statutes of the State of*

New-York, 1:301, begins at "no authority," and ECS added the emphasis. ECS also cites earlier editions of the statutes, evidence perhaps that several collaborators supplied her examples.

3. Elisha P. Hurlbut wrote that men and women were equal before men took rights away from women. "Her submission exalts the throne of his power: her legal insignificance elevates his dignity, and her lost rights are appropriated to himself." (*Essays on Human Rights*, 148.)

4. Minerva, goddess of wisdom, was not born of a mother but sprang full grown, in armor, from the head of Jupiter.

5. The passage comes from a footnote in Hurlbut, *Essays on Human Rights*, 126. He refers to a widow's right to administer the estate of her deceased husband if he left no will to instruct otherwise. Hurlbut's sentences about Anne Clifford, countess of Dorset, Pembroke, and Montgomery (1590–1676), who inherited the office of sheriff from her father in 1643, are taken from a note on page 326 of the 1832 edition of Edward Coke, *The First Part of the Institutes of the Laws of England*.

6. ECS refers to article II, section 1 (not 2) about the qualifications of voters, which concluded: "And no person of color shall be subject to direct taxation unless he shall be seized and possessed of" real estate sufficient to make him a voter.

7. The emphasis here is on "our own peers." The state's bill of rights guaranteed that the trial by jury be "inviolate forever" in all the courts of New York, but only male inhabitants could be returned as jurors. (N.Y. Const. of 1846, art. I, sec. 2; *RSSNY, 1852*, 2:656, sec. 5.)

8. On trial for treason, Charles I (1600–1649), king of Great Britain and Ireland, refused to acknowledge the court's legitimacy because the House of Commons established it without the consent of either the king or the House of Lords. He was, nonetheless, condemned to death and executed.

9. Probably a reference to the plight of Puritans omitted from the amnesty at the time of the Restoration, when Charles II came to the throne.

10. ECS raises a difficulty in the law of marriage that plagued legal reformers and fueled intense debates about divorce. State law followed the common law in defining marriage as simply a civil contract, valid when entered into by two people willing and able to do so. But in practice, it was a contract like no other because the parties could not dissolve it by mutual consent. Blackstone acknowledged that common law addressed one legal dimension of marriage, while ecclesiastical law addressed another, "the holiness of the married state." In the sum of its parts, marriage was both civil contract and sacrament, but American society lacked the legal foundation for sacramental marriage. There were numerous critics of the legal inconsistency by 1854. In 1852 the Committee on the Judiciary of the New York Assembly noted, nothing in state law justified declaring marriage indissoluble. As the law stood, marriage was "entirely a matter of municipal regulation," and decisions about divorce should be matters of "expedience and policy" only. Writing in the same year,

Henry Stanton's friend Joel Bishop urged that the model of contracting marriage be abandoned and replaced with a secular concept, derived from natural law, that bound two people into a unique civil status. Other critics tilted in the opposite direction, looking for marriage to be returned to the churches and made "a wholly divine institution and a sacrament of the church, a contract irrepealable except for infidelity." Thus one Albany newspaper responded to ECS's description of a "half-human, half-divine institution." That mix of human and divine law, the editors continued, reflected well marriage's special character. (*RSSNY, 1852*, 2:321, sec. 1; Blackstone, *Commentaries on the Laws of England*, 1:345–46; "Report of the Committee on the Judiciary, on the Subject of Divorce," *New York Assembly Documents*, 2 March 1852, No. 73, p. 4; Joel P. Bishop, *Commentaries on the Law of Marriage and Divorce, and Evidence in Matrimonial Suits* [Boston, 1852], 25; unidentified clipping, SBA scrapbook 1, Rare Books, DLC; Michael Grossberg, *Governing the Hearth: Law and Family in Nineteenth-Century America* [Chapel Hill, N.C., 1985], 17–24.)

11. This comparison between the legal ages for contracting marriage and conducting business comes from Hurlbut, *Essays on Human Rights*, 152–53. New York, for a time, raised the age of consent to seventeen years for boys and fourteen years for girls, but the legislature repealed the law in 1830 and reverted to the provisions of the common law noted by ECS. (*RSSNY, 1829*, 2:138, sec. 2; *RSSNY, 1836*, 2:74; Tapping Reeve, *The Law of Baron and Femme, of Parent and Child, Guardian and Ward, Master and Servant, and of the Powers of Courts of Chancery*, 2d ed. [Burlington, 1846], 200.)

12. The target of criticism is the Married Women's Property Act of 1848 which provided woman no rights to her earnings while married nor to joint earnings acquired by husband and wife.

13. ECS enumerates the legal consequences of marriage for women as spelled out in the common law. The list can be found in Blackstone, *Commentaries on the Laws of England*, 1:355–66.

14. *Taming of the Shrew*, act 3, sc. 2, lines 217–24.

15. Diotima, who taught Socrates, in Plato's *Symposium*, and Mary, the mother of Jesus, in Matt. 2:9 and John 19:25.

16. Tapping Reeve thought it impossible to define precisely the husband's power over his wife's person in nineteenth-century America because the "refinements of modern times" were changing social customs and the law. He insisted that the laws recognized no right to chastise a wife, but he listed circumstances that allowed a husband to imprison her. As Elisha Hurlbut summed up the legal defense of male supremacy, the husband "may still lock her up in a closet; he may bind her with cords; but he may not whip her." (Blackstone, *Commentaries on the Laws of England*, 1:366; Reeve, *Baron and Femme*, 64–65; Hurlbut, *Essays on Human Rights*, 162–63; Myra C. Glenn, *Campaigns Against Corporal Punishment: Prisoners, Sailors, Women, and Children in Antebellum America* [Albany, 1984], 63–83.)

17. ECS quotes an unidentified digest of a decision rendered by Justice Willard of the New York Supreme Court in *Lovett agt. Robinson and Witbeck*. In order to satisfy the debts of Mr. Lovett, the sheriff of Rensselaer County seized millinery goods purchased by his wife for her business in Troy, and the court upheld the seizure. The court pointed out that the law of 1848 and the amendment of 1849, protecting the property of married women, applied only to inherited property and gifts or bequests, not to a wife's business. "Her credit, or business talents, belong to the husband," the justice concluded, and thus the goods were his and liable to seizure. (7 Howard's Practice Reports, 105 [1852].)

18. A letter of administration appoints the executor of an estate; a married woman might be entitled to administration as a daughter or sister of the deceased. With minor alterations, ECS cites *RSSNY, 1852*, 2:260, sec. 32.

19. The Married Women's Property Act of 1848 and amendments made to it in 1849.

20. ECS threatens men with the demeaning encounter between a wife and the commissioner of deeds whenever property was to be sold. To protect the wife's dower rights, the commissioner needed her certification that she signed a deed of sale free from "fear and compulsion of her husband."

21. The Married Women's Property Act of 1849 provided that wives could dispose of their separate property by will. Otherwise married women could write no wills to dispose of either real or personal property, and the will of a single woman was revoked by marriage. On the one hand, "All persons, except idiots, persons of unsound mind, married women, and infants, may devise their real estate, by a last will and testament, duly executed according to the provisions of this title." On the other hand, "Every male person of the age of eighteen years, or upwards, and every female not being a married woman, of the age of sixteen years, or upwards, of sound mind and memory, and no others, may give and bequeath his or her personal estate, by will in writing." If women write wills, ECS asks, will widowers find themselves limited as widows have been to gaining use of a spouse's property as a tenant for life rather than owner? Will he face all the same restrictions that men have imposed through their wills on their wives? (*RSSNY, 1852*, 2:241, sec. 1; 243, sec. 18; 246, sec. 37; 331, sec. 67.)

22. Two conditions determine the experience of ECS's widow: her husband died intestate, or without writing a will, and she was childless. In the absence of a will, the law protected her right to the use of one-third of the real property owned by her husband at any time during their marriage (her widow's dower), and it allowed her to "tarry in the chief house of her husband, forty days after his death" without paying rent. Of his personal property, the law guaranteed her a life interest in one-half and distributed the other half to her late husband's next of kin. The laws exempted from the estate only a small number of personal items that the widow could retain outright, like her spinning wheel

and loom, the family bible, her clothing, necessary dishes and kitchenware, and her bed. With only a life interest in the estate, the widow could not bequeath the property in her turn. (*RSSNY, 1852,* 2:149, sec. 1; 151, sec. 17; 269–70, secs. 9–10; 281–82, sec. 82.)

23. No man could write a will that left his widow less than her dower right to his real estate, but he could dispose of his whole personal estate without leaving her anything save the items exempted for her personal use. If his children were minors, the widow had additional use of property in order to care for the children. (*RSSNY, 1852,* 2:269–70, secs. 9–11.)

24. John Hancock (1737–1793) and Samuel Adams (1722–1803) of Boston were prominent advocates of rebellion against British colonial rule.

25. Lydia Maria Child told of Hindu widows burning themselves on the funeral pile of their husbands. She explained it was not a religious duty but a custom based on the belief that a widow thus ensured eternal life with her husband. (*History of the Condition of Women,* 1:111–17.)

26. The law required adult consent before males under twenty-one or females under eighteen could indenture themselves to work as clerks, apprentices, or servants, and it specified that the father should be that adult, provided he lived and was responsible for his family. In his absence the mother could consent, but if she refused, guardians and town officials could override her wishes. (*RSSNY, 1852,* 2:339, sec. 2.)

27. ECS cites the *Revised Statutes* of 1829. In the edition of 1852, her quotation appears at 2:334, sec. 1.

28. ECS overstates the law and judicial opinion in this instance, as if the common law rights of fathers to their children stood unchallenged. New York's revised statutes had opened the way for courts to award the custody of minor children to mothers, and the courts moved in that direction. In *People v. Chegaray*, a case involving a mother's petition for custody after separation, a state supreme court justice thought, "it can hardly be doubted that the father is entitled to the custody of his infant children," and the case did not warrant "the interference of the court." But he also wrote that the father's rights were not absolute. In other cases decided before ECS wrote her address, judges interpreted their statutory authority to award custody of the children "as may seem necessary and proper" to mean custody decisions based on the welfare of children. They could decide, in the words of one judge, that the mother was an "unobjectionable" guardian. Given how personal and unpredictable the judges' decisions were, ECS may have sought clearer guidelines from the legislature. (*RSSNY, 1852,* 2:330, sec. 63; 332–33, secs. 1–3; 18 Wendell's Reports 637 [1836]; Ahrenfeldt v. Ahrendfeldt, 1 Hoffman's Chancery Reports 497 [1840], and 4 Sandford's Chancery Reports 525 [1847]; Grossberg, *Governing the Hearth,* 234–56.)

29. A man's "power of restraining" his wife was described in terms of that

"moderation that a man is allowed to correct his apprentices or children." (Blackstone, *Commentaries on the Laws of England*, 1:366.)

    30. Matt. 7:12 and Luke 6:31.

·◁━━━━━▶·

76 ∾ SBA and ECS to Lucy Stone

Albany, Feb. 16, 1854

Dearest Lucy

Your letter of the 13th inst caused a bursting of the floods long pent up;[1] and I went straight to Mrs. Stanton and read her the outgushings of your innermost. If I have done wrong to you, pardon me. Mrs. S. had said much to me on the subject. She has passed a most bitter experience in the short dress; says she now feels a mental freedom among her friends, that she has not known for the two years past. But Lucy, if <u>you waver</u>, and talk, yea, and resolve to make a long dress, why then, who may not? If Lucy Stone, with all her reputation, her powers of eloquence, her loveliness of character, that wins all who once hear the sound of her voice, cannot bear the martyrdom of the dress, who, I ask, can? Mrs. Stanton's parting words were, "Let the hem out of your dress <u>to-day</u>, before to-morrow night's meeting." (Mrs. Rose speaks again to-morrow night, and we hope Mr. Channing will come up the river in the P.M. and be here too.)[2] I have not obeyed Mrs. S. but have been in the streets and printing offices all the day long; had rude, vulgar men stare me out of countenance, and heard them say as I opened the doors, "There comes my Bloomer!" Oh, hated name!

I have been compelled to do all the business pertaining to this convention, as I did to that at Rochester. The Cleveland reports have come this very day, too late for the convention, though. Oh, it is too, too, bad that neither Lucy Stone nor Phillips[3] were here.

Dear Lucy,[4]

I have just read your letter to Susan. Would that I could spend a brief time with you. I have but a moment to say, for your own sake, lay aside the shorts. I know what you suffer among fashionable people. Not for the sake of the cause, nor for any sake but your own, take it off. We put the dress on for greater freedom, but what is physical freedom compared with mental bondage? By all means have the new dress made long. We have had a fine convention, but oh! how sorry I was not to see you there! In haste, your friend

✍ *E. C. Stanton.*

✍ Transcript in hand of I. P. Boyer, Blackwell Papers, DLC. Above ECS's letter is written: "Mrs. Stanton writes on the same sheet." A variant transcript of ECS portion in *Film*, 7:996.

1. Stone complained about reactions to her reform dress, especially when she traveled. She had decided to have dresses both long and short and choose the one most comfortable for each occasion. (13 February 1854, *Film*, 7:962–64.)

2. As one in a series of meetings organized by SBA and Lydia Mott to keep the topic of woman's rights alive in Albany, Ernestine Rose and William H. Channing spoke at Association Hall on 17 February. (*Rochester Daily Union*, 17 February 1854.)

3. Wendell Phillips (1811–1884) became one of the great orators of the nineteenth century while he championed the rights of African Americans. Raised in one of Boston's old families, educated at Harvard, and trained in law, Phillips disrupted the social patterns of his life to collaborate with extremists like William Lloyd Garrison. After the Civil War and emancipation, he sought equal citizenship for the former slaves, and he became a harsh critic of the degradation of labor by American capitalism. As a delegate to the World's Anti-Slavery Convention in 1840, Phillips urged the admission of American women, and thereafter, he endorsed the movement for woman's rights, though he often disagreed with its leaders. (James Brewer Stewart, *Wendell Phillips: Liberty's Hero* [Baton Rouge, La., 1986].)

4. The variant transcription of ECS's note dates it 23 February at Seneca Falls and removes references to SBA and the convention.

·⟨⚊⚊⚊⚊⚊⚊⟩·

77 ✍ SBA TO LUCY STONE

Albany, Mar. 7, 1854

Dear Lucy:

Where are you, and why are you so long silent? We have had a most glorious hearing before our Assembly Committee, the one to whom was referred our Petition for the Just and Equal Rights of Women.[1] All the members, save one, are quite liberally disposed. Mr. Channing and Mrs. Rose were the only members of our committee who could be present at the hearing. Nettie was pre-engaged at Cleveland and Pittsburg that week, and S. J. May engaged in discussing the Trinity question with Rev. Luther Lee.[2] Mrs. Rose made one of her very best arguments. I enclose the written statements as published in the Tribune

After the presentations of the statement to the Senate by Channing, Mrs. R. and Mr. C. made good arguments—as good as they could under the circumstances. The Senate Committee were very frivolous and wanting in common politeness.[3] I read the document presented to the Assembly Committee. Mrs. Rose followed with an hour's close argument. We expected Mr. C. to follow her, but he thought best that the impression made by Mrs. R. should not be marred.

Nettie is to be here to-morrow and give her Bible Argument on the 9th inst. I enclose a notice from the papers,[4] also an editorial that appeared in yesterday's Register from which you can judge the agitation here.[5] The Evening Journal published an extract of Mrs. Rose's Hartford Bible Convention speech, and commented upon it.[6] The Knickerbocker replied, and asked if Mr. Dawson in speaking of the Political career of Thomas Jefferson, would allude to his having been the bosom friend of Thomas Paine. They thought it unjust to apply one rule to men and another to women.—[7] Dawson could find no fault with a word that Mrs. R. uttered here.

I send you an editorial from the Knickerbocker in reply to the Register. Lucy do write me here in care of L. Mott. I shall be here until the middle of next week, when I leave for Washington in company with Mrs. Rose who is going <u>first</u> to speak on the Nebraska Question as deduced from <u>human</u> <u>rights</u>, and then upon Woman's Rights. I go to do the outside work, she being unable to attend to it.

Lucy is not this a wonderful time—and era long to be remembered? How is your health? Are you recovered from your exhaustion? A letter from Nettie says she is better but hoarse yet. Lucy I have let down some of my dresses and am dragging around with long skirts. It is humiliating to my good sense of cleanliness and comfort. In love

✑ S. B. A.

✑ Transcript in hand of I. P. Boyer, Blackwell Papers, DLC.

1. The assembly's select committee, chaired by James L. Angle, met on the afternoon of March 2 to hear arguments in support of the women's petitions for just and equal rights. SBA opened the hearing with an enumeration of twenty specific revisions needed in the laws, and Ernestine Rose spoke to

justify the changes. (*Albany Argus*, 3 March 1854, and *New York Daily Tribune*, 7 March 1854, *Film*, 7:1014-24.)

2. Luther Lee (1800-1889), of Syracuse, a leading Methodist minister and first president of the antislavery Wesleyan Methodist Connection of America, preached at Antoinette Brown's ordination in 1853. He and Samuel J. May held public debates for eleven evenings and published their arguments in *Discussion on the Doctrine of the Trinity, Between Luther Lee, Wesleyan Minister, and Samuel J. May, Unitarian Minister* (1854). (*NCAB*, 25:101-2; Eliot, *Heralds of a Liberal Faith*, 3:244.)

3. In support of the petitions for equal suffrage, William Channing and Ernestine Rose presented a short statement from the February meeting to the senate's select committee on March 1. The *Evening Journal* described their appearance "before the Senate Committee of Bachelors"; "The only effect produced was—a determination more fixed than ever, in the minds of the Committee, to *remain* Bachelors in the event of the success of the movement. And who could blame them?" (*Albany Evening Journal*, 2 March 1854, and *New York Daily Tribune*, 7 March 1854.)

4. The *Albany Evening Journal*, 7 March 1854, announced that Antoinette L. Brown would give her "Bible argument in favor of Woman's equality with Man" at Association Hall.

5. After condemning the "propagandists of women's rights" in "short petticoats and long-legged boots" as "unsexed women, who make a scoff of religion, who repudiate the Bible and blaspheme God," the editorial attacked Ernestine Rose as an immigrant who exploited American liberty by "her efforts to obliterate from the world the religion of the Cross—to banish the Bible as a textbook of faith, and to overturn social institutions that have existed through all political and governmental revolutions from the remotest time." (Albany *State Register*, 6 March 1854.)

6. The *Journal* reprinted Rose's argument at the meeting called by abolitionists and spiritualists to discuss the social impact of belief in the divine inspiration of the Bible, held in Hartford, Connecticut, in June 1853. (*Albany Evening Journal*, 21 February 1854; *Lib.*, 17 June 1853.)

7. A distinguished journalist and devout Baptist from Scotland, George Dawson (1813-1883) was Thurlow Weed's associate editor at the *Journal*. Pertinent issues of the *Albany Knickerbocker* cannot be found. The point is that Thomas Paine (1737-1809), pamphleteer of the American Revolution, was, like Ernestine Rose, a freethinker. (*NCAB*, 2:204; George R. Howell and Jonathan Tenney, *History of the County of Albany, N.Y., From 1609 to 1886* [New York, 1886], 360-64.)

·◁━━━━━◈━━━━━▷·

78 ～ FROM THE DIARY OF SBA

[*21 March–28 April 1854*]

March 21 [*1854*]. [*Washington*] Called on Mrs. Melvin a friend of Mrs. Rose, a member of the M.E. Church South.[1] We talked on the Slavery question, she called the relation between master & slave, a Patriarchial one, said Slavery is a humane institution   My blood chilled in my veins at the thought of a professed Christian, thus so entirely losing sight of the great principle of love, the Golden Rule—

Called at Gerritt Smith's about two Oclock, Mrs. Smith alone, had a very pleasant chat with her, on the right of every individual to his own belief.

To day the Nebraska Bill in the House was referred to the Com. on the Whole by a vote of 110 to 65. thought to be virtually, death to the Bill.[2]

Miss Miner of the Colored Girls School[3] called on us after dinner a very interesting enthusiastic nature, expressed herself interested in the Woman's Rights question.

Mrs. Rose spoke in Carusis Saloon[4] to a small audience, not exceeding 100, 40 tickets only were sold, thus $10. was the amount of receipts—

The smallness of the audience was attributable to the fact that the subject has never been agitated here, Lucy Stone spoke last January to a small audience, had a rainy night.[5] Mrs. R's subject the Educational & Social Rights of Woman. [*Entries for 22–26 March omitted.*]

1. The proslavery Methodist Episcopal Church South congregated on Eighth Street Northwest.

2. On March 3 the Senate approved an act to organize the Kansas and Nebraska territories and sent it to the House. The House vote on March 21, on the motion of New York Democrat Francis Burkholst Cutting (1804–1870) to refer the bill to the Committee of the Whole rather than to the Committee on Territories, was intended to bury it beneath some fifty bills already referred. The vote was 110 yeas and 95 nays, closer than SBA thought. In fact, the ploy failed. Under tight leadership, the House voted to table the prior bills and in

May, reached the Kansas-Nebraska bill and passed it. (*BDAC*; *Congressional Globe*, 33d Cong., 1st sess., 701–3.)

3. Myrtilla Miner (1815–1864) was a teacher from New York State who founded the Colored Girls School in Washington in 1851 to educate black women as teachers. Harriet Beecher Stowe, Lucretia Mott, and Wendell Phillips were among the abolitionists who financed her work. (*NAW.*)

4. The saloon or assembly rooms of Gaetani Carusi at Eleventh and C streets was one of the chief sites for public gatherings in Washington.

5. Lucy Stone spoke at Carusi's on 19 January 1854. (*Lib.*, 24 February 1854.)

March 27. Weather moderated but still cold. After walking about two miles, visiting five printing offices   the Bill Printer, & Bill Poster, I returned & with Mrs. R. visited the Patent Office, the most remarkable curiosities there were the sword & Cane, the Coat, vest, & breeches of Gen. Washington worn at the time he resigned his Commission, his Camp Chest—with its appertenances—Tea Pot, Coffee Urn, Pepper dish, Salt—tea chest—Grid Iron, Tin Kettles for cooking &c, also the writing desk used by him during all his Campaigns—there too was a bit of the old Tent cloth—ragged & dirty—[1]

From the Patent Office we went to the Treasury department—thence to the State departments, here we were shown the identical letter Benedict Arnold, to Major Andre found in the pocket of Andre—signed Augustus & written as though Andre were a merchant—[2] Saw also the Original Constitution of the United States with the signatures of the delegates from the 13. States—it was beautifully penned on Parchment one two feet square, tied together with a deep blue ribbon—at the Pattent Office saw also the original Declaration of Independence, many of the signatures were nearly obliterated, on account of having been written with poor ink—

From State Departments we went to the Presidents House   took a peep into the East Room, splendidly furnished eight large gilt mirrors, in front of the White house in a beautiful park, is a very fine bronze Statue of Gen. Jackson, on horse back—mounted on a white marble pedestal—[3] then called at Mr. Aker's office to see the Bust of Mrs. Davis, a very fine one indeed—[4] After dinner walked on to Capitol Hill & called on Anne Royal, a woman 85 years of age—[5] She is indeed as Mrs. R. says, the Living Curiosity of Washington—was brought up by the Indians, married a Captain of the Army, he died, & she has printed a paper called the Huntress for the past 20 years— She has a fine, intellectual head— She lives in a small house, has two little boys whom she is educating, one boy she has instructed in Greek & Latin & Geometry— Said to me no one can know how to reason without studying Geometry learning to say Therefore, Wherefore & Because. We each of us subscribed for the Huntress, she gave us each two books, written by her many years ago— She is the most filthy specimen of humanity I ever beheld, her fingers look like birds claws, in color & attennuity, they shone as if glazed.

A great black New Foundland dog, old Cat & kittens sat at her feet— & Mrs. R. says eight years ago she had in addition to these 2 Guinea hens & two little pigs running about the floor— She was writing her editorial for this weeks paper

Said I to her what a wonderful woman you are, she answered me, "I know it." [*28-30 March omitted.*]

1. At Seventh and F streets, the Patent Office housed its historical and scientific curiosities on the second floor.

2. The Treasury and the State Department occupied buildings on Fifteenth Street. SBA saw the evidence of Benedict Arnold's treachery in the American Revolution: letters carried by Major John André, a British spy, to General Henry Clinton, with plans for surrendering West Point.

3. By the sculptor Clark Mills, this equestrian statue was unveiled in Lafayette Square in January 1853.

4. Paulina Wright Davis accompanied her husband to Washington when he took his seat as an antislavery Democrat in the Thirty-third Congress in December 1853. Thomas Davis served one term in Congress. Benjamin Paul Akers (1825–1861) had just arrived in Washington from Portland, Maine, in search of commissions for portrait sculptures. Among his customers during one year spent in the city were President Franklin Pierce and Gerrit Smith. (*BDAC*; Wayne Craven, *Sculpture in America* [New York, 1968], 281–84.)

5. Anne Newport Royall (1769–1854) was a vigorous proponent of the separation of church and state and the sovereignty of the people. She published the *Huntress*, dedicated to exposing government corruption and holding political men up to public scrutiny. She died penniless in October of the year. (*NAW*; Bessie Rowland James, *Anne Royall's U.S.A.* [New Brunswick, N.J., 1972].)

March 31 ↑Baltimore↓ Had a small meeting last night. The landlord agreed to see me started from Alexandria in time to connect with the 8 Oclock Train from Washington but he did not,—seemed to be perfectly indifferent to my request. There is no promptness no order, no anything about these southerners. I have had Pro Slavery People tell me just go South once, & see Slavery as it is, & then you will talk very differently. I can assure all such, that contact with Slavery has not a tendency to make me hate it <u>less</u>, <u>no</u>, <u>no</u>, the ruinous effect of the institution, upon the white man alone, causes me to hate it—

Arrived at Washington about 9 Oclock. Called on Mrs. Davis. The Globe of 29th March commented on Mrs. Rose Lecture on the Nebraska Question as deduced from Human Rights very favorably, but misrepresented her on remark—[1]

I came on to Baltimore on the 3½ P.M., called on Dr. J. E. Snodgrass[2] firstly & then went in search of a private boarding house, finally decided to take rooms at Mrs. Waters, 49 Hannover st.[3] Every thing is plain but so far seems cleanly. learned from the Chambermaid Sarah, that she & four others of the [*blank*] Servants were Slaves.—[4] It is perfectly astonishing to see what an array of Servants there is about every establishment, three northern girls, with the engineering of a northern boarding house keeper would do all the work of one Dozzen ↑of these↓ men, women & children, whether Slaves or free. Such is the baneful effects of Slavery upon labor. The free blacks who receive wages, expect to do no more work than do the Slaves, Slave labor is the Standard—& it need but a glance at southern life, to enable an Abolitionist to understand, why it is that the northern man is a more exacting Slave master than is a southern one—he requires of the Slave an amount of labor equal to that he has been accustomed to get from the well paid northern free laborer. Vain requisition that. [*Entries of 1–5 April omitted.*]

1. In a letter to William Lloyd Garrison on 6 April, SBA explained that the *Globe* confused Rose's summary of southern views with her own views, that Rose, in fact, boldly denounced slavery and advocated its abolition. (*Lib.*, 14 April 1854.)

2. Joseph Evans Snodgrass (1813–1880) lived at 103 North High Street. A physician, abolitionist, temperance advocate, and supporter of woman's rights, he met SBA at the meeting of delegates excluded from planning a World's Temperance Convention, and he returned to attend the Whole World's Temperance Convention in the fall of 1853. That same year he was listed as the professor of medical jurisprudence at Russell Trall's New York Hydropathic School, a school for practitioners of water-cure. (City directory, 1853–1854; Weiss and Kemble, *Great American Water-Cure Craze*, 36.)

3. The city directory for 1853 and 1854 lists a Mrs. E. D. Waters at 102 Hanover.

4. On April 4, SBA learned that Sarah was hired by Mrs. Waters from her master for eight dollars a month. Her master supplied her clothes, and she was allowed to keep her tips from the boarders.

Apr. 6   I lectured this evening, by invitation from the Marion Temperance ~~Meeting~~ Society of Baltimore, had a full house.[1] The meeting was called to order by the President of the Society & opened by prayer by an old Methodist man, who made the stereotye prayer of Stephen S. Foster's Slave holder—"O Lord we thank thee, that our lives have been cast in places & that we live in a land where every man can sit under his own vine & fig tree, & none dare to molest or make him afraid"   Oh, how did my blood boil within me, & then to go on with my lecture & not protest against a mans telling the Lord such terrible falsehoods.— Mrs Rose was invited to speak after I had finished, she did so & alluded to the necessity of substituting healthful amusements in the place of alcoholic stimulus.—

Several gentlemen desired me to speak again on Temperance—

Received a letter from Lydia Mott, enclosing Mr. Angles report on the Woman's Rights Petitions.[2] Reported <u>adverse</u>, but presented a Bill giving to married women, in case the husband does not provide for the family, the right to their own earnings, also requiring the written consent of the mother, to apprentice or will away a child. [*Entries of 7–8 April omitted.*]

1. J. E. Snodgrass represented the Marion Temperance Society at the conventions in New York the previous year.

2. The report of the select committee to consider the petitions for equal rights, chaired by James L. Angle. A one-term assemblyman from Monroe County, Angle (c. 1820–1891) reported that the inequalities between men and women were divinely ordained and beyond legislative power to correct. Progress, however, revealed some deficiencies in the customs of marriage, and while the committee denied the prayer of the petitioners, it proposed minor adjustments, as SBA notes, in the rights of married women. (*New York Assembly Document*, 27 March 1854, No. 129; *History*, 1:616–19; Basch, *In the Eyes of the Law*, 193; Peck, *History of Rochester and Monroe County, N.Y.*, 1:344, 362–63.)

April 9   Very pleasant morning. Mr. Wheadon called & accompanied us to the Universalist Church to hear a sermon on "Womans Sphere" from Mr. Flanders[1]   The hymns were beautiful, one verse of the 2^d ran thus

'Tis man alone who difference sees
And speaks of high & low
And worships those, & tramples these
While the same path they go.

The minister admitted the justice of the demand of Woman for her Rights, but denied that they were <u>identical</u> with man's. The sermon was a bundle of inconsistencies.

Mrs. R. & myself were talking of the "<u>Know Nothing</u>" organization,[2] when she criticised Lucy Stone & Wendell Philips with regard to their feelings toward foreigners. Said she had heard them both express themselves in terms of prejudice against granting to foreigners the rights of Citizenship. I expressed disbelief as to either of them having that narrow, mean prejudice in their souls. She then said I was blinded & could see nor hear nothing wrong in that clique of Abolitionists. She thought she being connected with no Society or association, either in religion or reforms could judge all impartially.— I then ventured to say that Kossuths non committal coure while in this country, it seemed to me, she did not criticise as she would an American— She thought she did, & could see reasons why he pursued the course he did.[3] Yes said I you excuse him, because you can see the causes why he acted & spoke thus, while you will not allow me to bring forward the probable causes of Lucy's seeming fault— It seemed to <u>me</u> that <u>she</u> could not ascribe <u>pure motives</u> to any of our Reformers, & while to her it seemed, that I was blindly bound to see no fault, however glaring— At length in the anguish of my soul, I said Mrs. Rose, "there is not <u>one</u> in the Reform ranks, whom you think true, not one but whom panders to the popular feeling—["] She answered I can't help it, I take them by the words of their own mouths. I trust all until their own words or acts declare them false to truth & right, & continued she, no one can tell the hours of anguish I have suffered, as one after another I have seen those whom I had trusted, betray falsity of motive, as I have been compelled to place one after another on the list of panderers to public favor— Said I, do you know Mrs. Rose, that I can but feel that you place <u>me</u> <u>too</u> on that list. Said she, I will tell you, when I see you untrue— A silence ensued, while I copied the verse from the hymn sung at Church this A.M., & subscribed it Susan B. Anthony, for her dear friend Ernestine L. Rose, as I handed it to her, I observed tears in her eyes. Said I Mrs. Rose, have I been wicked, & hurt your feelings. She answered, No, but I expect never to be understood while I live— her anguish was extreme I too wept, for it filled my soul anguish to see one so noble, so true (even though I felt I could not comprehend her) so bowed down, so overcome with deep swelling emotions— At length she said, no one knows how I have suffered from not being understood— I know you must suffer & heaven forbid that I should add a feathers weight to your burdens—

Mrs. Rose is not appreciated nor cannot be by this age— She is too much in advance of the extreme ultraists even, to be understood by them—

Almost every reformer, feels that the odium of his own Ultraisms is as much as he is able to bear & therefore shrinks from being identified with one ↑in↓ whose view their ultraism is sheer Conservatism—this fact has been most plainly brought home to me— Every says "I am ultra <u>enough</u> the mercy knows; I don't want to seem to be any more so by identifying myself with one whose every sentiment is so shocking to the public mind.["]

Dr. Snodgrass called to bid us Good Bye, said his wife had been called into the Country to attend the funeral of a friend & he should be obliged to stay at home with his boy. the Dr. is a well-meaning man, & would be very active in helping on the work of reform—he however seems wanting in tact & judgement, cannot seem to strike at the right time, & consequently makes himself very unpopular. I am sorry for him, for he has stood up bravely for <u>human</u> <u>freedom</u> in this Slave City & yet he is not welcomed to platform—has too high an estimate of his abilities. I regret not being able to meet his wife again, I am deeply interested in her.

Mrs. Rose spoke this evening in Committee Room of the Maryland Institute, seats about 500, the room was crowded & it is said hundreds went away, who could not get in— So much for a <u>free</u> <u>meeting</u>— She spoke most glorious upon Charity as deduced from the formation of Human Character—& concluded by briefly reviewing the morning Sermon— Many of Mr. Flanders people were present—[4] [*Entries of 10, 12 April omitted; no entries for 11, 13 April.*]

1. George T. Flanders was minister of the Calvert Street Universalist Church in Baltimore. (City directory, 1853–1854.)

2. Nativist Know-Nothings and their American party opposed immigration.

3. Rose's most notable expression of support for Louis Kossuth came at the Tom Paine birthday celebration in New York on 29 January 1852, when she advocated intervention on behalf of the Hungarian leader, "the embodiment of the European spirit of freedom." To her, the need to intervene against European oppression outweighed Kossuth's refusal to condemn slavery while he sought American aid. (*New York Herald*, 31 January 1852; Suhl, *Ernestine Rose*, 124–25.)

4. SBA left Baltimore early on April 10 for Philadelphia, where she spent a day sightseeing with Sarah Grimké.

Apr. 14. Friday, Dined at James Motts, Abbey Gibbons, Sarah Grimpke, Thomas Curtis, Griffith Cooper & Eliab Capron & wife Rebecca,[1] were invited guests. An Uncle of Thomas Motts wife, Mary Anna, from Texas was there—[2] We had a very chat—Spiritualism as usual being the principal topic, Mrs. Rose & Mr. Curtis believing the spirit inseparable from the body, of course, were on the unbelieving side, while Sarah Grimpke was all enthusiasm in the faith. Eliab Capron doesn't believe, he knows there is a reality in spirits disembodied, communicating with the living. The rest of the company, with myself, seemed not to know whether or not there is any truth in these modern manifestations. Mrs. R. returned to the Doctors[3] immediately after dinner to rest for the evening meeting to be held at Samson's Street Hall—[4] I remained & with Lucretia   Sarah Grimpke & myself on one side & Thomas Curtis on the other, had an argument as to the probable future existence of the mind or soul or spirit of man— Not an argument could one of us bring, other than an intuitive feeling that we were not to cease to exist, when the body dies, while Mr. Curtis reasoned, (as has Mrs. Rose often done with me) that all things in nature die, or rather that the elements of all things are separated & assume new forms, that if the soul, the vital spark of man lives eternally so must the essence of the tree, the animal, the bird & the flower. There certainly is no argument to be brought against such reasonings— But if it be true that we die like the flower, leaving behind, only the fragrance or the contrary while the elements that compose us, go to form new bodies, what a delusion has the race ever been in—what a dream is the life of man—

James & Lucretia accompanied me to the Hall, the rain fell rapidly— Not a score of persons were present & Mr Mott stated to that Mrs. Rose would not speak—just as we got to the foot of the stairs, found Mrs. R. in the Carriage, I got in with them & returned to the Dr.

Mrs. R. decided to stay over Sunday & speak at the liberals meeting[5]
[*No entries for 15–16, 18–23 April; entries of 17, 24–27 omitted.*]

1. The Motts lived at 338 Arch Street. Abigail Hopper Gibbons (1801–1893), the daughter of the distinguished abolitionist and prison reformer Isaac Hopper, followed her father's interests. She lived in New York City. (*NAW.*) Thomas Curtis left Philadelphia for Iowa in 1856, and by 1894 lived in California. An historian of free thought described him as "among our best speakers and brightest poets," who knew life needed "neither 'God' nor 'immortality' to make it any more glorious than it actually is." (Lucretia Mott to Martha Wright, 17 April 1856, Garrison Papers, MNS-S; Samuel Porter Putnam, *Four Hundred Years of Freethought* [New York, 1894], 713–14.) Griffith M. Cooper (c. 1790–1864), who was visiting Philadelphia from his home in Wayne County, New York, opened a school for the Seneca Indians in Cattaraugus in 1833. A Hicksite minister and abolitionist, he was removed from the Genesee Yearly Meeting in 1846. (*Friends' Intelligencer* 21 [1865]: 521; Hallowell, *James and Lucretia Mott*, 275.) Eliab Wilkinson Capron signed the Declaration of Sentiments in 1848 and reported the meeting for the Auburn *National Reformer*. He was disowned by the Farmington Monthly Meeting in 1846, and in 1850, he was active in the Waterloo Congregational Friends. Through his friendship with Amy and Isaac Post, he learned about the Fox sisters' communications with spirits and published *Singular Revelations. Explanation and History of the Mysterious Communion with Spirits, Comprehending the Rise and Progress of the Mysterious Noises in Western New-York, Generally Received as Spiritual Communications* (1850). In 1854 he worked in Philadelphia as a journalist. (City directory, 1854; Braude, *Radical Spirits*, 15–19; research by Christopher Densmore.)

2. Thomas Mott (1823–?), son of Lucretia and James, married his first cousin Mariana Pelham (1825–1872), the daughter of Martha Coffin Wright's first marriage. They shared the house on Arch Street with James and Lucretia Mott. (Cornell, *Adam and Ann Mott*, 325–26; Hallowell, *James and Lucretia Mott*, 278n, 326.)

3. SBA and Ernestine Rose stayed with William R. Wright, a physician and freethinker, at 544 Pine Street. (City directory, 1854.)

4. That is, the Sansom Street Hall.

5. SBA reached New York on April 17 to visit friends, stopped in Albany and Troy, and proceeded to the homes of her sisters in Washington County.

[April] 28 [*Battenville*] Friday Took tea at Julius Collins, Louis T. & Eliza McLean & Maria Whelden & Husband Mr. Pierce,[1] had not seen her in 10 years, time has made some marks, but yet she looks old fashion—

Some thing was said of Mr. Garrison, that he was a very bad man, I asked in what respects, said I thought him the most Christ like man I ever knew— Said Mr. Pierce, "does he <u>believe</u> in <u>keeping</u> the Christian <u>Sabbath</u>, does he <u>believe</u> the <u>Bible</u>?["] & various other like questions— I told Mr. P. he had not asked me for a <u>single</u> <u>scriptural</u> <u>evidence</u>, nor does the church require any other evidence, than to say you <u>believe</u> thus & so.— It is astonishing to see how wholly bound to creed & Dogmas are they. I exposed a good many of my heresies to great surprise of all present— Eliza T. said she would rather that I should be a Slave Holder or believe in Slave holding, than a disbeliever in the Plenary Inspiration of the Bible—thus is it <u>belief</u>—not Christian benevolence, that is made the modern test of Christianity— When will the world wake from its stupor & look <u>truth</u> strait in the face—

This A.M. the ground was white with snow & frozen rain, & all the buds & stems on the trees were encased with ice—there is great reason to fear that fruit must be injured by this severe frost & cold—[2]

1. Friends of her family, Julius Collins (c. 1808–?) and his wife Ann (c. 1807–?) farmed in Jackson, Washington County. Lewis T. McLean (c. 1818–?) was a cousin of Aaron McLean and a prosperous farmer in Greenwich with his wife Eliza (c. 1820–?) and three young children. (A. McLean to SBA, 11 January 1846, *Film*, 6:537–44; Federal Census, 1850.)

2. After recording the weather on April 29, SBA set aside her diary until December.

⤞ Bound volume, SBA Papers, MCR-S.

·⊏━━━◈━━━⊐·

79 ⤗ SBA TO MATILDA JOSLYN GAGE,[1] WITH ENCLOSURE

Rochester June 28/54

Dear Mrs. Gage

The Woman's Rights Cause, already greatly indebted to you for past services, solicits another favor at your hands. You will see by the enclosed ↑plan↓ of prosecuting the present campaign, what the cause now asks. You, I trust, agree with me, that the great work before us is the enlightening of Public Sentiment—& will take measures in your village, to raise a fund for the purchase & distribution of Mrs. Stantons Address—a copy of which I sent you last winter from Albany—

I know Slavery is the <u>All</u>-absorbing question of the day, still we must push forward this great <u>Central</u> question, which underlies all others, not excepting that of Slavery even— With much Love I am Yours for the Right

≈ *Susan B. Anthony*

≈ ALS, in the collection of Robert A. Baum, Woodland Hills, Calif.

ENCLOSURE

WOMAN'S RIGHTS.

Circulate the Petition

The Albany Woman's Rights Convention, held in February last, resolved to continue the work of Petitioning our State Legislature, from year to year, until the law of Justice and Equality shall be dispensed to the whole people, without distinction of sex.

In order to systematize and facilitate the labors of the friends who shall engage in the work of circulating the Petitions, a Committee was appointed to devise and present some definite plan of action.[2] In the estimation of that Committee, the first and most important work to be done is to enlighten the people as to the *real* claims of the Woman's Rights movement; thereby dispelling their many prejudices, and securing their hearty good will. To aid in the accomplishment of this first great object, the committee propose holding Woman's Rights Meetings in all the cities and many of the larger villages of the State, during the coming fall and winter, and gladly—could they command the services of Lecturing Agents—would they thoroughly canvass the entire State. But, since to do so is impossible, they would urge upon the friends in every county, town, village and school district, to hold public meetings in their respective localities, and, if none among their own citizens feel themselves competent to address the people, invite speakers from abroad. Let the question be fully and freely discussed, both pro and con, by both friends and opponents.

Though the living speaker cannot visit every hearth-stone throughout the length and breadth of the Empire State, and personally present the claims of our cause to the hearts and consciences of those who surround them, his arguments, by the aid of the invaluable art of printing, *may*. Therefore the committee have resolved to circulate as widely as possible the written statement of Woman's Political and Legal Rights, as contained in the Address, written by Elizabeth Cady Stanton, of Seneca Falls, N.Y., and adopted by the Albany Convention—presented to our Legislature, at its last session. This Address has been highly spoken of by many of the best papers in the State; and pronounced, by eminent lawyers and statesmen, an able and unanswerable argument. And the committee, being fully confident of its power to convince every candid enquirer after truth of the justice and mercy of our claims, do urgently call upon the friends everywhere to aid them in giving to it a thorough circulation.

There is no reform question of the day that meets so ready, so full, so deep a response from the masses, as does this Woman's Rights question. To ensure a speedy triumph, we have only to take earnest hold of the work of disseminating its immutable truths. Let us, then, agitate the question—hold public meetings—widely circulate Woman's Rights Tracts, and show to the world that we are in earnest—that we will be heard—that our demands stop not short of justice and perfect equality to every human being. Let us, at least, see to it, that this admirable Address of Mrs. Stanton is placed in the hands of every intelligent man and woman in the State, and thus the way prepared for the gathering up of a mighty host of names to our petitions, to be presented to our next Legislature. A mammoth roll, that shall cause our law makers to know that the *People* are with us, and that if our prayer be not wisely and justly answered by them, other and truer representatives will fill those Legislative Halls.

The success of our first appeal to our Legislature, made last winter, encourages us to persevere. That the united prayer of only 6000 men and women, should cause the reporting and subsequent passage in the House, of a bill granting two of our most special claims, that of the wife to her earnings, and the mother to her children, is indeed a result the most sanguine scarce dared to hope for. What may we not expect from our next appeal, that shall be 20,000, nay more, if we but be faithful, 100,000 strong. To the work, then friends, of renovating public sentiment, and circulating petitions. There is no time to be lost. Our Fourth of July gatherings will afford fit opportunity for both distributing the Address, and circulating the petitions. And Women of the Empire State, it is for you to do the work, it is for you to shake from your feet the dust of tyrant custom, it is for you to remember that "he who would be free, must himself strike the blow."[3]

The petitions to be circulated, are the same as last year—one asking for the *Just and Equal Rights of Women*, and the other for *Women's Right of Suffrage*. The petitions are to be signed by both men and women, the men's names placed in the right column, and the women's in the left. *All* intelligent persons must be ready and willing to sign the first, asking a revision of the laws relative to the property rights of woman, and surely, no true republican can refuse to give his or her name to the second, asking for woman the Right of Representation—a practical application of the great principles of '76.

It is desirable that there shall be one person in each county to whom all the petitions circulated in its several towns, villages and school districts, shall be forwarded, and who shall arrange and attach them in one roll, stating upon a blank sheet, placed between the petition and the signatures, the number of signers, the name of the county, and the number of towns represented, and forward them as early as the 1st of December next, to Susan B. Anthony, Rochester, N.Y. Where no person volunteers, or is appointed such county agent, the petitions, properly labeled, may be sent direct to Rochester.

Mrs. Stanton's Address is published in neat, pamphlet form, in large type, and may be had at the following prices: $2 per 100, 37½ cts. per dozen; or if sent by mail, $3 per 100, and 50 cts. per dozen. Packages of over 25, may be sent by express to all places on the line of the railroads, at a less cost than mail.

It is hoped that every person who reads this notice, and feels an interest in the universal diffusion of the true aim and object of the Woman's Rights agitation, will without delay, order copies of this address to distribute gratuitously or otherwise, among their neighbors and townsmen. Should there be any wishing to aid in this work, who cannot command the money necessary to purchase the address, their orders will be cheerfully complied with, free of charge.

The Committee have on hand a variety of Woman's Rights Tracts, written by S. J. May, Wendell Phillips, Elizabeth C. Stanton, Mrs. C.

I. H. Nichols, Ernestine L. Rose, T. W. Higginson, and others.[4] Also the Reports of the several National Woman's Rights Conventions, all of which may be had at very low prices.

All correspondence and orders for address, petitions, &c. should be addressed to Susan B. Anthony, General Agent, Rochester, N.Y. June 22, 1854.

❧ Circular, in the collection of Robert A. Baum, Woodland Hills, Calif. Published in *Rochester Daily Union*, 24 June 1854, and *Frederick Douglass' Paper*, 30 June 1854.

1. Matilda Joslyn Gage (1826–1898) took a small part in the woman's rights movement in the 1850s, while her four children were young, and became one of its leaders in the 1870s. Well educated by her abolitionist father and sent to the Clinton Liberal Institute near their home in Syracuse, she married Henry H. Gage, a merchant, in 1845, and they settled at Fayetteville in Onondaga County. She made her speaking debut at the convention in Syracuse in 1852. Gage joined the National Woman Suffrage Association at its founding in 1869, was its president in 1875, and was fiercely loyal to its pursuit of national citizenship through a federal amendment and its secular traditions. (*NAW*; Sally Roesch Wagner, "Introduction," in Matilda Joslyn Gage, *Woman, Church and State* [Watertown, Mass., 1980], xv–xxxix.)

2. The Albany meeting named SBA the general agent of a canvass to reach into every school district of the state with the petitions for just and equal rights and suffrage. Officers of the convention were to act as a committee to help her. (*Albany Evening Journal*, 15 February 1854, and *New York Daily Tribune*, 17 February 1854, *Film*, 7:965ff.)

3. Lord Byron, "Childe Harold's Pilgrimage," canto 2, stanza 76.

4. The absence of dates of publication on most of the early woman's rights tracts and the dearth of bibliographic attention to the tracts make it difficult to know which edition SBA offered in 1854. The titles that follow were available by 1853. Many of them went through at least two printings, at Syracuse in 1852 and Rochester in 1853, and most were reprinted at later dates. Samuel J. May, *A Discourse on the Rights and Condition of Women*, probably in the third edition, published at Syracuse in 1852; *The Speech of Wendell Phillips, to the Convention in Worcester, Oct., 1851*; *Letters from Mrs. E. C. Stanton—1st, to the Convention at Worcester, Oct. 1850; 2d, to the Convention at Syracuse, Sept. 1852*; *Speech of Mrs. C. I. H. Nichols to the Worcester Convention, Oct. 1851*; *Speech of Mrs. Ernestine L. Rose, to the Convention at Syracuse*; and T. W. Higginson, *Woman and Her Wishes: An Essay*. All but Higginson's tract were listed in the *Proceedings of Woman's Rights Convention, 1852*, back cover, as "in press."

·⊂══════⟫⟨══════⊃·

80 ≈ REMARKS BY SBA TO THE NEW YORK STATE
TEACHERS' ASSOCIATION

Editorial note: The ninth annual meeting of the State Teachers'
Association commenced at Oswego on 1 August 1854. As the usual
committees were named—for the business of the convention, location of the next meeting, nominations, and by-laws—men only were
selected. SBA introduced her resolutions on the afternoon of the
second day. Thereafter, two women were named to the board of
editors of the *New York Teacher*, and Henrietta Hughes of Syracuse
was elected a vice president.

[2 August 1854]

Miss Susan B. Anthony, of Rochester, offered the following resolutions:—

Resolved, That so long as woman be not appointed to fill any of the
offices of the Association, or act upon any of its committees, her
equality is ignored; and all resolves to the effect that woman is an
effective and efficient co-worker with man in the profession of teaching, and, therefore, freely admitted to all the rights and privileges of the
New York State Teachers' Association, are not only meaningless, but
insulting to her womanhood.

Resolved, That the Association instruct the committee on the nomination of officers, and Board of Editors for the *New York State Teacher*
for the ensuing year, to have woman represented in each of their
reports.

She said she did not desire to make a speech on this occasion. She
felt, and she presumed that every woman and every man with true
manly and womanly feelings felt that there was something wrong in the
management of this Association. There was a majority of women in the
Association, but not one said a word or did a thing in managing or
carrying on the affairs of the Association. <She thought it a shame that
all the business of such an Association should be transacted by men,
while so large a number of ladies were present, some of them of long
experience as teachers, and much more able to instruct in regard to a
teacher's duty, and suggest and act at a Teachers' Convention, than the
boys who generally undertook and carried on all the business con-

nected with it. She believed that while men were so ready to address honied words of compliment to the ladies, it would be much better to act as if they considered them as being capable of a higher destiny and more useful purpose, than mere wearers of silks and laces. And she thought that if women would speak out their honest thoughts and desires, they would be found almost universally anxious to have their sphere of action and of thought enlarged. But while many thus desire, lack of moral courage restrains them from expressing themselves on this subject.>[1] She did not desire to create discord; but she thought that according to the constitution of the Association, and the nature of the teacher's profession, that it was right and proper to give Woman a fair representation in the committees and in the list of officers. Her speech was eloquent and at least *one* of the most interesting of the session.

Mr. McElligott, of New York,[2] defended the Association. He said his business here was to waive entirely the discussion of the rights of women in general. He admitted the omission of women from the committee and offices. But could not concede that this was an insult to the sex. It was not so designed. He would not attempt an argument to prove there was no intention to insult the ladies. The idea was repulsive. There had been no instruction to select men rather than women. The ladies in the Association have all power and could confirm all committees or officers, or reject them. They have the right to vote, and can fill every office as they please. He was willing to hear from Miss Anthony or any other lady teacher on the subject of education. Ladies were better primary teachers than men, and if they are the equals of men in the higher departments, he, for one, was willing to admit it, but the world, and not the Association, was the best judge.

Miss Anthony—When women ask a right, who shall say whether she does it rightfully?

Mr. McElligott—The Association, of course.

Mr. Patchin[3] also insisted that the women here had power and did elect officers. <He proposed that the resolutions be referred to the ladies present for action, and he was willing to abide by the event.>[4]

⇠ *New York Teacher* 2 (September 1854): 265–66; *Oswego Times and Journal,* 3 August 1854.

1. From editorial, "Miss Anthony's Speech," *Oswego Times and Journal,* 3 August 1854.

2. James Napoleon McElligott (1812–1866) ran a private school in New York City and was active in the American Sunday-School Union. *McElligott's Manual, Analytical and Synthetical, of Orthography and Definition* (1845) won him the recognition of an M.A. from Yale, and his other textbooks included *The Humorous Speaker* (1853) and *The American Debater* (1855). (Kirk, *New York State Teachers*, 37–38; *NCAB*, 3:73; *ACAB*.)

3. Ira Patchin (1814–?), of Livonia, studied at the Genesee Wesleyan Seminary in Lima, New York, and was named superintendent of common schools in Livingston County in 1843. (James H. Smith, *History of Livingston County, New York* [Syracuse, N.Y., 1881], 133; *Biographical Review . . . of Livingston and Wyoming Counties, New York* [Boston, 1895], 381–82.)

4. From proceedings, *Oswego Times and Journal*, 3 August 1854.

---

81 ⇝ SBA TO SARAH PELLET

Rochester Aug. 8/54

Dear Sarah

I had long been asking my ↑self↓ where is Sarah Pellet & what is she busy about, for <u>busy</u> <u>she must be</u>—

I attended the Teachers Convention, & if you visit Lucy she will show you what I did there— The old Fogies were not a ↑little↓ troubled at my presence but the progressives out numbered them— Your letter was read, but did not hear it—[1]

I can tell you <u>exactly</u> what my business is the rest of this year—it ↑is↓ making arrangements for meetings in the large Cities of our State & securing such speakers as Nette & Lucy, Mrs Rose, & Mrs Stanton to Address them— I <u>may</u> speak some as time may dictate in smaller places, where an audience can be had by a speaker without a name— Now Sarah I can point ↑out↓ a work for you to do, but I fear it will be too <u>common place</u> it is that you come into this State & Canvas one or more Counties as time shall permit on Woman's Rights,—Lecture, raise funds for ~~Add~~ purchasing Mrs. Stantons Address for Distribution, get signatures to Petitions &c, and of the monies you raise, you shall receive a percentage that shall satisfy you as remuneration— What say you Sarah—here is a chance for you, (under the auspices of our State Committee) to make yourself thoroughly at home in the Lecture room— If you ever intend to make Lecturing your business, you surely need just such a discipline one cannot have a reputation as speaker, until they have <u>won</u> it, & simply giving a few Lectures to small audiences in large places will not win a name to one's self— You may think me mistaken, but nevertheless I am sure I am <u>right</u>— Lucy lectured faithfully for years & was scarcely heard of—she ↑got↓ her power by familiarizing herself with her subjects in small places—so must we all—

What say you, are you ready to come into this State—[2] We would like 40 women to work in the Counties— Mr. May says if Sarah Pellet was only in Syracuse, he should know who to name to raise Funds there, distribute Address & circulate Petitions or who would be the <u>leader</u> in the work— Mr. Channing I have not heard <u>from</u> this summer, but heard <u>of</u> his being at Brattleboro Vt.

I hope Mrs. Jenkins & Love[3] & many others will take to the work of Canvassing the State   Yours in Love

≈ *Susan B Anthony*

≈ ALS, Bella Clara Landauer Collection, MCR-S.

1. *New York Teacher* 2 [September 1854]: 270.

2. Sarah Pellet joined SBA and Matilda Gage at Saratoga Springs for a woman's rights meeting on 18 August, when the resort hosted several large meetings. Whigs opposed to the Kansas-Nebraska Act rallied on 16 August, and proponents of the Maine law gathered on 17 August. None of the well-known speakers accepted SBA's last-minute invitations to participate, and the three novice speakers were forever proud of their successful meeting. (Unidentified clipping from M. J. Gage Scrapbooks, *Film*, 8:64; *History*, 1:620–23; *Anthony*, 1:120–21; Jeter Allen Isely, *Horace Greeley and the Republican Party, 1853–1861: A Study of the New York Tribune* [Princeton, 1947], 90–98; Booraem, *Formation of the Republican Party*, 50–54.)

3. Mary Fenn Robinson Love (1824–1886), later Davis, grew up in western New York, attended college there, and married a schoolteacher named Samuel G. Love in 1846. When SBA met her in 1852, she lived at Randolph in Cattaraugus County. SBA carried a letter of introduction from Giles Stebbins, who wrote, "I know you will take Susan by the hand & do all possible." From the temperance work of 1852 and 1853, Mary Love moved into the woman's rights work of 1854 with a clear message about a woman's need to control her own person in marriage. Instead of touring with SBA in the winter of 1854, she journeyed to Indiana to divorce her husband and a year later, married Andrew Jackson Davis. Mary Davis returned to the woman's rights platform later in the decade, and she promoted ideas of woman's equality among spiritualists, where she was a recognized leader. After the Civil War Davis was active in

New Jersey's woman suffrage movement and supported the National Woman Suffrage Association. (*NAW*; Braude, *Radical Spirits*, 41–42, 58, 117–18; SBA diary and copybook, 1854 and later, p. 74, *Film*, 7:879ff.)

·⟨⟞⟝⟩·

82   Antoinette L. Brown to SBA

Henrietta[1] Nov. 5 '54

You are probably now enjoying a visit with Mr Garrison and other friends.[2] My mother[3] is too ill to allow me to accept your invitation to Rochester to day even if there were no other detaining causes

Next Thursday I am to go to Butler. Shall probably be in the city several hours. Will business or pleasure take you there the same day If so I should like to sit down under the flow of that torrent of talk which you have pent up in your soul. A thorough inundation of it would be quite refreshing

Lucy says you exceeded yourself at Phil.[4] Good! Will Mrs Rose be able to work in this state? How do the petitions come on? We must have a grand list. Will you let me have a hundred or two of Mrs Stantons address next Thursday—let them be left at your Fathers office if you cannot take them there yourself

Lucy was not engaged, when I left Cincinnati—nor do I believe she will ever be married to H. B. Blackwell & I know she will not to the brother.[5] For the rest you must get information from her. She wrote me only a short note ↑not↓ alluding to the subject of course, so my knowledge is intuitive or guesswork. Cordially

      ⤳ *Nette*

I had a good time in Cincinnati. Came back more rested than I went

Mrs Stanton could not do a better work than write for the Tribune & I am so glad she is going to N.Y. to <u>live</u>[6]

⤳ ALS, Blackwell Papers, MCR-S.

1. Antoinette Brown resigned her pastorate at South Butler, effective 20 July 1854, and returned to her parents' house for several months of rest. Doubts about her faith and fitness for the ministry produced what she described as severe mental conflict. Early in 1855 she pronounced herself quite

unorthodox and ready to resume preaching without pastoral duties. (Lasser and Merrill, *Friends and Sisters*, 89–90, 140–42; Cazden, *Antoinette Brown Blackwell*, 86–90.)

2. At Rochester.

3. Abigail Morse Brown (1793–1873).

4. At the Fifth National Woman's Rights Convention, held in Philadelphia, 18–20 October 1854. (*Film*, 8:68–70.)

5. Lucy Stone had, in fact, just agreed to marry Henry Browne Blackwell (1825–1909), an English-born hardware merchant, who lived near Cincinnati. Raised as an abolitionist and introduced to woman's rights by his remarkable sisters, especially the pioneer physician Elizabeth Blackwell, Henry Blackwell had pursued Lucy Stone since May 1853, promising her a marriage of equals. Antoinette Brown could speak knowledgeably about the brother, Samuel Charles Blackwell (1823–1901), because he was courting her. Sam Blackwell was in business with his brother. (*DAB*, s.v. "Blackwell, Henry Browne"; Lasser and Merrill, *Friends and Sisters*, 91–92; Cazden, *Antoinette Brown Blackwell*, 103–10.)

6. The convention in Philadelphia named ECS to a committee to "provide for the preparation and publication, in widely circulated journals, of facts and arguments relative to our cause." ECS began to write for the *Semi-Weekly Tribune* in November but did not move to New York. (*Lib.*, 12 January 1855; ECS to H. Greeley, [before 25 November 1854], and ECS to Editor, 25 November 1854, *Film*, 8:90–94.)

·◁━━━━▶·

83 ❧ SBA TO MATILDA JOSLYN GAGE

Rochester[1] Dec. 5, 1854

Dear Mrs. Gage

Your letter of the 20th Nov. was duly rec'd. I regret to learn that your children are ill & you thereby obliged to forego Lecturing for the present— Most assuredly do we need every one of our <u>small</u> number to help on the work. "The Fields are ripe unto harvest & the laborers are inded few—"[2]

I do but <u>little</u> in the way of getting signatures to petitions, get persons engaged to circulate them— Every where, numbers volunteer to do the work—

We intend to present the Petitions as early as the 2[d] week of the Session, that is all that shall be forwarded to me thus early—& after that, I hope the friends will continue sending them in to <u>Lydia</u> <u>Mott</u> <u>Albany</u> & we will continue reminding our Hon. Legislators from day to day, of the wants of the Women of the State— Therefore you will be in time, provided you are able to do any thing previous to the close of the Session—

It is easy, but not so pleasant as might be, to tell you what I am now doing, I am <u>snowed</u> in at Fairport—[3] Yesterday, Monday, A.M. I rode through the snow, 3½ miles to Depot, intending to go to Rochester by 7¼ Train, waited there until 5 O.C. P.M. & ↑no↓ train went west, then availed myself of a chance to stop at a Friends house, where I now am, with no prospect of getting away very soon— I have been lecturing since my return from Philadelphia, the 1st of Nov.— I do not succeed with door fees in small villages—the prejudice against a charge at the door is so very strong— I trust luck to Collections to defray my expenses, & <u>sell</u> the Books—Mrs. S. Address at 3 cts apiece & the bound tracts, got from Lucy at 25 cts apiece—she sold them at Phila at less than wholesale price—her printer Yerrington[4] charges me $16 per hundred— I believe I can get them printed for less money—to retail at 2/ they should wholesale at 1/—

We have decided not to hold a Convention in Albany this winter, but to present our Petitions quietly, thus avoiding to rouse the <u>Lion</u> of the <u>Pulpit</u> or the Press—

A note from Mrs. Jenkins a few days since, says she is ill & has been most of the Summer & Fall—therefore we can↑not↓ look to her for help—

This is an old fashion New-England Snow Storm, & ↑all↓ looks like the "<u>Snow scene</u>" paintings— If I were only at my own home, then could I write & prepare for future work— I am however among very pleasant people, & ought to be content, when thousands are overtaken by this Storm who have neither home or shelter nor friend—the sufferings of the poor sewing women must be extreme this winter— Yours Truly

❧ *Susan B. Anthony*

❧ ALS, Matilda Joslyn Gage Collection, MCR-S.

1. Written at Fairport, east of Rochester. SBA indicates how to address her letters.

2. SBA modifies Matt. 9:37–38 and Luke 10:2.

3. On 5 December the *New York Daily Tribune* was unable to give full particulars of this severe storm, "in consequence of the breaking down of telegraphs, the delay of railroad trains, the suspension of steamboat navigation; and the consequent failure of the mails." The storm was most severe in central and northern New York.

4. James Brown Yerrinton (1800–1866) printed the *Liberator* in Boston, along with his son James Manning Winchell Yerrinton (1825–1893). The son became a skilled phonographic reporter, in demand for meetings and lectures throughout the Northeast. (Garrison, *Letters*, 5:31–32.)

·⟨⸺⟩·

84 ❧ APPEAL BY ECS

Seneca Falls, Dec. 11, 1854.

TO THE WOMEN OF THE STATE OF NEW-YORK.

We purpose again, this winter, to send petitions to our State Legislature; one asking for the *Just* and *Equal Rights of Woman*, and one for *Woman's Right of Suffrage*. The latter, we think, covers the whole ground; for we can never be said to have *just and equal rights* until the *right of suffrage* is ours. Some who will gladly sign the former, may shrink from making this last demand. But be assured our cause can never rest on a safe, enduring basis until we get the right of suffrage. So long as we have no voice in the laws, we have no guarantee that privileges granted to us to-day, by one body of men, may not be taken from us to-morrow by another.

All man's laws, his theology, his daily life, go to prove the fixed idea in his mind of the entire difference in the sexes, a difference so broad, that what would be considered cruel and unjust between man and man, is kind and just between man and woman. Having discarded the idea of the oneness of the sexes, how can man judge of the needs and wants of a being so wholly unlike himself? How can he make laws for his own benefit and woman's too at the same time? He cannot! He never has, as all his laws relative to woman must clearly show. But when man shall fully grasp the idea that woman is a being of like feelings, thoughts, and passions with himself, he may be able to legislate for her, as one code would answer for both. But until then, a sense of justice, a wise self-love, impels us to demand a voice in his councils.

To every intelligent, thinking woman, we put the question, On what sound principles of jurisprudence, constitutional law, or human rights, are one-half of the people of this State disfranchised? If you answer, as you must, that it is done in violation of all law, then we ask you, when and how is this great wrong to be righted? We say *now*; and petitioning is the first step in its accomplishment. We hope, therefore, that every woman in the State will sign her name to the petitions. It is most humiliating to know that many educated women so stultify their consciences as to declare they have all the rights they want. Have you, who make this declaration, ever read the barbarous laws in reference to women, to mothers, to wives and daughters, which disgrace our statute books? Laws which are not surpassed in cruelty and injustice by any slave-holding code in the United States—laws which strike at the root of the glorious doctrine for which our fathers fought, and bled, and died, "no taxation without representation"—laws which deny a right most sacredly observed by many of the monarchies of Europe, "the right of trial by a jury of one's own peers"—laws which trample on the holiest and most unselfish of all human affections, a mother's love for her child, and with ruthless cruelty snap asunder the tenderest ties— laws which enable the father, be he a man or a minor, to tear the infant from the mother's arms, and send it if he choose to the Fegee Islands; yea, to will the guardianship of the *unborn* child to whomsoever he may please, whether to the Sultan of Turkey or the Imaum of Muscat— laws by which our sons and daughters may be bound to service, to cancel their fathers' debts of *honor*, in the meanest rum-holes and brothels in the vast metropolis—laws which violate all that is most pure and sacred in the marriage relation, by giving to the cruel, beastly drunkard, the rights of a man, a husband, and father—laws which place the life long earnings of the wife at the disposal of the husband, be his character what it may—laws which leave us at the mercy of the rumseller and the drunkard, against whom we have no protection for our lives, our children, or our homes—laws by which we are made the watch-dogs to keep a million and a half of our sisters in the foulest bondage the sun ever shone upon—which forbid us to give food and shelter to the panting fugitive from the land of Slavery.

If, in view of laws like these, there be women in this State so lost to self-respect, to all that is virtuous, noble and true, as to refuse to raise their voices in protest against such degrading tyranny, we can only say of that system, which has thus robbed womanhood of all its glory and greatness, what the immortal Channing[1] did of slavery: "If," said he, "it be true that the slaves are contented and happy—if there is a system that can blot out all love of freedom from the soul of man, destroy every trace of his divinity, make him happy in a condition so low and benighted and hopeless—I ask for no stronger argument against such a slavery as ours!" No! never believe it; woman falsifies herself and blasphemes her God when, in view of her present social, legal, and political position, she declares she has all the rights she wants. If a few drops of Saxon blood gave our Frederick Douglass such a clear perception of his humanity, his inalienable right, as to enable him, with the slaveholder's Bible, the slaveholder's Constitution, a southern public sentiment and education, all laid heavy on his shoulders, to stand upright, and walk forth in search of freedom, with as much ease as did Samson of old with the massive gates of the city,[2] shall we, the daughters of our Hancocks and Adams—we, in whose veins flows the blood of the Pilgrim Fathers—shall we never try the strength of these withes of law and gospel with which, in our blindness, we have been bound, hand and foot? Yes, the time has come,

> The slumber is broken, the sleeper is risen;
> The day of the Goth and the Vandal is o'er;
> And old Earth feels the tread of Freedom once more.

Fail not, Women of the Empire State, to swell our petitions. Let no religious scruples hold you back. Take no heed to man's interpretation of Paul's injunction to women. To any thinking mind, there is no difficulty in explaining those passages of the Apostle as applicable to the times in which they were written, as having no reference whatever to the Women of the nineteenth century.

"Honor the King," heroes of '76! Those leaden tea-chests of Boston harbor cry out, "Render to Caesar the things that are Caesar's."[3] When the men of 1854, with their Priests and Rabbis, shall rebuke the disobedience of their forefathers,—when they shall cease to set at defiance the British lion and the Apostle Paul in their national policy, then it will be time enough for us to bow down to man's interpretation of law touching our social relations, and acknowledge that God gave us powers and rights, merely that we might show forth our faith in Him, by being helpless and dumb.

The writings of Paul, like our State Constitutions, are susceptible of various interpretations. But when the human soul is roused with holy indignation against injustice and oppression, it stops not to translate human parchments, but follows out the law of its inner being, written by the finger of God in the first hour of its creation.

Our petitions will be sent to every county in the State, and we hope that they will find at least ten righteous women to circulate them. But should there be any county so benighted that a petition cannot be circulated throughout its length and breadth, giving to every man and woman an opportunity to sign their names, then we pray, not that "God will send down fire and brimstone upon it,"[4] but that the "Napoleons" of this movement will flood it with Women's Rights tracts and missionaries.

⮠ *Elizabeth Cady Stanton,*
Chair'n N.Y. Women's Rights Con.

⮠ *New York Semi-Weekly Tribune,* 26 December 1854. Published in *Frederick Douglass' Paper,* 22 December 1854; *Lily,* 1 January 1855; *Una,* January 1855.

1. That is, William Ellery Channing.
2. Judg. 16:1–3.
3. Matt. 22:21.
4. A recurring image of the Lord's wrath, after the destruction of Sodom and Gomorrah by fire and brimstone in Gen. 19:24, Ps. 11:6.

---

85 ⮠ FROM THE DIARY OF SBA

[*26–27 December 1854*]

Chataque County Woman's Rights Convention held Tuesday Dec. 26th 1854 at Mayville in the Court House.[1]

Marrietta Richmond of Columbia County[2] in company with self— stopped at the house of Cyrus Underwood—[3] The weather warm & rainy— Sleighing gone, & wagoning dangerous on account of the heavy snowdrifts—

Notwithstanding, the Towns of Chataque, Clymer, Ellicott Harmony Stockton, Sherman & Hartfield were represented—whole number of Towns in the County 24—

Though the meeting was small, there seemed an earnest seeking after the new Truth— By invitation I went to Sherman a distance of 9 miles & spoke to a large audience Wednesday evening— Never saw more enthusiasm on the subject, even the Orthodox Churches vied with each other, who should open their doors— [*No entry for 28 December; entries for 29–30 omitted.*]

1. SBA resumed use of the volume in which she kept the diary of her trip to Washington with this entry. Mayville was the seat of Chautauqua County.

2. Mary Etta or Marietta Richmond (1817–1890) grew up in Hillsdale, Columbia County, and lived there until her death. Little is known about her beyond references to her abolitionist activity and the fact that she joined SBA on this tour in 1854 and 1855. At woman's rights conventions at Saratoga Springs in August 1855 and again at New York City in May 1860 she served with SBA on the finance committees. (Federal Census, 1850; *Una*, September 1855, and *Proceedings of the Tenth National Woman's Rights Convention, Held at the Cooper Institute, New York City, May 10th and 11th, 1860* [Boston, 1860], 3, in *Film*, 8:277–78, 9:612ff; Joshua Bailey Richmond, *The Richmond Family, 1594–1896, and Pre-American Ancestors, 1040–1594* [Boston, 1897], 322; and assistance from Helen M. McLallen, Columbia County Historical Society.)

3. Cyrus Underwood (c. 1801–?), a farmer, lived in the town of Chautauqua. He and his wife Emaline, the same age, were both from Massachusetts. Their eight children living at home in 1850 were all born in New York. (Federal Census, 1850.)

❧ Bound volume, SBA Papers, MCR-S.

·⊂══⊃✕⊂══⊃·

86 ≈ ANTOINETTE L. BROWN TO ECS

Andover [*Mass.*][1] Dec. 28 '54

Dear Mrs. Stanton—

Did you think my last was a savage letter? Well perhaps it was! You will give me credit for plain speaking at least.[2]

I have heard nothing yet from you or Susan and so thought I would write again

Please dont think me captious, Mrs Stanton, if you can help it, for it really is not true; but I am very sensitive about fastening theological questions upon the <u>woman movement</u>. It is not that I am horrified at your calling St Pauls writings 'human parchments'; but because I think when it is done officially that it is really unjust to the cause. It is compelling it to endorse something which does not belong to it. When you write for yourself say exactly what you please, but if you write as Cha'n Woman's Rights Con. do not compell us to endorse any thing foreign to the movement

But enough of that I was very glad to know that you and Susan were taking hold of the work so full of energy. God bless you both. You will get a grand petition   You will help her hold meetings most of the time, cant you? I thought from what Mrs Rose said that she would also work earnestly

The New Englanders are looking with interest to see what <u>our state</u> will do.

I shall be home in January sometime; yet but very little reliance can be put upon me any way since I am 'laid up to dry.'

Last week I saw Lucy Stone at Boston and she partly promised to come here and spend Sabbath and new years day. She is really engaged now, and will be married in the Spring. Well I am glad. Arent you? Very happy she seems too, and as frank as the day about it. I like that. Dont you? I would not be ashamed of 'my Harry' if I had one; but am 'o'er glad' after all that I haven't 'got in love.'

A great many people were at the antislavery Bazaars last week   It was pleasant to have a general rallying—Mrs Child was there and had a table[3]   Cordially ever

❧ Nette L. Brown

Wont you send me a line here   Andover, Mass. if you write by the 8th of January which I hope you will, or if after that to Hopedale Mass for a week more.[4]

❧ ALS, Blackwell Papers, DLC.

1. Where she visited her brother William Bryant Brown, pastor of a free church.

2. Brown wrote this missing letter after reading the appeal to the women of New York.

3. That is, Lydia Maria Child.

4. Brown frequently visited this fraternal community of two hundred people at Milford, Massachusetts. Its residents, who called themselves Practical Christians, were active in abolition and other reforms. (Fogarty, *American Communal and Utopian History*, 10, 145, 183–84.)

87 ↝ ANNOUNCEMENT BY SBA

[5 January 1855]

WOMAN'S RIGHT—SUFFRAGE.

County Woman's Rights Conventions will be held as follows, to discuss all the reasons that impel Woman to demand her Right of Suffrage. At

Bath, Steuben Co.	Friday, Jan. 5.
Elmira, Chemung Co.	Monday, Jan. 8.
Penn Yan, Yates Co.	Wednesday, Jan. 10.
Canandaigua, Ontario Co.	Friday, Jan. 12.
Rochester, Monroe Co.	Monday, Jan. 15.
Albion, Orleans Co.	Wednesday, Jan. 17.
Lockport, Niagara Co.	Thursday, Jan. 18.
Buffalo, Erie Co.	Friday, Jan. 19.
Warsaw, Wyoming Co.	Monday, Jan. 22.
Geneseo, Livingston Co.	Wednesday, Jan. 24.
Batavia, Genesee Co.	Friday, Jan 26.[1]

The first sessions will commence at 1 o'clock P.M.; the second at 7 o'clock, evening.

The Rev. Antoinette L. Brown and Ernestine L. Rose will be in attendance at these meetings; Lucy Stone is also expected at some of them.

It is hoped that every town of each county will be largely represented, and that the friends everywhere will be diligent in circulating the Woman's Rights petitions, and send up long lists of signatures to our County Conventions.

↝ *Susan B. Anthony,*
General Agent, Rochester, N.Y.

↝ *New York Daily Tribune,* 5 January 1855.

1. For this meeting, see *Film,* 8:128.

·❮═════❮═❯═════❯·

88 ❧ FROM THE DIARY OF SBA

[*5–12 January 1855*]¹

Steuben Co. W.R. Convention held at Bath Friday Jan 5, 1855— Meeting in Court House

Did not succeed in getting the names of representatives from but 4 Towns— House Full in the P.M. & crowded in the evening, though an admission of 12½ cts was charged Mrs. Rose spoke full two hours— Every one we meet is ready to tell some fact under the cruel laws to woman—

A Mrs. Rose of Avoca acted as President—² Good attention & order— Mrs President a woman of Dignity & intelligence—had on the short dress as did two other ladies, brave women, it does my soul good to see them—

Six women of Cohocton sent their names & reasons why they demanded the right of suffrage—

Mrs. Rose spoke on Saturday eve the 6th to a good audience, then all took Cars for Corning at 9½ Oclock   Mrs. R. stopped at the Dickinson House   Miss Richmond & self at Mr. Lowers³—had a meeting in Concert Hall Sunday evening— None of the Ministers would give the notice of our meeting, which so incensed some of the men, that they went to the printing office, struck off handbills & had boys standing at the doors of the Churches to give them to the peopple as they passed out—had some 150 or 200 present—

In the evening, I could but ask "at whose day lay the sin of Sabbath breaking—at the Ministers who refused to read the notice, or their Laymen, who set the type & struck of the Bills—["]

1. Entries for 1–3 January are omitted. Ernestine Rose met SBA at Corning on the third and traveled with her to Bath.

2. Adeline Rose of Avoca presided and her husband, probably H. S. Rose, served as vice president, according to the coverage in the *Farmer's Advocate and Steuben Advertiser*, 10 January 1855, *Film*, 8:116–17.

3. SBA stopped with him on 3 January also.

Chemung County Woman's Rights Convention held in Ely Hall, Elmira Monday Jan 8th 1855.

Mrs [*blank*] Gleason[1] was elected President, A Mr. Peeble's Universalist Minister one of the Vice Pres.[2]—he sat on the Platform, & in the evening made a few remarks—

The meeting was not large, but two or three towns represented

Thomas K. Beecher attended part of the time—took ↑tea↓ at Mrs. Holbrooks, Mr Beecher in company—[3]

His Theology as set forth that evening is a dark & hopeless one— sees no hope for the progress of the race—does not believe that education will enable man to improve his own species—as it has that of the the Animal races—

Spent the night at Dr. Glasons— Mrs. Rose remained & spoke on Tuesday evening— I returned to Corning Tuesday A.M. at 9 Oclock & spoke there to a small house again—a perfect apathy seems resting upon the people of Corning— The Clergy are responsible for it— ~~returned~~ returned to Elmira, on the 10 Oclock evening Train— Found Mrs. Welling[4] just retired were up again at 4 Oclock A.M. to go to Pen Yan— Mrs. Rose' meeting was small again—

The Rev. Mr. Murdock,[5] preaches in one of their most popular churches & his bigotry is enough to enslave the whole community—

1. Rachel Brooks Gleason (1820-1905) and her husband Silas Orsemus Gleason (1818-1899), both of them doctors, opened the Elmira Water-Cure in 1852. A student of Lydia Folger Fowler at Central Medical College in Rochester, Rachel Gleason earned her medical degree in 1851, and her skillful combination of hygenic, hydropathic, and medical treatments attracted many female patients. (*American Women*; Jane B. Donegan, "*Hydopathic Highway to Health*": *Women and Water-Cure in Antebellum America* [Westport, Conn., 1986], 39-49; Weiss and Kemble, *Great American Water-Cure Craze*, 155, 157-60.)

2. James Martin Peebles (1822-1922), from Vermont, preached at Oswego in 1854, at Elmira in 1855, and in Baltimore in 1856. He became a prominent lecturer and leader among spiritualists. (Braude, *Radical Spirits*, 47, 167-68; assistance from the Unitarian Universalist Historical Society.)

3. Thomas Kinnicut Beecher (1824-1900), younger brother of Catharine Beecher and Harriet Beecher Stowe, became pastor of the Independent Congregational Church in Elmira in June 1854. Modern scholarship echoes SBA's summation of his theology. A heartbroken widower, Beecher was living with the Gleasons at the Elmira Water-Cure. The tea party may have occurred in the home of George W. Holbrook, a physician who lived on Church Street

near High. A "Mrs. Holbrook" signed the call to the state convention in 1853. (*DAB*; Marie Caskey, *Chariot of Fire: Religion and the Beecher Family* [New Haven, 1978], 249–83; City directory, 1857.)

4. Catherine E. Welling, age thirty-six, wife of local manufacturer G. Post Welling, and mother of three children. She signed the call to the state convention in 1853. (Federal Census, 1850.)

5. David Murdoch (1800–1861) was called to Elmira's First Presbyterian Church in 1851 and stayed until 1860, when a new Second Presbyterian Church called him. He was a graduate of the University of Glasgow. (Henry B. Peirce, *History of Tioga, Chemung, Tompkins, and Schuyler Counties, New York* [Philadelphia, 1879], 254, 257; City directory, 1857.)

Yates County W.R. Con. held in Wesleyan Methodist Church at Pen Yan, Wednesday Jan 10th 1855

Arrived here from Elmira, about 8 Oclock A.M.— Miss Richmonds Cousin met her at Depot & took her to his home— A Mr. Brigham also met us & took Mrs. Rose & self to the house of Mr. Curtis[1]—very fine family indeed—every thing in beautiful order—& the cooking scientifically done—oh the murderous work that is perpetrated in the culinary departments of nine tenths the establishments of the land— The domestic sphere, considered the only appropriate one for woman—& yet not one woman in ten taught the art of bread making even—

Here we came in collission with Elder Knapp, the great Baptist Revivalist[2]—he had been at work three weeks—still we had a full house, & great interest manifested

In the evening—had a full house again, & a full vote, asking Mrs. Rose to remain & speak again Thursday night[3]—but we were too tired to think of it—had been broken of our sleep so much for the week past—

1. Probably Samuel F. Curtis, a cabinet and chair maker born in Connecticut about 1800, his wife Mary, two years older and born in Massachusetts, and their two children. (Federal Census, 1850, 1860.)

2. Jacob Knapp (1799–1874), a popular, itinerant Baptist evangelist, preached wherever a church would have him and always drew large crowds.

3. A report of the meeting appeared in the *Yates County Whig*, undated clipping, *Film*, 8:123.

Ontario County W.R. Con. held at Bemus' Hall Canandaigua, Friday Jan. 12th 1855—

Miss Richmond left us at Pen-Yan to Lecture by herself   Too expensive to pay Fare for three— Mrs. R & I took carriage to Mrs. Sands,[1] who had written us to go directly to her house—when there, she took us into a little room not 11. feet square, containing bed, Cooking Stove, beauro, table & three or four chairs—on the stove was a pot boiling some kind of fresh meat—the floor was strewn with papers, chips & straws—gave evidence of not having felt the impress of a broom for weeks—

She & her husband have been in a quarrel for years about this property   Soon learned that he J. D. Sands had issued Bills, announcing that he would be at our meeting & give his experience in Womans Rights for the last five years— Suffice it to say that he did not speak— though called out in the eve at close of Mrs. Rose speech— We declared the meeting adjourned— After learning the state of things I went out & hired a carriage to take us to the Candaigua Hotel—then took Carriage & went to every school, & gave the notice of the meeting There was a great commotion about the Sand's affair— The poor man & his chums seemed to think we had gone there for the purpose of settling individual quarrels, instead of advocating great first principles—[2]

1. The Sandses signed the call to the woman's rights convention at Rochester in 1853, and Mrs. Sands attended, speaking "a few words of encouragement." James B. Sands was a farmer at Canandaigua, age forty-five in 1850 and married to Catherine, also forty-five years old. In 1850 they had a four-year-old son. (*Frederick Douglass' Paper*, 16 December 1853, *Film*, 7:844ff; Federal Census, 1850.)

2. After writing a heading for the Monroe County meeting on 14 January, SBA stopped keeping this diary.

⇜ Bound volume, SBA Papers, MCR-S.

·⟨⟨══════⟩⟩·

89 ⇒ SPEECH BY SBA AT MONROE COUNTY
      WOMAN'S RIGHTS CONVENTION

Editorial note: Only SBA and Ernestine L. Rose were on hand for the convention in Rochester's Corinthian Hall, where four hundred people met at 2 P.M. on 15 January 1855, and twelve hundred gathered in the evening. Local women, including Mary Hallowell and Rhoda DeGarmo, were made officers of the meeting.

[15 January 1855]

Miss Susan B. Anthony then took the floor, and addressing "Mrs. President," proceeded to lay before her hearers food for their reflection. She stated that the principal object in view at present, is to agitate the question of Woman's right of suffrage, and by means of petition to operate on the State Legislature. Last year a petition bearing six thousand names was presented to the Legislature at Albany, and had the effect to cause the passage of a bill in the Assembly, giving to Woman some of the rights claimed by the petitioners. The bill did not come up in the Senate, however, owing to its unfavorable position on the calendar. Now it is proposed to follow up the good already accomplished, and by the same means. A great change has taken place in public opinion during the past year. In districts where it was almost impossible to get a name last year, scores are willing to sign now. Woman does not ask for any privileges; all she wants is her rights—to be placed upon an equality with man. If it be true that the nature of woman is different from that of man, no system of education, or position, can make them similar. This point was dwelt upon at length, and Queen Victoria, Joan of Arc, and numerous others, were alluded to in illustration. It was contended that woman is no less modest because she assists in the exercises of the dissecting room; that Antoinette L. Brown is no less refined, chaste, and lovely, because she officiates in the pulpit; and that women who fill various positions considered by many out of their sphere, are no less virtuous in consequence thereof. After alluding to the capabilities of woman, the speaker showed up the practice of cutting down their wages from the prices paid to men, when their work is performed full as well. The expense and value of female education, was next alluded to as compared with those of man, and the modern boarding schools for young misses handled without mittens. While the expense of educating the former was larger than that of the latter, the value received was the other way. The young man goes through a course of substantial studies and comes out a thinking being; the young lady is given a few lessons on the piano, a superficial knowledge of French and Italian, and comes out a frivolous butterfly—a mere plaything. To charge this difference upon the Creator is blasphemy; the evil lies in the systems of education. Woman wants honest employment and just compensation, and if means were contributed to this end, instead of buying and distributing tracts and bibles, and educating not over industrious young men for the ministry, much more real good might be accomplished. Miss Anthony concluded by suggesting the expediency of establishing in different localities Houses of Industry, where young women might learn trades and fit themselves for usefulness; and then, if there was any money to spare, try and do something for those helpless young men who are so anxious to enter the ministry.

～ *Rochester Daily Union*, 16 January 1855.

---

90 ～ ARTICLE BY ECS

[February 1855]

RUTH HALL.[1]

Some have been beaten till they know
What wood a cudgel's of by the blow;
Some kicked, until they can feel whether
A shoe be Spanish or neat's leather.[2]

By this same instinct some women know a true man from the creature that struts in whiskers, broadcloth and pantaloons as his representatives.

If by any unfortunate blunder in society she awakes to the consciousness that her legal protectors are her tyrants, in spite of all the beautiful things that have been written and said on conjugal, filial and fraternal devotion, her honest indignation will ever and anon boil up and burst forth in defiance of all ties of blood and kindred. In the name of womanhood, I thank Fanny Fern for this deeply interesting life experience. To me the tale of sorrow is beautifully and truthfully told. It matters not whether the selfish male monsters so graphically sketched in "Miss Hall," that compound of ignorance, formality and cant, are all of her own family,—enough that plenty of just such people live. This is some woman's experience. If it is her own life, so much the better. Heaven has witnessed these petty tyrannies in the isolated household long enough. When woman does at length divest herself of all false notions of justice and delicacy, and gives to the world a full revelation of her sufferings and miseries,—the histories of all other kinds of injustice and oppression will sink into utter insignificance, before the living pictures she shall hold up to the unwilling vision of domestic tyrants.

> Justice like lightning ever should appear
> To few men's ruin, but to all men's fear.[3]

Hardship and struggle always crush the weak and insignificant, but call forth and develop the true and noble soul. The great lesson taught in Ruth Hall is that God has given to woman sufficient brain and muscle to work out her own destiny unaided and alone. Her case, like ten thousand others, goes to prove the common notion that God made woman to depend on man, a romance, and not a fact of every-day life. Fanny Fern has been severely criticised for drawing her sketches from familiar scenes and faces. If her pictures are not pleasing ones, it seems to me the censure more justly belongs to the living subjects, than the artist who has too faithfully drawn the sketch. That she is truthful, is seen from the fact that the public readily pronounced her work an autobiography. Authors generally claim the privilege of writing about what they have seen and felt. Men have given us all their experience, from Moses down to the last village newspaper; and how much that is palatable have they said of woman? And now that woman has seized the brush, and brought forth on the canvas a few specimens of dwarfed and meagre manhood, lo! what a furor of love and reverence has seized our world of editors and critics! You who have ridiculed your mothers, wives and sisters since you first began to put pen to paper, talk not of "filial irreverence." This is but a beginning, gentlemen. If you do not wish us to paint you wolves, get you into lambs' clothing as quickly as possible. It is our right, our duty, to condemn what is false and cruel wherever we find it. A Christian charity should make me as merciful towards my enemy as my bosom friend; and righteousness would rebuke sin in either.

If there is anything galling in suffering and poverty, it is to be deserted by those who in sunny hours have shared our happiness and plenty. If all tyrannical parents, husbands and brothers knew that the fantastic tricks they play at the hearthstone, would in time be judged by a discerning public, no one can estimate the restraining influence of such a fear. Woman owes it to herself, to her sex, to the race, no longer to consent to and defend the refinements of degradation to which Christian woman is subject in the nineteenth century. We were sorry to see so severe a review of Ruth Hall, in an anti-slavery paper, as appeared in the "Anti-Slavery Standard." It was unworthy a place there, in columns that profess so much sympathy for humanity. The heart, if you have one, does sometimes hold the head in abeyance. Read "Ruth Hall," as you would read the life of "Solomon Northup," a Frederick Douglass,[4]—as you would listen to the poor slaves in our anti-slavery meetings. The story of cruel wrongs, suffered for weary days and years, finds sympathy in every breast. What is grammar, or rhetoric, rules of speech, or modes of thought, when a human soul pours forth his tale of woe to his fellow man! Among the "good old books"[5] you read, cold critic of the Standard, have you one on Nature? The next *mulatto slave* that comes North, and gets upon a platform, to tell of the cruelty and injustice of his *father and brethren*, hiss him down,—read him the laws of the Mohammedans and Christians on "filial irreverence"; "tell him his speech has no literary merit,"—"that he had better turn his attention to something else than oratory."[6] Because a villain for his own pleasure, has conferred on me the boon of existence, by what law, other than the Christian one—"Love your enemies"—am I bound to love and reverence him who has made my life a curse and a weariness, and who possesses in himself none of the Godlike qualities which command my veneration? We love our Heavenly Father, because he is just and good, and not because he is God. The blessed name of father does not belong to every man who merely begets a child. It takes love and kindness and sympathy to make a man my father. The law of affinity goes deeper than blood. What is it to me whether the man who robs me of my God-given rights, is a father, a brother, a husband, or a Southern slave-holder? Is my loss less, because the blow is struck at the hearthstone? It is my privilege, in either case, to throw myself on the great heart of Humanity, and to plead my cause wherever I can find a court to listen. Resistance to tyrants is obedience to God.[7] If the son is not taught at home, that there is a limit to his rights, he will never learn it elsewhere.

If woman had done her duty to her sires and sons, think you it would have taken them nearly one hundred years, after giving to the world a declaration of rights that made every king in Europe tremble beneath his crown, to see that a woman has a right to the property she inherits, and to the wages she earns with her own hands?

Pray, do not let the teaching come from anti-slavery men, that there are spots on this green earth, where tyranny may vent itself unknown and unrebuked. What are the strokes, the paddle or the lash, to the refined insults, with which man seeks to please or punish woman?

> Think'st thou there is no tyranny but that
> Of blood and chains?—The despotism of vice—
> The weakness, the wickedness of luxury—
> The negligence—the apathy—the evils
> Of sensual sloth—produce ten thousand tyrants.[8]

❧ E. C. S.

❧ *Una*, February 1855.

1. *Ruth Hall: A Domestic Tale of the Present Time* (1855) is a fictionalized autobiography by Fanny Fern that tells the story of a woman's search for self-fulfillment, not in marriage but in the financial independence she achieves as a writer. Fern's former publisher, William U. Moulton, revealed her secret identity in December 1854, and her unflattering but recognizable portraits of family and friends prompted controversy and critical reviews.

ECS replied to a review in the *National Anti-Slavery Standard*, 13 January 1855, which characterized *Ruth Hall* as "upon the whole, a very stupid book." The reviewer reserved his most serious criticism for Fern's angry portrayal of her father and brother. He was "indignant" that she could "so far forget a Christian law and a natural instinct" as to hold her own father and brother up to public "ridicule and contempt." "The Mohammedans," he continued, "pronounce their most dreadful anathema upon him who is guilty of filial irreverence."

2. Samuel Butler, "Hudibras," pt. 2, canto 1, lines 221–24.

3. *Swetnam, the Woman-hater, Arraigned by Women*, act 4, sc. 1, lines 89–90.

4. *Twelve Years a Slave* (1853) recorded the experience of Solomon Northup (1808?–1863), a free black man from New York who was kidnapped and sold into slavery in Louisiana in 1841. His narrative of the experience sold well in American and European editions. *Narrative of the Life of Frederick Douglass, an American Slave; Written by Himself* was published in 1845. (*DANB*.)

5. The reviewer had never before read Fern's work because, "[t]here are so many good old books to read that one of limited leisure seldom finds much time for new ones."

6. The reviewer wrote that *Ruth Hall* had "very little literary merit" and echoed a character in the book in urging Fanny Fern to "'turn her attention to something else than literature.'"

7. Epigram attributed to Thomas Jefferson.

8. Lord Byron, *Sardanapalus*, act 1, sc. 2, lines 66–70.

·❪━━━━━❄❅❄━━━━━❫·

91 ❧ ANNOUNCEMENT BY SBA

[7 February 1855]

Woman's Rights Meetings. County Woman's Rights Meetings, to discuss all the reasons that impel Woman to demand her rights of suffrage, are to be held as follows:

Albany, Albany Co..	Tuesday and Wednesday Evenings, Feb. 13 and 14.
Troy, Rensselaer Co.,	Friday, Feb. 16.
Schenectady, Schenectady Co.,	Friday, Feb. 16.
Salem, Washington Co.,	Monday, Feb. 19.
Ballston Springs, Saratoga Co.,	Monday, Feb. 19.
Caldwell, Warren Co.,	Wednesday, Feb. 21.
Schoharie, Schoharie Co.,	Wednesday, Feb. 21.
Elizabethtown, Essex Co.,	Friday, Feb. 23.[1]
Fonda, Montgomery Co.,	Friday, Feb. 23.
Plattsburgh, Clinton Co.,	Monday, Feb. 26.
Johnstown, Fulton Co.,	Monday, Feb. 26.
Malone, Franklin Co.,	Wednesday, Feb. 28.
Herkimer, Herkimer Co.,	Wednesday, Feb. 28.
Canton, St. Lawrence Co.,	Friday, March 2.
Morehouseville, Hamilton Co.,	Friday, March 2.

The first session of these meetings will commence at 1 o'clock P.M.; second at 7 o'clock evenings.

Ernestine L. Rose, the Rev. Antoinette L. Brown, Mrs. E. O. Smith,[2] and the Rev. S. J. May, will be in attendance at the Albany, Troy and Schenectady meetings, and some one or more of them at all the others.

It is hoped that every town of the Counties will be largely represented by self-appointed Delegates.

Afternoon Sessions, Free; Evening Session, One Shilling[3] admission.

By order of the N.Y. State Woman's Rights Committee.

❧ *Susan B. Anthony,*
General Agent.

❧ *New York Daily Tribune*, 7 February 1855.

1. For this meeting, see *Film*, 8:150.
2. Elizabeth Oakes Smith.
3. A coin worth 12½ cents.

·⊂════╳╳════⊃·

92 ❧ SPEECH BY SBA AT ALBANY COUNTY WOMAN'S RIGHTS CONVENTION

Editorial note: Antoinette Brown and Ernestine Rose accompanied SBA to the county meeting at the Albany Universalist Church on 13–14 February 1855. Despite bad weather, "quite large and respectable audiences" attended the meeting and heard "a style of oratory that would do infinite credit to any of the male sex." (*Albany Argus*, 15 February 1855.)

[13 February 1855]

Miss Anthony stated the object of the meeting to be the formation of a county society, to advocate and advance the rights of women. Since November, nineteen associations of a similar character have been organized, and the cause was acquiring new friends and advocates in every quarter. Miss A. depicted the wrongs which woman suffers, and by examples, illustrated the inequality in the rights of the opposite sex. In Rochester, said Miss A., there are sixteen public schools, eight of which are superintended by females. The same studies are pursued, and the progress made by the students in the schools under the care of females, is acknowledged to be greater than by those under the supervision of the male teachers. And yet the males receive salaries of $700 each, per annum, while the equally deserving, and the better qualified females, are paid but $250 yearly. Again, a man tailor receives from $4 to $10 for making a coat; a woman from $2 to $4; a male cook from twelve to twenty shilling per day, while a female, equally skilful, is fortunate to receive as much per week.

Miss A. further claimed that a most grievous wrong existed in that woman was not entitled to her own earnings. She met the argument, that woman, if allowed the rights claimed for her, would be less womanly in her nature; and by numerous examples, endeavored to prove the fallacy of the objection. She alluded to Queen Victoria, Joan of Arc, the Maid of Saragossa,[1] Miss Herschell, Miss Mitchell,[2] Comptroller Flagg's daughters,[3] and others, to disprove the allegation, and as a closing example related the heroic daring of the wife of Capt. Mitchell,[4] who, within a year past, her husband being taken suddenly ill, assumed the command of his vessel, for several days, during a most terrific gale, managed the ship—standing at the tiller herself—with the most daring intrepidity.

⇐ *Albany Argus*, 15 February 1855.

1. A heroine of the Spanish resistance to Napoleon's armies, Augustina, the maid of Saragossa, entered the battle and held the fort when her lover was shot. Lord Byron celebrated her daring in "Childe Harold's Pilgrimage," canto 1, stanzas 54–59.

2. That is, the astronomers Caroline Herschel and Maria Mitchell. Mitchell (1818–1889), born on Nantucket, discovered a new comet in 1847. In 1848 she was the first woman elected to the American Academy of Sciences in Boston, and in 1850 was elected to the American Association for the Advancement of Science. She joined the faculty of Vassar when it opened in 1865. (*NAW*.)

3. In her manuscript of this speech, prepared the previous summer, SBA noted that the daughters of New York's comptroller Azariah Cutting Flagg (1790–1873) worked as clerks in his Albany office. Flagg served from 1834 to 1839 and again from 1842 to 1846. (*DAB*; SBA, Lecture on the Rights and Wrongs of Woman, *Film*, 7:1075–113.)

4. In the manuscript speech, SBA explained that the sea captain's wife brought a ship safely into Boston harbor during a terrible storm.

·⊂══════⟩·

93 ⇒ SBA TO ANSON BINGHAM, WITH ENCLOSURE[1]

Rochester June 20/55

Mr. Bingham

Enclosed is a form of Petition as drawn by Mrs. Stanton— Does it meet your approbation? Is it ~~in~~ properly addressed? Would it not be well to in-sert after undersigned in the last paragraph the words <u>Men</u> & <u>Women</u> Petition— Please make such suggestions as you think best—

Enclosed also is the Call for our Saratoga W.R. Convention—[2] If convenient for you, will you call the attention of your Editors to the notice—they will without doubt publish it gratuitously—all of our Editors have done so. I hope to see you & Mrs. Bingham at our Saratoga meeting— Yours Respectfully

❧ *Susan B. Anthony*

❧ ALS, SBA Papers, NRU.

ENCLOSURE

To the Honorable the Senate & House of Representatives.

We the Women of the State of New York demand our "Right of Suffrage" a right which involves all the rights of Citizens, & which you cannot justly withhold now that we no longer consent to remain wholly unrepresented in this government.

We ~~therefore~~ the undersigned therefore Petition that you now take the necessary steps so to revise & improve our State Constitution that all her citizens may stand on equal grounds.[3]

❧ Ms in hand of SBA, SBA Papers, NRU.

1. Anson Bingham (1811–1882), a lawyer residing at Nassau, in Rensselaer County, wrote about woman's rights for the *Lily* and other papers under the name "Senex." He gained legal prominence in the anti-rent cases, brought after 1852 against the feudal rights claimed by owners of the Van Rensselaer manor lands. In order to work closely with Andrew J. Colvin, another lawyer with an anti-rent practice, he moved his office to Albany about 1856. Bingham won election as a Republican to the assembly in 1859, and, from his position on the judiciary committee, he supported new reforms in the property rights of married women. He married Laura McClellan (c. 1815–?) of Nassau. (William D. Murphy, *Biographical Sketches of the State Officers and Members of the Legislature of the State of New York in 1861* [New York, 1861], 158–60; Theodore A. Bingham, *The Bingham Family in the United States. Especially of the State of Connecticut* [Easton, Pa., 1930], 2:88, 312; Federal Census, 1860; New York State Census, 1855; SBA diary and copybook, p. 74, *Film*, 7:879ff.)

2. Enclosure omitted. The New York State Woman's Rights Committee called a second meeting at Saratoga Springs at the height of the summer season "to discuss woman's right to suffrage." (*Film*, 8:277–80.)

3. The final text read, in part, "Whereas the Women of the State of New York are recognized as citizens by the Constitution, and yet are disfranchised on account of sex only,—we do respectfully demand for them the right of suffrage;—a right which involves all other rights of citizenship, and one which cannot justly be withheld." (*Una*, September 1855.)

·❮━━━━❯·

94 ❧ ECS TO MARTHA COFFIN WRIGHT

[Seneca Falls] Monday morn [*17? December 1855*]

Dear Martha,

I have written my answer to cousin G.[1] but before copying it for the press I should like to take counsel with you & add any good things that you may have thought of. As I am rather larger than you, suppose you come to me instead of my going to you. Come over in the first train some morning this week & we will criticize together. "Two heads are better than one" especially when one head is full of baby clothes & labour pains. I have a month grace still. yours in haste

❧ *E. C. Stanton.*

❧ ALS, Garrison Papers, MNS-S.

1. Gerrit Smith. ECS was preparing an answer to his open letter to her, dated 1 December 1855, published in *Frederick Douglass' Paper* and circulated as a broadside, in *Film*, 8:323-26.

·❮━━━━❯·

95 ❧ ECS TO GERRIT SMITH

Seneca Falls, Dec. 21 [*1855*]

Gerrit Smith—Dear Friend:

Your letter on the "Woman's Rights" Movement, I have thoroughly read and considered.[1] I thank you, in the name of woman, for having said what you have on so many vital points. You have spoken well for a man whose convictions on this subject are the result of reason and observation; but they alone whose souls are fired through personal experience and suffering can set forth the heighth and depth, the source and centre, of the degradation of women; they alone can feel a steadfast faith in their own native energy and power to accomplish a final triumph over all adverse surroundings, a speedy and complete success. You say you have but little faith in this reform, because the changes we propose are so great, so radical, so comprehensive; whilst they who have commenced the work are so puny, feeble and undeveloped. The mass of women are developed at least to the point of discontent, and that, in the dawn of this nation, was considered a most dangerous point in the British Parliament, and is now deemed equally so on a Southern plantation. In the human soul, the steps between discontent and action are few and short indeed. You, who suppose the mass of women contented, know but little of the silent indignation, the deep and settled disgust with which she contemplates our present social arrangements. You claim to believe that in every sense, thought and feeling, man and woman are the same. Well, now, suppose yourself a woman. You are educated up to that point where one feels a deep interest in the welfare of her country, and in all the great questions of the day, in both Church and State; yet you have no voice in either. Little men, with little brains, may pour forth their little sentiments by the hour, in the forum and the sacred desk, but public sentiment and the religion of our day teach us that silence is most becoming in woman. So, to solitude you betake yourself, and read for your consolation the thoughts of dead men; but from the Bible down to Mother Goose's Melodies, how much complacency, think you, you would feel in your womanhood? The philosopher, the poet and the saint, all combined to make the name woman synonymous with either fool or devil. Every passion of the human soul, which in manhood becomes so grand and glorious in its results, is fatal to womankind. Ambition makes a Lady Macbeth, love an Ophelia;[2] none but those brainless things, without will or passion, are ever permitted to come to a good end. What measure of content could you draw from the literature of the past?

Again, suppose yourself the wife of a confirmed drunkard. You behold your earthly possessions all passing away; your heart is made desolate; it has ceased to pulsate with either love, or hope, or joy. Your house is sold over your head, and with it every article of comfort and decency; your children gather round you, one by one, each new comer clothed in rags and crowned with shame; is it with gladness you now welcome the embrace of that beastly husband, feel his fevered breath upon your cheek, and inhale the disgusting odor of his tobacco and rum? Would not your whole soul revolt from such an union? So do the forty thousand drunkards' wives now in this State. They, too, are all discontented, and but for the pressure of law and gospel would speedily sunder all these unholy ties. Yes, sir, there are women, pure and virtuous and noble as yourself, spending every day of all the years of their existence in the most intimate association with infamous men, kept so by that monstrous and unnatural artifice, baptized by the sacred name of marriage. I might take you through many, many phases of a woman's life, into those sacred relations of which we speak not in our conventions, where woman feels her deepest wrongs, where in blank despair she drags out days, and weeks, and months, and years of silent agony. I might paint you pictures of real life so vivid as to force from you an agonized exclamation: How can women endure such things! We who have spoken out, have declared our rights, political and civil; but the entire revolution about to dawn upon us by the acknowledgement of woman's social equality has been seen and felt but by the few. The rights to vote, to hold property, to speak in public are all important; but there are great social rights, before which all others sink into utter insignificance. The cause of woman is, as you admit, a broader and a deeper one than any with which you compare it; and this to me is the very reason why it must succeed. It is not a question of meats and drinks, of money and lands, but of human rights, the sacred right of a woman to her own person, to all her God-given powers of body and soul. Did it ever enter into the mind of man, that woman too had an inalienable right to life, liberty and the pursuit of her individual happiness? Did he ever take in the idea that to the mother of the race, and to her alone, belonged the right to say when a new being should be brought into the world? Has he, in the gratification of his blind passions, ever paused to think whether it was with joy and gladness that she gave up ten or twenty years of the hey-day of her existence to all the cares and sufferings of excessive maternity? Our present laws, our religious teachings, our social customs on the whole question of marriage and divorce are most degrading to woman; and so long as man continues to think and write, to speak and act, as if maternity was the one and sole object of a woman's existence—so long as children are conceived in weariness and disgust—you must not look for high-toned men and women capable of accomplishing any great and noble achievement. But when woman shall stand on an even pedestal with man, when they shall be bound together, not by these withes of law and gospel, but in holy unity and love; then and not till then shall our efforts at minor reforms be crowned with complete success. Here, in my opinion, is the starting point; here is the battle ground where our independence must be fought and won. A true marriage relation has far more to do with the elevation of woman than the style and cut of her dress. Dress is a matter of taste, of fashion; it is changeable, transient, and may be doffed or donned at the will of the individual; but institutions, supported by laws, can be overturned but by revolution. We have no reason to hope that pantaloons would do more for us than they have done for man himself. The Negro slave enjoys the most unlimited freedom in his attire, not surpassed even by the fashions of Eden in its palmiest days; yet in spite, of his dress and his manhood too, he is a slave still. Was the old Roman in his toga less of a man than he now is in swallow-tail and tights? Did the flowing robes of Christ himself render his life less grand and beautiful? In regard to dress, where you claim to be so radical, you are far from consistent.

Believing as you do in the identity of the sexes, that all the difference we see in tastes, in character, is entirely the result of education—that "man is woman and woman is man"—why keep up these distinctions in dress?[3] Surely, whatever dress is convenient for one sex must be for the other also. Whatever is necessary for the perfect and full development of man's physical being, must be equally so for woman. I fully agree with you that woman is terribly cramped and crippled in her present style of dress. I have not one word to utter in its defence; but to me it seems that if she would enjoy entire freedom she should dress just like man. Why proclaim our sex on the housetops seeing that it is a badge of degradation and deprives us of so many rights and privileges wherever we go. Disguised as a man, the distinguished French woman "George Sand" has been able to see life in Paris, and has spoken in political meetings with great applause, as no woman could have done.[4] In male attire, we could travel by land or sea; go through all the streets and lanes of our cities and towns by night and day, without a protector; get seven hundred dollars a year for teaching, instead of three, and ten dollars for making a coat instead of two or three, as we now do. All this we could do without fear of insult, or the least sacrifice of decency or virtue. If nature has not made the sex so clearly defined as to be seen throughout any disguise, why should we make the difference so striking? Depend upon it, when men and women in their every day life see and think less of sex and more of mind, we shall all lead far purer and higher lives. Your letter, my noble cousin, must have been written in a most desponding mood, as all the great reforms of the day seem to you on the verge of failure. What are the experiences of days and months and years, in the lifetime of a mighty nation? Can one man in his brief hour hope to see the beginning and end of any reform?

When you compare the public sentiment and social customs of our day with what they were fifty years ago, how can you despair of the temperance cause? With a Maine Law, and divorce for drunkenness, the rumseller and drunkard must soon come to terms. Let woman's motto be "No union with Drunkards," and she will soon bring this long and well fought battle to a triumphant close.

Neither should you despair of the anti-slavery cause; with its martyrs, its runaway slaves, its legal decisions in almost every paper you take up, the topic of debate in our national councils, our political meetings and our literature, it seems as if the nation were all alive, on this question. True, four millions of slaves groan in their chains still, but every man in this nation has an higher idea of individual rights than he had twenty years ago. As to the cause of woman, I see no signs of failure. We already have a property law, which in its legitimate effects must elevate the *femme covert* into a living breathing woman—a wife into a property-holder, who can make contracts, buy and sell. In a few years we shall see how well it works.

It needs but little forethought to perceive that in due time these large property holders must be represented in the government; and when the mass of women see that there is some hope of becoming voters and law-makers, they will take to their rights as naturally as the Negro to his heels when he is sure of success. Their present seeming content is very much like Sambo's[5] on the plantation. If you truly believe that man is woman, and woman is man; if you believe that all the burning indignation that fires your soul at the sight of injustice and oppression, if suffered in your own person, would nerve you to a life-long struggle for liberty and independence, then know that what you feel, I feel too, and what I feel, the mass of woman feels also. Judge by yourself, then, how long the women of this nation will consent to be deprived of their social, civil and political rights; but talk not to us of failure. Talk not to us of chivalry, that died long ago. Where do you see it? No gallant knight presents himself at the bar of justice to pay the penalty of our crimes. We suffer in our own persons, on the gallows and in prison walls. From Blackstone down to Kent, there is no display of gallantry in your written codes. In social life, true, a man in love will jump to pick up a glove or boquet for a silly girl of sixteen, whilst at home, he will permit his aged mother to carry pails of water and arms-full of wood, or his wife to lug a twenty pound baby, hour after hour, without ever offering to relieve her. I have seen a great many men priding themselves on their good breeding—the gentlemen, born and educated, who never manifest one iota of spontaneous gallantry towards the women of their own household.

Divines may preach thanksgiving sermons on the poetry of the arm chair and the cradle; but when they lay down their newspapers, or leave their beds a cold night, to attend to the wants of either, I shall begin to look for the golden age of chivalry once more. If a short dress is to make the men less gallant than they now are, I beg the women at our next convention to add at least two yards more to every skirt they wear. And you mock us with dependence, too. Do not the majority of women in every town support themselves, and very many their husbands, too? What father of a family, at the loss of his wife, has ever been able to meet his responsibilities as woman has done? When the mother dies, the house is made desolate, the children are forsaken—scattered to the four winds of heaven—to the care of any one who chooses to take them. Go to those aged widows, who have reared large families of children, unaided and alone, who have kept them all together under one roof, watched and nursed them in health and sickness through all their infant years, clothed and educated them, and made them all respectable men and women, ask them on whom they depended. They will tell you on their own hands, and on that never dying, never failing love, that a mother's heart alone can know. It is into hands like these,— to these, who have calmly met the terrible emergencies of life—who, without the inspiration of glory, or fame, or applause, through long years have faithfully and bravely performed their work, self-sustained and cheered, that we commit our cause. We need not wait for one more generation to pass away, to find a race of women worthy to assert the humanity of women, and that is all we claim to do. Affectionately yours,

❧ *E. C. Stanton.*

❧ Broadside, *A Letter From Mrs. Stanton to Gerrit Smith*, (Rochester, n.d.); from SBA scrapbook 1, Rare Books, DLC. Reprinted from *Rochester Tribune*, n.d., Matilda Joslyn Gage Scrapbooks, Rare Books, DLC. Published too in *Frederick Douglass' Paper*, 4 January 1856 (unavailable), and reprinted in *Woman's Advocate*, 2 February 1856, and in *Lily*, 15 February 1856. Also in *History*, 1:839–42.

1. In his long, rambling, and, as ECS notes, despondent letter, Smith explained "why I have so little faith in" the woman's rights movement. "[I]t is not in the proper hands; and . . . the proper hands are not yet to be found." To achieve woman's independence would be the most difficult of all reforms. Yet "the mass of women" were "content in their helplessness and poverty and destitution of rights," while their leaders donned "a dress, which imprisons and cripples them," "that both marks and makes their impotence." Smith conceded "that the dress of woman is not the primal cause of her helplessness and degradation." It was, however, "the outgrowth and symbol" of "false doctrines and sentiments"; if women would reject their irrational costume, they could present themselves to men as equals. (G. Smith to ECS, 1 December 1855, *Film*, 8:323–26; also in *History*, 1:836–39.)

2. Characters in William Shakespeare's *Macbeth* and *Hamlet*, these women were opposites in all respects.

3. The goal, Smith wrote, is for men and women to believe "that, with exception of that physical difference, which is for the multiplication and perpetuity of the race, man is woman, and woman is man." But, he added, "however much the dresses of the sexes should resemble each other, . . . they should be obviously distinguishable from each other."

4. Born Armandine Aurore Lucille Dupin, the French novelist took the name George Sand (1804–1876) when she published her first work in 1832, and she brought to Paris her childhood practice of dressing in men's attire.

5. Derived from a common African name and used in lieu of a personal name, "Sambo" referred to a black man.

---

96   ⇝   SBA TO GERRIT SMITH

Rochester Dec. 25, 1855—

Hon. Gerrit Smith   Dear Friend

Mrs. Stanton has just sent me her reply to your letter addressed to her— It will be published in next weeks Douglas' Paper.

I would very much like that Mrs. Stantons reply should be read by all who have seen your letter— Our little Rochester Tribune will publish Mrs. Stantons on Friday or Saturday of this week, & they would put their type in letter form & strike off copies, provided I could pay them for doing the work— This I cannot—for I have already incurred a debt of $120. for printing tracts—and $100. for the Services of Frances D. Gage of Missouri— She has been lecturing & circulating our Petition the last six weeks— We have a Committee on Lecturing Agents, but they have never held themselves responsible for the <u>salaries</u> of Agents— If you think best to have Mrs. Stanton's letter published in letter form for distribution—perhaps you would like to contribute to defray the expense—

Frances D. Gage has answered you too—her letter will appear in <u>this</u> weeks Douglas' Paper—[1] I stand alone in my opinion of the <u>dress</u> question— I can see no business avocation, in ↑which↓ woman, in her present dress <u>can</u> <u>possibly</u> earn <u>equal</u> <u>wages</u> with man—& feel that it is <u>folly</u> for us to make the demand until, we adapt our dress to our work— I every day, feel more keenly the terrible bondage of these long skirts— I own that the <u>want</u> of <u>Moral</u> <u>Courage</u>, caused <u>me</u> to return to them— And I can but doubt my own strength, in that it has failed me in one instance—& why should I marvel that <u>man</u> should doubt— I cannot think you meant to say aught that ↑should↓ <u>discourage</u> even the most feeble worker—& I thank you for having written that letter, if for no other reason, that it has roused our women from their seeming lethargy, & will make them put forth new efforts to prove that they can accomplish great things in long skirts even— With Love to Mrs. Smith & Mrs. Miller   I am yours with Hope

≈ *Susan B. Anthony*

≈ ALS, Smith Papers, NSyU.

1. Frances D. Gage thought Smith's argument "ridiculous," but because he was "the almost oracle of a large portion of our reformers, it becomes worthy of an answer from every earnest woman in our cause." Her reply was straightforward: "We *must own ourselves, under the law*, first—own our bodies, our earnings, our genius, and our consciences; then we shall turn to the lesser matter of what shall be the garniture of the body." (*Frederick Douglass' Paper*, 28 December 1855 [unavailable], reprinted in *Lib.*, 4 January 1856; also in *History*, 1:842–44.)

·⟨⬥————⬥————⟩·

97   ⮞   LUCY STONE TO SBA

[*Cincinnati, Ohio*] Wednesday Jan. 16—1856

Dear Susan

Yours of the 28th ult came duly— Thank you for it— But Susan d[ear?] you must be <u>sure</u> and work <u>moderately</u>, but I am afraid you dont know what moderation is. T'will be a <u>great</u> pity for you to lose those "10 years younger," and the extra 19 lbs. If you work at all, you will see so much to do, that you wont stop for yourself. Suffrage is <u>sure</u> to come to women, God will <u>wait</u> for it, and so may you, working only when you can, in justice to yourself.[1]

You are in debt too, for Aunt Fanny, & the tracts— Well if your plan adopted at Saratoga, does not help you out (I mean that of writing to Gerrit Smith & others able & willing to make offerings to the cause) I will try and send you something tho' my lectures have paid very little this winter comparatively— I am glad Aunt F. has done so well,—hope she has ~~got~~ procured "lots" of ~~subscribers~~ petitioners—

I hope you will not have another meeting at Albany when they are presented— It seems to me, that the cause will gain just as much— Our labor is not with the <u>Legislators</u>, but with those who <u>make</u> legislators—

I gave three lectures in Hamilton Ohio, last week, and set petitions for suffrage, in brisk circulation— Mrs. Swift[2] will do something at it, so much at least, as to get them before the assembly—and the newspapers will tell of it, and people will talk & think, and that will be this year's gain— <u>Somewhere in the future</u> the full equality awaits us—

I feel very proud of Mrs. Stanton's letter to Gerrit Smith— She is so strong and noble! If the Una ever goes out, when we have a new paper Mrs. Stanton <u>must be editor</u>. Gerrit Smith's letter, in some respects is unworthy of him— He had the blues when he wrote it— He puts effect for cause— Our dress is a consequence of our being what we are. When woman in her essential self, is larger than her dress—<u>it</u> will take the proper dimensions— I understand all that you feel about resuming the long skirts— We ought to have been richer than to do it, but I go every now and then, a long walk in the short skirt, and <u>hope</u> to keep up the habit— When we go from here, to a little retired home, I am going to wear trowsers & jacket for work, at home, "See if I dont"— I cant write my tract until it gets warmer— The thermometer at noon, is 10 degrees below zero. All my ideas are froze—you will have to wait— Tell Aunt F. that I accept her love, as large as a turnip, but that does not answer my long letter from Wisconsin— Is your anti slavery course of lectures doing well?[3] Douglass has not had so much <u>sense</u> in his paper since it started, as was in Mrs. Stanton's letter— Is'nt it fine to see how our northern men vote for Banks?[4] What a good speech Phillips made at Plymouth![5] With much love

❧ *Lucy Stone*

[*in margin on first page*] My husband would send love, but he is down at the store— I wish you had a good husband too— It is a great blessing

❧ ALS, Blackwell Papers, DLC. Bracketed letters obscured by ink blot.

1. SBA had worn herself out and developed back pains in the summer of 1855. After overseeing the woman's rights meeting at Saratoga Springs in mid-August, she headed to the Worcester Water-Cure Institution of her cousin Seth Rogers in Massachusetts and stayed east until the end of November. (SBA to Anthony family, 27 September 1855, and SBA to Amy K. Post, 1 October 1855, in *Film*, 8:284–87, 290–93; *Anthony*, 1:131–36; Weiss and Kemble, *Great American Water-Cure Craze*, 129–30.)

2. The *History of Woman Suffrage* gives her name as Adeline T. Swift, when quoting from coverage of the national convention at Cincinnati in 1855 and describing Ohio's campaign for woman's rights in the winter of 1860 and 1861. A different Mrs. Swift, Sarah F. Swift, took part in the Ohio movement in 1850 and 1851. In 1857 women's petitions produced modest results; a new law regarding married women's rights passed early in the year. (*History*, 1:164, 168; *The Woman's Rights Almanac For 1858* [Worcester, Mass., n.d.], 8–13, 16–17; Warbasse, *Changing Legal Rights of Married Women*, 265–66.)

3. SBA organized a course of lectures during the winter that brought William Lloyd Garrison, Theodore Parker, and Wendell Phillips to Corinthian Hall. (SBA to Amy K. Post, 1 October 1855, and W. L. Garrison to SBA, 1 March 1856, *Film*, 8:290–93, 385–88; *History*, 1:666; *Anthony*, 1:135, 140, 142; Garrison, *Letters*, 4:380–81.)

4. In the Thirty-fourth Congress, election of the Speaker of the House became a contest over slavery, when Nathaniel Prentiss Banks declared repeal of the Missouri Compromise an act of dishonor and galvanized southern opposition. After 132 ballots Banks became Speaker in early February. President of the Massachusetts constitutional convention in 1853, Banks (1816–1894)

was elected to Congress the same year and became governor in 1858. During the Civil War, he was a major general of volunteers in the Union army and returned to Congress in 1865. (*BDAC*; *DAB*; *History*, 3:9–10.)

5. At the Pilgrim Society's dinner in Plymouth, Massachusetts, on 21 December. (*Lib.*, 28 December 1855.)

·⊱━━━━━⊰·

98 ⇝ ANTOINETTE L. BROWN TO SBA

Henrietta Jan. 23/56

Dearest Susan

Will you ever forgive me? You must now I am very penitent! They say all things are fair in love.

When we had the long talk that night at Mrs. Stantons I told you the real truth and nothing but the truth. Among other things we talked of Sam'l C. Blackwell and said what <u>at the time</u> was felt,[1] that I should drop the correspondence with him entirely, which it is needless to say now was never done. At Boston I own up to hoaxing you and Lucy and Ellen[2] all of you—yet even then the matter was not decided but was just at the crisis where it <u>must</u> be decided for weal or woe at once, and I was more than half in earnest in the proposition that you should make his acquaintance for there were no two people that I liked much better than both of you. You can guess now who that lady love was in the East! After more than a weeks visit with him the scales predominated decidedly in his favor. When you asked me that night at Rochester whether I should not 'feel bad when Sam was married' I came near shaking you on to the floor with laughing at the joke for he was in the city then and was going up to spend the week at Fathers.[3] Now will you forgive me?

Well he is to be married tomorrow at half past 10 A.M. Yes I shall feel bad. Do not doubt it!

Susan, darling, I love you a little better than ever and would ask you to wedding only that absolutely no one is invited my mothers health is so feeble. She is not nearly so well as she has been. We go to Cincinnati for a few weeks, then return to New York to locate there permanently. The Blackwells have disposed of their business and will all leave Cincinnati in the spring— You may be sure of my continued interest and future cooperation in our N.Y. movement, and in every other good cause. I go right on with the writing, and even lecturing some more this winter. Write me, wont you? Yours ever

↜ *Nette.*

↜ ALS, Blackwell Papers, MCR-S.

1. Samuel C. Blackwell began courting Antoinette Brown in 1853, and in 1855 rumors that he would soon marry spread before anyone knew that Antoinette, at last, had agreed to marry him. (Cazden, *Antoinette Brown Blackwell*, 102–8.)

2. Brown, Lucy Stone, and SBA attended a woman's rights convention together in Boston on 19 and 20 September 1855. Ellen Blackwell (1828–1901), christened Sarah Ellen, was the youngest family member and an artist. (*NCAB*, 9:125.)

3. Joseph Brown (1784–1877) was a farmer at Henrietta.

·⊂━━━━⋙⋘━━━━⊃·

99 ↜ ECS TO SBA

[*Seneca Falls*] Thursday eve. [*24 January 1856*]

Dear Susan,

What has been the fate of my letter. I corrected it & sent it straight back as you directed but I have never got the promised copies.

The errors in Douglas ↑paper↓ were dreadful, & I did hope to have a few corrected copies to send to friends. Where are you Susan & what are you doing. Your silence is truly appalling   Are you dead or married? Well I have got out the sixth edition of my admirable work, another female child is born into the world!

Last <u>Sunday</u> afternoon, Harriet Eaton Stanton, oh the little heretic, thus to desecrate that holy day, opened her soft blue eyes on this mundane sphere.[1]

Maggie's joy over her little sister is unbounded. I am very [smart?] & very happy, that the terrible ordeal is passed & that the result is another daughter. good night   yours

↜ *E. C. Stanton.*

↜ ALS, Papers of ECS, NPV. Excerpt in "Early Letters," 1189.

1. Born on 20 January 1856 and known as Hattie. She spelled her name Harriot.

·◁▭▬▭▷·

100 ⳕ Antoinette Brown Blackwell to SBA

Newark N.J.[1] March 12, [*1856*]

Dearest Susan

Your welcome letter was recieved at Philadelphia. What can be done with those Albanians. I can think of nothing but to send them new petitions every week and weary them with much coming.[2] The places you name will suit me as well as any, when I am ready to go with you on the lecturing trip.[3] But dont rely on me with <u>positiveness</u>. It wont do, and I a married woman! I have been holding a number of meetings lately—am to speak here Sunday evening on Temperance but my throat is still troublesome and I shall venture no more engagements till it is quite well.

How do you like <u>this</u> plan for the next National Convention—to get up a petition for <u>the right of suffrage</u> to be presented to each state in the Union, in the name of the Convention. The name of the President officially to head the list, followed by the other officers and then by the members   This will be appropriate for a National Con. and will do much with a little labor. I spoke to Mrs Mott and others about it. They like the idea.[4]

Congratulate Mrs Stanton from me for her highly satisfactory sixth Edition of her most valuable work. I wish we had the contemplated Paper for her especial benefit in these days, and am afraid it will be too late to accommodate her when we get it fairly established, which does not promise to be very soon. Lucy believes her talents lie in other directions and gives no approval to the plan <u>for herself</u>; but some day when the right time and people present themselves <u>we'll</u> have the ↑paper↓ wont we?

At present my first wish is to get a home in the right place—that is near N.Y. We <u>may</u> secure one this year. At least we hope to next. "Mr Sam" will either join me in a week or two or I shall go to him   Of course it takes longer to settle up business affairs always than one calculates upon. He hoped to be free about this time, but now thinks it may occupy a month or more longer. In that case it will possibly seem best to remain West for a whole year longer.

You suspect rightly that Lucy is free yet from any maternal prospects; and quite to the regret of several people! She and Harry love each other quite well enough; and I hope sincerely, that this one tie to their union may yet be completed.

I have nothing personal to report. And for you, Sue, I hear of a number of bachelors making inquiries about Susan B Anthony. This means something! I shall look out for another wedding before the year closes, among our sisternity. Get a good husband—thats all, dear.

If I return West probably I will stop on the way and hold those meetings with you   Write me <u>here</u>.

∽ *Nette L B B*

∽ ALS, Blackwell Papers, MCR-S.

1. After a short stay in Cincinnati with her new husband and his family, Blackwell left to lecture in the East until mid-April. (A. L. B. Blackwell to SBA, 14 February 1856, *Film*, 8:374–77; Cazden, *Antoinette Brown Blackwell*, 113–14.)

2. SBA's comments about Albany and the legislature in her missing letter can only be guessed. Since January, the assembly had referred dozens of petitions for equal rights and suffrage to its hostile judiciary committee, which ignored them. According to Ida Harper, SBA went to Albany in search of action, probably at the end of a recess for Washington's Birthday on 27 February. On March 14, the Committee on Judiciary issued a crude report authored by Samuel A. Foot, a distinguished lawyer and former judge of the Court of Appeals. It "set the whole House in roars of laughter," recommending that husbands who signed the women's petitions seek a law allowing them to wear the dresses in their families. It concluded "that if there is any inequality or oppression in the case, the gentlemen are the sufferers." "I hope you won't get discouraged," Lydia Mott wrote SBA on 15 March. (*Film*, 8:396; *Anthony*, 1:140; *JNYA*, 19, 30 January, 2, 4, 8, 13, 27 February, 5, 21 March 1856, pp. 119, 180, 203–5, 214, 252, 297, 383, 452, 605; *New York Times*, 28 February 1856; *History*, 1:629–30; "Report of Committee on Judiciary, on Sundry Petitions for Women's Rights," *New York Assembly Document*, 14 March 1856, No. 147; McAdam, *Bench and Bar of New York*, 1:331.)

3. Blackwell offered to lecture with SBA in spring or summer to help her recoup the money paid to Frances Gage.

4. At the national convention of 1856 Antoinette Blackwell, Ernestine Rose, and Lucy Stone were named a committee to draw up a memorial for the franchise to be sent to twenty-five state legislatures. Stone reported at the convention in 1858 that presentations were made in Maine, Massachusetts, and Pennsylvania during the year. (Memorial to state legislatures from the national woman's rights convention of 1856, SBA scrapbook 1, Rare Books, DLC; *New York Daily Tribune*, 15 May 1858, *Film*, 8:1125–26.)

·(⟨══════⟩ℳ⟨══════⟩)·

101 ❧ SBA to ECS

Rochester May 26/56

Dear Mrs. Stanton

Taking it for granted that you are at home once more, I'll say a word to you by way of "exhortation & prayer"— I ought ↑to↓ be more ↑pious↓ than formerly, since I travelled all the way from Seneca Falls to Schenectady in company with President Finney & Lady[1]—& heard Garison Parker & all of us Woman's Rights actors duly denounced as "Infidels" I told him our cause was Infidel to the popular Theology & popular interpretation of the Bible— Mrs. Finney took me to another seat & with much earnestness enquired all about, what we were doing & the growth of our movement— Said she you have the sympathy of a large proportion of ↑the↓ educated women with you— In my circle I hear the movement much talked of & earnest hopes for its spread expressed—but these women dare not speak out their sympathy—

What a shame that you don't live where I can run ↑in↓ & tell you all I know in five minutes & be back to my work again— I saw Lucy & almost made her promise to call on you—she has left Cincinnatti for all—was going to look at Orange, Chapaqua & other places in the vicinity of N.Y. for a home & if not suited, going to Wiscon to look— but I can't bear to have her & Nette settle in the far west—they ought to be at the Centre of Civilization— The Aniversary meeting was good— though the weather was very rainy—[2]

I attended the Anniversary of the "American Woman's Educational Association" headed by Catharine E. Beecher—it was at Prof. Websters 14. Lexington Avenue—[3] Some parts of the Secretarys report were very fine— I said to Mrs. W. I would rather see the weight of your influence exerted to open the doors of the existing colleges to woman— far greater good would be done for woman by such work, than by the establishment of separate Colleges. Said ↑she↓ that is my mind exactly—isn't it strange that such women as those, Miss Beecher, Mrs. Kirkland Mrs. Stevens, S. J. Hale[4] &c, &c, are so stupid, Yes so false as to work for any thing secondary—any thing other than their highest conviction—but of those women are all bound by the fashionable Church & dare not take sides with the unpopular— Mrs. W. said she knew one of our leaders very well, Mrs. Stanton of Senca Falls—

I am now just done with house fixing & ready to commence operations on that Report—[5] Don't you think it would be a good plan to first state <u>what</u> we mean by educating the sexes together—then go on to show how the few institutions that profess to give <u>equal</u> education <u>fail</u> ↑in the↓ Physical, Moral & Intellectual departments & lastly that it is folly to talk of giving to ↑the↓ sexes, <u>equal</u> <u>advantages</u>, while you <u>withhold</u> from them <u>equal</u> <u>motive</u> to improve those advantages— Do you please mark out a plan & give me as soon as you can— Oh, that I had the requisite power to do credit to woman hood in this emergency—why is nature so <u>sparing</u> of her gifts— When will you come to Rochester to spend those days, I shall be most happy to see whenever it shall be—only let me know a few days before—that I may be as much at leisure as may be—Amelia & the two babies of course & as many more as convenient— With Love

∽ *Susan B. Anthony*

∽ ALS, Scrapbook 1, Papers of ECS, NPV. Transcript in ECS Papers, NjR.

1. Charles Grandison Finney (1792–1875) was president of Oberlin College and a leading revivalist preacher. During the winter of 1855 and 1856, he returned to the scene of earlier triumphs in Rochester. His first revival at Rochester in 1830 swept Henry Stanton into a reformer's life. ECS, however, called Finney "a terrifier of human souls" who "worked incalculable harm to the very souls he sought to save." Elizabeth Ford Atkinson Finney (1799?–1863) was his second wife and the widow of a Rochester miller. After her marriage to Finney late in 1848, she joined him as a revivalist and promoted an active social and moral role for women. (*DAB*; *Eighty Years*, 41–43; Leonard I. Sweet, *The Minister's Wife: Her Role in Nineteenth-Century American Evangelicalism* [Philadelphia, 1983], 184–219.)

2. SBA and Lucy Stone attended the American Anti-Slavery Society meeting on 7 May, and a few weeks later Stone left for Wisconsin, where she and Henry Blackwell owned some six thousand acres of land.

3. On May 10. An instrument of Catharine Esther Beecher's social and educational thought, the American Woman's Educational Association promoted a "liberal education, honorable position, and remunerative employment" for women in colleges that trained teachers and homemakers. Throughout her career, Beecher (1800–1878), who resigned from the association at this meeting, proposed to improve woman's position by raising the social value of domesticity. This fourth annual meeting took place at the home of Horace

Webster (1794–1871) and Sarah Maria Fowler Webster. They moved to New York City from Geneva in 1848 for him to head the Free Academy. Sarah Webster, who grew up in Albany, was the association's treasurer. That she knew ECS as a member of the Cady family is suggested by her naming her youngest son Edward Bayard Webster, after ECS's brother-in-law. (Kathryn Kish Sklar, *Catharine Beecher: A Study in American Domesticity* [New Haven, Conn., 1973], 217–26; American Woman's Educational Association, *Fourth Annual Report, May, 1856* [New York, 1856]; *NCAB*, 19:320–21, s.v. "Webster, Horace.")

4. Members of the association's executive committee. Caroline Matilda Stansbury Kirkland (1801–1864), who taught school before her marriage, was a writer and editor, living in New York City. Marguerite Otheman Stevens married the Reverend Abel Stevens, an editor of Methodist journals, and pursued a minor literary career. Sarah Josepha Buell Hale (1788–1879) taught school before her marriage and, as editor of the influential *Godey's Lady's Book*, promoted opportunities for women's education within their sphere. (*NAW*, s.v. "Kirkland, Caroline M. S." and "Hale, Sarah J. B."; *DAB*, s.v. "Stevens, Abel"; Allibone, s.v. "Stevens, Marguerite O.")

5. SBA was "appointed to prepare an essay for our next annual meeting upon 'The Education of the Two Sexes together,'" by the New York State Teachers' Association meeting in 1855. (*New York Teacher* 5 [October 1855]: 56, *Film*, 8:275.)

·⊂━━━━━━⟫·

102 ⚡ SBA TO ECS, WITH ENCLOSURE

Private

Home getting along toward 12 Oclck
Thursday Evening 5th June [*1856*]—

And Mrs Stanton, not a word written on that Address for Teachers Con.— This week was to be leisure to me—& lo, our girl, a wife, had a miscarriage on Tuesday,—at eve one Lady Visitor came & to day a man & the mercy only knows when I can get a moment—& what is worse, as the Lord knows full well, is, that if I get all the time the world has—I cant get up a decent document, so for the love of me, & for the saving of the reputation of womanhood, I beg you with one baby on your knee & another at your feet & four boys whistling buzzing hallooing Ma Ma set your self about the work—it is of but small moment who writes the

Address, but of <u>vast moment</u> that it be <u>well</u> <u>done</u>— I promise you to work hard, oh, how hard, & <u>pay</u> <u>you</u> <u>whatever</u> <u>you</u> <u>say</u> for your <u>time</u> & <u>brains</u>—but oh Mrs. Stanton <u>don't</u> say <u>no</u>, nor <u>don't</u> <u>delay</u> it a moment, for I must have it all done & <u>almost commit</u> it to memory

Now let me tell you, Do you write all you think of ready to copy, & then you come out here, or I will come to you & <u>copy</u>—

The Teachers Con. comes the 5 & 6th Aug, the Saratoga W.R. Con. the 13 & 14th & probably the Newport[1] the 20 & 21st

~~Now~~ During <u>July</u> I want to speak certainly twice at Avon, Clifton & Sharon, & Ballston Springs & Lake George—[2] Now will <u>you</u> <u>load</u> <u>my</u> <u>gun</u>, leaving me only to pull the trigger & let fly the powder & ball—

Don't delay one mail to tell me what you <u>will</u> <u>do</u>—for I <u>must</u> <u>not</u> & <u>will</u> <u>not</u> allow those <u>school masters</u> to say—<u>see</u> these <u>women</u> <u>cant</u> or <u>wont</u> do any thing when we do give them a chance— <u>No</u>, they shant say that, even if I have to a get a <u>man</u> to write it—but <u>no</u> <u>man</u> <u>can</u> write from <u>my</u> <u>stand</u> <u>point</u>,—nor no woman but <u>you</u>—for <u>all</u> <u>all</u> would base their <u>strongest</u> argument on the <u>un</u>likeness of the <u>sexes</u>— Nette wrote me that she should, were she to make the Address—& more than any other place does the <u>difference</u> of sex, if there is any, need to be <u>forgotten</u> in the school room—

Have just ↑heard↓ that Lucretia was at ↑the↓ Waterloo Meeting— suppose she must have visited you—[3] Will give you every thought I have <u>scared</u> <u>up</u> on another slip— Now do I pray you give heed to my prayer—those of you who have the <u>talent</u> to do honor to ↑poor oh how poor↓ womanhood, have all given yourselves over to <u>baby</u> making, & left poor brainless <u>me</u> to battle alone— It is a shame,—such a body as I <u>might</u> be <u>spared</u> to <u>rock</u> <u>cradles</u>, but it is a <u>crime</u> for <u>you</u> & <u>Lucy</u> & <u>Nette</u>— I have just engaged to attend a Progressive Meeting in Erie Co. the 1st of Sept. just because there is no other woman to be had,[4] not because I feel in the least competent—oh dear, dear If the <u>spirits</u> would only just make me a <u>trance</u> <u>medium</u>[5] & put the <u>rights</u> into my mouth— You can't think how earnestly I have prayed to be made a speaking medium for a whole week— If they would only come to me thus, I'd give them a hearty welcome—

Now don't fail to write me— Is your sister with you—how I do wish I could step in to see you & make you feel all my infirmities,—<u>mental I mean</u>—

Friday P.M. Father is off & I haven't half written out the points I have thought of—but will send what I have to stir you up—do get all on fire, & be as <u>cross</u> as you please, you remember Mr. Stanton told how cross you always get in a speech   Good By

❧   *Susan B—*

❧ ALS, ECS Papers, DLC. Variants in ECS Papers, NjR, and *Stanton,* 2:64–66.

ENCLOSURE

Why the sexes should be
Educated together

Because their life work is so nearly identical

By such education they get true ideas of each other—the College Student associates with only two classes of women, the kitchen drudge & parlor doll— The Seminary girl has only stolen interviews, gets her idea of man mostly from works of fiction—

Because the endowment of ↑Educational Institutions↓ by both public & private munificence is ever for those for the male sex—while all the Seminaries & Boarding Schools for Females are left to maintain themselves as best they may by means of their Tuition Fees—consequently cannot afford a faculty of 1st class Professors—

Because there are already colleges enough established for all of both sexes—<u>Economy</u> favors it—

Not a school in the Country gives to ~~woman~~ ↑the girl↓ equal privileges with the boy—not Oberlin Lima McGrawville nor Antioch—[6] Prof Morgan of Oberlin[7] said to his class, the <u>half</u> of a↑n↓ ~~young mans~~ education is obtained from declamation & discussion   No school <u>requires</u> & but very few <u>allow</u> the <u>girls</u> to declaim & discuss side side with the boys—thus are they robbed of their right   the <u>one</u> <u>half</u> of education—

The grand thing that is needed, is to give the sexes <u>like</u> <u>motives</u> for acquirement— Very rarely a person studies closely, without hope of making that knowledge useful—as means of support or house or something to them

That man may learn from his boyhood that woman is his <u>intellectual</u>

equal & ~~thus~~ no longer look upon her as his inferior—oh, dear dear, there is so much to say & I am so without <u>constructive</u> <u>power</u> to put in symetrical order—

Because separation & restraint stimulates the desires & passions—[8]

⮐ AMs, ECS Papers, DLC.

1. William Hay and SBA scheduled another meeting at Saratoga Springs in August, but within the month they cancelled it because none of the best speakers could attend. No meeting in Newport occurred either. (SBA to Martha C. Wright, 6 June, 6 July 1856, M. C. Wright to SBA, 14 June, 4 July 1856, *Film*, 8:449–52, 457–60, 470–75, 476–79.)

2. All were resort towns built around mineral springs.

3. The Yearly Meeting of the Friends of Human Progress at Waterloo, 1–3 June 1856. Although Lucretia Mott stayed at Martha Wright's house for most of the summer, ECS did not see her. (M. C. Wright to SBA, 30 August 1856, *Film*, 8:564–66.)

4. The first meeting of the Friends of Human Progress in Collins, New York, a group that became strongly identified with spiritualism. (Barbour, *Quaker Crosscurrents*, 135.)

5. That is, the person through whom spirits communicated from the other world.

6. The four schools that offered coeducational collegiate instruction and degrees to women. Oberlin College in Oberlin, Ohio, welcomed female and African-American students and granted the first bachelor's degrees to women in 1841. However, public speaking and practice at debate were proscribed by the Ladies' Board of Managers. Nearby in Yellow Springs, Ohio, Antioch College opened in 1853. There Horace Mann put his ideas about coeducation into practice without forsaking his convictions about female delicacy. Located in Lima, New York, the Genesee Wesleyan Seminary, established by Methodists in 1831, became a college and seminary in 1840 and awarded its first bachelor of arts degrees to women in 1856. New York Central College at McGrawville was founded by antislavery Baptists and supported by abolitionists, particularly by Gerrit Smith. Interracial and coeducational since 1849, its faculty included African-American men and white women. (Carol Lasser and Marlene Merrill, eds., *Soul Mates: The Oberlin Correspondence of Lucy Stone and Antoinette Brown, 1846-1850* [Oberlin, Ohio, 1983], 1–9; Horace Mann, *Dedication of Antioch College and Inaugural Address of Its President, Hon. Horace Mann* [Yellow Springs, Ohio, 1854]; Matthew Simpson, ed., *Cyclopedaedia of Methodism* [Philadelphia, 1881], 403; *New York Daily Tribune*, 22 July 1856; Harlow, *Gerrit Smith*, 231–32; Carleton Mabee, *Black Education in New York State: From Colonial to Modern Times* [Syracuse, 1979], 89–91, 166–69.)

7. John Morgan (1803–1884) was the New Testament professor at Oberlin College. (*NCAB*, 2:465.)

8. The manuscript of "Educating the Sexes Together," in SBA's hand, bears her notation of a much later date, "Mrs Stanton wrote this speech." If true, ECS did a remarkable job of finding a voice harmonious with SBA's. There is only a short summary of SBA's address in reports of the meeting on 6 August. For a fuller report of one presentation of the lecture, see 2 February 1857 below. (*Film*, 8:498, 500–560.)

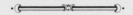

103 ⇝ ECS TO SBA

<Seneca Falls, 10 June 1856

Dear Susan>

Your servant is not dead but liveth. Imagine me, day in and day out, watching, bathing, dressing, nursing and promenading the precious contents of a little crib in the corner of my room. I pace up and down these two chambers of mine like a caged lioness, longing to bring nursing and housekeeping cares to a close.[1] <Is your speech to be exclusively on the point of educating the sexes together, or as to the best manner of educating women? Have you Horace Mann on that point?>[2] Come here and I will do what I can to help you with your address, if you will hold the baby and make the puddings. <Love to Antoinette and Lucy when you write them. Womankind owes them a debt of gratitude for their faithful labors in the past.> Let them rest in peace and quietness thinking great thoughts. It is not well to be in the excitement of public life all the time, so do not keep stirring them up or mourning over their repose. You, too, must rest, Susan; let the world alone awhile. We can not bring about a moral revolution in a day or a year. Now that I have two daughters, I feel fresh strength to work for women. It is not in vain that in myself I feel all the wearisome care to which woman even in her best estate is subject. <Good night. Yours in love,

⇝ *E. C. Stanton*>

⇝ *Anthony*, 1:142; typed transcript, ECS Papers, DLC. Additional variants in "Early Letters," 1189, and *Stanton*, 2:66–67. All are in *Film*, 8:453–56.

1. The transcript here adds: "I have other work on hand too. That you may see what it is, I send you Oliver Johnson's letter." The sentence was rewritten for *Stanton*: ". . . I send you the letters of Oliver Johnson and Samuel J. May." See *Film*, 8:403, 437–38.

2. Horace Mann (1796–1859), educational reformer and politician, served as congressman from Massachusetts from 1848 to 1853 before becoming president of Antioch College. ECS refers either to his *A Few Thoughts on the Powers and Duties of Woman*, or his *Dedication of Antioch College*. SBA's copy of the latter is in Rare Books, DLC. (*BDAC*.)

·◖━━━━━◗·

104 ❧ MARTHA COFFIN WRIGHT TO SBA

Auburn July 14th, 1856—

My dear Miss Anthony

My sister begs me to answer your note of Saturday, saying that she agrees with you, in the opinion that the <u>National</u> Convention had better <u>not</u> be postponed on acct. of ↑the↓ election in the Fall, and that is certainly my opinion—there will always be something of more importance than a <u>woman's convention</u> if <u>we</u> are willing to think so.[1] I hope therefore that we shall perseveringly re-iterate our demands, each year, until a more respectful answer is accorded than we received last year—there seemed good & sufficient reasons for giving up the meeting at Saratoga, but I do not agree with Mr P. that the place is an unfavorable one—our success last year in obtaining a hearing, at least, from those who wd. never have listened, elsewhere, was certainly encouraging— I am glad you are going to deliver yr. address there & that Mrs. Nicholls will speak on Kansas—[2]

It is pleasant to find that Lucy's interest is undiminished, tho' perhaps we ought, for her sake to wish that she might, for a time, have some of the engrossing cares that Mrs Stanton has— I was glad to hear of you with our bright cheerful friend at Seneca Falls.

As regards the time (1st & 2nd Oct) my sister says that if that time suits others, she is suited—

T. D. Weld's school at Raritan Bay opens on the 1st and I shall go with our children the day before.

Ellen[3] was pleased with your remembrance of her—she sends love— she has just returned from school, and is happy to be at home for awhile— She would be very glad to attend the Convention. Very truly Your friend

❧ M. C. Wright.

✒ ALS, Garrison Papers, MNS-S.

1. Lucy Stone, on 1 July, directed SBA to begin organizing the national convention by asking Wendell Phillips and Lucretia Mott "whether in view of the smoke from the Presidential election, our Convention had not better be deferred a year." The election, the first bid for national office by the new Republican party, was seen as a referendum on the Kansas-Nebraska Act and thus on the extension of slavery. (*Film*, 8:467–68.)

2. SBA changed her mind about delivering her address on coeducation, fearing to speak in a national convention and to preclude opportunities for paid lectures. Clarina Nichols moved to Baldwin City, Kansas, in April 1855, but she returned east to settle her husband's estate in January 1856 and found herself unable to return home because proslavery "ruffians" blockaded the Missouri River. Instead she lectured on Kansas. The territory was "bleeding"; the town of Lawrence was attacked by a proslavery federal marshall and posse in May; the Pottawatomie Massacre of proslavery men, under John Brown's leadership, occurred three days later; rival armies of free-state and proslavery settlers roamed the territory. (SBA to L. Stone, 19 October 1856, *Film*, 8:599–604; Potter, *Impending Crisis*, 199–224; Gambone, "Forgotten Feminist of Kansas," 255–57; *History*, 1:186–87.)

3. Ellen Wright (1840–1931), later Garrison, was the second daughter of Martha and David Wright. She attended Theodore Weld's Eagleswood School in the 1850s and studied music for a time before her marriage to William Lloyd Garrison, Jr., on 14 September 1864. Grown fond of SBA while still a teenager, Ellen Wright corresponded with her from 1858 until 1905 and, as Mrs. Garrison, provided her a home on visits to Boston. (Wright genealogy, Garrison Papers, MNS-S.)

· ⊱——•✕•——⊰ ·

105 ✑ Lucy Stone to SBA

Viroqua—Bad Ax Co. Wis July 22 1856

Many thanks, dear Susan for your good long letter, and for the extract from Mrs. Stanton, God bless her![1] She is partly right, and partly wrong— The <u>resentment</u> at the injustice, and meanness, is all right, but the serving the <u>highest right, for the sake of the right</u>, <u>whatever</u> may come to us, is still our duty, and the surest way, by its example of nobility, to teach men that we are fully worthy to be copartners with them in everything   The cause of Kansas, and of the country are still <u>our cause</u>, even tho, we <u>are</u> disfranchised & we shall suffur in all <u>its</u> wrong, and gain, in all <u>its</u> success. So, it is for <u>our interest,</u> to aid in securing justice for Kansas, but I have no desire to aid that "Illinois woman's" bah![2] I am every Sunday holding anti slavery meetings, and helping Kansas, by making anti slavery[3]   I sent the extract to Nettie.

I wrote you last,[4] asking you to do all about the Convention (if we had one,) for I felt then, and do now at times, that <u>every man</u>, who has helped us before, will be so in the anti slavery field, that we cant get them even for a single speech. Nettee wont be there. But we had better <u>have</u> the convention, but only <u>four</u> sessions. Let us have four <u>good</u> sessions, and it will be vastly better than <u>six</u>, of milk and water; and some of the cheap guns, will get no chance to fire, if there is no time— It is not possible, ~~now~~ to publish the speakers, even if it were worth while. I would send the notice to Tribune, and Womans Advocate,[5] asking friendly papers to copy— I expect to leave here for the east in two weeks, and then, when I get where there is a reliable mail that does not <u>creep</u>, I will at once take hold, and help all I can in getting up a good convention. Mr Higginson I see is in Missouri, looking after the interests of Kansas. God bless him too![6] I never knew Susan, till your last letter, that you are a <u>real</u> liar. It is <u>very</u> wicked— Dont all liars go up chimney, where Anannias did?[7] Why do you say the people wont hear you a bit, when you <u>know</u> you never made a speech, that was not <u>well</u> listened to? So grandly have you done, that you have acquired the name of <u>Napoleon</u>, and now you are making believe, that you cant do any thing—O Susan Susan, you naughty little liar! May God forgive you, as I do, ~~and give you more faith,~~ and give you as much faith in your <u>speaking</u>, as in your acting power— I am going to write Abby Foster and ask her to be the Prest. It is a good idea, and we must have a paper, ↑too↓ and dear brave sensible Mrs. Stanton, must be editor. When we can <u>talk</u>, we will counsel about it ~~and~~   Is it not good that the old quiet Episcopal Church, has a <u>live</u> man it, who has dared to move? This is certainly the most hopeful sign, I have seen—[8] What a bad letter Greeley[9] has written to Dan. F. Miller![10] He is not half an abolitionist. Neither Nettee or I shall settle west, but we are making us a farm here, on one of the most beautiful prairies, God ever made, and here we shall raise our wheat while our smaller farm East will raise all else we need except our clothes. Then, independent of the public, we shall say every true word we believe, and nobody can starve us— Harry has been absent three days at La Crosse. He should have been home before this, and I feel troubled, for there are a great many cut-throats, in this region. I am giving free lectures, every chance I can get. Harry does too— We get invitations from all quarters— It is too bad that the Saratoga Con. is lost. Could you not have done without Mrs. Mott?

⊱ AL, Blackwell Papers, DLC.

1. In her missing letter, ECS responded to suggestions that the woman's rights convention be postponed. Rescheduled twice, the Seventh National Woman's Rights Convention took place 25–26 November 1856.

2. Stone may refer to the relief for women in Kansas provided by sewing societies in Illinois through the Kansas Women's Aid and Liberty Association. In other words, to limit themselves to such traditional activity was to yield too much ground. (Arthur Charles Cole, *The Centennial History of Illinois*, vol. 3, *The Era of the Civil War, 1848–1870* [Springfield, Ill., 1919], 12.]

3. Stone no doubt intended to complete the sentence when she turned her sheet.

4. L. Stone to SBA, 1 July 1856, *Film*, 8:467–68.

5. Anne Elizabeth McDowell published the *Woman's Advocate* in Philadelphia from January 1855 perhaps until 1860, with women in all the jobs from reporter to typesetter. The weekly placed economic questions before suffrage, but its reporters attended woman's rights meetings, and SBA recommended the paper to her audiences. (*NAW*; *History*, 1:625.)

6. Back in Worcester by this date, T. W. Higginson was dispatched by the Kansas Aid Committee to investigate the fate of a party of emigrants who were disarmed on their way to Kansas by Missouri riflemen. (Edelstein, *Strange Enthusiasm*, 184.)

7. Ananais lied to the apostle Peter, "fell down, and gave up the ghost," in Acts 5:5.

8. Reference to reports about the Reverend Dudley Atkins Tyng, of Philadelphia's Church of the Epiphany, who preached against slavery on 29 June 1856. The vestry requested his resignation and resolved that he limit himself to "the simple preaching of Jesus Christ." (*New York Daily Tribune*, 3, 7 July 1856.)

9. Horace Greeley (1811–1872) was the most influential newspaperman in the country. In New York City his daily edition faced strong competition, but his semi-weekly and weekly editions dominated news in the state and the North. Greeley's personal interest in reforms shaped the *Tribune* into an important medium for reformers to publicize their ideas, and he lectured for causes, especially for temperance reform and improved public education. Never at the radical extreme in any cause, Greeley also infuriated reformers

who found him not abolitionist enough, not suffragist enough, or simply conservative about marriage and the family. In state politics, he was allied with the most powerful Whigs—with Albany's editor-lobbyist Thurlow Weed and Auburn's William Henry Seward. (*DAB*; Isely, *Horace Greeley and the Republican Party*.)

10. Daniel F. Miller, a Republican party activist in Fort Madison, Iowa, asked Greeley to clear up rumors that John C. Frémont (1813–1890), the Republican presidential candidate, owned slaves. In his reply, Greeley confirmed that Frémont owned no slaves, but he went on to say that slaveowning did not in itself disqualify a man from the Republican party. (*New York Daily Tribune*, 9 July 1856.)

106 ᕥ ACCOUNTS OF SBA WITH THE AMERICAN ANTI-SLAVERY SOCIETY

Editorial note: SBA kept accounts—personal accounts, woman's rights accounts, and antislavery accounts—in one daybook from November 1856 through 1860. She began the record when the executive committee of the American Anti-Slavery Society asked her to be the agent for their lecturers in New York. Her first tour, under the banner "No Union With Slaveholders," started at the end of November and continued until 20 February 1857. Charles Lenox Remond was the experienced lecturer on her team. It was the first tour for his sister Sarah P. Remond, the first antislavery tour for SBA, and Aaron M. Powell was, in William Lloyd Garrison's words, "comparatively a new lecturer in the field." The foursome headed into New York's northern counties, Clinton, Franklin, and St. Lawrence, and south toward Syracuse.

SBA recorded income on the left-hand page of her book (in a column headed "creditor"), and on the right-hand page she entered expenses charged against that income (in a column headed "debtor"). In the entries printed below, each income page precedes its companion page of expenses. (Samuel May, Jr., to SBA, 22 October 1856, *Film*, 8:606; *Lib.*, 14 November, 26 December 1856, 6 March 1857; *NASS*, 27 December 1856, 10 January, 14 March 1857; Aaron Macy Powell, *Personal Reminiscences of the Anti-Slavery and Other Reforms and Reformers* [New York, 1899], 169–71.)

[*5 November 1856–3 January 1857*]

[*verso*]

1856			Cr.
Nov.	25	C. B. Campbell[1]	2.00
"	30	Peru Union Con[vention][2]	43.88
Dec.	3	S. B. Anthony	44.15
"	2 & 3	Plattsburgh Convention	6.27
			96.30

[*recto*]

			Dr.
Nov.	5	To 40 stamps 25 Envelopes	2.00
"	6	" Postage on 200 Bills	2.00
"	15	" 25 stamp Envelopes	.80
"	"	" Postage on Bills to P[otsdam] & O[gdensburg]	.50
"	28	Albany to Keeseville	5.35
"	"	Baggage & Dinner	.50
		Bill at Ausable Hotel	.75
Dec.	3	C. L. Remond	20.00
"	"	S. P. Remond Expenses[3]	1.85
"	4	Printing 1000 Bills at Platts[burgh]	4.50
"	"	Bill, S. B. & Powell[4] Columbia Hotel	7.00
"	"	Rent Clinton Hall 2 Evening	8.00
"	"	Boy to circulating Bills	.63
"	"	Advertising Dem[ocrat] Paper	1.50
"	"	Dinners for two at Moores[5]	.50
"	4	Fare Plattsburgh to Cham.	.85
"	5	Champlain to Moores	.25
		Moores to Malone S. B. & Powell	2.70
		C. L. Remond going to Montreal	10.00
		Carried Over	69.68

[*verso*]

1856			Cr.
		Brot Forwd	96.30
Dec.	8	Kings Hall Malone[6]	4.01
"	11	Col[lection] Town Hall Pots.	3.00
"	12	Door " " Potsdam	5.41
"	"	[*blank*] Carpenter	1.00
"	15	Frances Jackson[7]	50.00
"	"	Door Lyceum Hall	5.12
"	16	" " "	4.00
			168.84

[*recto*]

			Dr.
		Bro't Forward	69.68
Dec.	6	Printing 500 Tickets	1.50
"	8	Door Tender & Bill dis[tribution]	1.50
"	"	Miller Hotel, S. B. & P.	7.50
"	"	Rent Kings Hall	5.00
"	"	Advertising Palladium	1.00
"	"	A. M. Powell	5.00
"	9	Malone to Potsdam	1.48
	13	Exchange Bill	4.50
	"	Pots. to Ogdensburgh S. B. & P.	2.50
	"	St. Lawrence Hotel	1.50
	"	Baggage	.25
"	15	Websters Board[8]	3.50
"	"	Advertising Ogd.	1.50
"	"	Boys Journal	1.00
"	16	A. M. Powell	12.00
		RR. Fare	.60
"	"	Lyceum Hall 2 Evenings	8.00
"	17	Washington Hotel S. B. & P.	4.00
			132.01

[*verso*]

1856

			Cr.
		Bro't Forward	168.84
Dec.	19	Joseph Savage[9]	5.00
"	22	Frances Jackson	50.00
			223.84

[*recto*]

			Dr.
		Bro't Forward	132.01
Dec.	17	Ogd[ensburg] to Watertown S. B & P.	5.85
"	"	C. L. Remond	14.00
"	18	Woodruff Hotel	3.00
"	"	Watertown to Rome	4.16
"	"	Omnibus & Baggage	.75
"	"	Rome to Albany, Powell	2.60
"	"	" " Syracuse S. B.	.77
"	"	Lunch & Carriage	.63
"	19	Syracuse to Oswego & return	2.00
"	"	Syracuse to Rochester	1.63

"	22 Lunch & Stationary	.56
"	" 25 Stamp Envelopes	.80
"	" C. L. 15 & S. P. Remond $10	25.00
"	24 Stamps & Envelopes	.98
"	25 Envelopes & Stamps	2.00
"	31 Postage on Handbills	1.30
Jan.	2 Rochester to Syracuse	1.62
"	3 Express on 4 Packages P.O.[10]	1.00
		201.66

↞ Daybook, pp. 4–9, SBA Papers, MCR-S. Letters in square brackets expand abbreviations.

1. Cornelius Bowman Campbell (1818–1890) studied with Beriah Green in New York and became a Congregational minister in Clinton, Iowa, sometime in the 1850s. In 1856 he married Phebe Thomas Wilbur, the widow of an abolitionist in Washington County, New York, and an acquaintance of SBA. The Campbells moved to Vineland, New Jersey, in 1863. SBA recorded his donation on the day of the national woman's rights convention in New York. (Frank D. Andrews, "Cornelius Bowman Campbell, A Biographical Sketch," *Vineland Historical Magazine* 12 [1927]: 190–93, 213–17, 247–49; research by Delight W. Dodyk.)

2. According to the *Standard*, the convention at Peru took place on 28 November.

3. Sarah Parker Remond (1826–1894) grew up in Salem, Massachusetts, in a family of abolitionists and, like her brother, crusaded against racial discrimination in public accommodations. She was an agent for the antislavery society for two years. Tired of discrimination and ambitious to obtain a medical education, she left the United States in 1858 to study in England and continued to lecture against slavery. In 1866 she moved to Florence, Italy, and built a medical practice there. After hearing her lecture on this tour, Garrison wrote, "She only needs practice to become a very useful lecturer." She "everywhere commanded the respect and secured the attention of her auditors." (*DANB*; *NAW*; *Lib.*, 6 March 1857.)

4. Aaron Macy Powell (1832–1899), the son of Quaker farmers in Ghent, Columbia County, worked for the American Anti-Slavery Society as early as 1852, and he led the New York State society at the end of the decade. Highly regarded as an able lecturer and agent, he suffered from poor health that often interrupted the tours he began. SBA worked closely with him from this date until the end of the Civil War, and Powell lived with her family in the fall of 1858. He became editor of the *National Anti-Slavery Standard* in 1865. (*NCAB*, 5:17; Powell, *Personal Reminiscences*; Franklin Ellis, *History of Columbia County, New York* [Philadelphia, 1878], 332, 346–47.)

5. SBA consistently misspells Mooers, a town in Clinton County.

6. After meetings in Malone on December 7 and 8, the local paper reported that SBA and Aaron Powell "held forth on that exaggerated form of politics—Abolitionism." Conceding that SBA "is possessed of considerable talents," the paper declared her "thoroughly fanatical in her opinions." The meetings were, it added, very small. (*Franklin Gazette*, reprinted in *Lib.*, 26 December 1856.)

7. She names Francis Jackson who sent her funds appropriated by the antislavery society. Jackson (1789–1861) was a prominent and wealthy Bostonian who supported William Lloyd Garrison, his family, and the *Liberator* and served as an officer of both the Massachusetts and the American antislavery societies. (Garrison, *Letters*, 4:328–70; *NCAB*, 2:318.)

8. At Ogdensburg, SBA and Powell were rejoined by the Remonds, only to find that Webster's Boarding-House, where rooms had been booked for them all, refused to entertain guests of color. The party departed and found rooms in a "fourth-rate hotel." (A. M. Powell to Editor, *Lib.*, 26 December 1856.)

9. Joseph Savage (c. 1803–?), a farmer living in Syracuse, supported antislavery work, signed the call to the First National Woman's Rights Convention at Worcester in 1850, and took part in the convention at Syracuse in 1852. On this date, SBA was in Syracuse to arrange for meetings later in the tour. (Federal Census, 1850; *Proceedings of Woman's Rights Convention, 1850*; *Proceedings of Woman's Rights Convention, 1852*; *Carson League*, 31 July 1851.)

10. The tour continued to the cities along the Erie Canal, to West Winfield and Herkimer, to Johnstown and Amsterdam. William Lloyd Garrison joined the party in February, and the group spoke in Rochester, Syracuse, Utica, and Hudson, before arriving in Albany on 20 February. Reporting for the *Liberator*, Garrison praised SBA's "executive talent and sound judgment" on the tour and added that her "cogent and impressive manner of address did excellent service." (6 March 1857.)

·❮━━━━━❯·

107 ❧ ADDRESS BY SBA ON EDUCATING THE SEXES TOGETHER

Editorial note: SBA used her report on coeducation to the state teachers' association as the basis for a public lecture. At Corinthian Hall in Rochester she spoke to a crowd variously estimated at two to five hundred "about equally divided as to sex," that included clergymen and the city's board of education. Alone on the stage, she began her talk without introduction. (*Rochester Daily Democrat*, 4 February 1857.)

[2 February 1857]

"Gentlemen *and* Ladies"—thus reversing the practice of persons of the opposite sex in speaking to a mixed assemblage. She divided her subject under three heads. First, The identity of the sexes. Before inquiring which is the best method for educating woman, it is necessary to find out what a woman is. With man she has always been either an angel or a devil, according to his love or his wrath. Centuries ago it was not believed possible that she could be taught to read or write, but it is different now. In mind there is no difference between man and woman. The only difference is sexual, but this does not change the head or heart. Man eats, drinks, loves, hates, is courageous, bold, &c., &c., and so is woman. In all the virtues and vices, joys and sorrows, man and woman are the same.

In country schools the distinction of sex is lost sight of. In their studies and in their sports, boys and girls labor and sport together—it is no uncommon thing to see girls assisting boys in their algebra, grammar, &c., or rubbing their faces in the snow. It has been said by an oft-quoted writer that intellectually woman is a man, having the same sensibilities and emotions. The work of education is therefore emphatically one. There is no fundamental difference between the soul of man and woman and should be no difference in education. There is no difference in the work of education and should be none in the way of doing it.

Secondly, the life purposes and destiny of man and woman are the same. Woman as well as man has guided nations. There is scarcely any place of power or trust that she has not occupied. We have woman physicians, divines and law students; Fourth-of-July orators, lecturers and type-setters; editors, authors, shoe-makers; &c., &c., &c. In Massachusetts alone there are 21,000 women who work on shoes. Women hold office, too. There are in the United States over 250 post mistresses and a great many more deputies. In Michigan there is a female deputy Light House Keeper. In Kentucky, Canada, and Michigan women vote on school matters and are chosen school trustees in some instances.[1] Our common school teachers are, five to one, women. The life purposes of the sexes are then essentially the same. To earn their bread and live is the work of both sexes. Every woman is born into the world alone and goes out of the world alone.

Next to body comes mind. The object of education is the highest happiness to the individual. It has always been the generally received opinion that man was made for himself, and woman for man. This is a great mistake. Woman was made for herself, and Miss Anthony claims for her the right to stand upon any height where her senses will not grow dizzy. Women are beginning to come down from their shirt making in the garrets and their scrubbing in the cellars, and are beginning to occupy more favorable positions. The mothers of the earth have a right to the fullness thereof, and they are beginning to see and appreciate that right. Every place is opening to them. If any portion of the race need to be educated it is the mothers.

We hear a great deal about woman, and wonders expressed as to what use she can possibly make of mathematics and other branches of learning, in washing her dishes or her babies. True, but who are to be the lucky ones? All women do not have husbands, and, besides, fathers and husbands die sometimes, and their wives and daughters may be obliged to earn a livelihood. Every father should educate his sons and daughters alike, for upon each may devolve the task of earning their own bread. And who would not rather see a woman occupying the most arduous position, if it is respectable, than to see her the gilded butterfly of some rich profligate or the drudging cook upon some sloop or canal boat?— Here Miss A.'s anti-slavery ideas broke forth. She wants to educate the women, and have the women educate their sons, with a view to teaching southern slaveholders a thing or two.

Thirdly. There are good colleges all over the country for boys, but no one has ever thought of establishing similar institutions for girls. Millions have been given to endow colleges for boys, but nothing to secure similar advantages to girls. Even women themselves give thus. An instance was cited where a woman died down in Massachusetts and left $100,000 to various institutions for the male sex.[2] Women give more in the direction, in proportion to their means, than men. Women will form societies and make pin cushions and the like to raise funds for the education of young men, but they never think of young women.

Oberlin, Ohio, and M'Grawville, in this State,[3] are the only institutions in the country where whites and blacks, males and females, are admitted upon a common footing. The educational needs of woman are imperative and must be attended to. The standard of woman's education has been too low and superficial, and it will take a long time

A PETITION

FOR

UNIVERSAL SUFFRAGE.

- - -

To the Senate and House of Representatives:

The undersigned, Women of the United States, respectfully ask an amendment of the Constitution that shall prohibit the several States from disfranchising any of their citizens on the ground of sex.

In making our demand for Suffrage, we would call your attention to the fact that we represent fifteen million people—one half the entire population of the country—intelligent, virtuous, native-born American citizens; and yet stand outside the pale of political recognition.

The Constitution classes us as "free people," and counts us *whole* persons in the basis of representation; and yet are we governed without our consent, compelled to pay taxes without appeal, and punished for violations of law without choice of judge or juror.

The experience of all ages, the Declarations of the Fathers, the Statute Laws of our own day, and the fearful revolution through which we have just passed, all prove the uncertain tenure of life, liberty and property so long as the ballot—the only weapon of self-protection—is not in the hand of every citizen.

Therefore, as you are now amending the Constitution, and, in harmony with advancing civilization, placing new safeguards round the individual rights of four millions of emancipated slaves, we ask that you extend the right of Suffrage to Woman—the only remaining class of disfranchised citizens—and thus fulfil your Constitutional obligation "to Guarantee to every State in the Union a Republican form of Government."

As all partial application of Republican principles must ever breed a complicated legislation as well as a discontented people, we would pray your Honorable Body, in order to simplify the machinery of government and ensure domestic tranquillity, that you legislate hereafter for persons, citizens, tax-payers, and not for class or caste.

For justice and equality your petitioners will ever pray.

NAMES.	RESIDENCE.
Elizabeth Stanton	New York
Susan B. Anthony	Rochester — N.Y.
Antoinette Brown Blackwell	New York
Lucy Stone	Newark N. Jersey
Joanna S. Morse	48 Livingston. Brooklyn
Ernestine L. Rose	New York
Harriet E. Eaton	6. West 14th Street N.Y.
Catharine C. Wilkeson	83 Clinton Place New York
Elizabeth R. Tilton	48 Livingston St. Brooklyn
Mary Fowler Gilbert	255 W. 19th St. New York
Mary S. Gilbert	New York
M. Griffith	New York.

On 29 January 1866, Thaddeus Stevens of Pennsylvania reluctantly submitted this petition to the House of Representatives, where it was referred to the Committee on the Judiciary (see document 211). The signers included leaders of the woman's rights movement, activists in the wartime Women's Loyal National League, and two of Elizabeth Cady Stanton's sisters.

(From National Archives, RG 233, 39th Cong., 1st sess., House 39A–H14.9.)

Elizabeth Cady Stanton announced the birth of her seventh child, Robert Livingston Stanton, to Susan B. Anthony in this letter dated 2 April. Stanton never wrote the year on her letters, and someone later added it here. The lines through the text direct a typist to the parts of the letter to omit in the edition by Harriot Stanton Blatch and Theodore Stanton after their mother's death.

(Courtesy of Special Collections, Vassar College.)

The signature, on this second page of the same letter, is one that Elizabeth Cady Stanton adopted in 1857. Susan B. Anthony used the left margin of this page to make note of the letter's author and a more complete date. After Stanton's death, Anthony returned her letters to the Stanton family.
(Courtesy of Special Collections, Vassar College.)

In this daguerreotype of Susan B. Anthony taken in 1848, while she taught at the Canajoharie Academy, she is no doubt modeling the dress she described to her mother (see document 16) as "plaid, white, blue, purple & brown, has two puffs around the skirt, cups to the sleeves, with puffs & buttons where they end & puff at the rist . . . & undersleeves I have made out of my linen wristlets . . . & a new colaret about my neck." (Department of Rare Books and Special Collections, University of Rochester.)

Elizabeth Cady Stanton, president, and Susan B. Anthony, recording secretary, signed this certificate of membership in the Women's New York State Temperance Society in January 1853. Anthony also worked as the society's agent, circulating petitions to outlaw the manufacture and wholesale of liquor, recruiting members, and distributing temperance literature. After eighteen months, she concluded that none of the local societies she organized could sustain themselves so long as women lacked rights to their property and wages. (Buffalo and Erie County Historical Society Archives, A00-558.)

This pen and ink cartoon, probably by Elizabeth W. McClintock, was drawn in 1849 when McClintock was denied a chance to learn the import business in Philadelphia. Elizabeth Cady Stanton helped McClintock write a satire about the merchants' fears of working alongside women (see document 36), and McClintock drew a number of cartoons about women's capabilities, including this image of their penmanship.
(Garrison Family Papers, Sophia Smith Collection, Smith College.)

This daguerreotype of Elizabeth Cady Stanton with one of her children dates from the late 1850s. Stanton delighted in her seven children, but their care constrained her public work. To Susan B. Anthony (see document 103) she described herself in 1856 as "a caged lioness," but reasoned, "it is not in vain that in myself I feel all the wearisome care to which woman even in her best estate is subject."
(Seneca Falls Historical Society.)

Lucy Stone (1818–1893), pictured here at the height of her success as an antislavery and woman's rights lecturer in the 1850s, helped to organize most of the major woman's rights conventions before the Civil War. Marriage to Henry B. Blackwell in 1855 and the birth of a daughter in 1857 then slowed her career until after the Civil War. From being one of Susan B. Anthony's best friends, Stone became her harshest critic by 1868, when she had resumed a leading position in the movement.
(Sophia Smith Collection, Smith College.)

Amelia Bloomer modeled the reformed dress known by her name for this engraving made in 1851. Originated by Elizabeth Smith Miller in 1850 and adopted by Elizabeth Cady Stanton, Susan B. Anthony, Lucy Stone, and many other reformers, the Bloomer costume drew ridicule and censure that wearied its proponents. Stanton gave up the short dress early in 1854 and urged Stone to do likewise, asking, "what is physical freedom compared with mental bondage?" Anthony thought it a sign of her moral cowardice that she returned to long dresses in 1854.
(*Boston Museum,* 28 June 1851, courtesy of the American Antiquarian Society.)

Martha Coffin Wright (1806–1875) lived in Auburn, New York, not far from Seneca Falls and Rochester, and she accompanied her sister Lucretia Mott to the first woman's rights convention in 1848. Both Susan B. Anthony and Elizabeth Cady Stanton turned to her for advice thereafter. Never a lecturer for reforms, Wright was often chosen to preside over the New York Anti-Slavery Society and the National Woman's Rights Conventions.
(Sophia Smith Collection, Smith College.)

Lucretia Coffin Mott (1793–1880) was the country's most esteemed abolitionist woman in 1840, when the World's Anti-Slavery Convention in London rejected her credentials. Her friendship had a profound influence on Elizabeth Cady Stanton's ideas about religious individualism, the universality of rights, and the public duties of women. Though she lived in Philadelphia, Mott traveled frequently to New York as a minister of the Society of Friends and a visitor to her sister Martha Wright.
(Sophia Smith Collection, Smith College.)

When Susan B. Anthony became an agent for the American Anti-Slavery Society in 1856, she managed first the team of Charles L. Remond, his sister Sarah Remond, and Aaron Powell on a lecturing tour into northern New York. She and C. L. Remond traveled together several more times before the war and again for equal rights in 1867. Powell became her close friend until they disagreed about manhood suffrage in 1866. Sarah Remond moved to Europe in 1859.

Aaron Macy Powell (1832–1899) (From A. M. Powell, *Personal Reminiscences of the Anti-Slavery and Other Reforms and Reformers,* courtesy of Rutgers University Libraries.)

Sarah Parker Remond (1826–1894) (Courtesy, Peabody Essex Museum, Salem, Mass.)

Charles Lenox Remond (1810–1873). (Courtesey, Peabody Essex Museum, Salem, Mass.)

*Antoinette Brown Blackwell (1825–1921), a college friend
and later sister-in-law of Lucy Stone, was ordained in
1853. Though her ministry lasted only a year, she preached
at different churches for many years. She often also toured
New York with Susan B. Anthony to deliver secular lectures
for woman's rights. She is pictured here with her daughter
Florence in 1857*
(The Schlesinger Library, Radcliffe College.)

Cartoon of the Ninth National Woman's Rights Convention, held 12 May 1859 at Mozart Hall in New York City. Susan B. Anthony presided over a gathering of seventeen hundred people. According to the New York Times *of 13 May 1859, "sundry voters" were "so intemperate in demonstrating their folly, rudeness, ignorance and indecency" that no one could "hear what they went to hear."*
(*Harper's Weekly,* 11 June 1859.)

Office of the Women's Loyal National League,
ROOM No. 20, COOPER INSTITUTE.

~ 119

New York, May 23 1864. 4

Hon. Charles Sumner
Dear Friend

We have now Eighty thousand Signatures to Petition—all rolled up ready to forward to you—If we knew Congress would not adjourn the 31st—we would hold on to them until we got the full hundred thousand—What say you, shall we send them immediate?

Is there a bill, for immediate & entire Emancipation before either Senate or House?—

Is it impossible to press such a bill to a vote this session?——Every member ought to be compelled to show his hand direct on the question—that his constituents may know whether they want him to be their representative another term—

I notice the final vote of the Senate on the Montana Amendment & rejoice that you so nobly insisted on adherence to principle as the vital question. You stand on the floor of Congress—the political arena, as does Phillips in our Convention—the reformers platform—the Representative of the "one idea"—that it is principles, not men, that we, as a Nation, have to settle—I never saw Phillips so grand, so earnest so impressive, as now—none but a god inspire hero, could thus stand & utter truths against the wish & the will of the leaders of Anti Slavery—Mr. Garrison's

Susan B. Anthony informed Senator Charles Sumner on 23 May 1864 about additional signatures to the Women's Loyal National League's petitions urging Congress to enact immediate emancipation of slaves.
(bMS AM 1, by permission of the Houghton Library, Harvard University.)

The league sold this badge, bearing its motto "In Emancipation is National Unity," to finance the petition campaign. Anthony described the image as a slave "breaking his last chain." The badge sold for $3.00 in solid silver, $2.00 in silver filled, and $1.00 in Britannia metal.
(The American Numismatic Society.)

Elizabeth Cady Stanton and Susan B. Anthony knew the white, male abolitionists pictured in this 1857 print, "Heralds of Freedom, Truth, Love, Justice," and all of them had a profound influence on their ideas about religion, reform, and equal rights. Pictured clockwise from the top are Ralph Waldo Emerson (1803–1882), Wendell Phillips (1811–1884), Joshua Reed Giddings (1795–1864), Theodore Parker (1810–1860), Gerrit Smith (1797–1874), and Samuel Joseph May (1797–1871). William Lloyd Garrison (1805–1879) is pictured in the center.
(Massachusetts Historical Society.)

to bring up the faculty of woman. Boys and girls must be educated together physically and intellectually. Even in those institutions where boys and girls are admitted, the latter are not allowed equal privileges with the former. The boys are allowed to ramble through the woods and fields, and over the hills, while the girls are kept housed up. Now the girls should be allowed to take fresh air and exercise as well as the boys. They need such things just as much. And if it is feared that it would be unsafe to allow them to ramble together, measures ought to be taken to prevent the girls from hurting the boys! or at least the boys ought to be imprisoned half the time. At Oberlin they have an absurd by-law which prevents girls from reading, the same as boys, the essays prepared by themselves. Lucy Stone, however, was too much for this by-law. She wouldn't allow anybody to read her essay; and Miss Antoinette Brown was allowed to discuss theology, perhaps owing to the lack of a by-law to prevent it.[4]

These colleges which are now calling for scholars should admit girls. Is it possible that boys and girls who have always associated together cannot go to college together? They take evening walks together, go to operas together, &c., &c., and surely they might be allowed to pursue their studies together. All who have tried this system like it. The sexes behave better and learn better together. Miss Anthony glanced at the charge often made that our colleges are sinks of iniquity, and she thinks the only way to redeem them is to send girls there for the happy influence they will exert.

It is objected that certain studies—anatomy and physiology—are not proper for woman to pursue. She cited the case of Elizabeth Blackwell, who went through a course at Geneva, and studied in France and England.[5] She was treated well while studying, and in the lecture room and dissecting room. The propriety of women performing the office of accoucher was dwelt upon. Miss A. dwelt at much length upon the advantages to be derived from the education of the sexes together, and answered many of the objections raised against such a system, but we have given enough to show the animus and the theory of the lecturer.

≈ Rochester Union and Advertiser, 3 February 1857. Also "Educating the Sexes Together," AMs, Film, 8:500–61, 819–22.

1. Kentucky permitted "any widow having a child between six and eighteen years of age" to vote for school trustees. Since 1850, women in Upper Canada who met the property qualifications had voted for trustees in country school

districts, and in Michigan women voted at school meetings in country districts. (*Woman's Rights Almanac For 1858*, 17-18; *History*, 3:515.)

2. Caroline Plummer of Salem died 15 May 1854, leaving $100,000 in bequests to Harvard College, the Salem Athenaeum, and a farm school. (Harvard University, *Endowment Funds of Harvard University, June 30, 1947* [Cambridge, Mass., 1948], 212-13; ECS to Editor, *New York Tribune*, undated clipping, *Film*, 8:341.)

3. That is, Central College at McGrawville.

4. When Lucy Stone graduated from Oberlin in 1847, she refused to write a graduation essay so long as the college denied her the right to read it. Antoinette Brown's fellow students in the Theological Course encouraged her to join their debates. (Lasser and Merrill, *Soul Mates*, 6.)

5. Elizabeth Blackwell (1821-1910), a sister of Henry and Samuel Blackwell, earned her medical degree in 1849 from Geneva College in New York. After additional training in England and France, she practiced medicine in New York City while she raised the money to open the New York Infirmary for Women and Children and later, the Woman's Medical College of the New York Infirmary. She retired to England in 1869. (*NAW*.)

---

108 ❧ SBA TO STEPHEN S. FOSTER AND ABIGAIL KELLEY FOSTER

Rochester Apr. 20/57

Dear Friends Stephen & Abbey

My will has been good to write you a long <u>long</u> time.— Ever since I left Worcester, and through Dutchess, Columbia & Herkimer Counties have been breathing the atmosphere of moral growth, which seems to me the result of <u>your</u> <u>early</u> <u>labors</u> in the vineyard of Anti Slavery, your spirits have hovered over me, & mine longed to go out to yours—[1]

At Clinton Corners, Dutchess Co,[2] a young girl, at the close of our meeting stepped in front of the stand, & with an earnest spirit, sang an Anti Slavery Song—there was a freshness, an out gushing of <u>soul</u> that seemed inspiration itself— I went to her & thanked her for her contribution to the Cause—learned her name—Shadbolt—her given name I have lost—said the tatterred song book she sang from was ↑one↓ she purchased of you—that she attended all your meetings, with her mother,— now passed from earth—that she was through and through an abolitionist— Her Father & James <u>Thorn</u>, with whom we stopped attended the Poughkeepsie Convention.[3]

Mr. Thorns wife is still insane, and the daughter <u>Frances</u>, what shall I say of her— I said to her—"You find some time for reading I suppose mid all your cares?["] She answered, "I have read ↑<u>more</u>,↓ I presume, than you will if you live to be ever so old,—and as to Philosophy I have philosophised more than you ever will if you live <u>two</u> life times—" She did not like the Liberator because it is too narrow & bigoted—did not sympathize with the Abolitionists, because they ~~were~~ ↑are↓ but agents of the British, &c, &c. A real <u>touch</u> <u>me not</u>—a Mono Maniac almost— in the direction of consummate egotism—but such a specimen of "house keeping"—such an exhibition of personal cleanliness & taste— I told Parker Pillsbury[4] of our descent upon them & he very much to my amusement <u>anticipated</u> me in my every effort to tell him the order of exercises—

But enough of that experience— Surely Nature must have had an odd streak, when she moulded such a genius— She remembered you very distinctly—

When at Worcester I told you of my <u>lone</u> visit to Winfield—[5] Aaron & I were completely snowed in there last week, under the hospitable ↑roof↓ of Good Mrs. Green & her sister Laura— We had an excellent time,—and Stephen, <u>Aaron</u> reports, that <u>Susan</u> was drawn on the <u>Anxious</u> <u>Seat</u> of <u>Spiritualism</u>—[6] Mrs. Green & her sister are both mediums—and we did have very wonderful demonstrations—and I have just written Lydia Mott, that I rather guess I am as far forward as the <u>foot</u> of <u>the</u> <u>Altar</u>—there surely <u>is</u> <u>intelligence</u> <u>not</u> <u>of</u> the minds present in the body—if it be not of disembodied spirits, as it purports, whence is it?— Thats the question—

Singular, quite, that I should have been intimate with those who first became believers, for the past Seven years—and never have my attention arrested, <u>seriously</u>, till this late day—

We had a dear good time at Winfield socially, with Mrs. Green & sister, Julius Bisby & Hiram Brown—[7] Green Thomas & family have moved to the far west— Our meetings were small, not more than Thirty persons present at any one— At Bridgewater,[8] the only aboli- tionist who lives there now, I forget his name, thought ↑it↓ of no use to <u>try</u> to hold a meeting there— The snow storm of Tuesday 14th prevented our meeting appointments at Cedar Ville & Cedar Lake—[9] When we left Winfield Thursday A.M. 16th the snow was <u>three</u> <u>feet</u> <u>deep</u>—had a <u>six</u> <u>hours</u> ride to Utica—and there resolved to abandon our appointments at Fairfield & vicinity—and Aaron went East & I westward—giving to the world a happy exhibition of a "Peaceful Dissolution of the Union—"

Thus has terminated our winter & spring Campaign— And I can truly say—<u>my</u> <u>spirit</u> <u>has</u> <u>grown</u> <u>in</u> <u>grace</u>, and that the experience of the past winter is worth more to me than all my Temperance and Woman's Rights labors— Though the latter were the school necessary to bring ↑me↓ into the Anti-Slavery work—

I am thinking to attend the Anniversary meeting at New York. How rejoiced was I to see Parker Pillsbury's name announced as one of the morning speakers—

Such burning, living words of truth as well forth from his great soul can but bless all who hear—

I wanted to see none but the <u>tried</u> <u>spirits,</u> the old <u>standard bearers,</u> brought forward at that <u>first</u> meeting— For <u>now</u> is the moment for the words of the Prophecies of Twenty-Five ago to be faithfully arrayed before the people, & they shown how even the so called wildest Fanaticisms have been more than fulfilled by the Monster Power of Slavery— And in addition to preaching the fulfilment of the old prophecies—to give to the world the <u>New</u> <u>Revelation</u>—that future generations may read & know that the Fathers & Mothers of this day are really the <u>Lords</u> <u>own</u> <u>Prophets</u>—

Stephen I have gone into a worldly speculation—have bought 5,000 Raspberry Roots—& am going to engage in the Raspberry Culture— Expect I shall prove a successful Gardener—

It has now snowed steadily for 36 hours—most of ↑it↓ melting as it falls— This will postpone the Plowing for two weeks or <u>one</u> at least— and I feel considerable interest now—as my roots are ordered to leave Milton Ulster Co. tomorrow P.M.— Aaron has gone into the experiment too— We shall have no fruit this year—but next year, we will see which will prove the most scientific Farmer— We get our roots of Sarah Hallock—[10]

If your nephew still lives & is with ↑you↓ give him my kind regards & earnest wish for his recovery— And the dear Alla[11] I have lots of love for her—have had to tell a great many people what I thought of <u>her</u>

during the last six weeks— Don't suppose I am hardly as extravagant in my estimation as Sallie Holley—but nevertheless, it is a good word only that I can speak for her— Yours Affectionately

❧ *Susan B. Anthony*

❦ ALS, Abigail Kelley Foster Papers, MWA.

1. SBA stopped in Worcester between February 23 and 27 en route to Bangor, Maine, and resumed her antislavery tour with Aaron Powell in mid-March along the Hudson River. (SBA daybook, pp. 23–27, *Film*, 8:620ff; *NASS*, 20 December 1856.)

2. The lecturers spoke in Clinton Corners, a Quaker community north of Poughkeepsie, on March 17–18 and in nearby Clinton Hollows on March 19. (SBA daybook, pp. 26–27.)

3. James Thorn (c. 1786–?) of Clinton Corners was a farmer, whose wife Sarah (c. 1789–?) was defined "insane" by the federal census taker. Their daughter Frances was about twenty-eight years old. The Poughkeepsie meeting occurred on 24 March. (*NASS*, 4 April 1857; Federal Census, 1850.)

4. Parker Pillsbury (1809–1898) grew up in New Hampshire and trained for the ministry before he became one of the American Anti-Slavery Society's most untiring agents, beginning in 1839 and continuing through the Civil War. He wrote hundreds of letters and articles for the antislavery press about public opinion and the movement's needs. Ralph Waldo Emerson wrote that Pillsbury "is fit to meet the barroom wits and bullies; he is wit and bully himself and something more; . . . [he] flings his sarcasms right and left, sparing no name or person or party or presence." He became one of SBA's best friends and valued teachers. Of the prominent male abolitionists, Pillsbury alone endorsed an all-out struggle for woman suffrage at the end of the Civil War, and he coedited the *Revolution* with ECS. In 1840 he married Sarah H. Sargent, who stayed in Concord, New Hampshire, raising their one child through his years of lectures and travel. (Pillsbury, *Acts of the Anti-Slavery Apostles*; Louis Filler, "Parker Pillsbury: An Anti-Slavery Apostle," *New England Quarterly* 19 [September 1946]: 315–37; Stacey Marie Robertson, "Parker Pillsbury, Antislavery Apostle: Gender and Religion in Nineteenth-Century U.S. Radicalism" [Ph.D. diss., University of California, Santa Barbara, 1994].)

5. After a stop in West Winfield, Herkimer County, on 16 January, SBA returned with Powell on April 11. (SBA daybook, pp. 12–13, 28–29.)

6. SBA employs the language of evangelical revivals to describe her conversion to spiritualism. Those anxious for their souls moved to the "anxious seats" to be the object of special prayers. To move to the "foot of the altar" was to declare one's salvation.

7. Julius Bisby (c. 1807–?), a merchant in Winfield, lived next door to Hiram Brown (c. 1805–?), a farmer. (Federal Census, 1850.)

8. South of Utica, Bridgewater and West Winfield are neighboring towns.

9. In Herkimer County.

10. Sarah Hull Hallock (1813–1886) farmed in Milton-on-Hudson. Married in the Society of Friends, she and her husband joined the Friends of Human Progress. She presided over the antislavery meeting at Poughkeepsie on 24 March 1857; she was also active in the Women's Loyal National League, the American Equal Rights Association, and the National Woman Suffrage Association. (Shirley V. Anson and Laura M. Jenkins, comp., *Quaker History and Genealogy of the Marlborough Monthly Meeting, Ulster County, N.Y., 1804–1900* [Baltimore, 1980], 60, 128, 131; Ulster County directory, 1871–1872.)

11. The nickname of Paulina Wright Foster, born in May 1847, the daughter of Abby and Stephen Foster.

---

109 ❧ PAPER BY ECS FOR THE YEARLY MEETING OF THE FRIENDS OF HUMAN PROGRESS

Editorial note: SBA read ECS's paper on marriage to the Waterloo Yearly Meeting of the Friends of Human Progress that opened on 7 June 1857. Mary F. Davis wrote the meeting's testimony on the rights of woman, urging full investigation and free discussion of the marriage relation, "that thereby woman may be rescued from personal bondage." The meeting published ECS's paper as well.

Seneca Falls, June 6th, 1857.

In the discussion of any Reform, the causes assigned for the abuse are as various as the minds that consider the subject, or the stages of development of any one mind.

In the review of woman's position—of her profitless labor—of her crippling, dwarfing dress—of her civil and legal disabilities—of her religious bondage—of her social degradation—we have by turns believed that in regulating any *one* of these abuses, we should reach *all* the rest. But, to those who in their own bodies and souls have borne the yoke of womanhood, who have groaned under all these abuses, a *new* revelation is made. They now clearly see that the most fatal step a woman can take, the most false of *all earthly relations*, is that under our present legal marriage institution.

The family is said to be the great conservator of national virtue and strength. The *true* one certainly is so. There the man and woman stand equal in dignity, honor and rights. There is no subjection except to principle; no sacrifice but of the soul to God.

If in such a family, children are born, it is by the wish and will of the mother, conceived with a holy purpose, stamped with a high and noble nature, and welcomed to the earth with rapture and hope; where each new creation is the product of love, friendship, passion, and sentiment. Then the woman would regard herself as an *Artist* about to give to the world a beautiful picture, realizing that her daily hourly life was all to be reflected back; that every transient thought and passion were but so many touches of the painter's brush, and that the atmosphere in which she lives is the light that falls upon the picture. The artist's *great* work is *done* before the world sees the result, and so it is with woman's; the child's character is *fixed* before its eyes are opened to the light.

The *true family* needs no laws or ordinances to bind it together; the Spiritual Union no force to make it enduring; no cement but that which love and friendship ever produce.

But what is woman, marriage and the family, as we now have it? Among all Christian nations woman is still regarded as an article of merchandise; she is given in marriage as an inferior; promises to "*obey*" and to "*cleave*" to *that one man* as *long* as he lives; no matter what his transformation or her development may be. If her soul, touched with living fire from the altar of God, should grow into the stature of an Archangel, henceforth the pleasure, the happiness, the well-being of the woman is not of the slightest consideration; the will of the husband is the absolute law of her life. What, says custom, has woman to do with happiness, health and life? Did not God make her for the one specific purpose of ministering to man's pleasure? And if in so doing she has wrecked herself body and soul, on whom shall we cast the blame—her Creator, her law-giver, or herself? We say, *herself*. Let no woman enter a relation where, by public sentiment, Church, and State, she at once becomes outlawed, civilly dead; where she can have no right to her own person, children, or property; into a relation declared by all our pulpits to be one of subjection and unquestioned obedience.

In the history of the past, has there ever been a movement for the elevation of woman? In his career of glory and fame, has man ever paused to consider the subtle causes of woman's weakness and degradation? Have the best Christian men in this nation ever felt the least compunction of conscience, as they have contemplated, year by year, the drooping form, the pale cheek, the sunken eye, the joyless, hopeless life of the self-sacrificing wife, the mother of six, eight or ten children? Whilst they still walk the earth, full of health and vigor, where are those rosy, happy girls they promised at the altar to love, cherish and protect?— *Victims all*, to the lust and selfishness of those to whom they looked for care and support—*dead*, or *suffering life*, with the excessive cares and anxieties of maternity!

And what body of Christians has ever yet protested against this wholesale system of murder and prostitution? The *Quaker* complacently refers you to his marriage ceremony, as one of *equality*.[1] But I shall believe he walks in the *spirit* of that compact when I shall cease to see in his household the exhausted wife, the mother of a troop of sickly children.

It is because woman is ignorant of her natural rights, that she submits without a murmur to these general forms of oppression.

The individuality of woman must be asserted and upheld, and she must ever hold in her own hands the means of self-support and protection. What we now demand is, the reorganization of our social institutions.

Marriage is the question before us. The Woman Movement has brought us to that point.

If marriage, as it now exists, is a divine institution, God will maintain it at all hazards. We can do no harm by a full and free discussion of the whole subject. Whatever has its foundation in truth, must ever remain immutable and secure.

If, on the contrary, it is of human origin, a transient institution, but a necessary step in the progress of development; if we have outgrown its authority and long to be relieved from the crushing power with which it holds both man and woman, blighting and withering the most noble and susceptible natures, let us cast it aside with other false institutions of the past. Let it *fall* with thrones and altars, with kings and priests; and let its symbols lie buried with the crown, the sceptre, the crucifix and cowl.

In a republican government, man claims to stand above all institutions. Whatever is in the way of his development, must be removed. If, in his political and civil life, he demands the greatest freedom of thought, word, and action, depend upon it, he will not always submit, in the holiest of all relations, to be the passive slave of forms and ordinances.

☞ *Proceedings of the Yearly Meeting of the Friends of Human Progress, Held the 7th, 8th and 9th of June, 1857, at Junius Meeting House, Waterloo, Seneca Co., N.Y.* (Rochester, 1857), 21–24.

1. The vows of bride and groom were the same because the duties of husband and wife were the same.

·(⸺⸻⸻)·

110 ☜ SBA TO LUCY STONE

[*Gates*] 16 June 1857

Lucy, I want this Convention to strike <u>deeper</u> than any of its predecessors.[1] It seems to me we have played on the <u>surface</u> of things quite long enough. Getting the right to hold property, to vote, to wear what dress we please, &c &c, are all good—but Social Freedom, after all, lies at the bottom of all—& until woman gets that, she must continue the slave of man in all other things.

I think the word spoken at the Waterloo Progressive Meeting the <u>true one</u>. Will send you report so soon as published. Mrs. Davis's & Mrs. Stanton's strong words are grand. That hour was a <u>sublime</u> one. God & the angels must have rejoiced, as did a <u>few</u> of us who saw & felt the force of the words.

The world, even the <u>religious</u> part of it, is ready to grant to woman her property rights—her Industrial & almost her Political— But in an <u>indissoluble</u> marriage she bows to man's passions.

When woman can be educated to assert her right to control her own person & affections—not only assert but <u>act</u> the traitor—then comes the <u>rub</u>—then comes the time for opposition.

There is more <u>real heroism</u> in the <u>lives</u> of <u>Mrs. Davis</u> & <u>Mrs Eddy</u>, than even <u>we</u> can begin to estimate.[2] I look upon <u>Mary F. Davis</u> as the <u>moral hero</u> of this generation—none greater. . . . Yes, it is good to look into the face of Lydia Mott—she is a glorious woman.

☞ Partial transcript in hand of A. S. Blackwell, Blackwell Papers, DLC; ellipses in original.

1. Planning for the next national convention had begun. See L. Stone to SBA, 11 June 1857, *Film*, 8:922–27.

2. Eliza Frances Jackson Merriam Eddy (1816–1881) was the daughter of Francis Jackson and active in the Boston Female Anti-Slavery Society. After the death of her first husband, she married James Eddy in 1848 but separated from him by 1857. According to Lucy Stone, Mr. Eddy had kidnapped their daughters and taken them to France. By her will Eliza Eddy left a large bequest to SBA and Lucy Stone for the promotion of woman's rights. (Garrison, *Letters*, 3:591n, 4:351n; Charles Henry Pope, *Merriam Genealogy in England and America* [Boston, 1906], 150, 250; Eddy, *Eddy Family in America*, 331; *History*, 3:312–15; Lucy Stone to SBA, 20 July 1857, *Film*, 8:953–60.)

·❲═════❳·

111 ↝ SBA TO LUCY STONE

Rochester Aug. 2, 1857—

Dear Lucy

A note from Mr. Higginson last night, says, if we can secure Mrs. Cutler,[1] Gage, Jones & Davis[2] for <u>Chicago</u> our Con. had better go there—though he cannot be <u>sure</u> to be there—he <u>must</u> attend the <u>Northern</u> Con. & may be <u>limited</u> as to the time of <u>leaving his wife</u>—[3]

I have written the above <u>women</u>, also Mr. Garrison & Phillips[4]— have deferred writing you, hoping to get replies from them— Mr. H. thinks we might announce the Con. at Chicago and <u>leave</u> the <u>time</u>, until after he has fixed the Disunion Con., which will be, he hopes very soon—

A line from Mrs. Rose, says she will attend the Convention, if her health will permit, wherever it shall be held—but thinks <u>New-York</u> the <u>only</u> place for it— I like N.Y. but not <u>this</u> <u>time</u>— I think we had better vote our National W.R. Con. into Anniversary week—then the time & place will always be <u>fixed</u>—

I leave for Binghampton tomorrow A.M. to attend the N.Y. State Teachers Association—shall return on Friday of this week—by that time I hope to find letters from every quarter that shall decide <u>the</u> <u>question</u> of <u>questions</u>—

Lucy for your own souls sake I rejoice at your prospects of becoming a <u>mother</u>—but, oh dear how <u>I</u> shall <u>miss you</u>— If you were not already tired of my wailings, I would tell ↑you↓ how sadly I feel about the prospect of success in a convention <u>without</u> <u>Lucy</u> Stone, or <u>Antoinette</u>

Brown— You <u>must</u> <u>let</u> <u>me</u> <u>feel</u> <u>lonesome</u>—I <u>can't</u> <u>help</u> it, <u>no</u> <u>how</u>—
though I rejoice with you & Nette from the very bottom of my heart—
and am exceeding glad that your souls may be warmed by a <u>Mothers</u>
<u>loves</u>—I nevertheless, <u>cannot</u> <u>shut</u> <u>my</u> <u>eyes</u> to the <u>fact</u>, that the <u>public</u>
<u>work</u> <u>will</u> <u>seem</u> to suffer from your <u>temporary</u> <u>withdrawal</u>—

Saturday Evening Aug. 8th— I returned from Binghamton Friday
(yesterday) A.M. at 10½ Oclock—travelled by night to save <u>time</u> & <u>heat</u>
& <u>dust</u>— I have ordered the "Binghamton Republican" sent to you, &
to Nette, from which you ↑will↓ get some idea of the proceedings of the
Teachers Convention— On the whole, there is great gain—a large
majority of the Convention was on the side of justice & equality, and
could the several questions have been <u>fairly</u> <u>discussed</u> & voted upon,
would every one of them been carried—but the Pres. was so <u>bitter</u>
against all reform, he <u>could</u> not <u>deal</u> <u>fairly</u>—[5] for instance—the Chair of
Com. on my "<u>Color</u>" Resolutions, sprung upon the Con. his <u>minority</u>
<u>report</u>—not one of ↑us↓ suspecting it—had kept perfectly hush in the
Com—and he had a man ready to move <u>its</u> adoption, in a twinkling, &
the Pres. <u>put</u> the question, while I stood on my feet crying <u>Mr</u> President—[6] thus was the cause & I cheated out my speech— I can't tell you
anything of the <u>mean</u> <u>insulting</u> ↑manner↓ of the President from ~~the~~
~~beginning~~ the beginning to the end.

Prof. Davies was told to his face, by one of the best men Teachers of
the State, that his Wednesday Evening speech, was the <u>most</u> <u>villainous</u>
<u>speech</u> ever made—[7] <u>Our</u> Prof. <u>Fowler</u> was the most "<u>logical</u>" man
altogether— On Compensation, he said Society paid the laborer ac-
cording his expenses—that womans were less than man's, therefore she
ought to be paid less—that the <u>demand</u> for woman's labor was <u>greater</u>
than the <u>Supply</u>—that Miss A.s statement that thousands were driven
in their desperation, because of <u>no</u> honest work—to eat the bread of
<u>shame</u>—he did not believe a word of— Oh, how I did wish <u>you</u> were
there to <u>dress</u> him <u>down</u>—but I did the best I could—[8]

Told the people the Prof. had not given us so powerful a reason,
why woman should not receive <u>equal</u> <u>pay</u> <u>for</u> <u>equal</u> <u>work</u>—as the Prof.
of Political Economy of Oberlin, gave to his Class—viz. that if ↑women↓
could get to themselves ~~equal~~ pecuniary indepence with man, they
<u>wouldnt</u> <u>marry</u>—[9] I rather Reckon the <u>Rev</u>.ds, on that platform came
to the conclusion that Miss A. didn't care a '<u>rye</u> <u>straw</u>' for their office or

title— I never spoke more to my own satisfaction in my life— And my prayer continually is that somebody's mantle may fall upon me & I be enabled to speak the needed word, wherever I may chance to be—

The last evening was a "Social["]   The Pres. called out Gent. after Gent. to speak the funniest word he knew—& at half past nine or ten, he said—the ladies had my views relative to Woman's Rights in my opening address but this is a Social Meeting, & if there is any lady present who has any thing to say she can now come forward & do so— I suppose he thought Miss Anthony would spring for the floor—but there he missed— the house rung with "Miss Anthony Miss Anthony" I simply stated that I had nothing to say— the fact was, I did not care to lash the Pres. & Old Fogy brethren any more, & would not speak merely to amuse—they might go, asking for more—

Mr. Higginson & Garrison say it is doubtful whether they go to Chicago—Phillips I have not yet heard from— Mrs. Jones will go to Chicago, or wherever the Con. shall be—   Aunt Fanny will go to Chicago, also M. F. Davis & Josephine Griffin—[10]

Another proposition:—Amy Post is very anxious to have the Con. in Rochester—thinks we might have an excellent one here—that the expense of Hall &c. would be less—

The only question with me is, should we get Higginson & Garrison to stop on their return route from the Dis. Con.—but both will go on to Chicago if sickness does not prevent— You ↑know↓ Mr. G. has a sick Aunt at his house—[11] The Women, we could have here as well as at C. at a cost but little more— What say you?— Is it best to make any change for Rochester now— We could not have an admission of over 10 cts for evening & 5 cts for day sessions, or day sessions Free, & evening 25 cts— What Fee could we have at Chicago— It seems to me there can be no doubt but we shall be able to get men speakers enough to go on to Chicago— What is your judgement Lucy? I really am at a loss to know what mine is—

I thought the Call would be here ere this—but if you can issue it & see to its insertion in all the Papers necessary I shall be very glad—since my head & hands are full of work— A. K. Foster writes me that the Ex. Com. are going to send a Strong force of speakers into Ohio & Western N. York, prior to the Disunion Con. and that I am desired to go to work the 1st of Sept. in Western N.Y. & North Western Pa.— For this I do not feel ready— I have written out but three Anti Slavery points—each,

15 minutes long—and not a line on Woman's Rights—[12] Why the summer seems hardly begun, & here I am to put on the harness for the winter three weeks from to day— I must confess I shrink from it—but the work needs to be done, & I must not be an idler— But I would like time to write out a few thoughts on W.R.— Why are there so few women workers?—why do we not have new women coming on to the stage of public action?

Please let me hear from you right speedily— If you can't attend to the Call, send it on to me— May you be blessed with a Second Lucy— and suffer as little as may be—& above all may you pass the ordeal of maternity, & be saved to work on for humanity— With best Love, Yours Truly

∾ Susan B. Anthony

(will you please let Nette see this as I can't write her of Binghamton—)

∾ ALS, Blackwell Papers 80-M227, MCR-S; Film, 45:347-57.

1. Hannah Maria Conant Tracy Cutler (1815-1896) was left a widow with three children to support in 1844 and began a career of writing and teaching. In 1851 she attended the woman's rights convention at Akron and a year later, was chosen president of the Ohio Woman's Rights Association. After marrying Samuel Cutler in 1852, she moved to Illinois. Cutler helped to canvass New York in 1859, campaigned in Illinois in 1860 with Frances Gage, and in 1861, returned to Ohio to campaign with J. Elizabeth Jones. (*NAW*; *History*, 1:111, 123, 3:561-62.)

2. Frances D. Gage, Jane Elizabeth Hitchcock Jones (1813-1896), and Mary F. Davis. Jones was recruited to the antislavery platform as a young woman by Abby Kelley Foster. In 1845 she joined a group of agitators at Salem, Ohio, and married her co-worker Benjamin Smith Jones in 1846. Together the Joneses edited the *Anti-Slavery Bugle* until 1849 and helped to build the Western Anti-Slavery Society. Elizabeth Jones participated in the woman's rights convention at Salem in 1850, and by the end of the decade was sought after as a woman's rights lecturer and organizer. She worked in the New York canvass of 1859, and she headed the campaign to rewrite Ohio laws in 1860 and 1861. (*NAW*; *History*, 1:168-70; Sterling, *Ahead of Her Time*.)

3. Variously called the "Northern Convention," the "Convention of the Free States," and "National Disunion Convention," this meeting was later scheduled for 28 October 1857 at Cleveland, "to consider the practicability, probability, and expediency of a separation of the Free and Slave States." Disunionism intensified in response to the Dred Scott decision, handed down by the Supreme Court on 6 March 1857. The Court ruled that slaves were not citizens of the United States and that Congress lacked authority to regulate

slavery in the territories. Mary Channing Higginson was invalid. (Edelstein, *Strange Enthusiasm*, 151–53, 197–201; Garrison, *Letters*, 4:454–58.)

4. See SBA to Wendell Phillips, 27 July 1857, and to Amy K. Post, 1 August 1857, *Film*, 8:967, 969–71.

5. The president was Thomas Weston Valentine (1818–1879), a Baptist lay preacher who headed a school in Brooklyn from 1855 until his death and helped to found the state teachers' association. In his opening address Valentine described woman's rights as an "apple of discord" in their meetings, and he warned that "if any lady attempts to drag in any extraneous subject, she should not, simply because she is a woman, be allowed to dash off into a senseless tirade on 'Woman's Rights' or 'Woman's Wrongs,' or any other subject foreign to the general objects of this Association." (*BDAmEd*; *Binghamton Republican*, 5 August 1857, *Film*, 8:977.)

6. SBA introduced resolutions on racial justice, urging the association to oppose "the exclusion of colored children from our public schools, academies, colleges and universities." Directed by a vote to refer the resolutions to a select committee, Valentine named five men, but he relented and added women after an uproar from the floor. When James H. Partridge reported for the committee the next day, he submitted both a majority report, that accepted SBA's resolutions, and his own minority report, that favored "equal advantages of education with the whites." Partridge (1810–1895) was a graduate of Union College, a teacher in New York City, and an author of several advanced mathematical texts. (Allibone; alumni files, NSchU; *New York Teacher* 6 [September 1857]: 540, 543–44; *Binghamton Republican*, 5, 6 August 1857; *Lib.*, 21 August 1857.)

7. Charles Davies denounced SBA's resolutions about opening all schools to women as well as men, as "the first step in that school which sought to abolish marriage—and behind the picture presented by them he saw a monster social deformity." (*Binghamton Republican*, 6 August 1857.)

8. Henry Fowler (1824–1872) taught political economy at the University of Rochester and in 1857 graduated from the Rochester Theological Seminary. The *Liberator* reported SBA's response: "'Where does Prof. Fowler live?' was the surprised rejoinder of Miss Anthony; and she proceeded to relate that in Rochester, where *she* lived, there were one hundred and twenty applicants for seventeen vacancies." (*ACAB*; *New York Teacher* 6 [September 1857]: 545; *Lib.*, 21 August 1857.)

9. Amasa Walker (1799–1875) taught political economy at Oberlin from 1842 to 1848. (*BDAC*.)

10. Josephine Sophia White Griffing (1814–1872) settled in Ohio after her marriage to Charles S. Griffing in 1835, and became active in the Western Anti-Slavery Society and the woman's rights movement. Abby Kelley Foster and Parker Pillsbury praised her ability and zeal as a lecturer and agent. During the war she lectured for the Women's Loyal National League, and she became an agent of the National Freedmen's Relief Association and an em-

ployee of the federal Freedmen's Bureau. In 1866 she was named a vice president of the American Equal Rights Association, and she presided over the District of Columbia Woman Suffrage Association. (*History*, 2:26–39, 869–75; Keith E. Melder, "Angel of Mercy in Washington: Josephine Griffing and the Freedmen, 1864–1872," *Records of the Columbia Historical Society of Washington, D.C.* [1963–1965]: 243–72; *NAW*.)

11. A sister of William Lloyd Garrison's mother, Charlotte Lloyd Newell lived with the Garrisons until her death on 2 October 1857. (Garrison, *Letters*, 4:70n.)

12. She refers no doubt to three of the following manuscripts, dated only by year: "Make the Slaves Case Our Own" and "What is American Slavery?" both 1857?, and a speech on No Allegiance to a Slave-holding Constitution and one titled "Judge Taney," both 1858?, *Film*, 8:1049–74; 9:163–99.)

·⟨══════⟩·

112 ❧ ECS TO SBA

[Seneca Falls, 20? August 1857]

Dear Susan

I did indeed see by the papers that you had once more stirred that pool of intellectual stagnation the educational convention What an infernal set of fools those school-<u>marms</u> must be!! Well if in order to please men they wish to live on air let them. The sooner the present generation of women die out the better, we have jackasses enough in the world now without such women propagating any more.

The Times was really quite complimentary[1] Henry amused me very much, he brought every notice he could see about you, well my dear, he would say another notice of Susan. "You stir up Susan & she stirs the world" I was glad you went to torment those devils. I guess they will begin to think their time has come. I glory in your perseverance. Oh! Susan I will do anything to help you on. If I do nothing else this fall I am bound to help you get up an antislavery address. I will write a letter to the Convention of course. This month my friends all visit me after they depart I will give you notice then you must come here a week or two & we will do wonders. Courage Susan this is my last baby & she will be two years old in January. Two years more & & &, time will tell what.— You and I have a prospect of a good long life we shall not be in our prime before fifty & after that we shall be good for

twenty years at least   If we do not make old Davies shake in his boots
or turn in his grave I am mistaken— I wish I knew what was in that
letter that I wrote to Lucy, for the last Convention.[2] I do not know what
the subject was. Write soon & often   good night yours   as ever

✍ *E. Cady Stanton*

✍ ALS, Papers of ECS, NPV; endorsed "August 1857" by SBA. The variant
in *Stanton*, 2:70–71 is dated 20 August.

1. The reporter for the *New York Times* wrote: "The Convention ought to
thank Miss Anthony for infusing a little healthful agitation among the body,
and preventing them from degenerating into the Mutual Admiration Society,
against which they have been warned by the President." (8 August 1857.)

2. For the Seventh National Woman's Rights Convention, ECS sent a letter
about marriage, similar to the one she sent in June 1856 to the Waterloo
Friends, but it arrived too late to be read. Lucy Stone published a part of the
text in the convention's report, *Film*, 8:807–8.

·⊂══════⊃·

113 ✍ SBA TO ECS

Collins[1] Sept. 29/57

Dear Mrs. Stanton

How I do long to be with you this very minute—to have one look
into your very soul & one sound of your soul stirring voice—

I did hope to call on you before embarking on this Western voyage—
but time & opportunity came not— How are you, & how comes on the
letter for <u>National</u> <u>Convention</u>— It seems impossible to array our
forces for effective action this Autumn— I, therefore, a few days since,
wrote Lucy Stone,[2] begging her to <u>Postpone</u> the Convention until <u>May</u>
<u>next</u>—then hold it Anniversary week, immediately following the Anni-
versary of the American A.S. Society   expect a reply from her at
Collins Centre Saturday Oct. 3^{d}— That Convention has been a heavy
burden to me, the last two months—nothing looks promising—nobody
seemed to feel any personal responsibility and, <u>alone</u>, feeling utterly
incompetent to go forward, unless sure of reliable & effective speakers
to sustain the Con.; could but grope in the dark—but I how hope Lucy
will say <u>amen</u> to my proposition—

Did I write you of Nette's visit at her Fathers—of my dear visit with her, of her darling Florence baby[3]—of her preaching in Unitarian Church in Rochester—of our excellent visit at my Fathers & at W. R. Hallowells, and how we wished <u>Mrs. Stanton</u> could be with us— I can't Remember whether I have answered your last letter or not—be that as it may, I well remember how good a word it brought to me and how it cheered me onward— Mrs. Stanton, I have <u>very</u> <u>weak</u> <u>moments</u>—and long to lay my weary head somewhere and nestle my full soul close to that of another in full sympathy— I sometimes fear that, <u>I</u> <u>too</u> shall faint by the wayside—and drop out the ranks of the faithful few—

There is so much, mid all that is so hopeful, to discourage & dishearten—and I feel <u>alone</u>   Still I know I am <u>not</u> <u>alone</u> but that all the true & the good souls, both in & out of the body, keep me company, and that the Good Father more than all is ever a host in every good effort

But you will see that this is <u>one</u> of my <u>tired</u> <u>moments</u>—so no more— but to the Cause thereof—

I left home the 1st of Sept. and commenced Anti-Slavery work at Binghamton in company with A. M. Powell & W. W. Brown[4]—had three weeks of cold hard labor among people not yet initiated into the first principles of true freedom— I returned home the 19th Sept— found <u>company</u> there—& company <u>came</u> & <u>came</u>— Our folks were in the midst of a heavy <u>Peach</u> harvest—my Mother was very feeble—the <u>Hibernian</u> unskilled—my <u>ward</u> robe in need of repair, my brain and body in need of rest— For a week I was in such a home <u>whirl</u>—on Friday the 25th I left for the "Collins Progressive Friends" Meeting— arrived Saturday A.M.—found Andrew J. Davis[5] speaking to the people, many more than could get into the Quaker Church—size of Waterloo house—he was proclaiming the <u>New</u> <u>Dispensation</u> that is being ushered in—that of Wisdom—that it ~~was~~ ↑is↓ one higher than that of Moses—the one of <u>force</u>—higher than that of Christ—the one of Love— that its mission is to <u>harmonize</u> the two—to make <u>Force</u> & ~~Wisdom~~ Love meet together—he is a very pleasant speaker but his thought rather strained—to me—

In the afternoon Mrs. Davis introduced a resolution on the Dress question— Some person remarked that he had Gerritt Smiths letter to the Dress Convention & moved that it be <u>read</u> & finally it was consigned to <u>me</u> to read—can you believe it?[6] I read that last letter through and then I could not but protest against its philosophy— It surely is a very weak letter—equalled only by Gerritts last position at the Cleveland Compensation Convention— Mrs. Davis, one other woman & several men followed— Then Mrs. D. from the Committee read a Paper on Womans Rights going back to Woman's position in marriage as the starting point— Mr. Davis spoke first—he set forth his idea of the nature of the sexes & their relation to each—spoke truthfully & nobly of re-production—of the abuses in marriage &c, &c.—but to his idea of the sexes—he said woman's inherent nature is Love & man's Wisdom—that Love reaches out to Wisdom man—and Wisdom reaches out to Love—woman—& the two meet & make a beautiful blending of the two principles— In other words woman starts with the Love Principle predominant & grows up into Wisdom—and man starts with Wisdom & grows up, into Love—he however most unphilosophically insisted that each could attain to equality in the two principles—

My soul was on fire—this is but a revamp of the Worlds idea from the beginning—the very same doctrine that consigned woman from the beginning to the sphere of the affections, that subjugated her to man's wisdom— Mrs. Davis was announced, immediately on his taking his seat— She read the same address she did at Waterloo—most excellent—lifting the curtain from the pollution & prostitution of all that is sacred in the marriage relation— Mr. Powell followed her with a most stirring word—& said this, the social question was the most important, & destined to work a greater revolution than any & all other questions—the question was called for—I must out—and said Mr. President—I must say a word—and I did say a word— I said women, if you accept the theory given you by Davis, you may give up all talk of a change for woman—she is now where God & Nature intended she should be— If it be a fact that the principle of Wisdom is indigenous in man, & Love an exotic, then the must Wisdom prevail—& so with woman, must Love prevail— Therefore woman must look to man for Wisdom—must ever feel it impossible for her to attain Wisdom equal to him— Such a doctrine makes my heart sink within me, said I— And did I accept it—I would return to my own Fathers house and never again raise my ↑voice↓ for Woman's right to the control of her own person, the ownership of her own earnings—the guardianship of her own children— For if this be true, she ought not to possess those rights— She ought to make final appeal to the wisdom of her husband

Father & brother— My word stirred the waters—and brought Davis to
↑his↓ feet again, but he failed to extricate himself from the conclusions
to which his premises philosophically lead— Well Sunday, there were
more than a <u>thousand</u> people congregated, hundreds more <u>out</u> than in
doors— In the P.M. I read the <u>basis</u> of my Educational Report—and
that evening until 10 or 11 Oclock, & all day yesterday, the likeness &
unlikeness of the sexes has been the topic of discussion[7]   Phillip D.
Moore of Newark N.J.[8] took sides with me—says <u>my</u> note at Waterloo,
last spring, was the <u>first</u> he ever heard sounded on that side—& there
he came forthwith to me & expressed his sympathy— Well, on the
Love & Wisdom side—we had Powell, George Taylor, Dr. Mary Taylor of Buffalo,[9] & a Mr. Lloyd of Pa.—the discussion has been loud &
long—and have I wished that <u>you</u> could be here— I tell you, Mrs.
Stanton after all, it is <u>very</u> <u>precious</u> to the soul of man, that <u>he</u> <u>shall</u>
<u>reign</u> <u>Supreme</u> <u>in</u> <u>intellect</u>—and it will take Centuries if not ages to
dispossess him of the fancy that he is born to do so

Mr. Moore & the Listeners, two women & one man, sound, sensible
people, say I sustained my position by <u>fact</u> & argument— The <u>Female</u>
<u>Doctor</u>—urged as a Physiological fact that <u>girl</u> <u>babies</u> have from their
birth less physical vigor, than the boy baby—then she claimed that
there is ever passing from the woman out to man a "<u>female</u> <u>orror</u>"[10]—
influence she meant—that thrills his soul—all unlike that of man to man
&c— Well then here is a fact, a girl dressed in boys clothes stands at a
type case side by side with a young man for three years—and this
"female orror" is never perceived, at least not sufficiently to cause the
recipient to suspect the <u>sex</u> at his side other than his own.

Take that same being, array her in womans dress, & tomorrow
morning place her at the same case while the tones of her voice, the
move of her hand the glance of her eye are all the same as yesterday—
her presence causes the sensuous thrill to rush to his very fingers &
toes ends— Now tell me the cause—is the "orror" in the being—does
it go out to that young man from the brain, the soul, the femininity of
that young woman—or is it in the flowing robes, and waving tresses—
in the <u>knowledge</u> of the <u>difference</u> of <u>sex</u>— the <u>latter</u> <u>I</u> <u>say</u>—at least to
a very great extent—but, say our opponents, such an admission is so
gross, so animal— Well I can't help that if <u>it</u> <u>is</u> <u>fact</u>—there it is—to me
it is not coarse or gross, it is simply the answering of the highest &
holiest function of the physical organism—that is that of <u>re-production</u>—

to be a <u>Mother</u> to be a <u>Father</u> is the last & highest wish of any human being—to <u>re-produce</u> <u>himself</u> or <u>herself</u>—the accomplish of this purpose is only through the inciting of the sexes— And when we come into the presence of one of the opposite sex, who embodies, what to us seems the true & the noble, & the beautiful, our souls are stirred, and whether we realize it or not,—it is a thrill of joy that such qualities are re-producible—<u>and</u> that we may be the <u>agents</u> the <u>artists</u> in such re-production—

It is the <u>knowledge</u> that the two together may be the instruments, of that shall execute a work so <u>God</u> <u>like</u>—

But I have wearied you already I fear, and surely have exhausted my moment of time— I must add that many women came to me & thanked me for the word I uttered in opposition to Davis said they—had you not spoken we should have gone home burdened in soul—

Oh Mrs Stanton how my soul longs to see ↑you↓ in the great Battle field—when will the time come—you say in two or three years— God & the Angels keep you safe from all hindrances—and free you from all mountain barriers— If you come not to the rescue, who shall?

Mrs. Stanton do write me a good long letter— I am to be at <u>Gerard</u> Pennsylvania,[11] Oct. 15th— If you write immediately on the receipt of this, it will be in time to reach me at <u>Gerard</u> Pa.

Don't fail to write me—it always does me so much good to get a letter from you— A Kiss for Maggie & Hattie, & Sadie[12]—and a kindly word for the boys— Tell Mr. Stanton that "<u>Powell</u>" is in company— With best Love

❧ *Susan B. Anthony*

❧ ALS, ECS Papers, DLC.

1. The southernmost town in Erie County. The Collins Yearly Meeting of Progressive Friends, on 26–28 September, coincided with SBA's antislavery tour with Aaron Powell and William Wells Brown. From Collins they headed into northwestern Pennsylvania and along Ohio's lakeshore to Cleveland.

2. See L. Stone to SBA, 29 September 1857, *Film*, 8:1022–24.

3. Florence Brown Blackwell was born 7 November 1856.

4. William Wells Brown (c. 1814–1884) escaped from slavery in 1834. While living in Buffalo, he became active in the Western New York Anti-Slavery Society, and within a few years won recognition as an effective speaker. This tour with SBA and Aaron Powell was only one of many he made for the American Anti-Slavery Society. Brown left his most enduring mark as a writer.

After publishing a *Narrative* of his life in 1847, he wrote histories, novels, drama, and essays. (*DANB*; William Edward Farrison, *William Wells Brown: Author and Reformer* [Chicago, 1969].)

5. Andrew Jackson Davis (1826–1910) was one of the best- known and most influential spiritualists. His analysis of spirit manifestations heralded a transformation of this world brought about by the spirits, the "new dispensation" to which SBA refers. Davis married Mary Robinson Love in 1855, and she joined him at the meeting. (*DAB*; Robert W. Delp, "Andrew Jackson Davis: Prophet of American Spiritualism," *JAH* 54 [June 1967]: 43–56; Braude, *Radical Spirits*, 33–37.)

6. Gerrit Smith wrote to the Dress Reform Association in June to say that women wasted their time pursuing rights so long as they continued to wear their "disgraceful and crippling dress." SBA likens this opinion to his argument at a meeting in August, that the North should compensate the South for emancipating slaves. (Gerrit Smith, *To the Dress Reform Association*, 18 May 1857, broadside, Smith Papers, NSyU; Harlow, *Gerrit Smith*, 371.)

7. The meeting resolved that a married woman "should be fully secured in her natural rights to property, to the legal custody of her children, and to the entire control of her own person, that thereby fewer and better children may be born, and humanity be improved and elevated." (Andrew Jackson Davis, *Memoranda of Persons, Places, and Events; Embracing Authentic Facts, Visions, Impressions, Discoveries, in Magnetism, Clairvoyance, Spiritualism* [Boston, 1868], 208.)

8. Philip D. Moore, an accountant, participated in meetings of the Friends of Human Progress at Waterloo from 1852 until at least 1861. During the Civil War he was a collector for the Internal Revenue, assigned to Olympia, Washington Territory, where he settled. (City directories, 1857 to 1864; Federal Census, New Jersey, 1860.)

9. George W. Taylor was a founder of the Progressive Friends in Collins. Under his leadership the meeting became a famous spiritualist gathering. Earlier in the summer of 1857 he attended the Friends of Human Progress at Waterloo. Dr. Mary Taylor, who also attended the Waterloo meeting, may be the same person who headed the female department at the Buffalo Cold Spring Water-Cure in the early 1850s. (Barrett and McCoy, *Cassadaga*, 11–13; Weiss and Kemble, *Great American Water-Cure Craze*, 178–79.)

10. This is probably a phonetic, or satirical, spelling of "aura."

11. Girard lies halfway between Erie, Pennsylvania, and the Ohio line.

12. Sadie still lived with or visited the Stantons in 1860, and Ellen Wright corresponded with her in 1864. See letter at 27 September 1860, below. Also, E. Wright to SBA, 4 August 1864, *Film*, 10:874–75.

·⟨⸻⟩·

114 ❧ CHARLES LENOX REMOND TO SBA

Cincinnati, Ohio, November 26, 1857.

My dear friend Susan B. Anthony,

By this you will learn the whereabouts of the Remond's and all there is of them, and after all it is not enough to make any fuss about. Still some editors and scribblers are foolish to do so, and if ↑it↓ does them any good I won't find fault. Now in the first place I want to hope you are, together with your entire family in the enjoyment of good health and a large share of worldly prosperity. Sarah is well and I find myself improved since our seperation in Cleveland in regard to meetings since that time, with the exception of a few places. I cannot say much, for the weather & travelling has every way unpleasant and uncomfortable, and getting money or subscribers seems out of the question.[1] We seperated with our friend Mr. Foss[2] on tuesday week past and started for this City by the way of Columbus, and whereat we held or tried to hold three meetings but all of which proved miserable failures, the entire citizens both colored & white gave us a rascally letting alone. And this you know uses me up a little quicker than any other demonstration, and if I could have got hold of about five hundred of the twice dead citizens on the last evening of our stay, I think I would have piled the epithets upon them pretty thick for I do consider it a little the most heartless place I ever visited. in this City we have held three meetings very well attended by the colored people and tomorrow (Friday) evening we hold our fourth and last, and on Saturday morning we start for Carrol and Harrison Counties[3] whereat we remain six or eight days, and then go into Pennsylvania on our way home, and shall probably reach home about the 20th of next month, and after being at home a few weeks shall be ready I hope to start again for another campaine. And do you know how our good friend Aaron is doing and if his health is improving? and will he be able to travell this winter? I shall be sorry if he cannot. At any rate please drop me a line intimating your plans for the winter. Its possible I am expected to spend the winter in Vermont but if what I hear is true of the climate of that state and among the mountains especially, I should not expose my health by going there, and I prefer Western N. York any how, at any rate if the party of Yourself—Aaron, Sarah and my self can be made I am in for it. So you can depend upon me if ↑you↓ wish as one who is willing to be a soldier under your generalship. now that ain't flattery greater than you can bear is it? for if it impresses you that way, I have not designed it.

From Mrs. Foster I have not heard anything since the Convention in Cleveland. And when I get home my promises made to her are more than fulfilled, and I am again at liberty, although I am anxious to know the plans for the season of the Boston Committee. Have you heard any thing from Messrs Howland Brooke—Brown & Mrs. Colman,[4] for I can not even learn their field of operations.

When you see Isaac & Amy[5] please give my love to them, and tell them I hope they will not allow Rochester to slumber or sleep through the winter but have the agitators in again who will torment them within an inch of their lives. Remember me also, very kindly to your parents and Sister Mary and in the meantime, I remain Very Truly, Yr friend

    ș   *C. Lenox Remond*

ș ALS, HM 10513, Ida Harper Collection, CSmH.

1. Remond alludes to the financial panic that hit the country in August 1857. He saw SBA at the Disunion Convention on 28 October. (*Anti-Slavery Bugle*, 7 November 1857.)

2. Andrew Twombly Foss (1803–1875), a Baptist minister, became an agent of the American Anti-Slavery Society in the 1850s. He too attended the Disunion Convention. (Garrison, *Letters*, 4:317n; Douglass, *Papers*, 2:446n.)

3. Carroll and Harrison are adjoining counties in east-central Ohio.

4. Another team of lecturers set out from Cleveland after the convention; they were Joseph Avery Howland, Samuel Brooke, William Wells Brown, and Lucy N. Colman. Howland (c. 1820–1889), of Worcester, Massachusetts, was an antislavery lecturer and an organizer of the Disunion Convention. (Garrison, *Letters*, 5:113n; *Boston Evening Transcript*, 21 December 1889.) Brooke (1808–1889) lived in Alliance, Ohio, and was general agent of the Western Anti-Slavery Society. (Garrison, *Letters*, 3:514n.) Lucy Newhall Danforth Colman (1817–1906) taught a school for black children in Rochester to support herself and a child and was active in abolitionism, efforts to integrate the public schools, woman's rights, and spiritualism. She allied herself with SBA in the state teachers' association and lectured for the American Anti-Slavery Society and for woman's rights. During the Civil War she was matron of the National Colored Orphan Asylum in Washington. She returned north to Syracuse to lecture and write on free thought. (*DAB*; *NCAB*, 4:229–30.)

5. Isaac and Amy K. Post.

·⟨⟞═════ш═════⟶⟩·

115 ⚘   SBA to Antoinette Brown Blackwell

Home [*Gates*] Apr. 22 1858—

Dear Nette

A note from Lucy last night, tells me that you have another <u>daugh-ter</u>—[1] Well so be it— I rejoice that you are safely passed the trial hour—had I known the fact I might have added your name to the list of speakers for the May Meeting—

Now Nette, <u>not another baby</u>, is <u>my</u> <u>peremptory</u> <u>command</u>—<u>two</u> will solve the <u>problem</u>, whether a <u>woman</u> <u>can</u> be any thing <u>more</u> than a <u>wife</u> and <u>mother</u> better than a half dozzen, or <u>Ten even</u>—

I am <u>provoked</u> at <u>Lucy</u>—just to think that she will attempt to speak in a Course with such intellects as Brady, Curtis and Chapin, and then as her <u>special</u> <u>preparation</u>, take upon herself in addition to <u>baby</u> <u>cares</u>, quite too absorbing for careful close & continued intellectual effort— the entire work of her house—[2] A Woman who <u>is</u> & <u>must</u> of necessity continue for the present at least, to the representative Woman, has no right to thus <u>disqualify herself</u> for such a <u>representative occasion</u>— I do feel that it is so foolish for ↑her↓ to put herself in the position of <u>maid of all work</u>, and <u>baby tender</u>— <u>What</u> <u>man</u> would dream of going before the public on such an occasion as the one of to night—tired & worn from such a multitude of engrossing cares— It <u>is</u> not best to have to many <u>irons</u> in the <u>fire</u> at one time—

Nette, I dont really want to be a <u>downright scolder</u>, but I can't help looking after the married sheep of the flock—a wee bit— I am sure it is folly for any human being to attempt to follow too many professions at the same time—

But I shall come and see you face to face to finish reading this Lecture— I go to New-York the first of May— Have just returned from Stantons— She is consoling herself that she is <u>doing</u> the work of rearing for the world <u>six</u> of <u>Mr</u> <u>Higginsons</u> model saints—<u>versus bod-ies</u>—[3]

She is preparing a history of the rise & progress of the W.R. Move-ment—which if I am President, which Lucy says I must be, I am going to read to the Convention at the opening session— She intends it to be printed with the <u>report</u>—how I wish she could go & read it herself— She says she shall go <u>next</u> year—

With best Love to you and your two little ones, and Kind regards to your husband I remain yours as ever

❧ *Susan B. Anthony*

❧ ALS, Blackwell Papers, MCR-S.

1. Mabel Blackwell was born 13 April.
2. Lucy lived with her baby, Alice Stone Blackwell, born 14 September 1857, on a farm in Orange, New Jersey, while Henry Blackwell worked in Chicago. She spoke on 22 April at New York's Mozart Hall in a series to benefit the Shirt-Sewers' and Seamstresses' Union, entitled "The Future of Woman in America." The series included some of the country's best-known lecturers: James Topham Brady (1815–1869), a prominent criminal lawyer, noted for eloquence; George William Curtis (1824–1892), popular author and lecturer; and Edwin Hubbell Chapin (1814–1880), a Universalist clergyman thought by some to be the nation's most eloquent man. (*New York Daily Tribune*, 1, 8, 15, 22, 23 April 1858; McAdam, *Bench and Bar of New York*, 1:266–67; *DAB*, s.v. "Curtis, George William" and "Chapin, Edwin Hubbell.")
3. A reference to T. W. Higginson's article, "Saints, and Their Bodies," a plea for physical culture in American education, in the *Atlantic Monthly* 1 (March 1858): 582–95.

·⟨⟩·

116 ❧ ADDRESS BY ECS TO THE EIGHTH
NATIONAL WOMAN'S RIGHTS CONVENTION

Editorial note: SBA presided over the Eighth National Woman's Rights Convention at Mozart Hall on 13–14 May 1858, and after welcoming the crowd, she read ECS's history of the woman's rights movement. ECS mentioned to Lucretia Mott her plans for such a history in 1848 (see above at 3 October 1848) and again in 1855, when she asked Mott to answer questions about the antislavery movement. This address later served ECS as a draft for the third chapter of the *History of Woman Suffrage*. SBA's reading copy is the only known source; the press barely noticed the address, and the convention voted not to publish a report. With its customary hostility, the *New York Herald* described it as "pitching into men generally, and especially into Christian men and anti woman's rights men, . . . and eliciting of course universal applause." (*New York Herald*, 14 May

1858, and L. Mott to ECS, 16 March 1855, *Film*, 8:200–204, 1134–35; *History*, 1:50–62.)

[13 May 1858]

We may date the Woman's Rights movement in this country, to the division in the Anti-Slavery ranks in 1840. Though, before that time, Frances Wright,[1] an English woman, and Ernestine L. Rose, a native of Poland, had spoken nobly on the Equality of the Sexes, and claimed for woman, at that early day, all that we now demand. In the formation of the first Anti-Slavery Society, man and woman labored unitedly, with earnestness & zeal, as has ever been the case in every moral movement. But in this, she did more than sew pin-cushions and ask alms; she proclaimed the living truths of the Gospel of freedom with her own voice, in the Halls of Legislation, as well as at the hearth-stone,—to grave & reverend seniors, as well as to her husband at home.

So absorbed, were these early reformers in the sufferings of the slaves, and the gross injustice, and horrible atrocities of the whole system, that all distinctions of sex and creed, of authority and tradition were, for a time, lost sight of;— But the Priest ever crafty and far-seeing, soon sounded the tocsin of alarm.

But from the adverse state of public sentiment, the praise and admiration they commanded by their presence, was well tempered [wi]th contumely and scorn. The Press, and the Pulpit exhausted the English language, to find execratives to express man's amazement and detestation, at so horrible a revelation, as a woman speaking in public, and maintaining her right to do so. If, said the Priest, Woman, in solving this great question of Human Rights, shall free herself from the trammels of tradition and superstition, if, in spite of the injunctions of Paul, and the discipline of the Church, she shall, with "uncovered head,"[2] minister at the altar, what becomes of us? Where shall we find new subjects who shall yield us the blind veneration and obedience, hitherto awarded us by women & children. An homage always grateful to those who hold and love power. In his secret councils, he then devised the plan, by which woman could be disposed of, and the attention of man turned from the bulwarks of the Church, which stood right in the way of Anti-Slavery. We will make it a political question, said he, we will set these hot reformers to work on the State;— The promise of a future hearing in our National Councils, will decoy them, at present, from our Religious Assemblies, Presbyteries and Synods. This, too, will relieve us, at once, from these misguided women. Beyond the moral sphere, they cannot go, for, most fortunately, all civil constitutions have, in their wisdom, restricted woman to that sphere for which nature designed her. The ball was at once set in motion. A Clerical Appeal was issued, denouncing those women, who dared to speak in public assemblies and calling on the Church, every where, to protest against the act, as unwomanly and unchristian.[3] Every Pulpit in New-England rung with a simultaneous shout of praise to those women who staid at home, obeyed their husbands, took care of their children, and prayed in their closets,—and portrayed in the darkest colors, the fearful results to the Family, the Nation, and the Church, for the Holy Spirit to utter its warnings or its comforts to a fallen race, through so weak a vessel as woman was declared to be.

Thus the memorable split in the American Anti Slavery Society, was effected by Priest-craft. The women were thrown overboard. The ship went down. The mass drifted away on the great ocean of life, and in the unceasing warfare against slavery in this country, have scarce been heard of since. And only those whose souls were buoyed up with the great truths of human rights, beheld the beacon light, and, struggling, reached the tower of strength and safety. On that solitary shore, the Liberator unfurled his banner to the breeze once more, a faithful few rallied around him, where they welcomed to their side the brave women, who, in that hour of peril, had seized the life boat, and followed in their wake. This little band, who, through twenty years of martyrdom, ever as true to humanity as the needle to the pole, have always demanded freedom, not only for the Negro, but for the mothers, wives and daughters of this Republic.

That last meeting of the American Anti Slavery Society, in New-York City, in 1840, ought to be familiar to the mind of every woman in our movement.[4] In no public assembly on record, did the ridiculous ever reach such a climax of absurdity. There were clergymen[5] urging women to vote on the question, whether, henceforth, woman should be permitted to vote in that organization,—calling on them to do there, what they declared it a sin for them to do anywhere. It was a stormy meeting, held that day, by the friends of the slave. And though he still groaned in his Southern house of bondage, they decided that woman's voice should not be heard in his behalf. Whilst, with one hand, they strove to loose the chains that clanked on the rice plantations in Georgia, with the other, they tried to force woman back into the narrow niche, where barbarism had found her. So partially does truth illume some minds, that even the colored man, too, was found voting to exclude woman from an Anti-Slavery Society.[6] Though a vote of the society at that meeting, shows a majority of one hundred in favor of woman's right to speak and to act in all business matters, that cannot be accepted as undoubted evidence of the true position of the immortal five hundred; for, in all popular assemblies, the mass follow their chosen leaders. And we can hardly believe, from the experience and observation of twenty years past, that at that early day, 500 men and women could be found to advocate a heresy so opposed to the Bible and its religion, as taught by the Church. Let the names of those men and women, who were true to womanhood in that hour of struggle, be embalmed in every heart. Let those who would fain have crushed her first efforts to rise above the clouds of prejudice, that had ever draped with darkness her earthly horizon, remain in that oblivion where narrow minds do ever so fittingly betake themselves.

At this crisis, a Worlds Anti-Slavery Convention was called to meet in London, whereupon, the Massachusetts and Pennsylvania societies saw fit to represent themselves in that august assembly by women delegates. But after going three thousand miles to attend a Worlds Convention, it was discovered, alas! that poor John Bull had a very vague idea of what a world was. Having always lived on a little island,— a fragment of a hemisphere,—his soul could take in but a fraction of the human family. In asking the friends of the slave from all parts of the world to meet in London, he never dreamt that woman, too, would answer to his Call. What, though the great idea of immediate emancipation was uttered by Elizabeth Heyrick in a moment of inspiration?[7] What though when Wm Lloyd Garrison first echoed back that glorious truth, New-England's women did quickly meet him heart to heart? What, though they stood firm, through all that martyr age, sacrificing caste, and family, and friends—those who had money, freely pouring it out—those who had courage, facing the merciless mob, and bravely standing between their champions and death? What though woman's soul was kindled with the same love of freedom that had made our Father's declarations so sublimely great and grand? What, though her unwonted lips had sent forth the fires of eloquence that flashed up from her burning soul, and electrified a nations heart? Could she sit in council with English men? Could she aid their deliberations with the lightening truths, that often flash through woman's mind? No!! Man had done the thundering so long, that he really believed himself the essential essence of all light and heat, force & attraction.

But, thank God! he cannot chain the lightening. The magnetic power of that "rod, not larger than a man's thumb," that proclaims itself on Statute books, and chimney tops,[8] does not always yield obedience to what he calls law. There are hidden mysteries of mind and matter, that often baffle him in his science, and confound him in his wisdom. Listen, and blush for your day and generation, at this fact. At the opening of the Worlds Anti Slavery Convention in London, on the 12th day of June 1840, delegates from the Massachusetts & Pennsylvania Societies were denied their seats, simply on the ground of sex. Remember this, and hand it down to your children's children for them to wonder at, and laugh over in the good time coming. This cool reception of the American women, can be attributed, in a great measure, to the unwearied exertions of a trio of Baptist Priests from America, who were unfriendly to the advanced positions of Garrison and his followers.[9] Infidelity, No Government, Woman's Rights, were the watchwords by which these cunning men[10] did make stout English hearts to quail. Nothing that bigotry could do, was left undone, in those days of woman's exodus, to drive her back into the sacred limits, where the tyrant Custom had ever held her.

The women delegates were plead with, in most piteous tones, to waive their rights, for the peace of the Convention,—that the harmony of the occasion might not be wrecked on a question of such minor importance. But, through their champion, Wendell Phillips, the women maintained that as they had been delegated by large and influential bodies, they must take their seats in the Convention, and discharge their high responsibilities, not only to those whom they immediately represented, but to the sad and speechless victims of American Slavery, unless forced to leave a sacred duty undone, by the vote of a Christian Convention.[11] Thus, the question was open for debate, and one entire day was occupied in the discussion of Woman's Rights, and when the vote was taken, not but few men in all that Anti-Slavery host were found true to the mother of mankind. Thus was Liberty struck dumb,—the right of speech denied one half the race,—the sacred rights of womanhood trampled in the dust, and spit upon by her ignoble sons. In sorrow she exclaims, if these, the champions of freedom, who proclaim the inalienable rights of the most degraded slave on Gods footstool, find in their souls no response to the just demands of woman,— if they will not help her to roll off the mountains of oppression that now grind her to the earth, where shall she look? With the setting sun that day, went down woman's hopes in man, but to rise again in God and in herself.

William Lloyd Garrison did not reach England until the third day of the Convention. When he learned that the women of Massachusetts had been refused their seats in the Convention, he declined to take his also,—his Anti Slavery principles being too broad to restrict human rights to color or sex. (Perhaps for his reputation, it is well that he was not there at the discussion, for he, too, might, unconsciously, have stabbed proud woman to the heart.)[12] Thank him, for his silent testimony. Alone, in the gallery, he sat a calm observer,—and what a spectacle did he look down upon. A body of Christian men, coming from all parts of the world to discuss the broad question of human rights, and then by their opening act repudiating the Bible truth that "in Christ there is neither male nor female."[13] Those surface reformers, who had come across the mighty Ocean, to weep over the atrocities of American Negro Slavery, whilst they mockingly laughed at the struggles of woman to vindicate her high descent,—to take that post of honor, that ever rightfully belongs to her, who gives to man his being, and the greatest sum of happiness he finds on earth. They came to strike off the chains that bound the black man down, but to rivet them more firmly on those who fain would rise themselves; for woman in demanding freedom for another, had tasted [o]f the tree of knowledge, and found that liberty was sweet. This sacrifice of human rights by an allied Priesthood, was offered up in the presence of such women as Lady Noel Byron, Mary Howitt, Anna Jameson,[14] and our own Lucretia Mott,—the latter, a delegate from one of the oldest and most efficient Anti-Slavery Societies in America. She, too, sat a silent spectator, though a public speaker, and a member of that sect of Christians, who believe in woman being moved by the Spirit. It was very considerate in the Spirit to make no move in that direction, for twelve long days, seeing that a Quaker occupied the chair.[15] Yes, women, such as these, listened, through one long day, to grave debates on woman's domestic virtues, and sacred sphere,—enshrined in the heart of man and home. How doubly dear she was to every man who spoke to save her from the burthen of her rights. But, his insults, couched in flattering terms, though heard in silence, roused the lasting indignation of those who felt themselves that day a mere target for mans irony and wit.

Our champions, on that occasion, fought our battle with bravery and skill. To stand alone, in that august assembly, and maintain the unpopular heresy of woman's equality, was a severe ordeal for a young man to pass through. Wendell Phillips, who generously took upon himself the odium of presenting this question, to the Convention, earned the everlasting gratitude of woman, by the eloquent and earnest manner in which he advocated her cause. (But, in giving him his due meed of praise, self-respect compels us to protest against a remark of his, after the vote was taken, in reply to George Thompson, who said, "I hope that as the question is now decided, it will never be again brought forward. And I trust that Mr. Phillips will give us the assurance that we shall proceed with one heart and one mind—" Mr. Phillips replied, "I have no doubt of it. There is no unpleasant feelings in our minds. I have no doubt, that the women will sit with as much interest behind the bar, as though the original proposition had been carried in the affirmative. All we asked, was an expression of opinion, and having obtained it, we shall now act with the utmost cordiality."[16] Would Mr. Phillips have made such a remark, had Douglas and Remond[17] been refused their seats in a Convention of Slaveholders in Baltimore? Think you, had they listened through one entire day, to debates on their peculiar fitness for plantation life, and unfitness for public assemblies and the forum, and then been refused their seats on the ground of color, they could have sat with as much interest in the convention, as if their rights had been acknowledged there? And, if it may not be too audacious to claim for ourselves the same feelings, that ebb and flow in the white man's breast, we might put our case to him, as well as the negro. Did Mr. Garrison, feel as "much interest" in that Worlds Convention, as he would have done, had he been free to take part in its discussions?)[18] Mr Phillips did but make the same mistake that has been made a thousand times by almost every man who has ever opened his mouth upon this question. Would proud saxon man but acknowledge that all human beings are governed by the same law of mind he would no longer blunder in dividing the rights & feeling of women & negroes.

The general character of the debates on this question was narrow, bigoted and deeply wounding to the self-love of woman. And her interest in the slave, was for a time swallowed up, in the grief and humiliation she felt, at such an outrage on her most sacred rights.

The injustice of excluding any delegates, on the ground of sex alone, touched a new and deeper chord, in many an English woman's heart. That one act of oppression, gave birth to Woman's Rights in England. The seed was sown. It took deep root.

The women of England have already established a Woman's Rights Journal, and petitioned Parliament for their rights of property. And their claims have been most forcibly maintained by Lord Brougham in the British House of Lords, and by (ascertain by who) in the House of Commons.[19]

And France too, is moving on this question. In spite of a tyrannical government, woman is there demanding a more enlarged liberty. They have a journal of their own, and so liberal and republican in its sentiments, that they are compelled to publish it in Italy, though it is clandestinely circulated in France.[20] In our own country, in 1848, a large body of men and women responded to a Call for a Woman's Rights Convention,—the first of the kind ever held.

The history of our movement from that time is too well known to all of you, to need rehearsal. The published reports of our Annual Conventions, afford abundant statistics for future history.

And how was the news of such a convention received, but ten short years ago? Why, the nation was convulsed with laughter, from Maine to Louisiana. So passingly ridiculous it did seem to all, that under this free government, any could complain of wrongs, much less "fair" woman. For in what other Country, said they, has she ever been treated with such profound respect as here? Has she not been worshiped, idolized, toasted at the mouth of the Cannon, every 4th day of July, for seventy long years? What more, can she ask? But soon, amazement took the place of merriment, as woman did, from time to time, assert and re-assert, that she had grievances to be redressed.

But when she learned with skilful tongue to set forth the story of her wrongs—to arraign man before the nations of the earth as a tyrant and usurper,—to point him to his unjust laws,—his grievous oppressions, and outrageous frauds on the weak and the defenceless, then did the Priest come forth, with Bible in hand, and did issue a mighty Bull, both long and loud, excommunicating this new order of being, not only from Church and state, but from her womanhood.[21]

With each new pressure, woman made new claims. And when she did, at length, declare her full equality with man, in Church and State, and at the fireside,—there were those who reeled with fear, at the frightful visions [tha]t did pass before their eyes,—Ghosts of families, without a head,—Legislators, draped in petticoats,—Altars, desecrated by Priests not of the order of Melchisedek.[22]

It is due to man to say, that, just so far as woman has proved her ability to vie with him in all the great works of life, he has ever promptly conceded to her the even plane of equality.

Does not the success of the Blackwells, and Beechers,—of a Hosmer, a Browning, a Bronte, a Martineau, and the unrivalled Rosa Bonheur, attest the power of genius to rise above all prejudice of sex.[23]

And whilst a galaxy of women, such as these, do vindicate our claims, in science, literature and art, the heroic virtues, too, have shone forth in the women of our day. Man cannot boast heroes more firm and brave than our own Patten and Nightengale.[24] Did it require more nerve to meet a Russian foe, when the blood was up, than in a calm and silent hour to gaze on all the horrors he had left behind, or, on the broad and trackless Ocean to control a crew and with an unpracticed hand to seize the helm and guide a vessel round Cape Horn?

Deeds, such as these, proclaim the truth,—there is no sex in mind. Strike off the fetters then! Let woman be all, and every thing she can. There is no sphere for sex. In nature's laws there is no clashing. Each planet has its circle. Each mind its sphere.

~ Ms in hand of SBA, SBA scrapbook 1, Rare Books, DLC. SBA wrote on the manuscript, at a later date, "From Elizabeth Cady Stanton—to the Eighth W.R. Con. held in Mozart Hall, New York—May 13 & 14, 1858—and read by Susan B. Anthony—" Margins clipped in scrapbook.

1. Frances Wright (1795–1852), born in Scotland and for many years a resident of the United States, was revered as the first woman to lecture on political subjects in America, and her picture graces the frontispiece of the *History of Woman Suffrage.* Her interests ranged from opposing slavery and racial segregation to promoting workingmen's politics and public education; she also advocated a clear separation of church and state and equal economic rights for women. (*NAW*; *History*, 1:35–36.)

2. 1 Cor. 11:5.

3. A series of clerical denunciations was issued in response to Sarah and Angelina Grimké's lectures in 1837. The first, from outside the antislavery movement, was the July 1837 "Pastoral Letter of the General Association of Massachusetts to the Congregational Clergy under their care." In August 1837 there followed the "Appeal of Clerical Abolitionists on Anti-Slavery Measures" and the "Appeal of Abolitionists of the Theological Seminary." (Lerner, *Grimké Sisters*, 188–204; Kraditor, *Means and Ends in American Abolitionism*, 41–47, 64; *History*, 1:81–86.)

4. Held in May 1840, this meeting was the last only in the sense that the American Anti-Slavery Society ceased to present a united front when conservatives withdrew to form the American and Foreign Anti-Slavery Society. Abby Kelley's nomination to the business committee occasioned the split. Conservatives objected that women, not being persons, were ineligible for full membership in the society, and several clergymen urged the women in attendance to vote against woman's right to office. Kelley's nomination was carried by a vote of 557 to 451. (Sterling, *Ahead of Her Time*, 102–5; Kraditor, *Means and Ends in American Abolitionism*, 51–52.)

5. SBA here cancelled the word "priests" and substituted "clergymen."

6. See *Black Abolitionist Papers*, 3:331–39.

7. The English Quaker Elizabeth Coltman Heyrick (1769–1831), a leader of the Leicester Ladies' Anti-Slavery Society, published *Immediate, not Gradual Abolition; or, an Inquiry into the Shortest, Safest and Most Effectual Means of Getting Rid of West-Indian Slavery* in 1824.

8. A play of words on the lightning rod and the provision in the common law that a man could beat his wife provided he used a rod not larger than his thumb and not of iron.

9. The Reverends Nathaniel Colver (1794–1870), Elon Galusha (1790–1855), and Henry Grew (1781–1862) had opposed women's equality since 1837. The debate over women's part in the convention began when Wendell Phillips proposed preparation of a membership list to include "all persons bearing credentials from any Anti-Slavery body." Grew and Colver objected. Admitting women to membership would be, Grew pronounced, a "violation of . . . the ordinance of Almighty God." Galusha amended the motion to deny membership to women. Phillips rose several times to affirm the justice of the women's claim and he declined an appeal from George Thompson, that the women withdraw their request for membership and avoid a vote. The vote was taken, and women's credentials were rejected. (*Proceedings of the General Anti-Slavery Convention, 1840*, 23–46; *DAB*, s.v. "Colver, Nathaniel"; Brown, *Mary Grew*, 13–14, 27; Douglass, *Papers*, 1:110n.)

10. SBA cancelled the word "priests" and entered "men."

11. SBA struck out the word "professedly" before "Christian Convention."

12. Parentheses were added in another pen.

13. Gal. 3:28.

14. A blank space was left after Jameson's name for additions to the list, and ECS added the names of Amelia Opie and Elizabeth Fry in the *History of Woman Suffrage*. Not previously identified are Mary Botham Howitt (1799–1888) and Anna Brownell Murphy Jameson (1794–1860). Howitt, an English Quaker, was a prolific writer, often in joint productions with her husband William Howitt. She became well known for her English translations of Fredrika Bremer's novels and Hans Christian Andersen's tales. Jameson wrote books on art, travel, and women. Separated from her husband and self-supporting, she turned her attention to the condition of working women and lectured on their economic needs. The names of Howitt and Jameson headed the petition for property rights presented to Parliament in 1856. (*DNB*.)

15. ECS probably refers to Joseph Sturge who chaired the meeting on the first day.

16. *Proceedings of the General Anti-Slavery Convention, 1840*, 46.

17. That is, Frederick Douglass and Charles Lenox Remond.

18. Again parentheses were added. The remainder of this paragraph, after the parentheses, was copied in an unknown hand and marked for insertion here.

19. The *English Woman's Journal* published its first issue in March 1858 under the editorship of Bessie Rayner Parkes. Lord Henry Brougham (1778–1868) was a champion of the antislavery cause in the House of Lords and supporter of reforming married women's property law. He presented the women's petition in March 1856. Thomas Erskine Perry (1806–1882) presented petitions in the House of Commons in 1856 and 1857, and he introduced a married women's property bill. (*DNB*; Ray Strachey, *The Cause: A Short History of the Women's Movement in Great Britain* [1928; reprint, London, 1978], 72–76, 89–94.)

20. ECS relies here on a speech by Ernestine Rose at the national convention in 1856, reprinted in the *Woman's Rights Almanac For 1858*. Speaking about the suppression of the French woman's rights movement after 1851, under the imperial government of Napoleon III, Rose explained that the women could not publish their ideas at home but had to print them in Sardinia. She dared not mention the women's names. (*History*, 1:646.)

21. ECS shifts her perspective to the clerical appeals of 1837, not to events in 1848.

22. According to the apostle Paul (Heb. 5:6–10), Christian priests share the blessing and promise given by God to Jesus Christ: "Thou art a priest for ever after the order of Melchizedek."

23. The accomplished women are Elizabeth Blackwell and her sister Emily Blackwell (1826–1910), also a medical doctor, who practiced with Elizabeth in New York City, and Catharine Beecher and her sister, the successful novelist Harriet Beecher Stowe (1811–1896). (*NAW*.) An American sculptor, Harriet Goodhue Hosmer (1830–1908) moved to Rome in 1852. She received critical acclaim for her "Beatrice of Cenci," commissioned by the St. Louis Mercantile

Library and exhibited at the British Royal Academy in 1857. (*NAW.*) An English poet, Elizabeth Barrett Browning (1806–1861) gained immense popularity among women in 1857 with her poem "Aurora Leigh," about a woman's attempt to be an independent artist. (*DNB.*) A French painter, Rosa Bonheur (1822–1899) exhibited at the Paris Salon in 1841 and won a medal at the International Exposition of 1855. (*DBF.*)

24. Mary A. Patton, the wife of Captain Joshua P. Patton of the ship *Neptune's Car*, took charge when her husband came down with "brain fever" and guided the ship from the straits of La Maire to San Francisco. (*New York Times*, 12 January, 18 February 1857.) Florence Nightingale (1820–1910) led British nurses to the battlefields of the Crimean War in 1854 and raised the standards of military medicine. Celebrated on her return to England in 1857, she founded a training school for nurses. (Banks, *Biographical Dictionary of British Feminists*; Strachey, *The Cause*, 19–29, 85–87, 395–418.)

<hr>

117 ❧ MARTHA COFFIN WRIGHT TO SBA

Auburn   June 8th 1858

My dear Susan—

I suppose you are at home now, weeding that acre of Antwerp Raspberries, so I will venture to write a few lines to say to you how disappointed I felt, at being obliged to part so abruptly at the close of the Convention—

You were too much engrossed for me to venture to interrupt you, and I was obiged to leave almost immediately for the sake of an escort, feeling too much a stranger in N.Y. to venture to walk alone up Broadway to 12th. at so late an hour— I wanted very much to talk over the Convention with you— It was too bad, with such an array of Reporters that better justice was not done— I owe you an apology for not performing my part better the last day, but the impure air of that ante room gave me such a severe head ache that I was scarcely able to do anything, ~~but~~ I hope ↑however, that↓ Miss Booth covered my deficiencies—[1]

I was rather sorry for all that was said about "unwilling maternity" because that is a subject that no Conventional or Legislative action can ever reach, & therefore it is better let alone, with the hope that as people become more enlightened, all those evils that have arisen from that source may be avoided—[2] As to that Mr. Pearl Andrews, that Lizzie Gay was so shocked at your permitting to open his mouth,[3] I suppose he was as much a stranger to you as to some of the rest of us, when he began, & I did not know him from "the Pure Pearl of Diver's Bay"— A free platform is always subject to such annoyance— I really do not think it so great an infliction as interminable prosy essays that weary the patience of <u>the very elect</u>, and frighten away half the audience—

It is delightful to see a young man like Curtiss willing to identify himself with an unpopular cause— His speech was beautiful, his tribute to Garrison very eloquent, I wish the speech had been reported—[4] With remembrance to yr. sister Mary, I am very sincerely Yr friend

❧ *M. C. Wright*

P.S. I hope if you are anywhere near here, that you will stop & see us— Ellen desires love—she is pursuing her studies at home, as well as she can, without a teacher.

❧ ALS, Garrison Papers, MNS-S.

1. Mary Louise Booth (1831–1889) served as secretary in Wright's place at the woman's rights convention. She filled that post in 1855 at Saratoga Springs and again at the national meeting in 1860. As a school teacher in Brooklyn, she joined SBA's efforts to shake up the state teachers' association, but she turned to translation and writing and published the *History of the City of New York* in 1859, the first book on the subject. She was named editor of the new *Harper's Bazar* in 1867. (*NAW*; M. L. Booth to SBA, [before 5 August], October? 1856, and *New York Teacher* 6 [September 1857]: 539–47, 7 [September 1858]: 533–48, *Film*, 8:490, 618, 972–76, 9:35–43.)

2. Wright refers to discussions launched by Stephen Pearl Andrews and Henry C. Wright and labeled "free love" by the local press. Andrews, who acknowledged that his theories might not be welcomed, asked if women intended to talk about their right to control "the maternity of the coming generation." This was "the vital point of woman's rights." Wright introduced a resolution, "that the most sacred of woman's rights was the right to decide for herself who, how often, and under what conditions she should assume the responsibilities and be subjected to the cares and sufferings of maternity." Committed to an open platform, SBA allowed Andrews to introduce the topic. The result was, in the word of the *Herald*, a "sensation." The city papers suggest that scheduled speakers regained control of the floor and returned the discussion to legal and economic rights. (*New York Herald*, 14, 15 May 1858, *Lily*, 1 June, 1 July 1858, in *Film*, 8:1124–37.)

3. Martha Wright wrote Lucretia Mott that "Susan handed me a letter from Lizzie Gay, lamenting in quite strong terms that she had permitted such a man to come on to the platform— I penned a little note on to it saying—'Why doesn't Lizzie Gay come here & do her part toward keeping the platform straight?'" The matter did not die, and in June SBA characterized the papers as saying, "all of Miss Anthonys friends are pained at her decision that Pearl Andrews had a right to the floor." (SBA to Lucy Stone, 8 June 1858, *Film*, 9:1-5; M. C. Wright to L. C. Mott, 17 May 1858, Garrison Papers, MNS-S.)

4. George William Curtis delivered an address, "Vindicating the Right of Woman to the Elective Franchise," in which he paid tribute to Garrison as the "solitary husbandman" who "planted" the "seed" of the antislavery movement. The *Lily* carried his speech on 1 July 1858. (*New York Herald*, 15 May 1858.)

·⊂══════⊃·

118 ⇝ REMARKS BY SBA TO NEW YORK STATE
TEACHERS' ASSOCIATION

Editorial note: President George Farnham called the thirteenth annual meeting of the State Teachers' Association to order at Lockport on 3 August 1858. SBA touched off an angry debate by asking that women be added to two of the committees he named. The next day she proposed, "That the quantity and quality of work done, not sex, should govern the price paid the teacher"; the motion was tabled. As the meeting neared its close on 5 August, no time remained to discuss her final resolutions about providing equal education to all the children of the state. But one convention member paid her tribute: "Miss Anthony had said more good things than anybody here. He admired the stand she had taken for fair play. The ghost of woman's rights was worse for some gentlemen, than that of Banquo was to Macbeth." (*Lockport Daily Advertiser and Democrat*, 6 August 1858, *Film*, 9:48–49.)

[3 August 1858]

Miss Anthony moved an amendment, that Miss Mary C. Vosburgh of Rochester, and Miss Mary A. Booth,[1] be added to the Committee on Editors of the *Teacher*, and that the same number of women be added to the Committee on Location of next Annual Meeting.

Mr. Cruikshank[2] asked if it was competent to add to the committee now.

The President[3] thought the Association had the power, and requested Miss Anthony to renew her motion.

Miss Anthony made a few explanations. She would not trouble the Convention unless a question of principle was at stake. She did not care a straw who acted on committees. But she did care whether the women who composed three-fourths of this body be ignored. They should be represented upon all committees; there was no justice in shutting women's mouths in this convention.

Mr. Danforth[4] rose to a point of order.

Miss Anthony resumed, appealing to the women in the Convention to vote upon the question, and demand their rights. She had hopes, from what she had heard of Lockport, that the result on such questions as these would be different from what it had been heretofore. <Miss Anthony went on and said she had battled for five years for this principle, and she wanted the Convention to consider it.> She attributed the motion of Mr. Bulkley, in the resolution inviting Messrs. Reid and Patterson[5] to act as the Committee on Music, to a determination, on his part, to disregard the claims and courtesies due to the ladies of the Association, and thought women should also have been named on the committee.

<Mr. Cavert[6] thought a re-consideration of the question, necessary.

The President remarked that he thought the Association had power to add the names proposed, and should put the vote unless an appeal was taken.>

Mr. Bulkley <was willing to concede all that was proper, but when woman steps out of her sphere, and when she calls in question the motives of the mover, he felt called upon to respond.> [He] arose to vindicate himself, and remarked that remembering the services of these gentlemen on former occasions, he deemed them suitable persons to have the matter in charge, and associate with themselves such other persons, ladies or gentlemen, as they might elect. He had made the motion in good faith, and would not have opposed the nomination of ladies on the committee.

<He had been requested by a lady to have the business of the Association transacted by the men—treat the ladies properly, and go on without this eternal jangle about "Woman's rights." There is no charge that the Committees were not capable of discharging the duties imposed upon them.>

Mr. Heffron[7] of Utica thought this discussion was foreign to the business of the Association, and contemplated on the part of Miss

Anthony, the subject of "Woman's Rights," and nothing less. Mr. H. would not derogate from Woman's Rights in their place. <[He] hoped for one that the proposed addition would not be made. He had no objection to a woman being on the Committee, but after it was made he was opposed to yielding to this cry of woman's rights. He did not believe one fourth of the women present, thought themselves aggrieved by the action of the Committee. He regretted to say that every dodge was practiced to bring in this question of woman's rights, at every meeting of the Association. It had come to be a stench in the nostrils of many prominent educational men.>

Miss Anthony wanted to ask a question. Suppose that our President had placed five women on each of these committees, wouldn't four out of five of the men have felt aggrieved? It was a poor rule that would not work both ways. Men flatter women when they wish them to add to their enjoyment in the small talk and frivolities of life; but when it comes to the question of practical life, involving the rights of women, they talk differently.

Mr. Bulkley rose to a question of order. The lady was not talking to the question.

Miss Anthony wished to be thoroughly understood.

The Chair hoped Miss Anthony would confine herself to the question before the house.

Miss A. had a suspicion that an effort was making to put down the rights of women. <[She] thought if the proposition had been made for two male additions, nothing would have been said.

(Cries of question, question!)

Mr. Valentine[8] hoped not. We might as well take the "bull by the horns" now as any time. Thirteen years ago the Association was organized. Where was woman then? Did she come forward then? No. For eight years they never came forward until the men coaxed them and put them forward. He was sorry that the question was not yielded at once. He should like to be associated with ladies. He did not think the women proposed could pass a school teacher's examination.

Miss Anthony called the gentleman to order.

Mr. Valentine begged leave to say that he meant nothing personal and hoped the question would be carried.

Mr. Clinton[9] thought a favorable vote on this subject would be no reflection on the President.

The question being taken, the President declared the question lost.
The second question was declared lost.

A count was called, and the motion was lost.>

❧ *New York Teacher* 7 (September 1858): 535–36; *Lockport Daily Courier*, 4 August 1858.

1. Mary C. Vosburg (or Vosburgh) was one of several members of her family to be active in the association. The Vosburgs opened a coeducational academy in Rochester in 1858 to train young people in business skills. Mary Louise (not A.) Booth is already identified. (W. H. McIntosh, *History of Monroe County, New York, 1788–1877* [Philadelphia, 1877], 107.)

2. James Cruikshank (1831–1917) attended Union College. In 1855 he joined the state Department of Public Instruction to supervise teachers' institutes and in 1856 became editor of the *New York Teacher*. He moved to Brooklyn and held a variety of jobs in that city's public schools. (Kirk, *New York State Teachers*, 41–42; *NCAB*, 10:232–33; alumni files, NSchU.)

3. George Loomis Farnham (1824–?) was the superintendent of schools in Syracuse until 1863. In 1860 he coauthored a report for the association with Mary Anthony and Elizabeth Powell in support of equal access to schools regardless of sex or race. After moving west, he kept up with SBA's career and in 1892 invited her to speak at the normal school he headed in Peru, Iowa. (Kirk, *New York State Teachers*, 33–34; *Anthony*, 2:728.)

4. Edward Danforth began his career in Erie County, as a teacher, principal, and school commissioner. Though he had moved to Grand Rapids, Michigan, to organize the public school system by 1859, he returned to New York to take part in meetings of the association. (Kirk, *New York State Teachers*, 71–72.)

5. John Williams Bulkley (1802–1888) was the first superintendent of public schools in Brooklyn from 1850 to 1873 and a founding member and past president of the State Teachers' Association. William N. Reid, of Newburgh, and Moses B. Patterson, of Yonkers, sang with the association's Quartette Club at the annual meeting. (*BDAmerEd*.)

6. Michael P. Cavert of Watertown.

7. Daniel S. Heffron (c. 1818–?) was superintendent of schools in Utica. (Federal Census, 1850, 1860.)

8. That is, Thomas W. Valentine.

9. George D. Clinton of Buffalo.

·⟨⟞————⟝⟩·

119 ❧ SBA TO ANTOINETTE BROWN BLACKWELL

Home [*Gates*] Sept. 4, 1858

Dearest Nette

Your "pet plan" is worthy "Napoleon" herself—[1]

Your proposal fills me with new hope and new energy to rush into the battle—though my friends urge †me↓ and I almost incline, to lay down the public "shovel and de hoe"[2] for the entire winter—but, how can I—"back or no back"— I wish I only knew, whether, by work, I am bringing to myself long years of helplessness—that questioned settled in the negative, and I should allow no present discomfort of the refractory member to deter me for a moment—but I am better now—

Nette, I had a plan something like yours—minus the three speakers,—for the coming winter— My idea was, to defer the matter until after the election—then, if the people vote for the Calling of a Convention to revise our State Constitution[3]—we must put out to sea, and spread every sail to run up a mammoth petition to that body—demanding, not "humbly praying" that the new Constitution shall recognize the equality of all the citizens of the State— With such a definite object in view, I had felt that I could go forth alone and stump the state, declaring the truth, getting signatures to Petition, and †arousing &↓ urging the voters, the people to the work of electing no man to that Convention, except he be an out & out democrat—a full believer in the declaration that "all men (& consequently woman) are born free & equal & endowed with a right to life, liberty &c.["]— And if I felt I could work single handed & alone—what think you, I now feel may be done, with the quartette you propose—but ah me!! ah me!!! alas!! alas!!!! Mrs. Stanton!! is embarked on the rolling sea—three long months of terrible nausea are behind and what the future has in store—the deep only knows—

She will be able to lecture however up to January—provided she will only make her surroundings bend to such a work—but her husband, you know does not help to make it easy for her to engage in such work—and all her friends would throw <u>mountains</u> in her path— Mr. Stanton will be gone most of the Autumn—full of <u>Political Air Castles</u>— and so soon as Congress sits, at Washington again—he was gone 7 <u>months</u> last winter—the whole burden of home & children, therefore falls to her, if she leaves the post—<u>all</u> is afloat— I only <u>scold</u> <u>now</u> that for a <u>moments pleasure</u> to herself or her husband, she should thus increase the <u>load</u> of <u>cares</u> under which she already groans— But there is no remedy now— Mrs. S. never said a single word to me about your plan[4]

Tuesday [*September*] 7th

Dear Nette—

The fates have been most unpropitious—my letter did not get to the Office yesterday—

One fact—A. J. Davis & wife Giles Stebbins & a Mrs. Brown[5] travelled in the west last winter, holding meetings & Conventions— they paid for travelling expenses Halls printing &c, &c. over $2,000— netted $3,500— They are going into the West again this winter—

Now the question for us to take into consideration is—~~what~~ how will the interest, or novelty of our troupe ~~compare~~ and the subject we carry to the people, compare with that of Davis'— M. H. Hallowell thinks we might do as well, ditto Henry C. Wright[6] who is now at De Garmo's— but I hardly think it possible—there is a mysticism about spiritual & Davis himself that makes people curious to see & hear but we <u>can at least try</u> as you say—& if we find ourselves too much <u>out</u> of <u>pocket</u>, we <u>can</u> <u>skip</u> surely—

If you & Mrs. Rose <u>wholly</u> disapprove the Memorial—how would it do to for Mrs. S. to send it with her name as Chairman of the Committee—[7]

I will send another copy to Mr. Higginson, for his criticism & signature—thus save time— How I do wish I could see you face to face, & talk over all matters with you— What was the matter with your darling Mabel?[9] We are all sad for you—but the little spirit is <u>not</u> <u>far</u> away from its Mother, no, no,— Lovingly & Sympathingly

∽ *Susan*

∽ ALS, Blackwell Papers, MCR-S.

1. Antoinette Blackwell broached her plan to Lucretia Mott, who mentioned

it to Martha Wright, who quoted Mott in a letter to SBA. "Did I write of A L Brown Blackwell's urging me to go with her & E. L. Rose on a lecturing tour thro' Canada & St. Louis?" (4 October 1858, *Film*, 9:114.)

2. The phrase appears in Stephen Foster's song "Dolly Day," copyrighted in 1850.

3. At the general election in November 1858, New Yorkers voted against calling a constitutional convention in 1859.

4. Though the manuscript ends here, it is likely that the following text, filed separately, completes it.

5. Andrew Jackson and Mary Davis were joined by Giles Badger Stebbins (1817–1900), the husband of Catharine Fish Stebbins, who began as an antislavery lecturer with Stephen and Abigail Kelley Foster and lectured also on spiritualism. (Garrison, *Letters*, 5:326n; Hewitt, *Women's Activism and Social Change*, 118; Stebbins, *Upward Steps of Seventy Years*.) Hannah F. M. Brown edited the spiritualist *Agitator* in Cleveland in 1858 and 1859. Relocated to Chicago by 1865, she wrote for the *Revolution* and was one of its midwestern agents, before heading to California as a spiritualist missionary and lecturer on woman suffrage in 1870. (*Film*, 1:264; *History*, 3:754–55; Braude, *Radical Spirits*.)

6. Henry Clarke Wright (1797–1870) was an early abolitionist and pacifist with an enormous following among spiritualists. After introducing his ideas about maternity into the woman's rights convention in May, he headed for the Rutland Free Convention, a gathering of several thousand spiritualists and radicals in June, and made the same proposals to a more receptive audience. (*NCAB*, 2:232; Braude, *Radical Spirits*, 70–71.)

7. In May T. W. Higginson proposed a committee of one person from each state and territory, "whose duty it shall be to frame a memorial in behalf of suffrage for women—to cause it to be presented to their respective legislatures at the next session, and to ask for a hearing there upon." The plan moved slowly. First, a list of committee members disappeared. Next, Higginson refused to help because he felt his resolution had been misunderstood. Finally, no one could agree what the memorial should say. Higginson, Caroline Severance, Ernestine Rose, and Antoinette Blackwell all disapproved of drafts circulated in the summer. Although a near final draft, about to be set in print, existed by September, no memorial from 1858 has been found. (*New York Daily Tribune*, 14, 15 May 1858, SBA to Lucy Stone, 8 June, 22 August 1858, L. Stone to SBA, 26 August 1858, Martha C. Wright to SBA, 24 June, 13 September 1858, all in *Film*, 8:1124ff, 9:1–5, 16–18, 50–55, 57–58, 84–86.)

8. Mabel Blackwell died in August 1858, age three months.

·⟨⟩⟫⟨⟫·

120 ⇝ WENDELL PHILLIPS TO SBA AND LUCY
STONE

Boston, Nov. 6, 1858.

Dear Friends: I have had given me five thousand dollars, to be used for
the Woman's Rights cause; to procure tracts on that subject, publish
and circulate them, pay for lectures, and secure such other agitation of
the question as we deem fit and best to obtain equal civil and social
position for woman.[1]

The name of the giver of this generous fund I am not allowed to tell
you; the only condition of the gift is, that the fund is to remain invested
in my keeping. In other respects, we three are a Committee of Trustees
to spend it wisely and efficiently.

Let me ask you to write me what plan strikes you as best to begin
with. I think some agitation specially directed to the Legislature very
important. It is wished that we should begin our efforts at once. Yours
truly,

⇜ Wendell Phillips.

⇜ History, 1:667. Also a variant transcript in Blackwell Papers, DLC, Film,
9:137.

1. Francis Jackson made this gift anonymously. A bequest in his will in 1861
augmented the fund. (History, 1:743; Jackson Fund Account, Wendell Phillips,
National American Woman Suffrage Association Papers, DLC.)

·⟨⟩⟫⟨⟫·

121 ⇝ ECS TO SBA

Seneca Falls Dec 1st [1858]

Dear Susan

I can think of nothing better at the first blush that lectures & tracts.
Emily Howland would get up a course in N.Y. at once could she feel
sustained.[1] Antoinette is ready to work all winter, why not send her to

every city in the union, & to London at some future time, where you might hold a <u>world's</u> woman's <u>convention</u>. It would be a great thing for the women of England   France & America to meet in London & have Lucretia preside there just where it was decided that she did not belong to the world. I should like to have Lucy Stone & Antoinette lecture in England   I never felt so thankful in the days of my life as when I read Phillips letter. Now our Napoleon can do something Praise the Lord!! we must save all the toe nails of the saint who has thus blessed us. Emily Howland is a worker you ought to know her. I say <u>no</u>, emphatically to your question. I cannot go to R. I cannot even visit you I am too unwell to travel. I was really thankful to get home.[2]

Do come down & see me & mine   The boys are doing well in Geneva[3]   they are contented & happy. They would be glad to hear from you   Henry goes to Washington to morrow morning   Come down, yours as ever

∿ *E Cady Stanton*

∿ ALS, HM 10515, Ida Harper Collection, CSmH.

1. Emily Howland (c. 1830–?), who lived with her parents at 78 Tenth Street, New York City, was the daughter of a wealthy merchant, Benjamin Howland, and she, like her brothers and sisters, was born in South Carolina. She organized the lectures by Lucy Stone, James T. Brady, and George William Curtis in 1858. (New York City directory, 1858; Federal Census, 1860; *History*, 1:666, 688; M. C. Wright to ECS, 12 September, and to SBA, 13 September 1858, *Film*, 9:79–86.)

2. ECS left Seneca Falls after 25 September for Baltimore to attend the birth of Harriet Eaton Brown's first child in late October. While she stopped with the Motts in Philadelphia on her way north, robbers broke into her trunk and stole jewels and clothes. With a patched trunk and diminished wardrobe, she proceeded to New York by 30 October and was still there on 4 November. (ECS to George W. Curtis, 25 September 1858, ECS to Charles W. Slack, 4 November 1858, *Film*, 9:93–94, 133–35; Lucretia Mott to Martha Wright, 3 November, 28 November 1858, Mott MSS, PSC-Hi.)

3. The older boys, Neil and Kit, attended Dr. Reed's school in Geneva, New York. Gat joined them in 1860.

·❮———❯·

122 ❧ ECS to Elizabeth Smith Miller

Seneca Falls, December 1, 1858.

Dear Julius:[1]

Why did I not fulfill my engagement in Boston?[2] I made the engagement in good faith and prepared myself, expecting fully to be there at the appointed date, which would have been in the fifth month—maternally, not quakerly, speaking—at which time I always have felt well and heroic. But my present experience differed from all its antecedents. I grew worse instead of better,—sick, nervous, timid, and so short-breathed that it was impossible for me to read one page aloud. You see I had a good excuse for not going. I selected the trunk episode as an excuse. I could not give the other to strangers. I knew if I told Mrs. Severance my dilemma, she would have to repeat it, and as the maternal difficulty has always been one of the arguments against woman entering public life, I did not like the idea that I, who had a hundred times declared that difficulty to be absurd, should illustrate in my own person the contrary thesis. It was all too humiliating to be disclosed. So the trunk it was! I hope I shall never meet on earth Mr. Slack; in heaven he could appreciate the nicety of the case. Your devoted

❧ *Johnson*.

❧ Typed transcript, ECS Papers, DLC.

1. ECS explained that the names "Julius" for Miller and "Johnson" for herself, dating back at least to 2 July 1851, began after they saw the Christy Minstrels in Albany and ably mimicked the show for Gerrit Smith. Julius was the wit, while Mr. or Missur Johnson played the philosopher. The Christy Minstrels, founded in 1842 in Buffalo, appeared in May 1844 at the Albany Museum. The Stanton children transcribed Johnson's title as "Massa," reading in the handwriting a word common in white imitations of African-American vernacular. But ECS wrote "missur," either slurring "mister" or mocking "monsieur." (*Film*, 7:90–93; *Eighty Years*, 418–19; *Stanton*, 2:31–32n; H. P. Phelps, *Players of a Century. A Record of the Albany Stage* [Albany, N.Y., 1880], 236–37.)

2. Charles Wesley Slack invited ECS to be the first woman to lecture in Boston's prestigious Fraternity Lecture Course, in a season that included

Ralph W. Emerson, Theodore Parker, George William Curtis, and more. She accepted early in September and was announced to speak on 16 November. Her decision to cancel the engagement brought a flurry of objections from Caroline Severance and other women on the lecture committee. Slack (1825–1885) was a Boston abolitionist, writer, and president of the Fraternity Lecture Course. (C. W. Slack to ECS, 2 September, C. M. Severance to ECS, 24 October, ECS to C. W. Slack, 4 November, C. W. Slack to ECS, 9 November, and C. C. Thayer to ECS, 11 November 1858, all in *Film*, 9:65–66, 132–35, 140–42. ECS to C. W. Slack, 4 September 1858 is in private hands and unavailable.)

123 ❧ SBA TO ANTOINETTE BROWN BLACKWELL

[Rochester, December? 1858]

Dear Nette

If Lucy is gone, don't send my outpouring of wrath on the devoted head of one of our women chieftains into the far west—[1] But to lose such a golden moment to say the word, which Mrs. Stanton professes she so longs to utter, is wholly unaccountable to me— When she wrote me ↑she↓ had accepted the invitation, she said <u>Mr</u>. <u>Stanton</u> was <u>delighted</u> with the idea— My vision finds no <u>mountain</u> in the way, but the <u>individual women</u>—

Nette, Institutions, among them marrige, are justly chargeable with social & individual ills—but after all, the <u>whole</u> <u>man</u> or <u>woman</u> can & <u>will</u> rise above them— I am sure my <u>"True Woman"</u>[2] will never be crushed or even dwarfed by them— Woman must take to her soul a <u>purpose</u>, & then <u>make</u> circumstances to meet that purpose—instead of this <u>lacadasical</u> way of doing & going, if, & <u>if</u> & if— Nette, I'd give the <u>half</u> my kingdom for a day with you & Lucy now—& <u>that</u> is large—for I am "Monarch of all I survey"[3]—Mother is spending some months East—& I keep the Castle alone—

❧ *S. B. A.*

❧ ALS, Blackwell Papers, MCR-S. Date falls after SBA learned that ECS cancelled her lecture in Boston.

1. Lucy traveled to Chicago with her husband and daughter.
2. A reference to SBA's lecture, "The True Woman," which she was writing at this time, in *Film*, 9:435–500.

3. William Cowper, "Verses, Supposed to be Written by Alexander Selkirk, During His Solitary Abode in the Island of Juan Fernandez," line 1.

·⟨══════⟩·

124 ❧ APPEAL BY SBA

Albany, Feb. 22d, 1859.

To the Readers of the *National Anti-Slavery Standard* in the State of New York.

Have you signed your names to the Petition to our State Legislature for a law to prevent the capture and return of fugitive slaves?[1] Have you solicited the names of all your neighbors and sent them up to Albany? If you have not already done so, I pray you lose no time, but copy the petition below—which is now in the hands of a Select Committee, who will this week report a Personal Liberty bill, virtually like that of Vermont—and go about the work in earnest.[2] Plead with every man and woman to give you their names and their influence, as you would do were the outraged, fleeing fugitive one of your own household. Especially do I appeal to *women* to circulate the petition, remembering that one-half the slaves are women, helpless, defenceless creatures, with no law, no religion, no public sentiment to shield them from the sensual Legrees who hunt them.[3]

Mothers! I appeal to you to devote the *present* hour, day and week to this work. Nerve yourselves up to go from house to house, from office to office, and roll up long lists of signatures, as you would do were it your own loved daughters you would rescue from the auction-block. Daughters! work as if it were your precious mothers you would save from the terrible sundering of every bond of affection. How can women remain quietly in their pleasant homes, or carelessly go about, doing their accustomed visiting, while such a momentous question is pending in our State Legislature? What if you *should* meet the chilling, hard-hearted look of indifference and contempt; what if you *should* be told that you had better go home and mind your own family; the consciousness that you are but doing the simplest act of kindness that you would have others do for you, were you the sufferer; the knowledge that your own best nature, the good angels and God approve your work, will cause all opposition and hatred of the slave to fall powerless before you. If you are disheartened, and feel that the cause of freedom is retrograding, then all the more urgent is my appeal to you to take the petition in hand, and go forth among the people. The many hearty "God-speeds" will cheer and encourage you; the many recognitions of the slave's right to freedom, on our own soil, at least will bring hope to your spirit, and strengthen your faith in the sure triumph of the right. If you *profess* love for the slave, make it manifest *now* by your *actions*. Send up to Albany your own name, and as many others as you can obtain, and thus contribute your mite toward making the Legislature feel that *the people* demand that New York shall be free, in fact as in name.

Members of the Legislature friendly to the enactment of a law of freedom to every human being, the moment he sets foot on New York soil, express no doubt of the passage of the bill in the House, and even have strong hope that it may pass the Senate.

Send in your petitions without delay. Direct to the Chairman of the Committee, Hon. Shotwell Powell, Albany, N.Y.[4]

Copies of the Petition may be had by addressing Lydia Mott, Albany, N.Y. Remember to enclose stamps to pay return postage.

❧ *Susan B. Anthony*

❧ *NASS*, 26 February 1859. Also in *Lib.*, 25 February 1859.

1. The petition, printed with this appeal, asked for a personal liberty law that would bar state and federal officers in New York from delivering slaves to anyone claiming their services. In 1857, the Republican assembly, but not the senate, approved a similar bill. At the antislavery meeting in Albany, 31 January to 2 February 1859, Wendell Phillips and William Lloyd Garrison both advocated the law as an assertion of state sovereignty in opposition to a federal government dominated by slavery's supporters. The first petitions were delivered to the assembly on February 2, but appeals were made for more signatures until the session ended in April. SBA spent six weeks in and around the capital, working with Aaron Powell, to keep the legislature informed about campaigns in other states, supply the members with copies of abolitionist speeches, and organize lectures. A select committee of the assembly reported a bill on 26 February, and it passed on 8 April. The senate took no action. (SBA daybook, pp. 54–55, 106–9, 204–5, and SBA to W. L. Garrison, 28 February, 8, 19 March 1859, in *Film*, 8:620ff, 9:223–31; *NASS*, 8 January, 12, 26 February 1859; *Lib.*, 22 February 1859; *JNYA*, 2 February, 8 April 1859, pp. 243, 1182; Morris, *Free Men All*, 182–85, 190–92; Norman L. Rosenberg,

"Personal Liberty Laws and Sectional Crisis: 1850–1861," *Civil War History* 17 [March 1971]: 37–39.)

2. "An act to secure freedom to all persons within this state" became law in Vermont in November 1858. It promised freedom to any slave who entered the state and threatened slave hunters with incarceration. (Wilbur H. Siebert, *Vermont's Anti-Slavery and Underground Railroad Record* [1937; reprint, New York, 1969], 64–65; Rosenberg, "Personal Liberty Laws," 39.)

3. A reference to Simon Legree, the despicable slaveowner in *Uncle Tom's Cabin*, who kept the slave Cassy as his mistress.

4. Shotwell Powell (1818–?) was a Quaker farmer from South Bristol, Ontario County, and a Republican member of the assembly. He presented the abolitionists' petitions and chaired the select committee formed to consider them. Powell reintroduced the measure in 1860. (William D. Murphy, *Biographical Sketches of the State Officers and Members of the Legislature of the State of New York in 1859* [Albany, 1859], 212–13; Morris, *Free Men All*, 192.)

---

125 ⇒ ECS TO SBA

[Seneca Falls] April 10th *[1859]*

Dear Susan

You need expect nothing from me for some time   I have no vitality of body or soul. All I had & was has gone into the developement of that boy.[1] It is now four weeks since my confinement & I can scarcely walk across the room   You have no idea how weak I am & I have to keep my mind in the most quiet state in order to sleep   I have suffered so much from wakefulness.

I am always glad to hear from you & hope to see you on your way to N.Y.[2] When you write to Antoinette give my love to her   If she starts in her meetings we will take Cousin G's $20. every little helps[3]   in haste   your friend

⇒ E. C. S.

⇒ ALS, Papers of ECS, NPV; someone's editorial deletions marked on manuscript. Version in "Early Letters," 1190.

1. Robert Livingston Stanton was born on 13 March 1859 at Seneca Falls.

2. For anniversary week and the Ninth National Woman's Rights Convention on 12 May.

3. Antoinette Blackwell sought funds to rent a hall in New York City where

she could preach. Lucy Stone thought this an appropriate use of the woman's rights fund but hoped the money could be raised from another source. While waiting to hear how Wendell Phillips voted, SBA asked ECS to solicit money from Gerrit Smith. Although Phillips at first denied the request, his accounts of the fund show that Blackwell received $150 on 19 March 1860. (L. Stone to SBA, 24 March 1859, ECS to SBA, 2 April 1859, SBA to A. B. Blackwell, 6 April 1859, *Film*, 9:235–38, 243–44, 249–63; Lasser and Merrill, *Friends and Sisters*, 151–59; Jackson Fund Account, Wendell Phillips, National American Woman Suffrage Association Papers, DLC.)

---

126 ᦥ DANIEL R. ANTHONY TO SBA

Leavenworth Kan June 10th [*1859*]

Dear Sister

Your letter of late come to hand.[1] Shall I draw on Wendell Phillips for the $200. when same is drawn from me—by the WR Association have sent Mrs C I H Nickols 25. she wants $25. more— It cost to much to have conventions in Kansas & people have to much else to occupy their minds—two or three lectures would do—one at Wyandott at time of constitutional convention—all else is money thrown away—without practical effect—

The cost of every thing here is enormous—and I would caution them to be prudent in their operations here—

You can spend the money at once or keep it on hand for future use—

ᦥ D R Anthony

ᦥ ALS, Letters of Daniel R. Anthony, KHi. Anthony wrote "1860."

1. SBA had arranged for her brother to advance money to underwrite a petition drive in preparation for the Kansas constitutional convention. Wendell Phillips would repay him from the woman's rights fund. Susan E. Lowe Wattles and Clarina Nichols had both contacted D. R. Anthony already, and he expressed his opinion to SBA that Kansans had "enough to attend to besides Woman's Rights just now—" Nichols intended to hold a few meetings and put petitions in circulation but reserve her main work for the convention itself. She was ready, she wrote, "were it not that I have lost so much time waiting for D R Anthony to remit expense money." (D. R. Anthony to SBA, 3, 13 June 1859, and C. I. H. Nichols to SBA, 18 June 1859, in *Film*, 9:313, 323,

328-31; *History*, 1:189-94; William Ansel Mitchell, *Linn County, Kansas: A History* [Kansas City, Mo., 1928], 336-37; Gambone, "Forgotten Feminist of Kansas.")

·⊂══════⊃⊂══════⊃·

127 ≫ APPEAL BY ECS

[*c. 12 July 1859*][1]

TO THE WOMEN OF THE EMPIRE STATE.

It is the desire and purpose of those interested in the Woman's Rights Movement, to send up to our next Legislature, an overwhelming petition, for the Civil and Political Rights of Woman.[2] These rights must be secured just so soon as the majority of the women of the state make the demand. To this end we have decided thoroughly to canvas our state before the close of the present year. We shall hold conventions in every county, distribute tracts and circulate petitions, in order, if possible, to arouse a proper self respect in woman.[3]

The want of funds has heretofore crippled all our efforts, but as large bequests have been made to our cause during the past year, we are now able to send out agents and to commence anew our work which shall never end until in church and state, and at the fire-side, the equality of woman shall be fully recognized.[4]

We hope much from our Republican Legislators. Their well known professions encourage us to believe that our task is by no means a hard one. We shall look for their hearty co-operation in every effort for the elevation of humanity. We have had Bills before the Legislature for several years, on some of which, from time to time, have been most favorable reports. The property bill of '48 was passed by a large majority. The various bills of rights, to wages, children, suffrage, &c., have been respectfully considered. The Bill presented at the last Session, giving to married women their rights to make contracts, and to their wages, passed the House with only three dissenting voices, but owing to the pressure of business at the close of the session, it was never brought before the Senate.[5]

Whilst man, by his legislation and generous donations, declares our cause righteous and just—whilst the very best men of the nation—those who stand first in church and state, in literature, commerce and the arts, are speaking for us such noble words and performing such God-like deeds, shall woman, herself, be indifferent to her own wrongs, insensible to all the responsibilities of her high and holy calling? No! No!! Let the women of the Empire State now speak out in deep and earnest tones that cannot be misunderstood; demanding all those rights which are at the very foundation of Republicanism—a full and equal representation with man in the administration of our State and National Government.

Do you know, women of New York, that under our present laws married women have no right to the wages they earn? Think of the 40,000 drunkards' wives in this state—of the wives of men who are licentious—of gamblers—of the long line of those who do nothing; and is it no light matter that all these women who support themselves, their husbands, and families, too, shall have no right to the disposition of their own earnings? Roll up, then, your Petitions on this point, if no other, and secure to laboring women their wages at the coming session.

Now is the golden time to work. Before another Constitutional Convention be called, see to it, that the public sentiment of this state shall demand suffrage for woman. Remember, "they who would be free must *themselves* strike the blow."[6]

❧ *E. Cady Stanton,*
Chairman Central Committee.

❧ Circular, Matilda Joslyn Gage Scrapbooks, Rare Books, DLC. Also in *Rochester Union and Advertiser*, 12 July 1859, *Film*, 9:341; *Seneca County Courier*, 25 July 1859; *Sibyl*, 1 August 1859.

1. Though undated, the circular was published in newspapers by 12 July 1859.

2. Petition omitted. In addition to suffrage, the petition sought "laws securing to married women the full and entire control of all property originally belonging to them, and of their earnings during marriage; and making the rights of the wife over the children the same as a husband enjoys, and the rights of a widow, as to her children, and as to the property left by her husband the same that a husband has in the property and over the children of his deceased wife."

3. SBA and Antoinette Blackwell began this canvass on July 13 in Niagara Falls and traveled together until September 22 at Oswego. Acting as general agent, SBA arranged further engagements through the fall and winter for Frances Gage, Hannah Cutler, J. Elizabeth Jones, and Lucy Colman. At the

woman's rights meeting in May 1860 she reported that the canvass reached forty counties and 150 towns. (*NASS*, July–December 1859; *Anthony*, 1:175–78; *History*, 1:689–92; Lasser and Merrill, *Friends and Sisters*, 155–59; SBA daybook, pp. 121, 125, *Film*, 8:620ff, 9:370–73.)

4. In addition to the anonymous woman's rights fund, the movement received a bequest from Charles F. Hovey in 1859. His will, proved on 30 May, stipulated that the residue of his estate be placed in a special trust to be spent, at a rate of eight thousand dollars annually, to promote the antislavery cause and "other reforms, such as Woman's Rights, Non-Resistance, Free Trade and Temperance." (*History*, 1:667–68; "Extracts From the Will of the Late Charles F. Hovey, Esq.," broadside, SBA scrapbook 1, Rare Books, DLC.)

5. The New York State Assembly considered "an act for the protection of the property in trade and earnings of married women" in 1859 and passed it overwhelmingly on April 8. The measure did not come to a vote in the senate. (Basch, *In the Eyes of the Law*, 194; *JNYA*, 8 February, 2 March, 1, 4, 5, 6, 8 April 1859, pp. 292, 477, 921, 1014, 1035, 1090, 1147; *JNYS*, 9 April 1859, p. 715.)

6. Byron, "Childe Harold's Pilgrimage," canto 2, stanza 76.

·⊂━━━━✕━━━━⊃·

128 ✐ ECS TO SBA

[*Seneca Falls*] July 15th [*1859*]

Dear Susan,

Well here is the tract.[1] I think it is about right now seeing that the best part is all cut out. I should have sent it long ago, but I have had to change servants. Mary[2] went into the factory as she was tired revolving round the cook stove & Susan got sick & went home   so imagine me with strage servants   my boys home in their vacation & excuse my seeming negligence of all your epistles. When you come I shall try & grind out what you say <u>must</u> be done   I expect to get my inspiration facts & thoughts from you. I will engage to dress all the children you bring.

I am in no situation to think or write, but the occasion demands that I exert myself to do all I can   so come on, we have issued bulls under all circumstances. I think you & I can still do more even if you must make the puddings & carry the baby. Oh! Susan! Susan! Love to Nette. I embrace her with my soul I am too happy that she has brought her thunder into our state. I hope she will strike the Legislature to their hearts core with her <u>lightn</u>ing so that not one man shall dare to wag his jaw against our demands   Now if Antoinette will get our right of suffrage within two years she shall have her pick of a boy or girl from my flock & that will save her the trouble of another experiment!! Generous offer!! good night   your friend

❧ *E Cady Stanton.*

Can I correct proof of this tract, or do you think you can get all right?

❧ ALS, Papers of ECS, NPV. Endorsed "July 15th/59" by SBA.

1. Enclosure missing. Since her appeal to the women of New York appeared in print three days earlier, ECS probably refers here to *It is So Unladylike*, a tract published in 1859 with the funds given for woman's rights work. In it ECS attacked men's attitudes toward training women for occupations. (*Film*, 9:505–8.)

2. Probably Mary Leary, eighteen years old in 1860, who worked again for the Stantons the next year and moved with the family to New York City. (Federal Census, 1860.)

·◖══════◗·

129 ❧ Clarina Howard Nichols to SBA

Con^l Hall, Wyandott [*K.T.*] July 21 [*1859*]

Dear Susan

I am still here laboring with members and outsiders—directly or indirectly as seems most politic—to advance our cause.[1] Defeated as we are bound to be on the suffrage question—we will get better terms on legal securities. Our right to hold, acquire and defend property independent of husbands & to equal control of children <u>during their</u> (entire) <u>minority</u> is passed in a provision adopted ↑(1st reading)↓ and without a single "<u>nay</u>."[2] There will be an effort to change ~~to the securing of~~ ↑on a second reading↓ by inserting "equal legal rights" as under that phraseology we can reach the whole subject of settle^t of estates ~~&c &c~~ taxation &c &c.

I have again secured the promise of an effort to get an exemption from taxes; also the friends are prepared to try again for suffrage submission thro' the Legislature. One branch of our friends contend that our case is provided for under a provision adopted, making a

<u>majority</u> vote of the Legis^e competent to submit any question of amendment to the people.[3] It is conceded that we can easily get a majority vote of the Legis^e to submit the question of suffrage— I believe this; nothing but the fear that the Con^n will be voted down preventing our enfranchisement by Con^l provision. Twice have the repub^ns in causes cast a majority vote (of the whole Con^n) in its favor. No such fear will prevent action by the Legis^e

I propose to go out in two weeks again & canvass the towns with reference to the election of a right Leg^e; & preparing the people & women for the practical ~~application~~ ↑use↓ of their school rights.[4]

I shall get collections when I can, & rely on the friends to secure my ex^s and a <u>small</u> compensation at least; as my daughter has to leave her school to keep house while I spend my time &—[5]

By urgent requests from all directions (members & citizens) I speak here again tomorrow evening.[6] They say I have accomplished a great change in public sentiment. I tell you because of <u>our</u> mutual interest in the <u>cause</u>. O Susan I thank God daily that with renovated strength, my capability & consequent success in the lecture field is increased. I did poorest in Leavenworth—indeed I felt at home every where else. It is the hardest place & yet the Ed. of the Ledger who made a disparaging notice of our movement before my visit, noticed my lecture saying he had not listened 10 minutes before he was woman's rights man &c.[7]

We want $25. of W.R. Tracts your brother I learn from Mr Wattles has reserved that much for the same. Mrs Wattles[8] wishes me to write— & select the Tracts— Please send the 5 you have stereotyped, & any additional you think best.

Whatever the friends appropriate to Kansas will be faithfully & economically used. We have our first Con^n in Moneka (Southern Kansas) 7 Sept. & from that to other Counties, organizing associations &c—

We have 12 men, <u>thorough</u> <u>reformers</u> in this Con^n. One of these says he has so long stood alone on the Wom. question that he feels almost doubtful of himself as if he had receded—to find public sentiment coming to his side. Affec^y

❧ *C I H Nichols*

P.S. I will drop a line often as any thing is <u>done</u> of interest in our direction

The poor colored man & the indian have been cut off by "white"—
the Con[n] ruling that all are white in whom <u>the white-blood preponder-
ates</u>! I think they will find trouble here tho' they cited, as precedents
the decisions of Ohio judges as according with this view.[9] But what is
not put in block characters on the page of the Con[n] I believe will be of
doubtful title with a negro-hating people as in ~~some~~ ↑the↓ river Counties the majority are. The indians will find lenient expounders of the
constitutional ~~limit~~ "<u>white</u>." The persistent efforts of the Democrats to
get a law excluding negroes from the State & from the Schools has been
resisted by large majorities.

✒ ALS, Clarina I. H. Nichols Papers, MCR-S.

1. She wrote from Constitutional Hall in Wyandotte, where the territory's
constitutional convention met 5–29 July 1859. Nichols stayed at the convention throughout its sessions to present petitions, draft provisions for the
constitution, lobby the delegates, and twice address them. Although women
petitioned for suffrage, Nichols and her allies on and off the convention floor
intended to ease the way for universal suffrage at a later date rather than to risk
statehood on fights over suffrage either for blacks or for women. (C. I. H.
Nichols to SBA, 18 June, 16 July 1859, *Film*, 9:328–31, 346–53.)

2. Reported on 20 July, this provision was adopted as article XV, section 6,
without the further changes Nichols sought: "The Legislature shall provide
for the protection of the rights of women, in acquiring and possessing property, real, personal and mixed, separate and apart from the husband; and shall
also provide their equal rights in the possession of their children." The
Committee on the Judiciary reported against woman suffrage on 14 July, and
the special committee to receive the women's petitions reported without
recommendation on 20 July. (Kansas, Constitutional Convention, 1859, *A
Reprint of the Proceedings and Debates of the Convention which Framed the
Constitution of Kansas at Wyandotte in July, 1859* [Topeka, 1920], 169–70,
329, 588, 693.)

3. Several different tactics were pursued by Nichols and her allies to make
the extension of suffrage likely and easy under the new constitution. In one
approach she wrote a resolution to instruct the Committee on Preamble and
Bill of Rights to declare the principle of no taxation without representation.
Although the committee ignored that resolution, its draft bill of rights included a phrase barring "constitutional distinctions on account of sect or
sex." Those words were removed by vote of the convention on 18 July. On 19
July the convention considered language that would allow the introduction of
woman suffrage without constitutional amendment, by enabling the legislature at any time to submit the question of female suffrage to a vote of all
persons twenty-one years of age and older, to be carried by a simple majority.

This measure was tabled. On the same day an attempt was also made to amend the article on constitutional amendments to read that a majority of the legislature, rather than two-thirds, could submit amendments to the voters. That, too, was rejected. (C. I. H. Nichols to SBA, 16 July 1859; Kansas, *Proceeding and Debates*, 188, 290, 307–8, 324.)

4. Nichols reported earlier to SBA her success with the legislative committee of the convention in providing for women to have, in her words, "an equal voice in the <u>organization</u> and conduct of the Common Schools of the State." This became article II, section 23: "The Legislature, in providing for the formation and regulation of schools, shall make no distinction between the rights of males and females." Under this section women gained suffrage in school elections. (C. I. H. Nichols to SBA, 16 July 1859; Kansas, *Proceedings and Debates*, 122, 135–37, 580.)

5. Birsha Clarina Carpenter (whose given name is variously spelled) was the first child of Nichols's first marriage and her mother's only daughter. She went to Theodore Weld's Eagleswood School in 1853, perhaps as a teacher, and she taught in Kansas. During the Civil War, she joined her mother in Washington and worked with freedwomen and at the Internal Revenue. Her mother's obituaries identified a surviving daughter, Mrs. Frank Davis of Cavendish, Vermont. (C. I. H. Nichols to SBA, [before 14 August 1853], *Film*, 7:807–10; *NAW*, s.v. "Nichols, Clarina I. H."; family notes, Nichols Papers, MCR-S.)

6. On 13 July, the convention voted to hold a special, evening session of the committee of the whole to consider the petitions for woman's rights and invited Clarina Nichols to speak. At the request of petitioners from Wyandotte, she spoke again on the evening of 22 July. (Kansas, *Proceedings and Debates*, 72, 383.)

7. Nichols spoke at Leavenworth on 29 June. George Washington McLane edited the *Ledger*. (Gambone, "Forgotten Feminist of Kansas," 420n; Henry Miles Moore, *Early History of Leavenworth City and County* [Leavenworth, 1906], 134–43.)

8. John Otis Wattles (?–1859) and his sister-in-law Susan E. Lowe Wattles were abolitionists and activists for woman's rights. John Wattles grew up in Ohio and helped his brother Augustus organize schools for African Americans in Cincinnati. Their families migrated together to Kansas in 1855, and they organized the town of Moneka in Linn County in 1857. Augustus Wattles recruited Susan Lowe from New York in 1835 to teach in his schools, and the two were married. She remained active in the woman suffrage movement in Kansas. (Gambone, "Forgotten Feminist of Kansas," 418n; Mitchell, *Linn County, Kansas*, 135–40; Mrs. O. E. Morse, "Sketch of the Life and Work of Augustus Wattles," *Collections of the Kansas State Historical Society* 17 [1926–1928]: 290–99; *History*, 2:255, 3:697, 4:294.)

9. The Republican party, with advice from Horace Greeley, agreed in advance of the convention to limit suffrage to white males, and article V,

section 1 of the constitution read: "Every white male person of twenty-one years and upwards . . . shall be deemed a qualified elector." But in the debate, there were numerous attempts by Democrats and Republicans to draw a different line. On 18 July, the sides vied to redefine "white," either to include or exclude Indians, blacks, and mulattoes of both groups. These additional precautions were not redundant, the Democrats explained, because the supreme court of Ohio had ruled that "white" meant a preponderance of white blood. A motion to strike out "white" also failed on 18 July. (*New York Daily Tribune*, 31 May, 2 June 1859; Kansas, *Proceedings and Debates*, 294–95, 300–304.)

·◉━━━━◆━━━━◉·

130 ❧ SBA TO JOHN J. ORMOND[1]

[*2 October 1859*]

Enclosed is a copy of our woman's rights memorial.[2] Will you give me a full report of the action taken upon it? . . . I hope you and your daughters arrived home safe. Say to the elder I shall be most happy to hear from her when she shall have fairly inaugurated some noble life work. I trust each will take to her soul a strong purpose and that on her tombstone shall be engraved her own name and her own noble deeds instead of merely the daughter of Judge Ormond, or the relict of some Honorable or D.D. When true womanhood shall be attained it will be spoken of and remembered for itself alone. My kindest regards to them, accompanied with the most earnest desire that they shall make truth and freedom the polar star of their lives.

❧ *Anthony*, 1:183; ellipses in original. Ormond's acknowledgement noted the date of SBA's letter, 17 October 1859, *Film*, 9:400.

1. At meetings in Saratoga Springs on 16 August, SBA met John James Ormond of Alabama and his daughters. Ormond (1795–1866) was a prominent lawyer, a former Whig legislator, and a former justice of the Alabama Supreme Court. Though retired from the court in 1849, he returned to public service to prepare Alabama's Code of 1852. He had three daughters: Mary Elizabeth, Margaret Cornelia, and Catherine Amanda. (*Daily Saratogian*, 17, 18 August 1859, *Film*, 9:372–73; Willis Brewer, *Alabama: Her History, Resources, War Record, and Public Men, From 1540–1872* [1872; reprint, Tuscaloosa, Ala., 1964], 557; James Edmonds Saunders, *Early Settlers of Alabama* [1899; reprint, Baltimore, 1969], 260–68.)

2. Printed with space to write in a state's name, this memorial to state legislatures, sent by a committee appointed at the May 1859 meeting, asked, "Where, under our Declaration of Independence, does the white Saxon man get his power to deprive all women and negroes of their inalienable rights?" It demanded that future legislation "secure to Woman all those rights and privileges and immunities which in equity belong to every citizen of a republic," and that the word 'male' be expunged from the state constitution. (*Proceedings of the Ninth National Woman's Rights Convention, Held in New York City, Thursday, May 12, 1859* [Rochester, 1859], 3, *Film*, 9:278ff; *History*, 1:674–75.)

·⟨══════⟩·

131 ᠅ ANTOINETTE BROWN BLACKWELL TO SBA

Newark [*N.J.*] Oct 25th '59

Dear Susan

So you wonder at my unaccountable silence. Poor child! Then listen, pity "a poor married woman"[1] and forgive. The ordeal which I have passed through! a house to clean, four different sewing women, each giving about two days each, and the numberless buttons to sew on, tucks to let down, and little dresses to make larger which no body could be found to attend to properly except the poor mother of them all, and you will see how it is. Remember that a little three year old[2] is capable of growing out of every thing it wears once in three month— just the time of my absence—and fancy me set down in a <u>very</u> dirty house just on the outside edge of cold weather with a child minus one decent or comfortable winter suit, a husband whose garments, as well as himself, have been deserted the whole season, and ones own wardrobe the worse for wear. Then there is a winter store of coal, provisions, &c to be taken in, a garden to be covered up from the frost; seeds to save, label & put up for spring; bulbs to store away, shrubs to transplant; &c &c. To help you in all this you have one good-natured stupid Irish girl, and said three year old who must have a hand in every possible thing which goes forward from scrubbing kitchen floors to making boquets for the parlors. This, Susan, is woman's sphere! In addition fancy me spending four mortal days from morning till night tramping up and down NY streets & stairs; intersperced with omnibus rides; in search of a suitable hall to preach in; then fancy me setting down in the midst of it all to write an appropriate introductory sermon, going in by the Sunday afternoon boat, preaching it, and coming home to breakfast and to a dress maker next morning, and you have a fair history of my doings & surroundings since we parted, only if all the items were to be enumerated I suppose all the letter paper in the house would not contain them. Of course then if some things must be done and some could be neglected I let the latter class wait, and writing to you was one of these. Now congratulate us, for we are getting on famously! My hall is just below Grace Church, on the opposite side. It was packed with a good listening audiance, & many went away; but the room is small, and we'll see what they'll do after a while! You have doubtless seen the advertisement before this, and are satisfied on that point.[3]

I am in good health & spirits and about as hopeful as when I saw you last. Now about yourself. You are tried with those Western women and it's too bad; but I think Lucy is not to blame.[4] You know I wrote her to ask Phillips to give Mrs. Johnes money, with your sanction. Afterwards you thought it better to get them into N.Y state. Lucy merely asked Phillips if he could give the 1000 to Mrs. J. for Ohio, if he thought best for her & the rest to work there. He said yes; but when I told her you expected them in NY & Mrs. Cutler was already there, she said, "Oh well then they had better not have the money for Ohio!" I think she has no choice in the matter & only wants a good understanding & the work carried on. Aaron Powel spent Sunday here & we all walked over to Orange   That is the only time I have seen Lucy & there was no time then for much talk; but I shall see her again soon & will report. Aaron made us a pleasant visit; but after an 8 miles walk I was too tired to walk down to hear him speak in the evening. Sam reported is as well done. I <u>know</u> that Phillips <u>expects</u> you <u>to spend</u> the 1000, and I would do so, if necessary, without scruple. 12 dollars <u>is</u> <u>very</u> <u>very</u> small compensation, if a woman is to break up her home at all for the moneys sake, and this time having no personal axe to grind, please let me say I should rather give it to them, yourself included, than to return it to Phillips. If you really havent it thats another thing. Couldnt you tell them they are pledged 12 but that <u>if</u> there is money <u>left</u> at <u>the close of the campaign</u> you will give something more. But do as you like. I only write as it seems to me.

I have many things to say to you but am interupted every 5 minutes by some one   Dress makers are nuisances at the best; but when one is remodling <u>Old</u> <u>Clothes</u> its still worse. However this one is a regular Miss Prisy[5] and my old blue & black silk is coming out as good as new. So I wont complain. Now dont really think that I am cumbered with much sewing. The sermons will not suffer. Probably they will be all the better for my being compelled to give attention to other things   My sister Rebecca has just come so you see half the interuptions are of a very friendly class.[6] Besides we are in the process of "doing up our chores" for the winter so next time you think of me imagine me setting peacefully with folded hands under my own vine & fig tree with nothing to disturb or make busy.

There is Sams ring   So good night but let me insert our list of debt & credit.[7] Be of good cheer and God speed thee in thy work!

Write me just what you are doing thinking & feeling at the time even though it results in describing such a medley as this   Very lovingly

~ *Nette.*

~ ALS, Blackwell Papers, MCR-S.

1. Probably a play on "A poor lone woman," in Shakespeare, *Henry IV, Part Two*, act 2, sc. 1, lines 31–32.

2. Her daughter Florence.

3. She preached weekly at Hope Chapel, 691 Broadway. (*Anti-Slavery Bugle*, 5 November 1859.)

4. Lucy Stone moved back to Orange, New Jersey, in the fall of 1859. At issue was the expenditure of woman's rights funds—whether to concentrate resources in New York or Ohio during the coming winter. The funds went to New York in 1859 and 1860 and to Ohio in the winter of 1860 and 1861.

5. Prissy, or finicky.

6. Rebecca Brown (1812–1898), the oldest of Antoinette's sisters, taught school near Henrietta.

7. Enclosure omitted. Blackwell wrote out her accounts with SBA for eleven weeks of lecturing and showed she was still owed $6.85, after payments of $184.

·◁═══◆═══▷·

132 ❧ ECS TO SBA

[*Seneca Falls, c. 15 December 1859*][1]

Indeed it would do me great good to see some reformers just now. The death of my father, the worse than death of my dear cousin Gerrit, the martyrdom of that great and glorious John Brown, all conspire to make me regret more than ever my dwarfed and perverted womanhood.[2] In times like these every soul should do the work of a fullgrown man. When I pass the gate of the celestials and good Peter asks me where I wish to sit, I will say: "Anywhere so that I am neither a negro nor a woman. Confer on me, great angel, the glory of white manhood, so that henceforth I may feel unlimited freedom."

❧ *Anthony*, 1:181–82. Also in "Early Letters" and a transcript in ECS Papers, DLC, both of which omit the reference to Gerrit Smith. Also incorporated into another letter, dated 23 December, in *Stanton*, 2:74–75, where Smith is restored. *Film*, 9:421–22, 424.

1. As dated on the transcript in ECS Papers, DLC. It could fall later in the month of December.

2. ECS probably responds to an invitation to join SBA at the antislavery meetings she arranged for January 1860. The two spoke together at Auburn on 12 January. Daniel Cady died on 31 October at Johnstown. John Brown (1800–1859), a longtime foe of slavery who fought in Kansas in 1856, led a band of twenty-one men against the federal armory at Harper's Ferry on 16 October 1859. Taken prisoner after two days of fighting, he was tried and hanged for treason against the state of Virginia on 2 December 1859. Gerrit Smith was committed to the State Asylum for the Insane at Utica on 7 November and stayed until the end of December. Letters in John Brown's possession at the time of his capture in mid-October exposed Smith's complicity in the raid, as friend and financier, and the risks and guilt of his position drove him temporarily insane. (Stephen B. Oates, *To Purge This Land with Blood: A Biography of John Brown*, 2d ed. [Amherst, Mass., 1984]; Harlow, *Gerrit Smith*, 411, 413.)

133 ❧ JOHN J. ORMOND TO SBA

Tuscaloosa, [*Ala.*] 26th Dec., 1859.

Madam—In redemption of my promise to you to inform you of the fate of the 'Woman's Rights Petition' to our Legislature, I have the honor to inform you that it was virtually rejected, being laid on the table. I interested a distinguished member of our Senate in its presentation, and, in addition, wrote a letter which, under ordinary circumstances, would have insured its respectful consideration, having expunged the word 'black' from the petition; as no one, I apprehend, would suppose that the Legislature of a State in which slavery was established by law would, for a moment, tolerate a petition based upon the supposition that the African race had equal political rights with the white race. But, after your petition was forwarded, came the treasonable and murderous invasion of John Brown. The atrocity of this act, countenanced as it manifestly was by a great party at the North, as shown by the sympathy felt for him and the honors paid to his memory, has extinguished the last spark of fraternal feeling for the people of the North. We now look upon you as our worst enemies. Whilst we are all living under a Constitution which secures to us our right to our slaves, the results of which in truth are more beneficial to the whole North, and especially to the New England States, than to us, you are secretly plotting murderous inroads into our peaceful country, and endeavoring to incite our slaves to cut the throats of our wives and children. Can you believe that this state of things can last? We now look upon you as our worst enemies, and are now ready to separate from you. Measures are now in progress as far as possible to establish non-intercourse with you, and to proscribe all articles of Northern manufacture or origin, including New England teachers. We can live without you. It remains to be seen how you will get along without us. You will probably find that fanaticism is not an element of national wealth, or conducive to the happiness or comfort of the people.

In conclusion, let me assure you this is written more in sorrow than in anger. I am not a politician, and have always until now been a strenuous friend of the Union. I am now in favor of a separation, unless you immediately retrace your steps, and give the necessary guarantees, by the passage of appropriate laws, that you will faithfully abide by the compromises of the Constitution, by which alone the slaveholding States can with safety or honor remain in the Union. But that this will be done, I have very little hope, as 'madness seems to rule the hour'; and as you have thus constituted yourselves our enemies, you must not be surprised at finding that we are yours.

ᴥ *J. J. Ormond.*

ᴥ *Lib.*, 2 March 1860, from proceedings of the New York State Woman's Rights Convention, 4 February 1860, *Film*, 9:522–23. Variant in *Anthony*, 1:184. Elizabeth Powell read this letter aloud on 5 February.

·⟨══════❦══════⟩·

134 ᴥ TRACT BY ECS

[*1859*][1]

"I HAVE ALL THE RIGHTS I WANT."

We have allowed this saying from the mouth of woman to pass quite long enough unrebuked, seeing that it is utterly and entirely false, and every woman who utters it knows in her own soul that it is so.

The slave on the southern plantation will tell you he is happy in slavery until he sees some chance of being free; but when he feels sure of freedom, behold how his soul leaps for joy! The satisfaction he felt in his chains is very much like that woman feels under the present condition of things.

Go watch the daily life of fortune's most favored woman. She has father, husband, brothers, sons, all willing and happy to minister to every wish and want. Luxurious and elegant are her surroundings, peace and plenty seem to mark out every path; but she is not happy— her life is objectless—there is no scope or freedom for the acting out of her womanhood. Who that has mingled with this class, is ignorant of the senseless round, the utter vacuity of such an existence. The woman who has no fixed purpose in her life is like a traveller at the depot, waiting hour after hour for the cars to come in—listless, uneasy, expectant—with this difference, the traveller has a definite object to look for, whereas the woman is simply waiting for something to "turn up." If she should follow the holy instincts of her nature, she would leave undone many things that mere conventionalism now says she should do, and do many things she ought not to do.

There is many a woman who, in spite of husband, rich clothes, gay equipage and home, longs for something more beyond it all. The soul lives not in the outward, and if the only legitimate object of a woman's pursuits *is* love and marriage, has she "all the rights she wants," when her love even may not be voluntary? When law and gospel, judge and juror, all agree that a man calling himself husband, has the right not only to the custody of her person, but to the guardianship of the holy affections of a young and trusting heart—affections, which, in his grossness, he never seeks to concentrate on himself—satisfied that he holds the outward woman.

If a woman make a blunder in her marriage, where shall she find happiness? In her children? Maternity has its penalties, many and severe. Bearing children without love is not the highest happiness of which a woman even is capable. What woman, who for peace' sake, has become the mother of five, ten or fourteen children, heirs ofttimes to poverty, disease and suffering, can say with truth, "I have all the rights I want!"

In ambition? Man ignores all publicity for woman, except where she appears for his amusement or necessity. He greets her with applause in the Theatre and the Opera, and as an angel of mercy in the wars of the Crimea, and the By-lanes of our vast metropolis. She may bind up the wounds and bruises of the flesh, perform any and every menial office, but he suffers her not to teach in the Church. She may face poverty, contagion and death; meet man anywhere and everywhere but on his Mount Sinai—in his highest offices as Priest and Law-giver. Perhaps he thinks the holy radiance that there surrounds him may prove too much for woman's weak vision.

She may write books, but they are popular only so far as they echo back man's thunder, hence our literary women instead of dealing stout blows for their own sex, are all trimming their sails to the popular breeze, for those who depend on their books for bread must guide their pens cautiously. Starvation and excommunication are stern penalties in the way of truth. Had our literary women "all the rights they want," we should have better books from them on subjects which they understand and feel most deeply.

Go ask the poor widow, childless and alone, driven out from the beautiful home which she had helped to build and decorate, why strangers dwell at her hearthstone, enjoy the shade of trees planted by her hand, drink in the fragrance of her flowers, whilst she must seek some bare and humbler home? Will she tell you she has "all the rights she wants," as she points you to our statute laws, which allow the childless widow to retain a life interest merely in "one-third the landed estate, and one-half the personal property of her husband?"[2]

Go ask the sister of the noble Kossuth, who kept a boarding house in New York City, what she thought when all her furniture and hard earnings were seized to pay the debts of a worthless husband.[3] In speaking of her troubles to a friend, she remarked that the laws of New York State in regard to married women were worse than those of poor, oppressed Hungary. When remonstrating with her husband on his extravagance, he in triumph pointed her to our revised statutes with the remark, "remember you are not in Hungary now." Whilst basking in the sunshine of our republic, whose laws enabled a European tyrant to seize on all she had—to send her forth a beggar in a strange land, and mock her with the justice of his claims, was *she* ever heard to say "I have all the rights I want?"

Go ask the wife and mother, who, weary of the heavy yoke of a discordant marriage, in obedience to the holy instincts of true womanhood, sunders the tie that binds her to one she does not love—behold her stripped of children, property and home, for law, in case of separation, gives all these to the husband, will *she* tell you in her days of poverty, desolation and loneliness, "I have all the rights I want?"

Go to any and every class of women who have had their own bread to earn—the Teacher, the Seamstress, the Drunkard's wife, the Outcast, any who have found out by personal experience the injustice of our laws, and the tyranny of our customs, and none will repel your sympathy, or underrate the importance of our demands, with the silly motto, "I have all the rights I want."

But suppose there are some women who actually have all the rights *they* want, surely that is no reason why they should not feel and plead for those who have them not. Because their soft white hands have never labored, is that a reason why they should not demand a right to wages

for those who spend their days in honest toil? When famine has reduced any of the human family almost to starvation, shall I refuse them
food because I am not hungry? If I have all I want for body and soul, is
it not the best reason in the world why I should generously aid all those
who are oppressed, suffering, destitute, friendless and alone? Lives
there a woman whose nature is so hard, narrow and selfish, that she can
pity no sorrows but those which she has felt in her own person? Or can
there be one woman in this nation so ignorant that she really thinks she
is already living in the full possession of all the rights that belong to a
citizen of a Republic?

❧ *I Have All the Rights I Want* (n.p., n.d.).

1. Published anonymously and without a date, this tract was advertised for
sale in October 1859. ECS used the same title for an article published in the
Una, March 1855, *Film*, 8:206.

2. *RSSNY, 1852*, 2:149, 281.

3. Emilia Siremleke Kossuth Zsulavszky (c. 1817–1860) came to the United
States in 1852, while her brother was in the country, and settled in New York.
Obliged to support her family, she opened a boardinghouse with the patron-
age and aid of sympathizers, but her abusive and alcoholic husband caused
the business to fail. She died in June 1860, and her four sons served in the
Civil War. (Odon Vasvary, *Magyar Amerika* [Szeged, 1988], 92–94; Edmund
Vasvary, *Lincoln's Hungarian Heroes: The Participation of Hungarians in
the Civil War, 1861–1865* [Washington, 1939], 88–89; assistance from August
Molnar, American Hungarian Foundation, New Brunswick.)

---

135 ⇝ SBA TO MARTHA COFFIN WRIGHT

[*Albany, 15 February 1860*][1]

Mr. Bingham, the chairman of the Judiciary Committee, will bring
in a radical report in favor of all our claims, but previous to his doing so
he wishes our strongest arguments made before the Committee, and he
says Mrs. Stanton must come.[2] I write her this mail, but I wish you
would step over there and make her feel that the salvation of the Empire
State, at least the women in it, depends upon her bending all her
powers to moving the hearts of our law-makers at this time. Mr. Bingham
says our Convention here has wrought wondrous changes with a large
number of the members who attended, and so says Mr. Mayo, of the

Albanians;[3] indeed our claims are so patent they need only to be known to be approved. Mrs. Stanton must move heaven and earth now to secure this bill, and she can, if she will only try. I should go there myself this very night, but I must watch and encourage friends here. The Earnings Bill has passed the House, and is in Committee of the Whole in the Senate. Then a Guardianship Bill must be drafted and put through if possible.[4] I returned from New York last evening; have taken the "Cooper Union," for our National Convention in May. Saw Miss Howland; she said Mr. Beecher's lecture is to be in this week's *Independent*.[5] Only think how many priestly eyes will be compelled to look at its defiled page. Theodore Tilton[6] told me that Mr. Beecher had had a severe battle to get into *The Independent*.

⪻ *History*, 1:678–79.

1. Dated by SBA's return to Albany on 14 February, noted in a letter to James F. Clarke, *Film*, 9:524–28.

2. In January, SBA and other activists carried their woman's rights campaign to the legislature, working closely with Anson Bingham, chair of the assembly's judiciary committee, and Andrew J. Colvin, his law partner and a Democratic member of the senate judiciary committee. SBA reports on one stage of drafting the act concerning the property of married women, passed in March 1860. Bingham steered an amendment to the bill of 1848 through the assembly to protect property in trade and earnings. SBA refers to this as the "Earnings Bill," passed by the assembly on February 10 and scheduled for debate in the senate at the end of the month. But SBA, Bingham, and Colvin wanted to substitute a bill under consideration in Massachusetts that would add more rights, and Bingham sought ECS's help getting the new text through his committee. In the senate, Colvin substituted the Massachusetts bill for his original one when debate began in the committee of the whole. The senate passed the more comprehensive bill on February 29 and sent it to the assembly, where it underwent considerable revision before passage on March 15. ECS did not go to Albany in time to affect the bill's outcome.

The Married Women's Property Act of 1860 greatly expanded a woman's economic autonomy. In addition to gaining control of "her sole and separate property" in wages, trade, or business, she could enter into contracts, carry on business, and sue and be sued in her own name. The assembly's revisions added that she could be "the joint guardian of her children . . . with equal powers, rights and duties in regard to them, with the husband." Further it made equal the rights of surviving spouses to a life interest in one-third of the family's property, and it ensured that if no will specified otherwise, the surviving spouse with minor children would possess all real estate during the children's minority. (*JNYA*, 13, 16, 27 January, 7, 10, 29 February, 15 March

1860, pp. 102, 112, 205, 308, 334, 454–55, 661–64; *JNYS*, 11, 19, 27 January, 11, 23, 24, 27, 28 February, 16 March 1860, pp. 57, 89, 130, 221, 261, 270, 282, 300–301, 446–47; Albany *Atlas and Argus*, 12, 14, 17, 28 January, 6, 8, 13, 24, 25, 28, 29 February, 1, 16, 17, 19 March 1860; Basch, *In the Eyes of the Law*, 164–65, 194–99; *History*, 1:686–88.)

3. Amory Dwight Mayo (1823–1907), minister of Albany's First Unitarian Society on Division Street from 1856 to 1863, attended the New York State Woman's Rights Convention in Albany 3–4 February. (*DAB*.)

4. A guardianship bill was introduced in the senate on March 16, but the assembly amended the property bill to incorporate equal custody for mothers.

5. Henry Ward Beecher (1813–1887) spoke in a lecture series at the Cooper Institute, organized by Emily Howland to publicize the campaign in Albany. Pastor of Plymouth Church in Brooklyn and one of the best-known ministers in the country, Beecher had issued periodic pronouncements on woman's rights that indicated a growing acceptance of her capacities but not of her equality. In "Women's Influence in Politics," he declared that men and women had the same right of suffrage. (*History*, 1:688; *DAB*; *Independent* 12 [16 February 1860]: 2.)

6. Theodore Tilton (1835–1907) was managing editor of the *Independent* and a member of Plymouth Church. He joined the staff of the Presbyterian *New York Observer* in the 1850s, with the assignment to report Beecher's sermons. From there he moved to the *Independent*, a journal more in tune with his abolitionism, and took over as editor in chief in 1862. Under his leadership until 1871, the paper grew into one of broad appeal and influence and became a forum for advocating a radical reconstruction. (*DAB*; Altina L. Waller, *Reverend Beecher and Mrs. Tilton: Sex and Class in Victorian America* [Amherst, Mass., 1982], 38–53.)

·⊂――――∞――――⊃·

136 ≋ AMORY D. MAYO TO ECS

[*Albany*] Monday Evening [*19 March 1860*]

My Dear Mrs. Stanton,

I regret not finding you in this evening, and most briefly announce our decision on the re[pet]ition of the address. M[iss M]ott, (whose instincts on such things I very much respect) feels strongly that nothing should be done in any way to mar the beautiful impression made this P.M.[1] The whole gathering, the day, the character of the audience, the general impression, <u>could not</u> be reproduced. We feel that it would be better to leave a thing perfectly done and not try to reproduce it.

May I not hope to see your speech in print. It is the first time I have listened to you; and you will not accuse me of flattery when I say that the hearing has confirmed my previous suspicion that you are 'the head and front of'[2] this offence against the oppressors of woman[kind?].[3] I only trust that you will again appear before the Legislature, and never rest till your idea prevails.

All this is clumsily said, and <u>execrably</u> written & blotted (for which charge the hotel stationary)   But it must do until I can have a 'long talk' over all these interesting themes   Mrs Mayo[4] was equally interested with myself— Truly Yrs

❧ *A D Mayo*

❧ ALS, ECS Papers, DLC. An inkblot obscures letters in the opening sentences.

1. ECS spoke before a joint session of the judiciary committees of the assembly and senate on behalf of woman suffrage, while the new bill on married women's property awaited the governor's signature. Though her speech was not reported at the time, she delivered it again at the woman's rights convention in May. "What is the right to property," she asked, "without the right to protect it? The enjoyment of that right to-day is no security it will be continued to-morrow, so long as it is granted to her as a favor by a privileged class, and not secured as a sacred right." She conceded that new rights to property and children now distinguished the woman from the slave. But with respect to "civil rights," she said, in New York "the prejudice against sex is more deeply rooted and more unreasonably maintained than that against color." (*Proceedings of the Tenth National Woman's Rights Convention, Held at the Cooper Institute, New York City, May 10th and 11th, 1860* [Boston, 1860], 34–46, *Film*, 9:612ff; *History*, 1:679–86, incorrectly dated; *New York Times*, 21 March 1860.)

2. *Othello*, act 1, sc. 3, lines 80–81.

3. Cramped at the margin, Mayo's ending to this word is illegible.

4. Lucy Caroline Clarke Mayo, the second wife of Amory Mayo, took part in the woman's rights convention in Albany in February. (*DAB*, s.v. "Mayo, Amory Dwight.")

·⊂━━━━⟩✕⟨━━━━⊃·

137 ➴ ADDRESS BY ECS TO THE AMERICAN ANTI-
SLAVERY SOCIETY

Editorial note: At the invitation of William Lloyd Garrison, ECS
spoke to an audience of 1,500, on the first morning of the American
Anti-Slavery Society anniversary at the Cooper Institute in New
York City. The phonographic report of her speech by James Yerrinton,
printed in the *National Anti-Slavery Standard*, is the source text;
significant differences from ECS's manuscript are recorded in the
notes. Sarah Pugh wrote that ECS "laid herself open to the charge of
'lugging in extraneous topics,'" but she understood why, "on her
first appearance on the platform of the Nat. Soc. she should wish to
testify to what its principles & associations had done for her." (W. L.
Garrison to ECS, 23 March 1860, *Film*, 9:549; S. Pugh to Mary Anne
Estlin, 22 June 1860, Estlin Papers, Dr. Williams's Library, London.)

[8 May 1860]

Mr. President, and Gentlemen and Ladies: This is generally known
as the platform of one idea—that is negro slavery. In a certain sense this
may be true, but the most casual observation of this whole anti-slavery
movement, of your lives, conventions, public speeches and journals,
shows this one idea to be a great humanitarian one. The motto of your
leading organ, "The world is my country and all mankind my countrymen,"[1] proclaims the magnitude and universality of this one idea,
which takes in the whole human family, irrespective of nation, color,
caste or sex, with all their interests, temporal and spiritual—a question
of religion, philanthropy, political economy, commerce, education
and social life, on which depends the very existence of this republic, of
the state, of the family, the sacredness of the lives and property of
Northern freemen, the holiness of the marriage relation, and the perpetuity of the Christian religion. Such are the various phases of the
question you are wont to debate in your conventions. They all grow
out of and legitimately belong to that *so-called* petty, insignificant,
annoying subject, which thrusts up its head everywhere in Church and
State—the "eternal nigger." But in settling the question of the negro's

rights, we find out the exact limits of our own, for rights never clash or interfere; and where no individual in a community is denied his rights, the mass are the more perfectly protected in theirs; for whenever any class is subject to fraud or injustice, it shows that the spirit of tyranny is at work, and no one can tell where or how or when the infection will spread. The health of the body politic depends on the sound condition of every member. Let but the finest nerve or weakest muscle be diseased, and the whole man suffers; just so the humblest and most ignorant citizen cannot be denied his rights without deranging the whole system of government.

It was thought a small matter to kidnap a black man in Africa, and set him to work in the rice swamps of Georgia; but when we look at the panorama of horrors that followed that event, at all the statute laws that were enacted to make that act legal, at the perversion of man's moral sense and innate love of justice in being compelled to defend such laws; when we consider the long, hard tussle we have witnessed here for near a century between the spirit of Liberty and Slavery, we may, in some measure, appreciate the magnitude of the wrong done to that one lone, friendless negro, who, under the cover of darkness and the star-spangled banner, was stolen from his African hut and lodged in the hold of the American slaver. That one act has, in its consequences, convulsed this Union. It has corrupted our churches, our politics, our press; laid violent hands on Northern freemen at their own firesides; it has gagged our statesmen, and stricken our Northern Senators dumb in their seats;[2] yes, beneath the flag of freedom, Liberty has crouched in fear.

That grand declaration of rights made by William Lloyd Garrison,[3] while yet a printer's boy, was on a far higher plane than that of '76. His was uttered with the Christian's view of the dignity of man, the value of the immortal being; the other but from the self-respect of one proud race. But, in spite of noble words, deeds of thirty years of protest, prayers and preaching, slavery still lives, the negro toils on in his weary bondage, his chains have not yet melted in the intense heat of the sun of righteousness; but in the discussion of this question, in grappling with its foes, how many of us have worked out our salvation; what mountains of superstition have been rolled off the human soul! I have always regarded Garrison as the great missionary of the gospel of Jesus to this guilty nation, for he has waged an uncompromising warfare with the deadly sins of both Church and State. My own experience is, no doubt, that of many others. In the darkness and gloom of a false theology, I was slowly sawing off the chains of my spiritual bondage, when, for the first time, I met Garrison in London; a few bold strokes from the hammer of his truth, I was free. Only those who have lived all their lives under the dark clouds of vague, undefined fears can appreciate the joy of a doubting soul suddenly born into the kingdom of reason and free thought. Is the bondage of the priest-ridden less galling than that of the slave, because we do not see the chains, the indelible scars, the festering wounds, the deep degradation of all the powers of the God-like mind?

To Garrison we owe, more than to any other one man of our day, all that we have of religious freedom. But for him I doubt whether our Cheevers,[4] our Beechers, would have yet found backbone enough to stand where they now do; for when he first called the American Church to its awful reckoning, it was as dead as the twelve apostles of solid silver which Cromwell melted into coin, and sent through the English nation to do the will of their master.[5]

I do not believe all history affords another such example as this so-called "Garrisonian Conspiracy"—a body of educated men of decided talent, wealth, rank and position, standing for a quarter of a century battling a whole nation, Church and State, law and public sentiment without the shadow of ever wavering, turning or faltering, as if chained to the great Gibraltar-truth of human freedom and equality. This unheard-of steadfastness can only be accounted for in the fact that woman too is represented in this "conspiracy." Yes, the Marys and the Marthas[6] have gathered round the prophets of our day. With noble words and deeds and holy sympathy they have cheered their exile from the love and honor of their own false countrymen. At their family altars they have been remembered, and unseen spirits of the brave and good have hovered o'er them and rejoiced in these true sons of earth. Yes, this is the only organization on God's footstool where the humanity of woman is recognized, and these are the only men who have ever echoed back her cries for justice and equality. I shall never forget our champions in the World's Anti-Slavery Convention; how nobly Phillips did speak, and how still more nobly Garrison would not speak, because woman was there denied her rights. Think of a World's Convention, and one-half the world left out! Shame on the women of this nation, who help to swell the cry of "*infidel*" against men like these! All time would not be long enough to pay the debt of gratitude we owe these noble men, who spoke for us when we were dumb, who roused us to a sense of our own rights, to the dignity of our high calling.

No, the mission of this Radical Anti-Slavery Movement is not to the African slave alone, but to the slaves of custom, creed and sex, as well; and most faithfully has it done its work. To appreciate the magnitude and benevolence of its mission, look but a moment at what fear has done from the beginning—at what an abject, hopeless slave man has ever been to this worst of tyrants! Behold how long, through ignorance, he crouched before the wonders of the solar system—the sun, the moon, the stars, the elements, the convulsions of nature, the accidents by sea and land, pestilence and famine; how long, in the follies and vices of man, he has seen the finger of God. In fact, we are but just now emerging from the savage idea that God is the special patron of all human calamities—of war, slavery, and governments of violence and force.[7] Who that sees a mind oppressed with the traditions of ages, in its first agonizings for life, and love and law, would dare to obstruct its vision?[8] Who would check its earnest longings with the cry, Behold a mystery? Who would bound its hopes, or deny its rights to explore the universe for facts and thoughts to feast the soul upon, or to find comfort, if it may, in one great law alone?

The weary traveller, long tossed about at sea, is filled with joy to find himself on land once more. How good it is to stand upright and firm—to feel no motion, swelling, heaving up and down, and

> Sweeter far than foothold firm on solid land
> Is to the soul a faith that it can understand.

As we rejoice this day in our deliverance from the sad train of fears and errors that have so long crippled and dwarfed the greatest minds of earth—as we thank the Lord that we are neither Hindoos, Hottentots, Mahomedans, or *New York Observer* Christians,[9] let us seek a new and holier baptism for the work that lays for each of us in the future.

The last fear from which man may hope deliverance is the fear of man. To this glorious freedom did the immortal John Brown arrive. He feared neither man nor God. He was made perfect in love; the future was bright and beautiful to him, for he had done the will of his Father, and with joy he went out to meet him. How grand, how calmly dignified, were his last days on earth! In his noble generosity and self-sacrifice, in his divine love for right and justice and humanity, how like a God he seemed among the petty tyrants who surrounded him. It has filled me with amazement to find any American citizen insensible to the holy grandeur of his life and death. Noble John Brown! thou wert true to thyself and thy race, and loyal to thy God. I ask no higher honor in the gift of this nation for any sons of mine than a gallows and a grave like thine! As these sons now gather round me and ask questions about different nations, governments and laws, think you it is with pride I read to them our constitutions, statute laws, and late judicial decisions on great questions of human rights? Ah, no! Mr. President, it is with the deepest sorrow that I check the budding patriotism in their young hearts—that I unveil to them our falsehood and hypocrisy, in the face of those grand and glorious declarations of freedom and equality which, when first proclaimed at the mouth of the cannon, raised us head and shoulders above the nations of the earth. It is all-important, in a republican government, that our laws be always on the side of justice. Here, where we have neither Pope nor King, no royal family, crown or sceptre, no nobility, rank or class, nothing outward to cultivate or command our veneration, Law, the immutable principles of right, are all and everything to us.

See to it, you who have the best interests of our republic in your care, that your laws keep pace with public sentiment. If you would have us teach our sons a sacred reverence for law, so frame your constitutions and your codes that, in yielding obedience to their requirements, they are not false to the holy claims of humanity—that they degrade not the mothers who gave them life. No one can be more awake than I am to all the blessings of a republican form of government, nor, as a mother, more apprehensive lest her sons should confound liberty with license. Here, where individual responsibilities are so great, and the influence of one so all-powerful, I fain would have them lovers of law and order, and meekly to suffer wrong themselves, if need be, to preserve it; but when the panting fugitive throws himself on our generosity and hospitality, I dare not check the noble, God-given impulses of their natures to place the man above all law. Yes, I must ever teach them that man alone is divine; his words and works are fallible; his institutions, however venerable with age and authority, his constitutions, laws and interpretations of Holy Writ may all prove false. That alone is sacred that can fully meet the wants of the immortal soul—that can stand the test of time and eternity.

On this platform are the only wise conservatives of the nation, the only men who would compel obedience to the laws by bringing them into harmony with the everlasting principles of right. These are the only "Union meetings"[10] that can effectually keep off dissolution, by dispelling that dangerous miasma of slavery, which has ever proved so fatal to republicanism, so deadly to all national virtue and strength.

Eloquently and earnestly as noble men have denounced slavery on this platform, they have been able to take only an objective view. They can describe the general features of that infernal system—the horrors of the African slave trade, the agonizing sufferings of the middle-passage, the auction-block, the slave pen and coffle, the diabolism of the internal traffic, the cruel severing of family ties, the hopeless degradation of woman; all that is outward they can see, but a privileged class can never conceive the feelings of those who are born to contempt, to inferiority, to degradation. Herein is woman more fully identified with the slave than man can possibly be, for she can take the subjective view. She early learns the misfortune of being born an heir to the crown of thorns, to martyrdom, to womanhood. For while the man is born to do whatever he can, for the woman and the negro there is no such privilege. There is a Procrustean bedstead[11] ever ready for them, body and soul, and all mankind stand on the alert to restrain their impulses, check their aspirations, fetter their limbs, lest, in their freedom and strength, in their full development, they should take an even platform with proud man himself. To you, white man, the world throws wide her gates; the way is clear to wealth, to fame, to glory, to renown; the high places of independence and honor and trust are yours; all your efforts are praised and encouraged, all your successes are welcomed with loud hurrahs and cheers; but the black man and the woman are born to shame. The badge of degradation is the skin and sex—the "scarlet letter"[12] so sadly worn upon the breast. Children even can define the sphere of the black man, and the most ignorant Irishman hiss him into it, while striplings, mere swadlings of law and Divinity, can talk quite glibly of woman's sphere, and pedant priests at the altar discourse most lovingly of her holy mission to cook him meat, and bear him children, and minister to his sickly lust.

In conversation with a reverend gentleman, not long ago, I chanced to speak of the injustice done to woman. Ah! said he, so far from complaining, your heart should go out in thankfulness that you are an American woman, for in no country in the world does woman hold so high a position as here! Why, sir, said I, you must be very ignorant, or very false. Is my political position as high as that of Victoria, Queen of the mightiest nation on the globe? Are not nearly two millions of native-born American women, at this very hour, doomed to the foulest slavery that angels ever wept to witness? Are they not doubly damned as immortal beasts of burden in the field, and sad mothers of a most accursed race? Are they not raised for the express purposes of lust? Are they not chained and driven in the slave-coffle at the crack of the whip of an unfeeling driver? Are they not sold on the auction-block? Are they not exposed naked to the coarse jests and voluptuous gaze of brutal men? Are they not trained up in ignorance of all laws, both human and divine, and denied the right to read the Bible? For them there is no Sabbath, no Jesus, no Heaven, no hope, no holy mission of wife and mother, no privacy of home, nothing sacred to look for, but an eternal sleep in death and the grave. And these are the daughters and sisters of the first men in the Southern States! Think of fathers and brothers selling their own flesh on the auction-block, exposing beautiful women of refinement and education in a New Orleans market, and selling them, body and soul, to the absolute will of the highest bidder. And this is the condition of woman in republican, Christian America, and priests dare look me in the face and tell me that for blessings such as these my heart should go out in thankfulness! No, proud priest, you may encase your soul in holy robes, and hide your manhood in a pulpit, and, like the Pharisee of old,[13] turn your face away from the sufferings of your race; but I am a Christian—a follower of Jesus—and "whatsoever is done unto one of the *least* of these my sisters is done also unto me."[14] Though, in the person of the poor, trembling slave mother, you have bound me with heavy burthens, most grievous to bear—though you have done all you could to quench the spark of immortality which, from the throne of God, quickened me into being— though you have left me no vehicle of thought—though you have made the letters of Cadmus,[15] the whole English language, as dead to me as Egyptian hieroglyphics, yet can I still talk with God.[16] From majestic rivers and mighty forests I have learned his power, while gentle murmuring waters and the music of the woods have told me of his love. Yes, outside of my sad, hard slave life, in gay flowers and songs of happy birds, in the spicy breezes and sweet orange groves of my Southern home, I sometimes feel the pulsations of the great heart of God. He comes to me in all his works; I have worshipped him in the glorious sun, and moon, and stars, and laved my soul in their silent majesty and beauty. I have asked the everlasting hills, that in their upward yearnings seem to touch the heavens, if I, an immortal being, though clothed in womanhood, was made for the vile purposes to which proud Saxon man has doomed me, and in solemn chorus they all chanted NO! I have turned my eyes within, I have asked this bleeding heart, so full of love to God and man, so generous and self-sacrificing, ever longing for the pure, the holy, the divine, if this graceful form, this soft and tender flesh was made but to crawl and shiver in the cold, foul embrace of Southern tyrants, and, in stifled sobs, it answered, No! Thank you, oh Christian priests, meekly I will take your insults, taunts and sneers. To you my gratitude is due for all the *peculiar blessings* of slavery, for you have had the morals of this nation in your keeping. Behold the depths into which you have plunged me—the bottomless pit of human misery! But perchance your head grows dizzy to look down so far, and your heart faints to see what torture I can bear! It is enough!

But, Mr. President, I rejoice that it has been given to woman to drink the very dregs of human wretchedness and woe. For now, by an eternal law of matter and of mind, when the reaction comes, upward and upward, and still upward, she shall rise. Behold how far above your priestly robes, your bloody altars, your foul incense, your steepled synagogues, she shall stand secure on holy mounts, mid clouds of dazzling radiance, to which, in your gross vision, you shall not dare even to lift your eyes.[17]

⪻ *NASS*, 12 May 1860. Also *Lib*., 18 May 1860, and ECS's manuscript, *Film*, 9:567–71, 579–611.

1. The *Liberator*'s motto: "Our Country is the World—Our Countrymen are all Mankind."

2. ECS refers to the "gag rule" in force in the House of Representatives between 1836 and 1844, which tabled all matters relating to slavery, and to an assault on Senator Charles Sumner. Sumner (1811–1874) was elected senator from Massachusetts in 1851 and served until his death. A founder of the Free

Soil party, he was an outspoken abolitionist, and in 1858 South Carolina congressman Preston Brooks attacked and injured him on the floor of the Senate. A leader among radical Republicans after the Civil War, Sumner was the nation's most eloquent spokesman for building the republic on the basis of the equal rights of individuals. (*BDAC*; David Donald, *Charles Sumner and the Rights of Man* [New York, 1970.])

3. That is, his early commitment to immediate and total abolition of slavery, as in the American Anti-Slavery Society's *Declaration of Sentiments. Adopted at the Formation of said Society, in Phil., on the 4th of Dec., 1833* (New York, 1833).

4. George Barrell Cheever (1807–1890) was pastor of the Church of the Puritans, Union Square, New York, from 1846 to 1867, and a founder of the Church Anti-Slavery Society. (*DAB*.)

5. During the English Civil War, Parliament, under the leadership of Oliver Cromwell (1599–1658), appointed a committee to demolish "monuments of superstition and idolatry" in Westminster Abbey, and many of the church's ornaments were sold or melted down to pay parliamentary expenses. (Arthur Penrhyn Stanley, *Historical Memorials of Westminster Abbey* [New York, 1888], 3:143–44.)

6. Mary and Martha, sisters of Lazarus, were disciples of Jesus. (John 11.)

7. Here, in a passage marked off in parentheses, the manuscript continues the theme of emancipation from religion. Nature has nothing to compare with the "inflictions on the human family . . . which man has conjured up for himself," with his "vain speculations of an eternal hell, a royal Heaven an aristocracy of saints, an arch fiend to torment & a God who laughs at our calamities."

8. The *Standard* printed "mission," but the manuscript clearly reads "vision."

9. ECS groups readers of the conservative, Presbyterian *New York Observer* with non-Christian, and in her view, equally unenlightened people.

10. Northern moderates convened "Union meetings" after John Brown's raid and execution to reassure the South that they opposed extremism and disunionism.

11. From Procrustes, son of Poseidon, the term came to mean a requirement for strict conformity.

12. From Nathaniel Hawthorne, *The Scarlet Letter*, published in 1850.

13. Luke 14:1.

14. ECS substitutes "sisters" for "brethren" in Matt. 25:40.

15. In Greek mythology, Cadmus, King of Thebes, was credited with inventing the alphabet.

16. ECS originally wrote this sentence and the remainder of the paragraph in first person plural. After the convention, the *Liberator* published a protest against the speech from a man who did not like to see "the cause of the slave burdened with a topic so entirely foreign," but Garrison pointed out that she

spoke of slave women, not white women, in this conclusion to her speech. (*Lib.*, 18 May 1860.)

17. An additional paragraph in the manuscript reveals that behind "our fans & banjo's," the woman and the black man "laugh at least" at how poorly the white man uses his freedom, "at his awkward somersets in church & state," and his failure "in all the acts of war & government & social life."

138 ↝ TENTH NATIONAL WOMAN'S RIGHTS CONVENTION

Editorial note: The Tenth National Woman's Rights Convention also met at the Cooper Institute, where Martha Wright presided over an audience of one thousand people, on 10 and 11 May 1860. As secretary of the central committee, SBA reported on the year's work and the legislative victories in New York. Wendell Phillips delivered an elegant argument for woman suffrage, and ECS asked the crowd to "please resolve yourselves into the 'Gentlemen of the Judiciary'" in order to listen to the address to the legislature she had delivered in March. It was on the second day that ECS carried out her intention to speak about marriage and divorce.

[11 May 1860]

Mrs. Elizabeth Cady Stanton then presented the following resolutions, in support of which she purposed to address the Convention:

1. Resolved, That, in the language (slightly varied) of John Milton, "Those who marry intend as little to conspire their own ruin, as those who swear allegiance, and as a whole people is *to an ill government*, so is one man or woman *to an ill marriage*. If a whole people, against any authority, covenant or statute, may, by the sovereign edict of charity, save not only their lives, but honest liberties, from unworthy bondage, as well may a married party, against any private covenant, which he or she never entered, *to his or her mischief*, be redeemed from unsupportable disturbances, to honest peace, and just contentment."[1]

2. Resolved, That all men are created equal, and all women, in their natural rights, are the equals of men; and endowed by their Creator with the same inalienable right to the pursuit of happiness.

3. Resolved, That any constitution, compact or covenant between human beings, that failed to produce or promote human happiness,

could not, in the nature of things, be of any force or authority;—and it would be not only a right, but a duty, to abolish it.

4. Resolved, That though marriage be in itself divinely founded, and is fortified as an institution by innumerable analogies in the whole kingdom of universal nature, still, a true marriage is only known by its results; and, like the fountain, if pure, will reveal only pure manifestations. Nor need it ever be said, "What God hath joined together, let not man put asunder,"[2] for man could not put it asunder; nor can he any more unite what God and nature have not joined together.

5. Resolved, That of all insulting mockeries of heavenly truth and holy law, none can be greater than that *physical impotency* is cause sufficient for divorce, while no amount of mental or moral or spiritual *imbecility* is ever to be pleaded in support of such a demand.

6. Resolved, That such a law was worthy those dark periods when marriage was held by the greatest doctors and priests of the Church to be a *work of the flesh only*, and almost, if not altogether, a defilement; denied wholly to the clergy, and a second time, forbidden to all.

7. Resolved, That an unfortunate or ill-assorted marriage is ever a calamity, but not ever, perhaps never, a crime;—and when society or government, by its laws or customs, compels its continuance, always to the grief of one of the parties, and the actual loss and damage of both, it usurps an authority never delegated to man, nor exercised by God himself.

8. Resolved, That observation and experience daily show how incompetent are men, as individuals, or as governments, to select partners in business, teachers for their children, ministers of their religion, or makers, adjudicators or administrators of their laws; and as the same weakness and blindness must attend in the selection of matrimonial partners, the dictates of humanity and common sense alike show that the latter and most important contract should no more be perpetual than either or all of the former.

9. Resolved, That children born in these unhappy and unhallowed connections are, in the most solemn sense, of *unlawful birth*,—the fruit of lust, but not of love;—and so not of God, divinely descended, but from beneath, whence proceed all manner of evil and uncleanness.

10. Resolved, That next to the calamity of such a birth to the child, is the misfortune of being trained in the atmosphere of a household where love is not the law, but where discord and bitterness abound;

stamping their demoniac features on the moral nature, with all their odious peculiarities;—thus continuing the race in a weakness and depravity that must be a sure precursor of its ruin, as a just penalty of long-violated law.

ADDRESS OF MRS. E. C. STANTON.

Mrs. President,—In our common law, in our whole system of jurisprudence, we find man's highest idea of right. The object of law is to secure justice. But inasmuch as fallible man is the maker and administrator of law, we must look for many and gross blunders in the application of its general principles to individual cases.

The science of theology, of civil, political, moral and social life, all teach the common idea, that man ever has been, and ever must be, sacrificed to the highest good of society; the one to the many—the poor to the rich—the weak to the powerful—and all to the institutions of his own creation. Look, what thunderbolts of power man has forged in the ages for his own destruction!—at the organizations to enslave himself! And through those times of darkness, those generations of superstition, behold all along the relics of his power and skill, that stand like milestones, here and there, to show how far back man was great and glorious! Who can stand in those vast cathedrals of the old world, as the deep-toned organ reverberates from arch to arch, and not feel the grandeur of immortality? Here is the incarnated thought of man, beneath whose stately dome the man himself now bows in fear and doubt, knows not himself, and knows not God,—a mere slave to symbols,—and with holy water signs the Cross, whilst he who died thereon declared man God.

I repudiate this popular idea. I place man above all governments, all institutions—ecclesiastical and civil—all constitutions and laws. (Applause.) It is a mistaken idea, that the same law that oppresses the individual, can promote the highest good of society. The best interests of a community never can require the sacrifice of one innocent being—of one sacred right. In the settlement, then, of any question, we must simply consider the highest good of the individual. It is the inalienable right of all to be happy. It is the highest duty of all to seek those conditions in life, those surroundings, which may develop what is noblest and best, remembering that the lessons of these passing hours are not for time alone, but for the ages of eternity. They tell us, in that future home—the heavenly paradise—that the human family shall be sifted out, and the good and pure shall dwell together in peace. If that be the heavenly order, is it not our duty to render earth as near like heaven as we may?

For years, there has been before the Legislature of this State a variety of bills, asking for divorce in cases of drunkenness, insanity, desertion, cruel and brutal treatment, endangering life.[3] My attention was called to this question very early in life, by the sufferings of a friend of my girlhood, a victim of one of those unfortunate unions, called marriage.[4] What my great love for that young girl, and my holy intuitions, then decided to be right, has not been changed by years of experience, observation and reason. I have pondered well these things in my heart, and ever felt the deepest interest in all that has been written and said upon the subject, and the most profound respect and loving sympathy for those heroic women, who, in the face of law and public sentiment, have dared to sunder the unholy ties of a joyless, loveless union.

If marriage is a human institution, about which man may legislate, it seems but just that he should treat this branch of his legislation with the same common sense that he applies to all others. If it is a mere legal contract, then should it be subject to the restraints and privileges of all other contracts. A contract, to be valid in law, must be formed between parties of mature age, with an honest intention in said parties to do what they agree. The least concealment, fraud, or intention to deceive, if proved, annuls the contract. A boy cannot contract for an acre of land, or a horse, until he is twenty-one, but he may contract for a wife at fourteen.[5] If a man sell a horse, and the purchaser find in him great incompatibility of temper—a disposition to stand still, when the owner is in haste to go—the sale is null and void, the man and his horse part company. But in marriage, no matter how much fraud and deception are practised, nor how cruelly one or both parties have been misled; no matter how young, inexperienced or thoughtless the parties, nor how unequal their condition and position in life, the contract cannot be annulled.[6] Think of a husband telling a young and trusting girl, but one short month his wife, that he married her for her money; that those letters, so precious to her, that she had read and re-read, and kissed and cherished, were written by another; that their splendid home, of which, on their wedding day, her father gave to him the deed, is

already in the hands of his creditors; that she must give up the elegance
and luxury that now surround her, unless she can draw fresh supplies
of money to meet their wants! When she told the story of her wrongs to
me,—the abuse to which she was subject, and the dread in which she
lived,—I impulsively urged her to fly from such a monster and villain,
as she would before the hot breath of a ferocious beast of the wilderness. (Applause.) And she did fly; and it was well with her. Many times
since, as I have felt her throbbing heart against my own, she has said,
"Oh, but for your love and sympathy, your encouragement, I should
never have escaped from that bondage. Before I could, of myself, have
found courage to break those chains, my heart would have broken in
the effort."

Marriage, as it now exists, must seem to all of you a mere human
institution. Look through the universe of matter and mind,—all God's
arrangements are perfect, harmonious and complete! There is no discord, friction, or failure in his eternal plans. Immutability, perfection,
beauty, are stamped on all his laws. Love is the vital essence that
pervades and permeates, from the centre to the circumference, the
graduating circles of all thought and action. Love is the talisman of
human weal and woe,—the *open sesame* to every human soul. Where
two beings are drawn together, by the natural laws of likeness and
affinity, union and happiness are the result. Such marriages might be
Divine. But how is it now? You all know our marriage is, in many cases,
a mere outward tie, impelled by custom, policy, interest, necessity;
founded not even in friendship, to say nothing of love; with every
possible inequality of condition and development. In these heteroge-
neous unions, we find youth and old age, beauty and deformity, refinement and vulgarity, virtue and vice, the educated and the ignorant,
angels of grace and goodness, with devils of malice and malignity: and
the sum of all this is human wretchedness and despair; cold fathers, sad
mothers, and hapless children, who shiver at the hearthstone, where
the fires of love have all gone out. The wide world, and the stranger's
unsympathizing gaze, are not more to be dreaded for young hearts than
homes like these. Now, who shall say that it is right to take two beings,
so unlike, and anchor them right side by side fast bound—to stay all
time, until God shall summon one away?

Do wise, Christian legislators need any arguments to convince them
that the sacredness of the family relation should be protected at all

hazards? The family, that great conservator of national virtue and strength, how can you hope to build it up in the midst of violence, debauchery and excess? Can there be any thing sacred at that family altar, where the chief priest who ministers makes sacrifice of human beings, of the weak and the innocent? where the incense offered up is not to the God of justice and mercy, but to those heathen divinities, who best may represent the lost man in all his grossness and deformity? Call that sacred, where woman, the mother of the race,—of a Jesus of Nazareth,—unconscious of the true dignity of her nature, of her high and holy destiny, consents to live in legalized prostitution!—her whole soul revolting at such gross association!—her flesh shivering at the cold contamination of that embrace,—held there by no tie but the iron chain of the law, and a false and most unnatural public sentiment? Call that sacred, where innocent children, trembling with fear, fly to the corners and dark places of the house, to hide themselves from the wrath of drunken, brutal fathers, but, forgetting their past sufferings, rush out again at their mother's frantic screams, "Help, oh help"? Behold the agonies of those young hearts, as they see the only being on earth they love, dragged about the room by the hair of the head, kicked and pounded, and left half dead and bleeding on the floor! Call that sacred, where fathers like these have the power and legal right to hand down their natures to other beings,—to curse other generations with such moral deformity and death?

Men and brethren, look into your asylums for the blind, the deaf and dumb, the idiot, the imbecile, the deformed, the insane; go out into the by-lanes and dens of this vast metropolis, and contemplate that reeking mass of depravity; pause before the terrible revelations made by statistics of the rapid increase of all this moral and physical impotency, and learn how fearful a thing it is to violate the immutable laws of the beneficent Ruler of the universe; and there behold the terrible retributions of your violence on woman! Learn how false and cruel are those institutions, which, with a coarse materialism, set aside those holy instincts of the woman to bear no children but those of love! In the best condition of marriage, as we now have it, to woman come all the penalties and sacrifices. A man, in the full tide of business or pleasure, can marry and not change his life one iota; he can be husband, father, and every thing beside: but in marriage, woman gives up all. Home is her sphere, her realm. Well, be it so. If here you will make us all supreme, take to yourselves the universe beside; explore the North Pole;[7] and, in your airy car, all space; in your Northern homes and cloud-capt towers, go feast on walrus flesh and air, and lay you down to sleep your six months' night away, and leave us to make these laws that govern the inner sanctuary of our own homes, and faithful satellites we will ever be to the dinner-pot, the cradle, and the old arm-chair. (Applause.)

Fathers, do you say, let your daughters pay a life-long penalty for one unfortunate step? How could they, on the threshold of life, full of joy and hope, believing all things to be as they seemed on the surface, judge of the dark windings of the human soul? How could they foresee that the young man, to-day so noble, so generous, would in a few short years be transformed into a cowardly, mean tyrant, or a foul-mouthed, bloated drunkard? What father could rest at his home by night, knowing that his lovely daughter was at the mercy of a strong man drunk with wine and passion, and that, do what he might, he was backed up by law and public sentiment? The best interests of the individual, the family, the State, the nation, cry out against these legalized marriages of force and endurance. There can be no heaven without love, and nothing is sacred in the family and home, but just so far as it is built up and anchored in love. Our newspapers teem with startling accounts of husbands and wives having shot or poisoned each other, or committed suicide, choosing death rather than the indissoluble tie; and, still worse, the living death of faithless wives and daughters, from the first families in this State, dragged from the privacy of home into the public prints and courts, with all the painful details of sad, false lives.[8] What say you to facts like these? Now, do you believe, men and women, that all these wretched matches are made in heaven? that all these sad, miserable people are bound together by God? I know Horace Greeley has been most eloquent, for weeks past, on the holy sacrament of ill-assorted marriages;[9] but let us hope that all wisdom does not live, and will not die, with Horace Greeley. I think, if he had been married to the *New York Herald*, instead of the Republican party, he would have found out some Scriptural arguments against life-long unions, where great incompatibility of temper existed between the parties.[10] (Laughter and applause.) Our law-makers have dug a pit, and the innocent have fallen into it; and now will you coolly cover them over with statute laws, *Tribunes*, and Weeds,[11] and tell them to stay there, and pay the life-long penalty of having fallen in? Nero[12] was thought the chief of tyrants, because he made laws and hung them up so high that his subjects could not read them, and then punished them for every act of disobedience. What better are our Republican legislators? The mass of the women of this nation know nothing about the laws, yet all their specially barbarous legislation is for woman. Where have they made any provision for her to learn the laws? Where is the Law School for our daughters?—where the law office, the bar, or the bench, now urging them to take part in the jurisprudence of the nation? But, say you, does not separation cover all these difficulties? No one objects to separation when the parties are so disposed. Now, to separation there are two very serious objections. First, so long as you insist on marriage as a Divine institution, as an indissoluble tie, so long as you maintain your present laws against divorce, you make separation, even, so odious, that the most noble, virtuous and sensitive men and women choose a life of concealed misery, rather than a partial, disgraceful release. Secondly, those who, in their impetuosity and despair, do, in spite of public sentiment, separate, find themselves in their new position beset with many temptations to lead a false, unreal life. This isolation bears especially hard on woman. Marriage is not all of life to man. His resources for amusement and occupation are boundless. He has the whole world for his home. His business, his politics, his club, his friendships with either sex, can help to fill up the void made by an unfortunate union or separation. But to woman, marriage is all and every thing; her sole object in life,—that for which she is educated,— the subject of all her sleeping and her waking dreams. Now, if a noble, generous girl of eighteen marries, and is unfortunate, because the cruelty of her husband compels separation, in her dreary isolation, would you drive her to a nunnery; and shall she be a nun indeed? Her solitude is nothing less, as, in the present undeveloped condition of woman, it is only through our fathers, brothers, husbands, sons, that we feel the pulsations of the great outer world.

One unhappy, discordant man or woman in a neighborhood, may mar the happiness of all the rest. You cannot shut up discord, any more than you can small-pox. There can be no morality, where there is a settled discontent. A very wise father once remarked, that in the government of his children, he forbid as few things as possible; a wise legislation would do the same. It is folly to make laws on subjects beyond human prerogative, knowing that in the very nature of things they must be set aside. To make laws that man cannot and will not obey, serves to bring all law into contempt. It is very important in a republic, that the people should respect the laws, for if we throw them to the winds, what becomes of civil government? What do our present divorce laws amount to? Those who wish to evade them have only to go into another State to accomplish what they desire. If any of our citizens cannot secure their inalienable rights in New York State, they may in Connecticut and Indiana.[13] Why is it that all agreements, covenants, partnerships, are left wholly at the discretion of the parties, except the contract, which of all others is considered most holy and important, both for the individual and the race? This question of divorce, they tell us, is hedged about with difficulties; that it cannot be approached with the ordinary rules of logic and common sense. It is too holy, too sacred to be discussed, and few seem disposed to touch it. From man's stand-point, this may be all true,—as to him they say belong reason, and the power to ratiocinate. Fortunately, I belong to that class endowed with mere intuitions,—a kind of moral instinct, by which we feel out right and wrong. In presenting to you, therefore, my views of divorce, you will of course give to them the weight only of the woman's intuitions. But inasmuch as that is all God saw fit to give us, it is evident we need nothing more. Hence, what we do perceive of truth must be as reliable as what man grinds out by the longer process of reason, authority, and speculation.

Horace Greeley, in his recent discussion with Robert Dale Owen,[14] said, this whole question has been tried, in all its varieties and conditions, from indissoluble monogamic marriage down to free love; that the ground has been all gone over and explored. Let me assure him that but just one-half of the ground has been surveyed, and that half but by one of the parties, and that party certainly *not* the most interested in the matter. Moreover, there is one kind of marriage that has not been tried, and that is, a contract made by equal parties to live an equal life, with equal restraints and privileges on either side. Thus far, we have had the man marriage, and nothing more. From the beginning, man has had the sole and whole regulation of the matter. He has spoken in Scripture, he has spoken in law. As an individual, he has decided the time and cause for putting away a wife, and as a judge and legislator, he still holds the entire control. In all history, sacred and profane, the woman is regarded and spoken of simply as the toy of man,—made for his special use,—to meet his most gross and sensuous desires. She is taken or put away, given or received, bought or sold, just as the interest of the parties might dictate. But the woman has been no more recognized in all these transactions, through all the different periods and conditions of the race, than if she had had no part nor lot in the whole matter. The right of woman to put away a husband, be he ever so impure, is never hinted at in sacred history. Even Jesus himself failed to recognize the sacred rights of the holy mothers of the race.[15] We cannot take our gauge of womanhood from the past, but from the solemn convictions of our own souls, in the higher development of the race. No parchments, however venerable with the mould of ages, no human institutions, can bound the immortal wants of the royal sons and daughters of the great I Am,—rightful heirs of the joys of time, and joint heirs of the glories of eternity.

If in marriage either party claims the right to stand supreme, to woman, the mother of the race, belongs the sceptre and the crown. Her life is one long sacrifice for man. You tell us that among all womankind there are no Moses, Christs, or Pauls,—no Michael Angelos, Beethovens, or Shakespeares,—no Columbuses or Galileos,—no Lockes or Bacons. Behold those mighty minds attuned to music and the arts, so great, so grand, so comprehensive,—these are our great works of which we boast! Which, think you, stands first, the man, or what he does? By just so far as Galileo is greater than his thought, is the mother far above the man. Into you, oh sons of earth, go all of us that is great and grand. In you centre our very life-thoughts, our hopes, our intensest love. For you we gladly pour out our heart's blood and die. Willingly do we drink the cup in the holy sacrament of marriage, in the same faith that the Son of Mary died on Calvary,—knowing that from our suffering comes forth a new and more glorious resurrection of thought and life. (Loud applause.)

Editorial note: When ECS was done, Antoinette Blackwell spoke first, evoking the tradition of free discussion and opposing divorce. She proposed that marriage "must be, from the nature of things, as permanent as the life of the parties" and that "all divorce is naturally and morally impossible." In agreement with ECS that the laws made subjection of women the main idea of marriage, Blackwell would raise society up to the moral level required for a marriage of equals.

Ernestine Rose replied that Blackwell had delivered a "sermon" about what "ought to be"; in an imperfect world, divorce should be available. Marriage was a human institution and must serve the needs of real men and women. Wendell Phillips objected "to entering these resolutions upon the journal of this Convention." The entire discussion had no place in a woman's rights meeting, where discussion should be limited to "the laws that rest unequally upon women, not those that rest equally upon men and women." Abigail Hopper Gibbons seconded Phillips's motion to suppress the resolutions. William Lloyd Garrison reminded the audience that discussions of slavery often wandered away from the central point. Marriage, he believed, was "at least incidental to the main question of equal rights of woman." Antoinette Blackwell took the floor one final time to insist that the question of marriage "*must* come upon this platform" because it bears unequally on women. SBA then spoke.

I wish to say, in the first place, that I hope Mr. Phillips will withdraw his motion that these resolutions shall not appear on the records of the Convention. I am very sure that it would be contrary to all parliamentary usages in Conventions of this kind to say, that when the speech which enforced and advocated the resolutions is reported and published in the proceedings, the resolutions shall not be placed there. And as to the point that this question does not belong to this platform,—from that I totally dissent. Marriage has ever and always been a one-sided matter, resting most unequally upon the sexes. By it, man gains all—woman loses all; tyrant law and lust reign supreme with him—meek submission, and cheerful, ready obedience, alone befit her. Woman has never been consulted; her wish has never at all been taken into consideration as regards the terms of the marriage compact. By law, public sentiment, and religion, from the time of Moses down to the present day, woman has never been thought of other than as a piece of property, to be disposed of at the will and pleasure of man. And this very hour, by our statute-books, by our (so called) enlightened Christian civilization, woman has no voice whatever in saying what shall be the terms of the marriage compact. She must accept marriage as man proffers it, or accept it not at all. Therefore, in my opinion, this discussion of the marriage question is perfectly in order on this Woman's Rights platform. I hope, at any rate, that the resolutions, which embody the ideas of the persons, at least, who presented them, will be allowed to go out to the public, that there may be a fair understanding and a fair report of the ideas which have actually been presented here upon these subjects, and that they shall not be left to the mercy of the secular press. I therefore hope that the Convention will not vote to forbid the appearance of these resolutions with the proceedings.

Editorial note: The motion of Wendell Phillips was put to a vote and was lost.

☞ *Proceedings of the Tenth National Woman's Rights Convention, Held at the Cooper Institute, New York City, Thursday and Friday, May 10th and 11th, 1860* (Boston, 1860), 65–73, 90.

1. ECS modifies a passage from John Milton's "The Doctrine and Discipline of Divorce" to make it gender neutral.

2. Matt. 19:6.

3. Bills to allow divorce for cruel treatment and abandonment had been introduced into the legislature every year since 1850, except 1856, but few of them ever made it out of committee, and those that did were defeated.

4. ECS may elaborate upon the predicament of her cousin Cornelia Smith Cochran Barclay (1825–1890), a niece of Gerrit Smith. Married in 1847 to Henry A. W. Barclay, of a prominent New York family, Cornelia soon discovered that she had an abusive and alcoholic husband. Just a year after her marriage, Cornelia's brother reported that Henry did not support his wife and baby and was using up not only his wife's estate, but that of her sisters. After the birth of at least one more child, Cornelia was evicted from a boarding-house because of Henry's "unusually abandoned conduct." She finally moved to Peterboro until Henry died in 1857. (R. Burnham Moffat, *The Barclays of New York: Who They Are and Who They Are Not,—and Some Other Barclays*, rev. ed. [New York, 1904], 128; John Cochrane to Gerrit Smith, 19 June, 25 July 1848, 3 October 1851, Ellen Cochran Walter to G. Smith, 27 September 1851, and Gerrit Smith's accounts with family members, Smith Papers, NSyU; Cornelia S. Barclay, *Mrs. Singleton* [New York, 1880].)

5. As she did in 1854, when addressing the legislature, ECS employs Elisha Hurlbut's comparison between the legal ages for contracting marriage and business. Though some states raised the age of consent, New York relied on the common law ages identified by ECS. (Hurlbut, *Essays on Human Rights*, 152–53.)

6. According to New York law, a marriage could be annulled "on the ground that the consent of one of the parties was obtained by force or fraud," unless, at any time before the suit, "there was a voluntary cohabitation of the parties as husband and wife." (*RSSNY, 1852*, 2:326, secs. 35, 36.)

7. There had been a number of Arctic expeditions by this time and, as ECS read her speech, Charles F. Hall was preparing yet another. (*New York Herald*, 15 May 1860.)

8. The sordid divorce case of Isaac and Mary Burch captured ECS's attention in the months preceding the convention. Mary, the niece and adopted
daughter of Erastus Corning of Albany, met Isaac Burch in 1842 when he was
a bank clerk and lived in her household. They married in 1848, moved to
Chicago, where Isaac became a successful banker, and purchased a mansion
on Michigan Avenue with her marriage dower. In January 1860 Isaac accused
Mary of committing adultery and produced her signed confession, obtained,
according to Mary, by force and deceit. Obliged to defend her honor in court
against these widely published charges, Mary accused her husband of neglect
and of marrying her for her money. Isaac had treated her well, she testified,
until her uncle withdrew his financial support of the couple following an
argument between the two men. Mary concluded that Isaac accused her of
adultery solely in order to obtain a divorce. (ECS, "Fashionable Women
Shipwreck," *Film*, 10:105–29; *New York Daily Tribune*, 13, 14, 21 February,
21, 30 April, 6 June 1860.)

9. Horace Greeley and Robert Dale Owen debated divorce in the *Tribune*.
Greeley opposed divorce "for any other cause than that recognized as sufficient by Jesus Christ," that is, for adultery. (*New York Daily Tribune*, 1, 5, 6,
12, 17, 28 March, 7, 21 April, 1 May 1860; *Divorce: Being a Correspondence
between Horace Greeley and Robert Dale Owen* [New York, 1860].)

10. The *New York Herald*, edited by James G. Bennett, was the *Tribune*'s
chief competition in New York City. An independent paper with Democratic
leanings, it was known for sensationalism and hostility to reformers.

11. Thurlow Weed (1797–1882), publisher of the *Albany Evening Journal*,
ruled New York's Whig and Republican parties for decades, employing patronage, lobbying, and probably graft to retain control over the state legislature. He opposed passage of a divorce bill in 1860. (*DAB*; Glyndon G. Van
Deusen, *Thurlow Weed: Wizard of the Lobby* [Boston, 1947]; *History*, 1:720.)

12. Nero, the tyrannic Emperor of Rome from 54 to 68 A.D.

13. Connecticut's and Indiana's short residency requirements and more
liberal grounds for divorce made these states havens for couples wishing to
escape unhappy marriages.

14. Robert Dale Owen (1801–1877) came to the United States from Scotland
in 1825, with his father, the socialist Robert Owen, to begin an experimental
community in New Harmony, Indiana. Both politician and reformer, the
younger Owen supported married women's property rights and liberal divorce laws. As a Democrat he at first opposed war with the South, but he
became a War Democrat and advocate of emancipation by 1862. In 1863 and
1864 he aided the Women's Loyal National League, and he fought for federal
guarantees for the rights of former slaves. (*DAB*; Richard William Leopold,
Robert Dale Owen: A Biography [New York, 1969]; *History*, 1:292–306, 2:50,
81.)

15. In Matt. 19:19 Jesus allowed a husband to divorce his wife if she committed adultery but did not accord the same privilege to a wife.

·⟨==========⟩·

Editorial note: ECS's resolutions preoccupied the New York press for several weeks after the convention. The *Evening Post* immediately warned that friends "will be disgusted with this new dogma" that equates marriage with a business contract. Such an "exceedingly loose view" of marriage would enable women to seek divorce whenever marriage became "distasteful." On May 14 the *Tribune*'s editorial, "Marriage As a Business," called the new doctrine "simply shocking" and marveled "that a modest woman should say" what ECS said. Traditionally contemptuous of woman's rights meetings, the *Herald* found it "difficult to believe that the speakers were females" and accused them of "preach[ing] revolt against the only discipline that imposes restraints upon their unruly tendencies." On May 16 the *Evening Post* called it "suicidal" for women to propose, as ECS had, "abolishing marriage," because marriage laws were written expressly to protect women. Characterizing the meeting as "infidel and licentious," the weekly *New York Observer* reported that resolutions "which no true woman could listen to without turning scarlet, were unblushingly read and advocated by a person in woman's attire, named in the programme as Mrs. Elizabeth Cady Stanton." They "would turn the world into one vast brothel." When ECS defended herself in the *Tribune* of 30 May, Sydney Gay's editorial response said that ECS had "thrown down the gage to the Christian world," advancing a doctrine that was "simply infernal." "In our view," he continued, "the fundamental idea of the State or Commonwealth is the subordination of individual to general well-being; and so we hold that the good citizen will cheerfully bear the ills of an unfit marriage rather than seek its dissolution at the cost of the general good." (New York *Evening Post*, 12, 16, 23 May 1860; *New York Daily Tribune*, 14, 30 May 1860; *New York Herald*, 16 May 1860; *New York Observer*, 17 May 1860.)

139 ❧ MARTHA COFFIN WRIGHT TO ECS

Auburn May 26th '60

My dear Mrs. Stanton

Your note and Susan's with the extracts from the papers, wh. I was glad to see, reached me in due time:—the pleasantest part was the assurance that you were thinking of coming here— Do come, for I have regretted so much the loss of that afternoon after the Con. It wd. have been such a satisfaction to talk over that exciting last session— It was very aggravating to have to pass your room door, and hear your voices, as I hastened to bed—

It was not easy to decline Susan's invitation to accompany her, but it seemed hardly fair to leave home again so soon— I am glad you have answered the absurd criticisms of the papers charging you with wishing to abrogate marriage laws— One would think from the howls of the press that there were no <u>Gay</u>[1] deceivers, and no wrongs under existing laws, that no license was ever found for licentiousness, no husbands and wives poisoned, no absconding parties from the Heaven ordained marriages now existing— It ill becomes the timid & wavering, who, by the success of our cause the past winter, have been reluctantly drawn to our platform, to criticise and protest—that they fled back, affrighted, takes not one feather's weight from the strength of our cause— I think Wendell Phillips' mature judgment, must condemn his hasty action, in proposing so arbitrary a measure, without having heard all the resolutions read— Of course there will be difference of opinion as to the wisdom of introducing the subject of divorce yet awhile, but that it must come up eventually, in conventions met for the discussion of all the rights and <u>all the wrongs</u> of woman, cannot be disputed— And it is the comparison of opinions, that gives life to a Convention— Even the saintly and dignified Evening Post maligns us, as you will see—asserts that the Resolutions were <u>adopted</u> wh. they never were and makes various false charges— I wish I cd. have been with you & Susan, those two days—I shd. have liked to see what you wrote— Be sure & come, when you can—

I have not seen Mrs. Seward & Mrs. Worden[2] yet— It was almost like a funeral in town, when the news of [*sideways on first page*] the nomination was recd. Mrs. Worden is very indignant at Greeley's course.[3] Do let me hear from you once in a while   very affy Yrs.

≈ *M. C. W.*

≈ ALS, Garrison Papers, MNS-S.

1. A pun on the names of Elizabeth and Sydney Gay. Elizabeth Gay, in a letter to the *Tribune*, expressed indignation that the "foreign" topic of divorce was introduced at the convention and insisted that Wendell Phillips's speech represented the views of the majority there. Sydney Howard Gay (1814–1888), editor of the *Standard* from 1844 to 1857, joined the staff of the *Tribune* in 1857 and was managing editor from 1862 to 1866. (*New York Daily Tribune*, 14 May 1860; *DAB*.)

2. Frances Adeline Miller Seward and Lazette Maria Miller Worden, good friends of Martha Wright and ECS, were among Emma Willard's first students at the Troy Female Seminary. Frances (1805–1865) married William Henry Seward when he was a young lawyer in her father's office, and the couple lived in Auburn. Though she was something of a recluse and rarely accompanied her husband to Washington during his long career in the Senate and the cabinet, Frances Seward was respected for astute political knowledge and advice. Her sister Lazette (?–1875), widow of Alvah Worden, lived with her. (*TroyFS*; *DAB*, s.v. "Seward, W. H."; John M. Taylor, *William Henry Seward: Lincoln's Right Hand* [New York, 1991]; *Eighty Years*, 194–99.)

3. At the Republican National Convention in Chicago in May, Horace Greeley, there as a delegate from Oregon because New York Republicans would not send him, helped to defeat William H. Seward's bid for the presidential nomination. (Alexander, *Political History of New York*, 2:286–93; Isely, *Horace Greeley and the Republican Party*, 280–86.)

---

140 ⇒ PARKER PILLSBURY TO ECS

[*May? 1860*][1]

What a pretty kettle of hot water you tumbled into at New York! Your marriage and divorce speeches and resolutions you must have learned in the school of a Wollstonecraft or a Sophie Arnaut.[2] You broke the very heart of the portly Evening Post and nearly drove the Tribune to the grave.

≈ *Anthony*, 1:195.

1. Dated with reference to the May convention.

2. Sophie Madeline Arnould (1740-1802) was a celebrated French actress and singer who, like Mary Wollstonecraft, opposed marriage.

·❮═══❯◗·

141 ✌ MARTHA COFFIN WRIGHT TO ECS, WITH ENCLOSURE

Auburn 5th July 1860

My dear Mrs. Stanton

I have just written a line to Susan, enclosing Mrs. Worden's letter,[1] for which I am much obliged—she shall not know I have seen it— It is very full and satisfactory & I am glad she sees so clearly, now if she will only try and see how much can be done in this 'sphere,' we may not have to wait till the next, before something is accomplished— I hope you will make the suggested visit, and that I may meet you there, as well as see you here. I have not seen Mrs. Worden since the wedding—she pussed thro the crowd, at Mrs. Watson's,[2] saying "Where is my strong-minded friend?" The wedding was quite a grand affair—Ch. crowded, a perfect jam in the house, boys & girls perched on every picket & the street thronged, near the house, to hear the music, and 'take a smell'— The garden was lighted with lanterns, & carpets spread— Mrs. Worden took a chair under the blue canopy and placed one for me, but I protested against the imprudence, & came in—was not out five minutes, but have been sick with sore throat ever since—

I copied a few lines from sister L.'s letter, thinking you might like to see what she says—

She says she has been writing to Dr. H. K. Hunt, who sent her bridal cards,[3] and asked a sentiment—wh. effort she dreaded— I wondered whether if some Boston Adonis of mature age should be accepted some day, it wd. be considered bigamy, and whether succeeding patients wd be less legitimate than previous ones— There is a "sentiment," but probably not the one prayerfully suggested to my sister—

Remember me to Mr. Stanton and to those fine boys & girls of yrs. Affectionately   Yr. friend

✍ M. C. Wright.

✍ ALS, Garrison Papers, MNS-S.

ENCLOSURE

EXTRACT FROM LUCRETIA MOTT'S LETTER

I was glad to have such a defence of the resolutions as the letter with the scraps of Parker Pillsbury's & S. B. Anthony's. I have great faith in Elizabeth Stanton's quick instincts & clear insight in all appertaining to woman's rights & [wron]gs, and the fullest confidence in the united judgment of herself & S. B. Anthony, with our sister Martha & P. Pillsbury to back them— I am glad they are all so vigorous for the work. Every word sent on the subject is most acceptable. I don't think Garrison wd exclude the marriage & divorce questi[on] [*page torn*] from the platform— He took sides in favor of all these subjects being discussed, when we met him at Miller's (MᶜKim's) 2 yrs ago.[4] I mean to read all to Miller MᶜKim when I have a chance, he is so dreadfully afraid of Free Love. How little patience he had, with Robt. Dale Owen's views, in that discussion with Greeley. As to Sydney Gay's article, I tho't it was Greeley's, & sd it was unfair, & no answer to E. C. S.— I shd. have liked to hear her answer the farmer at Junius[5]—& sorry was I, that thou could not go to that mg. We happen to know a good many fat wives of farmers in this region, so thy illustration wd. not be convincing, but then these are Quaker farmers—and they recipricate, dont they?

☞ Copy in hand of M. C. Wright, Garrison Papers, MNS-S. One entire word and parts of two other words are torn away at the margin.

1. M. C. Wright to SBA, 5 July 1860, enclosure missing, *Film*, 9:732–34.

2. The wedding of Janet McNeil Watson to William Henry Seward, Jr., on 27 June 1860. The bride's mother was Margaret Standart Watson. (Alvin Seaward Van Benthuysen, *The Seaward and Seward Families of America, Part II*, 2d ed. [Brooklyn, n.d.], 294.)

3. Harriot Kezia Hunt (1805–1875) celebrated twenty-five years of marriage to her profession with a silver anniversary party for which she wore a wedding dress and copied bridal customs. A successful physician in Boston, organizer of the Ladies Physiological Society in 1843, and a lecturer on women's health, Hunt was also a regular participant in national woman's rights conventions, and her annual protests against paying her property taxes were legendary. (*NAW*; *Woman's Journal*, 5 January 1875; *History*, 1:259–60.)

4. James Miller McKim (1810–1874) was a minister and founding member of the American Anti-Slavery Society, who worked closely with Mott in Philadelphia. Mott reported on 6 July 1858 that McKim "thinks conservatism is needed, and that I ought to read and understand the views of those ultra

free-love people, so as to give my influence against them." (*DAB*; Hallowell, *James and Lucretia Mott*, 382.)

5. At the Yearly Meeting of the Friends of Human Progress in June, ECS and SBA served on the business committee, which introduced resolutions on marriage and divorce similar to the ones ECS presented at the national convention. Abram Pryne raised objections, but the resolutions were adopted. (*Proceedings of the Twelfth Yearly Meeting of the Friends of Human Progress, Held at Waterloo, Seneca Co., N.Y. The 1st, 2d, and 3d days of June, 1860* [Cortland, N.Y., 1860], *Film*, 9:690ff.)

·⟨══════⟩·

142 ❧ ECS TO MARTHA COFFIN WRIGHT

[*Seneca Falls, after 12 July 1860*][1]

Anything that is outward, all forms and ceremonies, faiths and symbols, policies and institutions, may be washed away, but that which is of the very being must stand forever. Nothing, nobody could abate the all-absorbing, agonizing interest I feel in the redemption of woman. I could not wash my hands of woman's rights, for they are dyed clear through to the marrow of the bone.

Those sad-faced women who struggled up to press my hand, who were speechless with emotion, know better than the greatest of our masculine speakers and editors who has struck the blow for them in the right place. I shall trust my instinct and my reason until some masculine logic meets mine better than it has yet done on the point at issue.

❧ "Early Letters," 1194; at 2 June 1860, *Film*, 9:713. Variant at 9:714.

1. Dated by ECS's reference to a letter of 12 July 1860, in which Martha Wright told her that "Lizzie Gay washes her hands of the W.R. movement." (*Film*, 9:746–48.)

·〈━━━━※━━━━〉·

143 ❧ ECS to Wendell Phillips

Seneca Falls August 10ᵗʰ [*1860*]

Dear Friend,

I hold in my hand abundant evidence that you are still a subject for missionary effort. Here is a letter for "Susan Anthony to the care of Mrs H. B. Stanton." Only think of it! one of the noblest champions of freedom, at this late day denying to woman her own name. Now my dear friend, did you pen that insult?—or was it done by your private secretary?—a perfumed young man who never heard that women & negroes were beginning to repudiate the name of their masters?—& claiming a right to a life long name of their own? Perhaps I do injustice to your chirography & this "Mrs." may be Mr. after all, but if you are guilty I shall feel it my duty to make a special effort to convince you of the heinousness & criminality of your offence   But how shall I preach to you the new gospel of individual sovereignty! Not by pen—your benighted condition would require folios of paper! I cannot go to that part of the Lord's vineyard where you dwell, for I am anchored here, surrounded by numberless small craft, which I am struggling to tug up life's stream. May I hope that during the coming winter you will stay a few days in Central New York. Do accept all the Lyceum invitations you may get from this part of the state, that you may thereby place yourself in the way of being converted, to my idea of right & at the same time refresh us with your presence at many a breakfast & dinner too. You little know how sadly disappointed we all were, at not seeing you last winter, nor how many pair of blue eyes & rosy cheeks watched at the gate to herald your coming.[1]

From what I have said Mrs Phillips[2] must not infer that her Husband does not always do honour to the admirable home influence, which we all know he has, but in spite of the purest angelic influences, all Husbands & sons will occasionally let the old Adam stand out   With much love & admiration for Mrs Phillips, & yourself, (in spite of your shortcomings)   I am sincerely your friend

❧ *E. Cady Stanton.*

ALS, bMS Am 1953(1152), Wendell Phillips Papers, MH-H.

1. Phillips missed a breakfast with the Stantons in March, and ECS never let him forget it. (ECS to W. Phillips, 15 March 1860, *Film*, 9:536.)

2. Phillips married Ann Terry Greene (1813–1886) in 1837. A member of the Boston Female Anti-Slavery Society at the time she met Phillips, Greene converted him to abolitionism. She was an invalid at the time of her marriage and remained so the rest of her life. (Garrison, *Letters*, 2:490–91n; Stewart, *Wendell Phillips*, 43–51.)

·❮════❯·

144 ❧ WENDELL PHILLIPS TO ECS

August 21ˢᵗ [*1860*]

Mrs. Cady,

Thank you for your pleasant letter, my dear friend— I'm afraid my excuse will not bring you to the old Saint's state of mind—"such an excuse almost makes me glad you offended"—but will rather banish me still nearer the North pole of your dislike.

the Truth is I've no memory for <u>first</u> names, & specially girls names— Lizzie & Hattie—Sarah & Susan—Abby & Eliza mingle & melt in utter confusion— I'm not quite so bad as Old Presᵗ Quincy & Sidʸ Smith[1] who confess to have forgotten their own names—but I live next door, so far as women's <u>first</u> names are concerned— Now that note to S. B. Anthony—was scribbled where I had no means of concealing my ignorance by relying on others knowledge— I could not for the life of me be sure whether you were Lizzie Cady or Susie—or whatnot; & the more I thought the more I did not know— I thought I covered it up nicely by HB-ing it, for I always remember by the <u>eye</u> better than the ear—& H. B. S. lived on [that?] point in time—'the memory of man runneth not to the contrary'—[2] But hereafter you shall be Mrs Elizabeth Cady everywhere, at all times, & to all purposes intents & constructions whatever & I've hit on an excellent way never again to be in doubt— Queen Elizabeth, you know, redheaded & so jealous of her looks that she forbid all but two painters (by proclamation) to attempt painting her likeness— She will exactly bring <u>you</u> to my mind— Rely on me in future—

As to lectures: yes. I'll accept all I can near you & count on the break fasts <u>if</u> Ann's health allows me to plan going so far from home— But provided & it being fully understood & agreed—(as the dying man said—"If I die I forgive you, otherwise Look out, you scoundrel"—) that this breaking of——eggs & eating of hot cakes does in no wise make up our quarrel about your lugging onto our platform that noisy alien "M & Divorce"—which dispute I nowise abate, pretermit or smother even in toast dipped in the richest cream of Central New York—

Yea verily—the matter is of great moment & deserveth discussion— nathless it hath no right in our house— Let it go now & build for itself a lodging place & summon thereto the good men & honorable women not a few who take note thereof—& let there be light shed all about— But meanwhile let the interloping & unnaturalized alien avoid our Jerusalem—or she shall be, not privily, thrust out of the gates thereof— Selah—[3]

& so farewell—Mistress Elizabeth Cady—may no ill behaving cars prevent our next meeting—

With regards both to thee—/& H. B—/and the "blue eyes & rosy cheeks" I hope to see—/thine—W P.[4]

↝ ALS, ECS Papers, DLC. Word in square brackets is uncertain.

1. Josiah Quincy (1772–1864), Massachusetts politician and Harvard College president. Sydney Smith (1771–1845) was canon of St. Paul's Cathedral, London, and a droll and witty writer and speaker on reform topics.
2. A legal phrase for custom.
3. "Selah" is a term of uncertain meaning in the Psalms and may be a musical direction for a pause.
4. Slashes added to indicate Phillips's line breaks in this closing verse.

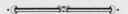

145 ↝ SBA TO ECS

Worcester[1] [*Mass.*] Aug. 25, 1860

Dear Mrs. Stanton

I learn through Stephen Foster and Lydia Mott of your invitations to attend Political Anti Slavery Conventions in Cleveland and Worcester—[2] I would be delighted to Women attend, and speak & act with them—but of course it can be only those who really feel that it is best for men, even, at this moment, to stop to <u>organize</u> the <u>mere</u> <u>handful</u> of voters, who would cast their ballots for <u>principle</u>—& not for what they deemed the "<u>least of the two evils</u>," one of which the nation must surely have in the presidential chair— You see Stephen is but <u>repeating</u> the <u>Liberty</u> <u>Party</u> <u>Experiment</u>— Men who cannot or will not bear their testimony against the two great Political Parties, by <u>non</u> voting, can not & will not by voting for a man for principles sake—~~for~~ whose election is not possible

It requires precisely the same material to make a true Political abolitionist—that it does to make a non voting Disunion Abolitionist— the only difference is the <u>mode</u> of expressing opposition to the prevailing pro slavery action—

Antoinette Brown is the only woman who could go into Fosters Movement with right good will—for she is a politician in philosophy— while you & I & others are agitators to <u>make</u> public sentiment— So it seems to me— But if you feel right for the work go ahead— Stephen wants you to read an address on the true government at ↑one of↓ their evening sessions, & to act on their business Committee— Parker Pillsbury, in the Hovey Committee, when Stephen asked an appropriation to pay your expenses to his Convention—said, "I have great faith in Mrs. Stanton, & would vote her expenses to any place where there was an audience for to address, no matter by whom or for what called together—sure that her word would be true & grand anywhere["]— Why dont you go to the Liberty Party Convention at Syracuse—Stephen expects to be there, to try & get Goodell[3] & Gerritt Smith & all to join him—they make nominations & the Worcester Convention endorse their nominees—

I wish Henry would go & report to the Tribune & the World,[4] without scandal prejudice or irony—just what they propose & do— I hope they may unite—Stephen thinks Frederic Douglas will unite with him— I hope he will—for he stands so isolated alone now—[5] If you go to Syracuse, you'll get an idea of what Stephen's plan is & can then decide whether you had better go to Worcester— If you see you way clear to help both Woman & the Negro, or only the Negro—then go by all means—

Write me at Albany Care Lydia Mott— We got the Money voted for our Albany Depository[6] Love to All—

✒ *S. B. Anthony*

« ALS, Scrapbook 1, Papers of ECS, NPV.

1. SBA attended a meeting of the Hovey Committee in Boston and stopped in Worcester on her return.

2. Abolitionists called several political conventions in late summer of 1860 and invited women. The first was in Syracuse on August 29, where Gerrit Smith was nominated for president. The second, organized by Stephen Foster, was held in Worcester on September 19, to consider founding an antislavery party. The third convention took place on October 3 in Oberlin, Ohio. Though invited to them all, ECS attended only the Syracuse convention. (*Principia*, 15 September 1860; Sterling, *Ahead of Her Time*, 326–27; John M. Sterling to ECS, 17 August 1860, ECS to G. Smith, [after 17], 24, 30 August 1860, and S. S. Foster to ECS, 21 August 1860, all in *Film*, 9:785–98, 807–10, 817–19.)

3. William Goodell (1792–1878), a founder of the American Anti-Slavery Society and the Liberty party, edited the *Principia*, an abolitionist paper. Though an ally of Smith's for twenty years, Goodell stayed away from the Syracuse convention and repudiated its candidates. (*DAB*; *Principia* 15, 22 September, 6 October 1860.)

4. Henry Stanton. The daily New York *World* began publication in July 1860. It became a leading Democratic paper.

5. Fearing for his life after John Brown's raid, Douglass fled to Canada in October 1859 and then to England, where he remained until the spring of 1860. After his return he did not resume public speaking until August. Moreover, Garrison still maligned him and made it difficult for him to find a place among white abolitionists. (McFeely, *Frederick Douglass*, 198–202, 207–8; Garrison, *Letters*, 4:693–95.)

6. The Hovey Committee agreed to fund the Anti-Slavery Depository at 15 Steuben Street, Albany, for the sale of books and tracts promoting antislavery, temperance, woman's rights, and other reforms, under the direction of Lydia Mott. (*Lib.*, 21 September 1860; SBA to Antoinette B. Blackwell, September? 1860, and SBA to G. Smith, 2 December 1860, *Film*, 9:851–53, 945–54; Sterling, *Ahead of Her Time*, 325.)

146 » SBA TO HENRY B. STANTON, JR., AND GERRIT S. STANTON

Seneca Falls Sept. 27, 1860

My Dear Kitt & Gatt

Has any body told of the grand affair that came off here at your Castle last Monday evening—[1]

In the first place Theodore, your Cousin Nellie Eaton,[2]—the most beautiful & lovely of young women,—and myself, walked over to Union Hall to a "<u>Wide Awake</u>" meeting—expecting to hear a grand speech from the <u>Hon</u>. <u>H</u>. <u>B</u>. <u>Stanton</u>—but lo, it was only a "<u>Wide awake drill</u>"—& Miss Eaton & I shortly left them, and returned home— presently the <u>Hon</u>. H. B. S. came—with Tribune, and <u>letters</u> for <u>Susan B. Gatt</u>— We were all reading & talking, when the sound of martial music struck our ears.— Soon it was decided that the "<u>Wide Awakes</u>" were coming down upon us—what was to be done for their reception— the House & Grounds should be illuminated, the person in whose honor the torch light visit was, should be prepared to give them a speech of welcome, and all should give them a most cordial greeting—

Your Mother produced the two wide awake lamps from the garrett— lamps & candles were set in all the windows—your Mother & Miss Eaton,—each with wide awake torch in hand,—took their stand on the circle mound, between the two front gates—& the Hon. H. B. and S. B. stood guard to them—

Down marched the Wide awakes with steady tramp, & strait into the gate in single file they came—until our Quartette were completely encircled with the caped, capped, torch lighted host— then rang their Captain's[3] cry—"<u>halt</u>"—and ↑then a↓ silence, for the space of a half minute—when the Hon. H. B. doffing his hat, & bowing most gracefully, said, "Gentlemen Wide awakes—we welcome ↑you↓ to our home— You are here in honor of Mrs. Stanton, and she no doubt is ready to extend to you a hearty greeting— I have the pleasure of introducing you to Mrs. Stanton"— Then Mrs. Stanton said, "Gentlemen Wide Awakes, I give you welcome, but ↑being↓ unable to make an impromptu speech—I delegate to <u>Mr</u>. Stanton the pleasant duty"— Then the Hon. H. B. again said, "Gentlemen Wide Awakes, we welcome you here—& something about their lamps being kept trimmed & burning &c, &c," and soon came to the final pause— Then, their Captain Failing made a speech to your Mother, Mrs. Stanton—↑told↓ how sorry he was that he was absent when she presented the banner and speech to the Wide awakes—then he called <u>three cheers</u> for Mrs. Stanton—and "<u>hip-hip</u>" and away went the ringing hurrahs— Some one then halloed, <u>three cheers</u> for <u>Mr</u>. Stanton—"hip, hip," and away they went—and yet again another voice—"three cheers for the <u>little Stantons</u>,"— Some one said how many of them—the cry was <u>seven</u>— The Hon. H. B. cried ["]for

mercy ↑sake↓ take them all in a lump"—and so they cheered again—
Then Susan B. was Anthon*e* was called on for a speech— She briefly
told them she hoped they'd not only keep Wide awake to the
inauguration↑e↓ of Abram Lincoln[4]—but also to go to the aid of the
Slaves, in case of an insurrection, or another John Brown invasion in
Virginia— Then spoke the Hon. H. B. again, most eloquently of Old
Abe—then followed three cheers for Miss Anthony—three cheers for
Miss Eaton—the daughter of Major Eaton of the United States Army—
& lastly three cheers for Old Abe— Then they marched around the
house to the tap of the drum, & passed down the Canal way to Mr.
Murrays,[5]—then to the Congressional nominee's, Mr. Chamberlain—[6]

We had but fairly got settled, when again a ↑a second↓ torch light
invasion occurred—Soon the sound of music discovered it to be a
serenade—again we lighted up the windows— Your Mother & Miss
Eaton Waltzed & Polkaed on the piazza while they played—then the
Glee Club was invited into the parlor & regaled with pears and mel-
ons— When all were gone & silence again reigned—lo, where was
Theodore—gone with the Wide awakes— Near Eleven Oclock—he
came—escorted by Abe Leary & his Mother—[7] thus ended the Grand
Gala in honor of your Mothers splendid banner speech to the Wide
↑Seneca↓ Falls Wide Awakes—

Yesterday morning your Father—the Hon. H. B. Stanton left for a
Republican Mass Meeting at Amsterdam— To day your Mother—
Elizabeth Cady—and Nellie, the Major's daughter—have gone to Au-
burn to call on Mrs. Seward and Mrs Wright— Robbie is better &
better every day—it is now 7.30 evening—Maggie, Hattie & Robbie in
bed & asleep—Sadie and Mary & Eliza gone down town[8]—and Sadie
& I sitting at the parlor table—with nice fire on the hearth—Sadie
playing with the Cards—& I writing to Kitt & Gatt of the Wide awake
& Glee Club invasion, last Monday night—expecting your Mother &
Nellie every minute—

Nellie is to leave for New-York tomorrow—I shall stop yet a few
days—

And now dear boys Good Night, and pleasant dreams to you, both
waking & sleeping, resolve only to live better, & grow wiser & nobler
as each setting sun shines over your precious heads   Affectionately
yours

⫷ *Susan B. A.*

❧ ALS, Scrapbook 1, Papers of ECS, NPV.

1. The "grand affair" of 24 September was a response to ECS's 10 September speech to the Seneca Falls Wide Awakes, a marching club of young Republicans. On behalf of the town's Republican women ECS presented a banner to the club with a speech urging them to the "highest ideal of Republicanism," the abolition of slavery. (*New York Herald*, 19 September 1860; *New York Times*, 3 October 1860; and *Film*, 9:826–42.)

2. Ellen Dwight Eaton (1832–?) was the oldest child of ECS's cousin Amos Beebe Eaton (1806–1877) and had recently met ECS for the first time. ECS once described Ellen, who lived with her parents, as an invalid. Her father, a graduate of West Point, served as a commissary officer for most of his career, with assignments in New York, Michigan, and California. In 1860 he was the depot commissary at New York City. During the Civil War he was promoted to commissary general with the rank of brigadier general. (Allen, *Descendants of Nicholas Cady*, 175; ECS to Ann G. Phillips, [before 9 January 1866], *Film*, 11:265–70; *New York Times*, 22 February 1877; Ezra J. Warner, *Generals in Blue: Lives of the Union Commanders* [Baton Rouge, 1964].)

3. Probably William Failing, a painter, age twenty-nine in 1860 and a married head of household, though the name was common in Seneca Falls. (Federal Census, 1860.)

4. Abraham Lincoln (1809–1865), an Illinois congressman and the Republican presidential nominee in 1860, became the sixteenth president of the United States.

5. John B. Murray (c. 1823–?), a lawyer, replied on behalf of the Wide Awakes to ECS's speech of 10 September. (Federal Census, 1860.)

6. Jacob Payson Chamberlain (1802–1878), who signed the Declaration of Sentiments at Seneca Falls in 1848, won election to the Thirty-seventh Congress. A leading citizen of Seneca Falls, who operated several mills, organized the village's first savings bank, and was a member of its board of education, Chamberlain was active in organizing the Free Soil party, and as a Republican, he won election to the New York State Assembly in 1859. (*BDAC*; *History of Seneca Co., N.Y.*, facing p. 120; *New York Times*, 6 October 1878; research by Judith Wellman.)

7. Abram Leary, age thirteen, and his mother Elizabeth, age forty-seven, were neighbors of the Stantons. (Federal Census, 1860.)

8. Mary and Eliza Leary, ages eighteen and twelve, were the sisters of Abram. Mary worked as a servant in the Stanton household. (Federal Census, 1860.)

·⟨⟩═══⟨⟩═══⟨⟩·

147 ❧ ARTICLE BY ECS

Seneca Falls, N.Y. [16 November 1860]

MRS. DALL'S FRATERNITY LECTURE.[1]

"The women of Boston," said Mrs. Dall, "in advocating the cause known by the distasteful name of 'Woman's Rights,' have chosen to confine themselves to three points: Education, Vocation, and Civil Position. They regard a present consideration of the subject of Marriage and Divorce as premature and unwise, apart from the fact that these subjects are equally the concern of both sexes."

In the consideration of any subject, how can an earnest soul, in search of truth, set bounds to its investigations? How can a philanthropist with a cold intellection divide up a great humanitarian question; select certain points as proper for thought, reason and feeling, and at the dictate of a worldly wisdom ignore all that remains?

It would be "premature and unwise," and impossible, for the women of Boston to bring forth a thought that had never agonized their souls, and quite as impossible for the women of New York to repudiate the utterance of a truth, when to them the time had fully come.

If to any one is given a clear perception of an egregious wrong, as no one holds a lease of life, *now* is always the time to cry aloud and spare not. Perhaps the American nation thought the "Printer's Boy"[2] "premature and unwise" when, thirty years ago, he proclaimed the doctrine of "immediate and unconditional emancipation," for even the friends of the slave who gathered round him stood appalled at the boldness and rashness of his declaration. In the passing of generations, in the life-time of a nation, the loss of caste or influence to the individual is of little consequence, compared to the good to the race in the utterance of a sublime truth,—the opening of the way to health and happiness and heaven.

As the Christian rises above the mists and dark clouds of tradition and authority, and learns a deeper and truer philosophy of life; as he catches new glimpses of truth, a holy love impels him to fly back in haste with the gospel of glad tidings to the helpless, ignorant and oppressed. The good Father makes his face to shine on those who will reflect his glory. He reveals his truth to those only who will bravely and generously give it back to man. There is no surer way to shut the soul against all heavenly influence than ever in its onward, upward way to pause, and put the question to itself, "What now will be said of me?" They who would wish a holy consecration, would devote themselves to the good of the race, must let the weal and the woe of humanity be all and every thing to them, but their praise and their blame of no effect.[3]

How can the women of Boston discuss the civil position of woman, without touching the subject of Marriage and Divorce? Woman, as woman, has nothing to ask but the right of suffrage. All the special statutes of which we complain, all the barbarities of the law, fall on her as wife and mother. We have not yet outlived the old Feudal idea—the right of property in woman. The term marriage expresses the nature of the relation in which man alone is recognized. It comes from the Latin "*Maris*,"[4] husband. Hence, as you look through the statutes and old common law, you find constant mention of "marital rights," the rights of the husband. Here and there, through the endless labyrinth of authorities, you will be refreshed with a bit of benevolence for the wife in the form of protection. You never hear of "uxorial rights," but the "widow's dower," the "widow's incumbrance," "the wife's alimony."

That "marriage is the concern of both sexes" is certainly no reason why we should not discuss it. The education and vocation of woman are equally the concern of both sexes. In fact, whatever promotes the happiness and development of woman, affects man as deeply as it does herself. If, on the Woman's Rights platform, we are to discuss nothing that concerns man as well as woman, we shall be dumb indeed. Imagine an editorial in the *Liberator* twenty years ago, saying, "In the discussion of slavery on our platform, we shall confine ourselves to the religious, political and commercial view of this question, but we deem it 'premature and unwise' to touch on the social relations of the slave; for the wholesale concubinage that prevails at the South concerns the master equally with the slave." If, however, we are to have a right to discuss all inequalities, religious, political, civil and social, we may most assuredly discuss marriage, for therein is the greatest inequality between man and woman;—an inequality that meets her in Church and State, and at the fireside, and even in her final resting place, where she lies a nameless thing, but the relict of some Saxon lord. Now, do you tell us that a relation which strips woman of her name, her legal existence, her moral responsibility, her property, wages, children, home,—that gives the woman to the man as an article of merchandise, though baptized at the altar with apostolic hands heavy with the authority of ages,—as an ordinance of God, shall not be sifted, through and through, by those who have for centuries been the blind and innocent victims of this civil and religious conspiracy? While hundreds of our sex, this very hour, at happy firesides and dim cathedral altars, decked in white robes and orange blossoms, are taking vows of obedience, on trembling lips, to this Moloch[5] of the flesh, shall we not teach those who soon shall fill our vacant places, that unquestioned obedience, blind submission and silent endurance suit not the rightful dignity, equality and freedom of the true mother of the race? I would have woman repudiate marriage utterly and absolutely, until our tyrants shall revise their canons and their codes, and by the talisman of justice transform the "*femme covert*" into an equal partner, the "weaker vessel"[6] into a morally responsible being, the "angel of the family altar,"[7] now sued on bended knee, into a noble woman, whose love would dignify and not degrade the man. What wickedness, for a whole class of beings deliberately to make such shipwreck of their liberties;— to hold in such low esteem their sacred, God-given rights,—rights baptized in blood by the Fathers of the Revolution,—rights, the maintenance of which is even now rocking to their very foundations the kingdoms of the Old World! If woman were sufficiently developed to love and appreciate freedom, nothing could tempt her to accept the kind of marriage man now offers. What man, with his eyes open, would take a position so hemmed in with disabilities? Suppose the tables turned, and some woman should offer marriage, as now set forth in our church services and statute laws, to Charles Sumner: could the most gifted and beautiful, with power to lay at his feet the wealth of the Indies, induce him to give up his name, his legal existence, his moral responsibility, to be known no more but in and through his legal representative,—on his return to Washington to be introduced in the Senate as *Mr. Jane Smith*,—with no rights of person, property, wages, children, home,—a mere dependent on the bounty of his "fair" owner— the victim of her whims, caprices, tyranny and abuse—held there and thus till death, by the mighty pressure of public sentiment? No! no!! If the man were necessarily buried in the husband, few men could be coaxed into that endearing relation. It seems immensely important to me that woman should be made to feel the monstrous compromise she makes with custom when she consents to bury the woman in the wife.

Some of our noble women have gone into their graves under "legal protest," declaring they were not dead, and would not be buried, and their own names should mark their monuments. But what's all that to Paul and Petersdorff?[8] They still declare the husband is the head—to him belong the person and the purse. When Church and State combine, no protest under chains can set the captive free.

To my mind, the matter calls not only for discussion, but for outspoken rebellion.

⤠ *E. C. S.*

⤠ *Lib.*, 16 November 1860.

1. ECS responds to and quotes from a lecture, "The Progress of the Woman's Cause," by Caroline Wells Healey Dall (1822–1912), printed in the *Liberator* on 26 October 1860. Dall grew up in Boston and married a Unitarian minister. After her husband left her in 1854, she threw herself into organizing meetings, lecturing, editing the *Una*, and writing for the woman's rights movement. She made a speciality of detailed progress reports on changes in the law, education, and employment. Her lectures on women's status became her most important book, *The College, the Market, and the Court; or Woman's Relation to Education, Labor, and Law*, published in 1867. (*NAW.*)

2. That is, William Lloyd Garrison.

3. A motto of Hugues Félicité Robert de Lamennais.

4. ECS's Latin is incorrect; "maritus" is the word for husband.

5. Meaning that which demands terrible sacrifice, from the name of an ancient god of the Ammonites to whom children were sacrificed, in Amos 5:26 and Acts 7:43.

6. 1 Pet. 3:7.

7. Perhaps a reference to Coventry Patmore, "The Angel in the House," published between 1854 and 1856.

8. A reference to the church and state, to the apostle Paul and to Charles Erdman Petersdorff (1800–1886), a British judge and author of an abridgement of the common and statute law of England.

148 ∾ SBA TO ECS

Newport, N.Y., November 23, 1860.[1]

My dear Mrs. Stanton:

What a grand advertisement the Albany Argus and New York Express have given "Mrs. E. Cady Stanton's Slaves' Appeal,—the wife of Henry B. Stanton, a leading Republican orator."[2] Parker Pillsbury, who is with me, has taken the papers on to Wendell Phillips. By the way, what think you of Mrs. Child's "Appeal"?[3] It is good, but so long as to repel the common mind.

Parker wished yours were "more argumentative." I told him it was not intended for an argument, but precisely what it is. Lydia Mott insists we need appeals to the heart more than to the intellect. I am sure yours will have a powerful effect on our people and will prove a firebrand at the South. Lydia is mailing them to every Southern Member of Congress, as well as to the Northern Members, and to every member of our Legislature, etc., etc. Parker said to me: "Tell Mrs Stanton I think she has power to shake the world, and if she only is true to the light within, I am sure she'll do it." He read your Liberator letter[4] to a parlour full of women in Michigan, and they all rejoiced in your call for "outspoken rebellion," and he read it to a number of us in Albany, with power and holy unction. Never has he read the word so needful and that too at this very hour. In speaking to him of your Wide-Awake speech, he said: "I am very choice of Mrs Stanton. I watch over her with great and constant anxiety."

Does Henry feel compromised by your "Slaves' Appeal?" How shamefully weak and trembling the Republicans are,—even more than the Abolitionists foreshadowed. Weed on his knees for endorsing the Helper book![5] Affectionately yours,

∾ S. B. Anthony

∾ Typed transcript, ECS Papers, NjR.

1. In Herkimer County, where SBA, Aaron Powell, and Beriah Green stopped on a tour for immediate emancipation.

2. *The Slave's Appeal*, published in November by the Anti-Slavery Depository and printed by Weed, Parsons and Company, supported a personal liberty law. The *Atlas and Argus* thought it evidence of the North's continued war against the South and its editorials attacked Thurlow Weed for printing the tract. The *Express* called it "a sharp, bitter, incendiary pamphlet." (*Film*, 9:936–40; Albany *Atlas and Argus*, 19, 20 November 1860; *New York Evening Express*, 19 November 1860.)

3. Lydia Maria Child, *The Duty of Disobedience to the Fugitive Slave Act: An Appeal to the Legislators of Massachusetts* (1860), which was thirty-six pages long.

4. See previous document.

5. Thurlow Weed and other prominent Republicans endorsed and financed a compendium of Hinton Rowan Helper, *The Impending Crisis of the South: How to Meet It* (1857) for the campaign of 1860. (*New York Daily Tribune*, 16 March 1859.)

·(⊂══⊃)·

149 ⇝ LYDIA MOTT TO ECS

Albany Nov 28 1860

Dear Mrs Stanton

I dont think I shall be able to send you the Journal which noted the article in Atlas and Argus[1]   I can give you the substance   That "Weed and Parsons did not hold themselves responsible for matter printed in their Jobbing office, that they had sometimes printed the Atlas and Argus to oblige their neighbours, never for a moment supposed that they were responsible for what they printed"   I dont read the Journal regularly   am told that Weed has behaved very badly indeed   has recommended yeilding to the South so far as to pay them for the Slaves ~~who~~ ↑which↓ have escaped   If that is so, we have nothing to hope from him   The fact is he is too old to keep up with public opinion at the same time entirely devoid of any fixed moral principle, very kind and benevolent in his feelings   It was capital the little excitement created by your appeal   When Congress meets I shall send every member a copy of your appeal, I have attended to your directions in letter received yesterday   We all felt just as you feel in regard to ~~those~~ ↑the↓ positions of those articles in Liberator[2]   I think that article of yours as unanswerable as any thing I ever remember to have seen from your pen

I guess Phillips will think with you ↑too↓ it will require more than "Cream toast" to smother your convictions of right. Where is poor Mrs Dall that we did not hear from her last week? I am inclined to think that hereafter they will let N.Y. alone   I have not thought of it until this moment I wonder if it would not be a good idea to invite Mrs Dall to come to our convention this winter[3]   Do you believe she would come? It would at events teach them a good lesson that we are not affraid to have all sides of the question pro and con discussed— I dont know but she has so much self conceit that she might think her presence a necessity which I am sure is not the case—

I have just written a line to Susan ↑on business↓ and enclosed your note as I knew that she would like to see any thing that you might say to me   I find quite enough to do—have already mailed more than a thousand single copies of the appeal not any of the womens[4] yet   Shall commence soon   yours Truly

⇝ *L. Mott*

had a pleasant little call from your husband enroute to N.Y. [*sideways in margin*] will send appeals before he returns if you wish them

⇝ ALS, ECS Papers, DLC.

1. Thurlow Weed and his partner John D. Parsons defended their printing of ECS's tract in the *Albany Evening Journal*, 20 November 1860.

2. Mott's reference is unclear.

3. The state woman's rights convention in Albany.

4. The *Appeal to the Women of New York*, issued by the New York State Woman's Rights Committee, in November 1860. SBA attributed it to ECS. (*Film*, 9:941–44.)

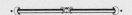

150   ⇝   SBA TO ECS

Albany Dec. 23, 1860

Dear Mrs. Stanton

I hope your "Liege Lord" handed the letter from Lucretia Mott—he just dropped into the Office Saturday noon, about a half minute— Isn't it good that we are to have Lucretia— Then I have a real old fashioned letter from Phillips—saying, "You are doing grandly,—Go ahead—I'll come to Albany if I <u>possibly</u> can"— So I shall advertise him— We have a tremendous force of speakers engaged— Mrs. Rose will come if we don't all "<u>dissolve</u>" before that time—she never felt so strong to speak on Anti Slavery— Antoinette is to give to the world a <u>new</u> <u>live</u> volume the first of January—she finds more ready publishers for that, than for her Sermons & poems—so we shan't have her—but all promises well here—

Now about my stopping at the Falls next Saturday— If I stop till Monday, I shall have only Tuesday at home—for I must go to Buffalo Wednesday—[1] If you say it is <u>absolutely</u> <u>essential</u>, then I'll stop, from the 3 P.M. to the 8 P.M. train—but I must go into Rochester Saturday night—and cant leave for the West till after <u>Friday</u> <u>evening</u>—↑as↓ <u>that</u> <u>eve</u>, I am to address the Montgomery County Teachers Institute at Canajoharie—am to give my Education of the Sexes together—

I rattled off a hundred things to Mr. Stanton to tell you—but they only slipped off like water from a ducks back—all about Johnstown &c. &c—but I cannot tell ↑now↓ only that on the whole, we had a good time—the rain poured & I didn't call on your Mother but saw Mrs. McMartin & Wilkinson at the meeting[2]—they kept the order—we left at 7.30 Friday A.M.—

Will ↑you↓ be at Buffalo <u>Thursday</u> or <u>Friday</u>— I want to know so as to have Mr. May[3] there the day you are not—hadn't you better stop <u>through</u> <u>that</u> Convention—so as to get initiated into the <u>mysteries</u> thereof— Enclosed is the January list of Conventions—[4] Let me hear from you soon—how you found the <u>Wee</u> <u>ones</u>—& how you get on—

good night—[5] Lydia sends Love and is very glad you can join in the work this work this winter & feels with me that ~~very much of~~ our ↑prospects↓ success in getting the <u>ears</u> of the people are greatly enhanced by the addition of your name— I tell you it looks good on our bills—when I get one, I'll send you copy—but tell me all about yourself—how you feel & hope & all—

✎ S. B. A.

✎ ALS, ECS Papers, DLC.

1. SBA began a tour for "No Compromise with Slaveholders" at Buffalo on 3 January and finished it at the annual convention in Albany on 5 February 1861. Between Abraham Lincoln's election in November and his inauguration in March, President Buchanan advocated compromise with the South and

specifically repeal of personal liberty laws. New York Republican governor Edwin Morgan agreed. South Carolina seceded nonetheless on 20 December.

2. Margaret Cady McMartin and Catharine Cady Wilkeson attended SBA's antislavery meeting in Johnstown on 20 and 21 December.

3. Samuel J. May, who joined the tour at Rochester.

4. Enclosure missing.

5. SBA wrote "Susan" below this closing and struck it out to continue her letter.

⋅⟨══════⟩⋅

151 ⇒ SBA TO MARTHA COFFIN WRIGHT

Albion[1] Jan. 7, 1861—

Dear Mrs. Wright—

Here we are—Mrs. Stanton, Green & I—alive—after the Buffalo Mob—[2]

I have forgotten whether I have asked you to have the Auburn Convention published in your weekly papers to date—so send this—[3] We have dispatched notes of the Buffalo riot—to Tribune, Standard & Liberator & hope some of them will get out to the world—

There was a more determined union to put down a speech, not to the mind of the masses—but we must face it through—

Mrs. Stanton's pen is scratching on free speech—[4] She is getting a grand speech—& we are doing nicely, only want to see the faces of Powell & May—[5] Good Bye—

⇒ S. B. A.

P.S. Dont your folks get up a scare about the Hall, they have at Utica & at Rochester—but we shall go through—

⇒ ALS, Garrison Papers, MNS-S.

1. The second stop on the "No Compromise with Slaveholders" tour, the meeting at Albion, Orleans County, took place 8–9 January in the dining room of a hotel because "neither hall, church, nor school-house could be obtained." (*NASS*, 29 December 1860; *History*, 1:467.)

2. Mobs took over the meetings in Buffalo's St. James Hall on 3 and 4 January. See local coverage and ECS's description for the press in *Film*, 9:978–82, 1025.

3. Enclosure missing. The meeting at Auburn was scheduled for 31 January.

4. ECS delivered this address at the Albion, Rochester, Auburn, and Albany meetings in the face of further opposition. She argued that attacks on free speech and individual rights were a far greater threat to the future of the republic than antislavery meetings. (*Free Speech: by Elizabeth Cady Stanton, at the Fourth Annual N.Y. State Anti-Slavery Convention* [Albany, 1861], *Film*, 9:1092–95.)

5. Aaron Powell and Samuel J. May joined the tour at Rochester, 11–13 January.

·⊂══════╳═══════⊃·

152 ⟫ HENRY B. STANTON TO ECS

Washington House,[1] Washington, Jan. 12, 1861

My dear Elizabeth:

I see by the papers to night, that Susan, Mr. May, & you, I presume, had a riotous time at Rochester last night. I do'nt know whether you were there, as your name is not mentioned in the despatch.[2] If you were, I hope that no harm befel you, nor indeed any of the rest of those who desired to hold the meeting.

Of course, these mobs are wrong, wicked, & ought to be put down. But, in the present temper of the public mind, it is of no use to try to hold abolition meetings in large cities. I think you risk your lives; & in cities of the size & character of Buffalo, Albany, Boston & New York, where there is so much rowdyism, the mobocrats would as soon kill you as not.

These rioters are not union-savers now, so much as of yore, but are rather secessionists, who desire to break up the union. Pray don't stand in their way: for they are doing a good work.

I am here at the center of political commotion, & I assure you this union is going to destruction as fast as it can. Four states are already out. Four more will be soon.[3] Civil war is close upon us. Military troops are here & coming here to try & protect the public buildings & save the seals of office & the symbols of power from being siezed by the Revolutionists. The Republican party will have as much as it can do to even get possession of these symbols on the 4th of March,[4] even with the aid of U.S. troops.

I believe all the slave states with 2 or 3 exceptions will secede before

Lincoln comes in. In a word, <u>we are in the midst of a Revolution</u>—& I do sincerely fear that the bloodshed, & pillage, & arson, will not all be confined to the South. I fear that prominent republicans & abolitionists will be victimized all thro the North.

You have no idea of the temper of things here. Gen. Scott,[5] & other officers are here, the Regiment of Flying Artillery[6] is here, & troops are being ordered to this City, to prevent its falling into the hands of the Revolutionists.

Now, I advise you, & Susan, & all friends, to keep quiet & let the Revolution go on. You must not hope to get any additional liberty bills <u>now</u>. When these ↑Southern↓ states have all gone, then we shant need any. Half the negroes will run away, & there will be no fugitive slave law to stop them—for there will be no slave States in <u>our</u> Union.

You can't make any impression now in the way of personal liberty bills. The minds of the people are too much absorbed with the main Revolution, to look after these details. They are mere eddies in the grand current which is sweeping Slavery to perdition. Stand out of the way & let the current run.

Tell Daniel, the Zouave,[7] that if Gov. Morgan[8] calls out our Militia to go Southward, & put down Secession, or to come here & protect the Capital, I shall look to see his gallant corps rallying among the foremost.

By the by, before the Zouave takes the field, I wish he would write me about how he gets along with Arithmetic, wood-chopping, &c. A thousand and loves to all. Your affectionate

⟶ *H. B. S.*

⟶ ALS, ECS Papers, DLC.

1. At the corner of Pennsylvania Avenue and Third Street.

2. Mobs prevented ECS from delivering her speech on 11 January but she succeeded the next day. (Rochester *Evening Express*, 14 January 1861, *Film*, 9:1059.)

3. Following the lead of South Carolina, Mississippi, Florida, and Alabama seceded on 9, 10, and 11 January 1861. Georgia, Louisiana, and Texas seceded by 1 February. Tennessee rejected secession on 9 February.

4. The day of Abraham Lincoln's inauguration.

5. Winfield Scott (1786–1866), commander of the army at the outbreak of the Civil War, arrived in Washington in December. He retired from the army later in 1861. (Warner, *Generals in Blue*.)

6. Horse-drawn cannon.

7. The Seneca Falls militia were known as the "Zouaves" for their brilliant uniforms. (*History of Seneca Co., N.Y.*, 115.)

8. Edwin Denison Morgan (1811–1883) was a founder of the Republican party and governor of New York from 1859 to 1862. Elected to the Senate as a Union Republican, he served from 1863 to 1869. (*BDAC.*)

·❮━━━❯·

153 ❧ SBA TO ECS

[*Utica? c. 16 January 1861*][1]

Mrs. Stanton

Your note came yesterday— Most sincerly do I regret that your household must give you such greeting on your return—it is a shame that those large boys, <u>young</u> men—do not begin to feel a pride in helping to keep good order— But I will only rejoice that you & the cause have had the little you have of this winters experience— I have sent you the Utica Papers—& hope you get them— We had two excellent meetings in Zions (Colored) Church, Rochester, on Sunday—[2]

Mrs. Stanton—The Hon. Phelps of Boston[3] is determined to execute the law on me— I pray you <u>impart</u> nothing of <u>my action</u> to the sister Mrs. Garnsey— I'd like you to get her account of the whole affair especially her testimony as to Mrs. Phelps <u>sanity</u>—but on no account reveal her whereabouts—moreover tell her, if any thing—that I know it not—

I have a letter from Mr. Garrison, begging me to reveal her hiding place[4]—he says there is not spot or blemish on Phelps character—get Mrs. Garnsey's opinion on his <u>chastity</u> to his Marriage Vow— You will of course slip over to Auburn one of the days—

It is a shame that you can never be released from constant presence at your home— I shall make a contract with the <u>Father</u> of my children to watch & care for them <u>one half</u> the <u>time</u>

I cannot write much— Mr. Green was down yesterday—bright & pure as ever and fresh for the wars spiritual—

Garrison is clearly with us says they expect a sever time—but shall go on as if there was nothing but sunshine in prospect—& such is more

& more clearly our duty— Poor dear Mr. Mays philosophy, is just the one to best please his satanic Majesty—& we can even <u>spare</u> [↑]the test for[↓] <u>Syracuse</u>—[5] No, no, that city of loud[↑]est[↓] pretentions must be put to the test— I hope you may steal down there one day—

≈ *A.*

[*upside down on first page*] P.S. I have asked Lydia to see Ramsey about the Divorce hearing before the Judiciary—[6]

⇐ ALS, Scrapbook 1, Papers of ECS, NPV.

1. Written after newspapers reported on the Utica meeting of 14 January. ECS returned home before the Rochester meetings were done. (*Utica Morning Herald*, 15 January 1861; Utica *Evening Telegraph*, 15 January 1861.)

2. After the proprietor refused to rent Corinthian Hall on Sunday, 13 January, William Watkins offered the Memorial African Methodist Episcopal Zion Church for Sunday's meeting. (*New York Daily Tribune*, 19 January 1861; *NASS*, 26 January 1861.)

3. Phoebe Harris Phelps, wife of Charles Abner Phelps of Boston and the sister of prominent New York lawyers and politicians, approached SBA in Albany in December 1860 for help in her flight from her husband. On Christmas day SBA accompanied Phoebe Phelps and one daughter to New York City, where Abby Hopper Gibbons and the writer Elizabeth Ellet concealed the fugitives until they moved on to Philadelphia. Charles Phelps (1820–1902), who graduated from Union College in 1841 and Harvard Medical School in 1844, practiced medicine with his father. A successful political career began with election to the Massachusetts legislature in 1855. Meanwhile, his wife, who worked at the Albany Female Academy before her marriage, raised their three children and published several children's books on religious themes. By her account, Charles Phelps became abusive and unfaithful before 1858, and when she confronted him, he committed her to the McLean Lunatic Asylum. After seventeen months of confinement, she got away to Albany. In one version she escaped; in another she was released to her brother's home, and the flight to New York occurred after several months of disputes over visits with the children. In Philadelphia Phoebe Phelps supported herself by writing and sewing until, after ten months of safety, agents of her husband seized their daughter and returned her to Boston. Phoebe Phelps followed and with help from friends found a safe place from which to file for divorce. She published one more religious book in 1865. When Charles Phelps died in 1902, his obituary named his wife but said nothing more about her. Their daughters, both single, lived in Boston. SBA kept clippings about the case in her scrapbooks and identified the principals. (*ACAB*, s.v. "Phelps, Abner"; William Stewart Wallace, comp., *Dictionary of North American Authors Deceased before 1950* [Detroit, Mich., 1968], 355; *NCAB*, 1:414, s.v. "Harris,

Hamilton," and 2:96, s.v. "Harris, Ira"; obituary of Charles Phelps, from *Boston Globe* files, courtesy of Lynn Sherr; *Anthony*, 1:200–205; unidentified clippings, SBA scrapbook 1, Rare Books, DLC.)

4. Ida Harper quoted a letter from Garrison, telling SBA to avoid "any hasty and ill-judged, no matter how well meant, efforts" of her own because she was identified with abolitionism and woman's rights. Wendell Phillips insisted that Phoebe Phelps return to her relatives and told SBA "that our movement's repute for good sense should not be compromised by any such mistake" as helping her. Harper also quoted SBA's reply: "as I ignore all law to help the slave, so will I ignore it all to protect an enslaved woman." (*Film*, 9:1080–84.)

5. Samuel J. May's biographer describes his mood after Lincoln's election as apprehensive and depressed about the country's future. He did, however, consent "to go forward and leave the responsibility of free speech or its suppression with the people of the places we visit—" Syracuse produced the worst riots of the trip. After stopping the meetings, the mob paraded the streets with effigies of May and SBA in the act of sexual intercourse. (SBA to W. L. Garrison, 18 January 1861, *Film*, 9:1071–72; *Anthony*, 1:210–11; Samuel J. May, *Some Recollections of Our Antislavery Conflict* [1869; reprint, New York, 1968], 392–95; Powell, *Personal Reminiscences*, 69–72; Yacovone, *Samuel Joseph May*, 170–71.)

6. SBA asked Lydia Mott to visit Joseph H. Ramsey (1816–?), Republican senator from Schoharie and Delaware counties, who introduced a divorce bill in the senate on January 7. It would allow parties who had lived in the state for at least five years to file for divorce in cases of desertion after three years and for cruel and inhuman treatment after one year. On 8 February, ECS, Ernestine Rose, and Lucretia Mott obtained a hearing before the judiciary committee. ECS recalled that Mott deemed marriage "a question beyond the realm of legislation, that must be left to the parties themselves." The bill reached the floor of the senate in mid-February and was defeated. (Murphy, *New York State Officers, 1861*, 103–5; *JNYS*, 7, 12 January, 12, 14, 15 February 1861, pp. 40, 60, 168–69, 180–84; *History*, 1:745–46; *NASS*, 16 February 1861; Albany *Atlas and Argus*, 8 February 1861; *Address of Elizabeth Cady Stanton, on the Divorce Bill, before the Judiciary Committee of the New York State Senate, in the Assembly Chamber, Feb. 8, 1861* [Albany, 1861], *Film*, 9:1101–9; *Eighty Years*, 217.)

·⊂══════⊃·

154 ⇌ ECS TO WENDELL PHILLIPS

Albany Feb 5th [*1861*]

Wendell Phillips   Dear Friend,

It is a great disappointment not to meet you here   The Mayor is behaving very well. His letter to the citizens of Albany is admirable.[1] He was present during the entire meeting last evening. We were however very much disturbed & compelled to give way at last to the tumult. Cousin Gerrit is to have a hearing in the Capitol to morrow[2] & we shall struggle through the remaining time, as best we can   We have some fears that our woman's rights convention may be disturbed also, as the same persons must figure on both occasions.[3] You have so much to meet in Boston[4] that it is too bad to urge you to come here, but if you can possible come it would be a great pleasure to all of us to listen you, to see how you look out of the union.

I must confess to one fraud that I have been extensively practising, that is to using your "clown" "with his arrow["] & "eagle" in my "Free speech" speech.[5] But if Dan Rice's clown[6] may travel over the states why not yours. We all feel exceedingly proud of you. You are spoken of in all the journals as the leader of "<u>those people</u>"   No other party can in my opinion boast a leader so noble & brave & true as ours.

Much love to Mrs Phillips. I am sorry to hear that her health is so delicate   adieu your friend   sincerely

⇌ *E Cady Stanton.*

⇌ ALS, bMS Am 1953(1152), Wendell Phillips Papers, MH-H.

1. George Hornell Thacher (1818–1887) was the Democratic mayor of Albany from 1860 to 1862. In response to petitions that he prohibit the meeting of abolitionists, he wrote a public letter about his duty to protect the rights of free speech and peaceful assembly. At the meeting he sat on the platform with the antislavery speakers and used the police to clear the gallery when disorder threatened. (Howell and Tenney, *County of Albany, N.Y.*, 578–79, 665; Union University, *Centennial Catalog, 1795–1895, of the Officers and Alumni of Union College in the City of Schenectady, N.Y.* [Troy, N.Y., 1895], 64; *Lib.*, 15 February 1861, and *NASS*, 23 February 1861, *Film*, 9:1078–79, 1085–87.)

2. Gerrit Smith spoke against repeal of the personal liberty laws.

3. The New York State Woman's Rights Convention met on 7–8 February but received very little notice from the press. (Albany *Atlas and Argus*, 8 February 1861; unidentified clipping, SBA scrapbooks, *Film*, 9:1100.)

4. Phillips, who continued to demand disunion as the southern states seceded, was the target of mob attacks in Boston in the winter of 1861. (Stewart, *Wendell Phillips*, 212–15.)

5. ECS modified a passage from his speech "The Pulpit," in which he said, the "idea that agitation was needless is like the clown in the old classic play two thousand years ago, who seeing a man bring down with an arrow an eagle floating in the blue ether above, said, 'You need not have wasted that arrow, the fall would have killed him.'" (Wendell Phillips, *Speeches, Lectures, and Letters*, 2d ser., ed. Theodore C. Pease [Boston, 1891], 272; ECS, *Free Speech*, 4, *Film*, 9:1092–95.)

6. Dan Rice (1823–1900) was a circus clown and showman at the height of his popularity. (*DAB*.)

---

155 ↠ SBA to ECS

Albany Feb. 20, 1861—

Terrific Mrs. Stanton

What a cruel thing you are to make <u>me</u> <u>beg</u> money of your sisters— but I've done it—and they'll doubtless curse me for it—[1]

I have given up going to Ghent—& take 7.30 train tomorrow A.M. for Rochester   Parker Pillsbury is coming into the State the 2ᵈ of March and then I must ↑to the↓ work with him[2]—and any farther delay <u>now</u> for visiting, robs ↑me↓ of any visit or rest at home— Then, my Mother has been a severe sufferer from this terrible epidemic cold for several weeks—

Shall Parker speak at the Falls a sunday night or afternoon— Would it pay—that is would there be enough to hear him to ~~make~~ pay for ~~his~~ ↑the↓ tax on him— I must make business that shall fasten him at the Falls until we get all the resolutions & planning for next May that we[3] I am so glad that you are in for raking the <u>Courts</u>—[4]

I do wish you would get up a speech on that point— It is Eleven Oclock—& I ache in every bone & muscle of me—came last night & have written & worked & run all day—to go at 7.30— Tell you sister

Mrs. Wilkinson[5]—I am sorry but I shall surely get to see her some-time— Aaron is but little—but Matrimony he intends to perpetrate the 13th of April—God Willing—[6] Then he wants me there—& to give in brief my views of marriage as it should be and the degradation of it as it is— Oh the world is so full of work for those who work at all— I see no old fashioned <u>heaven</u> for me—to sit & sing & glorify   so Good Night— Lydia sends love & so do I to all—

⇝ S. B. A.

⇝ ALS, ECS Papers, DLC. Above the salutation SBA wrote Mrs. M. M[c].

1. SBA was collecting money for the American Anti-Slavery Society. (*Lib.*, 22 February 1861.)

2. SBA and Parker Pillsbury began a series of antislavery meetings in Seneca Falls on 14–15 March and ended in Union Village on 31 March. They were also scheduled for Junius, Brockett's Bridge, North Easton, and Easton. (*Lib.*, 15 March 1861.)

3. Line ends without explanation.

4. The Burch divorce trial and other well-publicized cases provoked ECS into attacking the courts and the legal system in general. After reading about the trial of a man for poisoning his wife, in which the judge prohibited women from hearing some of the evidence because he believed the testimony was too lurid for their delicate natures, ECS wrote to Martha Wright asking, "instead of the authorities turning the women out of the courtroom . . . would it not have been better to put women on the bench and exclude the men?" She wrote a speech on the same theme in 1861, entitled "Fashionable Women Shipwreck." (ECS to M. C. Wright, 10 February 1861, and ECS, "Fashionable Women Shipwreck," *Film*, 9:1111, 10:105–29; *New York Daily Tribune*, 9 February 1861.)

5. Catharine Cady Wilkeson, whose name SBA misspelled consistently.

6. Aaron Powell married Judith Anna Rice of Worcester, Massachusetts, on 15 April 1861 in Ghent. Following the ceremony, the couple recorded a protest against the marriage laws, stating that the "marriage contract is formed in ignorance, inequality, and injustice, in the making of which one of the parties becomes at once civilly dead and legally buried." (Ellis, *History of Columbia County, N.Y.*, 332.)

156 ⁂ ECS TO ANTOINETTE BROWN BLACKWELL

[*Seneca Falls*] March 13th [*1861*][1]

Dear Nette,

How many times I have thought of you since reading your pleasant letter to Susan. I was so happy to hear that you had another daughter.[2] In spite of all Susan's admonitions I do hope you & Lucy will have all the children you desire. I would not have one less than seven in spite of all the abuse that has been heaped upon me for such extravigance Just as soon as I can summon the courage to enter my cold garret & overhaul the trunks of summer clothing you shall have all that remains of my baby wardrobe. Parker Pillsbury & Susan are spending a few days with me Can we depend on you for a speech at our coming anniversary, no fail!! We want to know just how many we may depend on that we may determine whether to hold over two days or not.

I suppose you must be very busy making butter & cheese on your little farm.[3] Churning is capital exercise I shall expect to see you wonderfully developed across the chest & lungs. I have no doubt you will be able to fill Cooper Institute without the least difficulty this year. On what point will you speak "Education & Vocation"? Let me hear from you soon. Susan sends love as ever your friend

E Cady Stanton

ALS, Blackwell Papers, MCR-S.

1. Pen appears to have blotted the second digit of date.
2. Edith Brown Blackwell was born in December 1860.
3. The Blackwells had moved from Newark, New Jersey, to more rural Millburn.

157 ⇝ ECS to Caroline Healey Dall

Seneca Falls   March 15th [*1861*]

My dear Mrs Dall,

May we depend on you for a speech at our coming anniversary? Rest assured though I differ with you on some points, I have no feeling but of hearty good will towards every man & woman earnestly engaged in the reforms of the day.

I am impatient to make the acquaintance of the noble women in Boston who are with me on this question of woman's rights. If we could meet face to face, I feel sure [th]ere would be no diff[er]ence between us. Every true woman must feel the same necessities & aspirations.

With the earnest desire of soon meeting you I am your friend sincerely

⇝ *E Cady Stanton.*

⇝ ALS, C. H. Dall Collection, MHi. Page torn.

158 ⇝ Henry B. Stanton to ECS

Washington, April 18/61

My dear Love:

A sense of danger makes me wish I was with you. I am surrounded by soldiers on all sides; & the report comes to us, seemingly well founded, that the Virginia troops are rallying at Alexandria, a dozen miles away.[1] I was at the Treasury Dept. to night, & when coming down the stairs to leave it, I had to step aside to let eighty armed soldiers go in up who were going to be on guard there to night. The same is true of all the other departments—War, Navy, Post Office, &c. &c.

I am closing up some business, & hope to get away tomorrow. I have earned about $1000 by doing some business, but alas, on account of this war cannot get my money now, as I should otherwise have done, & may lose it entirely! However, if we can only have a war that will destroy Slavery I shall be content to lose all the little I am worth.

Things look very much like a conflict here in the course of a few weeks. A thousand troops came in from Pa. to day; & tomorrow 1000 to 1500 come from Mass., & on Saturday N.Y. sends 1000. In ten days there will be 8 or 10,000 troops here.[2] And then, if the South don't back down, will come the tug. May God wipe out the last vestige of Slavery!

Hope to be home by Monday. A thousand loves to the chicks. Your devoted

≽ *H. B. Stanton*

≼ ALS, ECS Papers, DLC.

1. Virginia seceded on 17 April, five days after the firing on Fort Sumter and two days after President Lincoln issued a proclamation calling 75,000 militiamen into service. On 16 April one thousand Virginia troops assembled at Harper's Ferry. (James M. McPherson, *Ordeal by Fire: The Civil War and Reconstruction* [New York, 1982], 149–51.)

2. Governor John Andrew of Massachusetts sent troops to Washington on 17 April, but they were mobbed in Baltimore on 19 April. By the end of April ten thousand troops were in the capital. (McPherson, *Ordeal by Fire*, 150–52.)

·⊂══════⟩·

159 ≽ SBA TO WENDELL PHILLIPS

Seneca Falls Apr. 29, 1861—

Dear Friend

I slipped down to confer with Mrs. Stanton this morning— She is decided, that it is best to postpone our W.R. Convention—says it is impossible for her to think or speak on anything but the War—and I have, according to her counsel, written letters to go by this mail to the friends whom I knew were intending to go—telling ↑them↓ that the Con. is postponed— Oliver, I have again written to announce the postponement in Standard—[1]

Mrs. Stanton is delighted with your War speech[2]—says it convinces her that her own feelings were right— She is very enthusiastic— What a glorious revolution we are in—emancipation must come out of it—

I have said to Oliver, if the Cooper Institute Agent refunds the $30. advanced, to return it to you—if does not—it will be so much gone I suppose—& that will be too bad—still what we could not foresee & and could not help— Sincerely yours—

⇴ *Susan B. Anthony*

⇴ ALS, on folio with call to woman's rights convention, bMS Am 1953(213), Wendell Phillips Papers, MH-H.

1. The call for the Eleventh National Woman's Rights Convention at the Cooper Institute appeared in the *Standard* on 13 April 1861. But on 27 April the *Standard* announced that the American Anti-Slavery Society cancelled its meeting and suggested that the woman's rights convention follow suit. SBA telegraphed Oliver Johnson to prepare a notice of cancellation and await further word from herself or Wendell Phillips, and she wrote to Phillips for advice. Without the antislavery audience and speakers, she explained, there was little hope of a good woman's rights convention. SBA's notice of the postponement appeared in the issue of 3 May 1861. (SBA to W. Phillips, 28 April 1861, *Film*, 9:1149–50.)

2. Phillips delivered his "Discourse on the War" at the Boston Music Hall on 21 April 1861, "under the stars and stripes." He reversed his disunionist position, acknowledged himself a citizen of the United States, and welcomed the war. (*Lib.*, 26 April 1861; Stewart, *Wendell Phillips*, 220–24.)

·⊂══════⊃·

160 ⇴ ANTOINETTE BROWN BLACKWELL TO SBA

Millburn [*N.J.*] April 30 '61

Dear Susan

When shall you be in New York? Will you come to Millburn? Ask Lydia Mott, Phoebe[1] & any of the rest of our Albanians to come here if they can. I should like to talk with some body before the meeting for inspiration. I suppose Parker and the rest of you got up those resolutions. What is the gist of them? I went through Albany in the night, and returning, came from Fathers to Rondout in one day, speaking in the evening.[2] Of course there was no time to stop, which I much regretted.

I tried to write on "The Home and the Workshop" for May—

planned the whole thing and half prepared it; but could not go on in these times of present interest and peril, and am preparing now upon "The Relation of the Woman Question to our National Crisis["] Every one will of course harp on the same theme; but they can scarcely come in each others way, and it is the topic of the day. I only ask to speak before Phillips who will sweep every thing clean; but for any one else do not mind.

When do we meet and where for consultation? If I stay over night must take Florence in with me; and if I am there in the evening shall be obliged to remain all night. There is no late train   The child would be delighted to go, and would give little trouble. I could leave her here; but prefer not. I suppose we are to take quarters together; but if she would be in the way, doubtless I can send her to her aunties at the hospital.[3] What have you planned? let me hear from you.

So Mrs Stantons two boys have "gone to the wars" So has my nephew Willie.[4] More when we meet   Very affectionately

⪼ A. L. B. B.

Number 2

My letter was written, signed, and sealed, when lo! here comes yours saying the convention is postponed. Doubtless it may be well. 2 days ago I should have said amen right heartily; but I have written these two days on my speech and it of course gives me a pang that it is all to go for nothing, still it is not finished and there is little lost. The war news occupies my whole thought also. I cannot write on any thing else and do not feel equal to sermonising of those topics. I had fully planned to give several sermons this spring in N.Y. but it is utterly useless to speak on any other topic than that of the times, and with all my cares I am not equal to the emergency I fear. So I must ever wait unless the spirit comes over me, if it does I will speak yet a few times   My lectures were all well recieved and I had a fine trip

Give best thanks to your people for looking after my telegraphic despatches. The great snow storm and an unexpected lecture prevented my keeping my engagement with your father, and the best that could be done was telegraphing. I spent only one day at home and had to take a carriage out in a snow storm to do that. It is not probable that I shall go home again this summer, if all are well. How I do wish you could visit here   Nette [*at top of first page*] I will make careful inquiries for your niece[5] and wish her the greatest success

❧ ALS, Blackwell Papers, MCR-S.

1. Phebe Hoag Jones (1812–1881), a close friend of Lydia Mott and a political activist in Albany, married Eleazer Jones of Troy in 1832 and had one daughter, born in Florida. When her husband died suddenly, Phebe Jones supported herself and child by running a linen manufactory in Troy. She also helped to organize that city's first Unitarian society. In 1856 she moved to Albany. (SBA speech at funeral, *Film*, 22:38; unidentified clipping, SBA scrapbook 9, Rare Books, DLC; Federal Census, 1850.)

2. Blackwell's parents still lived in Henrietta, just outside of Rochester. Rondout is a village on the Hudson near Kingston.

3. Elizabeth and Emily Blackwell's New York Infirmary for Women and Children was located at Second Avenue and Eighth Street.

4. ECS's two oldest sons, Daniel and Henry, joined the Nineteenth New York Volunteer Infantry, or "Seward Regiment." William M. Brown (1843–?), Blackwell's nephew, was the son of William Bryant Brown and his wife Mary O. Messinger. (*History of Seneca Co., N.Y.*, 58–59; *Lib.*, 10 May 1861, *Film*, 9:1147; alumni files, OO-Ar.)

5. Probably Ann Eliza McLean (1840–1864), the daughter of Guelma Anthony McLean. (Anthony, *Anthony Genealogy*, 182.)

·⊂━━━━✕●━━━━⊃·

161 ❧ SBA TO MARTHA COFFIN WRIGHT

Rochester May 28/61

Dear Mrs. Wright

Are you at home yet?— If yes—then I hope to see you at the Waterloo meeting—Friday—Saturday & Sunday next—[1] I now think I shall go down Friday A.M. train that arrives there at 8 Oclock— I have written Mrs. Stanton begging her to be there—

It seems to be the only not postponed meeting of the year—hence may be our only chance of meeting & talking over the affairs of the nation— The Abolitionists, for once, seem to have come to a perfect agreement with all the world—that they are emphatically out of time & place—hence should hold their peace—no longer torment this wicked nation before its time, by their keen rebukes & scorching anathemas—

Our position, to me, seems most humiliating—simply that of the political world—one of <u>expediency</u> not principle—

Oliver's long twaddle in answer to Beriah Greens unanswerable signs of the Times is sorrowfully weak & wicked—[2]

I have not yet seen <u>one good</u> reason for the abandonment of all our meetings—& am as time lengthens, more & more ashamed & sad that even the little apostolic number have gone over to the worlds motto that the means must be sacrificed to the end—

I hope you will be at Waterloo—they, last year, had stage at the 8½ A.M. & Noon trains—to take the friends out to the meeting house— Yours Sincly & Affectionately

❧ *Susan B. Anthony*

A letter from Mr. Pillsbury spoke of you—that he sent you a <u>book</u> to Phil, care Mrs. Mott—a long time ago—but had not heard a word from you— How ~~is~~ ↑are↓ Ella & Eliza[3] & the boys—tell Mr. Wright my raspberries are finely—the cherry currants nice— All fruit, but the peaches, grand— S. B. A

❧ ALS, Garrison Papers, MNS-S.

1. The Yearly Meeting of the Friends of Human Progress. Neither Martha Wright nor ECS attended.

2. In a letter to the *Standard*, Beriah Green criticized the decision to cancel the annual antislavery meeting and denounced the war. He was unimpressed by the North's new patriotism and accused supporters of the war of "preferring pelf to principle." In reply Oliver Johnson admitted that most northern supporters were fighting against the South's rebellion; nonetheless, "the very process of stopping the rebellion will . . . set half the slaves free, and cure the Northern soldiers of the delusion that it is in their interest to help continue the enslavement of the other half." (*NASS*, 18, 25 May 1861.)

3. Eliza Wright Osborne (1830–1911), a daughter of Martha and David Wright, lived in Auburn with her husband David Munson Osborne, a manufacturer of agricultural implements. A lifelong friend of SBA and ECS, she was active in the New York State Woman Suffrage Association after the war. (Garrison, *Letters*, 6:214n; *Woman's Journal*, 12 August 1911.)

·◁═════◆◈◆═════▷·

162 ~ ECS to Ellen D. Eaton

Seneca Falls June 23rd [1861]

Dear Nellie

I spent yesterday with Mrs Seward. I had a charming visit   She spoke of you, when you come we will visit her again. I write to day to urge you to come & make me a good long visit   You have no idea how lovely this spot is in the leafy month of June. I expect Cady Eaton[1] to visit me sometime this month, then you & I together, will give him a series of lectures on love & marriage. Have you read Legouvè on ["]moral history of woman" traslated from the French by Palmer   published by Rudd & Carleton, 130. Grand st. New York.[2] Do read it! Now Nellie will you come immediately whilst our strawberries are in their height   Just pack what you want, you need no finery & come.

Mr Stanton goes to Washington next week to be abroad sometime, it would be a great pleasure to have you here when entirely deserted Remember those midnight talks. Only think of them by moonlight instead of ↑over↓ an air tight.[3] My address on Divorce has been published by the Hovey Committee. I send you a copy. You will be charmed with Legouvè.

Remember me to your Father & Mother sister brother[4] & lover if you have such an appendage. If you are not particular to have that sentiment expressed through some young sprig of manhood, to gratify your soul, know that it ↑love for you↓ is deep & strong in the heart of gray headed woman, yes Nellie I love you very much   in fact I conceived a kind of passion for you last fall   you seemed to me like my idea of Jane Eyre. Come & see me. I want you to visit Johnstown & Peterboro. adieu your friend & cousin

~ E Cady Stanton.

~ ALS, Alice Paul Papers, MCR-S.

1. This Daniel Cady Eaton (1837–1912) was ECS's nephew and Ellen Eaton's cousin. News of his engagement to Alice Young (?–1920) met opposition from some family members, but ECS invited the couple to visit Seneca Falls. They were married 17 December 1861. (ECS to E. D. Eaton, 2 July 1861, *Film,*

10:48–51; Allen, *Descendants of Nicholas Cady*, 175; *WWW1*; *New York Times*, 5 May 1921; D. Cady Eaton Papers, CtY.)

2. Ernest Legouvé (1807–1903), French author and dramatist, published *Histoire morale des femmes* in 1849, a work translated as *The Moral History of Women* by J. W. Palmer in 1860. Legouvé was critical of the lack of protection given to women by the legal system and was an advocate of female education, but his feminism was limited; he believed that women had no place in politics, and he could not conceive of a family that was not ultimately patriarchal. (Moses, *French Feminism in the Nineteenth Century*, 136–39.)

3. A heating stove that admitted very little air.

4. Nellie's mother, Elizabeth Selden Spencer Eaton (1796–1868), widow of Joseph Spencer, married Amos Beebe Eaton in 1831. They had three children: Ellen, another Daniel Cady Eaton (1834–1895), and Frances Spencer Eaton (1836–?), who married Charles Atwood White in 1861. This Cady Eaton graduated from Yale in 1857 and taught botany at his alma mater from 1864 until his death. In 1866 he married Caroline Ketcham of New York. (Allen, *Descendants of Nicholas Cady*, 175; Nellie Zada Rice Molyneux, comp., *History Genealogical and Biographical of the Eaton Families* [Syracuse, 1911], 223, 749; Sophie Selden Rogers, Elizabeth Selden Lane, and Edwin van Deusen Selden, *Selden Ancestry. A Family History* [Syracuse, 1931], 167, 198.)

·⟨⟩———✦———⟨⟩·

163 ≈ ECS TO GERRIT SMITH

Seneca Falls   Dec 16ᵗʰ [*1861*]

Dear Cousin,

I am obliged for your letters to Croswell & Stevens.[1] I read them with great pleasure & fully agree with you in your estimate of our ↑President↓. I really blushed for my country when I read that message But all his messages have been of the most mamdy-pamby order. He certainly does not dignify the office he fills. Did you notice that memoria of John Brown in the last Standard from the Times?[2] Do you know who wrote it? It is certainly very fine. I suppose the voyagers are nearing old England by this time.[3] Every night when I lay down in comfort I think of them rocking & tumbling about on the ocean. We have had beautiful weather ever since they sailed, so we have reason to think they have had a pleasant voyage. How impatient you must be to hear of their safe arrival. Will it not be grand to have Phillips, Cheever & Beecher thunder in Washington,[4] tho' I hope Beecher will not take his old constitutional gun down there. If all the ink & wind that has been expended to prove that constitution a most lucid & transparent document, had been used to denounce slavery we should have need of no armies to crush a rebellion at this hour.

I am actually nauseated with the word constitution   It is used as a cover for such base fraud & hypocracy. I remember Treadwell,[5] witnessed his vain efforts to get up meetings in Boston & have been bored with him ↑by the hour↓. My soul has [*sideways in margin of first page*] literally groaned under constitutional s̶o̶ logic so long that I dread the subject as a "burnt child does the fire"   yours affectionately,

⪜ *E. C. S.*

When you write to me again please let by name be recognized in the direction thus

E Cady Stanton

I am not tenacious about the Mrs. but E. C. is no name   suppose I should write to you

Mr. G. S. Fitzhugh

You see my dear cousin you have not taken in the whole idea of woman's degradation. When Cuffy[6] leaves the plantation he always takes a name, it is a symbol of individuality   of freedom. I have been obliged to call even the noble Phillips to task for a similar blunder, & when he showed a proper sense of the wrong I forgave him as I will you

⪜ ALS, Smith Papers, NSyU.

1. Gerrit Smith praised former editor of the Democratic *Albany Argus* and New York City businessman Edwin Croswell (1797–1871) for his endorsement of the confiscation of slaves for service in the Union army. In a second public letter, to Thaddeus Stevens (1792–1868), the leading radical Republican in the House of Representatives, Smith attacked President Lincoln's annual message to Congress of 3 December as "twattle and trash." Responding to Lincoln's statement that he would not interfere with slavery in the South, Smith criticized him for rigid adherence to the Constitution. Stevens, from Pennsylvania, was first elected to Congress in 1848 and served from 1849 until 1853. He was elected again as a Republican in 1859 and served until his death. On 5 December 1861 he offered a resolution urging emancipation under the war powers. At the war's end, he opposed the reconstruction policies of presidents Lincoln and Johnson, believing the southern states should revert to territorial status. (*Lib.*, 6 December 1861; *NASS*, 21 December 1861; *NCAB*, 10:31; Richard Nelson Current, *Old Thad Stevens: A Story of Ambition* [1942; reprint, Westport, Conn., 1980].)

2. On 14 December the *Standard* printed a tribute to John Brown from the *New York Times*, dated 1 December, one day before the second anniversary of Brown's death. It argued that the events of the past two years vindicated Brown.

3. Ann Smith and Elizabeth Miller sailed to England in December 1861. Elizabeth Birney stayed with Gerrit Smith during their absence.

4. Wendell Phillips, George Cheever, and Henry Ward Beecher were among those invited to speak in a series of antislavery lectures at the Smithsonian early in 1862. (*NASS*, 14 December 1861.)

5. This is the first of two references ECS makes to a supporter of an antislavery interpretation of the Constitution. Perhaps she refers to Seymour Boughton Treadwell (1795–1867), author of *American Liberties and American Slavery* (1838), editor of the *Michigan Freeman*, and organizer of the Liberty and Republican parties. (*ACAB*; Birney, *Letters*, 2:816.)

6. Cuffy, a generic and often patronizing term for a black man and also a form of brotherly address among African Americans, was in common use among both whites and blacks before the Civil War. (*Random House Historical Dictionary of American Slang*; Clarence Major, ed., *Juba to Jive: A Dictionary of African-American Slang* [New York, 1994].)

---

164 ❧ SBA and ECS to Martha Coffin Wright

Seneca Falls Jan. 30, 1862

Dear Mrs. Wright

Here I am once more, on my way to the Albany Anti Slavery Convention— You will of course go— Who shall we have for President? there is no one but Mrs. Wright—hence you must go— I left all invitations of speakers, and all arrangements for Convention entirely to Powell this time—he may have written you ere this—but you never need to be invited—you officially belong to the Albany meetings—[1]

Mrs. Stanton says you must come over & see us, before I go— I shall stop till next Wednesday—as she is trying to write a slaves appeal to the powers that be—[2] I shall hardly have time, to spend a day with you & Ellen until my return— I hope you & Ellen too will come & pronounce upon the forth-coming proclamation from Mrs. Stanton— Love to Ellen yours—

❧ *S. B. Anthony*

Dear Martha,

I hope you will be able to come over & see us. Suppose we say Monday & Tuesday that we may get something ground out for ↑which↓ you to ↑may↓ sit in Judgement.

I have not put pen to paper yet but Susan says I must   I hope you will go to Albany. I cannot   my cares are too pressing. I have just written to Cousin G. urging him to go & I think he will,[3] then if Phillips & Garrison & Pillsbury are there you must have a grand meeting & a good time socially. Lydia stopped a day on her return from the West.[4] With kind regards to Mr Wright I am as ever yours

≈ *E Cady Stanton.*

≈ ALS, Garrison Papers, MNS-S.

1. Wright presided at the 1860 and 1861 annual meetings but did not attend the 1862 meeting held in Albany 7–8 February.
2. ECS's address to the "People of the North," read by SBA at the meeting of the New York Anti-Slavery Society. (*Film*, 10:157–62.)
3. ECS to Gerrit Smith, 30 January 1862, *Film*, 10:140–48.
4. That is, Lydia Mott.

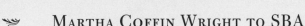

165 ≫ MARTHA COFFIN WRIGHT TO SBA

Philadelphia   March 31st, 1862

My dear Susan

There was neither heading nor date, to your letter just recd. forwarded from Auburn,[1] but of course it was from Rochester, and I hasten to answer it, fearing it may have been waiting some time for D's[2] return from Rochester, where he was attending Court. He, and several of the lawyers & Judges were at Fredk. Douglass' lecture, & were well pleased— You were doubtless there, also—[3]

Judge Johnson[4] said Douglass was the ablest living representative of Va. and that she would one day, claim him ↑with pride↓ as one of her sons. I should have enjoyed hearing him—

And now as to calling a National Woman's Rights Convention. I have felt that it[5] would be very unwise, at this time, when the nation's whole heart & soul are engrossed with this momentous crisis— It is true, as you say, that we "should not forget our principles, or fail to declare them because the majority do not, or cannot recognize them"; but it is useless to speak if nobody will listen—and every body now is absorbed in watching the course of our politicians, calculating the effect of every action on the future of the nation, reading with anxiety the acct of battles, in wh. so many of us have a personal interest— How then is it possible to think of a Convention   I[6] have hoped that it would be given up until the War is over, & the question of a revision of the Constitution, makes it necessary for us to assert our claim to a voice in the matter— Sister L. fully agrees with me in this opinion, and David says we should be crazy to think of such a thing—

This I say, in answer to your question and not with any expectation of changing the opinion of those who have come to a different conclusion— Still, I think, by writing to others, you will find a majority, opposed to a Convention this year— Should anything occur, in the future, to make it imperative, one could be called at any time— Let me know your decision—I shall be at home in the course of two or three weeks— I wanted to see Mrs. Stanton again, before leaving home, and Eliza was going with me, but we were prevented— Remember me to her, affectionately, when you write— We had the pleasure of listening to Mr Phillips' lecture here, and hearing, at home, an account of his visit to Washington—[7] He made his home here, (at Thomas Mott's).*
Very sincerely   Your friend

❧ *M. C. Wright*

* We can see by the treatment of Mr. P. at Cincinnati,[8] just what we may all expect in the future, if the dreadful Slave power is again in the ascendant as it surely will be, unless the force of circumstances compels the President to declare Emancipation, under the war power.— I dont see how any one can praise his milk & water message which was only intended to stop the debates in Congress, & quiet the radical Anti Slavery party[9]—a sop to Cerberus—[10]

❧ ALS, Garrison Papers, MNS-S.

1. Neither this nor other letters about a woman's rights convention in 1862 has been located.

2. That is, David Wright.

3. At Corinthian Hall in Rochester on March 25, Frederick Douglass argued that only by destroying slavery could the nation be united and liberty ensured. (Douglass, *Papers*, 3:508–21.)

4. Probably Alexander Smith Johnson (1817–1878), a Utica lawyer who had served on the New York Supreme Court and Court of Appeals. (*DAB*; McAdam, *Bench and Bar of New York*, 1:373.)

5. Changed to "We have felt that this" by another hand.

6. Again, "I" changed to "We" by another hand.

7. In Washington by 15 March, Wendell Phillips spoke at the Capitol and the Smithsonian, was guest of honor at a dinner hosted by Speaker of the House Galusha Grow, and had a private interview with Lincoln. He then traveled to the Midwest, stopping in Philadelphia, where he spoke at Concert Hall. (*NASS*, 29 March, 5 April 1862; Stewart, *Wendell Phillips*, 233–38.)

8. In Cincinnati on 24 March, Phillips was attacked by an egg-throwing mob.

9. Lincoln recommended to Congress a joint resolution offering cooperation and compensation to "any State which may adopt a gradual abolishment of Slavery." (*New York Daily Tribune*, 7 March 1862.)

10. A bribe.

---

166 ≫ SBA TO LYDIA MOTT

[Rochester? after 10 April 1862][1]

Dear Lydia: Your startling letter is before me. I knew some weeks ago that that abominable thing was on the calendar, with some six or eight hundred bills *before it*, and hence felt sure it would not come up this winter, and that in the meantime we should sound the alarm. Well, well; while the old guard sleep the young "devils" are wide-awake, and we deserve to suffer for our confidence in "man's sense of justice," and to have all we have gained thus snatched from us. But nothing short of this can rouse our women again to action. All our reformers seem suddenly to have grown politic. All alike say, "Have no conventions at this crisis"! Garrison, Phillips, Mrs. Mott, Mrs. Wright, Mrs. Stanton, etc., say, "Wait until the war excitement abates"; which is to say, "Ask our opponents if they think we had better speak, or, rather, if they do not think we had better remain silent." I am sick at heart, but I can not carry the world against the wish and the will of our best friends. But what can we do now, when even the motion to retain the mother's joint guardianship is voted down? Twenty thousand petitions rolled up for that—a hard year's work!—the law secured!—the echoes of our words of gratitude in the capitol have scarce died away, and now all is lost![2]

ᵚ *History*, 1:748–49.

1. Dated with reference to passage of the amendment to the Married Women's Property Act of 1860 on 10 April 1862.

2. On 27 February 1862, SBA mentioned the proposed amendment in a letter to ECS and urged her to speak out. A few of its provisions clarified the distinction between the property of husbands and wives by limiting the liability of husbands for their wives' debts and freeing women from the necessity of having their husbands' consent when they conveyed real property. Thus they strengthened the independence of married women. But in other respects, the amendments were a step backward. Women lost equal guardianship of their children with their husbands and were left with only a veto power over decisions on apprenticeship and the appointment of testamentary guardians. In addition, the provisions of the 1860 law which made husbands and wives equal with regard to realty in cases of intestacy were overturned, restoring the privileges husbands had previously enjoyed. (*Film*, 10:171–73; Basch, *In the Eyes of the Law*, 207–8, 236–37; *Laws of New York, 1862*, chap. 172.)

·⟨⟨════⟩⟩·

167 ᵚ ELLEN WRIGHT TO SBA

Auburn, Sept. 18—1862—

Dear Susan—

How much I should like to accept my share of your kind invitation to come & see you—but Mother seems to think we must decline. Mrs. Stanton wrote that you might stop here, on your way home,[1] & I have been looking for you, & wanting very much to see you— It is a long time since you were at Auburn—

I remember with delight, our visit at your house, two years ago—ᵗwhichᶜ dear Parker Pillsbury, helped to make pleasant— I wish he would write me a letter—but famous people are so busy—

I have seen notices of his movements & yours, in the Liberator which seemed the only means of finding out what you were doing—[2] And Mr. Powell—how indefatiguable he is! why didn't he send me his wedding cards, I wonder!—

You dont think the nation is going to rack & ruin, do you? People hereaway have been doleful to the last degree; & our friends in Phila. half expect to be scalped in their beds. Our Willy, writes cheerful letters from Sugar Loaf Mt.[3]

Dont you think that Abraham the Honest, will begin to emancipate, before we are grey?— Then it will be Womans Rights turn, wont it?—

Will you let me travel around with you, to take tickets?

Sept. 25th— After having written the foregoing, I found that Mother had sent her letter to you, without mine, which was such a shock to my feelings, that I locked this up, sternly determined never to finish it; but since then, we have received the box of peaches, you were so kind as to put up for us, & I have concluded to thank you in our family name, for them, even upon this despised sheet— I am sure, with all your cares, we are very grateful to you, for remembering us—

Mother thinks the President's Proc. of Emancipation no such great things after all[4]—& she would like to say with Artemus Ward—"A. Lincoln—adoo"—[5]

We have heard through our cousin Mrs. Brown, of your being at Milton—& Mr. Pillsbury too—I should choose above many things, to see him! There is a New Hampshire Dr. Hall (Keene) here, who reminds me of him.—

Is Lizzie Powell, ready to be married yet?[6] I dont exactly like nonresistants, in these times! Have you a program made out, for this winter?

I wish you would tell me what it is.

Please remember me to Mary & your father & mother— Goodbye— Affectionately

～ *Ellen Wright*

～ ALS, Garrison Papers, MNS-S.

1. ECS left Seneca Falls in May 1862 and settled her family in Brooklyn.

2. SBA attended the American Anti-Slavery Society meeting in New York in May and proceeded to Boston for the annual meeting of the New England society. After a trip home, she traveled to Framingham, Massachusetts, for the annual Fourth of July antislavery festivities, and in August she and Parker Pillsbury held some antislavery meetings in the lower Hudson valley at Ellenville and Milton. (*Lib.*, 13 June, 11, 18 July 1862; *NASS*, 7 June, 13 September 1862.)

3. William Pelham Wright (1842–1902), son of Martha and David Wright, enlisted as first lieutenant in Captain T. J. Kennedy's independent battery, which was mustered into service in November 1861, and was part of the Army of the Potomac. He wrote home from Sugar Loaf Mountain, Maryland, about thirty miles northwest of Washington and a good location from which to observe the city. Union troops had recently taken control of Sugar Loaf from Confederate troops. (Elliot G. Storke, *History of Cayuga County, New York*

[Syracuse, 1897], 103, 114, 134–36; Wright genealogy, Garrison Papers, MNS-S; *New York Daily Tribune*, 12 September 1862.)

4. Throughout the summer of 1862, Lincoln urged border states to accept his offer of compensated emancipation. When his appeals were rejected, he drafted an emancipation proclamation in July but waited until 22 September, after the Union victory at Antietam, to issue it. The proclamation, effective 1 January 1863, freed slaves in the states still in rebellion, but left slavery in the border states and in areas under federal control untouched. (McPherson, *Ordeal by Fire*, 272, 278–79, 292–93.)

5. Artemus Ward was the pseudonym of Charles Farrar Browne (1834–1867), a humorist who published *Artemus Ward—His Book* in 1862. At the end of a visit with the president-elect, showman Ward parted with the words "A. Linkin, adoo!" Ward, who was disgusted by political corruption, expressed confidence in Lincoln's ability. Apparently Martha C. Wright was less sanguine.

6. Elizabeth Macy Powell (1841–1926), later Bond, a sister of Aaron Powell, grew up in Ghent, New York, graduated from the State Normal School at Albany, and pursued a career in education and reform. After the war she directed the department of physical culture at Vassar College and, in 1886, became dean of Swarthmore College. She married Henry Herrick Bond in 1872 but was widowed in 1881. (*NCAB*, 6:365; Ellis, *History of Columbia County, N.Y.*, 347; Emily Cooper Johnson, *Dean Bond of Swarthmore, A Quaker Humanist* [Philadelphia, 1927].)

· ⟨━━━━━✸✦✸━━━━━⟩ ·

168 ❧ SBA TO THEODORE TILTON

[*Ontario County*] Jan. 30, 1863—

My Dear Friend Tilton

Your two most welcome letters[1] have been long, too long, waiting reply. To the first, what could I say, both tongue & pen still falter over the sad event that called it forth. For thirty years the unwelcome messenger had had no errand to my Fathers household[2]—and now thus rudely to strike the very head, brings a shock not easily or soon to be recovered from— I did ↑not↓ write, because I could not— And your more recent note came just as I was trying to gather up conscience & courage to go out to do battle for freedom & justice, as I was wont to do before the departure of my dear Father— Now for two weeks I have been out in the World again— Last night, here in this little hollow in the very South of Ontario Co. I had a country church full to suffocation, quite one half Seymourites—called here "<u>Secesh</u>"[3]—& to come in contact with such heathen gives little hope of success to our armies—

Yes, I <u>am</u> thankful for the Proclamation, & shall be vastly more thankful when I see the men & the means in actual work of executing its provisions to the letter & the spirit.

But the adage, "it is hard to learn old dogs new tricks" is most strikingly exemplified in the slow & feeble moves out of the traces of Slavery—to turn freedomward seems the work of ages, when we take into view the blood & treasure poured out to save slavery inviolate—& yet, the Nation <u>does</u> move in that direction, & we will hope—

Thank you for telling me that my name was taken upon lips so glorious as your own & Phillips— To be approved by such, is second only to my own hearts just estimation—[4]

I always meant to have dropped you a line, when I failed to see you before I left New-York— You and Oliver[5] go to dinners together yet— & have good times generally— I would like a good chat—the better though in your own dear home, it is such a blessing Theodore Tilton to have a <u>real</u> <u>home</u>—may you & your charming noble wife realize the bliss—[6]

I have note from our Friend Lydia Mott of Albany—and Parker Pillsbury—in both, <u>your</u> name is mentioned as one of the "sine qua non's" of our Albany Convention—the last week of February— I suppose Powell will write you—but I must send my hope that you will say yes— <u>Albany</u> must not be left without our presence this winter—

I am glad you like Mrs. Stanton, & hope you may continue to—

I have scribbled this on my knee, with the good people of the house buzzing about—& now must leave for my next post—six miles hence— Anything directed to Rochester will reach me—

Love to your loved & loving wife & little ones—& Oliver—I often think of—but haven't written in a long long time—nor has he spoken to me in an age— Good Bye Your friend

☙ *S. B. Anthony*

☙ ALS, James Fraser Gluck Collection, Rare Book Room, NBu.

1. See 11 January 1863, *Film*, 10:375. Tilton wrote to console SBA after the sudden death of her father on 25 November 1862.

2. SBA refers to the death of her sister Eliza T. at age two in 1834. (Read Genealogical Ms., SBA Papers, MCR-S.)

3. "Secesh" or secessionists described supporters of Horatio Seymour

(1810–1886), elected Democratic governor of New York in the fall of 1862. A powerful symbol of a political reaction against the war and Lincoln's conduct of it, Seymour believed that the North lacked constitutional authority to subjugate the South, and he opposed the Emancipation Proclamation. (Alexander, *Political History of New York*, 3:31–52, 61–64.)

4. In his letter, Tilton confided to SBA that in a recent conversation, Wendell Phillips called her "one of the salt of the earth."

5. That is, Oliver Johnson.

6. Elizabeth Richards Tilton (?–1897) attended the Brooklyn Female Seminary before she married Theodore Tilton in 1855 at Henry Ward Beecher's Plymouth Church. Her daughters Florence and Alice were born in 1858 and 1859. (*DAB*, s.v. "Tilton, Theodore"; Waller, *Reverend Beecher and Mrs. Tilton*, 38–63.)

Editorial note: On 10 April 1863 ECS and SBA issued a "Call for a Meeting of the Loyal Women of the Nation." In this "crisis," it read, it was the duty of citizens to defend and preserve republican institutions. It was "high time for the daughters of the revolution, in solemn council, to unseal the last will and testament of the Fathers,—lay hold of their birthright of freedom, and keep it a sacred trust for all coming generations." Slavery was not named.

By addressing "loyal" women, ECS and SBA appropriated a term with wide currency in the winter of 1863. Peace Democrats mounted bold challenges to the war and emancipation, making overtures to Confederate leaders about peace, proposing that the Midwest secede from the antislavery East, and declaring in Congress that "the Union as it was be restored" with slavery intact. Loyalty connoted patriotism over partisanship, unqualified condemnation of northern traitors, and, in some quarters, unconditional support of the Union. It marked common ground where War Democrats, Republicans, and abolitionists could cooperate to mobilize the North, as they did in New York's Loyal Publication Society, founded in February, and in the Loyal Union League and Loyal National League, both founded in March. Responding to the mood of urgency, northern women organized their own loyal leagues that winter, in cities as far apart as Madison, Wisconsin, and Hartford, Connecticut. Though loyalty did not by common usage encompass emancipation, many abolitionists saw in the loyal leagues a chance to preach their cause; in New York Sydney H. Gay, Theodore Tilton, Henry Stanton, and Gerrit Smith all worked with the leagues.

The call published early in April was ambiguous about the meeting's purpose. To some extent that was an accident. At the end of March, after SBA moved to the Stantons' house in Brooklyn, ECS recast for a general audience an appeal she had written to abolitionist women in February, but she waited weeks for the *Tribune* to publish it. (See below at 24 April 1863.) She had intended, she wrote Sydney Gay on 20 April, that the appeal to end slavery set the context for the call. But an ambiguous purpose also helped ECS and SBA reach and mobilize a new constituency of loyal women. (Frank Freidel, "Introduction," *Union Pamphlets of the Civil War, 1861–1865* [Cambridge, Mass., 1967], 1:1–26; Frank L. Klement, *Copperheads in the Middle West* [Chicago, 1960], 40–42, 87–95; Sidney D. Brummer, *Political History of New York State During the Period of the Civil War* [1911; reprint, New York, 1967], 295–302; Harlow, *Gerrit Smith*, 432–33; Rice, "Henry B. Stanton," 394–95; McPherson, *Ordeal by Fire*, 347–48; *NASS*, 7 March 1863, and ECS to S. H. Gay, 20 April 1863, in *Film*, 10:385–89, 420–21.)

·⇐══════❊══════⇒·

169 ⇝ SBA TO AMY KIRBY POST

Anti Slavery Office—Beekman st. New York Apr. 13, 1863—

My Dear Friend

The enclosed will tell you that we have resolved to make an opportunity for Woman to speak her thought on the War—

I hope you can be present— Mrs. Stanton has an address to the Women of the Republic in type, in the Tribune Office—if only it shall ever be published, you may get sight of it—

I have been with Mrs. Stanton five weeks tomorrow— We shall prepare an address to the President, to be adopted by the meeting—Lucy & Antoinette, & Mrs. Rose will be on the spot—Anna Dickinson[1] and Mrs. J. E. Jones too I hope—

It seems a long, long time since I left Rochester—but I see no chance for me to return until after the Anniversaries— I think of you all very often—and of my own lonely farm home—but it can never be made whole again— Truly & Affectionately

⇝ *Susan B. Anthony*

[*sideways*] P.S.—your Brother Joseph[2] is just come in—reports all well at home—looks as fresh & joyous as ever—

❧ ALS, on folio with "Call for a Meeting of the Loyal Women of the Nation," Post Papers, NRU.

1. Anna Elizabeth Dickinson (1842–1932), known as the Joan of Arc of the Union cause, rose to fame during the Civil War for her spellbinding, fiery oratory. Within the span of three years, she went from working in the United States mint in Philadelphia to addressing the House of Representatives, with President Lincoln in the audience. In the winter of 1863 she campaigned for Republican candidates in New Hampshire and Connecticut. The party credited her with their success against popular Peace Democrats and relied on her help for the next decade. On 3 April SBA invited her to the meeting of loyal women, *Film*, 10:402–3. (*NAW*; James Harvey Young, "Anna Elizabeth Dickinson and the Civil War: For and Against Lincoln," *MVHR* 31 [June 1944]: 59–80; Giraud Chester, *Embattled Maiden: The Life of Anna Dickinson* [New York, 1951].)

2. Joseph Post (1803–1888) of Westbury, Long Island, was a brother-in-law of Amy Post and a Quaker abolitionist. (*ACAB*, s.v. "Post, Isaac.")

·(⸺⸺⸺)·

170 ❧ ABIGAIL KELLEY FOSTER TO SBA

Worcester, [*Mass.*] April 20, 1863.

Dear Susan: I see your call to the loyal women. Will you let me know distinctly if you propose to commit yourselves to the idea of loyalty to the present Government? I can not believe you do. But to me there is something equivocal in the call, if it does not mean that. I am sorry it is not explicit on that point.

You and I believe if the present Administration had done its duty, the rebellion would have been put down long ago. Hence, we hold it with its supporters responsible for the terrible waste of treasure and of blood thus far, and for that which is to follow. It needs strong rebuke instead of unqualified sympathy and support. Hastily, yours as ever,

❧ *Abby Kelley Foster*

❧ *History*, 2:877.

171 ≫ APPEAL BY ECS

New-York, [24 April 1863][1]

TO THE WOMEN OF THE REPUBLIC.

When our leading journals, orators, and brave men from the battle-field complain that Northern women feel no enthusiasm in the war, the time has come for us to speak—to pledge ourselves loyal to Freedom and our Country.

Thus far there has been no united public expression from the women of the North as to the policy of the war. Here and there one has spoken and written nobly. Many have vied with each other in acts of generosity and self-sacrifice for the sick and wounded in camp and hospital. But we have, as yet, no means of judging how and where the majority of Northern women stand.

If it be true that at this hour, the women of the South are more devoted to their cause than we to ours, the fact lies here. They see and feel the horrors of the war; the foe is at their firesides; while we, in peace and plenty, live and move as heretofore. There is an inspiration, too, in a definite purpose, be it good or bad. The women of the South know what their sons are fighting for. The women of the North do not. They appreciate the blessings of Slavery; we do not the blessings of Liberty. We have never yet realized the glory of those institutions in whose defense it is the high privilege of our sires and sons this day, to bleed and die. They are aristocrats with a lower class, servile and obsequious, intrenched in feudal homes. We are aristocrats under protest, who must go abroad to indulge our tastes, and enjoy in foreign despotisms the courts and customs which the genius of a republic repudiates and condemns.

But, from the beginning of the Government, there have been women among us, who, with the mother of the immortal John Quincy Adams, have lamented the inconsistencies of our theory and practice, and demanded for *all* the people the exercise of those rights that belong to every citizen of a Republic.[2]

The women of a nation mold its morals, religion, and politics. The Northern treason, now threatening to betray us to our foes, is hatched at our own firesides, where traitor snobs, returned from Europe and the South, out of time and tune with independence and equality, infuse into their sons the love of caste and class, of fame and family, wealth and ease, and baptize it all in the name of Republicanism and Christianity.

Let every woman understand that this war involves the same principles that have convulsed the nations of the earth from Pharaoh to Abraham Lincoln—Liberty or Slavery—Democracy or Aristocracy—Christianity or Barbarism—and choose, this day, whether our republican institutions shall be placed on an enduring basis, and an eternal peace secured to our children, or whether we shall leap back through generations of light and experience and meekly bow again to chains and slavery.

Shall Northern freemen yet stand silent lookers-on when through Topeka, St. Paul, Chicago, Cleveland, Boston and New York, men and women, little boys and girls, chained in gangs, shall march to their own sad music, beneath a tyrant's lash? On our sacred soil shall we behold the auction block—babies sold by the pound, and beautiful women for the vilest purposes of lust; where parents and children, husbands and wives, brothers and sisters shall be torn from each other and sent East and West, North and South? Shall our free presses and free schools, our palace homes, colleges, churches and stately capitols all be leveled to the dust? Our household gods all desecrated, and our proud lips, ever taught to sing paeans to Liberty, made to swear allegiance to the god of Slavery? Such degradation, and more than words can tell, shall yet be ours, if we gird not up our giant freemen now to crush this Rebellion, and root out for ever the hateful principle of caste and class. Men who, in the light of the Nineteenth Century, believed that God made one race all booted and spurred, and another to be ridden; who would build up a government with Slavery for its cornerstone, cannot live on the same continent with a pure democracy.

To counsel grim-visaged war seems hard to come from woman's lips; but better far that the bones of our sires and sons whiten every Southern plain, that we do their rough work at home, than that Liberty, struck dumb in the Capital of our Republic, should plead no more for man. Every woman who appreciates the grand problem of national life, must say war, pestilence, famine, anything but an ignoble peace.

We are but co-workers now with the true ones of every age. The history of the past is but one long struggle upward to equality. All men, born slaves to ignorance, superstition, lust and fear, crept through centuries of darkness, discord and despair—now one race dominant then another—but in this ceaseless warring, ever wearing off their chains and the gross material surroundings of a mere animal existence, at last the sun of civilization and Christianity dawned on the soul of man, and the precious seed of the ages, garnered up in the Mayflower, was carried in the hollow of God's hand across the mighty waters and planted deep beneath the snow and ice of Plymouth Rock with prayers and thanksgiving. And what grew there? Men and women who loved liberty better than life. Men and women who believed that not only in person but in speech, should they be free, and worship the God who had brought them thus far, according to the dictates of their own conscience. Men and women who like Daniel of old defied the royal lion in his den.[3] Men and women who repudiated the creeds and codes of despots and tyrants, and declared to a waiting world that all men are created equal. And for rights like these the Fathers fought for seven long years, and we have no record that the women of that revolution ever once cried "hold, enough," till the invading foe was conquered and our independence recognized by the nations of the earth.

And here we are, the grandest nation on the globe. By right no privileged caste or class. Education free to all. The humblest digger in the ditch has all the civil, social, and religious rights, with the highest in the land. The poorest woman at the wash-tub may be the mother of a future President. Here all are heirs apparent to the throne. The genius of our institutions bids every man to rise, stand upright, perfect and use all the powers that God has given him.

It cannot be, that for blessings such as these, now twice baptized in blood, the women of the North do not stand ready for any sacrifice.

A sister of Kossuth,[4] with him an exile to this country, in conversation one day, called my attention to an iron bracelet, the only ornament she wore. In the darkest days of Hungary, said she, our noble women threw their wealth and jewels into the public treasury, and clasping iron bands around their wrists, pledged themselves that these should be the only jewels they would wear till Hungary was free.

If darker hours than these should come to us, the women of the North will count no sacrifice too great. What are wealth and jewels, home and ease, sires and sons, to the birthright of freedom, secured to us by the heroes of the Revolution—liberty to universal man? Shall a priceless heritage like this, be wrested now from us by Southern tyrants, and Northern women look on unmoved, or basely bid our freemen sue for peace? No! No!! The vacant places at our firesides, the void in every heart says No!! Such sacrifices must not be in vain!! The cloud that hangs o'er all our Northern homes is gilded with the hope, that through these present sufferings the nation shall be redeemed.

➢ *Elizabeth Cady Stanton.*

➢ *New York Daily Tribune,* 24 April 1863. On film at 30 March 1863. Reprinted as *Address of Mrs. Elizabeth Cady Stanton to the Women of the Republic,* broadside (n.p., n.d.), *Film,* 10:391-94.

1. Dated 30 March by ECS, this is the date of publication.
2. The outspoken letters of Abigail Smith Adams (1744-1818), wife of President John Adams and mother of John Quincy Adams, were published by her grandson as *Letters of Mrs. Adams, the Wife of John Adams,* ed. Charles Francis Adams, in 1840.
3. A test of faith in Dan. 6.
4. Louis Kossuth had four sisters, three of whom are known to have come to the United States: Emília Zsulavsky, Lujza Ruttkay, and Zsusánna Mezléyin. (Vasvary, *Magyar Amerika,* 92-94; assistance from August J. Molnar, American Hungarian Foundation, New Brunswick, New Jersey.)

·⟨————⟩⟨⟩·

172 ～ ECS TO ELIZABETH SMITH MILLER

New York, May 10, 1863.

Dear Julius:

Your boys arrived safely,[1] and with mine are on the go continually. They are crazy on the base ball question. Yesterday they saw the game between the Atlantics and the Eckfords, the best players in the United States,[2] and your Gat is confounded with such skill. He says Yankeeland has nothing like it. They will see games every day this week. This morning, after breakfast, they all agreed to go to Central Park, lunch with me afterwards and then go over to Brooklyn. Accordingly, I ordered a nice repast; but in my absence, they changed the programme, walked off to visit the Custom House,[3] and left word that they would eat the lunch at nine o'clock tonight! Such is man even in embryo. Last evening, they had a talk about life and came to the conclusion that books are a weariness. Your Gat held that Baker with his garden and flowers is happier than Cousin Gerrit in his library with his books. Even Dudley, struggling on the lounge with an overdose of oysters and ice cream, joined in these absurd propositions, while I maintained against all the young masculinity, the superiority of the intellectual pleasures. If only I could have had a chairman to keep them in order, I think I could have floored them all. But as it is, mistaking bluster for logic, I imagine they went off believing themselves triumphant. As ever,

~ *Johnson.*

~ Typed transcript, ECS Papers, DLC.

1. Gerrit Smith Miller (1845–1937) and Charles Dudley Miller, Jr. (1847–1894) visited the four-story brownstone at 75 West 45th Street in New York to which ECS moved in late April. Gerrit, known as Gat, who attended the Epes Sargent Dixwell School in Boston from 1860 to 1865, had an early interest in baseball. While still in Peterboro, he organized the Bobolink Base Ball Club, and at the Dixwell school, he joined the Lowell Base Ball Club of Boston. His brother Dudley also attended the Dixwell school. (ECS to Gerrit Smith, 20 April 1863, *Film*, 10:422–25; *New York Times*, 11 March 1937; Winthrop S. Scudder, ed., *Gerrit Smith Miller: An Appreciation* [Dedham, Mass., 1924], 16–25; Genealogical scrapbook, Smith Papers, NSyU.)

2. The Atlantics and the Eckfords were well-known Brooklyn baseball clubs at a time when the Brooklyn teams dominated baseball. In 1862 the two teams played each other for the championship. (Melvin L. Adelman, *A Sporting Time: New York City and the Rise of Modern Athletics, 1820–1870* [Urbana, Ill., 1986], 125, 132, 146, 157.)

3. In August 1861, Henry Stanton was appointed deputy collector of the New York Custom House and procured a job there for his son, Daniel.

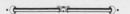

173 ~ MEETING OF THE LOYAL WOMEN OF THE REPUBLIC

Editorial note: SBA called the meeting of the loyal women to order on 14 May 1863 at the Church of the Puritans and nominated Lucy Stone to preside. The morning session was dominated by speeches and the reading of letters in support of the convention. Both ECS and

Angelina Grimké Weld addressed the large, mostly female, audience. "[H]ardly any of the speakers were heard for lack of voice,"
William Lloyd Garrison wrote his wife that afternoon, "and, on the
whole, the meeting was almost a dead failure—resolving itself, in fact,
into a Woman's Rights Convention. It has not been wisely got up."
(Garrison, *Letters*, 5:154.)

[14 May 1863]

Susan B. Anthony, on behalf of the Business Committee,[1] reported
the following resolutions:

Resolved, 1. That the present war between slavery and freedom is but
one phase of the irrepressible conflict between the aristocratic doctrine
that power, not humanity, is statute-maker, and the democratic principle that self-government is the inalienable right of the people.

Resolved, 2. That we heartily approve that part of the President's
Proclamation which decrees freedom to the slaves of rebel masters, and
we earnestly urge him to devise measures for emancipating all slaves
throughout the country.

Resolved, 3. That the national pledge to the freedmen must be redeemed, and the integrity of the Government in making it vindicated at
whatever cost.

Resolved, 4. That while we welcome to legal freedom the recent
slaves, we solemnly remonstrate against all state or national legislation
which may exclude them from any locality, or debar them from any
rights or privileges as free and equal citizens of a common Republic.

Resolved, 5. That it is in the same class favoring aristocratic interest
that the property, the liberty, and the lives of all slaves, all citizens of
African descent, and all women, are placed at the mercy of a legislation
in which they are not represented. There never can be a true peace in
this Republic until the civil and political equality of every subject of the
Government shall be practically established.

Resolved, 6. That if Northern women lack enthusiasm in this war, it
is because they have not seen its real nature and purport. If the wife or
mother cheerfully lays her loved ones on the altar, she must be impelled to it by a living faith in the justice of her cause.

Resolved, 7. That the women of the Revolution were not wanting in
heroism and self-sacrifice, and we, their daughters, are ready in this
war to pledge our time, our means, our talents, and our lives, if need
be, to secure the final and complete consecration of America to freedom.

The President: Before the resolutions shall be discussed, the Hutchinsons will give us one of their songs. General McClellan[2] was not willing that they should sing on the other side of the Potomac, but we are very glad to have them sing here.

A song was then given by the Hutchinsons, entitled "The Contraband Song."

The President: The resolutions may now be discussed, either by those friendly or those opposed to them—even copperheads, so they have good ideas, are quite welcome to discuss them.

Susan B. Anthony: Mrs. President, there is great fear expressed on all sides lest this war shall be made a war for the negro. I am willing that it shall be; I am ready to admit that it is a war for the negro. It is a war to found an empire on the negro in slavery, and shame on us if we make it not a war to establish the negro in freedom! It is a war for the elevation of humanity. And the negro, the portion of humanity most down-trodden in this country—the negro, against whom the whole nation, North and South, East and West, in one mighty conspiracy, has been combined from the beginning—must now be made the exponent of the war. There is no name given under heaven wherewith to break, and for ever crush out this wicked conspiracy, save that of the negro.

Great care has been taken, ever since the war began, to keep the negro and slavery out of sight and hearing. But my position has ever been, that instead of thus suppressing the real cause of the war, it should have been proclaimed, not only by the people, but by the President, Congress, Cabinet, and every Military Commander. And when the Government, military and civil, and the people, acknowledged slavery to be the cause of the war, they should have simultaneously, one and all, decreed its total overthrow. Instead of President Lincoln's waiting two long years before calling into the field and to the side of the Government the four millions of allies whom we have had within the territory of rebeldom, it was the first duty of the first decree he sent forth. Every hour's delay has been a sin and a shame registered against him, and every life sacrificed to the Moloch of war, up to the Proclamation that called the slave to freedom and to arms, was nothing less than downright murder by the Government. For by all the laws of common sense—to say nothing of laws military or national—if the President, as Commander-in-Chief of the Army and Navy, could have devised any possible means whereby he might hope to suppress the rebellion, without the sacrifice of the life of one loyal citizen, without the sacrifice of one dollar of the loyal North, it was clearly his duty to have done so. Every interest of the insurgents, every dollar of their property, every institution, however peculiar, every life in every rebel state, even, if necessary, should have been sacrificed, before one dollar or one man should have been drawn from the free States. How much more, then, was it the President's duty to confer freedom on the four million slaves, transform them into a peaceful army for the Union, cripple the rebellion, and establish justice, the only sure foundation of peace! I therefore hail the day when the President, the Government, and the people shall recognize that it is a war for the negro and for his freedom.

For if there is a God in heaven, if there is a law of justice in the earth, if there is a law of cause and effect in the universe, this war can never be suppressed, this nation can never know peace, until slavery—the cause of the war—is wholly and for ever removed. (Applause.) It is impossible. We talk about returning to the old Union—"the Union as it was," and "the Constitution as it is"—about "restoring our country to peace and prosperity—to the blessed conditions that existed before the war!!"[3] I ask you what sort of peace, what sort of prosperity, have we had in this country? We have had no peace, but constant war from the beginning. Since the first slave-ship sailed up the James River with its human cargo, and there, on the soil of the *Old* Dominion, it was sold to the highest bidder, we have had nothing but war. When that pirate captain landed on the shores of Africa, and there kidnapped the first stalwart negro, and fastened the first manacle, the struggle between that captain and that negro was the commencement of the terrible war in the midst of which we are to-day. Between the slave and the master there has been war, and war only, from the beginning. This is only a new form of the war. No, no; we ask for no return to the old conditions. We ask for something better than the old. We want a Union that is a Union in fact—a Union in spirit, not a sham Union. (Applause.) I just remembered[4] that it is the women of the North who are assembled here to-day—the women who have been wont to consider themselves irresponsible for the conduct of the affairs of the nation. And indeed they have no direct responsibility, for they have been content to accept whatever conditions of politics or morals the ruling class has been pleased to make. From the commencement of the Government, political intriguers have given to the entire nation not only its political code, but its moral and religious codes.

By the Constitution as it is—that is, as it has been interpreted and executed from the beginning—the North has stood pledged to protect slavery in the states where it existed. We have been bound, in case of slave insurrections, to go to the aid, not of those struggling for liberty, but to the aid of the oppressors. It was politicians who made the pledge at the beginning, and who have renewed it from year to year to this day. These same politicians have had control of the churches, the Sabbath-schools, and all religious influences; and the women, in this department, have been a part and party in complicity with slavery. The women have made the large majority in all the different religious organizations throughout the country, and have without protest even, in obedience to the behests of politics and trade, fellowshipped the slaveholder as a Christian, accepted pro-slavery preaching from their pulpits, suffered the words "slavery a crime" to be expurgated from all the lessons taught their children, listened to the perversion of the Golden Rule, "Do unto others as you would that others should do unto you." For all these years, women, mothers, have thus sat silent lookers-on, while their sons and daughters were being educated in forgetfulness of every law of right and justice to the slave. They have had no right to vote in their churches, and, like slaves, have merely accepted whatever of morals and religion the selfish interest of politics and trade dictated.

The point I wish to make here is this, that the hour is fully come, when woman shall no longer be the passive recipient of whatever morals and religion the trade and politics of the nation may decree; but that she shall now assume her God-given responsibilities, and make herself what she is clearly designed to be, the educator of the race. Let her no longer be the mere reflector, the echo of the worldly pride and ambition of the other half of the race. (Applause.) Had the women of the North studied to know and to teach their sons the law of justice to the black man, as the white, regardless of the frown or the smile of pro-slavery priest and politician, they would not now be called upon to offer the loved of their households to the bloody Moloch of war.

And now, women of the North, I ask you to rise up with earnest, honest purpose, to speak the true word and do the just work, in season and out of season. I ask you to forget that you are women, and go forward in the way of right, fearlessly, as independent human beings, responsible to God alone for the discharge of every duty, for the faithful use of every gift, for the multiplying tenfold every talent the good Father has given you. Forget conventionalisms; forget what the world will say, whether you are in your place or out of your place; think your best thoughts, speak your best words, do your best works, looking only to suffering humanity, your own conscience, and God for approval.

Ernestine L. Rose: I rise simply to make one remark, and I know my friend who has just taken her seat will have no objection. I know what she meant, but some may misunderstand her. No. Woman should never forget herself that she is a woman. It is because she remembers that she is a woman that she is in duty bound to go for everything that is right, for everything that is just, for everything that is grand and noble, and consequently for human freedom. (Applause.)

Mrs. Hoyt of Wisconsin:[5] Thus far this meeting has been conducted in such a way as would lead one to suppose that it was an anti-slavery convention. There are ladies here who have come hundreds of miles to attend a business meeting of the Loyal Ladies of the North; and good as anti-slavery conventions are, and anti-slavery speeches are, in their way, I think that here we should attend to our own business.

> Editorial note: SBA and ECS took very little part in the subsequent, lengthy debate, spearheaded by Elizabeth Hoyt, about the fifth resolution. That resolution, Hoyt argued, with its reference to women's civil and political equality, introduced an unpopular and divisive subject into a meeting ostensibly called to "assist the Government in its struggle against treason." Sarah Hallock disagreed with Hoyt but she was willing to drop references to women if by doing so, the league could garner more support for African-American political rights. Ernestine Rose objected to such a bargain; our goal, she reminded the meeting, is "to promote human rights and human freedom." Angelina Weld, Lucy Stone, Lucy Colman, and SBA all endorsed the idea that the rights of women and blacks were inextricably linked. The indefatigable Hoyt, who rose again and again to answer this cast of well-known lecturers, carried some portion of the meeting with her. The resolution about rights passed but only by a majority.

⇜ Women's Loyal National League, *Proceedings of the Meeting of the Loyal Women of the Republic, Held in New York, May 14, 1863* (New York, 1863), 15-19.

1. SBA, Antoinette Blackwell, Ernestine Rose, Amy Post, and Annie W. Mumford.

2. General George Brinton McClellan (1826-1885) was named general in chief and commander of the Army of the Potomac in November 1861. Extremely cautious, he spent the next several months preparing his army but taking no action. Lincoln removed him from supreme command in March 1862 and from command of the Army of the Potomac that November. (Warner, *Generals in Blue*.)

3. Copperhead slogans.

4. Text reads "I just remember me."

5. Elizabeth Orpha Sampson Hoyt (1834-?) wrote essays and poems for children. Originally from Ohio, she taught mathematics and metaphysics at Worthington Female Seminary before her marriage in 1854 to John Wesley Hoyt. In 1857 she moved with her husband to Madison, Wisconsin, where, in the early months of 1863, she may have helped to organize the Ladies' Union League, which claimed to be the first in the nation. (*ACAB*, s.v. "Hoyt, John Wesley"; William Coyle, ed., *Ohio Authors and Their Books* [Cleveland, Ohio, 1962]; *Proceedings of the Loyal Women, 1863*, 73-74.)

·⊂══════⊃·

174 ⇝ MEETING OF THE WOMEN'S LOYAL NATIONAL LEAGUE

Editorial note: A business meeting on the afternoon of 14 May began the work of creating the Women's Loyal National League by electing ECS for president and SBA for secretary, but time ran out, and delegates from various local leagues and societies met again on the following afternoon.

[15 May 1863]

The business Committee of the Loyal League of Women, with a number of ladies who take an interest in the formation of such a society, met yesterday afternoon in the Lecture Room of the Church of the Puritans, for the purpose of agreeing upon some definite platform and of determining the future operations of the League.

Miss Susan B. Anthony, as President of the Business Committee, took the chair, and at 3 o'clock called the meeting to order.

Mrs. Elizabeth Cady Stanton rose to decline accepting the nomination she had received on Thursday, as President of the League. She could not pledge herself to unconditional loyalty to the Government—certainly not if the Government took any retrogressive step. As President of a National League many might object to her. She desired the vote by which she had been made President might be reconsidered.

Miss Anthony thought the best way to elucidate the matter would be to ascertain how many wished to become members of National and how many of Local Leagues. She thought there were fears of the Government retrogressing in the policy of Freedom. The question is every day discussed in the papers as to on what terms the South shall be received back again. She could not be Secretary to a League which was pledged to unconditional loyalty to the Government. Miss Anthony then read the following Pledge and Resolutions which had, on Thursday, been partially agreed to.

THE PLEDGE.

We, the loyal women of ——, do hereby pledge ourselves loyal to justice and humanity and to the Government in so far as it makes the war a war for freedom.

RESOLUTIONS.

Resolved, That we rejoice in the local women's leagues already formed, and earnestly recommend their organization throughout the country; and that we urge the women everywhere to take the highest ground of loyalty to our country, right—not wrong.

Resolved, That we hail the conscription[1] as necessary for the salvation of the country, and cheerfully resign to it our husbands, lovers, brothers and sons.

Miss Anthony went on to explain what a national league was, and what the business and pecuniary responsibilities it entailed.

Mrs. A. G. Weld suggested that before entering on other matters, the question of offices should be settled.

Miss Anthony—Will some one put the motion?

Mrs. Loveland,[2] took the floor. She stated that she had come there the day before with one idea—only one—and that she retained that one idea still. Mrs. Loveland trusted that the League would co-operate with the laws of the land, and strengthen the hands of the President in his efforts to vigorously prosecute the war. She thought the Government had made great advances in the path of progress. If the pledge required the war to be waged for Freedom, that was all that was necessary. It would be desirable to secure the experience and ability of Mrs. Stanton and Miss Anthony in the offices to which they had been elected; yet if harmonious action could not be had in a National League, perhaps it would be better to organize local Leagues.

Miss Willard of Pa.[3] thought there was a way to get over the difficulty. The pledge is conditional, to the extent of requiring the war to be a war for Freedom. Miss Willard said she was a true patriot. She loved her country. She had borne with its defects, though she confessed she had sometimes desired to remove them. She believed in sustaining the Government; though if Vallandigham[4] should chance to be elected President she really didn't know what she should do.

Incredulity was very generally manifested as to the possibility of Vallandigham ever becoming President, but Miss Anthony exclaimed that "the next President would probably be something like him."

Miss Willard seemed to think that the pledge offered would do under the existing Administration. When there is a change they can have another League. <[I]f any event occurred that rendered that duty unpleasant they could change their constitution. Even the Constitution of our country could be changed.

Mrs. Stanton—And improved.

Mrs. Weld—I hope so.

Miss Willard>[5] believed if the President was slow he was sure, and that he was the Moses who was to lead this people to their promised land of freedom.

> Editorial note: A few more remarks about presidential prospects followed. SBA read the pledge, and it was adopted without opposition. She then read the resolutions again, and a general discussion of conscription followed.

Mrs. Weld then read an address from the League to the soldiers, which, at the request of the Business Committee, she had prepared. Hereafter, when revised, this address will be published.[6]

Mrs. Loveland hoped the sailors would be included in the address. They never refused to go aloft because a black man was going at the same time.

After some remarks by Mrs. Stanton, Miss Anthony offered for discussion what may be called

THE PLATFORM OF THE LEAGUE.

Resolved, That our work as a National League is to educate the nation in the true idea of a Christian Republic.

This is how the resolve was finally adopted. Considerable preliminary debate, in which many Ladies joined, took place on details of form and phraseology. The resolve as it stands was constructed by Mrs. Stanton, with the exception of the word "Christian."

<There was an earnest discussion on the introduction of the word Christian; some argued that a *true Republic*, where every human being's rights were recognized, could but be Christian. A Mrs. M'Farland[7] seemed to settle the question, by stating a fact of history, that in olden times there were Pagan Republics.

Miss Anthony said: No matter if it were a mere tautology: it required repetition to make this nation, so steeped in crime against humanity, understand. She then spoke of the awful lie of this nation, in naming itself Civilized, Republican, Christian, while it had made barter of men and women, bought and sold children of the Good Father, and paid their price to send missionaries to the Fejee Islands and the remotest corners of the earth, while it stood bound to fine and imprison any man or woman who should teach any one of *four millions* of its own citizens at home to read the letters that spell the word God.[8] It would take long years to educate this nation into the idea and *practice* of a true, Christian Republic. It was a momentous work the women of this National Loyal League had undertaken. And she hoped one and all would take in its full import, and dedicate themselves fully and earnestly to the work.>[9]

❧ *New York Daily Tribune*, 16 May 1863; *New York Times*, 16 May 1863. Also reported in Women's Loyal National League, *Proceedings of the Meeting of the Loyal Women of the Republic, held in New York, May 14, 1863* (New York, 1863), 53–54.

1. On 3 March Congress passed the Enrollment Act of 1863, which set enlistment quotas based on population within congressional districts. If a district could not meet its quota by volunteer enlistments within fifty days, a draft was imposed. Drafted men could avoid service by hiring a substitute or

by paying a commutation fee of three hundred dollars. (McPherson, *Ordeal by Fire*, 356.)

2. Mrs. Loveland identified herself as a sailor's wife.

3. Fannie W. Willard, one of two delegates elected by the women of the Pennsylvania State Normal School in Millersville to represent them at the convention, was a vice president of the meeting on 14 May.

4. Clement Laird Vallandigham (1820–1871), Ohio Democrat, was a notorious Copperhead who was arrested in May 1863 for acting to benefit the enemy. (*BDAC*.)

5. This bracketed passage comes from the *New York Times*, 16 May 1863.

6. Angelina Grimké Weld's address to the "Soldiers of Our Second Revolution" expressed gratitude to the soldiers and appealed to them to welcome the aid of black troops and to continue fighting for the "victory of free government, sacred rights, justice, liberty, and law, over the perfidies, perjuries, lying pretenses, and frantic revelries in innocent blood, of the most foulest national crime that ever reeked to Heaven." (*Proceedings of the Loyal Women, 1863*, 51–53.)

7. This could be Abby Sage McFarland (1837–1900), later Richardson, who lived in New York in 1863 giving dramatic readings and studying to be an actress under the patronage of Horace Greeley's sister. Abby McFarland's divorce, remarriage, and custody battle, between 1867 and 1870, were the centerpiece of a mass protest by women against the laws of New York State. (*WWW1*; "Mrs. Richardson's Statement," *New York Tribune*, 11 May 1870, and clippings December 1869–May 1870, SBA scrapbook 1, Rare Books, DLC.)

8. Many southern states passed laws in the 1830s prohibiting anyone from teaching slaves to read.

9. Longer than any newspaper report, this bracketed passage comes from *Proceedings of the Loyal Women, 1863*, 53–54.

·⟨══════⟩·

175 ➳ MEETING OF THE WOMEN'S LOYAL
NATIONAL LEAGUE

[29 May 1863]

At a meeting of the Women's Loyal National League, held at the Cooper Institute yesterday afternoon,[1] the following resolutions were adopted:

Resolved, That the following be the official title and the pledge of the League—the pledge to be signed by all applicants for membership:

WOMEN'S LOYAL NATIONAL LEAGUE,
ORGANIZED IN THE CITY OF NEW YORK, MAY 14, 1863.

We the undersigned, Women of the United States, agree to become members of the Women's Loyal National League, hereby pledging our most earnest influence in support of the Government in its prosecution of the War for Freedom and for the restoration of the National Unity.

Resolved, That for the present this League will concentrate all its efforts upon the single object of procuring to be signed by one million women and upward, and of preparing for presentation to Congress, within the first week of its next session, a petition in the following words, to wit:

"*To the Senate and House of Representatives of the United States.*

The undersigned, women of the United States above the age of 18 years, earnestly pray that your honorable body will pass, at the earliest practicable day, an act emancipating all persons of African descent held to involuntary service or labor in the United States."[2]

Resolved, That in furtherance of the above object, the Executive Committee of this League[3] be instructed to cause to be prepared and stereotyped a pamphlet, not exceeding four printed octave pages, briefly and plainly setting forth the importance of such a movement at the present juncture; a copy of the said pamphlet to be placed in the hands of each person who may undertake to procure signatures to the above petition; and for such further distribution as may be ordered by the said Executive Committee.

Resolved, That to a committee of nine, to be hereafter appointed by the President and Secretary of this League, be entrusted the duty of procuring subscriptions to defray the expenses connected with the preparation, and signature, and presentation of the said petition.

Resolved, That the initiation fee for membership be either one dollar, or, at the option of the applicant, a petition for Emancipation, signed by not less than one hundred names.

Remarks were made by Miss Anthony, Mrs. Stanton, Mrs. Hague and others. A determination was manifested to add a million of names to the proposed petition.

❧ *New York Daily Tribune*, 30 May 1863.

1. According to the New York *World*, ECS chaired the meeting at the

league's new office, Room 20, Cooper Institute, and SBA acted as secretary. Thirty females and two males were present. (30 May 1863, *Film*, 10:504.)

2. At its weekly meeting on 12 June 1863, the league resolved to collect men's signatures as well. When the *Commonwealth*, a weekly published in Boston, acknowledged the league's work in October, it credited Robert Dale Owen with writing this petition. (*New York Daily Tribune*, 13 June 1863, *Film*, 10:508; *Commonwealth*, 2 October 1863.)

3. The original committee consisted of Mattie Griffith, B. Peters, Clemence S. Lozier, Mary A. Halsted, Laura M. Ward, and Mary F. Gilbert. Rebecca K. Shephard was added at the meeting of 5 June. (*Proceedings of the Loyal Women, 1863*, 54, 79, *New York Daily Tribune*, 6 June 1863, *Film*, 10:434ff, 505.)

---

176 ❧ SBA TO EDWIN D. MORGAN

New York, [*July*] 1863[1]

Hon. E. D. Morgan   Dear Sir

I wrote you, some days since, asking you to confer a favor on the "Women's Loyal National League" by way of franking letters and documents for them.[2] Getting no reply, I venture to address ↑you↓ a second time, feeling sure, either that my request was not sufficiently explicit, or that you have not received it. For, it cannot be that you are indifferent as to the success or failure of ↑the↓ present undertaking of our League to secure a full expression of the wish & the will of the entire people of the North, & the Union Army so far as possible, as to whether there shall be left, to be engrafted in the new order of things— in the new Union—one single germ of the System of human chattelism, there to sprout & grow, and upheave & overturn our future's hope of peace and order, so surely as the little seed planted by the Fathers of the first revolution, grew into the Mighty Rebellion that now divides, desolates & drenches in blood the promised land of the free, they bequeathed to us.

You will see, Sir, by our plan of a penny contribution with each signature to Petition[3] we cannot expect aid from the people generally, until the return of our Petitions, and they, surely, cannot be returned until sent out. Our hope of success, therefore, lies in first getting liberal contributions from generous men & women who feel the importance of our work, that shall enable us to scatter our petitions like Snow flakes all over the Free States.

Gerrit Smith of Peterboro N.Y. & Schieffelin Brothers of this City, have recently sent us <u>one</u> <u>hundred</u> dollars each,[4] which added to the numerous small contributions ~~has~~ ↑have↓ enabled us to despatch several thousands packages like the enclosed.[5]

Trusting, Sir, that you will feel it a privilege to aid us in this vast enterprise, either by a Contribution of your frank, or if ↑you↓ do not like to confer that,—a contribution of money— I am   Respectfully Yours

⪼ *Susan B. Anthony*
Sec'y Women's L.N. League

⪻ ALS, on loyal league letterhead, 1863, Edwin D. Morgan Papers, Manuscripts and Special Collections, N. In *Film* as after 24 June 1863.

1. Though undated, this letter follows SBA's to Morgan on 24 June, and it mentions contributions received between 1 and 18 July. (*Film*, 10:516–17.)
2. Senator from New York, Morgan enjoyed free postage as a perquisite of his office.
3. This plan was adopted at the weekly meeting of 26 June, *Film*, 10:522.
4. SBA acknowledged Smith's donation on 1 July. Schieffelin Brothers, the drug firm of Samuel Bradhurst, Sidney A., William H., and Bradhurst Schieffelin, located at 170 Williams Street in New York, contributed one hundred dollars in early July. (SBA to G. Smith, 1 July 1863, and *New York Daily Tribune*, 21 July 1863, *Film*, 10:529–32, 542; City directory, 1862–1863.)
5. Enclosure missing.

177 ⪼   SBA TO SAMUEL MAY, JR.[1]

New-York, Sept. 21st 1863

Dear Friend May

Your letter with names & one dollar came duly— Thank you for all—

We, the Leauge, are <u>alive</u> and planning a most vigorous prosecution of <u>our</u> <u>war</u> of <u>ideas</u>—not bullets & bayonets—

I have decided to go to Boston by Wednesday nights boat—and would like to meet ~~as many of~~ the Anti-Slavery men & women of the several Committees—the American Society—the Massachusetts, the Hovey & Jackson—& as many <u>not</u> <u>of</u> those committees, as may be—on Friday morning at such hour as t̶h̶e̶ ↑you think↓ the friends can be at the Anti Slavery Office—

Mrs. Stanton & I are writing several to be there, Angelina Grimpke, Mrs. Child & others—[2] We must have <u>concert</u> of action—in some <u>one</u> <u>practical</u> <u>direction</u>. The honest, earnest people of the country are asking what can we do to help save the nation to freedom—the hour of <u>adjustment</u>—of reconstruction is coming, and it is <u>our</u> duty to educate the people to demand justice ↑as the↓ first—the chief corner stone—

I want to see you all together— Will you notify such of the friends as are earnest to be at work & can help point out the most efficient way—

All the lecturing agents need to be of the circle too, they have felt the pulse of the people & will be able to advise as to ways & means.— But you know all the <u>live</u> workers in & out of the lecture field—& will I know call them around the council board at 221 Wash. St.[3]

I write Stephen & Abby Foster— If you know where Parker Pillsbury is will you please inform him—

All this seems presuming in me—but surely our Leagues aim & purpose cannot be understood or it would be more heartily responded to by the true & tried   I am not after <u>money</u>, settle that point, but to secure cooperation— Truly Yours

⚞ *Susan B. Anthony*

⚞ ALS, on loyal league letterhead, 1863, Papers of SBA, NPV.

1. Samuel May, Jr. (1810–1899), a cousin of Samuel J. May, was named general agent or general secretary of the American Anti-Slavery Society in 1847, and he managed the society's agents and business until 1865. (Eliot, *Heralds of a Liberal Faith*, 3:235–38; Garrison, *Letters*, 4:7–8n, 5:38n.)

2. The Weld and Grimké household moved from New Jersey to the suburbs of Boston in the fall of 1863. See L. M. Child to ECS, 28 September 1863, *Film*, 10:562–63.

3. Both the Massachusetts Anti-Slavery Society and the *Liberator* had offices at 221 Washington Street, Boston.

·◁═══╳═══▷·

178 ∾ SBA to ECS

Worcester [*Mass.*] Oct. 10, 1863   Saturday P.M.

Dear Mrs. Stanton

Here I am with Stephen & Abby Kelly Foster— Left Boston last Monday in <u>despair</u> of securing any general cooperation from the A.S. Committees & old lecturers— But Stephen & Abby said it must not be— So Thursday P.M. he went in to Boston to see Garrison & Phillips, & yesterday returned with hopeful word— Meetings of the Hovey Committee, the Mass. and American A.S. Comittees, are to be held next Tuesday— We propose to have the American Society Ex. Com. issue an address to the people, setting forth the importance of the North's demanding <u>immediate</u> <u>emancipation</u>—& the danger of delay— that we must make the passage of an ↑act of↓ <u>entire</u> Emancipation the <u>peoples</u> <u>first</u> & most imperative demand of the coming Congress—¹

I wish you could be at the meeting—221 Washington st. Boston—at 9½ Oclock A.M. Tuesday the 13th—& then the address is to wind up with a <u>terrific</u> appeal to every friend of <u>our</u> <u>Country</u> <u>right</u>—<u>free</u>—to immediately send in his & her largest possible donation to carry forward the work of making a thorough canvass of the free states by lectures, conventions, & Petitions— We have thought of <u>twelve</u> lecturers—who will make <u>four</u> lecturing <u>corps</u>—to undertake four different districts or states—hold single lectures in all small towns of a given circuit, & then meet in a grand mass meeting at some central point— We want in each corps a <u>white</u> man, <u>black</u> man & a woman— And to make the <u>woman</u> possible, we must have <u>Lucy</u> <u>Stone</u> & Lizzie Jones— The Fosters commission me to make sure of Lucy— If she will go, she shall choose ~~her~~ ↑the↓ <u>white</u> <u>man</u> & <u>black</u> <u>man</u>—for ↑her↓ company—² I hope she can be prevailed upon to forget the <u>old</u> <u>Lucy</u> <u>Stone</u> & her <u>oratorical</u> <u>powers</u>—so beyond match—and resolve to throw just what she is to do, more or less, into the travelling for freedom— I know the old fires are in her—or, if not the <u>old</u> <u>ones</u>—still brighter and grander ones—which she nor the world will ever believe until she permits them to come in contact with the <u>orators</u> <u>oxygen</u>—the <u>great</u> <u>heart</u> of the

<u>people</u> met together to demand a nation <u>free</u> & equal to all mankind—
The Committee will write her as soon as plans are fixed—& may the
powers of all the good & true & earnest help her to say <u>yes</u>—<u>I go</u>—

The second step—is to have <u>all</u> <u>the</u> <u>lecturers</u> who will join in the
work—meet in Boston, have resolutions stating the precise points to
press in our meetings, fully discussed & adopted—so that we shall
drive at the same end—avoiding all <u>side</u> issues— I can't yet see the day
to return to New-York—but I do hope you go down to the Office and
see <u>exactly</u> <u>what</u> is <u>being</u> <u>done</u>—<u>don't</u> <u>allow</u> us to be <u>turned</u> <u>wholly</u> into
a <u>praying</u> <u>machine</u>—[3] I have heard nothing from there in a week or
more— I see by yesterday's Tribune that Mr. <u>Goodell</u> entertained the
Office Thursday evening—[4]

Do you get you best thoughts in a speech—all written & ready to
help—for we must have a good meeting in New York & towns near
there— Love to the whole household—Good

⇝ S. B A—

⇝ ALS, on loyal league letterhead, 1863, "New York" struck out, ECS Papers,
DLC.

1. The executive committee of the American Anti-Slavery Society, after
concluding that the federal government had the authority to abolish slavery,
decided to put agents in the field to solicit men to petition for universal
emancipation. Its pronouncement, which ran in both the *Liberator* and the
Standard from October to December, praised the loyal league for work by and
among women, extended "the heartiest co-operation," and asked loyal men to
be "equally zealous" in delivering a message to Congress. The Hovey Committee also voted a salary of twelve dollars a week for SBA. (*Lib.*, 23 Octo-
ber-4 December 1863; *NASS*, 24 October-19 December 1863; *Anthony*, 1:234.)

2. Nothing as elaborate as SBA's scheme can be documented. At least four
universal emancipation tours by the society's agents took place in the fall and
early winter in New England and eastern New York. In New York City the
league increased its local presence with lectures at Cooper Institute and the
Church of the Puritans and weekly speakers at its office. In the Midwest
Josephine Griffing and Hannah Cutler became paid lecturing agents for the
league in the summer of 1863. (*NASS*, 8 August 1863; *Lib.*, 6, 13 November, 11,
25 December 1863; William Lloyd Garrison to Aaron M. Powell, 31 October
1863, Garrison, *Letters*, 5:168-70; Wendy Hamand Venet, *Neither Ballots nor
Bullets: Women Abolitionists and the Civil War* [Charlottesville, Va., 1991],
118-19; *History*, 2:81.)

3. In addition to weekly business meetings, members of the league held
prayer meetings on Wednesday afternoons. (*NASS*, 3 October 1863.)

4. William Goodell spoke on 8 October on "Politics as they are and as they should be." (*New York Daily Tribune*, 9 October 1863.)

·⚞————⚞⚞————⚟·

179 ⚘ MARY GREW TO SBA

[*Philadelphia, before 28 November 1863*]

I regard this work of moving Congress, by petition or otherwise, as the last great act of our anti-slavery enterprise—the decree of universal emancipation as *the* work of the hour for Abolitionists. And I rejoice that the Women's Loyal League has set itself to the task, and that our American A.S. Society is about to summon its agents into the field to make a mighty, and, as we trust, a last effort for this end. I shall be *especially* busy until after our Decade meeting;[1] but, though even then, I look for no leisure, I must make anything which I can do in this department of our cause my chief work. Verily, the end is nigh; the victory at hand. I can scarcely believe it, cannot realize it.

⚘ *NASS*, 28 November 1863.

1. The American Anti-Slavery Society's thirtieth anniversary meeting, held in Philadelphia 3–4 December 1863.

·⚞————⚞⚞————⚟·

180 ⚘ SPEECH BY SBA TO THE AMERICAN ANTI-SLAVERY SOCIETY

Editorial note: The American Anti-Slavery Society celebrated its third decade in Philadelphia's Concert Hall on 3–4 December 1863. Confident that politicians would complete the abolition of slavery, William Lloyd Garrison urged abolitionists to turn their attention to the welfare and schooling of former slaves. Henry Wright, after consulting with Senator Charles Sumner on the eve of the meeting, proposed instead a petition campaign for a constitutional amendment to prohibit slavery. Wright's proposal matched the temper of the crowd and won favor. Though no one spoke directly about the relationship between this new campaign and the one already launched by the Women's Loyal National League, league women distributed their petition, endorsed its work in their speeches, and referred often to the long tradition of women petitioning against slavery. (Donald, *Charles Sumner and the Rights of Man*, 147–48; Venet, *Neither Ballots nor Bullets*, 119–20; *Lib.*, 22 January 1864.)

[4 December 1863]

SPEECH OF SUSAN B. ANTHONY.

Among the early lessons which I learned upon the abolition platform was this: That it was our distinctive work to educate the heart of the people of this nation into a full recognition of the humanity of the black man; that we were to so educate the people of the North that they would refuse to aid the Government in holding the black man in chains; and I suppose that is precisely our work to-day. I remember that I had thought fugitive-slave work was very important and really anti-slavery; and I also remember that one of the first lessons I had to learn was, that the fugitive slave would be aided by common philanthropy and benevolence, and that we, who called ourselves Radical Abolitionists, should give our attention, our thought, our efforts, to the removal of the cause which compelled the fugitive, with bleeding feet, to cross the Free States of the North to the British domain. It seems to me that the Sanitary Commission work, the Freedmen's Association, the Freedmen's Educational work, are to-day common charity, common benevolence, and the world will look after it. Here, in this third decade of the American Anti-Slavery Society, are assembled, from different parts of the Free States, the representatives of a little handful of men and women over the country, who have for these thirty years been working to undermine the law of the nation which allows the holding of property in man. Precisely this is the work which I think we should abide by at this hour, leaving to the grand masses of the world, whose attention is now called to the question of liberty—to the question of saving this nation, to the question of emancipation even— leaving it to them to take care of the freedmen, to take care of the sick and wounded upon the battle-field. Let us go on with our primitive and fundamental work of removing the laws which allow of the existence of slavery.

That is the specific work to which the Association of which I have been a member for the last six months (the Woman's Loyal League) has specially devoted itself. We aim to circulate throughout the entire

North a petition, to be presented to the next Congress, asking that body to enact a law of Universal Emancipation. As women, we felt that it was especially fitting for us to work in this way, because as women we could have no voice as to what should be the basis of reconstruction of this government, save through the one right which the nation has left to us, the right of petition. Women can neither take the ballot nor the bullet to settle this question; therefore, to us, the right to petition is the one sacred right which we ought not to neglect. I appeal to women here to-day to set themselves about this work when they shall return to their homes; to circulate this emancipation petition themselves, and to urge upon their neighbors and friends to engage in the work.

I know there are women here who would like to know something of the progress of this petition movement. I am sorry not to be able to make an enthusiastic and encouraging report; but the fact is, that wherever our petitions have been sent, from vastly too many places the responses have come back, "What do you mean by asking us to circulate a petition for emancipation? Is not the work already done? Has not the President proclaimed freedom? Is he not doing the work as fast as he can?" This has been the one great obstacle, the one great discouragement, which we have had to meet. Those who have hitherto occupied the highest places in our estimation have seemed the most indifferent, and to feel as if this was really an unnecessary work. Why should we, who have been at work for these long years, endeavoring to move slavery out of the way, when it has been the cause of all the national disasters and national strifes and discords which we have had, be afraid, in this last struggle, of doing too much?

The petitions to-day are being returned rapidly. Day before yesterday, one mail brought four or five thousand signatures. I only hope that the people, at this hour, will begin to feel that there is need of a public expression. There is an important question to come before the next Congress—the question of reconstruction. I have no doubt that Senator Wilson himself would say to you this morning, if he were to speak, that the signatures of a million of the men and women of the North, poured in upon Congress, will do much to encourage the members to stand fast by their principles.[1] The Congress needs to know that the people, their constituencies, stand by them, and will demand of them the strictest faithfulness to freedom, and will not abide the slightest compromise of principle. It is for us to make them feel this.

☞ American Anti-Slavery Society, *Proceedings of the American Anti-Slavery Society, at its Third Decade, Held in the City of Philadelphia, Dec. 3d and 4th, 1864 [1863]* (New York, 1864), 73–75. Also in *Lib.*, 15 January 1864, *Film*, 10:581.

1. Henry Wilson (1812–1875), radical Republican senator from Massachusetts and chair of the Senate Committee on Military Affairs, arrived at the meeting just before SBA spoke. In an address that evening, he praised abolitionists for their political successes and warned that Peace Democrats and the South still posed a significant threat to ending slavery forever. (*BDAC*; *Lib.*, 25 December 1863.)

---

181 ⇝ ECS TO THE EDITOR, *LIBERATOR*

New York, Dec. 13, 1863.

Dear Garrison, I was sorry to hear that, at the Decade meeting in Philadelphia, you passed a resolution to petition Congress to amend the Constitution.[1] I hope, on consideration, you will see the bad policy of all specific petitioning,—either to amend the Constitution, impeach the Judges of the Supreme Court,[2] or to place the black and white soldiers on equal ground.[3] The petition for universal emancipation covers all these specific abuses. Slavery abolished, no one will pass behind the fair face of the Constitution for a heart of blackness and villainy.

When not a slave breathes in this republic, we care not for the decisions of Judge Taney or Grier; and when black men have a chance to show themselves the heroes they are, they will soon settle the question of equality. Our work is to secure to them freedom at the earliest possible day. We propose to send in the first instalment of [*blank*] on the 14th day of January,[4] and shall continue to roll up the petitions throughout the entire Union, and so long as slavery exists and there is one man or woman to protest against that execrable crime. The enthusiasm that is steadily growing out of this movement is indeed promising. The petitions are coming in daily by hundreds and thousands. Yesterday, one came in from Wisconsin with the signatures of 900 men and 900 women, all collected by one poor, infirm widow who has lost her husband and two sons in the war. In her letter she says, "I have registered the names, too, of every man and woman that will not sign the petition, that they may be handed over to the future scorn they so well deserve." In many of the petitions for women, the place assigned to the residence is filled with facts of husbands, brothers, and sons, who have died in the struggle for freedom. Such is the feeling among the mothers, wives, and daughters of the West. Where they dwell is to them of but little consequence, while they live in the memory of those brave men who have been true to their country. One mail brought petitions from Maine, Delaware, Kansas, and New Orleans, with hundreds of names.

As we keep the petitions from each State distinct, there is a chance to prove "State rights" in this race for freedom! At the last counting, New York was ahead! We who have watched this work in its beginnings, through months of struggle, doubt and discouragement, are now cheered and surprised with the genuine enthusiasm of the people everywhere. What we want is the united expression of the friends of freedom against slavery, from Maine to Louisiana. Inasmuch as the petition demanding universal emancipation covers the whole ground, and is already in circulation North and South, do not let us distrust the public, or weaken our action, by changing the form of our petition. Yours, truly,

❧ *E. Cady Stanton.*

❧ *Lib.*, 1 January 1864.

1. The society's petition was sent out with a cover letter from Samuel May, Jr., dated 26 December 1863 and addressed "Dear Sir." "The Petition is sent extensively to clergymen," May explained, and he entreated them to preach sermons on the subject. (SBA scrapbook 1, Rare Books, DLC.)

2. In the fall of 1863 abolitionists feared that the southern majority on the Supreme Court would find the Emancipation Proclamation unconstitutional. Roger Brooke Taney (1777–1864), author of the Dred Scott decision, still served as chief justice, and Robert Cooper Grier (1794–1870), who wrote a concurring opinion in the case, still sat on the Court as an associate justice. (Carl B. Swisher, *The Taney Period, 1836–64*, vol. 5, *History of the Supreme Court of the United States* [New York, 1974], 936–39.)

3. The fact that African-American soldiers received lower pay than white soldiers was creating a crisis in the fall of 1863. Two Massachusetts regiments refused any pay rather than accept short pay. Secretary of War Edwin Stanton asked Congress in December to enact a law for equal pay, Thaddeus Stevens introduced the bill, and abolitionists organized to press for its passage. (James

M. McPherson, *The Struggle for Equality: Abolitionists and the Negro in the Civil War and Reconstruction* [Princeton, N.J., 1964], 213-15.)

4. SBA told Charles Sumner on 18 December that the league hoped to present petitions with fifty thousand names on 14 January 1864. (*Film*, 10:587-89.)

·⪥⪤⪦·

182 ⪼ ECS TO HORACE GREELEY

[*New York*] Jan. 18th [*1864*]

<u>Private</u>

Mr Greeley,

Will you my dear friend be careful in your <u>editorial</u> <u>statements</u> in reference to my Husband[1]

In this hour of the deepest sorrow of my life I ask not mercy, but justice

I do not wish you for the sake of any individual to conceal a single <u>fact</u>, for I feel with you, that the salvation of our country depends on the virtue & moral probity of our public officers; & any man who in this hour is false to a public trust, is unworthy the name of an American citizen.

I do fully believe there is a determination in some quarters to <u>undermine</u> not openly accuse Mr Stanton.

Insinuations can never be met. When his persecutors can find their facts be sure they will be published & I trust fairly met. With an unwavering confidence in your integrity & a sincere regard   I am your friend

⪥ *E Cady Stanton.*

⪥ ALS, Horace Greeley Papers, Manuscript Division, NN.

1. ECS responded to an editorial in the *Tribune* about fraud uncovered in the New York Custom House, during a struggle between rival factions of the Republican party over control of this patronage plum. Though he had not yet been accused of wrongdoing, Henry Stanton resigned his position in mid-December 1863, and the House Committee on Public Expenditures began investigating charges of misconduct in mid-January. (*New York Daily Tribune*, 15 January 1864; Rice, "Henry B. Stanton," 422-62; Harry J. Carmen and Reinhard H. Luthin, *Lincoln and the Patronage* [New York, 1943], 245.)

·❮━━━━━❯·

183 ❧ ECS TO FRANCES MILLER SEWARD

New York, Feb 15th [*1864*].

My dear Mrs Seward,

You will see by the Washington Globe that Mr Sumner presented the "emancipation petition" last week, made a good little speech which called out some discussion, & that the petition instead of being thrown under the table was referred.[1] Now we desire to send in just such a petition every month during the session, but to do this the friends of freedom must do their uttermost. I write to ask you & Mrs Worden to set the ball in motion in Auburn. It is surely very little for us to ask our friends to write their names in a good cause. You have quite a circle of acquaintances among the coloured bretheren & sisters!! Could you not hire some bright mulatto boys & girls to canvass your city & send us 10,000 from that region round about   I send you a petition. Please read the Appeal on the back, that you may appreciate our work.[2] You see we propose, not only to bind up the wounds of our soldiers, & clothe our freedmen but to remove the cause of all our woe viz slavery. Do let me hear from you occasionally. I have had several interviews lately with Weed,[3] & I must say I admire him exceedingly   When we all meet again at Judge Sacketts[4] I think I shall be with him on the Weed question.

Who is to be our next President   I should like to hear Mrs. Worden expatiate on public matters, for my part I know not what to say or think, & so I work to the one point of ending slavery [*sideways in margin*] your friend sincerely

❧ *E Cady Stanton.*

❧ ALS, on loyal league letterhead for 1863, unaltered, William Henry Seward Collection, NRU.

1. On 4 February, league secretary Charlotte Beebe Wilbour shipped the petitions with 100,000 signatures in a trunk to Senator Charles Sumner. On 9 February, according to Ida Harper, two large African-American men delivered the enormous bundle to Sumner's desk on the Senate floor. When

Sumner presented the petitions, the Senate referred them to the Select Committee on Slavery and Freedmen, created at his request in January. (ECS, SBA, and C. B. Wilbour to C. Sumner, 4 February 1864, and *Congressional Globe*, 38th Cong., 1st sess., 536–38, 1247, in *Film*, 10:716–21, 740; *Anthony*, 1:235.)

2. Enclosure missing. The appeal of February 1864 was also published in *NASS*, 27 February 1864, *Film*, 10:724.

3. As the leader, with William Seward, of a powerful faction of the state's Republican party, Thurlow Weed took a personal interest in the distribution of patronage. ECS sought his help with her husband's troubles, but Weed may have been the author of their woes. Stanton was allied with a rival faction, led by Secretary of the Treasury Salmon P. Chase, and Weed wanted the Chase men out of the Custom House. (ECS to T. Weed, 26 January 1864, T. Weed to ECS, 3 February 1864, *Film*, 10:712, 715; Rice, "Henry B. Stanton," 448–53; Alexander, *Political History of New York*, 3:85–86; Brummer, *Political History of New York State*, 394–95.)

4. Gary Van Sackett (1790–1865), a Seneca Falls lawyer, former judge of the court of common pleas, farmer, and friend of Daniel Cady, was also a friend and ally of William Seward and Thurlow Weed. (Janet Cowing, "Genealogical and Biographical Sketch of Gary V. Sackett," *Occasional Papers of the Seneca Falls Historical Society* [1905]: 65–70; G. V. Sackett to ECS, 8 March 1864, *Film*, 10:797–99.)

·⟨⟨══════⟩⟩·

184 ⇜ SBA TO CHARLES SUMNER

New York, March 1, 1864.

Hon Charles Sumner Dear Sir

The hundred thousand signatures forwarded to you during my absence,[1] with the <u>twenty</u> <u>thousand</u> toward our second installment, now here in office, are the result of our <u>first</u> effort— We ↑then↓ sent out <u>6,000</u> Petition packages—they returned us 120,000 signatures—

We are unwilling to give up our promise of the Million—and are now preparing to make a new planting of 25,000 petitions, with a direct personal appeal to the President of every Soldier's & Freedmen's relief society to aid us in our work to kill the <u>Cause</u> of all our national troubles— At least we will make one more bold effort—

The Paper & Printing trades of this City—have kindly pledged to donate us the <u>paper</u> & <u>printing</u>—we now lack only the <u>Postage</u>— Can you tell me any way we can ↑get↓ M.C. franks— I see the objections to you or other prominent A. Slavery members giving yours—but are there not some new converts in Congress who will frank for us— Or, if you think the effect better to have no franking, Can you not say the word to some of the best members that shall move them to send us contributions in money to aid us in paying our postage—

Your speech at the time of presenting our Petition was most excellent— What a stupid Washington Correspondent the Tribune must have there, that he did not forward it entire for the ↑next↓ mornings paper—[2] With our 25,000 Petitions we shall send out a circular letter— or appeal—& on same sheet print your speech entire— I enclose the Globes copy of it—if there ↑are↓ any changes you would like—please make them—

Mr. Sumner, Could you not send us all the scattering petitions that are & have been presented in the Senate & House— We very much wish to roll ↑up↓ every name in our Mammoth petition—if you cannot send them to us, will you not carefully stow every one with or in the trunk we sent—so that at the end of this session we may count them up & thus swell the lists—

And, Mr Sumner, is there not a word on the importance of the people's registering their names for entire & immediate abolition by Congress & by Constitution— The people cannot believe the little thing of signing a Petition worth doing—they need to be told by members of Congress—

Our new petitions include the demand for Constitutional amendment—so hereafter we shall pray for the two safeguards—

George Thompson's Reception last evening was a glorious triumph— not to him alone—but to freedom & Fremont—[3] With deepest gratitude   Yours

⇜ *Susan B. Anthony*

⇜ ALS, on loyal league letterhead for 1863, date corrected, bMS Am 1(67–104), Charles Sumner Papers, MH-H.

1. SBA returned to Rochester in January to help her mother prepare for the wedding of Daniel R. Anthony and Anna E. Osborne on 21 January.

2. See *New York Daily Tribune,* 10 February 1864. The *Congressional Directory* for this session lists no Senate reporter for the *Tribune.*

3. John C. Frémont presided at a reception at the Cooper Institute in honor of British abolitionist George Thompson. Frémont explained that though he

was not a veteran of the antislavery struggle, he represented the new, armed phase of the same fight. As commander of the Western Department in the war, he placed Missouri under martial law in 1861 and freed the slaves of rebels. When Lincoln revoked the order, Frémont became a symbol of abolitionist frustrations with the administration and a possible presidential candidate in 1864. (*New York Daily Tribune*, 1 March 1864; McPherson, *Struggle for Equality*, 72–74, 264–65.)

·⊂━━━━━━⊃·

185 ∿ SBA TO CHARLES SUMNER

New York, March 6 1864.

Dear Friend

We dispastached a thousand envelopes by to days Express—

Your note came duly— thank you for your prompt & cheerful attention to our work—when almost every-body thinks & says it is too late— slavery is already dead—it is really very cheering to get cordial aid from members of Congress—[1] In every package is a copy of the enclosed—[2] I wish we could send your little speech to be read at every fireside throughout the Country—it is the best word on the subject we have been able to get—though we have had several tracts written specially for our need—[3] Yours Truly

∿ *Susan B. Anthony*

P.S.—Our office is to be honored on Friday evening next by a meeting of young <u>working</u> <u>men</u> of this City to organize the first "<u>Freedom & Fremont</u> Club"—[4] I rejoice in any movement that asserts the right to examine & pronounce upon <u>the administration</u>—the tendency to despotic rule—<u>all treason</u>, that dissents from Lincoln—must be checked— Let the <u>young working men</u> demand larger installments of freedom—& lets see if <u>the people</u> will not say amen— S. B. A.

∿ ALS, on loyal league letterhead for 1863, date corrected, bMS Am 1(67–114), Charles Sumner Papers, MH-H.

1. Sumner replied on 2 March, with corrections in the text of his speech and the explanation that the league's mailings could be franked if they were sent from Washington. On 24 March he reported that he had franked the third and fourth installments sent him by SBA, and he had presented more petitions to the Senate. The Senate began to consider what became the Thirteenth

Amendment at the end of March and passed it on 8 April. In the House of Representatives in June, the measure failed to win a two-thirds majority. Throughout this period, the loyal league continued to circulate petitions; it sent more than 85,000 new signatures at the end of May and neared a total of 400,000 signatures when the session ended in July. (Donald, *Charles Sumner and the Rights of Man*, 149–50; *Congressional Globe*, 38th Cong., 1st sess., 1313, 1490; Venet, *Neither Ballots nor Bullets*, 146–47, 192n; C. Sumner to SBA, 2 March, 24 March 1864, SBA to C. Sumner, 23 May 1864, ECS to C. Sumner, c. 28 May, 23 June 1864, *Film*, 10:731–33, 818–19, 821, 839, 45:360.)

2. Enclosure missing.

3. On 7 April, the league published *The Prayer of One Hundred Thousand*, with Sumner's speech and the new petition seeking a constitutional amendment. (*Film*, 10:746–49.)

4. The Freedom and Frémont Club, or the Frémont Campaign Club, was organized at the league's offices on 18 March.

·❈·

186 ✑ ECS TO CAROLINE HEALEY DALL

New York, [*c. 22 April 1864*].[1]

Dear Mrs. Dall,

Enclosed find our call.[2] Do you intend to be here during anniversary week? If so we should be glad to hear from you in the convention, on the political questions of the day.

Woman will undoubtedly be a power in the coming Presidential campaign, & is already speaking on all phases of the question, hence the importance that we know whereof we speak.

I am opposed to the reelection of Lincoln, on two grounds

1st I do not believe in the two term principle, especially in time of war when under military power a man can do so much

2nd He has proved his incapacity for the great responsibilities of his position.

I want the women of the nation to give some expression of their desire in favour of a complete overthrow of the present dynasty.

Why do not you Boston women galvanize Mr Garrison into something higher & better than an admirer & adulater of Abraham with the foul serpent of slavery coiled up in his bosom.[3] I say Butler[4] or Fremont or some man on their platform for the next President & let Abe finish up his jokes in Springfield We have had enough of "Nero fiddling in Rome" in times like these, when the nation groans in sorrow, & mothers mourn for their first born. If you cannot come write a good letter, your friend sincerely

～ *E Cady Stanton.*

＜ ALS, on 1863 letterhead folio, unaltered, with call to the loyal league's anniversary, C. H. Dall Collection, MHi. In *Film* after 14 April.

1. Dated with reference to ECS to William Lloyd Garrison, 22 April 1864, which contains several of the same phrases, in *Film*, 10:761–65.
2. To the first anniversary of the Women's Loyal National League, on 12 May at the Church of the Puritans. It urged women to participate in "the reconstruction of the nation on the basis of justice and equality," to "infuse into the politics of the nation a purer morality and religion," and to make themselves "a *power for freedom* in the coming Presidential Campaign."
3. In an editorial in the *Liberator* on 18 March, Garrison threw his support to Lincoln because a more radical candidate would split the Republican party. ECS admonished him, "[y]ou must still be a leader of public sentiment & when you find easy sailing with the majority rest assured your face is down stream." (ECS to W. L. Garrison, 22 April 1864.)
4. Benjamin Franklin Butler (1818–1893), a former Democratic politician in Massachusetts, was a major general in the Union army. While commander of Fort Monroe in 1861, he sheltered runaway slaves within his lines, for the first time calling them "contraband of war." Appointed military governor of New Orleans in May 1862, he was widely suspected of corruption and condemned for his infamous order that labeled as whores any southern women who insulted Union soldiers. He was removed as governor in December 1862. (*DAB*; McPherson, *Ordeal by Fire*, 380–81; Warner, *Generals in Blue*.)

187 ～ WENDELL PHILLIPS TO ECS

Ap^l 25 '64

Dear friend,

Your S. B. A thinks she is very cunning!! As if I did not see a monstrous large, huge pussy under that meal![1]

She has been so modest, humble, ashamed, reluctant, apologetic, contrite self accusing, whenever, the last ten years, she has asked me to do anything, go anywhere, speak on any topic!! Now she makes <u>you</u>

pull the chestnuts out of the fire & thinks I do not see her waiting behind!![2] Ah, the hand is the hand of Esau the voice is the voice of Jacob, wicked—sly—skulking, mystifying Jacob![3] why dont "Secretaries" write the official letters? How much they leave the "President" to do! naughty idlers those secretaries!

Well first thank Miss Secretary Anthony for her gentle consideration, then let me say I'll try to speak as you say fifteen minutes—but I cannot consent to take part in nominating our Fremont— He is my choice but I cant see any benefit to our canvas in nominating then & there—the machinery is working to give him a fair chance   My judgment is to leave his name to come out naturally from Conventions met to nominate— But still if you think better to do so dont let me stand in the way— But for very good reasons, I think, I would ask then to be excused from speaking— We shall confine the American Anniversary to individual expressions of opinion but let the Society keep uncommitted if we can so far direct its action. My judg^t would be for your league to do the same. Is it quite fair to turn into a partisan machine something meant for a specific & definite object

Understand me I do not presume to dictate— But I must act myself on my own convictions   Remember me defiantly to S. B. A. & Believe me faithfully

❧ *W Phillips*

❧ ALS, Alma Lutz Collection, MCR-S. "Dear Mrs. Stanton" added in a different hand. Also in *Anthony*, 1:237.

1. ECS assumed SBA's secretarial duties to invite speakers to the league's anniversary meeting.

2. A reference to an old fable about a monkey who used the cat's paw to draw chestnuts from the fire. To become a cat's paw, thus, is to become the instrument of another.

3. Thus Isaac responded when his son Jacob disguised himself as his twin brother Esau. (Gen. 27:22.)

·⟨═══≈⟨═══⟩·

188 ≫ ECS TO WENDELL PHILLIPS

[*New York*] 26th April, [*1864*]

Dear Phillips,

As Susan is in Albany I may now be supposed to write what is in my own brain, & I say I was glad to hear from you that you would speak for us, if we would only be ladylike, politic & puristic in our Convention. We will be everything that you desire, everything that is best for the triumph of Fremont

We fully agree with you in what you say is best, but we were very strongly urged, to declare ourselves for Fremont by some of his special friends,[1] but we did not see the matter clear & it was to fortify our <u>own</u> opinions that in solemm counsel "Pussy" & "Paw" decided to sound you & to all that the silver voiced oracle saith, ever clear as a bel<u>l</u>e, I say Amen. As to my proper functions, when Lincoln condescends to walk in the streets may not I write letters? especially if I desire the autography of great men. You will never talk to me,—always run away with somebody else never accept my invitations, & now you coolly hint that it is improper for me to write you, inasmuch as you prefer to correspond with people who have brains of their own. sorrowfully,

≫   "Cats paw"

Dear Lydia Mott & her sister are very ill, & Susan is with them. Jane will not recover, her physician so decides.[2] Kind regards to Mrs Phillips—

≫ ALS, bMS Am 1953(1152), Wendell Phillips Papers, MH-H.

1. One among their friends of Frémont was his wife, Jessie Benton Frémont, who contributed to the league and consulted SBA and ECS in the spring of 1864. (ECS to J. B. Frémont, April 1864, and *New York Daily Tribune*, 28 May 1864, *Film*, 10:774, 810; *NAW*.)

2. Jane Mott (1796–?) was the older sister of Lydia Mott. A week later SBA wrote to a friend, "I left the Miss Mott's of Albany somewhat improved & hope they may be restored ere long." (SBA to George W. Lord, 5 May 1864, *Film*, 10:779–82.)

·❮══════❯·

189 ❧ ECS to Caroline Healey Dall

New York, May 7, 1864.

My Dear Friend—I regret that any misapprehension, on your part, of the nature and purposes of the "Woman's National League," should have caused you the confusion your letter manifests.[1]

In your invidious insinuation of a concealed purpose, you reveal your man of straw, alone vulnerable to your attack.

The *Call* for the Convention was legitimately open for a public reply; but the League is in no way responsible for my private letters. Your paradoxical letter of fragmentary thoughts, thrown together without logic or arrangement, I have pondered as I would a Chinese puzzle;[2] and after adjusting and readjusting its conflicting assertions, the following propositions are discernable:—

1st. You deny woman's political rights; she may "interest herself in national questions," but she may not "dictate."

2d. Her sphere is morals; she may not descend into vulgar politics.

3d. She is ignorant of the science of government—wholly incompetent to judge of the political fitness of a tried man for the Presidency, while, with the accuracy of a thermometer, she measures a man's moral altitude the moment he enters her presence.

4th. She must not enter the political arena until *invited*; "an unauthorized interference never produces any good results."

5th. Our Presidents are made by the direct fiat of Heaven; not like Moses, to lead the people, but like the golden calf of the Israelites, to be adored and borne on our shoulders, wherever the popular tide may flow.

6. You say Mr. Garrison's stand-point for the last thirty years has not been the best one for sound political judgment of men and measures.

Now, on all these points I take issue with you, and gladly embrace this opportunity to reassert rights I had supposed settled, long ago, in all advance minds.

1. I believe the best interests of the nation demand the united, equal power and influence of man and woman, in politics, religion and social

life; and woman will never "interest" herself in national questions until she feels she has a right to be heard. Experience and reason alike prove that the right to dictate, in all the practical affairs of life, belongs not to them only who are crowned with the glory of manhood.

2. For the moral position of the "Woman's National League," I refer you to our report and resolutions, in which you will find that we, so far from descending into an electioneering caucus or political cabal, by the enunciation of principles, have lifted politics into the sphere of morals and religion. Our League, formed one year ago, pledging its members loyal to freedom, with the avowed object of educating the nation into the idea of a true republic, is the first and only organization of women for the declared purpose of influencing politics. In petitioning Congress for an act of emancipation, we began with the a, b, c, of human rights, and have thus made ourselves a power for freedom with the people and their representatives.

We differ from you in that, as we near the point of reconstruction, we see "reason for renewed effort in the coming Presidential campaign." However faithful you may have been in the past, we, with the mass of Northern women, must mourn our want of vigilance—must plead guilty to the charge, that we have not guarded the tree of liberty with the care and earnestness they of the South have shown for their "peculiar institution." Because a careful housewife has always guarded against fire and sparks and candles, is certainly no reason why she should "not sound a special reveille" when her house is in flames.

3. The great difficulties in the exercise of civil power, "not yet surmounted by man even after years of experience," should, you say, "make woman pause before assuming responsibilities God has not conferred." To my mind these difficulties are not traceable to the intricacy of the problem of government, for justice is a simple thing, but to the blindness of man in not seeing that freedom and equality are the cornerstones of all just and stable governments. Perchance, with woman's help, he might more easily have unrolled the tangled skein that has so sorely perplexed him unaided and alone.

As to woman's ignorance of the science of government, we Americans are proverbial for our knowledge of politics and its machinery. When the wife of old John Adams rebuked him for the fatal compromises with slavery made in the Constitutional Convention, did she not show the higher statesmanship?

In the exciting campaign of "Tippecanoe and Tyler too,"[3] who so firmly and eloquently kept up the standard of freedom—who so thoroughly understood the momentous issues of that hour, as did Abby Kelley Foster?—a name I ever speak with reverence.[4] Have not women for the last twenty years taught our legislators higher laws of justice, and compelled them to clean their books of many barbarous statutes? What man did more than Anna Dickinson to save the election in Connecticut and Pennsylvania? The best word yet spoken on the vexed question of retaliation is by a Connecticut woman, in the *Independent* of May 5.[5]

In dooming woman to modest silence, then commanding her to arraign her rulers before the judgment seat of the people by "moral rebukes," "the stern stand and deliver," your logic is like that of a fond mother who bade her son "never go near the water till he had learned to swim"; and your cruelty is only surpassed by the rude men in Titus Andronicus, who cut out the tongue and cut off the hands of the royal daughter, then bade her "go call for water, and wash her hands."[6]

In judging of our public men, I am at a loss to know by what plummet you sound their moral depths. You praise President Lincoln, who holds millions of human beings in slavery, with its wholesale licentiousness and concubinage, and denies the right of suffrage to free black citizens, while you scorn the name of Gen. Butler, whose policy is freedom—the recognition of the manhood of the slave. Remember, in the black man we are settling the fundamental principles of morals and government. It is not a question merely of what shall we do with four millions of Africans, but what are the rights of man. President Lincoln's proclamations are a dead letter, unless backed up by the immortal declaration, "All men are created equal," and our revolution to no purpose, unless in the reconstruction we realize that sublime utterance of the Fathers.

4. What progress should we have made in government if men had always waited for an invitation to take their rights and privileges? Would there have been a House of Commons in the English Parliament if the people had waited for the Lords to inaugurate the movement? Would our revolutionary Fathers ever have founded a republic, and repudiated the monarch and his throne, had they waited for the permission of George III? Did Massachusetts or New York propose to give their women their rights of property, children and wages, before

we ourselves made the demand? "No, no, an aristocracy never seeks to share its privileges."

5. "If, through the uncertainties of politicians and the quarrels of demagogues, God led Abraham Lincoln to the executive chair" to clog the wheels of civilization, a dead weight on the people for education at the very moment they needed a pillar of light to go before them in the wilderness, who should say that Pierce[7] and Buchanan were not given for the same purpose; and thus involve God in the absurdity of changing his politics once in four years, and dividing the heavenly hosts into Republicans and Democrats? To my mind, thus to bring God and the angels down into the "muddy pool of politics" would be far worse than for the daughters of the Pilgrims, "unauthorized," even to share all the dangers and difficulties of this earthly sphere.

The day has passed for making Providence the scape-goat for all our ignorance and folly. Our duty is to study the immutable principles of right, and bring ourselves and the nation into tune with them. We do not propose to leave the next Presidency to chance, or guess, or wire-pullers, under the very shadow of executive patronage, but that the people, in mass convention, shall decide, for themselves, whom they will have of the men already tried. We do not want "an unknown man, pledged to nobody and nothing." Neither do we want one pledged to slavery, as President Lincoln has ever been. Had I been asked who should be President in '61, I should have said, William H. Seward.[8] Gen. Fremont was not thought of in that campaign, though a candidate in '56. The emergencies of the war have placed Generals Butler and Fremont before the nation, admired for their military genius, their statesmanship, their executive ability, and their broad views of human rights. If Gen. Butler should be chosen for our next President, your position would be a very painful one; for four long years you would not be able to write or speak the name of the executive of the nation;[9] but under such Providence, perhaps you might "patiently learn the lesson" of the one term principle.

6. They who, outside the excitement and competition of a game, calmly watch the moves and chances, often see the results more clearly than those who play. In the conventions of politicians, in the speeches of acknowledged statesmen, either in our day or the past, where do you find deeper, broader, higher principles of policy and government than have been uniformly enunciated in our Anti-Slavery conventions? For

the last thirty years, they have been the nation's school, where new measures have been candidly and severely criticised, and where our most liberal Christians, clearest logicians, earnest orators, and wisest statesmen, have taken their best lessons for the practical work of life. Who can say that Wendell Phillips, the advance man of this hour, would not be a safer pilot at the helm of government than Thurlow Weed, the American Talleyrand,[10] and skilled as he is in all the arts of diplomacy and management? Yours, sincerely,

≺   *E. Cady Stanton.*

≺ *Lib.*, 3 June 1864. Also printed in *NASS*, 11 June 1864, with changes in placement of quotation marks.

1. Written in response to Caroline Dall's published letter to ECS, dated 1 May, answering ECS's letter at c. 22 April, above. Dall proclaimed that "if the women of the advance owe one duty to their country more than another, it is the duty of *modest* service in this hour of trial." She did not want women, inexperienced in politics, to turn the convention into "an electioneering caucus" and "forfeit forever a moral stand-point which is *fully* their own." More specifically, she did not want the convention to endorse Butler or Frémont for president. ECS quotes and paraphrases extensively from her letter. (*NASS*, 7 May 1864, *Film*, 10:775–77; *Lib.* 6 May 1864.)

2. An intricate puzzle, specifically one made up of interlocking shapes.

3. The campaign slogan of William Henry Harrison and John Tyler, the Whig presidential and vice-presidential candidates of 1840.

4. Abby Kelley opposed both parties in the 1840 election because of their toleration of slavery.

5. A Connecticut woman who signed herself "H. M." urged the federal government and the individual states to grant suffrage and equal rights to African Americans in retaliation for the Fort Pillow massacre of black Union soldiers who had already surrendered. Such a response would send the message that freedmen were the equals of northern whites and strike a blow to the very heart of the Confederacy. (*Independent* 16 [5 May 1864]: 1.)

6. *Titus Andronicus*, act 2, sc. 4, line 6.

7. Franklin Pierce (1804–1869), fourteenth president of the United States.

8. William Henry Seward (1801–1872), former New York governor and senator, served as secretary of state in the cabinets of Abraham Lincoln and Andrew Johnson. He was an unsuccessful candidate for the Republican presidential nomination in 1856 and 1860. (*DAB*; Taylor, *William Henry Seward.*)

9. In her letter, Dall refused to "soil" her paper with Butler's name because of his immorality.

10. ECS compares Thurlow Weed with Charles Maurice Talleyrand Périgord (1754–1838), a French statesman and diplomat, renowned for his skills in negotiation and political survival.

·◁━━━━▨━━━━▷·

190   SBA TO ECS

69 North Street[1]   Rochester May 30/64

Dear Mrs. Stanton

I am safe home—stopped at Albany until 10.45 P.M.—then took train in company with Pillsbury to Rochester—other <u>Cleveland</u> Pilgrim in company[2]—also Maria Giddings taking home the body of her dear Father—[3]

She said he never seemed brighter or more beautiful in spirit than but a very few moments before he dropped—it is delightful to go thus—

Found all well here— P. P. came to Mothers with me after dinner— I went with him to Hallowells[4] & he left for Cleveland this A.M. in first best spirits— Phillips send splendid <u>letter</u> by him—but will go on to day if he possibly can—[5] Oh such times as they had at Boston last week— I wish you could have been with us—but you will have to read <u>under</u> the ink in the report in this weeks paper— You will see that Pillsbury's Resolutions were adopted & Garrisons "<u>substitutes</u>" stripped of their "<u>bald</u> lie"—as Stephen Foster said they carried on their face— & then adopted. The "<u>lie</u>" was that this government <u>had</u> recognized the equal manhood of the negro—[6]

Please to observe that <u>Gay</u> did <u>not</u> put our financial appeal with our Report in the supplement—though I sent a note to him Friday asking him <u>not</u> to fail to do it—[7] I wish you would make see that he has <u>cheated</u> us ⸢out⸣ of the very end we aimed at— ~~Whenever you~~ But I am going

❧ AL, incomplete, Smith Papers, NSyU. Was enclosure in ECS to G. Smith, 2 June 1864.

1. The *Standard* noted on 28 May that SBA's address was now Rochester. Sixty-nine North Street was the home of her mother.

2. Parker Pillsbury was on his way to the convention in Cleveland on 31 May, called for the purpose of nominating John C. Frémont for president.

3. Joshua Reed Giddings (1795–1864) of Ohio, one of the earliest abolitionists in the House of Representatives, died in Montreal, where he served as consul general to the British North American Provinces, on 27 May 1864. Lura

Maria Giddings (1825–1871) was his oldest daughter. An antislavery activist herself, she contributed to Ohio's woman's rights movement. (*BDAC*; George Washington Julian, *The Life of Joshua Giddings* [Chicago, 1892], 25; *History*, 1:114.)

4. That is, Mary and William Hallowell.

5. Wendell Phillips sent a letter endorsing Frémont, criticizing Lincoln's reconstruction policies, and calling for citizenship and suffrage for African-American men. (*NASS*, 11 June 1864.)

6. At the New England Anti-Slavery Society meeting. Garrison praised the advance of antislavery sentiment and called on Congress to abolish slavery. As evidence of progress, he offered "the recognition of the citizenship of all native-born colored inhabitants," a point Stephen Foster disputed and the meeting rejected. (*Lib.*, 3 June 1864.)

7. The league's executive committee presented a report on the year's work at the meeting of 12 May. The *Daily Tribune Supplement* printed it on 28 May, but the league's appeal for funds appeared in the regular edition on 26 May. (*Film*, 10:810, 820.)

·◁▭▭▭✦▭▭▭▷·

191 ❧ ECS TO GERRIT SMITH

June 2^d [*1864*]   New York.

Dear Cousin Gerrit,

Well has not John spoken brave words at Cleveland,[1] how it does rejoice my heart to see him at last so thoroughly entrenching himself in eternal principles. Yes it is true under this weak administration our most sacred rights have been slowly but surely drifting away. Even here where the civil courts have all been open citizens have been thrown into Fort Lafayette with ↑out↓ notice or trial. There is some reason for the exercise of arbitrary power in the army & on the high seas but none in this Metropolis.[2]

I have been asked many times how you stood on the Presidential question. as I did not know exactly I have always said, you were right as you were ever for "principles not men"[3]   I had a long letter yesterday from Wendell Phillips   he says they had a most stormy time in the New England convention, but he conquered, Garrison was voted down in Boston. Phillips spoke grandly here, Garrison's special pleading was most pitiful.[4] Beside hearing them speak several times in public I had several private conversations with each separately, & feel sure that Phillips occupies the higher ground. How I should like to see you to know just what you think, are you not coming down soon?

Phillips says this administration has as yet failed to recognize the <u>manhood</u> of the negro & until that is done all special proclamations & privileges are but a mockery, an insult. I see the point & feel it. What is a man's love! his tenderness! his care! what though he picks up my fan, carves my food, clothes me in purple so long as he denies my equality— & regards me as property! When we demand suffrage for the negros we make freedom a fact. If John stops at Peterboro on his return conjure him never again to lower his standard. He occupies the advance ground now, may he redeem the errors of the past by earnestness & devotion to principle,—thus do we make age happy & beautiful. We need a grand army of freedom to defend with pen & voice the sacred rights of habeas corpus free, speech, & press.— I enclose a scrap from a letter of Susan Anthony. Much love to all. Has Cousin Nancy read Cudjo's cave?[5] It is very thrilling & has some beautiful love scenes & sentiments. We are all well. I have all the boys in good places. Neil is doing well with George Livingston wholesale commission house[6]   Kit & Gat in law offices, where they study & write making $5. a week. The burthen of life is nothing to those who have hope & courage   Love to Charly Julius & Greene.[7] I was sorry not to see Greene when he was sick here but it was in the midst of our small pox dispensation. I sent Neil down to invite him up to my hospital but he declined.

⇒ AL, Smith Papers, NSyU.

1. John Cochrane (1813–1898) was a lawyer and a formidable Democratic politician. A son of Gerrit Smith's sister, Cornelia Smith Cochran, John changed the spelling of his surname in 1855. From 1856 to 1861 he served in the House of Representatives, and until the eve of the war, he supported states rights and blamed the North for divisions that threatened the Union. The attack on Fort Sumter, however, jolted him into joining the army where he served until 1863. Cochrane was elected attorney general of New York and in 1864, he presided at the convention to nominate John C. Frémont for president. There he condemned the Lincoln administration's suspension of *habeas corpus* and other infringements of civil rights; "never upon any plea or occasion," he declared, "can the rights of the citizen be suffered to be unwarrantably invaded, and without due process of law." He was selected as Frémont's running mate. (*BDAC*; Warner, *Generals in Blue*; *New York Daily Tribune*, 1 June 1864; Alexander, *Political History of New York*, 2:272, 3:4–10, 25, 75–76, 90–92; Smith Papers, NSyU.)

2. Suspension of the writ of *habeas corpus* by the president was a bone of contention throughout the war, especially when it affected civilians whose crimes were political ones. ECS may refer to the military seizure of the New York *World* and the *Journal of Commerce* and their editors in May 1864. (James G. Randall, *Constitutional Problems Under Lincoln* [New York, 1926], 147-53, 496-99.)

3. Smith answered ECS in a public letter dated 6 June 1864, saying that his primary concern was to keep out of power "a man who would make any other terms with the rebels than their absolute submission." (*Lib.*, 17 June 1864, *Film*, 835-36.)

4. Wendell Phillips and William Lloyd Garrison spoke at the May meeting of the American Anti-Slavery Society. Phillips criticized the administration for seeking to crush the rebellion without acknowledging that the future security of republican institutions depended upon the abolition of slavery and guarantees of equal civil and political rights. Garrison contended that Lincoln deserved reelection because he was committed to enforcement of the Emancipation Proclamation. (*Lib.*, 20, 27 May 1864.)

5. *Cudjo's Cave*, by John Townsend Trowbridge, published in 1864.

6. Daniel Cady Stanton left his job as a clerk at the Custom House in disgrace, accused even by his father of improper, perhaps illegal, conduct. George H. Livingston, merchant, lived in Brooklyn and had his business at 58 Broad Street in New York. (Rice, "Henry B. Stanton," 424, 429, 446; New York City directory, 1863-1864.)

7. Green Smith (1842-1886), who enlisted in the Fourteenth New York Heavy Artillery in 1860, was suffering from congestion of the lungs. (Harlow, *Gerrit Smith*, 308-9, 423-24, 489; Gerrit Smith to ECS, 20 August, 19 November 1864, *Film*, 10:881-82, 916; Smith Papers, NSyU.)

192 ❧ SBA TO ECS

Rochester, June 12, 1864.

Dear Mrs. Stanton:

Isn't the spirit of the Lincoln press on Fremont and the abolitionists diabolical? I have seen nothing kindly and manly save the New York *Evening Post*.[1] I hope Fremont will just hold on in patience to the day of election. Already the desired effect is apparent. Baltimore gave us a better platform and Old Abe a more explicit letter of acceptance.[2] Fremont's platform ought to have said fully and frankly, "equal civil and political rights to black men."[3] That is really the one and only point at issue between the parties to-day. I am starving for a full talk with somebody posted, not merely pitted for Lincoln. I wish I could see Fremont. I was a little disappointed in Fremont's letter of acceptance; and yet it is good.[4] But it did not electrify as I had expected it would. These men don't see the right way to express themselves. What a pity that they should take the ground that "slavery is dead." It requires explanation. It is in the process of dying. Our papers are publishing all of Garrison's eulogies on Lincoln and calling the attention of all abolitionists and radical republicans to them. In their eyes, Mr. Garrison is now a sound philosopher and wise statesman.[5] Yours sincerely,

❧ *Susan B. Anthony.*

❧ Typed transcript, ECS Papers, DLC.

1. The *Evening Post* did not endorse Frémont, but it described him as a man of "ability and patriotism," whose criticism of the administration's violations of civil rights expressed the "prevailing public sentiment." (1 June 1864.)

2. The platform of the Baltimore National Union Convention, held by the Republican party, called for the abolition of slavery by constitutional amendment, enlistment of former slaves into the Union army, and "full protection of the laws of war" for Union soldiers, "without regard to distinction of color." Lincoln approved the demand for an amendment "to prohibit slavery throughout the nation." (*Lib.*, 17 June 1864.)

3. The Cleveland convention resolved that "the Rebellion has destroyed Slavery, and the Federal Constitution should be amended to prohibit its reestablishment, and to secure to all men absolute equality before the law." Parker Pillsbury failed to persuade the delegates to endorse suffrage for African Americans. (*New York Daily Tribune*, 1 June 1864; McPherson, *Struggle for Equality*, 270.)

4. Although Frémont endorsed an amendment ending slavery, he focused attention on the administration's usurpation of power. (*Lib.*, 10 June 1864.)

5. After Garrison attended the Baltimore convention, he had an interview with Lincoln in Washington. (McPherson, *Struggle for Equality*, 271-72.)

·⟨══════⟩·

193 ≈ ECS TO GERRIT SMITH

New York July 3rd [*1864*]

My dear Cousin,

Your letter to Henry was like balm to his wounded spirit as every expression of kindness & confidence is. That infamous report was bought![1] The chairman (Hurlbut of St. Lawrence)[2] told me <u>after the testimony had all gone in</u> there was nothing implicating Henry   He told Fenton[3] & Wilkeson the same thing. The moment that report appeared in the Tribune I went to every editor, in the city, made a full statement & urged them not to publish the report until they had Mr Stantons reply. It was not published in a single paper. The World even waited for the reply & then published a few extracts from both. Raymond has taken no notice of the affair from the beginning & told me he never should believing it to be a miserable raid.[4] I have had a new phase of life in the last eight months with Investigating Com. marshalls, grand jurors, editors & Lawyers & Weeds & have been surprized to find how small the sons of Adam are   The grand & great in Nature grows more so at each advancing step, but man ever greater in the distance

> "And thus our idols perish one by one
> In knowing what we once adoreed"

Lest you being a great man should take this insidiously, let me say sub rosa that I have never felt that disappointment in the sage of Peterboro. I expect Duncan McMartin down this week & then we shall try to bring this matter to a head, that Henry may feel at ease.[5] I am glad Chase has resigned, this is the first shock in the wreck of this rotten administration under which we may already write justice obsolete, in the republic.[6] A man in high position said to me a few days since, the short way of settleing all this matter is for Mr Stanton to buy his peace. That said I he will never do with my consent   I should scorn to buy any advantage that could not be secured to the humblest citizen of the Republic. I am glad our Governor has laid his hand on these arbitrary arrests, that question better be tested before we drift into a hopeless despotism, & he has nicely chosen one of the highest officials Gen Dix, for the criminal, unlike the crafty Abraham who seeks obscurity for <u>his</u> vengence.[7] I had letters from Cate & Sam yesterday. Frank[8] is visiting them in Washington, he has been made second Lieut. in the same company Bayard fell, in the regular army. How does Mrs Birney bear her affliction?[9] if she is with you give her my love & sympathy. This war in one form or another must try us all, & we have not yet neared the bitter end. Blessed are those who with hope & philosophy know how to bear earth's trials bravely but on all they leave their scars. Mama was well when Harriet last wrote. Gat went up last week with my little girls. Mr & Mrs Brown sail from Liverpool on the 16th & hope to spend Hatties birthday in Johnstown.[10] Cady & Alice have been there for a few weeks   Mr McMartin has just returned from Iowa where he owns a large tract of land he is charmed with that western country. Neil has been promoted in his business ~~he is doing very well~~, George Livingston speaks very well of him. I can already see many blessings under the dark cloud now passing over us. Much love to each & all. Why does Julius write no loving words to Johnson in the hour of trial. I do not remember to have received a letter in months though I know it is from ↑no↓ want of affection. What did Cousin Nancy think of my charming Nelly? [*in margin of first page*] She must tell me herself. adieu your Cousin

⪼ *E. C. S.*

⪼ ALS, Smith Papers, NSyU.

1. The House Committee on Public Expenditures issued its report on fraud in the New York Custom House on 15 June. It concluded that Henry Stanton was guilty of "no common carelessness if not culpable complicity" in the abstraction of bonds and other misconduct. Stanton's biographer concludes that, no doubt careless in administering his office, Stanton was sacrificed to protect Collector of the Port Hiram Barney. (*New York Daily Tribune*, 16, 17 June 1864; Rice, "Henry B. Stanton," 441–45, 453–58; Frederick J. Blue, *Salmon P. Chase: A Life in Politics* [Kent, Ohio, 1987], 232–35.)

2. Calvin Tilden Hulburd (1809–1897), Republican congressman from St. Lawrence County, chaired the House Committee on Public Expenditures. (*BDAC*; Rice, "Henry B. Stanton," 452–53.)

3. Reuben Eaton Fenton (1819–1885), a founder of the Republican party, was the congressman from Chautauqua County. He was elected governor of New York in 1864. (*BDAC*.)

4. The New York *World* published extracts from the report and Henry

Stanton's reply on 17 June 1864. Henry Jarvis Raymond (1820–1869) was editor of the *New York Times*.

5. Though Duncan McMartin's specific role is not evident, the family's legal talent had been mobilized in Henry Stanton's defense. John Cochrane was his counsel, and Samuel Wilkeson acted as messenger between his brother-in-law and the congressional committee. (Rice, "Henry B. Stanton," 425.)

6. Lincoln accepted the resignation of Secretary of the Treasury Salmon Portland Chase (1808–1873) on 30 June. Chase lost the Republican nomination to Frémont in 1856 and to Lincoln in 1860. An ally of the radical Republicans, he let his name be considered for nomination in 1864. Lincoln later appointed him chief justice of the Supreme Court. (*BDAC*; Blue, *Salmon P. Chase*.)

7. Governor Horatio Seymour determined to prosecute those responsible for arresting the editors of the *World* and the *Journal of Commerce*, and at the time ECS wrote, warrants had been issued for the arrest of General John Adams Dix (1798–1879). (Randall, *Constitutional Problems Under Lincoln*, 496–99; *BDAC*.)

8. Frank Wilkeson (1848–1913), the second son of Samuel and Catharine Cady Wilkeson, lied about his age to enlist in the Second New York Independent Battery after the death at Gettysburg of his older brother Bayard (1844–1863). (*ACAB*; *WWW4*; *Military Order of the Loyal Legion of the United States Commandery of the State of Kansas*, printed circular, KHi.)

9. Fitzhugh Birney died of pneumonia on 17 June. ([Cutler], *Fitzhugh Birney*, 34.)

10. Harriet Cady Eaton, widowed herself, often stayed with her widowed mother in the Cady family house in Johnstown, to which ECS sent her children for summer visits. Harriet Eaton's children—Cady, his wife Alice, his sister Harriet Eaton Brown—gathered there as well. In 1857, young Harriet married George Stewart Brown (1834–1890), head of the international banking house Alexander Brown & Sons of Baltimore. Her birthday fell on 4 August. (*NCAB*, 1:474–45; *Biographical Cyclopedia of Representative Men of Maryland and District of Columbia* [Baltimore, 1879], 74–75; Frank R. Kent, *The Story of Alex. Brown & Sons* [Baltimore, 1950].)

·〈══════〉·

194 ⮌ ECS to Wendell Phillips

75. West 45th   New York   Sept 25th [*1864*]

Dear Mr Phillips,

Returning in the cars yesterday from the West a gentleman asked me what your position would be during the Presidential campaign   What

should I have said? What did I say? "I do not know" would undoubtedly ↑have↓ been the wise & proper answer, but I am not proper & so
I said I presume his position will be what it ever has been a terror to evil
doers   He will criticise both Lincoln & McClellan & vote for neither.[1]
You are mistaken said he, "both Phillips & Freemont will take the
stump for Lincoln next month." What shall I say the next time that
question is put to me? If you are not satisfied with my answer give me
a better one   in haste   your friend

ᐁ   E Cady Stanton.

ᐁ ALS, bMS Am 1953(1152), Wendell Phillips Papers, MH-H.

1. The Democratic National Convention in Chicago in August nominated
George B. McClellan for president and adopted a platform acceptable to
Peace Democrats. The nomination united Republicans and many abolition-
ists behind Lincoln as the only candidate who could defeat McClellan. John
Frémont withdrew from the race on 22 September, in return for the resigna-
tion of conservative Postmaster General Montgomery Blair.

·⊂══════⟫·

195   ᐁ   WENDELL PHILLIPS TO ECS

Sept 27th Tuesday [1864]

Dear friend

Yours just come. You answered correctly. I would cut off both
hands before doing any thing to aid Mac's election— I would cut off
my right hand before doing any thing to aid A. L.'s election— I wholly
distrust his fitness to settle this thing—indeed his purpose   de Retz
said "feeble men always reluct at the means necessary for their ends"—[1]
A. L. wishes the end, wont consent to the <u>means</u>—

our friends (honesty) have quitted the old platform— we used to
hold "that it is always <u>safe</u> to do <u>right</u>"— they dont dare to do what
they confess wd be absolute right now— we used to say "let the
potsherds of the earth contend"[2]—no matter of ours— H. Mann offered
us in 1850 half the loaf–we refused even tho' he warned us we risked
democratic <u>success</u> by our opposition.[3] I still rejects A L's quarter loaf
at the same hazard— <u>Justice</u> is still more to me than <u>union</u>   Yrs

ᐁ   Wendell Phillips

❧ ALS, ECS Papers, DLC.

1. Jean François Paul de Retz (1613–1679), a French cardinal, is best known for his *Memoirs of Cardinal de Retz*, first published in 1717, full of succinct and colorful phrases and anecdotes.

2. Paraphrase of Isa. 45:9.

3. Horace Mann sought abolitionists' support when he ran for reelection to Congress as a candidate of the Free Soil party in 1850.

·⊂══════⚭══════⊃·

196 ❧ ECS to Wendell Phillips

Sunday eve. [*6 November 1864*]

Dear Friend,

Did you see Beechers last sermon[1] He speaks grandly & truly of you. How good & broad he is the only public man who has yet dared to give you unqualified praise. Now be sure & read that to your wife, that she may know you have more than "one admirer in New York," that would be too proud a position for me to claim the only worshipper (admirer is too tame) of the best & bravest man of the land I am especially proud of you as everybody says your wife is the power behind the throne hence you represent the moral excellence & sagacity of womanhood combined with manly reason & courage. Well all I have to say I wish all men could be so compounded I read the report of your speech in the Herald & like it thoroughly.[2] Henry read it too & pronounced it the best of the season. I have seen Tilton since, I think he is under conviction & would gladly stand with you if he had the courage.

Beecher calls you Abraham's "counterparts." Do you feel magnetically attracted to him. I trow not. Well ere you get this the voice of the nation will have reelected Lincoln[3] It will be a satisfaction to us in the future to feel that we did what we could to lift the nation higher, & that no word or thought or prayer of ours has been without its influence, though none see it now.

To walk by faith, is the highest path for man. When we forsake principle for expediency all is doubt & bewilderment I hope you are as thoroughly self sustained as your friends are satisfied with you Darker days are coming—"the Lion's den" & "Fiery Furnace"[4] may yet be yours, that you may come through all as safely & soundly as through this fearful campaign is my sincere wish. Your friend & worshiper

⇝ *E Cady Stanton.*

⇝ ALS, bMS Am 1953(1152), Wendell Phillips Papers, MH-H.

1. Following his sermon on 30 October, Henry Ward Beecher praised Phillips as "the ablest speaker on the continent; a man of the profoundest political convictions," whose purpose was to "go ahead of the people" and prepare the way. (*Independent* 16 [3 November 1864]: 1.)
2. At Cooper Institute on 26 October, Phillips continued his criticism of the Lincoln administration. (*New York Herald*, 27 October 1864.)
3. The election took place Tuesday, 8 November 1864.
4. ECS refers to two tests of faith recounted in chapters three and six of the Book of Daniel.

---

197 ⇝ WENDELL PHILLIPS TO ECS

Nov 10th [*1864*]

Dear friend—

Thank you for remembering the silent but best member of the Firm. She deserves it. Those words of Beecher were very generous & very <u>profoundly</u> appreciated just now, the <u>partiality</u> of the estimate only proved the half blind affection which gave birth & their highest worth to them.

Now our common duty is to throw all <u>personal</u> matters behind us & rally together to claim of the <u>Repub</u> party the performance of their pledge (amend^{ts} of the Cons^{tn}) that puts <u>things</u> beyond <u>men</u> in all time to come & is a barrier against men & parties— On that issue the canvass was conducted, & now we have rights to demand the "bond"— ↑& they ve a right to demand that we shall help them to the ability of granting it↓ My kind regards to your husband. I pity him if you imposed on him a <u>New Yorker</u> in such a <u>month</u>, the reading of even a quarter of what the generous Herald gave me Yrs truly

⇝ *Wendell Phillips*

⇝ ALS, ECS Papers, DLC.

198   ⮞   SBA TO ECS

Leavenworth, Kansas— Tuesday Feb. 14, 1865—

My Dear Mrs. Stanton

Your letter of Jan. 23^d found me in the above City & State & in my brother D. R.'s home, with his little fat wife—he being absent in Washington D.C.—[1]

I arrived here Jan. 31st—about two weeks previous there came invitations too solid to be resisted by way of R.R. Tickets & bank check— So I waited only to have <u>my</u> <u>tip</u> <u>top</u> Rochester dress maker make the new five dollar silk of last winter, you remember— Stopped a few days in Chicago—but did not call on the League women—weather too ↑cold↓

I like Leavenworth much better than I expected, & so far the fat wife is all she promised at first sight—she has a splendid black ("Stallion") horse—"Bill" is his name—& a nice carriage & drives, <u>herself</u>, every pleasant day—last week she took me out every P.M.—the weather very like our warm <u>April</u> days—bright & beautiful, though a sharp wind— but most delightful—they have had such beautiful weather with but two or three cold or rainy days, since Christmas—the roads are dry & smooth as summer—I am quite taken captive— one day we called on Gen. Curtis, at the Fort.—three miles north of the City—but much to my regret he had left that very morning for his new head-quarters at Milwaukie—but we saw his wife & daughter-in-law—[2] The Gen. is universally loved here— They don't know about their new one—Gen. Dodge,—[3] What a world to talk over, in the worlds Political and Military— Don't you begin to <u>bend the knee to Abraham yet</u>?— Gen. Sherman's negro plan for South Carolina is better than Gen. Banks— but smacks too much of the white man's "<u>protection</u>"—which means giving to a few military favorites the sole privilege of fleecing from the faithful blacks—[4]

In this City there are Four-thousand ex-Missouri slaves—who have sought refuge ↑here,↓ within the three past ~~three~~ years— I make it a point to enter into conversation with every one I meet—I want to see the real genuine "niggers" that loves Slavery better than freedom—the ignorant, stupid ones—but so far every man woman & child of them, is brimful of good common sense, & knows more than any ten of the same class of Irish population— I have but just called at the Freedman's home—where they shelter, feed & clother the new refugees, both black & white, until they can find employment—found there a Miss or Mrs. Mead of Hillsdale Mich.[5] who said she Dined at Gerritt Smiths with you & me—the time we spoke there one Sunday—she wears curls—

Brother Dan owns a paper, which he wants me to help edit—he wants to make it the most radical mouth-piece of Kansas—but you know I can't get off anything when I think it is to go into print— I wish I could talk through it, the things I'd like to say to this young martyr state—

The Legislature gave but six votes for negro suffrage the other day— I would like to say the right say on that subject—the idea of Kansas refusing her Loyal negroes—[6]

I hear you say, how long are you going to stay in Kansas? I can't tell—6 months or a year if I like it—& six weeks or less if I don't— nothing fixed— I find promise of an added member to the household, some three of four months hence— But the prospective ↑mother↓ is as gay as a lark—plays & sings & laughs as merrily as ever & trips up & down and drives her "Bill" as fearlessly & freely as ever— How I wish you were here & free with me to travel & see & be seen— A little bit of a house—like your Irish Ann's at Seneca—rents $250. per year—Flour $16.50—Potatoes & apples 4 & 5 dollars a bushel other articles of food not far from Rochester prices—

Brother Daniel has a neat little ↑snow white↓ cottage, with green blinds—↑the very same he told you you might have—↓with Hall, Parlor, library and nursery on first floor, with piazza on ↑(East)↓ front & South side—two large nice bedrooms above—cellar, dining, kitchen & servants room in basement—located on the esplionade—most delightful—they have a real Aunt Chloe in the kitchen, & a little ("Darkie") boy for errands & table waiter—[7] I never saw the girl to match—save your Mary Leary—& the more I see of the race the more wonderful they are to me— So let me hear from you often— I am very sorry about Kitt—what violation of physical law has he been so guilty of that he must thus suffer—only think—his mother's "Flower"—& the one Susan always bragged over— The Fosters failed, the Weld's failed, & now Mrs. Stanton's largest promise fails—ah me—how very little we know after all of health & life—[8]

Lydia Mott asks me what she shall do with the box of your "<u>Divorce</u>" tracts—says she cannot afford to pay cartage on them for any more moves— I have written her to send them to you 75 West 45th & that you would pay Express & take charge of them—the time will come when they will be of service,—But if you don't want them, write Lydia not to send them to you— I would have said send them to me at Rochester—but Mother broken up house-keeping & she & Mary are boarding at brother McLeans—have splendid airy, large front chamber, for parlor & large bedroom & closet—then sister Hannah has moved into a neat, new brick house next door—so all are there together—we moved the last of December, & sister H the last of January—[9] This arrangement left me "<u>free</u> <u>to roam</u>"—hence I am in Kansas as a beginning—

Do tell me all about everything & every body—I am all out of the way of those I love to talk with—

Your enclosed letter from some good woman, needs only a kind word of encouragement or silence— We can't tell of any organization plan— With love to Governor & your children one & all & to Mary Leary—I am yours affectionately

❧ *S. B. A.*

❧ ALS, ECS Papers, DLC.

1. Daniel, or D. R., Anthony and his wife Anna E. Osborne Anthony (1845–1930) lived on Main Street. Their political and social lives reflected D. R.'s short but colorful war record, as lieutenant colonel in the Seventh Kansas Volunteer Cavalry. While in command of his regiment in June 1862, he ordered his troops not to return fugitive slaves, in defiance of his commanding officer. Arrested and charged with disobedience of orders, he resigned in September 1862. He returned to Leavenworth a hero of antislavery sentiment and was elected mayor the next year. His efforts to bring order to the city included burning down its "houses of ill-repute," arresting a local editor with whose articles he disagreed, and defying the imposition of martial law by General Thomas Ewing, Jr. When SBA arrived, Anthony was the city's postmaster, where he employed Annie's brother, John P. Osborne (c. 1848–?) as a clerk; publisher of the Leavenworth *Evening Bulletin*, which he purchased in 1864; an insurance agent; and the mayoral candidate of the radical Republican faction. (City directory, 1865–1866; Federal Census, 1870; *U.S. Biographical*

Dictionary: Kansas Volume, 58–59, 61; Stephen Z. Starr, *Jennison's Jayhawkers: A Civil War Cavalry Regiment and Its Commander* [Baton Rouge, 1973], 172–75, 180, 252–53, 318–24, 379.)

2. Samuel Ryan Curtis (1805–1866) commanded the Department of Kansas, headquartered at Fort Leavenworth, until 7 February 1865, when he took up command of the Department of the Northwest, at Milwaukee. He married Belinda Buckingham of Mansfield, Ohio, in 1831. His daughter-in-law was the widow of Major H. Zarah Curtis. (Mark Mayo Boatner, III, *The Civil War Dictionary* [New York, 1959], 215, 601–2; *DAB*; Daniel W. Wilder, *The Annals of Kansas* [Topeka, 1875], 349.)

3. Grenville Mellen Dodge (1831–1916) was given command of the Department of Kansas from February through June 1865. (Boatner, *Civil War Dictionary*, 242–43, 556.)

4. SBA contrasts the orders of William Tecumseh Sherman (1820–1891) and Nathaniel Banks. Completing his march across the South, Sherman ordered in January that land within thirty miles of the coast between Charleston and Jacksonville be distributed to freed families in allotments of forty acres. His plan prohibited whites other than authorized military personnel from entering the area. When Banks arrived in New Orleans as commander of occupation forces in December 1862, he ordered all able freedmen to work on plantations or public projects. (McPherson, *Struggle for Equality*, 208, 257–58, 289–90.)

5. The Freedmen's Home consisted of two large buildings to house refugees, including about thirty children. Mary Jane Ford Mead (1822–1902), a widow, came to Leavenworth to assist there. After the war Mead taught among the freedmen in Selma, Alabama. (Laura Haviland, *A Woman's Life-Work: Labors and Experiences of Laura S. Haviland* [Chicago, 1887], 361–79; Mitchell Public Library, Hillsdale, Mich.)

6. A resolution to amend article V, section 1 of the state constitution which restricted the vote to white males was rejected by the senate on 2 February. (*Kansas Senate Journal*, 13, 16, 27 January, 2 February 1865, pp. 40, 47, 140, 203–4.)

7. SBA compares the black servant Emily Robinson (c. 1810–?) to Aunt Chloe, a slave in *Uncle Tom's Cabin*. Robinson's children Lucinda, age twelve, and John, age ten, also lived in the household. (Kansas State Census, 1865.)

8. At age eleven, Stephen and Abby Foster's daughter Alla developed curvature of the spine. Theodore and Angelina Grimké Weld's son Theodore suffered from a mental illness. Kit Stanton's condition at this time is unknown. He apparently recovered, for he lived a productive life. (Sterling, *Ahead of Her Time*, 242, 316; Lerner, *Grimké Sisters*, 288, 345–49.)

9. At 7 and 9 Madison Street in Rochester.

·⟨⟩⟨⟩·

199 ⤳ FROM THE DIARY OF SBA

[*4 March–17 April 1865*]

SATURDAY, MARCH 4, 1865. [*Leavenworth*] Beautiful day— President
Lincoln begins his new term— The day is observed as a national
holiday—

In P.M. Annie & self made calls ⌈on⌊ Mrs. Dr. Mayer,[1] Mrs. Parker,
Mrs. Earle, Mrs. Wise & Mrs. Bally— Mrs. Mead of the ["]Home"
called—she told us of the almost universal infection of the ex-slave
women—child born last week one mass of corruption   dead of course
& one living still

Letter from sister Hannah— [*in margin*] Went to market in the
A.M.—

   1. The wife of Martin Mayer, a German physician.

SUNDAY, MARCH 5, 1865. Splendid day— Went to Colored Sabbath
school at Christian Church[1]—Mr. Crane,[2] formerly of Osawatomie is
superintendent— Went to Congregational Church with Mr. Brown
and his sister Mrs. Hand—[3] Col. Hoyt[4] of the old Kansas 7th was to
dine with us, but did not come— D. R. and Annie took a long ride in
the afternoon— Got letter from Mother Gula & Aaron—all well &
happy in their new arrangements—

also letter from Lucy Stone

   1. There were also black Sunday schools at the African Methodist Episcopal Church, the black Baptist Church, and three at the Freedmen's Home.
(City directory 1865–1866; Haviland, *Woman's Life Work*, 372.)

   2. Perhaps Charles H. Crane, a lawyer. (City directory, 1865–1866.)

   3. Jeremiah Root Brown (1819–1874), half-brother of John Brown, was an
agent of the United States Sanitary Commission in Leavenworth in 1865 and
oversaw a soldier's home for white refugees and freedmen. His sister was Sally
Marian Brown Hand (1811–1894). (City directory, 1865–1866; Haviland, *Woman's
Life Work*, 361; Guide to the Samuel Lyle and Florella Brown Adair Family
Collection, KHi.)

   4. George Henry Hoyt (1837–?), one of John Brown's defense attorneys in
1859, edited the Leavenworth *Conservative* after the war and became attorney

general of Kansas. (David W. Hoyt, *Genealogical History of the Hoyt, Haight, and Hight Families* [Providence, 1871], 600; Wilder, *Annals of Kansas*, 463.)

MONDAY, MARCH 6, 1865. Bright & warm— Annie called at Mrs. Parkers— Eliza Ann (colored) began plain sewing— Did pretty well, but not nice enough for the little dresses

TUESDAY, MARCH 7, 1865. Leavenworth   Growing cold— Went shopping in the afternoon—
    Eliza Ann sewed this day & took home with her to make 1 sheet & 3 pair of pillow cases

WEDNESDAY, MARCH 8, 1865. Leavenworth   Coldest morning of the season—10 deg. below zero—such sudden transitions from bright spring days to the intensest cold—

THURSDAY, MARCH 9, 1865. Leavenworth   Cold & windy but relaxing—

FRIDAY, MARCH 10, 1865. Leavenworth   Quite warm & pleasant—
Called at Primary Colored School (Mrs Douglas')[1] in the morning—
    In afternoon visited Mr. Langston's school[2]—200 scholars in one room—two departments & two Teachers
    Called at Rev. Mr. Mitchells[3]—he was out—

    1. In the black Baptist Church. Sattira A. Steele Douglas (1840–?) was sent to Leavenworth by Chicago's Colored Ladies Freedmen's Aid Society and its Women's Loyal National League to teach the slaves held there as contraband. The daughter of free parents, she grew up in Chicago, became active in antislavery work, and married H. Ford Douglas. After his death in 1865, she resettled in Chicago. (*Black Abolitionist Papers*, 5:167–68n; Joseph A. Walkes, Jr., "Charles Henry Langston: First Black School Teacher of Leavenworth, Kansas," 106, KHi.)
    2. Charles Henry Langston (1817–1892) organized a school for contraband children in the Christian Church, where he taught seventy-five students, according to the Board of Education. The son of a Virginia planter and his freed slave, he was one of the first black students in the preparatory department of Oberlin College, and he became a leader in Ohio's African-American community before moving to Leavenworth during the war. (*Black Abolitionist Papers*, 5:214n; Walkes, "Charles Henry Langston.")
    3. Daniel P. Mitchell (1821–1881), minister of the First Methodist Episcopal Church. (Andreas, *History of Kansas*, 2:1259.)

SATURDAY, MARCH 11, 1865. Leavenworth—beautiful spring day—cleaned house with alcohol & brushed furniture all the A.M—

Mr. Langston called in P.M— D. R. and Annie took a ride—

In eve read in the "Atlantic" for March "The Popular Lecture"—& "Causes of Foreign hate toward america["]—[1]

1. *Atlantic Monthly* 15 [March 1865]: 362–75.

SUNDAY, MARCH 12, 1865. Leavenworth—A bright, warm day— Attended the Colored Sunday School—Mr. Crane of Osawatomie—Superintendent— Gov. Arney of New Mexico[1] present—had not slept in bed for the last four weeks—rode in stage for a thousand miles—going to Washington to negotiate about the Hopi Indians & Unadillas

Bible Society in P.M. at Laings Hall—[2] In evening wrote letters to Mother & Lucy Stone & Lydia Mott—

1. William Frederick Milton Arny (1813–1881), a former Kansas legislator, was appointed an Indian agent in New Mexico in 1861 and secretary of the territory in 1862. He was acting governor in 1865 and 1866. (Lawrence R. Murphy, *Frontier Crusader—William F. M. Arny* [Tucson, Ariz., 1972].)

2. Laing's Hall was the most elaborate of Leavenworth's public halls, located on the northwest corner of Delaware and Fourth streets and seating about one thousand.

MONDAY, MARCH 13, 1865. Leavenworth Heavy Thunder Shower in the ↑last↓ night— wrote an article on the Bible Society in the forenoon— In afternoon made second apron for John— Annie sewed all day and it rained all day— In evening, read Beecher on "Negro Suffrage"—[1] Wrote S. H. Camp—asking him to give Phillips his testimony of Port Hudson & Gen Banks—[3]

1. In a series on the importance of black suffrage to Reconstruction, the *Standard* published a sermon by Henry Ward Beecher in which he said that African Americans had earned suffrage by their heroic conduct during the war. (*NASS*, 3 March 1865.)

2. In the spring of 1863 General Nathaniel Banks led African-American troops against the Confederate stronghold of Port Hudson, Louisiana. The soldiers' courageous performance changed the minds of many people opposed to arming black men for the war. Stephen Henry Camp (1837–1897), a chaplain of a black regiment at Port Hudson, was minister to a Unitarian church in Toledo, Ohio. SBA repeated this sentence in the next entry. (Dudley Taylor Cornish, *The Sable Arm: Negro Troops in the Union Army, 1861–1865* [New York, 1966], 142–43; Eliot, *Heralds of a Liberal Faith*, 3:57–58.)

TUESDAY, MARCH 14, 1865. Leavenworth Another heavy Thunder shower last night—partly cleared off during the day

P.O. boy brought me the home letter—Sister Mary, Mother, Gula and Aaron the writers—also a letter from Parker Pillsbury[1] and a package of the "Broken Fetter" from Detroit[2]

1. Perhaps the one dated March? 1865, *Film*, 11:160.
2. The *Broken Fetter* published daily in Detroit from 28 February through 1 April 1865, during the Ladies' Michigan State Fair for the Relief of Destitute Refugees and Freedmen.

WEDNESDAY, MARCH 15, 1865. Leavenworth   Snowed all day   Annie sewed very steady all day— [*16–20, 22, 24 March omitted; no entries for 21, 23, 25 March.*]

SUNDAY, MARCH 26, 1865. Leavenworth   Had Miss Norris' Class at the colored Sabbath School in A.M.— Went to Fort—with Mrs. Douglass— to spend day—saw Colored Battery drill in morning—dined with Lieut. Wm Mathews[1]—and in P.M. saw Colored Battery on dress parade with a Wisconson Veteran Battery—two Rock Island Rebel companies & other white companies—here black & white are equal   Lieut Mathews marched off in line to salute acting Col.[2] Found letter from Mrs. Stanton—[3]

1. The Kansas Independent Battery of United States Colored Light Artillery, organized at Fort Leavenworth in December 1864, was the army's only all black military unit. First Lieutenant William D. Matthews (1828–?), the second ranking officer, moved to Kansas from Maryland in 1858 and became superintendent of the contrabands for the Kansas Emancipation League. (*Black Abolitionist Papers*, 5:287n, 332n; Wilder, *Annals of Kansas*, 369.)
2. Lieutenant Colonel W. R. Davis of the Sixteenth Kansas Cavalry, was commander of Fort Leavenworth from September 1864 until March 1865. (Elvid Hunt, *History of Fort Leavenworth, 1827–1927* [1926; reprint, New York, 1979], 224.)
3. This may be the letter dated March? 1865, *Film*, 11:159.

MONDAY, MARCH 27, 1865. Leavenworth   Rainy in morning   Called at Mr. Burnhams found Lieut Miner[1] dead—then called on Rev. Mr. Caldwell[2] (Baptist)—his wife said my dear Father ~~had~~ made them visits when in Leavenworth four years ago— Called also at brother Turners[3] (Methodist Col'd) & talked about Free Schools
City primary meeting went strong for D. R. for Mayor—

1. William H. Burnham (c. 1820–?), an African-American barber, was married to the sister of Second Lieutenant Patrick Henry Minor, the third ranking

officer of the Kansas Independent Battery, who died on 22 March. Minor attended Oberlin College and came to Leavenworth in 1862 with an Ohio regiment. His funeral service was conducted at St. Joseph's, the German Catholic church. The Burnham household also included Charles Langston. (Kansas State Census, 1865; City directory, 1865–1866; Leavenworth *Evening Bulletin*, 30 March 1865; Wilder, *Annals of Kansas*, 369.)

2. Robert Caldwell or Colwell organized Leavenworth's black Baptist Church. (Andreas, *History of Kansas*, 1:432; City directory, 1863–1864, 1865–1866.)

3. John Turner was minister of the African Methodist Episcopal Church, organized in 1861. (Andreas, *History of Kansas*, 1:432.)

TUESDAY, MARCH 28, 1865. Leavenworth   Attended funeral of Lieut. Patrick Henry Miner of Capt. H. Ford Douglass'[1] (Col'd) Battery— burried with Military Honors—Lieut. W[m] Mathews in Command—

Daniel. R. nominated for Mayor by the regular Republican delegation Convention [*Entries of 29–31 March, 1–2, 9–12 April omitted; no entries for 3–8 April.*]

1. Hezekiah Ford Douglas (1831–1865), husband of Sattira Douglas, escaped from slavery in 1846. One of the few African Americans to serve with a white regiment in the war, he recruited the Kansas Independent Battery in 1864 and was commissioned captain early in 1865. Mustered out of service in July, he died in November. (*Black Abolitionist Papers*, 4:78–79n; Robert L. Harris, Jr., "H. Ford Douglas: Afro-American Antislavery Emigrationist," *Journal of Negro History* 62 [July 1977]: 230.)

THURSDAY, APRIL 13, 1865. First gun fired on Sumter four years ago to day— Spent forenoon in office—

FRIDAY, APRIL 14, 1865. Leavenworth   Fort Sumter Flag raising to day—just four years since it was furled   both done by Maj Gen. Anderson   Beecher the high-priest—[1]

Weather warmer but clouding up for rain—

1. In command of Fort Sumter when South Carolina seized it from Federal forces at the start of the war, Robert Anderson (1805–1871) returned to raise the flag at war's end. Henry Ward Beecher delivered an oration at the ceremony.

SATURDAY, APRIL 15, 1865. Morning Telegram reported President Lincoln assassinated at Fords Theatre in Washington—and Sec. Seward stabbed in his sick bed—

Stunning— Soon another that Lincoln was dead—

Vice President Johnson[1] immediately sworn in

1. Andrew Johnson (1808–1875). As military governor of Tennessee before he became vice president, Johnson worked to make it a free state and promised to lead the slaves to freedom. Some abolitionists believed he would be a stronger ally than Lincoln.

SUNDAY, APRIL 16, 1865. D. R. went to M.E. Church—Mitchell gave a stirring word— John Osborn went to the Irish Catholic[1] they did not mention the occurrence— I went to the Episcopal[2] merely mentioned the fact— In eve I called at Colored M.E. & Colored Baptist—but the jam was too great—

1. Probably the Church of the Immaculate Conception.
2. The Church of St. Paul.

MONDAY, APRIL 17, 1865. Wilkes Boother[1] the murderer—Seward not dead

Sent letter to Gula & Mother and Lydia Mott and received letter from Merritt and Mrs. Wright of Auburn—rainy— [*18–21 April omitted; no entry for 22 April.*]

1. John Wilkes Booth (1838–1865).

☞ Pocket Diary 1865, printed by Willy Wallach, New York, SBA Papers, DLC.

·⟨═══════⟩·

200 ✥ SBA TO ECS

Leavenworth [*Kan.*] Apr. 19/65

Last but not Least   My dear Mrs. Stanton

I have this second finished a note to dear ever glorious Phillips,[1] and just before, one to Parker Pillsbury—on the Official resignations of the heads of our Anti Slavery Society—[2] Told Phillips "if the people had been assembled to consult as to the ability of the Vice President to take forward the Government, the vast majority would have shaken their heads in doubt—but the terrible blow came—the office was vacant—Johnson takes it—and the people already feel him the chosen of God to end the war.["] That I believe the same would prove true with the A.A.S. Society, though it now seems that no other men could fill the posts of Garrison, Quincy[3] and Johnson, yet with Wendell Phillips in the chair of the ~~President~~ ↑Society↓ and Parker Pillsbury in that of the Standard the machinery would move on with scarce a jar. I wonder if there is a "Special Providence" too, in the fact that I cannot be in New York this spring!—

Of course, with all who really feel their Anti Slavery work done, it is done—no votes of society, to pleadings of friends for them to keep up the appearance can galvanize them into any more efficient work— Therefore, the Society should disband, unless the men & the women who see work still to do, will put shoulder to the wheel. The one great question is the money—and I suppose that has not a little weight in causing this move— I have written Parker that I hope he will allow nothing to prevent him from recording his testimony on the state of things, in the last meeting of the Society, in form of resolutions— I hope you are settled & have a spare bed, and feel impressed that the best service you can do the cause of humanity is to invite him to your home, and help him to write out just the word that the Prophets of the Lord should speak at this fearfully tragic hour. Was there ever a more terrific command to a nation to "Stand still and know that I am God"[4] since the world began— The Old Book's terrible exhibitions of Gods wrath sinks into nothingness— And this fell blow just at the very hour he was declaring his willingness to consign those five millions faithful brave, only loving loyal people of the South to the tender mercies of the ex-slave lords of the lash—[5]

Dear a me—how over-full I am, and how I should like to be nestled into some corner away from every chick & child, with you once more—

I am writing now every forenoon at my brothers Office—put in one or more items every day—[6] Will send you a weekly, that you may see— it seems doing so little—my soul longs to go out to do battle for the Lord once more— The Church folks called a union meeting at the Largest Hall last Sunday P.M. for general expression of all the people— but alas Priests took the platform, read the Bible, gave out the hymn, said the prayer and called out one man to speak—& with two priests word—and dismissed— My soul was full—but the flesh not equal to stemming the awful current, to do what the people have called, make an exhibition of myself— So quenched the spirit and came home ashamed of myself[7]

Do have your work out of the way, so as to attend every session of the May Meeting, and give me the spirit of things you know the papers give only the dry bones— Tell Lucy & any who inquire after me that I ~~am not one of the~~ ↑sorrow not as↓ one without hope—for I am full of the faith that reconstruction on Lincoln's basis is stayed for a time, if not wholly stopped— Do write me often—your last letter was so good— and I over↑heard↓ the Dan's Annie telling him all you said to her & of her— She is bright as a bird yet—though she cannot have another month—

≈ *S. B. A*

[*sideways in margin on first page*] Love to one and all—are you moving or moved—no I can not see a place for <u>you</u> here—it is such an isolation from all our workers—if you & I had the means to carry on some reform work in New York or here all would be right—

≈ ALS, ECS Papers, DLC.

1. SBA summarizes her letter to Wendell Phillips here. (19 April 1865, *Film*, 11:165–68.)

2. The *Standard* of 8 April carried the executive committee's proposal that the American Anti-Slavery Society dissolve. William Lloyd Garrison believed that the society's work would be done with passage of the Thirteenth Amendment, and Edmund Quincy and Oliver Johnson announced that they would resign as editors of the *Standard* after the May meeting. Wendell Phillips, Parker Pillsbury, and Frederick Douglass, among others, insisted that the society's work would not be complete until equal civil and political rights for African Americans were secured. (McPherson, *Struggle for Equality*, 301–3; *NASS*, 8 April 1865.)

3. Edmund Quincy (1808–1877), an editor of the *Standard* since 1844 and a member of the society's executive committee, was a loyal supporter of Garrison. (Garrison, *Letters*, 5:18n.)

4. Paraphrase of Job 37:14.

5. In his final speech on 11 April, Lincoln defended his plan to readmit Louisiana to the Union without requiring that African Americans be enfranchised.

6. Most of SBA's unsigned articles are not identified.

7. The meeting at Laing's Hall, called to allow the people "to give vent to their feelings on the President's death," was addressed by the Reverend Daniel P. Mitchell, the Reverend Winfield Scott, and Colonel Cloud. According to the *Evening Bulletin*, "the people did not feel at liberty to participate freely." (17 April 1865.)

·⊂━━━━⋙⫍⊂━━━━⊃·

201 ∾ REMARKS BY SBA AT MEMORIAL SERVICE
FOR ABRAHAM LINCOLN

Editorial note: Daniel P. Mitchell opened the meeting at Laing's
Hall, where SBA was joined by Hiram Griswold, H. Ford Douglas,
and Daniel R. Anthony.

[23 April 1865]

I was reading the President's last speech when the stunning telegram
of his assassination reached me. I was pausing and pondering over the
paragraph, that may now be called his dying plea for Louisiana. My
soul was sad and sick at what seemed his settled purpose—to consign
the ex-slaves back to the tender mercies of the disappointed, desper-
ate, sullen, revengeful ex-lords of the lash—to disarm and send home
the entire rebel army—to disband and send home the 200,000 brave,
black Union soldiers—re-arming the former, our enemies, with the
ballot, the mightiest weapon for good or for evil, in the gift of the
nation, disarming and disfranchising our loyal black soldiers—men to
whom the nation is largely, if not altogether, indebted for its triumphs
in the field over the rebellion—all power to protect themselves or the
Government. To me it looked the crime of crimes, and hence my first
thought was that God had spoken to the nation in His thunder tone to
"stand still and know that I am God."

So far the interpretation of this awful tragedy, by press and pulpit, is
only to visit the whole penalty of the law upon the heads of the traitor
chiefs. Not one leading influential voice has yet cried out against the
awful crime of building up the Union on the disfranchisement of a
whole loyal race—a crime, in view of the light and knowledge of this
day, and the faithful, heroic service of the race to the nation; vastly
more black and damning, than was that of the Fathers in permitting
their enslavement one hundred years ago. God's one great purpose, is
that this nation shall establish and practice His law of the perfectly
equal humanity of all races, nations and colors. And though not a
prophet, yet it is made to include the African race, and thus cease to be
a mere glittering generality.

∾ Leavenworth *Evening Bulletin*, 24 April 1865.

·❬═══════✠═══════❭·

202 ➽ FROM THE DIARY OF SBA

[*23 April–18 July 1865*]

SUNDAY, APRIL 23, 1865. State Fast day for the Death of Lincoln—
Heard Liggitt[1] in the A.M. attended Peoples meeting at Laing's Hall in
the P.M. Colored people took front seats—the pro Slavery anti-negro
people dreadfully shocked & outraged

1. James D. Liggett of the American Home Missionary Society was pastor
of the First Congregational Church for ten years. (Andreas, *History of Kansas*,
1:432.)

MONDAY, APRIL 24, 1865. Took tea at H. Griswold's[1]—with J. R.
Brown and Sister—Mrs. Hand—& Rev. Mr. Woodward & wife—[2] It is
perfectly shocking how few of the Republicans are ready to give euqual
rights to black men— [*25 April omitted*]

1. Hiram Griswold (1808–1881), a lawyer who represented John Brown in
1859, came to Leavenworth from Ohio with his wife Eleanor A. G. Griswold
in 1863. He was appointed register in bankruptcy of the United States District
Court in 1864. (Federal Census, 1870; Kansas Biographical Scrapbooks,
57:290–92, KHi; Wilder, *Annals of Kansas*, 379, 462.)
2. George Simeon Woodward (1821–1892) became pastor of Leavenworth's
First Presbyterian Church in 1863. He married Eliza Miller Tyler in 1853.
(Andreas, *History of Kansas*, 1:456; Bowdoin College, *General Catalogue of
Bowdoin College and the Medical School of Maine . . . 1794–1950* [Brunswick,
Me., 1950], 86.)

WEDNESDAY, APRIL 26, 1865. Writing article on Special Providences[1]—
at dusk called on Mrs. Haviland[2] at the Home   she is quite ill.
Standard came   read Phillips Card against disbanding A.S. Societies at midnight[3]—he is right—it is sad—

1. *Evening Bulletin*, 27 April 1865.
2. Laura Smith Haviland (1808–1898), educator, antislavery activist, and
advocate for the freedmen, was an agent of the Freedmen's Aid Commission of
Michigan. She had charge of the Freedmen's Home in Leavenworth until she
closed it in May 1865. (*NAW*; Haviland, *Woman's Life Work*, 361–79.)
3. *NASS*, 15 April 1865.

THURSDAY, APRIL 27, 1865. Sewed all day didn't go out   read A.S.

Standard   The disbanding of the American A.S. Society is fully as untimely as Gens. Grant and Sherman's granting Parole & Pardon to the whole rebel armies—[1] [*28 and 30 April omitted; no entries for 29 April, 1–3 May*]

1. When Confederate General Robert E. Lee surrendered to General Ulysses S. Grant (1822–1885), Grant permitted the rebel soldiers and officers to return home on parole. On 18 April, General William T. Sherman offered more generous terms to General Joseph E. Johnston: guarantees of southerners' "political rights and franchises, as well as their rights of person and property." (McPherson, *Ordeal by Fire*, 482, 485.)

THURSDAY, MAY 4, 1865. This afternoon spoke at a meeting of the Colored people at Turners Hall[1]—in evening spoke at the African M.E. Church [*Entry of 5 May omitted; no entry for 6 May.*]

1. The hall of the German Turners Society.

SUNDAY, MAY 7, 1865. Did not go to Church—tried to write all day but didn't get but one sentence— Congressman Sidney Clarke dined here[1]—also Mr. Isbell of the Conservative—[2]

1. Sidney Clarke (1831–1909), Republican congressman from Kansas from 1865 to 1871, purchased the *Evening Bulletin* with D. R. Anthony in 1864. (*BDAC*; Albert Castel, *A Frontier State at War: Kansas, 1861–1865* [Ithaca, N.Y., 1958], 178–79.)
2. George T. Isbell edited the *Leavenworth Conservative* until October 1865 and again in 1870. (City directory, 1865–1866; Wilder, *Annals of Kansas*, 348, 428, 520.)

MONDAY, MAY 8, 1865. D. R. set W. P. Allen[1] (a bright mulatto) to work setting type this A.M.— Two boys dropped work & left—soon a call for a Printers Union meeting came—all left & voted the man must not be allowed to work. They wont admit him to their union, and wont allow him to work because he isn't a member—

1. Probably William Allen (c. 1805–?), a soldier. (Kansas State Census, 1865; City directory, 1865–1866.)

TUESDAY, MAY 9, 1865. No hope that Mr. Allen will get work— It is a burning, blistering shame—time however will surely right the wrong.

Got a letter from Parker Pillsbury,[1] from Albany also a note from Lydia Mott—all going to N. York— To day is the business meeting that decides the fate of the American A.S. Society—[2] Mailed letter to mother this A.M.[3]

1. See *Film*, 11:184.

2. The business meeting lasted a day and a half, during which Wendell Phillips accused the executive committee of merely standing "on the level of the Republican party," and William Lloyd Garrison questioned his loyalty. Phillips called on the society to put "the liberty of the negro beyond peril," and Garrison's resolution to dissolve was rejected by a vote of 118 to 48. He relinquished the leadership, and Phillips was elected president. At the society's public meeting, Phillips called for land, the ballot, and guarantees of citizenship for African Americans. He would not, he said, yet ask for woman suffrage; "One question at a time. This hour belongs to the negro." In a letter that survives only in published form in *Stanton*, dated 25 May, ECS asked him, "Do you believe the African race is composed entirely of males?" There is no indication that ECS attended the meeting. (McPherson, *Struggle for Equality*, 303–7; *Lib.*, 19 May 1865; Ellen Carol DuBois, *Feminism and Suffrage: The Emergence of an Independent Women's Movement in America, 1848–1869* [Ithaca, N.Y., 1978], 59–60; *Film*, 11:186.)

3. SBA remained in Leavenworth until 30 June but made only scattered entries in her diary between mid-May and her departure. Her niece Maude Anthony was born 29 May.

SATURDAY, JULY 1, 1865. [*Topeka*] Spoke to full house in M.E. Church[1]— Col. Richie[2] President of meeting—negro suffrage

1. The Methodist Episcopal church organized in 1855 and erected a building in 1860. SBA spoke at a hastily organized meeting on "Reconstruction and Suffrage." Her address, reported to be "well-timed and able," argued against giving rebels the vote without also granting it to blacks. (Leavenworth *Evening Bulletin*, 8 July 1865, *Film*, 11:189.)

2. John Ritchie (1817–1887), a farmer and abolitionist, supported African-American and woman's rights in the Kansas constitutional convention of 1859. He was a captain of the Fifth Kansas Cavalry and colonel of the Second Indian Home Guards. In 1867 he served as a vice president of the Kansas Impartial Suffrage Association. (Andreas, *History of Kansas*, 1:575; Boatner, *Civil War Dictionary*, 701; Gambone, "Forgotten Feminist of Kansas," 528.)

SUNDAY, JULY 2, 1865. Spoke to the Colored Sabbath School—

MONDAY, JULY 3, 1865. [*Ottumwa*] Had pleasant stage ride—grand old prairies are perfectly splendid—and the timber-skirted creeks are delightful—crossed the Maria De Leigne 12 miles from source and 40 above Ossawatomie—[1]

1. The Marais des Cygnes was made famous by the 1858 massacre along its banks in the free-state community of Blooming Grove.

TUESDAY, JULY 4, 1865. Ottumwa Celebration—grand mass gathering, Hon. Sid. Clarke M.C. the Orator. I spoke just a hour on Pres. Johnsons Mississippi reconstruction Proclamation—[1] [*Entries for 5–17 July omitted.*]

1. At the Fourth of July celebration of Lyon, Greenwood, and Coffey counties, SBA read the president's proclamation of 13 June, which used Mississippi's old constitution as the basis for a new government. She pointed out that his policy would bar poor whites, all blacks, and women from a voice in reconstruction and leave rebels in charge. She also called upon the people of Kansas to demand black suffrage of their representatives in Washington and Topeka; no government would be truly republican, she reminded them, until women too were granted the vote. (Burlington *Kansas Patriot*, 8 July 1865, and SBA, "Reconstruction," *Film*, 11:190–98.)

TUESDAY, JULY 18, 1865. [*Leavenworth*] Got letter from Mrs. Stanton from Johnstown—sent one from Phillips to her—he say "tell ↑Susan↓ to come east—there is work for her to do["]— [*No entries for 19-22, 24 July; 23, 25-31 July omitted.*]

❧ Pocket Diary 1865, printed by Willy Wallach, New York, SBA Papers, DLC.

·⊂══❧══⊃·

203 ❧ ARTICLE BY ECS

[29 July 1865]

UNIVERSAL SUFFRAGE.[1]

The experiment of class legislation has been so long and thoroughly tried by the human family, under every form of government and in every latitude and longitude, that we need no argument to prove that one class cannot legislate for another.

Despotisms, monarchies, and republics have alike shown its fallacies. The facts of centuries with their sad results, and the protest of far-seeing men in all ages are against the principle of aristocracy. Justice and logic clearly show that there is no safe resting point in legislation this side of universal suffrage.

No honest mind can present a plausible argument in favor of any class legislation, that does not logically go back to a monarchy, a royal family, an order of nobility; in fact to a form of government and social life directly opposite to the genius of true republican institutions.

The question for to day is not how or where to limit the right of suffrage, but where did the privileged few get their power to deprive the masses of their inalienable right to life, liberty and the pursuit of happiness?

Where does the aristocrat get his authority to forbid poor men, ignorant men, and black men, the exercise of their rights? The cool impudence of these pirates in civil rights, who look in the faces of disenfranchised citizens and talk of the dangers of extending the privileges they claim for themselves, is only equalled by the boldness of their reasoning.

All this talk about education and property qualification is the narrow assumption of a rotten aristocracy. How can we grade wealth and education?

Shall he who is rich in ideas and noble deeds be denied the right of suffrage because he hoards no gold in his coffers?

Shall a man of sound judgment and executive talent who can thread his own way through the world of matter or thought, whose touch is genius turning alike pig-iron, potter's clay, or cotton to gold,—shall he be disfranchised because he never had time to learn the signs of Cadmus, or because by the statute laws of his State he was forbidden to read and write, or amass property in his own name?

Let leading minds beware how they invoke the popular thought in such absurdities. We have tried class legislation and found it a dead failure.

No country ever has had or ever will have peace until every citizen has a voice in the government. Now let us try universal suffrage. We cannot tell its dangers or delights until we make the experiment. At all events let us leave behind us the dead skin of class legislation which, in the progress of civilization, we have, at last, outgrown.

❧ *E. C. S.*

❧ *NASS*, 29 July 1865.

1. Advocacy of black suffrage preoccupied abolitionists in the summer of 1865, but not everyone agreed that the franchise should be made universal, without any literacy or property requirements. Proponents of impartial suffrage

accepted the idea of restricting voting rights so long as blacks and whites were equally, or impartially, affected. By summer's end a further difference became evident in interpretations of the term universal: did universal suffrage encompass the voting rights of women as well? (McPherson, *Struggle for Equality*, 326-28.)

·⊂══════◊══════⊃·

204 ≈ FROM THE DIARY OF SBA

[*1 August–25 December 1865*]

TUESDAY, AUGUST 1, 1865. [*Leavenworth*] fine day   31 years to day since Emancipation took effect—and 27 since total & immediate—in the British W. Indies—   Large gathering at the Grove—not a speaker there save myself—spoke mainly of the changed condition of the colored people & their new rights & new duties—very attentive   walked up & back—

WEDNESDAY, AUGUST 2, 1865. Called this A.M. at Brother Turner's & Caldwell's   began raining [*No entry for 3 August.*]

FRIDAY, AUGUST 4, 1865. Raining still   Hon Sidney Clarke to dinner— he advised me <u>not</u> to bring in W. Rights—   I showed I had done so only by of illustrating the point that <u>no class</u> can be trusted to legislate for another though that other be wife, daughter, mother, etc

SATURDAY, AUGUST 5, 1865. [*Atchison*] Raining—warm showers   Took stage at 10.30—very rough—had a long wait at the western R.R. Station—   Found Planters Hotel[1] full—sent note to Mr. Adams Editor Free Press,[2] he came & took me to John M. Crowells—an ex-Mayor of Atchison—right cordial welcome[3]   began to feel my mercury rise— Senator S. C. Pomeroy[4] called—said I must speak before I left—

1. The Planters' House, on Commercial Street.
2. Franklin George Adams (1824–1899), editor of the *Atchison Free Press* between 1864 and 1868, was appointed United States Indian Agent for the Kickapoos in March 1865. He became the first secretary of the Kansas State Historical Society in 1876. (Andreas, *History of Kansas*, 1:554.)
3. John M. Crowell (1829–1902), who moved to Kansas in 1857, was mayor of Atchison from May 1863 until May 1865 and again one year later. (Andreas, *History of Kansas*, 1:375; Kansas Biographical Scrapbooks, KHi.)

4. Samuel Clarke Pomeroy (1816–1891) escorted Clarina Nichols into Kansas in 1854, as an agent of the New England Emigrant Aid Company, and won election to the Senate in 1861. A consistent supporter of woman suffrage, he presided over the Universal Franchise Association in 1868. (*BDAC*; *History*, 1:185, 3:810.)

SUNDAY, AUGUST 6, 1865. Atchison   Went to Pomeroy's Church in A.M. sat with him— In P.M. spoke to a fine audience of the colored people—six of them subscribed for Anti Slavery Standard[1]

1. In the afternoon at the Congregational church, SBA told her audience that they would be admitted to the privileges of free American citizens. At the church on Monday, her topic was "Reconstruction in the Rebel States." (*Atchison Daily Free Press*, 7 August 1865, *Film*, 11:206.)

MONDAY, AUGUST 7, 1865. Atchison   Spoke to the white people this evening—not a colored person came—they don't venture—except specially invited—never crowd themselves   Had a hard time thoughts, nor words would come—but I staggered through— It was too bad— had a large sprinkling of Secesh—[1]

1. The diary records her tour to St. Joseph, Chillicothe, Macon City, and St. Louis, where she arrived on the eighteenth.

SATURDAY, AUGUST 19, 1865. St. Louis   Called on Emile Pretorias[1]— not in—sent card to I. H. Sturgeon, Pres. N.M.R.R.[2] Frank Robinson called to say his wife had gone east with her Father Mr. Turner—[3] Rev. M. M. Clarke[4] called—am to speak in his Church tomorrow Sunday P.M.—

1. Emil Preetorius (1827–1905), editor of the *Westliche Post*, was active in John C. Frémont's bid for the presidency. He left Germany in 1853, settled in St. Louis, and served in the legislature from 1862 to 1864 as a Republican. (*DAB*.)
2. Isaac Hughes Sturgeon (1821–1908), who dined with SBA at her brother's house on 12 April, was president and general superintendent of the North Missouri Railroad. As a Democrat, he served as state senator and United States assistant treasurer before the war but allied himself with Republicans when the war began. (*Sketch of the Incidents in the Life of Isaac H. Sturgeon Written by Himself in January, 1900* [n.p., n.d.].)
3. Frank Roberson or Robinson was an African-American barber. His wife was the daughter of Henry Turner, a partner in a coal and wood yard. (City directory, 1864, 1865.)
4. Molson M. Clark or Clarke (c. 1794–1874), former editor of the *Christian*

Recorder, was minister of St. Paul's Chapel, an African Methodist Church, built, according to SBA, "by actual slaves with money they earned working odd hours allowed them by their masters." (City directory, 1864, 1865; Douglass, *Papers*, 1:447–48n; SBA to Unknown, [after 20 August 1865], *Film*, 11:210.)

SUNDAY, AUGUST 20, 1865. St. Louis   at Mrs. Drummon's—208 7th street[1]   Mr. Elliot—Unitarian in A.M.—[2] In P.M. spoke to the Color'd people in their old <u>Slave</u> church— In eve, went back to Planter's House—best economy to pay most money—no letters from Leavenworth—

   1. Elizabeth Drummond or Drummons, the wife of Samuel, an African-American riverman. (City directory, 1864, 1865; memoranda in back of diary.)
   2. William Greenleaf Eliot (1811–1887) was minister of the Unitarian Church of the Messiah. During the war he directed the Western Sanitary Commission. (*DAB*.)

MONDAY, AUGUST 21, 1865. Planter's—S. Louis   Called on Sturgeon and Pretorius—both out— Visited Freedmens rooms[1] & the St. Louis Library   Saw Harriet Hosmer's Cenci Enone & Puck[2]—wrote letters to Rochester & Leavenworth
   Had very small meeting—had sudden attack of Direahea while speaking—had to close suddenly—& all night thought of Dear Ann Eliza—[3]

   1. The offices of the Freedmen's Relief Society.
   2. After studying anatomy in the city, Harriet Hosmer was commissioned to sculpt for the St. Louis Mercantile Library Association. The library displayed "Oenone," her first full-length figure in marble, "Beatrice Cenci," and "Puck."
   3. Her niece Ann Eliza McLean died in 1864.

TUESDAY, AUGUST 22, 1865. St Louis   Mr. Sturgeon gave me a pass to go to Chicago via Alton & Springfield— Mrs. Henry Turner made calls with me in P.M. Mr. Clark called & gave me $3. as compensation for lectures— [*23 August omitted.*]

THURSDAY, AUGUST 24, 1865. Chicago   Took Cars at 8 last evening— a woman thief pressed up to me & took from my pocket this book—I grabbed her arm not very gently & told her to deliver—she stoutly denied, but the book dropped to the platform—
   Arrived at Uncles[1] about 7 Oclock—called in P.M. at Mrs Loomis[2] [*25 August omitted.*]

   1. Ann Eliza Anthony (1814–1886), the youngest of Daniel Anthony's sis-

ters, married Albert Franklin Dickinson (1809–1881) in 1836 and moved from Albany to Chicago in 1854 or 1855. Ann Eliza Dickinson was an elder of the Chicago Meeting of Friends at the time of her death. Her husband founded the very successful Albert Dickinson Seed Company, a major dealer in grains, and was one of the first members of the Chicago Board of Trade. Six of their ten children lived into adulthood. SBA mentions their second daughter, Melissa (1839–1910), who attended college in New York but kept house for her family. Melissa later joined her brothers in business. (Anthony, *Anthony Genealogy*, 218; Elinor V. Smith, comp., *Descendants of Nathaniel Dickinson* [n.p., 1978], 233–34; *Friends' Intelligencer* 43 [1886]: 184; Alfred Theodore Andreas, *History of Chicago, From the Earliest Period to the Present Time* [Chicago, 1885], 2:356; *Chicago Tribune*, 9 March 1881; unidentified clipping, SBA scrapbook 9, Rare Books, DLC.)

2. Elizabeth Jane Edwards Loomis, the second wife of James W. Loomis, worked for the Northwest Sanitary Commission and directed the Chicago Soldiers' Home in 1865. She was a member of the Chicago branch of the Women's Loyal National League and active in the fight for universal suffrage. (Elias S. Loomis, *Descendants of Joseph Loomis in America* [1908; reprint, Fresno, Calif., 1981], 441–42; unidentified clipping, SBA scrapbook 1, Rare Books, DLC; *History*, 3:565, 569, 572, 589; Andreas, *History of Chicago*, 2:312–13.)

SATURDAY, AUGUST 26, 1865. Called at Mrs. Loomis— Mrs. Douglass[1] called with me at Freedmen's Commission Office—[2]

1. That is, Sattira Douglas.
2. The Northwestern Freedmen's Aid Commission.

SUNDAY, AUGUST 27, 1865. Chicago   Uncle A. walked with me almost to Mrs. Loomis'— Found Mrs. Tracy Cutler there—she is the same managing woman—found the Liberator here—& one very good Editorial from Mr. Garrison—[1] Heard Gen Howards lecture in Bryan Hall on the Freedmen[2]

1. "The Spirit of the South," *Lib.*, 25 August 1865.
2. Oliver Otis Howard (1830–1909), commissioner of the new Bureau of Refugees, Freedmen and Abandoned Lands, or Freedmen's Bureau, spoke in Bryan Hall, site of the city's great war meetings and sanitary fairs. (*DAB*; *Chicago Tribune*, 27 August 1865.)

MONDAY, AUGUST 28, 1865. Chicago   Called at Sherman House[1]—saw Gen. Howard—supertd of Freedmen's Beauro—talk with Mrs. Haviland & Cutler & Copp on Freedmen & Poor Whites— Had fine Audience in Quinn's Chapel[2]—"Republican" reported my speech—[3]

1. A six-story marble hotel completed in 1861.

2. An African Methodist Episcopal church.

3. The *Chicago Republican*'s report has not been recovered. SBA told her largely African-American audience that Johnson's reconstruction policy would make it "impossible to secure negro suffrage, and that by the present inauguration of the governments of the southern states there is not an earthly chance for the loyal black man of the south." (*Rochester Union and Advertiser*, 31 August 1865, *Film*, 11:212.)

TUESDAY, AUGUST 29, 1865. Chicago Went from Mrs. J. W. Loomis—462 State street to Uncle A. F. Dickinson's 113 S. Green st

Had a talk at eve with Melissa & Aunt A. E. on the duty of all women to get themselves an <u>independent</u> purse—that it was poor enconony for Melissa to just help manage home when she could earn 8 or 10 dollars a week by teaching—&c &c—to my utter surprise found I had hurt Aunt A. E's feelings badly

1. The diary records SBA's visits with relatives in Illinois and Michigan between 30 August and 19 September. She arrived in Rochester on 22 September.

TUESDAY, OCTOBER 10, 1865. Rochester to Clifton Springs & Auburn—Dined at Cousin Malintha Howe's[1]—& left for Auburn at 3 P.M. on way freight train— Found Mrs. Wright well—Mr. Wright had a severe attack of Rheumatism near the heart—they feel constant alarm—

1. Malintha Howe (1805–1869), daughter of Lucy Anthony's sister Amy, married Nathan Patchen and Isaac Stotenburg. (Howe, *Howe Genealogies*, 200.)

WEDNESDAY, OCTOBER 11, 1865. Auburn to P[alatine] Bridge Delightful visit with Mrs. Wright and call at her daughter Eliza Wright Osborns—Mrs. W. would be glad to have woman's rights revived but fears it will be impossible—

Took train 12. noon—just saw Charles Mills[1] at Syracuse Depot—found all well at Uncles—Sarah cleaning Parlors[2]

1. Charles de Berard Mills (1821–1900) settled in Syracuse in 1852, attracted to the city by fellow abolitionist Samuel J. May. For many years he presided over meetings of the Progressive Friends in Waterloo. (William A. Beauchamp, *Past and Present of Syracuse and Onondaga County, New York* [New York, 1908], 2:362–69.)

2. That is, at the home of Joshua and Mary S. Read, where she found Sarah B. Read.

THURSDAY, OCTOBER 12, 1865. Palatine Bridge to Albany   Had pleasant visit with Uncle & Aunt—took train 2 P.M. arrived at Albany at 4 P.M.—found Phebe & Margaret[1] well, also Lydia & Jane & their Sister Phebe Willis[2]—P[arker] P[illsbury] not expected till tomorrow P.M.—

1. That is, Phebe Hoag Jones and her daughter, Margaret (c. 1835–1870). (Unidentified clipping, SBA scrapbook 9, Rare Books, DLC; Federal Census, 1850.)

2. Phebe Mott Willis (1805–?), sister of Lydia and Jane Mott, married Henry Willis in 1839 and settled in Battle Creek, Michigan. (Cornell, *Adam and Ann Mott*, 219; Garrison, *Letters*, 4:272n.)

FRIDAY, OCTOBER 13, 1865. Albany   Bright & beautiful   L. Mott & self called on Hon. A. J. Colvin[1] & talked of work for Woman's Right to suffrage in N.Y. Mr. C. recommends immediate work—separate & apart from the negro question—Mr. Bingham is ill—
Got no tidings of my shawl— P. P. came at 5 P.M.

1. Andrew James Colvin (1808–?) was the law partner of Anson Bingham, a former district attorney of Albany, a Democrat, and the chief senate advocate of the Married Women's Property Act of 1860. In anticipation of a state constitutional convention, he advised SBA to campaign for woman suffrage, keeping her work separate from the campaign already underway to remove from the constitution the property qualification for black voters. Although the legislature failed to call a convention for 1866, the next session would try again to pass the measure. (Murphy, *New York State Officers, 1861*, 42–45, 159; Charles Z. Lincoln, *The Constitutional History of New York* [1906; reprint, Buffalo, 1994], 2:234, 241.)

SATURDAY, OCTOBER 14, 1865. Albany   P. P. spent Thursday night at Ghent—report Lizzie—all Right—[1] We Dined at Lydia's   Tea at P. H. Jones   All went to Troy to hear Senator Wilson of Mass.—he made a pitiable speech—never said negro suffrage—[2] [*15 October omitted.*]

1. That is, Elizabeth Powell.
2. Campaigning against Democrats, Senator Henry Wilson was willing to readmit southern states without requiring that blacks be enfranchised, and he expressed confidence that Andrew Johnson intended to protect the rights of freedmen. (*New York Daily Tribune*, 16 October 1865.)

MONDAY, OCTOBER 16, 1865. New York   Found Mrs. Stanton at 464 West 34th st. well, and had a cordial welcome from the entire household—had an all days chat—in P.M. Mrs. Wilkerson called—in eve, we attended Dr. Loziers opening medical lecture[1]—then called at Dr.

Hudsons[2]—found P. P. & all out—at Opera [*Entries for 17–19 October omitted.*]

1. Clemence Sophia Harned Lozier (1813–1888), a graduate of Syracuse Medical College, was founder and dean of the New York Medical College and Hospital for Women, chartered in 1863, and a lifelong activist for woman's rights. During the war, she served as an officer of the loyal league, and later, she helped finance the *Revolution* and presided over the New York City Woman Suffrage Society. (*NAW.*)

2. Erasmus Darwin Hudson (1805–1880), an abolitionist agent and writer in New England in the 1840s, was an orthopedic surgeon who designed prothetic devices for Union soldiers. (*ACAB.*)

FRIDAY, OCTOBER 20, 1865. New York   Mary Caldwell Warren[1] came to Stanton's—I took her to Dr. Lozier—she examined found an ulcer on neck of womb—man Doctor experimented on her for six years—then Mary lunched with me at Stantons—

1. The daughter of Joseph and Margaret Caldwell, Mary was one of the children with whom SBA lived in Canajoharie. Various Caldwells had moved to New York. (City directory, 1865–1866.)

SATURDAY, OCTOBER 21, 1865. At Mrs Stantons   Wrote at Mrs Stantons

SUNDAY, OCTOBER 22, 1865. At Mrs. Stantons   Wrote on the appeal to Women of the State for Constitutional Amendt to give women the right of suffrage[1] [*No entries for 23–24 October.*]

1. When SBA attended the West Chester Anti-Slavery Society meeting near Philadelphia on 27 October, she took with her an address by ECS about reviving the campaign for woman suffrage but found little support. Lucretia Mott wrote to Martha Wright, "It is well for yr. state to revive the quest[n] as the time for revis[g] the constitut[n] is near—but as a general move, it w[d] be in vain, while the all-absorb[g] negro quest[n] is up—" (2 November 1865, Garrison Papers, MNS-S.)

WEDNESDAY, OCTOBER 25, 1865. At Mrs. Stantons all day— at eve went to Cooper Institute to hear Wendell Phillips—fine audience and Splendid speech—title "South Victorious"[1]   Saw Dale Owen, Mattie Griffith[2] & Mrs. Gilbert—[3] [*26–31 October, 1–15, 19–24 November omitted; no entries for 16–18 November.*]

1. According to Phillips, the South had won because it had abandoned none of the principles for which it seceded and yet, the North seemed willing to readmit southern states to the Union. (*NASS*, 28 October, 11 November 1865.)

2. Martha, or Mattie, Griffith (c. 1833–1906) freed the slaves she inherited from her family and moved north, after publishing the fictional *Autobiography of a Female Slave* in 1856. Active in abolitionist circles in New York, she served on the executive committee of the loyal league and held office in the American Equal Rights Association, until her marriage to Albert G. Browne in 1867. (Garrison, *Letters*, 5:117n; *Woman's Journal*, 9 June 1906.)

3. Mary Fowler Gilbert lived at 293 West 19th Street according to SBA, the address of Arad Gilbert. The assumption has been made, however, that she might be the wife of Edward Gilbert, the lawyer, abolitionist, and ally of George Cheever. She was prominent in the loyal league and in the drive for universal suffrage. (City directory, 1865–1866; memoranda in back of diary; DuBois, *Feminism and Suffrage*, 68.)

SATURDAY, NOVEMBER 25, 1865. [*Brooklyn*] Spent forenoon with cousin Semantha[1]—and after dinner all with P[arker] P[illsbury] went to Roseville N. Jersey[2] to visit Lucy Stone   Cousin S. seemed to enjoy their talk

    1. That is, Semantha Vail Lapham.
    2. Lucy Stone moved to Roseville, a section of Newark, in early 1865.

SUNDAY, NOVEMBER 26, 1865. At Lucy Stone's at Roseville— Phebe Jones, Lydia Mott—Parker Pillsbury and myself—had pleasant day—

MONDAY, NOVEMBER 27, 1865. Lydia, Phebe and P. P. went into N.Y. with Mr. B[lackwell] Lucy & I visited   (L. told me that Mrs. S. last summer gave her ↑[such love?]↓ experience)—[1] Antoinette called in P.M.— every body who has husband, home & children to look after has enough without public work [*28 November omitted.*]

    1. Parentheses added in a different pen.

WEDNESDAY, NOV. 29, 1865. Called at Dr. Cheever's—dined at Mattie Griffiths   Dale Owen not in—Mattie bright and true as ever

THURSDAY, NOVEMBER 30, 1865. The Evening Post refused to print Mrs. Stanton's word of Robert Dale Owen's letter for Constitutional amendment—[1] Took it Tribune—Gay not in— Dined at Dr. Cheevers & also P. P. then went to meeting the Doctor's Memorial to Congress is capital[2]

    1. The *Evening Post*, 25 November 1865, published Owen's proposal to meet the constitutional guarantee of a republican form of government in the states by setting federal qualifications for voters in presidential and congressional

elections. He thought that voters should be able to read the Constitution, but he would bar exclusions based on race.

2. About one hundred people met at the Church of the Puritans to hear a memorial to Congress written by George Cheever, Parker Pillsbury, and Edward Gilbert. It detailed constitutional grounds for Congress to refuse to seat members from the southern states until the civil and political rights of African Americans were guaranteed. States did not have the right to destroy voting rights, it concluded, and the federal government had the power to protect the rights of all citizens. (*New York Daily Tribune*, 1 December 1865; Harold M. Hyman, ed., *The Radical Republicans and Reconstruction, 1861–1870* [Indianapolis, 1967], 273–88.)

FRIDAY, DECEMBER 1, 1865. Decided to go to Worcester to see A. K. Foster—on A.S. and W.R. business— called at Dr. Cheever's—Dr. Hudson & A.S. office—found P. P. out—back to lunch at Mrs. Stantons— P. P. did not come to boat—the Norwich line—the N.Y. City steamer Found Hannah [Thurl?] & her mother on board— [*2 December omitted.*]

SUNDAY, DECEMBER 3, 1865. Boston called at Dr. H[arriet] K. Hunts— found her ready for a W.R. work— Found Dr. Zackshefskah gone[1]— took dinner at Mr. Garrisons—poor Mrs. G. has never fully recovered her shock of two years ago—[2] Giles & Kate Stebbins there— Fannie & Willie[3] going on to Philadelphia to Wendells Wedding on the 6th—[4]

1. Marie Elizabeth Zakrzewska (1829–1902), who left Germany in 1853 to pursue medical training, received her M.D. in 1856 and worked with Elizabeth Blackwell. In Boston she taught at the New England Female Medical College and opened the New England Hospital for Women and Children. (*NAW*.)

2. William Lloyd Garrison was on his way back from a western tour. Helen Eliza Benson Garrison (1811–1876) suffered a severe stroke at the end of 1863. (Garrison, *Letters*, 1:277–78, 5:133, 353–54.)

3. Known as Fanny, Helen Frances Garrison (1844–1928) was a lifelong friend of SBA and woman suffrage. She married the journalist Henry Villard in 1866. William Lloyd Garrison, Jr. (1838–1909), a wool broker, married Ellen Wright in 1864. (*NAW*; *New York Times*, 13 September 1909.)

4. Wendell Phillips Garrison (1840–1907) married Lucy McKim on 6 December 1865. Literary editor of the *Nation* from 1865 until 1906, he and his younger brother prepared a four-volume biography of their father. (Garrison, *Letters*, 5:9n, 356.)

MONDAY, DECEMBER 4, 1865. Called At A.S. Office—saw Whipple[1] May, and Walcutt[2]—then went Wendell Phillips house—found him— he consented to use $500. W.R. fund—[3] Talked of Mr. P. P. and Mr.

S. not fully harmonizing in the A.S. office at New York—[4] [*5 December omitted.*]

1. Charles King Whipple (1808–1900) served on the Hovey Fund Committee. He was later a trustee of the Francis Jackson bequest. (Garrison, *Letters*, 2:438n, 5:31n, 6:79n.)

2. Robert Folger Wallcut (1797–1884), bookkeeper for the *Liberator* from 1846 until 1865, later worked for the Freedmen's Commission. (Garrison, *Letters*, 3:343n, 5:46n.)

3. On this date the Thirty-ninth Congress began its first session, faced with decisions about readmitting the southern states and with pressure for black suffrage from radical Republicans and abolitionists. It assigned the business to a Joint Committee on Reconstruction, chaired by Congressman Thaddeus Stevens and Senator William Fessenden. Members immediately introduced scores of resolutions to amend the Constitution to prevent southern domination of Congress and rebel control of southern states. (Eric Foner, *Reconstruction: America's Unfinished Revolution, 1863–1877* [New York, 1988], 228–39; Joseph B. James, *The Framing of the Fourteenth Amendment* [Urbana, Ill., 1965], 21–23; *New York Daily Tribune*, 4 December 1865.)

4. George Washburn Smalley (1833–1916), the husband of Wendell Phillips's adopted daughter and a journalist, worked at the *Standard*. (*DAB*; McPherson, *Struggle for Equality*, 438.)

WEDNESDAY, DEC. 6, 1865. <u>West Newton</u>   delightful day with Mrs Severance—she is earnest for work for women

THURSDAY, DECEMBER 7, 1865. National Thanksgiving Day at Mrs. C. M. Severance's West Newton—Mass. The daughter Julia went into Boston with her affianced   The three sons—Seymour Sibley & Pierre at home—[1] Snow fell all day—had pleasant visit with Mrs. Severance— read Ruskin's letter on woman—also some in Mrs. E. W. Farnham's Woman & her Era— Mr. R. takes something the same view of Mrs F. the superiority or total unlikeness of the sexes—[2] [*8 December omitted.*]

1. The Severance sons were James Seymour (1842–1936), Mark Sibley (1846–1931), and Pierre Clarke (1849–1890). Julia Long (1844–?) married Edward C. Burrage in 1866. (John F. Severance, comp., *The Severance Genealogical History* [Chicago, 1893], 61, 73; alumni files, MH-Ar.)

2. John Ruskin (1819–1900), English social critic, published *Sesame and Lilies* in 1865; Eliza Wood Burhans Farnham (1815–1864), prison reformer and lecturer, published *Woman and Her Era* in 1864.

SATURDAY, DECEMBER 9, 1865. [*Worcester*] bright & cold again   the day passed & no chance for talk—Abby busy about house and Stephen gone to the city all day

SUNDAY, DECEMBER 10, 1865. at Fosters

MONDAY, DECEMBER 11, 1865. Returned to New-York—and commenced W.R. work in earnest— [*No entries for 12–23 December.*]

SUNDAY, DECEMBER 24, 1865. writing and folding and addressing petitions—

MONDAY, DECEMBER 25, 1865. Christmas   Mrs S. and I wrote all the A.M. at 2 P.M. I went to Brooklyn—found Cousins Geo & Aaron Vail there—Oliver Lapham married[1]—and a general jolly time there was at Lucien Squier's—[2]

1. George Otis Vail (1817–1880), SBA's second cousin, was in business with his brother Aaron in Buffalo. Oliver Keese Lapham was a first cousin of the Vails. A New York leather dealer, he married Caroline Gooding and in 1866 lived in Brooklyn with Lucien Squier. (Vail, *Moses Vail*, 221, 223–24; Aldridge, *Laphams in America*, 109; New York City directory, 1865–1866; Brooklyn city directory, 1866–1867.)

2. Lucien Bertrand Squier (1829–1904), the husband of SBA's first cousin Ellen Hoxie (1833–1904), entered the oil business in New York in 1855. (*Friends' Intelligencer* 61 [16 January 1904]: 40; Anthony, *Anthony Genealogy*, 191, 197; *Quaker Genealogy*, 3:173.)

⭢ Pocket Diary 1865, printed by Willy Wallach, New York, SBA Papers, DLC. Letters in square brackets expand initials or indicate doubt in transcription.

·⬤━━━◆━━━⬤·

205   ⤳   SBA TO CAROLINE HEALEY DALL

Standard Office—48 Beekman st.   New York Dec. 26, 1865

Dear Mrs. Dall

I send you three copies of our petition to Congress by same mail— I send a package to Mrs. C. M. Severance this week in A.S. Standard package to care of Mr. Walcutt—

On farther looking over the ways & means we decided to scatter a thousand copies of the form of petition, and get it published in as many newspapers as possible—and thus leave every representativ[e] woman to lead off in her own neighborhood and send a few names on each into Congress at the earliest day possible—

I hope the petition will not shock your good taste though it is not up to my hope—the printer & I together making some blunders— You will see the petition assumes that Congress will move to amend the Constitution to prohibit negro disfranchisement—and then to admit woman is to give <u>Universal</u> <u>Suffrage</u>—

To me the broad ground of republicanism is the one true place for all advance minds to occupy—

Gratz Brown is probably our best man in the Senate—that is the nearest ready to make the whole demand—[1] I don't know about Sumner—though all his bills are worded so as not to add any new limitations to suffrage[a] which cannot be said of R. Island Jenckes bill—saying—"Male citizens" and none others shall vote &c—[3]

I was very sorry not go to your delightful home that night—but it was chilly, and I was so far out as Mrs. Severances, and to say the least one half sick— I meant, surely, to have written my poor reason— I did wish very much to get more of your idea how we should proceed—and shall be glad of any suggestions you may make— Our N.Y. State work we will postpone a little, until the Constitutional Con. is called by the Legislature— Hastily but Truly yours

❧ *Susan B. Anthony*

❧ ALS, C. H. Dall Collection, MHi. Square bracket marks letter supplied at margin.

1. Benjamin Gratz Brown (1826–1885), Democratic senator from Missouri from 1863 to 1867, included women in his definition of universal suffrage, offered in a well-publicized speech in September 1865. The rights of women, he asserted, being "intrinsically the same with those of men, may not be consistently denied." (*BDAC*; Benjamin Gratz Brown, *Universal Suffrage; an Address by Hon. B. Gratz Brown Delivered at Turner Hall, St. Louis, Mo., September 22, 1865* [St. Louis, 1865].)

2. On 4 December Charles Sumner introduced resolutions on reconstruction, representation, and suffrage, including a bill to prohibit restrictions on suffrage in the District of Columbia "by reason of race or color," and one to guarantee republican government in the southern states. However, Sumner supported a joint resolution, submitted on the same day, to apportion representation according to the number of male voters in each state. (*The Works of Charles Sumner*, [Boston, 1874], 10:5–37.)

3. Thomas Allen Jenckes (1818–1875), Republican congressman from Rhode Island from 1863 to 1871, introduced a resolution on 11 December to amend the Constitution to allow for the direct election of president and vice president and to restrict voters to literate male citizens age twenty-one and over. (*BDAC*; *New York Daily Tribune*, 14 December 1865.)

·⟨⟞━━━⟝⟩·

206 ≈ ECS to the Editor, *National Anti-Slavery Standard*

New York, Dec. 26, 1865.

"THIS IS THE NEGRO'S HOUR."[1]

Sir, By an amendment of the Constitution, ratified by three-fourths of the loyal States, the black man is declared free.[2] The largest and most influential political party is demanding Suffrage for him throughout the Union, which right in many of the States is already conceded. Although this may remain a question for politicians to wrangle over for five or ten years, the black man is still, in a political point of view, far above the educated women of the country.

The representative women of the nation have done their uttermost for the last thirty years to secure freedom for the negro, and so long as he was lowest in the scale of being we were willing to press *his* claims; but now, as the celestial gate to civil rights is slowly moving on its hinges, it becomes a serious question whether we had better stand aside and see "Sambo" walk into the kingdom first.

As self-preservation is the first law of nature, would it not be wiser to keep our lamps trimmed and burning, and when the Constitutional door is open, avail ourselves of the strong arm and blue uniform of the black soldier to walk in by his side, and thus make the gap so wide that no privileged class could ever again close it against the humblest citizen of the Republic?

"This is the negro's hour." Are we sure that he, once entrenched in all his inalienable rights, may not be an added power to hold us at bay? Have not "black male citizens" been heard to say they doubted the wisdom of extending the right of Suffrage to women? Why should the African prove more just and generous than his Saxon compeers?

If the two millions of Southern black women are not to be secured in their rights of person, property, wages, and children, their emancipation is but another form of slavery. In fact, it is better to be the slave of an educated white man, than of a degraded, ignorant black one. We who know what absolute power the statute laws of most of the States give man, in all his civil, political, and social relations, do demand that in changing the status of the four millions of Africans, the women as well as the men should be secured in all the rights, privileges, and immunities of citizens.

It is all very well for the privileged order to look down complacently and tell us, "This is the negro's hour; do not clog his way; do not embarrass the Republican party with any new issue; be generous and magnanimous; the negro once safe, the woman comes next." Now, if our prayer involved a new set of measures, or a new train of thought, it would be cruel to tax "white male citizens" with even two simple questions at a time; but the disfranchised all make the same demand, and the same logic and justice that secures Suffrage to one class gives it to all.

The struggle of the last thirty years has not been merely on the black man as such, but on the broader ground of his humanity. Our Fathers, at the end of the first revolution, in their desire for a speedy readjustment of all their difficulties, and in order to present to Great Britain, their common enemy, an united front, accepted the compromise urged on them by South Carolina, and a century of wrong, ending in another revolution, has been the result of their action.[3]

This is our opportunity to retrieve the errors of the past and mould anew the elements of Democracy. The nation is ready for a long step in the right direction; party lines are obliterated, and all men are thinking for themselves. If our rulers have the justice to give the black man Suffrage, woman should avail herself of that new-born virtue to secure her rights; if not, she should begin with renewed earnestness to educate the people into the idea of universal suffrage.[4]

⇜ *E. Cady Stanton.*

⇜ *NASS,* 30 December 1865.

1. The phrase credited to Wendell Phillips in his speech to the May antislavery meeting.

2. The Thirteenth Amendment was ratified on 18 December 1865.

3. A reference to the constitutional compromise by which representation to Congress was based on the population of free inhabitants plus three-fifths of the slave population.

4. In the same issue the editor explained that printing ECS's letter did not pledge the paper to the advocacy of woman's rights. Parker Pillsbury, who left

his post at the *Standard* in December, did not write this piece; the author was probably Wendell Phillips. At this hour, he wrote, "it is certainly perilous and may be fatal to relax any energy hitherto devoted to [the negro's] emancipation, or to allow any fraction of our strength to be diverted to another issue." Women's enfranchisement was not "entitled to equal effort at this moment." "Causes have their crises," he concluded, and "that of the woman's rights movement has not come." (Lillie Buffum Chace Wyman and Arthur Crawford Wyman, *Elizabeth Buffum Chace, 1806–1899: Her Life and Its Environment* [Boston, 1914], 1:287.)

·◁═══✶═══▷·

207 ∾ Appeal by ECS and SBA

December 26, 1865.

Dear Friend: As the question of Suffrage is now agitating the public mind, it is the hour for woman to make her demand.

Propositions have already been made on the floor of Congress to so amend the Constitution as to exclude Women from a voice in the Government.* As this would be to turn the wheels of legislation backward, let the Women of the Nation now unitedly protest against such a desecration of the Constitution, and petition for that right which is at the foundation of all Government—the right of representation.

Send your petition when signed to your representative in Congress. In behalf of the National W.R. Com.

∾   *E. Cady Stanton,*

∾   *S. B. Anthony,*

∾   *Lucy Stone.*

* See Bill of Mr. Jenckes, of Rhode Island.

To the Senate and House of Representatives:

The undersigned, Women of the United States, respectfully ask an amendment of the Constitution that shall prohibit the several States from disfranchising any of their citizens on the ground of sex.

In making our demand for Suffrage, we would call your attention to the fact that we represent fifteen million people—one half the entire population of the country—intelligent, virtuous, native-born American citizens; and yet we are the only class who stand outside the pale of political recognition.

The Constitution classes us as "free people," and counts us *whole* persons in the basis of representation; and yet are we governed without our consent, compelled to pay taxes without appeal, and punished for violations of law without choice of judge or juror.

The experience of all ages, the Declarations of the Fathers, the Statute Laws of our own day, and the fearful revolution through which we have just passed, all prove the uncertain tenure of life, liberty, and property so long as the ballot—the only weapon of self-protection—is not in the hand of every citizen.

Therefore, as you are now amending the Constitution, and, in harmony with advancing civilization, placing new safeguards round the individual rights of four millions of emancipated slaves, we ask that you extend the right of Suffrage to Woman—the only remaining class of disfranchised citizens—and thus fulfil your Constitutional obligation "to Guarantee to every State in the Union a Republican form of Government."[1]

As all partial application of Republican principles must ever breed a complicated legislation as well as a discontented people, we would pray your Honorable Body, in order to simplify the machinery of government and ensure domestic tranquility, that you legislate hereafter for persons, citizens, tax-payers, and not for class or caste.

For justice and equality your petitioners will ever pray.

↜ *NASS*, 30 December 1865. The *Standard* placed the petition first.

1. U.S. Const., art. IV, sec. 4.

·⟨━━━━━⟩·

208 ↝ FROM THE DIARY OF SBA

[26–31 December 1865]

TUESDAY, DECEMBER 26, 1865. [*Brooklyn*] Called on Beecher—too late—must get there before 9 A.M.

Ex. Com. meeting in Boston—Pillsbury and Powell there

WEDNESDAY, DEC. 27, 1865. Theodore Tilton called at A.S. Office— talked of an "Equal rights" Committe or Society—& the "National Standard" its organ[1]

1. The *History of Woman Suffrage* adds that he proposed Wendell Phillips be president. On this day the executive committee of the Pennsylvania Anti-Slavery Society discussed letters from SBA and Parker Pillsbury, written in anticipation of a special meeting of the American society, about "the expediency of so altering the name of the Society as to be more in accordance with the changed character of slavery and to add suffrage for women as one of its objects." (*History*, 2:92; Pennsylvania Anti-Slavery Society Minute Book, 1856–70, pp. 99–100, PHi.)

THURSDAY, DECEMBER 28, 1865. Took tea at Cousin Semantha's— Aaron and George Vail there—slept at Cousin Nellies—

FRIDAY, DECEMBER 29, 1865. Beecher found Beecher He will give us Tuesday the 30th Jan./66 for Universal suffrage movement—[1]

1. No record of this speech can be found.

SATURDAY, DECEMBER 30, 1865. Sever snow storm Lucy Stone called at Office—Cousin Aaron Vail called—
[*on same page*] 31 Mrs. S. & self called at Mattie Griffith saw R. D. Owen

⚮ Pocket Diary 1865, printed by Willy Wallach, New York, SBA Papers, DLC.

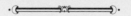

209 ⚮ ECS TO GERRIT SMITH

464. West 34th N.Y. Jan 1st [*1866*]

Dear Cousin G.

Do you see what the sons of the Pilgrims are doing in Congress? Nothing less that trying to get the irrepressible "male citizen" into our immortal Constitution.

I am glad that the men who are doing so base an act are named Schenck[1] & Jenckes. Say their names slowly & see how indicative the sound is of pettiness & cruelty. I hope the oleaginous festivities of Christmas may soften their strong hearts & that they may return from the discussion of turkey joints with a renewed grace for "Joint resolutions" I had a long talk with Robert Dale Owen yesterday & he gave me a copy of all the resolutions before Congress on suffrage

What a shame it would be to mar that glorious bequest of the Fathers, by introducing into it any word that would recognize a privileged order. As our Constitution now exists, there is nothing to prevent women or negroes from holding the ballot, but state legislation, but if that word "male" be inserted as now proposed by Broomall[2] Schenck & Jenckes, it will take us a century at least to get it out again As you have your hand in now, dressing the Chicago Tribune,[3] suppose you take a round with this base trio. The Knights of old thought themselves honoured in striking brave blows for woman   shall it be said in this republic, chivalry has died out, that our noblest & best will not rush unasked to recant this foul insult to the mothers of the republic? Sage of Peterboro unsheath your sword & to the rescue. The United States Constitution has always been one of your pet themes, save it now from this desecration by the recreant sons of the Fathers.

Note too that "National equal suffrage association" recently formed at Washington.[4] With such a grand title look at the 2nd article of their Constitution proposing to give "all men" suffrage. What impudence to call such an association national!! equal! Did these men spring from the brains of their Fathers,[5] armed & equipped with Joint resolutions, & Articles, that they thus presume to ignore 15 000 000 native born, taxpaying virtuous intelligent, citizen women?

Oh! my cousin! heal my bleeding heart with one trumpet note of manly indignation

I have just written to Greeley imploring him to say one word of rebuke for this republican action which is quite probably of his own concocting[6]   I am just going up to see Cousin Nancy.[7] Tell Julius that I was sorry not to see more of <u>him</u>. Love to all   Your loving Cousin

≈ E Cady Stanton.

≈ ALS, Smith Papers, NSyU.

1. Robert Cumming Schenck (1809–1890), Ohio Republican, who served in the House before the war and again from 1863 to 1871, introduced a resolution to base congressional representation on "the number of male citizens over twenty-one years of age, having the qualifications requisite for electors of the most numerous branch of the state legislature." This proposal met opposition from representatives of eastern states with large populations and high percentages of women and children. (*BDAC*; *Independent* 18 [14 December 1865]: 1; *Congressional Globe*, 39th Cong., 1st sess., 407, 409.)

2. John Martin Broomall (1816–1894) of Pennsylvania served in the House

from 1863 to 1869. His resolution based representation on the number of electors in a state, not population. Although he later retreated from this proposal in the interest of passing an amendment, he doubted, he told Congress, "that the East is entitled to count its women and children in its basis of representation unless it gives them a voice in the Government, any more than the people of South Carolina ought to count their negroes without giving them a voice in the Government." (*BDAC*; *Congressional Globe*, 39th Cong., 1st sess., 10, 433.)

3. In December 1865, Gerrit Smith filed a libel suit against the *Chicago Tribune* for its statements about his confinement to a mental hospital during John Brown's trial. (Harlow, *Gerrit Smith*, 450-54.)

4. William D. Kelley, congressman from Pennsylvania, was president of this organization, formed to secure "to every man of suitable age, unconvicted of crime, the right to vote at our municipal, state, and national elections." (*NASS*, 6 January 1866; *New York Daily Tribune*, 12 March 1866.)

5. A reference to the goddess Minerva.

6. ECS may refer to the text published in the *Tribune* and the *Standard* on 6 January, *Film*, 10:259, 264.

7. Ann Smith was visiting their son Green.

---

210 ❧ ECS TO WENDELL PHILLIPS

[*New York*] Jan 12th [*1866*]

Dear Mr Phillips

You ask "How a course of lectures in <u>one place</u> can help your movement"[1]

Should a course be given in the Fegee Islands it might not, but in the metropolis of the nation with a dozen or more reporters to send your words the world over, it would be a grand time for you & Beecher & Carl Shurtz to say the right word on suffrage

Everybody is befogged on that question & a little light might dissipate the thick clouds

Please do not bow me out until I introduce myself & make known my errand.

What good are our petitions so long as such women as Martha Wright & Mrs Wendell Phillips Garrison[2] will not sign them? & why will they not? because they feel that our antislavery priesthood are opposed to them.

In regard to blocking the wheels of action for the black man, I have not heard one leading republican express the slightest hope that suffrage could be [secured?] for the negro during this session. I do sincerely believe the shortest way to get justice for him is to educate the people now into the true idea   Your argument against the reading qualification given here in one of your speeches struck me as admirable,[3] & confirmed me in my intuition on the same side of that question, & no arguments that I have since heard in its favour has changed my opinion one iota.

Where did you find in my letter to your good wife a "deprecating remark"?[4] Could I so violate good manners as to write in that tone to a man's wife? Oh! no, that must be a ruse of yours to draw out more compliments, but I am too full of wrath against Schenck & Jenckes to worship any "white male citizen" profoundly.

Mr Pillsbury has arrived in good spirits. Are we not to say the word woman in the Standard   Pray be merciful to us miserable sinners Yours sincerely

≈ E Cady Stanton.

≈ ALS, bMS Am 1953(1152), Wendell Phillips Papers, MH-H. Square brackets indicate text in doubt.

1. Phillips declined an invitation from SBA to lecture in New York and asked, "do you need more than a few good sized petitions just to awaken Congress & block wheels that are only too willing to be blocked?" (W. Phillips to ECS, [between 9 & 12 January 1866], Film, 11:273–75.)

2. Martha Wright later signed the petition. Lucy McKim Garrison (1842–1877), the daughter of abolitionist James Miller McKim and the wife of Wendell Phillips Garrison, told her husband she would not sign because it was "out of time." A music student at the Eagleswood School, she was an editor of Slave Songs of the United States (1867). (ECS to M. C. Wright, 6, 20 January 1866, Film, 11:263, 297; Dena J. Epstein, "Lucy McKim Garrison, American Musician," Bulletin of the New York Public Library 67 [October 1963]: 529–46.)

3. Speaking in May to the American Anti-Slavery Society, he dismissed "book learning" as a qualification for voting; "It is by work, not reading, that good voters are made." (New York Times, 10 May 1865.)

4. Phillips himself forgot what he meant by these words. ECS had asked Ann Phillips's advice about her "silver tongued tyrant or slave as the case may be" and particularly about his willingness to speak for women or to assure her "that we shall have no frown from that quarter, in speaking for ourselves." (ECS to A. G. Phillips, [before 9 January 1866], W. Phillips to ECS, 14 January 1866, Film, 11:265–70, 283–86.)

·⟨══════⟩·

211 ⇝ SBA TO JAMES BROOKS[1]

Standard Office, 48 Beekman Street, New York, January 20, 1866.

Dear Sir: I send you the inclosed copy of petition and signatures sent to Thaddeus Stevens last week. I then urged Mr. Stevens, if their committee of fifteen could not report favorably to our petition, they would, at least, not interpose any new barrier against woman's right to the ballot.

Mrs. Stanton sent you a petition; I trust you will present that at your earliest convenience. The Democrats are now in minority. May they drive the Republicans to do good works—not merely to hold the rebel States in check until negro men shall be guarantied their right to a voice in their governments, but to hold the party to a logical consistency that shall give every responsible citizen in every State equal right to the ballot.

Will you, sir, please send me whatever is said or done with our petitions? Will you also give me names of members whom you think would present petitions for us?[2] Respectfully yours,

⇝ Susan B. Anthony.

⇐ Congressional Globe, 39th Cong., 1st sess., 23 January 1866, 380; printed with petition signed by ECS, SBA, Antoinette Blackwell, Lucy Stone, Ernestine Rose, Joanna S. Morse, Elizabeth R. Tilton, Ellen Squier, Mary Fowler Gilbert, Mary E. Gilbert, and Mattie Griffith. Also in History, 2:97.

1. James Brooks (1810–1873) was editor of the New York Express, a Democratic congressman from the city, and his party's leading debater against Thaddeus Stevens. At the opening of the Thirty-ninth Congress, Brooks fought hard to seat the southern delegates and to block formation of the Joint Committee of Fifteen. Clashes with Stevens and the radical Republicans continued through the session. To help the suffrage campaign, Brooks used his congressional frank to mail out the woman's rights petitions. (DAB; Current, Old Thad Stevens, 222–23.)

2. On 23 January, Brooks asked the Clerk of the House to read aloud SBA's letter and petition, and he announced his intention to amend various proposals before the House to read that congressional representation would be reduced if the elective franchise were denied "on account of race or color or sex." Pressed by Stevens to say whether he favored woman suffrage, Brooks

replied, yes, if negroes were to vote; "I am in favor of my own color in preference to any other color, and I prefer the white women of my country to the negro." Stevens finally introduced the petition he received from ECS on 29 January. (*Film*, 11:326–29.)

·⟨⟩·

212 ⟩⟩ SBA TO SIDNEY CLARKE

Standard Office—48 Beekman st— New York Jan. 21, 1866

My dear Friend

I send you enclosed petition[1] with but few signatures—but enough to remind Congress that true republicanism cannot disfranchise any class of intelligent citizens. If you do feel like presenting it—please hand it to some ~~pers~~ Member who will—

I have sent to Thad. Stephens freighted with our old Woman's Rights Workers names—with a letter urging his Committee not to put up new barriers against Woman—if they could not report favorably to our petition— But it will be weak & cowardly, if not wicken and craven for the "White Male citizens" to again vote themselves the government of this republic. The good spirits spare them from so sad a record of themselves—

I go to Boston tomorrow— We of New York state are about organizing a "N.Y. State Equal Rights Association"—[2] The time for Nego or Woman specialties is passed—and we proposed to step on to the broad platform of equality & fraternity— Truly your Friend

⟩⟩ *Susan B. Anthony*

⟩ ALS, Carl Albert Center Archives: Sidney Clarke Collection, Western History Collections, OkU.

1. Enclosure missing.
2. The officers were Theodore Tilton, ECS, Frederick Douglass, Aaron Powell, and SBA. In accepting his office Douglass wrote, "I have about made up my mind that if you can forgive me for being a negro—I cannot do less than to forgive you for being a woman." (ECS and SBA to Caroline Dall, 31 January 1866, ECS to Wendell Phillips, 10 February 1866, F. Douglass to ECS, 16 February 1866, *Film*, 11:335–38, 343–47, 367.)

·❪━━━━❖━━━━❫·

213 ❧ SBA TO WENDELL PHILLIPS

Standard Office—48 Beekman st. New York Jan. 28, 1866—

Dear Friend Phillips

I learned of the women when in Boston last week—that they were getting up a new and different petition from the one we ↑have↓ sent out—[1] I dont know as they will ask our W. Rights, or the Hovey Com. for money to print their new form—but I wish to put in my protest against spending a dollar of either ↑fund↓ on mere phraseology—our form will awaken the public to the fact of ↑that↓ woman demands political recognition in the new order of things—and that is the point we should aim at— Moreover, Mrs. Dall, Mrs. Severance and Dr. Hunt were each asked ↑at first↓ to prepare the petition and each deferred the work to Mrs. Stanton and myself—not one of them ↑even↓ suggested that it should be a <u>mere</u> <u>protest</u> against <u>backward</u> legislation—hence, after the cost of <u>sixty</u> <u>dollars</u> for paper, printing and envelopes—and the petitions actually in the hands of women in every northern state, it would be worse than waste, both of money & time to print new petitions—

You have doubtless seen how splendidly Gratz Brown of Mo. presented our petition in the Senate[2]—and ↑with↓ what skill Brooks managed to get it before the House—

Those Boston Meetings were very refreshing to every abolitionist present, and I hope the report of them may go out to those who were absent, so full, and so perfect that every reader of the Standard shall take on new life and new zeal to work to the end—[3] The first work now seems to me to get every abolitionist to subscribe for the Standard— I have written both Stearns and Whipple about the Liberator list of subscribers[4]—and hope it ↑may↓ reach me here at the earliest moment—as it will be quite a job to compare the lists so as to send only to those who do not already take the Standard— If Stearns fails us—wont Mr. Wolcott give it to us?—

Several ↑new↓ subscriptions came in yesterday in response to Mr. Pillsbury's appeal—[5] Do you ↑know↓ I brought back forty new subscribers?— Cant you give this weeks Standard the round figures of the Festival receipts?—[6] I want <u>this</u> number to be <u>extra wide awake</u> that it may stir every person who gets it to subscribe for it— did we have none of the speeches reported?— I hope we did—for the country abolitionists are anxiously waiting to learn the spirit of those at the helm of our old ship—

Will you please send me another hundred dollars of the W.R. Fund— less <u>ten dollars</u>—which $10. I wish given to Mrs. Sargent[7] as my Festival Contribution— Pardon this long letter Sincerely yours

❧ *Susan B. Anthony*

[*upside down on last page, in ECS's hand*] Do Susan & I bore you? I fear you look upon us very much as abolitionists used to regard Mellen[8] & Treadwell on the constitution.

❧ ALS, bMS Am 1953(213), Wendell Phillips Papers, MH-H.

1. SBA attended special meetings of the American Anti-Slavery Society in Boston on 24 January and the Massachusetts society the next day. Caroline Dall explained that the Boston petition would protest the addition of the words "male citizen" to the Constitution but not ask for woman suffrage. (*History*, 2:101–2n; SBA to C. H. Dall, 30 January, and ECS to C. H. Dall, 31 January 1866, *Film*, 11:330–38.)

2. On 24 January 1866. Brown described those who signed it as "some of the most intelligent and accomplished women of our land." They shared the hardships of the Civil War, he said, and held "their claim in abeyance" until the slave was freed; now, fearing a constitutional amendment granting rights to blacks might block their own rights, "they feel no longer content to remain silent." (*Congressional Globe*, 39th Cong., 1st sess., 390, *Film*, 11:309.)

3. The plan to join the antislavery and woman's rights causes in a single society came up for discussion at the meeting, suggested by Theodore Tilton and Stephen Foster. Charles Remond and Abby Foster opposed it; the focus should be kept on negro suffrage. Reiterating his familiar position, Phillips would not "engraft female suffrage" on the society's platform. SBA did not join this discussion; her remarks to the meeting concerned reviving the antislavery society and its newspaper. (*NASS*, 3 February 1866, *Film*, 11:306–8; *Anthony*, 1:256.)

4. George Luther Stearns and Charles K. Whipple. Stearns (1809–1867) was an accomplished publicist for the cause of black suffrage, with a vast mailing list for his many pamphlets and newspapers. (*DAB*; McPherson, *Struggle for Equality*, 322–26, 338.)

5. In the issue dated 6 January 1866, Parker Pillsbury wrote a tribute to the retiring William Lloyd Garrison and urged readers of the *Liberator* to subscribe to the *Standard*.

6. The National Anti-Slavery Subscription Anniversary on January 24 raised $2,834.70, a sum "much larger than we had reason to expect." (*NASS*, 3 March 1866.)

7. Mary Elizabeth Fiske Sargent (1827–1904) was the second wife of Boston abolitionist John Turner Sargent and a manager of the festival. (Emma Worcester Sargent and Charles Sprague Sargent, comps., *Epes Sargent of Gloucester and His Descendants* [Boston, 1923], 162–63.)

8. George W. F. Mellen (c. 1804–1875), a Boston regular at antislavery meetings, published *An Argument on the Unconstitutionality of Slavery* in 1841 and persistently confronted Garrisonians with his conclusions. Henry Stanton thought him insane. (Garrison, *Letters*, 3:241n; Stanton, *Random Recollections*, 2d ed., 76.)

·⊏━━━━━▶◀━━━━━▷·

214 ⪼ ECS TO THE EDITOR, *NATIONAL ANTI-SLAVERY STANDARD*

[*New York, before 17 February 1866*]

DOUGLASS AND JOHNSON.

"The white man was permitted to vote before government was derived from him."—*A. Johnson*[1]

Sir: Does not the "old serpent" hide himself as cunningly under the word "white" in the United States as he does under "class" in the Old World? Who were those privileged white men that voted in the beginning, before governments were? For what did they vote?

Did Adam vote himself out of Paradise, or did Noah and his compeers vote themselves into the ark? Have no black men ever had nations, votes or governments? Have all "white men," even in France, England and the United States, been permitted to vote from the beginning? Did Mr. Johnson never hear of black votes deciding an election in a northern State? There have been changes in the fortunes of voters, as in all other privileges.

Jefferson and Adams told us a century ago, that all just governments were derived from the consent of the governed; but now, the President of the United States tells us, that the "white man" is the author of government, and that he voted before governments were.

If there ever was a time when Abolitionists might feel proud of a race they have sought to elevate, it was when Frederick Douglass and Andrew Johnson stood face to face.

There met a negro and a poor white, both having escaped from the bondage of ignorance at the same time. They learned their letters at the age of twenty-one. Douglass wishing to see men under other phases, went beyond Mason and Dixon's line, to study republican institutions in a Northern institute; while Johnson, regarding himself as the future Moses of the oppressed African, decided to remain in his native land, "to sacrifice his life, property and ambition to the welfare of the colored race." But the most apparent and lamentable sacrifice he has made, if we may judge from this interview, has been of his own powers of discrimination.

Who that reads the speeches of the colored delegation, and the President's, can help seeing how much better Douglass understands the philosophy of social life and republican institutions than the President?

This may be partly due to his Northern education, and partly to superior original powers of thought.

As he measured himself with the best man the liberal party could find to represent them as Vice-President, it must have been a proud moment for Douglass. After such an exhibition of white intelligence and statesmanship, he must have felt fresh confidence in his own race, for surely any slave on a Southern plantation could have given a better solution of the problem of Southern life.

That interview illustrates the power of the ballot. Had Douglass been enfranchised when Johnson was, he too could have remained South, and by a constant "sacrifice of life, property and ambition," in the same manner, found his way to the White House, not as a suppliant, but perchance as President of the United States. Talk of educating men for suffrage. That right itself makes manhood; the dignity and responsibility it confers is education.

Why did Andrew Johnson dare to talk in that sneering tone to Frederick Douglass, one of the ablest men in the Empire State? Simply because he represented no power to vote him back to "his property in Tennessee now occupied by his slaves."

⪢ E. C. S.

⪢ *NASS*, 17 February 1866.

1. From the interview at the White House between President Andrew Johnson and a delegation from the Colored Men's Convention on 7 February. Frederick Douglass was among thirteen men who requested legislation to enforce the Thirteenth Amendment and guarantee black suffrage. Johnson defended his policies on race and suggested that if African Americans were unhappy in the South, they should emigrate. If the poor white and the black were "thrown together at the ballot-box, with this enmity and hate existing between them," he argued, "a war of races" would begin. The interview was published in the Washington *Evening Star* and widely reprinted. (Douglass, *Papers*, 4:96–106.)

·⊂━━━✕━━━⊃·

215 ✧ THOMAS W. HIGGINSON TO ECS

Newport, R.I. May 2, 1866

Dear Mrs. Stanton

I have been delayed by excess of writing on other matters, & by doubt what to say.

I never go to Conventions, now, & dislike public speaking. A letter I will <u>try</u> to write.[1]

My <u>convictions</u> as to the political rights of woman are unchanged. My <u>faith</u> is clogged by two things. 1st Lucy Stone's entire absorption in her own household & admission that the mother of young children must during her prime of life be so absorbed, & 2nd my deep impression, at the South, of the impossibility of a race of <u>contented</u> slaves. I had always taken the ground that the acquiescence of the vast majority of women was like that of slaves, but observation has taught me that no such phenomenon is to be found among slaves. The acquiescence of women—for it is not an unwilling, coerced ~~illegible~~ ↑dogged↓ submission,↓—is an argument hard to answer <u>for a man</u>. Certainly men can never secure ~~their~~ ↑woman's↓ rights vicariously for them. Hence a sort of chill of discouragement, for it is no more.

With increased respect for women like yourself who <u>are</u> dissatisfied I am   Cordially yours

✧ *T. W. Higginson*

✧ ALS, Scrapbook 1, Papers of ECS, NPV. ECS intended this letter to be published somewhere. She wrote: "print ——'s instead of Lucy Stone. Read carefully & see that every word is right, some are obscure but you can study them."

1. See T. W. Higginson to SBA, 14 May 1866, *Film*, 11:513.

·⊂━━━━━━⊃·

216 ↝ REMARKS BY ECS TO THE AMERICAN ANTI-SLAVERY SOCIETY

Editorial note: The American Anti-Slavery Society held its meeting in the Church of the Puritans in New York on 8–9 May 1866, with Wendell Phillips presiding. At the end of April Congress reached agreement on wording the Fourteenth Amendment, basing representation on population and threatening to reduce the representation of states that excluded male voters on the basis of race. It postponed a decision about black suffrage until after the mid-term elections in November. The antislavery society resolved that Congress should make the African American "the absolute equal of the white man before the law" and secure him "his political rights, especially the right of suffrage." Furthermore, Congress should "assert as a principle of national law definitively settled by the defeat of the rebellion in the field, that no State is *Republican* in a constitutional and national sense which makes any distinction in civil or political rights among its citizens on account of race or descent." During debate on the resolutions on 9 May, Aaron Powell made a new proposal. The *Standard* omitted the ensuing discussion from its report of the meeting. (*NASS*, 19 May 1866.)

[9 May 1866]

Mr. Aaron M. Powell then offered the following resolution:

Resolved, That we urgently call upon the people of the State of New-York to improve the favorable opportunity offered by the approaching Constitutional Convention for the revision of the State Constitution to secure the repeal of the word white and the property qualification for colored voters as an urgent and unchristian, and a formidable obstacle to the progress of National reconstruction upon a just and true basis.

Mrs. Stanton moved to amend the resolution, by inserting the words "a republican form of government," which would strike out the words male and white. (Laughter.) Why should they go about this State and ask for suffrage for the negro, and not demand it for herself? <In a

cause for which women had labored for thirty years she did not see the justice of securing suffrage to the negro and denying it to women.>

Mrs. [Abby Kelley] Foster said it would be an insult to ask a woman to go over the State and make such a demand for the negro, and not include herself. But that is simply an act of her own volition. She did not think such a subject should be introduced into an Anti-Slavery meeting. They had other organizations for the advocacy of those rights. Just as soon as the civil rights of the negroes are secured in the South, we cease to be an Anti-Slavery Society, and then I am ready for an organization for universal suffrage.

Mr. Willcox (Staten Island)[1] moved an amendment, to insert "Democratic" in place of "Republican."

<The Chairman, Wendell Phillips, with some acerbity, said Mrs. Stanton's amendment was out of order, because it was not consistent with the constitution.

Robert Purvis, of Philadelphia,[2] said he would appeal from the chairman's decision. He believed it was the business of this society to resist all oppression—the oppression of women, as well as others.

Old Mr. [Stephen] Foster, who was stated to be the husband of Abby Kelley Foster, wanted to know wherein the amendment was out of order.

Mr. Phillips said the sole object of this society was the abolition of slavery in the United States.

Mrs. Stanton said her motion was merely that the Constitution of the State of New-York should be amended so as to give it a republican form of government, and she had expressed her opinion that that would strike out the word "male."> Mrs. Stanton said that as long as any form of oppression was tolerated, even Mr. Phillips himself was not secure in his liberty.

A vote sustaining the chair was obtained, and

Mr. Foster moved to strike from the constitution all restrictions of the right of suffrage, and to insert a "republican form of government."

Mr. A. M. Powell said that we owe to the colored people of the State a hearty expression of our opinions in reference to the striking out of "white," and all the paragraphs relative to a property qualification.

Mr. Stephen S. Foster (Worcester), Mass.—We have been drawn into a question on which the life of this society depends. Some who have worked with us for thirty years say that our time as an Anti-

Slavery Society has passed away. We are now a small body, and if we have another division it will be very apt to totally destroy us. I object to the restriction of the time of speaking here.

On motion of Mr. Theo. Tilton, it was argued that Mr. Foster be allowed unlimited time to make whatever statements he pleased.

> Editorial note: Discussion was interrupted for the nominating committee to submit a slate of officers. Charles Remond took the chair, while the executive committee left the room.

Mr. Foster then rose and continued: The question now arises, is there any common ground on which we can all stand and preserve our unity? My conviction is that there is such a ground on which we can stand and not sacrifice our principle or our union. Mr. Phillips says on this platform we can demand only the right of the negro to the suffrage. But, you can demand everything that goes to secure that suffrage to the negro. Twenty-five years ago it was asked if woman had a right to speak in public in behalf of the slave. That right was conceded, although it caused a division of the Society. The question now comes, has woman a right to strike off the shackles of the slave by her vote, as well as by her tongue. I say she has. (Applause.) I will fight to the death for it, and I tell you that you will never see the negro voting until woman cast her ballot for him. Is liberty an incident of sex? I should despise myself if I asked woman to help me in securing my right to the ballot-box and deny it to her. I will never vote until I shall be able to carry my wife there and drop her ballot with mine. This is no narrow question of Constitutional technicalities. I did not bring this question into our debates. Mr. Frothingham said yesterday that it was the all and all of Americans.[3]

Mr. Prince[4] asked whether black women ought not to be entitled to vote, in order to secure their liberty on the same ground.

Mr. Foster—I have never made a discrimination. I have demanded the ballot for all classes and sexes, and when I make that demand, I make an appeal to the conscience. If you limit me here to any partial measure, this is no plan for me. What difference does it make to the negro that you ask for his rights singly or in company with the rights of others? We keep an eye on the negro when we demand that woman unloose her tongue and cast her ballot for him. Until you admit woman to the ballot-box, you are exercising a rank tyranny. The same despotism which tramples on the negro will trample on woman, and revolution after revolution shall go on, until we have established our institutions on the broad basis of justice to all classes and colors. Now, how is this in opposition to your Constitution? If it is so, trample on your Constitution; put your heel on it. Exclude from it nothing that can be of any good. I shall work for you on the Anti-Slavery platform; but if there is a broader platform on which I can stand for liberty for all, there shall I plead also.

Mr. Lee said that he believed the most intense hatred of the negro in this city was felt by the women. In the theater, the omnibus, the church, everywhere, was this manifested. The most fiendish outrages in the time of our riots were perpetrated by the women.[5] And so on through the Rebellion. Still I have a respect for the women, for I remember that my mother was a woman (laughter); but though I am in favor of woman's rights, I think it is right that they should have the truth told of them.

Mr. Prince—It has been asserted that the black man should have the right to vote because he is not sure of his freedom without it. If this is the case, why should not the women who were lately slaves have the same right? Why should we be afraid of this question? The greater includes the less. I think it reasonable that we should incorporate it. This is not a foreign question here; it belongs to this society.

Mrs. Stanton said that the women who are so prejudiced against the black men are not the women who now demand universal suffrage. She entertained Frederick Douglass or Charles Remond the same as she would any other gentleman of education and culture. There is a broad difference between giving the ballot to the negro and to women. In order to have a government perfect you need to have women in it. Until woman stands on an equal platform with us, all man's enunciations are cold, barren and of no account until vitalized by her influence.

Mr. George W. Smalley—When I heard the remarks of a gentleman, somewhere in the lower part of the room, relative to the prejudices of woman against the negro, I certainly did not expect that a reply would be made to anything so contemptible and unworthy; but inasmuch as Mrs. Stanton has seen fit to reply, a word from one who is not a woman may not be out of place. If women do act here in such a way, in the theater and in the church and elsewhere, it is because we have men among us who prompt them to such a course. (Applause.)

Mr. [Edward M.] Davis made a few remarks in favor of embodying Woman's Rights in the Anti-Slavery platform, after which

Mrs. Stanton said that it was simply a question of time. It was only demanding it for the negro on Thursday and for woman on Friday.

The resolution was then adopted.

❧ *New York Tribune*, 10 May 1866; New York *World*, 10 May 1866. Square brackets show expanded versions of the speakers' names.

1. Albert Oliver Willcox (1810–c. 1897) was a New York merchant living on Staten Island who played minor roles in the antislavery movement for several decades. A Democrat, he was a conspicuous supporter of woman suffrage from 1866 until his death. (*ACAB*; *History*, 4:295.)

2. Robert Purvis (1810–1898) was a founding member of the American Anti-Slavery Society, and, from 1845 to 1850, president of the Pennsylvania Anti-Slavery Society. Born free in South Carolina and raised in Philadelphia, Purvis was especially active in aiding fugitive slaves and protecting and extending the civil and political rights of northern blacks. He and his wife Harriet Forten Purvis, herself a prominent abolitionist, joined the American Equal Rights Association in 1866. (*DANB*.)

3. Though the *Tribune* reported Foster as saying "Mr. Nottingham," he refers to the statement by Octavius Brooks Frothingham, that the former slave "must have the ballot . . . because he is entitled to it under the natural law of absolute right." Frothingham (1822–1895) was pastor of a Unitarian church in New York City and an influential intellectual. Finding Unitarianism too orthodox, he became a founder of the Free Religious Association in 1867 and its president until 1878. (New York *World*, 9 May 1866; *DAB*.)

4. Charles Prince resided in Connecticut. Active in the American Equal Rights Association, he was named one of its vice presidents in 1869. (*History*, 2:378n.)

5. A reference to the draft riots in New York in 1863.

·❮━━━━━━━❯·

217 ❧ ELEVENTH NATIONAL WOMAN'S RIGHTS CONVENTION

Editorial note: The Eleventh National Woman's Rights Convention met in the Church of the Puritans on 10 May 1866, ECS presiding. Major addresses were delivered by ECS, Henry Ward Beecher, and Frances Ellen Watkins Harper, and the body adopted an Appeal to Congress to recognize that "[t]he only tenable ground of representation is *Universal Suffrage*."

[10 May 1866]

Susan B. Anthony presented the following resolution, and moved its adoption:

Whereas, By the act of Emancipation and the Civil Rights bill,[1] the negro and woman now hold the same civil and political *status*, alike needing only the ballot; and whereas the same arguments apply equally to both classes, proving all partial legislation fatal to republican institutions, therefore

Resolved, That the time has come for an organization that shall demand *Universal Suffrage*, and that hereafter we shall be known as the *"American Equal Rights Association."*

Martha C. Wright seconded the motion, and Miss Anthony said: Our friend Mrs. Mott desires me to explain the object of this change, a work she would gladly do but for a severe cold, which prevents her from making herself heard. For twenty years the Woman's Rights movement has pressed the claims of woman to the right of representation in the government. The first National Woman's Rights Convention was held in Worcester, Mass., in 1850, and each successive year, conventions were held in different cities of the Free States—Worcester, Syracuse, Cleveland, Philadelphia, Cincinnati, and New York—until the rebellion. Since then, till now, we have held no conventions.

Up to this hour, we have looked to State action only for the recognition of our rights; but now, by the results of the war, the whole question of suffrage reverts back to Congress and the Constitution. The duty of Congress at this moment is to declare what shall be the basis of representation in a republican form of government. There is, there can be, but one true basis; and that is that taxation must give representation; hence our demand must now go beyond woman—it must extend to the farthest bound of the principle of the "consent of the governed," the only authorized or just government. We, therefore, wish to broaden our Woman's Rights platform, and make it in *name*— what it ever has been in *spirit*—a Human Rights platform.

It has already been stated that we have petitioned Congress the past Winter to so amend the Constitution as to prohibit disfranchisement on account of sex. We were roused to the work by the several propositions still to permit negro disfranchisement in the rebel states, and at the same time to put up a new bar against the enfranchisement of women.

As women we can no longer *seem* to claim for ourselves what we do not for others—nor can we work in two separate movements to get the ballot for the two disfranchised classes—the negro and woman—since to do so must be at double cost of time, energy and money.

The State of New York is to hold a Constitutional Convention the coming year. We want to make a thorough canvass of the entire State, with lecturers, tracts and petitions, and, if possible, create a public sentiment that shall send genuine Democrats and Republicans to that Convention who shall strike out from our Constitution the two adjectives "*white male*," giving to every citizen, over twenty-one, the right to vote, and thus make the Empire State the first example of a true republican form of government. And what we propose to do in New York, the coming eighteen months, we trust to do in every other State, so soon as we can get the men, and the women, and the money, to go forward with the work.

Therefore, that we may henceforth concentrate all our forces for the practical application of our one grand, distinctive, national idea—*Universal Suffrage*—I hope we will unanimously adopt the resolution before us, thus resolving this Eleventh National Woman's Rights Convention into the "*American Equal Rights Association*."

The Resolution was unanimously adopted, after which Miss Anthony proposed a list of officers for the new Society.

> Editorial note: Stephen Foster moved an adjournment until four o'clock to prepare a constitution. Lucretia Mott reviewed the movement's history, and the meeting adjourned.

The Convention reassembled at four o'clock in the Lecture Room of Dr. Cheever's Church.

Susan B. Anthony took the Chair and said, the first thing, in order to complete the new organization, would be to fix upon a form of Constitution.

Parker Pillsbury, from the Business Committee, reported the following, which was considered article by article and adopted.

There was an interesting discussion relative to the necessity of a preamble to the Constitution, in which the majority sympathized with

Lucretia Mott, who expressed herself specially desirous that there should be a preamble, and that it should state the fact that this new organization was the outgrowth of the Woman's Rights movement. Mrs. Stanton gave her idea of what the preamble should say—and Mrs. Mott moved that Mrs. Stanton be appointed to write out her thought, and that it be accepted as the preamble of the Constitution. The motion was adopted.

CONSTITUTION OF THE AMERICAN EQUAL RIGHTS ASSOCIATION.

Preamble.

Whereas, by the war, society is once more resolved into its original elements, and in the reconstruction of our government we again stand face to face with the broad question of natural rights, all associations based on special claims for special classes are too narrow and partial for the hour; Therefore, from the baptism of this second revolution—purified and exalted through suffering—seeing with a holier vision that the peace, prosperity and perpetuity of the Republic rest on *Equal Rights to All*, we, to-day, assembled in our Eleventh National Woman's Rights Convention, bury the woman in the citizen, and our organization in that of the American Equal Rights Association.

> Editorial note: The constitution, omitted here, defined offices and provided for other equal rights associations to become auxiliaries of the American. ECS headed the slate of officers proposed to the meeting.

Mrs. Stanton thanked the Convention for the honor proposed, but said she should prefer to see Lucretia Mott President; that thus that office might ever be held sacred in the memory that it had first been filled by one so loved and honored by all. I shall be happy as Vice-President to relieve my dear friend of the arduous duties of her office, if she will but give us the blessing of her name as President. Mrs. Stanton then moved that Mrs. Mott be the President, which was seconded by many voices, and carried by a unanimous vote.

Stephen S. Foster then escorted Mrs. Mott to the Chair. On taking the chair, Mrs. Mott remarked that her age and feebleness unfitted her for any public duties, but she rejoiced in the inauguration of a movement broad enough to cover class, color and sex, and would be happy to give her name and influence, if thus she might encourage the young and strong to carry on the good work.

On motion of Theodore Tilton, Mrs. Stanton was made first Vice-President. The rest of the names were approved.

Mrs. Stanton said, It had been the desire of her heart to see the Anti-Slavery and Woman's Rights organizations merged into an Equal Rights association, as the two questions were now one and the same. With emancipation, all that the black man asks is the right of suffrage. With the special legislation of the last twenty years, all that woman asks is the right of suffrage. Hence it seems an unnecessary expenditure of force and substance, for the same men and women to meet in convention on Tuesday to discuss the right of one class to the ballot, and on Thursday, to discuss the right of another class to the same. Has not the time come, Mrs. President, to bury the black man and the woman in the citizen, and our two organizations in the broader work of reconstruction?

They who have been trained in the school of anti-slavery, they who, for the last thirty years, have discussed the whole question of human rights, which involves every other question of trade, commerce, finance, political economy, jurisprudence, morals and religion, are the true statesmen for the new republic—the best enunciators of our future policy of justice and equality. Any work short of this is narrow and partial, and fails to meet the requirements of the hour. What is so plain to me, may, I trust, be so to all before the lapse of many months, that all who have worked together thus far, may still stand side by side in this crisis of our nation's history.

James Mott said, he rejoiced that the women had seen fit to re-organize their movement into one for equal rights to all, that he felt the time had come to broaden our work. He felt the highest good of the nation demanded the recognition of woman as a citizen. We could have no true government until all the people gave their consent to the laws that govern them.

Stephen S. Foster said, Many seemed to think that the one question for this hour was negro suffrage. The question for every man and woman, he thought, was the true basis of the reconstruction of our government, not the rights of woman, or the negro, but the rights of all men and women.

Suffrage for woman was even a more vital question than for the negro; for in giving the ballot to the black man, we bring no new element into the national life—simply another class of men. And for one, he could not ask woman to go up and down the length and breadth of the land demanding the political recognition of any class of disfranchised citizens, while her own rights are ignored. Thank God, the human family are so linked together, that no one man can ever enjoy life, liberty or happiness, so long as the humblest being is crippled in a single right. I have demanded the freedom of the slave the last thirty years, because he was a human being, and I now demand suffrage for the negro because he is a human being, and for the same reason I demand the ballot for woman. Therefore, our demand for this hour is equal suffrage to all disfranchised classes, for the one and the same reason—they are all human beings.

Martha C. Wright said, Some one had remarked that we wished to merge ourselves into an Equal Rights Association to get rid of the odious name of Woman's Rights. This she repudiated as unworthy and untrue. Every good cause had been odious some time, even the name Christian has had its odium in all nations. We desire the change, because we feel that at this hour our highest claims are as citizens, and not as women. I for one have always gloried in the name of Woman's Rights, and pitied those of my sex who ignobly declared they had all the rights they wanted. We take the new name for the broader work, because we see it is no longer woman's province to be merely a humble petitioner for redress of grievances, but that she must now enter into the fulness of her mission, that of helping to make the laws, and administer justice.

Frances D. Gage remarked that she did not agree with Wendell Phillips's morning speech.[2] It was very difficult for one belonging to the privileged order to understand what an incubus on the soul of woman our present creeds, and codes, and customs are. How difficult it is for women, with opposing forces on every side, for even the bravest to demand their true position.

Mrs. Josephine S. Griffing agreed with Mrs. Gage. She could not understand Mr. Phillips. Yesterday, he said the ballot, in the hand of the negro, was a talisman to bring to him every weal, and ward off every woe, while, to-day, he said it was nothing in the hand of woman. That

Albany can do nothing for us; that we must go home and go to work for ourselves.

Aaron M. Powell remarked, I fully agree with the view Mr. Phillips took this morning, and I have no doubt it will have the effect to rouse many women from their apathy and indifference.

Mrs. Stanton said Mr. Phillips's position this morning was true—that he had spoken noble words for woman the last twenty years. His record dated farther back than this morning. His object was to show women the need of doing for themselves, and she felt his guns were turned on the worst enemies of our cause—women themselves. If the women of this nation could be provoked, even, to thought and action by any view of their case from Mr. Phillips, she should begin to think the day dawned, and thank him for his seeming severity.

Mr. Powell presented the following resolution:

Resolved, That in view of the Constitutional Convention to be held in the State of New York the coming year, it is the duty of this Association to demand such an amendment of the Constitution as shall secure equal rights to all citizens, without distinction of color, sex or race.

Miss Anthony seconded the resolution, and urged the importance of making a thorough canvass of the State with lectures, tracts and petitions. Mr. Powell, Mrs. Gage, and others, advocated the concentration of all the energies of the Association for the coming year on the State of New York; after which the resolution was adopted.

❧ *Proceedings of the Eleventh National Woman's Rights Convention, Held at the Church of the Puritans, New York, May 10, 1866* (New York, 1866), 48–49, 52–56.

1. Early in April, Congress overrode Andrew Johnson's veto to pass the Civil Rights Act, which defined persons born in the United States as national citizens with fundamental rights that the federal government should guarantee when the states did not. Though it omitted political rights, the act provided freedmen and freedwomen with access to federal courts to enforce their emancipation and freedom.

2. In an impromptu speech, Wendell Phillips called women the greatest obstacle to their own emancipation. "The singularity of this cause," he said, "is that it has to be argued against the wishes and purposes of its victims." If women agreed to change the fashion and tone of society, their enormous influence would do more than any legislation to open jobs and schools and implement reforms. "Albany is nothing," he insisted, "compared with Fashion." (*Proceedings of Woman's Rights Convention, 1866*, 37–43.)

·⊂══════⚭══════⊃·

218 ✽   SBA TO EDWIN A. STUDWELL[1]

Rochester Aug. 20, 186[6]

Friend Studwell

Enclosed is order for fifty dollars, on Mr. Patton—to be paid to the printer R. J. Johnston—[2] Will you sign it—then get Powell's name— If our four names will not do—will you pass it on to Mrs. Winchester[3] 23 Gramercy Park—Mrs. Mary F. Gilbert—I think her number is 17 West 11th street—Wendell Phillips Garrison—Nation office— But I should think Mr. P. would consider our four names all sufficient— It is too bad to keep Mr. Johnston waiting thus long—

Mrs. Stanton's letter to Gerritt Smith—sent to the Standard two weeks ago, does not appear—hence I suppose it is rejected— The gate is shut, wholly, it would seem against any <u>question</u> of the present position of Gerritt Smith, Wende[ll] Phillips and the American Anti Slavery Society—[4] Wel[l] all there is to be said is "<u>it an't as it used to was</u>"— Time was when we boasted of <u>inviting</u> criticism from <u>friend</u> as well as foe— Time was when we professed to have a <u>free platform</u> but surely those proud days are not now— I am sorry—that the good old ship has ↑thus↓ anchored in a harbor of non-intervention

I was sorry I didn't insist on your stopping over night—to be frank, the real reason was, <u>both</u> my sisters houses were <u>full</u> to overflowing— I wanted so much to decide about starting a paper— I hav[e] a note from Parker Pillsbury, saying he will be here, this week Friday night—how I wish you could be here too— If we launch a new Equal Rights paper—it should be by the first of January 1867—should it not— Might it not be well just to make it a campaign paper—for the Constitutional Convention—there will be no paper in the state through which we can urge <u>our</u> claim for <u>equal</u>, <u>impartial</u> suffrage—no—not one— If you and Mrs. Wells,[5]—of Fowler & Wells—could insure advertisements enough to pay cost—or nearly so—I sho'ld feel it best to go ahead— Our first number should contain <u>our</u> (not Henry J. Raymond's) address to the people of the State[6]—statement of our aim & purpose—agencies &c,

and testimonies of Stuart Mill[7] & all our best & noblest men & women on both sides the Atlantic—in <u>favor</u> of universal suffrage—in fine, it should be a splendid sheet—then we should strike of at least 50 thousand copies, and scatter them like Snow flakes all over the state—and the nation too— We could get G. L. Stearn's 50,000 names—the Liberator 2,000—The Standards 3,000—the Principia & National Era list[s]—the Phrenological Journal list—&c &c— I think we could hit a good many <u>solid</u> <u>heads</u>—with fifty thousand random [*illegible*] But what say you? shall we try the experiment— Please give me your judgement—that I may submit it to Mr. Pillsbury

How I do wish we had Powell to put in ↑his↓ right hand, head and heart work with us—it is my first experience, since we first began work together, in getting along without counseling with him—but it is of little avail to go through the form—when I know his every power of body and mind is pledged to a society and a paper that should, but wont, do the very work I most wish to accomplish— However good his wish & will to help us—he can't do more than he has already on his hands— So we must get on the best we can without ~~him~~ ↑his↓ active aid— Cordially Yours

⇴ *Susan B. Anthony*

P.S. Will you see that the Patton Pledge of $50. gets to Mr— Johnston—

⇴ ALS, SBA Papers, NRU. Square brackets surround characters worn away at margin.

1. Edwin A. Studwell (1837-?) was connected with his family's boot business in New York City and lived in Brooklyn, where he was active in antislavery and Republican politics. He was named to both the executive and finance committees of the American Equal Rights Association and served as an officer until 1870. A Quaker, he was a critical one; the prospectus for his journal the *Friend*, launched in 1866, promised "to wage war, if needful, upon the misconstrued" teachings of the Friends, "by which so much of the true Religious spirit of the Society is marred." (Garrison, *Letters*, 5:186–88, 410–12, 461; *Quaker Genealogy*, 3:226, 305; New York City directory, 1866–1867; *NASS*, 31 March 1866.)

2. To pay Robert Johnston's bill for printing the report of the May meeting, signatures of executive committee members were needed on Ludlow Patton's bank order. Patton (1825–1906), treasurer of the association, was a wealthy stockbroker and speculator who employed his Orange, New Jersey, neighbor Henry Blackwell during the war and again in 1866. He married Abigail

Hutchinson of the singing family in 1849. Johnston was the printer of the *National Anti-Slavery Standard* in New York and became a member of the equal rights executive committee himself in 1869. (Henry Whittemore, *The Founders and Builders of the Oranges* [Newark, N.J., 1896], 271–74; Kerr, *Lucy Stone*, 114, 116, 120; *New York Times*, 7 September 1906; New York City directory, 1866–1867.)

3. SBA names members of the executive committee, beginning with Aaron Powell. Margaret E. Winchester was married to Jonas Winchester of New York, owner of a drug company. A donor to the association at the May meeting, she was an active member for several years and hosted executive committee meetings at her house. (City directory, 1865–1866.)

4. ECS sparred in print with Gerrit Smith—her "target through which to rebuke other men's sins"—about advocating African-American rather than universal suffrage. In "Build a New House," she said it was not enough to ask "that races . . . shall stand equal before the law." Anything less than individual rights violated the republican idea. Smith replied that Reconstruction had nothing to do with "making a new Constitution for the nation, or laying anew the foundation stones of republican government." Keeping the peace was the sole purpose; war "will break out again if suffrage is withheld from the black man." The same could not be said of female suffrage. ECS sent another "thunderbolt" to the *Standard* on 6 August. (*NASS*, 21 July 1866, 4 August 1866, and ECS to G. Smith, 6 August 1866, *Film*, 11:558, 559–61.)

5. Charlotte Fowler Wells (1814–1901) was the sister of the phrenological Fowlers and wife of Samuel Robert Wells. A phrenologist and an astute businesswoman, she and her husband bought out her brothers in 1855 and ran the publishing firm together. (*NAW*.)

6. On 17 August the newspapers carried an "Address to the People of the Country," read by Henry J. Raymond at the National Union Convention in Philadelphia. Declaring the war over and the need for military powers at an end, it called for completing "the restoration and peace which the President of the United States has so well begun."

7. Elected to Parliament in 1865, John Stuart Mill presented a petition seeking women's enfranchisement in June 1866.

·(⊏━━━━⟨Ж⟩━━━━⊐)·

219 ⇝ APPEAL BY ECS

New York, Oct. 10, 1866.

ELIZABETH CADY STANTON FOR CONGRESS.

TO THE ELECTORS OF THE EIGHTH CONGRESSIONAL DISTRICT.

Although, by the Constitution of the State of New York, woman is denied the elective franchise, yet she is eligible to office; therefore I present myself to you as a candidate for Representative to Congress. Belonging to a disfranchised class, I have no political antecedents to recommend me to your support, but my creed is *free speech*, *free press*, *free men*, and *free trade*—the cardinal points of democracy. Viewing all questions from the stand-point of principle rather than expediency, there is a fixed uniform law, as yet unrecognized by either of the leading parties, governing alike the social and political life of men and nations. The Republican party has occasionally a clear vision of personal rights, while in its protective policy it seems wholly blind to the rights of property and interests of commerce; while it recognizes the duty of benevolence between man and man, it teaches the narrowest selfishness in trade between nations. The Democrats, on the contrary, while holding sound and liberal principles in trade and commerce, have ever in their political affiliations maintained the idea of class and caste among men; an idea wholly at variance with the genius of our free institutions and fatal to a high civilization. One party fails at one point and one at another. In asking your suffrages—believing alike in free men and free trade—I could not represent either party as now constituted.

Nevertheless, as an Independent Candidate, I desire an election at this time, as a rebuke to the dominant party for its retrogressive legislation, in so amending the Constitution as to make invidious distinctions on the ground of sex.

That instrument recognizes as persons all citizens who obey the laws and support the State, and if the Constitutions of the several States were brought into harmony with the broad principles of the

Federal Constitution, the women of the nation would no longer be taxed without representation, or governed without their consent. One word should not be added to that Great Charter of Rights to the insult or injury of the humblest of our citizens. I would gladly have a voice and vote in the Fortieth Congress to demand *universal suffrage*, that thus a republican form of government might be secured to every State in the Union.

If the party now in the ascendency makes its demand for "negro suffrage" in good faith on the ground of natural right, and because the highest good of the State demands that the republican idea be vindicated, on no principle of justice or safety can the women of the nation be ignored.

In view of the fact that the Freedmen of the South and the millions of foreigners now crowding our Western shores, most of whom represent neither property, education or civilization, are all, in the progress of events, to be enfranchised; the best interests of the nation demand that we outweigh this incoming pauperism, ignorance and degradation, with the wealth, education, and refinement of the women of the republic. On the high ground of safety to the nation and justice to its citizens I ask your support in the coming election.

❧ *Elizabeth Cady Stanton.*

❧ *NASS*, 13 October 1866. Also published in New York *World*, *New York Tribune*, *New York Herald*, and other city papers on 11 October 1866.

---

220 ❧ REMARKS BY SBA AT THE CONVENTION OF COLORED CITIZENS OF NEW YORK

Editorial Note: The Convention of Colored Citizens of New York met at the First African Baptist Church in Albany on 16–17 October to call for a constitutional convention to remove the property qualifications for black voters. SBA and Andrew Colvin attended, and Colvin was made an honorary delegate. After an acrimonious debate, the group opposed granting the same status to SBA but indicated a desire to hear her speak during the meeting. In the evening of the second day, the delegates considered endorsing the acts of Congress in regard to Reconstruction, "notwithstanding their work so far is only the beginning of the great end." (*NASS*, 29 September 1866;

New York Tribune, 18, 19 October 1866; *New York Herald*, 17, 18 October 1866; William Henry Johnson, *Autobiography of Dr. William Henry Johnson* [1900; reprint, New York, 1970], 210–11.)

[17 October 1866]

Miss Susan B. Anthony said that if she were to address the Convention at any time, she would like to speak before a vote should be taken upon this resolution.

Miss Anthony was given permission to address the Convention. She spoke substantially as follows:

Mr. President[1] and Gentlemen of the Convention: I felt that when this resolution was placed before me I could no longer keep silence. To-day my eye fell upon the address of the Committee appointed by the Southern Loyalists Convention to visit the North and the tomb of Abraham Lincoln.[2] These men say to us that the one great impending danger to this country is in the temptation to the North to commit itself to the Constitutional Amendment. Fellow-citizens for I am to be a citizen some day, I fully expect it—it is not for you who have come here into convention, it is not for you to indorse such an amendment as this. It is a wicked compromise—one of the most wicked ever submitted to the people—a compromise by which the advocates of Slavery will hold the 4,000,000 of people hitherto slaves in a vassalage worse than the original Slavery from which they have emerged. It is a compromise by which these former oppressors of the slave will have power to say whether the brave Robert Small or the gallant Sutton[3] shall have the right to vote or no. Therefore I could not keep silent when a resolution for the indorsement of such an amendment was submitted to this Convention. No, never let the colored men of New-York say Amen to that constitutional Amendment. Such action is simply helping to place the halter round your neck—helping to place you in a condition worse than Slavery—worse, for in Slavery the slave-owners had a sort of selfish interest in the physical well-being of the slave. Now even this will go. Therefore I beg you not to indorse this amendment. If it had added suffrage to the negroes it would have been well. But in this Congress failed. This and reconstruction might have been gained in a much simpler way. One of the few things Congress need have done was the striking out of the three-fifths representation clause from the Constitution. Many of the good and loyal people hesitate in this matter;

they say grant so and so, and the South will enfranchise the negroes. The South will not do this. The South, having the negroes in their power will never give them the franchise. The amendment is a political trap. Place yourselves upon the plantations and consider what would be your decision upon this measure. Think well before you give your sanction to such a scheme.[4]

⬿ *New York Tribune*, 19 October 1866.

1. William Howard Day (1825–1900) presided. A classmate of Lucy Stone's at Oberlin, he was active in Ohio before the war as an abolitionist and journalist. In 1863 he moved to New York City and edited the *Zion Standard* for the African Methodist Episcopal Zion Church. He also served the Freedman's Bureau as a superintendent of schools. (*Black Abolitionist Papers*, 4:79–80n.)

2. The Convention of Southern Loyalists at Philadelphia in September named a committee to visit the tomb of Abraham Lincoln in Springfield, Illinois. Their address to the people warned the North that the Fourteenth Amendment provided insufficient protection for the rights of southern loyalists, black and white, and would leave the unreconstructed states in the hands of rebels. (*New York Tribune*, 16 October 1866.)

3. Robert Smalls (1839–1915), born a slave in South Carolina and hired out to pilot the *Planter*, became a war hero in 1862, when he turned the vessel over to the Union and continued as its pilot. After the war he was elected a delegate to South Carolina's constitutional convention, a state legislator, and a congressman. (*DANB*.) Robert Sutton, a former slave on the St. Mary's River in Florida, served as a corporal in the First South Carolina Volunteers under T. W. Higginson, who described him as "the wisest man in our ranks." (T. W. Higginson, "Up the St. Mary's," *Atlantic Monthly* 15 [April 1865]: 422–36; Garrison, *Letters*, 4:208n.)

4. Andrew Colvin spoke next. He urged the convention to call for universal suffrage, for men and women, black and white, and to apologize to SBA. "What right have you to say a woman shall not vote?" he asked. "As well might women say, these men shall not have the ballot."

·⊂══⟩·

221 ⬿ Ann Fitzhugh Smith to ECS

Peterboro Oct 21st 1866

My dear Lib

I have wanted so much to send you a word of encouragement ever since I saw your self-nomination for Congress—but I thought my approval could not have much weight. Still my heart urges me to say: "God speed you at every step." Some, while they do not question the lawfulness of your course, doubt its wisdom. This is not the day to pass judgement on it. It is noble and brave in you to take the lead here. Some one must "bear the brunt." Truth is ever born in a manger. Blessed are they who labor and <u>wait</u> for its triumph. If I lived in your Eighth District, I think I could go through a great deal squeezing and even pelting in an effort to cast a vote for you.[1] God bless you and give you each day an increase of goodness and wisdom. My love to all yours Ever in love

⇒ *Ann C. Smith*

⇒ ALS, ECS Papers, DLC.

1. The final tally in the Eighth Congressional District race was: James Brooks, Democrat, 13,816; Le Grand B. Cannon, Republican, 8,210; ECS, Independent, 24. (*History*, 2:181.)

⊰━━━⊱⊰━━━⊱

222 ⇒ SBA TO WENDELL PHILLIPS

464 West 34th street New York Nov. 4, 1866

Dear Friend Phillips

Will you speak at our Albany Convention Tuesday evening the 20th, on the duty of New York state at <u>this time</u> to make herself a genuine republican form of government?— If you ↑will,↓ please let me know immediately that I may add your name to our list of speakers— Mrs. Stanton has decided to devote the winter to lecturing—and will thus announce.

Lucy Stone and husband were here yesterday—they are very earnest to start a <u>Universal</u> <u>Suffrage</u> paper—both are ready to give their time & labor to the work—and only ask, that such friends as wish such a paper, t̶o̶ ↑shall↓ place behind them a fund of $10,000 that may be drawn upon in case the paper fails to pay cost—merely of paper & printing & contributions—nothing for editorial or publishing services— We <u>surely</u> <u>must</u> <u>have</u> a <u>paper</u> through which those who demand the <u>whole</u> <u>loaf</u> ↑of↓ <u>republicanism</u> may speak—

The Republican party has thrown overboard the question of Negro

Suffrage in the rebel states even—and the fight henceforth is to be with <u>the people</u> of each state—and it cannot be on any solid ground, but that of <u>right of citizens</u>— I still wish, as last Spring, that the good old <u>Standard</u> might take the lead in this new gospel; but if it can't—it can't—and I, as then, submit sorrowfully.

Mr. Powell announced to me that "henceforth all notices of our Equal Rights lecturers, if they went into the Standard, must be paid for, at the regular advertising prices,—that is, if <u>I</u> was not going ↑to↓ give my <u>personal efforts to the Standard</u>"— Of course I said, "I shall speak as always, that the Standard is true & uncomprosing for the Negro["]—but I can't say to my audiences, "subscribe for the Standard, it is the <u>one</u> & <u>only paper</u> that will bring to you from week to week <u>fresh instalments</u> of the <u>new gospel</u> I have endeavored to preach to you["]—and not being able to say <u>that</u>—all else I might say would be of no avail— One can't get subscribers for a paper—only on the assurance that it will take ↑to↓ them <u>more</u> of the very thought which has begun to stir their souls— Thus you will see, Mr. Phillips, that <u>I</u> <u>can't</u> <u>serve</u> the Standard efficiently, because the Standard doesn't serve ~~the~~ the idea which to me is the pivotal one. Would to God that it were otherwise—for the men & the women who stand by the Standard are, more than any others, educated to go forward to the new work.

I hope you are getting well & strong for the battle— I felt sad to see you looking ill at the Cooper Institute the other night—and as those needed warnings & rebukes went out to that earnest assemblage I prayed that you might be saved to do mighty battle to the end—[1] I was so glad of your strong protest against "<u>male</u>"— Sincerely yours

⚔ Susan B. Anthony

Mr. Phillips—If it is impossible for you to be at Albany, which I hope it is not—wont you give us a brief word by way of letter?— S. B. A

⚔ ALS, on folio with call to "Equal Rights Convention for New York State," bMS Am 1953(213), Wendell Phillips Papers, MH-H.

1. On 25 October 1866. He spoke on "The Peril of the Hour" or "Reject the Amendment—Depose the President." The proposed amendment, he said, would restore the South to its old place in the government and "engraft into the Constitution of the United States a new feature. . . . Yes, the timid and cowardly policy of a party bound only upon its own perpetuation undertakes to engraft into that Constitution the word 'male,' confining us in the onward

march of the suffrage question to one sex. I repudiate all limitations. (Applause.) Our fathers left it uncommitted to face the demands of the opening century. I would leave it uncommitted." (*NASS*, 3 November 1866.)

·⊂━━━⟐━━━⊃·

223 ⇝ NEW YORK STATE EQUAL RIGHTS CONVENTION

Editorial note: ECS welcomed a small crowd of one hundred and fifty people to Tweddle Hall in Albany at ten o'clock on the morning of November 20. In remarkable journalistic confusion, almost nothing about this two-day meeting is certain. Newspapers attributed the same speech at the morning session to three different people; there were divergent accounts of the order of discussion; ECS was called "Mrs. Anthony" but described in terms unmistakably aimed at her. This is more than a case of editorial predilection shaping how oral discussion was recorded; it is unusual chaos that cannot be reconstructed into a definitive narrative. Because none of the reports can be treated as a source text for the entire meeting, sources have been identified for each significant speech and discussion.

[20 November 1866]

Mrs. Stanton opened the Convention, regretting that the venerable President of the Society, Mrs. Lucretia Mott, was detained by ill health. She said as to the question they were met to consider was that of suffrage, lying at the foundation of all representative governments, the means were favorable to success. Many Republicans have lately given in their adhesion to woman suffrage. Much surprise is expressed when John Bright informs us that out of seven millions of people in that country only two millions are represented at the ballot-box;[1] but how many ever think of the fact coming nearer home, that only three-eighths of the people of this Republic are so represented? Five-eighths of our entire adult population is disfranchised. Massachusetts has nobly taken the lead in sending two negroes to the legislative halls;[2] let us hope that this State will take the lead in elevating woman to participate in the government. The speaker then introduced Lucy Stone as President of the Convention.

⤺ *New York Tribune*, 21 November 1866. Attributed to Lucy Stone in the *New York Herald*, 21 November 1866.

Editorial note: SBA read the call either before ECS spoke or after Lucy Stone welcomed the audience in her turn. According to the *Tribune*, in the only account that made sense of subsequent discussions, SBA followed her reading by complimenting the newspapers that gave readers favorable advance notice of the meeting. Her remarks, nowhere quoted, prompted ECS to speak.

I desire, before the Convention goes further, to insist that this body indulge in no fulsome adulation of the Republican party; and I tell that party that when we get the right of suffrage, which we will, that they will have no right to claim our votes as they do the negroes'. <She also protested against the use of the word "Copperhead," and looked to the Democrats quite as much as to the Republicans for the ballot.> The Democratic party has alone done anything in favor of an extended suffrage. The States that have ever given the blacks the ballot have been governed at the time by Democratic administrations.[3] Why, James Brooks was the only Congressman last winter that had the nerve and the decency to present the woman suffrage memorial to Congress. (Applause.)

❧ New York *World,* 21 November 1866; *New York Tribune*, 21 November 1866.

Frederick Douglass remonstrated against such a tribute being paid to the Democratic party, explained Brooks's advocacy of woman's rights as the trick of an enemy to assail and endanger the rights of black men. He did it to make a point against the liberal policy of the Republicans and to shame them out of their anti-Slavery principles. He (Douglass) desired harmony but if this eulogizing of the Democracy and bestowing encomiums on such men as James Brooks and Sunset Cox[4] are to be persisted in there would be trouble in our family. (Applause and merriment.)

❧ *New York Tribune*, 21 November 1866.

Editorial note: The enigmatic Henry Blackwell prompted the only debate over resolutions, when he introduced his own proposal for a new political party committed to "the expansion of the suffrage to all adult citizens." He argued that neither Democrats nor Republicans understood how universal suffrage would preserve their relative strength with the voters and how enfranchising only black men or only women would tip the balance, especially in the South. As a critique of congressional inaction on suffrage, his ideas won general approval.

However, at the next session, he added a resolution declaring that voting rights should be based on an educational qualification. In a long speech, according to the *World*, he pointed to the election of New Yorker John Morrissey to Congress as proof that if the incompetent voted, they elected their own kind.

Mrs. Stanton opposed the resolution. She was in favor of universal suffrage, but she did not believe in the educational qualification. <[She] opposed it on the ground that the negro at the South has not the free school, and cannot obtain it without first obtaining the ballot. To say that he must be educated before he votes, is to say that he shall not vote at all.> Reference had been made to the election of John Morrissey to Congress.[5] For one she was glad to see Mr. Morrissey elected, because she thought it might improve his morals. It would also give him an opportunity to learn to read and write if he had not done so before. She, however, thought that the State ought to have done its duty to Morrissey long ere he had been elected to Congress.

↞ *Albany Express*, 21 November 1866, SBA scrapbook 1, Rare Books, DLC; Philadelphia *Press*, 21 November 1866.

Fred. Douglass opposed it; he believes in no qualification beyond that of common humanity, manhood and womanhood. Some men regard our republican institutions as a failure. He wished they had less to justify it. Executive usurpations, bitter hostilities between Congress and the President, the serious troubles at Memphis and New Orleans,[6] and various other grave events gave reason for the fear. Our only safety is in the ballot in the hands of all. He closed with an eloquent appeal for this right.

Other speeches were made against the resolution, after which their further consideration was postponed until to-morrow morning, on motion of Mrs. Stanton, who, on making the motion, contrasted the loyal action of the uneducated black with the disloyalty of the West-Pointer.

↞ Philadelphia *Press*, 21 November 1866.

Editorial note: Before a large audience at an evening session, ECS read an address called "Bread and the Ballot."

The Constitutional Convention is now a fixed fact. Let the people decide what their representatives shall do when they assemble. In the twenty years' interval in which these conventions meet, it is right to suppose that the people will have outgrown many of their old ideas, and will demand some onward step. In the last convention "white" citizens made quite merry over the idea of placing the ballot in the hands of the negro. Now the nation is convulsed on that very question. As the proposed work of the convention is to be the extension of suffrage, all disfranchised classes should be represented there.[7] Seeing that we cannot be there in person we are deeply interested in the choice of the men who are to be there to act on this great question. Balls and dinners, receptions, &c., may now be turned to good account, if those who wield them, of the female sex, will use the social opportunities they afford in favor of their own interests. There has been but little said on woman's right during the war. We thought less of our claims[8] than of those of the black man. Moreover, as the disposition seemed to be to give the negroes the ballot on the score of humanity we thought the settlement of his claims logically included ours also. His manhood was proved when he showed his rights and ability to bear arms in the nation's behalf, and the question of his voting has become a certainty soon to be accomplished. Now, as women are the sole parties whose status is fluctuating, we demand attention on the part of the coming new formers of our Constitution. We appeal to the women of the State to organize into clubs in every school district for the circulation of tracts, petitions, and documents in favor of their rights. Let the men of the Convention look to it how they treat our claims now. Twenty years to come, when we are voters, we will pass upon theirs. The opportunity of placing the ballot in the hand of woman must not be let pass. Woman's right to life, liberty, and the pursuit of happiness, as well as to property, cannot be denied, for if we go back to first principles, where did the few get the right, through all time, to rule the many? From the same source that pirates had the right to make the ocean a sepulchre. Force and fraud took the place of right in both cases. Twenty years ago women in New-York State had no more rights than slaves on plantations; had no rights to person, children, wages, to make contracts, to sue or be sued, nor, in many cases, to testify in courts; much of this has been changed for the better, and an equal advance will secure us an affirmative hearing in the Constitutional Convention. All that we have received, however, have been favors secured by the will of an uncertain, varying majority. Mrs. Stanton continued at great length, and advocated the ballot for women, not only as a question of right in the abstract, but as required by her interests in the business of the country. She insisted that the only way to reclaim the sex from the helplessness, the frivolity, and in some cases the degradation into which they lapse, was to make them, above all, and first, independent. The lady insisted that no objection could be urged against it. People were only opposed to it because they did not think of it. On the score of judgment, justice, and intelligence, woman stood on an admitted level with man, and far above the negro. That she would exercise the right discreetly, could not be doubted; and that it would produce disorganization could no more be predicated, than it could of the fact that she worshipped at the same altar with man.

❧ New York *World*, 21 November 1866.

[21 November 1866]

Miss Anthony then, from the business committee, stated that the Association intended to canvass New-York State, through and through; intended to hold fifty county conventions within the next six months; and that these women meant to arouse all the other women to the dignity and necessity of the ballot. When they once found that voting gave them position, equal wages, and even a higher special distinction, then the apathy which her present condition of servitude effects would disappear. A big mass meeting is soon to be held in New-York to inaugurate the enterprise on a broad basis; Miss Anthony requests that all who in various parts of the State favor the cause send her their names and addresses, and that they will be put to work. Tens of thousands of petitions are to be circulated, of the following kind:

PETITION.

To the Constitutional Convention of the State of New-York:
We, citizens of the State of New-York, pray your honorable body, that in amending the Constitution you will so frame the section prescribing qualifications of electors as to secure the right of suffrage upon equal terms to both men and women.

❧ New York *World*, 22 November 1866.

1. John Bright (1811–1889) was a member of Parliament for forty-five years and an advocate of expanding the electorate in a country where, by one estimate, five out of every six males were disfranchised. (*DNB*.)

2. Edward G. Walker, a Boston attorney, and Charles L. Mitchell, a printer who worked in the *Liberator* office, won election to the Massachusetts General Court in 1866, becoming probably the first African Americans elected to a state legislature. (*DANB*.)

3. A Democratic paper but not the Republican papers reported these words. If the report is accurate, ECS stood on shaky historical ground, crediting Democrats with more generous views about black suffrage. More than antebellum Federalists or Whigs, Democrats favored expanding the electorate in general and recognizing the franchise to be a right of the citizen, not linked to property ownership. With regard to granting the right to African Americans, however, the best that New York Democrats could point to was a role in stopping full disfranchisement at the constitutional convention of 1821 by forging the compromise that linked black voting rights to property. In 1846 Democrats resisted proposals for equal suffrage. Democratic opposition to equality only intensified in the subsequent decades. (Phyllis S. Field, *The Politics of Race in New York: The Struggle for Black Suffrage in the Civil War Era* [Ithaca, 1982], 35–79.)

4. Samuel Sullivan Cox (1824–1889), a Copperhead from Ohio who served in the House of Representatives from 1856 to 1865, was a virulent opponent of black suffrage. His nickname "Sunset" dated from his days as a journalist with a penchant for descriptive writing. (*DAB*.)

5. John Morrissey (1831–1878), Irish immigrant, proprietor of gambling houses, and 1858 champion heavyweight boxer of the world, had just won election as a Democrat to the House of Representatives from New York City. (*BDAC*.)

6. Violent anti-black riots broke out in Memphis in early May and New Orleans in July of 1866, resulting in loss of property and many deaths.

7. When New York's legislators set the voting qualifications to elect delegates to the constitutional conventions of 1801 and 1821, they set aside all property requirements that limited the franchise in state elections. This gave men without suffrage rights a role in redrafting the constitution. The equal rights association sought a similar provision in 1867 that would allow all black men and all women to select convention delegates. (ECS, *Address in Favor of Universal Suffrage, for the Election of Delegates to the Constitutional Convention . . . January 23, 1867, Film*, 11:894–906.)

8. In this and the next sentence the *World* reported this word as "chains." "Claims" is the word reported by the *Tribune*.

·⟨━━━━━━✕❧━━━━━━⟩·

224 ❧ REMARKS BY SBA TO THE PENNSYLVANIA ANTI-SLAVERY SOCIETY

Editorial note: From Albany SBA traveled to Philadelphia to attend the annual meeting of the Pennsylvania Anti-Slavery Society at the Franklin Institute. There, James Mott, president, Edward M. Davis, secretary, and Lucretia Mott, of the board of managers, were the moving spirits of the meeting. In the afternoon of the meeting's first day, SBA spoke briefly at the invitation of Lucretia Mott, who wanted to hear her report of "the glorious Convention at Albany" and her thoughts on "the subject of suffrage for the freedmen." On the morning after the society adjourned, an informal meeting agreed to organize an equal rights association, after the plan set forth in Albany.

[22 November 1866]

I did not come exactly by the telegraph wires, as our friend Davis suggested this morning;[1] but I came by the telegraph lines, and I find that the wires have brought the news a little sooner than I could get here, for I find in the Philadelphia *Press* a report which does very full justice to the meeting. We had such a meeting at Albany as we never had before, either as Women's Rights or as Anti-Slavery women, in point of enthusiasm and every way. There was but one voice among us in regard to the question, that now is the hour, not only to demand suffrage for the negro, but for every other human being in the Republic. We felt for the first time in the Woman's Rights movement that we had actually the women with us. Mr. Greeley's everlasting answer to us for a number of years, has been that women will get the right to vote as soon as they ask it. I am sure the conclusion we reached at this meeting was, that the working women of the country are with us. Say to them that with the ballot in their hands they can secure equal pay for their work, and their demand for the ballot will be as strong as that of the black man to-day. But we also come to the conclusion that, whether the black man or whether women shall be intelligent enough to make the demand for themselves or not, it is the duty of every intelligent man who knows the value of the ballot by the position it brings to him, to make the demand for us. (Applause.)

❧ *NASS*, 1 December 1866.

1. Edward Davis's comment was not reported.

❧ Genealogies

THE FOLLOWING GENEALOGICAL CHARTS are designed to help the reader understand the relationships of family members who appear in this volume. They are not complete; only relatives mentioned in the documents are included.

In these documents ECS makes no mention of Stanton relatives. Her contact is only with the Cady and Livingston families, with siblings, cousins, nieces, and nephews. For her part SBA traveled within a wider circle of extended kin. Her many "cousins" included descendants of great-grandparents as well as of grandparents. Two genealogies of ECS's family are thus followed by three for SBA's family. The immediate families of both ECS and SBA are included only in the first of their respective charts, but both women reappear as individuals on subsequent charts in order to assist the reader in visualizing the lines of kinship.

FAMILY OF ELEAZER AND TRYPHENA BEEBE CADY

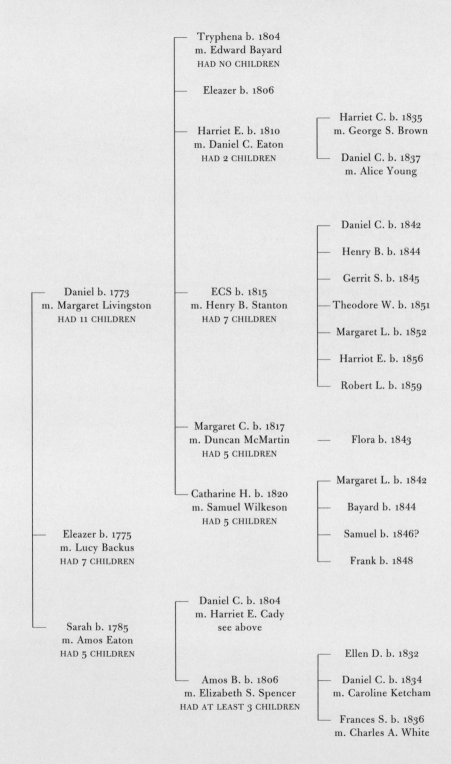

Tryphena b. 1804
m. Edward Bayard
HAD NO CHILDREN

Eleazer b. 1806

Harriet E. b. 1810
m. Daniel C. Eaton
HAD 2 CHILDREN

Harriet C. b. 1835
m. George S. Brown

Daniel C. b. 1837
m. Alice Young

Daniel b. 1773
m. Margaret Livingston
HAD 11 CHILDREN

ECS b. 1815
m. Henry B. Stanton
HAD 7 CHILDREN

Daniel C. b. 1842

Henry B. b. 1844

Gerrit S. b. 1845

Theodore W. b. 1851

Margaret L. b. 1852

Harriot E. b. 1856

Robert L. b. 1859

Margaret C. b. 1817
m. Duncan McMartin
HAD 5 CHILDREN

Flora b. 1843

Catharine H. b. 1820
m. Samuel Wilkeson
HAD 5 CHILDREN

Margaret L. b. 1842

Bayard b. 1844

Samuel b. 1846?

Frank b. 1848

Eleazer b. 1775
m. Lucy Backus
HAD 7 CHILDREN

Sarah b. 1785
m. Amos Eaton
HAD 5 CHILDREN

Daniel C. b. 1804
m. Harriet E. Cady
see above

Amos B. b. 1806
m. Elizabeth S. Spencer
HAD AT LEAST 3 CHILDREN

Ellen D. b. 1832

Daniel C. b. 1834
m. Caroline Ketcham

Frances S. b. 1836
m. Charles A. White

FAMILY OF JAMES AND ELIZABETH SIMPSON LIVINGSTON

Elizabeth b. 1773
m. Peter G. Smith
HAD 5 CHILDREN

Cornelia W. b. 1795?
m. Walter L. Cochran
HAD 8 CHILDREN

John b. 1813

Cornelia S. b. 1825
m. Henry A. W. Barclay
HAD AT LEAST 2 CHILDREN

Gerrit b. 1797
m. (1) Wealthy A. Backus
HAD NO CHILDREN
m. (2) Ann C. Fitzhugh
HAD 4 CHILDREN

Elizabeth b. 1822
m. Charles D. Miller
HAD 4 CHILDREN
Gerrit S. b. 1845
Charles D. b. 1847
William F. b. 1850
Anne F. b. 1856

Green b. 1842
m. Elizabeth Fitzhugh

Margaret b. 1785
m. Daniel Cady
HAD 11 CHILDREN
see Cady Descendants

ECS b. 1815

Richard M. b. 1787
m. Sarah Jacobs
HAD AT LEAST 1 CHILD

Mary b. 1812
m. John W. Olmstead

FAMILY OF HUMPHREY AND HANNAH LAPHAM ANTHONY

Daniel b. 1794
m. Lucy Read
HAD 7 CHILDREN

Guelma P. b. 1818
m. Aaron M. McLean — Ann Eliza b. 1840
HAD 4 CHILDREN

SBA b. 1820

Hannah L. b. 1821
m. Eugene Mosher
HAD 5 CHILDREN

Daniel R. b. 1824
m. Anna E. Osborne — Maude b. 1865
HAD 5 CHILDREN

Mary S. b. 1827

Eliza T. b. 1832

J. Merritt b. 1834
m. Mary A. Luther
HAD 4 CHILDREN

Hannah b. 1797
m. Isaac U. Hoxie
HAD 9 CHILDREN

Eliza H. b. 1823
m. (1) Edward B. Shove
m. (2) Merritt Cook

Ellen b. 1833
m. Lucien B. Squier

John b. 1800
m. Elizabeth Wadsworth
HAD 7 CHILDREN

Ann Eliza b. 1814
m. Albert F. Dickinson — Melissa b. 1839
HAD 6 CHILDREN

FAMILY OF JOSHUA AND HANNAH SHERMAN LAPHAM

Lydia b. 1751
m. Stephen Rogers
HAD 10 CHILDREN

Aaron b. 1776
m. Dinah Folger
HAD 12 CHILDREN

Seth b. 1823
m. Hannah Mitchell

Ruth b. 1787
m. John Vail
HAD 8 CHILDREN

Aaron R. b. 1810
m. (1) Sophronia Lapham
b. 1814
m. (2) Charlotte Hewitt

George O. b. 1817
m. Helen N. Shaw

Semantha L. b. 1826
m. Henry G. Lapham
b. 1822

Nathan b. 1761
m. Elizabeth Arnold
HAD 10 CHILDREN

Jesse b. 1788
m. Elizabeth Griffith
HAD 7 CHILDREN

Sophronia b. 1814
m. Aaron R. Vail b. 1810

Henry G. b. 1822
m. Semantha L. Vail
b. 1826

Oliver K.
m. Caroline Gooding

Cynthia b. 1790
m. John C. White

Anson b. 1804
m. (1) Anna D. Thorn
m. (2) Amy Ann F. Willets

Hannah b. 1773
m. Humphrey Anthony
HAD 9 CHILDREN
see Anthony Descendants

Daniel b. 1794

SBA b. 1820

Family of Daniel and Susannah Richardson Read

Amy b. 1777
m. Joseph Howe
HAD 7 CHILDREN

  Malintha b. 1805
  m. (1) Nathan Patchen
  m. (2) Isaac Stotenburg
  NO KNOWN CHILDREN

  Nancy b. 1811
  m. Lemuel Clark
  HAD 2 CHILDREN

    Emily
    m. Arthur I. Griggs

    Susan

Joshua b. 1783
m. Mary Stafford
HAD 3 CHILDREN

  Eleanor J. b. 1812?
  m. George Caldwell
  HAD 2 CHILDREN

    Joshua R. b. 1834

    Elisha S. b. 1837?

  Margaret A. b. 1820?
  m. Joseph W. Caldwell
  HAD 4 CHILDREN

    Mary E. b. 1840?
    m. —— Warren

    Theodore b. 1842?

    Albert S. b. 1845?

    Margaret R. b. 1849

  Daniel S. b. 1824?
  m. Sarah A. Burbeck
  HAD AT LEAST 1 CHILD

Joseph b. 1786
m. Lorinda Eddy
HAD 5 CHILDREN

  Carlos
  HAD 2 CHILDREN

    Lorinda?

Lucy b. 1793
m. Daniel Anthony
HAD 7 CHILDREN
see Anthony Descendants

  SBA b. 1820